DATE DUE

*British Modernist Fiction
1920 to 1945*

THE CRITICAL COSMOS SERIES

British Modernist Fiction 1920 to 1945

Edited and with an introduction
by *HAROLD BLOOM*
Sterling Professor of the Humanities
Yale University

CHELSEA HOUSE PUBLISHERS ◇ 1986
New York ◇ New Haven ◇ Philadelphia

© 1987 by Chelsea House Publishers, a division of Chelsea
House Educational Communications, Inc.
    133 Christopher Street, New York, NY 10014
    345 Whitney Avenue, New Haven, CT 06511
    5014 West Chester Pike, Edgemont, PA 19028

Introduction © 1986 by Harold Bloom

Printed and bound in the United States of America

∞The paper used in this publication meets the minimum
requirements of the American National Standard for
Permanence of Paper for Printed Library Materials,
Z39.48-1984.

Library of Congress Cataloging-in-Publication Data
British modernist fiction, 1920–1945.
    (The Critical cosmos)
    Bibliography: p.
    Includes index.
    1. English fiction—20th century—History and
criticism. 2. Modernism (Literature) I. Bloom,
Harold. II. Series.
PR888.M63B75   1986   823'.912'091   86-13611
ISBN 0-87754-987-7 (alk. paper)

Contents

Editor's Note

This book brings together representative essays on the fiction of the principal British novelists whose work centers itself in the span 1920 to 1945. Three essays each are given to James Joyce and to Virginia Woolf, and two to D. H. Lawrence, since they are, by common consent, the major figures of that era. The eighteen other novelists studied here receive only a single essay each, though E. M. Forster clearly is of an eminence far beyond that, say, of Wyndham Lewis.

The essays are arranged here in the order of the novelists' ages, from John Cowper Powys and Ford Madox Ford through Graham Greene and Henry Green. They are preceded by my introduction, which centers upon the three major figures —Joyce, Woolf, Lawrence —and which considers the originality of these powerful inventors.

I am grateful to Edward Vesneske for aid in researching this volume.

The first three novelists considered here are now largely out of favor, but John Cowper Powys, Ford Madox Ford, and Dorothy Richardson were intense and singular writers, richly rewarding if very demanding. Timothy Hyman describes Powys as a visionary of romance, who teaches his readers to accept ordinary reality only if it retains something of the aura of a higher, archetypal realm of consciousness. Arthur Mizener, Ford's biographer, gives an overview of *Parade's End*, Ford's series of novels whose hero, Christopher Tietjens, embodies the best values of a vanishing world of honor and fidelity. Dorothy Richardson, a novelist once linked in critical estimates with Joyce and with Proust, is analyzed by Stephen Heath with particular emphasis upon issues of language and of feminine representation.

We do not think of E. M. Forster as an innovating novelist, so it is particularly refreshing to include here a persuasive defense of his originality by Daniel R. Schwarz.

James Joyce, certainly the most eminent creator of prose fiction in the

English language in this century, is first studied in this book by Judith Spector, who rather ambivalently finds in *Ulysses* "the complete masculine aesthetic," an aesthetic presumably as vividly incarnated by *Hamlet* and by Dante's *Comedy*. *Finnegans Wake* is adroitly presented by Derek Attridge as a work ultimately extending and testing the limits of narrative digression, while simultaneously performing for itself the process of rhetorical demystification that critics now call "deconstruction." David Hayman follows, with a similarly advanced rhetorical analysis of aspects of both *Ulysses* and the *Wake*.

Wyndham Lewis, apocalyptic satirist and tendentious ideologue, is described by Terence Hegarty as having crucial affinities with Joyce, a judgment that is both suggestive and highly disputable.

In three essays on Virginia Woolf, we are given perspectives that reinforce without merely repeating one another. Michael Rosenthal, in a subtly balanced estimate, emphasizes her subjectivity and her necessarily personal art, which separates her from the narrative achievements and socio-psychological concerns of her strongest contemporaries. Nelly Furman, in an exegesis of *A Room of One's Own*, defends the book as the true manifesto of the literary feminism it prophesies. In Ian Gregor's essay, Woolf is seen as a novelist who dramatizes her own skepticism about her own created world.

Ivy Compton-Burnett, savage traditionalist and strangely destructive comic writer, is read by Frederick R. Karl as a moral chronicler of energetic monsters, humorous and tenacious.

Lawrence, the last of the major novelists studied in this volume, receives two very discerning treatments from Robert Kiely and Maria Di-Battista. Both center upon his finest novel, *Women in Love*, with Kiely defending Lawrence's apparent formal inadequacies, and DiBattista emphasizing Birkin's Lawrentian attempt to make the creative life into a mode of spiritual salvation.

Joyce Cary is described by Hazard Adams as a visionary pursuing a more intense reality, in the manner of Blake, and perhaps even of Wordsworth. A refreshing difference enters with Eliot A. Singer's investigation of Agatha Christie as a kind of riddle writer, and in another register with A. E. Dyson's analysis of Aldous Huxley's ironic dialectic of two nihilisms: hedonistic boredom and mystical negation of the common life and of the natural man or woman.

L. P. Hartley, at once traditionalist and modernist, is seen by Neil McEwan as a subtle mannerist who relies upon nuance, particularly in *The Go-Between*. John Zneimer, writing upon Liam O'Flaherty, finds in his work the aesthetic personalism of a sense of absurdity in existence, rather than a philosophical conviction of an Existentialist kind. C. S. Lewis, an orthodox Christian ontologist, is judged by Janice Witherspoon Neulieb as having reconciled the claims of art and the Divine Will, a rather generous estimate in my own opinion.

Two extraordinary women fiction-writers, Elizabeth Bowen and Stevie

Smith, are the subjects of two of the most vital essays in this volume, by Harriet S. Chessman and Hermione Lee, respectively. Chessman emphasizes Bowen's desire to imagine forms of language and of narrative that might overcome the distance "between those women who possess language and those who do not," while Lee integrates the rhetorical stances of Smith's lyrics with *Novel on Yellow Paper*'s fierce critique of male privileges.

Two important satirists, George Orwell and Evelyn Waugh, receive illuminating exegeses from Lynette Hunter and Alvin B. Kernan, respectively. Hunter recounts Orwell's search for an image of voice that would offer a positive alternative to the vicious politics he satirized, while Kernan genially and masterfully exposes Waugh's astonishing satiric genius in the fantastic exuberance of his early novels.

The Marxist critic Terry Eagleton provides a sympathetic if ideologically distant portrait of Graham Greene's "reluctant heroes." In a final consideration, the elusive Henry Green is analyzed by Bruce Bassoff as a lyrical novelist, a profoundly playful visionary of "surfaces and depths."

Introduction

I

It is an odd sensation to begin writing on Joyce on June 16, 1985, particularly if one's name is Bloom. Poldy is, as Joyce intended, the most *complete* figure in modern fiction, if not indeed in all Western fiction, and so it is appropriate that he have a saint's day in the literary calendar: Bloomsday. He is, thankfully, no saint, but a mild, gentle sinner; in short, a good man. So good a man is he that even the critic Hugh Kenner, who in his earlier commentary saw Poldy as an instance of modern depravity, an Eliotic Jew as it were, in 1980 could call Joyce's hero "fit to live in Ireland without malice, without violence, without hate." How many are fit to live, in fact or fiction, in Ireland or America, without malice, without violence, without hate? Kenner, no sentimentalist, now finds in Poldy what the reader must find: a better person than oneself.

Richard Ellmann, Joyce's biographer, shrewdly says of Poldy that "he is not afraid that he will compromise his selfhood." Currently fashionable criticism, calling itself "Post-Structuralist Joyce," oddly assimilates Joyce to Barthes, Lacan, Derrida; producing a Poldy without a self, another floating signifier. But Joyce's Poldy, as Ellmann insists, is heroic and imaginative; his mimetic force allies him to the Wife of Bath, Falstaff, and Sancho Panza, and like them his presence is overwhelming. Joyce's precursors were Dante and Shakespeare, and Poldy has a comprehensiveness and immediacy worthy of his ancestry. It is good to remember that, after Dante and Shakespeare, Joyce cared most for Wordsworth and Shelley among the poets. Wordsworth's heroic naturalism and Shelley's visionary skepticism find their way into Poldy also.

How Jewish is Poldy? Here I must dissent a touch from Ellmann, who says that when Poldy confronts the Citizen, he states an ethical view "more Christian than Judaic." Poldy has been unbelieving Jew, Protestant, and

Catholic, but his ethical affirmations are normative Jewish, as Joyce seems to have known better than Ellmann does. When Poldy gazes upon existence, he finds it good. The commonplace needs no hallowing for Poldy. Frank Budgen, taking the hint from Joyce, emphasizes how much older Poldy seems than all the other inhabitants of Joyce's visionary Dublin. We do not think of Poldy as being thirty-eight, prematurely middle-aged, but rather as living in what the Hebrew Bible called *olam*: time without boundaries. Presumably, that is partly why Joyce chose to make his Ulysses Jewish rather than Greek. Unlike a modern Greek, Poldy is in surprising continuity with a lineage of which he has little overt knowledge. How different would the book have been if Joyce had centered on a Greek living in Dublin? The aura of exile would not be there. Joyce, the Dubliner in exile, tasting his own stoic version of a Dantesque bitterness, found in Poldy as wandering Jew what now seems his inevitable surrogate. Poldy, not Stephen, is Joyce's true image.

Yet Poldy is certainly more like Homer's Ulysses than like the Yahwist's Jacob. We see Poldy surviving the Cyclops, but not wrestling with one among the Elohim in order to win a new name for himself. Truly Jewgreek, Poldy has forsworn the Covenant, even if he cannot escape from having been chosen. Joyce, too, has abandoned the Church, but cannot escape the intellectual discipline of the Jesuits. Poldy's sense of election is a little more mysterious, or perhaps it is Joyce's sense of his hero's election that is the true mystery of the book. At the end of the Cyclops episode, Joyce evidently felt the necessity of distancing himself from Poldy, if only because literary irony fails when confronted by the heroic pathos of a creation that defies even Joyce's control.

> —Are you talking about the new Jerusalem? says the citizen.
> —I'm talking about injustice, says Bloom.
> —Right, says John Wyse. Stand up to it then with force like men.

But that is of course not Poldy's way. No interpolated sarcasm, however dramatically wrought, is able to modify the dignity of Poldy's rejoinder:

> —But it's no use, says he. Force, hatred, history, all that. That's
> not life for men and women, insult and hatred. And everybody
> knows that it's the very opposite of that that is really life.
> —What, says Alf.
> —Love, says Bloom. I mean the opposite of hatred.

Twelve delirious pages of hyperbole and phantasmagoria follow, detailing the forced exit of the noble Poldy from the pub, and ending in a grand send-up indeed:

> When, lo, there came about them all a great brightness and they
> beheld the chariot wherein He stood ascend to heaven. And they
> beheld Him in the chariot, clothed upon in the glory of the bright-
> ness, having raiment as of the sun, fair as the moon and terrible

that for awe they durst not look upon Him. And there came a voice out of heaven, calling: *Elijah*! *Elijah*! And he answered with a main cry: *Abba*! *Adonai*! And they beheld Him even Him, ben Bloom Elijah, amid clouds of angels ascend to the glory of the brightness at an angle of forty-five degrees over Donohoe's in Little Green Street like a shot off a shovel.

It is all in the juxtaposition of "ben Bloom Elijah" and "like a shot off a shovel," at once a majestic deflation and a complex apotropaic gesture on Joyce's own part. Like Falstaff and Sancho Panza, Poldy runs off with the book, and Joyce's strenuous ironies, dwarfing the wit of nearly all other authors, essentially are so many reaction-formations against his love for (and identity with) his extraordinary hero. Homer's Ulysses may be as complete as Poldy, but you wouldn't want to be in one boat with him (you would drown, he would survive). Poldy would comfort you in every sorrow, even as he empathizes so movingly with the pangs of women in childbirth.

Joyce was not Flaubert, who at once was Madame Bovary and yet was wholly detached from her, at least in aesthetic stance. But how do you maintain a fixed stance toward Poldy? Falstaff is the monarch of wit, and Sancho Panza the Pope of innocent cunning. Poldy's strength, as Joyce evidently intended, is in his completeness. "The complete man" is necessarily a trope, but for what? On one side, for range of affect; like Tennyson's Ulysses, Poldy is a part of all that he has met. His curiosity, his susceptibility, his compassion, his potential interest—these are infinite. On another side, for cognitive activity; Poldy, unlike Stephen, is certainly not brilliant, and yet he has a never-resting mind, as Ulysses must have. He can be said to have a Shakespearean mind, though he resembles no one in Shakespeare (a comparison of Poldy and Shylock is instructive). Poldy is neither Hamlet nor Falstaff, but perhaps he is Shakespeare, or Shakespeare reborn as James Joyce, even as Stephen is the younger Dante reincarnated as Joyce. We can think of Poldy as Horatio to Stephen's Hamlet, since Horatio represents us, the audience, and we represent Shakespeare. Poldy is our representative, and it is Joyce's greatest triumph that increasingly we represent him, as we always have and will represent Shakespeare.

Post-Structuralist Joyce never wearies of reminding us that Poldy is a trope, but it is truer to say that we are tropes for Poldy, who as a super-mimesis of essential nature is beyond us. I may never recover from a walk through a German park with a dear friend who is the most distinguished of post-Structuralists. When I remarked to him, in my innocent cunning, that Poldy was the most lovable person in Western fiction, I provoked him to the annoyed response that Poldy was not a person, but only language, and that Joyce, unlike myself, knew this very well. Joyce knew very well that Poldy was more than a person, but only in the sense that Poldy was a humane and humanized God, a God who had become truly a bereft father, anguishing for his lost Rudy. Poldy is not a person only if God is not a person, and the God of the Jews, for all his transcendental sublimities, is also very much a person and a personality, as befits his immanent sub-limities. Surely the uniqueness of Yahweh, among all the rival godlings, is that Yahweh is complete. Yahweh is the complete God, even as Poldy is the complete man, and God, after all, like Poldy, is Jewish.

French post-Structuralism is of course only a belated modernism, since everything from abroad is absorbed so slowly in xenophobic Paris. French Hegel, French Freud, French Joyce are all after the event, as it were, just as French romanticism was a rather delayed phenomenon. French Joyce is about as close to the text of *Ulysses* and *Finnegans Wake* as Lacan is to the text of *Three Essays on the Theory of Sexuality* or Derrida to Hegel and Hei-degger. Nor should they be, since cultural belatedness or Alexandrianism demands the remedy of misprision, or creative misreading. To say that "meaning" keeps its distance from Poldy is both to forget that Poldy is the Messiah (though which Messiah is not clear) and that one name (Kabbal-istic) for Yahweh is "language." The difference between Joyce and French Joyce is that Joyce tropes God as language and the belated Parisians (and their agents) trope the Demiurge as language, which is to say that Joyce, heroic naturalist, was not a Gnostic and Lacan was (perhaps unknowingly).

As a knowing Gnostic, I lament the loss of Joycean heroic naturalism and of Poldy's natural heroism. Let them deconstruct Don Quixote; the results will be as sorrowful. Literary criticism is a mode which teaches us not only to read Poldy as Sancho Panza and Stephen as the Don, but more amiably takes us back to Cervantes, to read Sancho as Poldy. By a Borgesian blessing in the art of mistaken attribution, we then will learn to read not only *Hamlet* and the *Inferno* as written by Joyce, but *Don Quixote* as well, with the divine Sancho as an Irish Jew!

Joyce necessarily is closer to Shakespeare than to Cervantes, and Joyce's obsession with *Hamlet* is crucial in *Ulysses*. His famous reading of Hamlet, as expounded by Stephen, can be regarded as a subtle coming-to-terms with Shakespeare as his most imposing literary father in the English language. Ellmann, certainly the most reliable of all Joyce scholars, insisted that Joyce "exhibits none of that anxiety of influence which has been at-tributed to modern writers. . . . If Joyce had any anxiety, it was over not incorporating influences enough." This matter is perhaps more dialectical than Ellmann realized. Not Dante, but Shakespeare is Joyce's Virgil, as Ellmann also notes, and just as Dante's poetic voice matures even as Virgil fades out of the *Commedia*, so Shakespeare had to fade out of *Ulysses* even as Joyce's voice matured.

In Stephen's theory, Shakespeare is the dead king, rather than the young Hamlet, who becomes the type of the Romantic artist, Stephen himself. Shakespeare, like the ghost, has been betrayed, except than Anne Hathaway went Gertrude one better, and cuckolded the Bard with both his brothers. This sexual defeat has been intensified by Shakespeare's loss of the dark lady of the sonnets, and to his best friend, a kind of third brother. Shakespeare's revenge is to resurrect his own dead son, Hamnet, who enters the play as Prince Hamlet, with the purpose of vindicating his father's honor. Such a resurrected son appears to be free of the Oedipal ambivalences, and in Joyce's view does not lust after Gertrude or feel any jealousy, however repressed, for the dead father. So Stephen and Poldy, as two aspects of Shakespeare/Joyce, during the "Circe" episode gaze into a mirror and behold a transformed Shakespeare, beardless and frozen-faced ("rigid in facial paralysis"). I do not interpret this either as the view that Poldy and Stephen "amount only to a paralytic travesty of a Shakespeare" (W. M. Schutte) or that "Joyce warns us that he is working with near-identities, not perfect ones" (Ellmann). Rather, I take it as a sign of influence-anxiety, as the precursor Shakespeare mocking the ephebe Joyce: "Be like me, but you presume in attempting to be too much like me. You are merely a beardless version, rigid in facial paralysis, lacking my potency and my ease of countenance."

The obscene Buck Mulligan, Joyce's black beast, weakly misreads *Hamlet* as masturbation and Poldy as a pederast. Joyce himself, through Stephen, strongly misreads *Hamlet* as the cuckold's revenge, a play presumably likelier to have been written by Poldy than by Stephen. In a stronger misreading still, I would suggest that Joyce rewrites *Hamlet* so as to destroy the element in the play that most menaces him, which is the very different, uncannily disinterested Hamlet of Act V. Stephen quotes the subtle Sabellian heresy that the Father was Himself His Own Son. But what we may call the even subtler Shakespearean heresy (which is also Freudian) holds rather that the Son was Himself His Own Father. This is the Hamlet of Act V, who refers to his dead father only once, and then only as the king. Joyce's Hamlet has no Oedipus complex. Shakespeare's Hamlet may have had one, but it passes away in the interval between Acts IV and V.

Stephen as the Prince does not convince me; Poldy as the ghost of the dead king, and so as Shakespeare/Joyce, is rather more troublesome. One wishes the ghost could be exorcised, leaving us with the fine trinity of Shakespeare/Poldy/Joyce, with Poldy as the transitional figure reconciling forerunner and latecomer, a sort of Messiah perhaps. Shakespeare is the original Testament or old aesthetic Law, while Joyce is the belated Testament or new aesthetic dispensation. Poldy is the inter-Testamentary figure, apocryphal and apocalyptic, and yet overwhelmingly a representation of life in the here and now. Joyce went on to write *Finnegans Wake*, the only legitimate rival to Proust's vast novel in the Western literature of our time. More than the difficulties, both real and imaginary, of the *Wake* have kept Joyce's common readers centered upon *Ulysses*. Earwicker is a giant hieroglyph; Poldy is a person, complete and loving, self-reliant, larger, and more evocative even than his book.

II

In May 1940, less than a year before she drowned herself, Virginia Woolf read a paper to the Worker's Educational Association in Brighton. We know it as the essay entitled "The Leaning Tower," in which the Shelleyan emblem of the lonely tower takes on more of a social than an imaginative meaning. It is no longer the point of survey from which the poet Athanase gazes down in pity at the dark estate of mankind, and so is not an image of contemplative wisdom isolated from the mundane. Instead, it is "the tower of middle-class birth and expensive education," from which the poetic generation of W. H. Auden and Louis MacNeice stare sidelong at society. Woolf does not say so, but we can surmise that she preferred Shelley to Auden, while realizing that she herself dwelt in the leaning tower, unlike Yeats, to whom the lonely tower remained an inevitable metaphor for poetic stance.

It is proper that "The Leaning Tower," as a speculation upon the decline of a Romantic image into belatedness, should concern itself also with the peculiarities of poetic influence:

> Theories then are dangerous things. All the same we must risk making one this afternoon since we are going to discuss modern tendencies. Directly we speak of tendencies or movements we commit ourselves to the belief that there is some force, influence, outer pressure which is strong enough to stamp itself upon a whole group of different writers so that all their writing has a certain common likeness. We must then have a theory as to what this influence is. But let us always remember—influences are infinitely numerous; writers are infinitely sensitive; each writer has a different sensibility. That is why literature is always changing, like the weather, like clouds in the sky. Read a page of Scott; then of Henry James; try to work out the influences that have transformed the one page into the other. It is beyond our skill. We can only hope therefore to single out the most obvious influences that have formed writers into groups. Yet there are groups. Books descend from books as families descend from families. Some descend from Jane Austen; others from Dickens. They resemble their parents, as human children resemble their parents; yet they differ as children differ, and revolt as children revolt. Perhaps it will be easier to understand living writers as we take a quick look at some of their forbears.

A critic of literary influence learns to be both enchanted and wary when such a passage is encountered. Sensibility is indeed the issue, since without "a different sensibility" no writer truly is a writer. Woolf's sensibility essentially is Paterian, as Perry Meisel accurately demonstrated. She is hardly unique among the great Modernist writers in owing much to Pater. That group includes Wilde, Yeats, Wallace Stevens, Hart Crane, as well as Pound and Eliot. Among the novelists, the Paterians, however involuntary, include Scott Fitzgerald, the early Joyce, and in strange ways both Conrad and Lawrence, as well as Woolf. Of all these, Woolf is most authentically Pater's child. Her central tropes, like his, are personality and death, and her ways of representing consciousness are very close to his. The literary ancestor of those curious twin sensibilities—Septimus Smith and Clarissa Dalloway—is Pater's Sebastian Van Storck, except that Woolf relents, and they do not go into Sebastian's "formless and nameless infinite world, quite evenly grey."

Mrs. Dalloway (1925), the fourth of Woolf's nine novels, is her first extraordinary achievement. Perhaps she should have called it *The Hours*, its original working title. To speak of measuring one's time by days or months, rather than years, has urgency, and this urgency increases when the fiction of duration embraces only hours, as *Mrs. Dalloway* does. The novel's peculiar virtue is the enigmatic doubling between Clarissa Dalloway and Septimus Smith, who do not know one another. We are persuaded that the book is not disjointed because Clarissa and Septimus uncannily share what seems a single consciousness, intense and vulnerable, each fearing to be consumed by a fire perpetually about to break forth. Woolf seems to cause Septimus to die instead of Clarissa, almost as though the novel is a single apotropaic gesture on its author's part. One thinks of the death died for Marius by Cornelius in Pater's *Marius the Epicurean*, but that is one friend atoning for another. However unified, does *Mrs. Dalloway* cogently link Clarissa and Septimus?

Clearly the book does, but only through its manipulation of Pater's evasions of the figure or trope of the self as the center of a flux of sensations. In a book review written when she was only twenty-five, Woolf made a rough statement of the stance towards the self she would take throughout her work-to-come, in the form of a Paterian rhetorical question: "Are we not each in truth the centre of innumerable rays which so strike upon one figure only, and is it not our business to flash them straight and completely back again, and never suffer a single shaft to blunt itself on the far side of us?" Here is Clarissa Dalloway, at the novel's crucial epiphany, not suffering the rays to blunt themselves on the far side of her:

> What business had the Bradshaws to talk of death at her party? A young man had killed himself. And they talked of it at her party—the Bradshaws talked of death. He had killed himself—but how? Always her body went through it first, when she was told, suddenly, of an accident; her dress flamed, her body burnt. He had thrown himself from a window. Up had flashed the ground; through him, blundering, bruising, went the rusty spikes. There he lay with a thud, thud, thud in his brain, and then a suffocation of blackness. So she saw it. But why had he done it? And the Bradshaws talked of it at her party!
>
> She had once thrown a shilling into the Serpentine, never anything more. But he had flung it away. They went on living (she would have to go back; the rooms were still crowded; people kept on coming). They (all day she had been thinking of Bourton, of Peter, of Sally), they would grow old. A thing there was that

mattered; a thing, wreathed about with chatter, defaced, obscured in her own life, let drop every day in corruption, lies, chatter. This he had preserved. Death was defiance. Death was an attempt to communicate; people feeling the impossibility of reaching the centre which, mystically, evaded them; closeness drew apart; rapture faded, one was alone. There was an embrace in death.

The evasiveness of the center is defied by the act of suicide, which in Woolf is a communication and not, as it is in Freud, a murder. Earlier, Septimus had been terrified by a "gradual drawing together of everything to one centre before his eyes." The doubling of Clarissa and Septimus implies that there is only a difference in degree, not in kind, between Clarissa's sensibility and the naked consciousness or "madness" of Septimus. Neither needs the encouragement of "Fear no more the heat o' the sun," because each knows that consciousness is isolation and so untruth, and that the right worship of life is to defy that isolation by dying. J. Hillis Miller remarks that: "A novel, for Woolf, is the place of death made visible." It seems to me difficult to defend *Mrs. Dalloway* from moral judgments that call Woolf's stance wholly nihilistic. But then, *Mrs. Dalloway*, remarkable as it is, is truly Woolf's starting-point as a strong writer, and not her conclusion.

Critics tend to agree that Woolf's finest novel is *To the Lighthouse* (1927), which is certainly one of the central works of the modern imagination, comparable to Lawrence's *The Rainbow* or Conrad's *Victory*, if not quite of the range of *Women in Love* or *Nostromo*. Perhaps it is the only novel in which Woolf displays all of her gifts at once. Erich Auerbach, in his *Mimesis*, lucidly summing up Woolf's achievement in her book, could be expounding Pater's trope of the privileged moment:

> What takes place here in Virginia Woolf's novel is . . . to put the emphasis on the random occurrence, to exploit it not in the service of a planned continuity of action but in itself. And in the process something new and elemental appeared: nothing less than the wealth of reality and depth of life in every moment to which we surrender ourselves without prejudice. To be sure, what happens in that moment—be it outer or inner processes—concerns in a very personal way the individuals who live in it, but it also (and for that very reason) concerns the elementary things which men in general have in common. It is precisely the random moment which is comparatively independent of the controversial and unstable orders over which men fight and despair; it passes unaffected by them, as daily life. The more it is exploited, the more the elementary things which our lives have in common come to light. The more numerous, varied, and simple the people are who appear as subjects of such random moments, the more effectively must what they have in common shine forth.

The shining forth is precisely Pater's secularization of the epiphany, in which random moments are transformed: "A sudden light transfigures a trivial thing, a weathervane, a windmill, a winnowing flail, the dust in the barn door; a moment—and the thing has vanished, because it was pure effect." Woolf, like Pater sets herself "to realize this situation, to define, in a chill and empty atmosphere, the focus where rays, in themselves pale and impotent, unite and begin to burn." To realize such a situation is to set oneself against the vision of Mr. Ramsay (Woolf's father, the philosopher Leslie Stephen), which expresses itself in the grimly empiricist maxim that: "The very stone one kicks with one's boot will outlast Shakespeare." Against this can be set Lily Briscoe's vision, which concludes the novel:

> Quickly, as if she were recalled by something over there, she turned to her canvas. There it was—her picture. Yes, with all its greens and blues, its lines running up and across, its attempt at something. It would be hung in the attics, she thought; it would be destroyed. But what did that matter? she asked herself, taking up her brush again. She looked at the steps; they were empty; she looked at her canvas; it was blurred. With a sudden intensity, as if she saw it clear for a second, she drew a line there, in the centre. It was done; it was finished. Yes, she thought, laying down her brush in extreme fatigue, I have had my vision.

"An attempt at something" postulates, for Woolf, a center, however evasive. The apotheosis of aesthetic or perceptive principle here is Woolf's beautifully poised and precarious approach to an affirmation of the difficult possibility of meaning. *The Waves* (1931) is a large-scale equivalent of Lily Briscoe's painting. Bernard, the most comprehensive of the novel's six first-person narrators, ends the book with a restrained exultation, profoundly representative of Woolf's feminization of the Paterian aesthetic stance:

> "Again I see before me the usual street. The canopy of civilisation is burnt out. The sky is dark as polished whale-bone. But there is a kindling in the sky whether of lamplight or of dawn. There is a stir of some sort—sparrows on plain trees somewhere chirping. There is a sense of the break of day. I will not call it dawn. What is dawn in the city to an elderly man standing in the street looking up rather dizzily at the sky? Dawn is some sort of whitening of the sky; some sort of renewal. Another day; another Friday; another twentieth of March, January, or September. Another general awakening. The stars draw back and are extinguished. The bars deepen themselves between the waves. The film of mist thickens on the field. A redness gathers on the roses, even on the pale rose that hangs by the bedroom window. A bird chirps. Cottagers light their early candles. Yes, this is the eternal renewal, the incessant rise and fall and fall and rise again.
>
> "And in me too the wave rises. It swells; it arches its back. I am aware once more of a new desire, something rising beneath me

like the proud horse whose rider first spurs and then pulls him back. What enemy do we now perceive advancing against us, you whom I ride now, as we stand pawing this stretch of pavement? It is death. Death is the enemy. It is death against whom I ride with my spear couched and my hair flying back like a young man's, like Percival's, when he galloped in India. I strike spurs into my horse. Against you I will fling myself, unvanquished and unyielding, O Death!"

The waves broke on the shore.

"Incessant rise and fall and fall and rise again," though ascribed to Bernard, has in it the fine pathos of a recognition of natural harshness that does not come often to a male consciousness. And for all the warlike imagery, the ride against death transcends aggressivity, whether against the self or against others. Pater had insisted that our one choice lies in packing as many pulsations of the artery, or Blakean visions of the poet's work, into our interval as possible. Woolf subtly hints that even Pater succumbs to a male illusion of experiential quantity, rather than to a female recognition of gradations in the quality of possible experience. A male critic might want to murmur, in defense of Pater, that male blindness of the void within experience is very difficult to overcome, and that Pater's exquisite sensibility is hardly male, whatever the accident of his gender.

Between the Acts (1941), Woolf's final novel, can be read as a covert and witty subversion of late Shakespeare, whose romances Woolf attempts to expose as being perhaps more male than universal in some of their implications. Parodying Shakespeare is a dangerous mode; the flat-out farce of Max Beerbohm and Nigel Dennis works more easily than Woolf's allusive deftness, but Woolf is not interested in the crudities of farce. *Between the Acts* is her deferred fulfillment of the polemical program set forth in her marvelous polemic *A Room of One's Own* (1929), which is still the most persuasive of all feminist literary manifestos. To me the most powerful and unnerving stroke in that book is in its trope for the enclosure that men have forced upon women:

> For women have sat indoors all these millions of years, so that by this time the very walls are permeated by their creative force, which has, indeed, so overcharged the capacity of bricks and mortar that it must needs harness itself to pens and brushes and business and politics. But this creative power differs greatly from the creative power of man.

That last assertion is becoming a kind of shibboleth in contemporary feminist literary criticism. Whether George Eliot and Henry James ought to be read as instances of a gender-based difference in creative power is not beyond all critical dispute. Is Dorothea Brooke more clearly the product of a woman's creative power than Isabel Archer would be? Could we necessarily know that Clarissa Harlowe ensues from a male imagination?

Woolf, at the least, lent her authority to provoking such questions. That authority, earned by novels of the splendor of *To the Lighthouse* and *Between the Acts*, becomes more formidable as the years pass.

III

Art was too long for Lawrence; life too close.
—R. P. BLACKMUR

Lawrence no longer needs the kind of defense that he required in the 1950s, which was the age of critical formalism, when R. P. Blackmur, Allen Tate, and their precursor T. S. Eliot reigned over the world of letters. The Romantic tradition has been reinstated, and has its own ironical triumph. The poet Eliot is widely recognized now as one of its monuments, akin to his actual precursors, Whitman and Tennyson. And more ironically still, when I compare Blackmur and Tate to nearly any current critics, I see that Blackmur and Tate are to be praised as having more in common with Walter Pater than with my brethren.

Blackmur and Tate do not confuse poets with slumlords, as neo-Marxists do. They do not confuse poetry with post-Hegelian philosophy, do not read codes instead of poems, and do not worship a Gallo-Germano Demiurge named or troped as "Language." Unfortunately, they did mix poetry up with Eliot's version of theology, but at least they never forgot the claims of experience and of the aesthetic in itself, even though they frequently forgot that these claims took precedence over what Eliot had taught them was "the tradition." Eliot expelled Lawrence as a modern heretic in *After Strange Gods*, while confidently declaring the eminent orthodoxy of James Joyce. Lawrence was a Protestant apocalyptic, as religious as Blake, but also a personal mythmaker like Blake. If the churches are Christian, then Blake and Lawrence are not, though they are altogether religious in their visions.

Joyce, like his truest precursors, Dante and Shakespeare, was a poet of the secular world. Eliot's malign critical influence has given us the Joyce of Hugh Kenner and his disciples, for whom Joyce might as well be St. Augustine, and for whom poor Poldy is a benighted Liberal Jew, bogged in Original Sin. This is hardly the Joyce or the Poldy of Richard Ellmann and William Empson, or of the common reader. Joyce was not religious, not a believer, nor particularly fond of the Roman Catholic Church. As for Poldy, if you can still read, and still believe that writers can represent persons in their books, then Poldy—gently sinful, Jewish, liberal—remains the kindest, most humane, and altogether most lovable character in modern prose fiction.

Lawrence, hardly a libertine, had the radically Protestant sensibility of Milton, Shelley, Browning, Hardy—none of them Eliotic favorites. To say that Lawrence was more a Puritan than Milton is only to state what is now finely obvious. What Lawrence shares with Milton is an intense exaltation of unfallen human sexuality. With Blake, Lawrence shares the conviction that touch, the sexual sense proper, is the least fallen of the senses, which implies that redemption is most readily a sexual process. Freud and Lawrence, according to Lawrence, share little or nothing, which accounts for Lawrence's ill-informed but wonderfully vigorous polemic against Freud:

> This is the moral dilemma of psychoanalysis. The analyst set out to cure neurotic humanity by removing the cause of the neurosis. He finds that the cause of neurosis lies in some unadmitted sex desire. After all he has said about inhibition of normal sex, he is brought at last to realize that at the root of almost every neurosis lies some incest-craving, and that this incest-craving is *not the result of inhibition and normal sex-craving*. Now see the dilemma—it is a fearful one. If the incest-craving is not the outcome of any inhibition of normal desire, if it actually exists and refuses to give way before any criticism, what then? What remains but to accept it as part of the normal sex-manifestation?
>
> Here is an issue which analysis is perfectly willing to face. Among themselves the analysts are bound to accept the incest-craving as part of the normal sexuality of man, normal, but suppressed, because of moral and perhaps biological fear. Once, however, you accept the incest-craving as part of the normal sexuality of man, you must remove all repression of incest itself. In fact, you must admit incest as you now admit sexual marriage, as a duty even. Since at last it works out that neurosis is not the result of inhibition of so-called *normal* sex, but of inhibition of incest-craving. Any inhibition must be wrong, since inevitably in the end it causes neurosis and insanity. Therefore the inhibition of incest-craving is wrong, and this wrong is the cause of practically all modern neurosis and insanity.

To believe that Freud thought that "any inhibition must be wrong" is merely outrageous. Philip Rieff subtly defends Lawrence's weird accusation by remarking that: "As a concept, the incest taboo, like any other Freudian hypothesis, represents a scientific projection of the false standards governing erotic relations within the family." Lawrence surely sensed this, but chose to misunderstand Freud, for some of the same reasons he chose to misunderstand Walt Whitman. Whitman provoked in Lawrence an anxiety of influence in regard to stance and form. Freud, also too authentic a precursor, threatened Lawrence's therapeutic originality. Like Freud, Lawrence's ideas of drive or will stem from Schopenhauer and from Nietzsche, and again like Freud, Lawrence derived considerable stimulus from later nineteenth-century materialistic thought. It is difficult to remember that so flamboyant a mythmaker as Lawrence was also a de-idealizer with a reductionist aspect, but then we do not see that Freud was a great mythmaker only because we tend to believe in Freud's myths. When I was young, I knew many young women and young men who believed in Lawrence's myths, but they all have weathered the belief, and I do not encounter any Lawrentian believers among the young today.

Rereading *The Rainbow* and *Women in Love* after many years, I find them very different from what I had remembered. Decades ago I knew both books so thoroughly that I could anticipate most paragraphs, let alone chapters, but I too had half-believed in Lawrence, and had read as a half-believer. Now the books seem richer and stranger, clearly an audacious and relevant myth, and far more original than I had recalled. States of being, modes of consciousness, ambivalences of the will are represented with a clarity and vividness that are uncanny, because the ease of representation for such difficult apprehensions seems unprecedented in prose fiction. Lawrence at his strongest is an astonishing writer, adept at saying what cannot be said, showing what cannot be shown. *The Rainbow* and, even more, *Women in Love* are his triumphs, matched only by a few of his poems, though by many of his short stories. In the endless war between men and women, Lawrence fights on both sides. He is unmatched at rendering really murderous lovers' quarrels, as in chapter 23, "Excurse," of *Women in Love*, where Ursula and Birkin suffer one of their encounters upon what Lawrence calls "this memorable battlefield":

"I jealous! *I*—jealous! You *are* mistaken if you think that. I'm not jealous in the least of Hermione, she is nothing to me, not *that!*" And Ursula snapped her fingers. "No, it's you who are a liar. It's you who must return, like a dog to his vomit. It is what Hermione *stands* for that I *hate*. I *hate* it. It is lies, it is false, it is death. But you want it, you can't help it, you can't help yourself. You belong to that old, deathly way of living—then go back to it. But don't come to me, for I've nothing to do with it."

And in the stress of her violent emotion, she got down from the car and went to the hedgerow, picking unconsciously some flesh-pink spindleberries, some of which were burst, showing their orange seeds.

"Ah, you are a fool," he cried bitterly, with some contempt.

"Yes, I am. I *am* a fool. And thank God for it. I'm too big a fool to swallow your cleverness. God be praised. You go to your women—go to them—they are your sort—you've always had a string of them trailing after you—and you always will. Go to your spiritual brides—but don't come to me as well, because I'm not having any, thank you. You're not satisfied, are you? Your spiritual brides can't give you what you want, they aren't common and fleshy enough for you, aren't they? So you come to me, and keep them in the background! You will marry me for daily use. But you'll keep yourself well provided with spiritual brides in the background. I know your dirty little game." Suddenly a flame ran over her, and she stamped her foot madly on the road, and he winced, afraid that she would strike him. "And *I*, *I'm* not spiritual enough,

I'm not as spiritual as that Hermione —!'' Her brows knitted, her eyes blazed like a tiger's. "Then *go* to her, that's all I say, *go* to her, *go*. Ha, she spiritual—*spiritual*, she! A dirty materialist as she is. *She* spiritual? What does she care for, what is her spirituality? What *is* it?'' Her fury seemed to blaze out and burn his face. He shrank a little. "I tell you, it's *dirt*, *dirt*, and nothing *but* dirt. And it's dirt you want, you crave for it. Spiritual! Is *that* spiritual, her bullying, her conceit, her sordid materialism? She's a fishwife, a fishwife, she is such a materialist. And all so sordid. What does she work out to, in the end, with all her social passion, as you call it. Social passion—what social passion has she?—show it me!— where is it? She wants petty, immediate *power*, she wants the illusion that she is a great woman, that is all. In her soul she's a devilish unbeliever, common as dirt. That's what she is, at the bottom. And all the rest is pretence—but you love it. You love the sham spiritually, it's your food. And why? Because of the dirt underneath. Do you think I don't know the foulness of your sex life—and hers?—I do. And it's that foulness you want, you liar. Then have it, have it. You're such a liar.''

She turned away, spasmodically tearing the twigs of spindle-berry from the hedge, and fastening them, with vibrating fingers, in the bosom of her coat.

He stood watching in silence. A wonderful tenderness burned in him at the sight of her quivering, so sensitive fingers: and at the same time he was full of rage and callousness.

This passage-at-arms moves between Ursula's unconscious picking of the fleshly, burst spindleberries, open to their seeds, and her turning away, tearing the spindleberry twigs so as to fasten them in her coat. Birkin reads the spindleberries as the exposed flesh of what Freud called one's own bodily ego, suffering here a *sparagmos* by a maenad-like Ursula. It is as though Birkin himself, lashed by her language, becomes a frontier being, caught between psyche and body. Repelled yet simultaneously drawn by a sort of Orphic wonder, Birkin yields to her ferocity that is not so much jealousy as it is the woman's protest against Birkin's Lawrentian and male idealization of sexual love. What Ursula most deeply rejects is that the idealization is both flawed and ambivalent, because it is founded upon a displaced Protestantism that both craves total union and cannot abide such annihilation of individuality. Birkin-Lawrence has in him the taint of the Protestant God, and implicitly is always announcing to Ursula: "Be like me, but do not dare to be too like me!'' an injunction that necessarily infuriates Ursula. Since Lawrence is both Birkin and Ursula, he has the curious trait, for a novelist, of perpetually infuriating himself.

Lawrence compares oddly with the other major British writers of fiction in this century: Hardy, Conrad, Kipling, Joyce, Forster, Woolf, Beckett. He is primarily a religious writer, precisely apocalyptic; they are not, unless you count Beckett, by negation. His last book, *Apocalypse*, written as he died slowly in the winter of 1929–30, begins with Lawrence remembering that his own first feeling about the Revelation of John, and indeed of the entire Bible, was negative:

> Perhaps the most detestable of all these books of the Bible, taken superficially, is Revelation. By the time I was ten, I am sure I had heard, and read, that book ten times over, even without knowing or taking real heed. And without ever knowing or thinking about it, I am sure it always roused in me a real dislike. Without realising it, I must, from earliest childhood have detested the pie-pie, mouthing, solemn, portentous, loud way in which everybody read the Bible, whether it was parsons or teachers or ordinary persons. I dislike the "parson" voice through and through my bones. And this voice, I remember, was always at its worst when mouthing out some portion of Revelation. Even the phrases that still fascinate me I cannot recall without shuddering, because I can still hear the portentous declamation of a nonconformist clergyman: "And I saw heaven opened, and behold a white horse; and he that sat upon it was called"—there my memory suddenly stops, deliberately blotting out the next words: "Faithful and True." I hated, even as a child, allegory: people having the names of mere qualities, like this somebody on a white horse, called "Faithful and True." In the same way I could never read *Pilgrim's Progress*. When as a small boy I learnt from Euclid that: "The whole is greater than the part," I immediately knew that that solved the problem of allegory for me. A man is more than a Christian, a rider on a white horse must be more than mere Faithfulness and Truth, and when people are mere personifications of qualities they cease to be people for me. Though as a young man I almost loved Spenser and his *Faerie Queene*, I had to gulp at his allegory.

Yet by the end of his book, Lawrence has allegorized Revelation into "the dark side of Christianity, of individualism, and of democracy, the side the world at large now shows us." This side Lawrence simply calls "suicide":

> The Apocalypse shows us what we are resisting, unnaturally. We are unnaturally resisting our connection with the cosmos, with the world, with mankind, with the nation, with the family. All these connections are, in the Apocalypse, anathema, and they are anathema to us. We *cannot bear connection*. That is our malady. We *must* break away, and be isolate. We call that being free, being individual. Beyond a certain point, which we have reached, it is suicide. Perhaps we have chosen suicide. Well and good. The Apocalypse too chose suicide, with subsequent self-glorification.

This would seem to be no longer the voice of Birkin, who in effect said to Ursula: "We *must* break away, and be isolate," but who never learned how to stress properly his antithetical desire for connection. Lawrence, approaching his own end, is suddenly moved to what may be his single most powerful utterance, surpassing even the greatest passages in the fiction and the late poetry:

> But the Apocalypse shows, by its very resistance, the things that the human heart secretly yearns after. By the very frenzy with which the Apocalypse destroys the sun and the stars, the world, and all kings and all rulers, all scarlet and purple and cinnamon, all harlots, finally all men altogether who are not "sealed," we can see how deeply the apocalyptists are yearning for the sun and the stars and the earth and the waters of the earth, for nobility and lordship and might, and scarlet and gold splendour, for passionate love, and a proper unison with men, apart from this sealing business. What man most passionately wants is his living wholeness and his living unison, not his own isolate salvation of his "soul." Man wants his physical fulfillment first and foremost, since now, once and once only, he is in the flesh and potent. For man, the vast marvel is to be alive. For man, as for flower and beast and bird, the supreme triumph is to be most vividly, most perfectly alive. Whatever the unborn and the dead may know, they cannot know the beauty, the marvel of being alive in the flesh. The dead may look after the afterwards. But the magnificent here and now of life in the flesh is ours, and ours alone, and ours only for a time. We ought to dance with rapture that we should be alive and in the flesh, and part of the living, incarnate cosmos. I am part of the sun as my eye is part of me. That I am part of the earth my feet know perfectly, and my blood is part of the sea. My soul knows that I am part of the human race, my soul is an organic part of the great human soul, as my spirit is part of my nation. In my own very self, I am part of my family. There is nothing of me that is alone and absolute except my mind, and we shall find that the mind has no existence by itself, it is only the glitter of the sun on the surface of the waters.

Starting with the shrewd realization that apocalyptic frenzy is a reaction-formation to a deep yearning for fulfillment, this celebratory passage moves rapidly into an ecstasy of heroic vitalism, transcending the Zarathustra of Nietzsche and the related reveries of Pater in the "Conclusion" to *The Renaissance*. Lawrence may not have known that these were his ancestral texts in this rhapsody, but I suspect that he deliberately transumes Pater's "we have an interval, and then our place knows us no more," in his own: "But the magnificent here and now of life in the flesh is ours, and ours alone, and ours only for a time." Pater, hesitant and elaborate, skeptical and masochistic, added: "For our one chance lies in expanding that interval, in getting as many pulsations as possible into the given time."

Lawrence, truly apocalyptic only in his vitalism, aligns himself rather with Whitman and Blake in refusing that aesthetic one chance, in favor of the dream of becoming integral, rather than a fragment:

> What we want is to destroy our false, inorganic connections, especially those related to money, and re-establish the living organic connections, with the cosmos, the sun and earth, with mankind and nation and family. Start with the sun, and the rest will slowly, slowly happen.

Lawrence died four months short of his forty-fifth birthday, with every evidence that he was making a fresh start as poet and as visionary polemicist. As a novelist, he had suffered a decline, in the movement from the eminence of *The Rainbow* (1915) and *Women in Love* (1920) through the very problematical *Aaron's Rod* (1922) and *Kangaroo* (1923) on to the spectacular disaster of *The Plumed Serpent* (1926) and the somewhat tendentious *Lady Chatterley's Lover* (1928). Lawrence's greatest pride was in his achievement as a novelist, but it is the short novels and tales of his last decade, rather than the longer fictions, that persuade us how much was lost by his early death.

Despite the intense arguments of Dr. F. R. Leavis, Lawrence is not quite at home in any canon of the great English novelists, particularly when compared to Conrad. Even *The Rainbow* and *Women in Love* share more with Blake and Shelley, Whitman and Nietzsche, than they do with *Middlemarch* and *The Portrait of a Lady*. Beneath their narrative procedures, Lawrence's two great novels essentially are visionary prose poems, inhabited by giant forms acting out the civil wars of the psyche. In the penultimate chapter of *The Rainbow*, aptly titled "The Bitterness of Ecstasy," Ursula and Skrebensky suffer their final embrace together:

> Then there in the great flare of light, she clinched hold of him, hard, as if suddenly she had the strength of destruction, she fastened her arms round him and tightened him in her grip, whilst her mouth sought his in a hard, rending, ever-increasing kiss, till his body was powerless in her grip, his heart melted in fear from the fierce, beaked, harpy's kiss. The water washed again over their feet, but she took no notice. She seemed unaware, she seemed to be pressing in her beaked mouth till she had the heart of him. Then, at last, she drew away and looked at him—looked at him. He knew what she wanted. He took her by the hand and led her across the foreshore, back to the sandhills. She went silently. He felt as if the ordeal of proof was upon him, for life or death. He led her to a dark hollow.
>
> "No, here," she said, going out to the slope full under the moonshine. She lay motionless, with wide-open eyes looking at the moon. He came direct to her, without preliminaries. She held him pinned down at the chest, awful. The fight, the struggle for

consummation was terrible. It lasted till it was agony to his soul, till he succumbed, till he gave way as if dead, lay with his face buried, partly in her hair, partly in the sand, motionless, as if he would be motionless now for ever, hidden away in the dark, buried, only buried, he only wanted to be buried in the goodly darkness, only that, and no more.

He seemed to swoon. It was a long time before he came to himself. He was aware of an unusual motion of her breast. He looked up. Her face lay like an image in the moonlight, the eyes wide open, rigid. But out of her eyes, slowly, there rolled a tear, that glittered in the moonlight as it ran down her cheek.

He felt as if the knife were being pushed into his already dead body. With head strained back, he watched, drawn tense, for some minutes, watched the unaltering, rigid face like metal in the moonlight, the fixed, unseeing eye, in which slowly the water gathered, shook with glittering moonlight, then surcharged, brimmed over and ran trickling, a tear with its burden of moonlight, into the darkness, to fall in the sand.

Dreadfully impressive, this possesses both the force of an experiential representation, and the form of High Romantic mythology. It could be a warring coition of Blake's Los and Enitharmon, an instance of what Blake called a "Reasoning from the loins in the unreal forms of Beulah's night." Presumably Lawrence intended it as part of his prophecy against "sex in the head," but in this instance he wrought too much better, perhaps, than even he knew. The pathos of these paragraphs would be excessive, except for their mythic implications. Short as it was, life was too long for Lawrence, art too close.

The Modus Vivendi
of John Cowper Powys

Timothy Hyman

In surveying Powys's achievement, I want to focus on his work as being, above all, representative of a certain way of life.

If we take *Wolf Solent*, for instance, we see that the book is mainly about one man's method for living, and that the whole shape of the book is expressive of this method. Wolf is a man unable to accept any single reality, or any certain stable belief. Wolf conceives the world as a "multiverse" in which he will contrive to live by "no system at all." Wolf's passage between different versions of reality is the central theme of the book. The reader is therefore shown, in the course of the book, one reality, only to have it broken and substituted for another, which, it is implied, may itself transpire to be no less delusory. What should be emphasised is that, although it does resemble one, *Wolf Solent* is not a dialectical novel (on the lines of Thomas Mann's *Magic Mountain*, for instance). Wolf's passing from one reality to another is not a passing upwards, to wisdom or knowledge. Even at the end of the book, all values remain uncertain.

This is not the uncertainty of youth. *Wolf Solent* was Powys's first major work, yet Powys was almost sixty when he wrote it; and in each of the five long prose romances that followed over the subsequent twenty years he exhibits the same ambivalence. At eighty he was still uncertain.

It seems to me that in this apprehension of a fundamentally uncertain world is the essence of what Powys has to offer us. But it is also this ambiguous, anticlimactic element that makes his books such uncomfortable works of art, and that must probably bear the chief responsibility for his neglect.

Powys may have defined "Art" and "Life" by his own polarity of poet and philosopher. He had spent his earlier years mainly as a popular lecturer,

From *Essays on John Cowper Powys*. © 1972 by The Authors and the University of Wales Press.

travelling the length and breadth of the United States. Especially as a young man, he had written a good deal of verse; but parallel to this he had begun to develop a popular philosophy which he published under titles like *The Art of Happiness* and *A Philosophy of Solitude*.

Powys's verse had been somewhat derivative and aestheticising. Writing to a friend in 1909, when he was already thirty-seven, he asks:

> Have I, I wonder, been all this while on wrong tracks? asking of myself what do you admire most in literature and what therefore would you like to go further with?—instead of what do the secret boy-maids of your inner Self—the beautiful, coy Diapheneites of your hidden thoughts, of your real, native, unalloyed, untampered-with sensations—whisper, when you try to lay all 'literary' influences away and listen to them?

Although they are unstructured and repetitive, Powys's philosophical writings do convey a personal apprehension of life; and, for better or worse, this was the kind of achievement that was to interest Powys most. As he was later to write in his *Autobiography*:

> My writings . . . are simply so much propaganda, as effective as
> I can make it, for my philosophy of life.

It was, I think, a mistake for Powys to have attempted to present his "untampered-with sensations" in the form of philosophic discourse, which cannot really convey the kind of sharply contradictory and complex experience that we have seen to be characteristic of him. But by the time he had discovered the all-inclusive form of the long prose romance, a form that had "no system at all" and could reconcile all his previous activities, the balance had already turned against "Art."

The underlying values that make Powys's fiction, for all its convincing density of texture, so uncomfortable, can best be introduced by surveying his *Autobiography*.

The earlier chapters often recall *The Prelude* recording the "growth of a poet's mind" through a series of intimate, solitary experiences:

> The greatest event in my life at Cambridge was a very quiet event . . . it was a sort of Vision on the Road to Damascus. I remember the exact spot where it took place. Not far from Trumpington Mill—somewhere in the umbrageous purlieus to the rear of the Fitzwilliam Museum—there stands an ancient wall; and as I drifted along . . . I observed, growing upon this wall, certain patches of grass and green moss and yellow stone-crop. Something about the look of these small growths, secluded there in a place seldom passed, and more seldom noticed, seized upon me and caught me up into a sort of Seventh Heaven.
>   A few seconds ago, before touching my pen . . . I felt all that I have ever felt, of the burden of this extraordinary moment . . . I

would call it a *beyond sensation*, and it lies in my consciousness
now, like a sunken ship, full of fathom-deep treasure . . . *that*
impression, that vision of "Living Bread," that mysterious meeting
point of animate with inanimate, had to do with some secret underlying world of rich magic and strange romance. In fact I actually
regarded it as a prophetic idea of the sort of stories that I myself
might come to write.

It was exactly this kind of moment that was to form the foundation
for Powys's doctrine, expounded first in the philosophic books like *In Defence of Sensuality* (where "sensuality" is only of his diffuse and private
kind), and later in the romances, where the breaking through to some such
insight is the recurrent and central experience. The sensation is not easy
to pin down, but it often occurs in Powys together with the epithet "Saturnian": that is, it is a sensation which seems to hark back to a former
age, now vanquished, when all nature was reconciled, an Age of Gold.
Powys knew that one of the central questions that must form about his
work was that of evaluating this kind of sensation. It could so easily seem
too personal or too euphoric. But Powys never lost his belief that such
moments were universally felt and were of enormous power and value.

I know perfectly well that everybody born into the world has the
feelings I am describing, is visited by these indescribable and apparently causeless transports. I am not in the least suggesting that
I am peculiar in this. But why, in the Devil's name, then, do we
go on making a cult of everything else except these?

Powys's "cult" was, accordingly, a cult of these sensations, and it
becomes clear as the *Autobiography* progresses that Powys's great aim in life
is the day-to-day harvesting of such moments. The self of the *Autobiography*,
the peripatetic lecturer whose life is vested not in any single person or
activity but in the "diffusion" of his emotions across the face of the Earth,
is the perfect embodiment of the way of life Powys is proposing.

What I wanted was that kind of romantic struggle with things and
people, things and people always yielding as I advanced, *but not
too easily*, a struggle which takes place in an ideal region, hewn
out of reality and constantly touching but never quite identified
with reality, such as might be most conveniently described by the
expression, *a Quest*.

The development of the *Autobiography* is the steady intensification of
this sense of Quest, with a correspondingly increasing frequency of those
"transporting" moments that are the most real fruits of such a Quest. In
the final chapter, entitled "There's a Mohawk in the Sky!", Powys is at last
actually airborne and is able to see some pattern as he hovers above the
"unrolled map" of his life.

Powys's emphasis on "Quest," rather than on any "real" goal, on diffusion, rather than on focus, results in some extraordinary omissions. As with Rousseau in his *Confessions*, an apparent candour and intimacy deceives us into accepting a thoroughly selective and manipulative record.

There is very little mention of himself as a creative artist, let alone any discussion of individual works (although *Wolf Solent* and *A Glastonbury Romance* had already been written). More enigmatically, it is an *Autobiography* "without women." I believe that implicit in this mutilation of an experience that had included marriage as well as frequent women friends was the conviction that ordinary sexual activity was of small consequence, set beside "Saturnian" pleasures, and that unless sex eluded both the concrete and the domestic it would actually get in the way of these more valuable sensations. In his *Autobiography* Powys is attempting (like Rousseau) to construct a philosophic myth from the elements of his own life in order to preach what he calls elsewhere "the Gospel of the Aquarian Age." He could perhaps *imagine* an equivalent sexuality; but his own *experience* of women did not fit this Aquarian role.

In his fiction, however, Powys is able to accommodate sexuality as a central theme, and the sexual attitudes of his "Aquarian" characters are the most direct expression of their attitude towards the world in general.

What is confirmed in the romances is that sexual relations are indeed the "danger-area" for Powys's life-way. All the major novels share a basic pattern, a cycle in which a life-illusion is first betrayed, and then lost, and the chief agent of this betrayal is invariably some kind of sexual involvement. The sexual theme is especially clear in *Wolf Solent* and in *Maiden Castle*; and here, as in all the romances, the broken world is at the end of the book integrated anew by a "Saturnian" vision of the kind already described.

Experientially, then, sexual failure is the precipitate of the Saturnian vision; and this is, I think, part of the justification of Powys's tendency to evade the commitment involved in genital love. Freud, indeed, ascribes those Saturnian sensations of "universal" love (so important also to Traherne and to Wordsworth) to "infantile narcissism," and Powys never presents a "diffusionist" without a full critique accompanying him. But he simply believed the rewards of such a way redeemed its inadequacies.

But there is also another, "Aquarian," justification. In these individuals the sense of yearning for love in the most spiritualised sense remains ever present; and there is always the possibility that from such a yearning may yet be born with Rimbaud calls "un nouveau corps amoreux," a new amorous body that can be held without any of the deadening or destructive effect of most partnerships. In *Maiden Castle*, Powys suggests there is a basic confusion in genital "lust": there is the "lust" that is "excess of tenderness," but there is also "the 'lust' in a lover's embrace that is alien to love, and indeed may be *the opposite of love*." It is only by the consciousness of such a dissatisfaction that the human race might evolve to some new solution, or even some new mutation.

Wolf Solent is a man whose reality is almost entirely inward and archetypal. Wolf gives this inner life a corporeal identity, calling it his "mythology": it is the image of a plant that lives within him and is fed mostly by the "sensations" he collects on his long solitary walks (which may be seen as a ritualisation of his yearning).

At the outset, then, Wolf is a picaresque hero, armed with a walking stick, wandering into a world of mystery. To his detachment, each character presents himself as embodying some principle of Good or Evil. The obvious lack in Wolf's life of any personal or sexual focus is the whole source of its intensity.

Wolf then becomes entangled with two women, Gerda Torp and Christie Malakite, whose names signify clearly enough their polarisation. Gerda he sleeps with, and marries, but it is the far more elusive Christie who alone stirs his "mythology." Christie and Wolf can certainly share a great deal of one another's experience; but in a very harrowing episode, when their consummation seems already underway, Wolf discovers that he is paralysed. The obstruction is from the mythology itself tugging at him "like a chain fixed to a post," refusing to be trapped in such a decisive act. Subsequently, under terrible pressure from various kinds of failure, Wolf's "mythology" withers and dies.

The novel ends with Wolf's being cuckolded; but, at the moment when he has apparently lost everything, he enters at sundown a field transformed by the horizontal rays of the sun into a "golden sea," releasing an enormous wash of pleasure and illumination.

> What he longed to do was to plunge his own hands into this Saturnian gold, and to pour it out, . . . All . . . all . . . all would reveal some unspeakable beauty, if only this Saturnian gold were sprinkled upon them!

It is in the light of this vision that he can accept the environment revealed by the loss of his mythology, a world less dramatic, but more complex, than the patterns he had imposed upon it. The loss of the mythology is revealed as the only road to a complete perception of the world.

The Powys novel commits suicide, so to speak, in order to gain more life. It is the suicide of Prospero, a renunciation of "rough magic," of the polarities, a deliverance from the "barren island." And yet the taste Powys leaves in the reader's mouth is so different from that finality with which *The Tempest* comes to a close. Powys's ending is in some way abject: the reader feels cheated, he had been led to expect a solution. Like the typical Powys-hero, like Dud No-man in *Maiden Castle*, the Powys novel is impotent.

I have no doubt that this cheating of the reader is conscious and deliberate. Significantly the novel written just before *Wolf Solent* was entitled *Ducdame*: the cry of barren, melancholy Jacques in *As You Like It* (2.5). The scene opens with two stanzas of "Under the greenwood tree," treating of the simple life, to a chorus of "come hither." Jacques declares he has written a third verse; he sings:

> If it do come to pass
> That any man turn ass
> Leaving his wealth and ease
> A stubborn will to please
> Ducdame, ducdame, ducdame.

As he sings this outlandish word, the others begin to gather around him, peering at the paper from which he reads; he then walks out of their circle.

"What's that *ducdame*?" asks one of them; and Jacques explains:

> " 'Tis a Greek invocation to call fools into a circle."

In such a way does Powys draw us into Glastonbury or Weymouth or Dorchester, and in just such a way, when we ask: "What's that *Grail*?" or "What's that *Mythology*?" we discover the author outside it all, mocking us, telling us it was but a trick, so he could draw us together; so he could show us that any such simple meaningful world was a fraud, and that all escape would end in the chaotic complexity of Nature.

This conception of Nature is the theme of *A Glastonbury Romance*. The whole book is set up as an equivalence to Nature's balance between affirmation and negation. The reader is obliged to share in Powys's uncertainty, because those beliefs and doubts that were Wolf's in the earlier novel are here presented as concrete realities. Parallel to the explicit suspense, as to whether those within Glastonbury will be vouchsafed the Grail, is the uncertainty of the reader, as to whether the Grail, or any of the other enormous metaphysical powers the author so coolly introduces, have any existence at all. Our belief is immediately challenged when we encounter in the book's opening sentence the personality of the First Cause. (How many potential readers must simply have put the book down at this point?) But let this work from our knowledge of the individual, and the role of these powers will become obvious.

The obvious successor to Wolf, in Glastonbury, is John Crow. Both are determinedly detached in their experience. Says Wolf:

> I'll live in my own world to the end, . . . Nothing shall make me yield.

Says John, in an image that is often repeated:

> I'm a hard, round, glass ball, that is a mirror of everything, but that has a secret landscape of its own in the centre of it.

They both conceive themselves as able to escape commitment to any of the conflicting beliefs that surround them, by a process they call "dissolving." Says John:

I'll steer my life in a region of values totally unknown to any of them! . . . I'll become air, water, fire. I'll flow through their souls . . . I'll possess them without being possessed *by* them!

Their life method depends on a constant motion between their secret landscapes and their dissolving. As we hear of Wolf:

What he lived in was not any compact, continuous sense of personal identity, but rather *a series of disembodied sensations*, some physical, some mental, in which his identity was absolutely merged and lost.

Their metaphysic is equivalent to this; as Wolf sums it up:

anything suggestive of metaphysical unity is distasteful to me. It must be that my world is essentially a manifold world, and my religion, if I have any, essentially polytheistic! And yet, in matters of good and evil . . . I'm what they'd call a dualist . . . Directly one comes to putting feelings into words, one is compelled to accept hopeless contradictions in the very depths of one's being!

Wolf's and John's is the individual metaphysic externalised in the *Romance*. So long as he retains the "hopeless contradictions," Powys can introduce representatives of every conceivable shade of belief. Man gods, sun, moon, or star gods, stone gods, a First Cause, Greek, Celtic, or Christian gods, even "invisible watchers"—

> As in that crystal orb—wise Merlin's feat,—
> The wondrous 'World of Glass,' wherein inisled
> All long'd-for things their beings did repeat—
> (S. T. Coleridge, "The Pang More Sharp
> Than All")

amid so many symbols of order, the suspicion is always present in the reader's mind that there is really "no system at all." But it is clear what the Grail represents in such a world. It is that "distasteful" metaphysical unity which would resolve these "hopeless contradictions."

The Grail is described frequently as a "morsel," a "piece," or a "fragment of the Absolute." When Evans asks himself of the Fisher Kings:

"For what did (they) . . . seek . . . when they fished?" he answers:
"the Amalgam of the Is and Is-not."

The Grail retains this identity with the Fish throughout the book; that is, with the symbol of the Messiah, but also the symbol of Leviathan, the World Fish, who underlies all existence, and whom the Messiah will catch and divide among the Faithful at the Apocalypse. The appearance of a Messiah, and the commencement of the Apocalypse, are the ultimate hopes and expectations in the *Romance*. But just as any "metaphysical unity" would have destroyed the experience of the Powys-hero, so the appearance of the Grail would end the book.

Powys therefore builds into it a chaotic and undermining element. Much follows from his stance of reproducing a Natural process, rather than "artistically" telling a story. Squire Urquhart had explained to Wolf Solent:

> "What I want to do is to isolate the particular portion of the earth's surface called 'Dorset'; as if it were possible to decipher there a palimpsest of successive strata, one inscribed below another, of human impression. Such impressions are for ever being made and for ever being obliterated in the ebb and flow of events; and the chronicle of them should be continuous, not episodic."

But the attraction of such an impressionism, for Urquhart as perhaps for all others, is that it undermines any hierarchies of experience. Urquhart's is clearly a mocking and ironic book, in which equally, nothing or everything is holy.

The fundamental horizontality of the *Romance*—its length, its multi-centredness, the concreteness of thoughts and feelings within it—is a constant threat to any development of plot or action. Powys's narrative method resembles in its evasiveness the *modus vivendi* adopted by John and Wolf. On the brink of any resolution, Powys contrives always to "dissolve," and the reader finds himself transported into the "secret landscape" of one after another of his characters. A chapter begins to resemble a relay race —against the episodic, against meaning.

Powys likens human minds to "unknown planets, encountering and colliding," and we may relate these planets to John's "hard, round, glass ball" that is a mirror of everything, but that contains within itself a secret world. The penetration of that inner landscape by something from outside becomes the pattern of all mystic experience.

Glastonbury's name signifies the town, or island, of glass, and it is often felt as being enclosed beneath a roof of water; while Geard talks in his final speech of "the dream-world whose margins overlap ours." He explains of the Grail that, "Out of this deeper dream there fell of old upon our Glastonbury Something that bewilders and troubles us unto this day." Similarly, Sam describes Christ as "the Thing Outside breaking into our closed circle"; and both he and John experience their vision as the entry of some sharp thing from outside.

Powys's characters thus become at once a polarity to and an extension of his abstract themes. They afford a solidity, and a relief from his questioning, but eventually they reveal at their center the identical problems. Dissolving from the cosmic to the human scale, and then to the microscopic of thoughts and feelings, the image remains the same. All this activity, this constant flight through space, exists only so that Powys can perform a kind of jugglery, can keep his hard, round, glass balls in the air, through a thousand pages.

The action covers exactly a year, the first part beginning on March 5th, the day of the Spring Solstice, and ending on Midsummer's day, on a rising note, with all kinds of promises still in the air. When the second half opens, it is already autumn: and the last three chapters enact a wintry betrayal of all the reader's hopes.

It has been seen that the revelation of the Grail is that which would end the book (because it would resolve the doubt on which it rests); but, when (in the chapter called "The Grail") Sam sees the Grail and tells people of his vision, there is no relief for us. Sam's vision is too personal an experience to have any public resonance. No one is excited, much less do they disbelieve him.

The senseless melodrama of "The Iron Bar" continues this anticlimax. It mercilessly rids the book of nine of its characters, including the "Aquarian" lovers, the cousins John and Mary Crow, whose love is to some extent a flowering of the Grail. They had met in Norfolk, in the uncertain consciousness that they were reliving a childhood romance (uncertain because John suspects it was a boy, Tom Barter, and not Mary, who initiated him in the bottom of a boat). Barter is Mary's closest friend in Glastonbury.

> What John and Mary really did was to make love like vicious children; and this was due to the fact that they were both very nervous and very excitable but not in the faintest degree tempted to the usual gestures of excessive human passion.

John follows Mary to Glastonbury; far into the book we ascertain that she is still a virgin. The melodrama concerns the attempted murder of John; but in the event the victim is only Barter, the archetype of banality in the book. There is no satisfaction for the reader either in the crime, or in its result. John and Mary return to a normal domestic marriage in Norfolk's flat fields, carrying

> not only the corpse of Tom Barter but the corpse of their stillborn, never-returning opportunity of touching the Eternal in the enchanted soil where the Eternal once sank down into time!

In the final scene in a monstrous anticlimax every hope is overwhelmed, with Geard drowning in the midst of a flood. One feels the heartsinking described (a great many pages earlier) as being felt by poor Barter:

> It was just a day dying out; of no more interest, of no more importance, than a bonfire of cabbage stalks, over which some one has thrown a bucket of water.

There is, however, a last all-important complexity. Just as the book dies on the day it was born, the day of the Spring Solstice, so, it is implied, will something be born from this wreck. For Geard could be said to have *drowned himself*,—recalling Merlin's vanishing into "Esplumeoir,"

some "Great Good Place," some mystic Fourth Dimension, or Nir-
vanic apotheosis, into which the magician deliberately sank, or
rose; thus committing a sort of inspired suicide; a mysterious dying
in order to live to live more fully.

Moreover, Geard drowns in sight of the Tor, and we seem to understand
that in his final moments he sees the hill metamorphosed to a swelling
chalice, to the Grail itself . . . But the novel is already ended. The Duality
that has dominated the book is already leaving Glastonbury Tor for some
other "particular spot," and the revelation of her presence is only the
prelude to her passing, and the book's ending. She

moves through the generations from one twilight to another . . .
until she finds the land that has called her and the people whose
heart she alone can fill. . . .
    For She whom the ancients named Cybele is in reality that beau-
tiful and terrible Force by which the Lies of great creative Nature
give birth to Truth that is to be. . . .
    Thus she abides; her Towers forever rising, forever vanishing,
Never or Always.

Weymouth Sands is much briefer than *A Glastonbury Romance*, but it
conveys far more convincingly the multi-centred and communal experience
that the earlier book attempted. It is a world bound in a consciousness of
romantic love, the kind of romantic love I have already called "Aquarian,"
whose watery essences find a marvellously literal projection in the actual
landscape of beach and pier, island and causeway, saltmarsh and harbour
and cliff, all the various forms water has brought into existence.
    Of this love the archpriest is Sylvanus Cobbold, who preaches on
Weymouth Esplanade, of whom we hear that:

He was always trying to make clear to himself what he really was
after in his dealings with women; but this seemed to be the evasive
point in his days. He could not formulate it or define it. In fact he
could not understand it. He only knew that he was driven more
and more obstinately by some secret urge within him to do what,
as he actually experienced it, he felt to be a gathering up of wom-
en's most secret responses to life; as if some half-crazed Faust had
found the magic oracles of those Beings he called 'the Mothers' in
the nerves and sensibilities of every ordinary young Gretchen he
encountered.

A succession of ordinary young Gretchens thus become his disciples and
supply a half-comprehending audience for his mystical monologues (in
which Powys parodies his own nature-mysticism). In his distant house on
Portland, Sylvanus communes with the Absolute all through one night,
holding to him, like Mephistopheles' key, the sleeping body of Marret
Jones, the Punch and Judy girl who has followed him from the sands.
Marret explains later,

We sleep together, you know, and he presses me to him, . . . but *he never does anything*. He never seems to want to, and I don't think he ever will.

In one form or another, the use of unconsummated sexuality as the means of "breaking through" is common to most of Powys's central characters. Across all Powys's fiction, whether in Wolf's vision of gold "behind the pigsty," or Cordelia's rain vigil in Carbonek, or Sam's vision of the Grail by the old post, we hear again and again the echo of Powy's experience at Cambridge. The intensity of yearning experienced by young girls, or in a one-sided passion; the solitary craving of the sadist; the sexual mortification of the religious ascetic: all these are shown as having their due rewards, and are to some degree equated, because in Powys the reward always takes the same form.

But the issue of responsibility is not avoided, and Sylvanus's kind of love, which catches up its objects in a game which they are not equipped to play, is shown in all its social imperfection. Marret leaves him in a fury at his essential selfishness; but while Sylvanus attempts to sleep away his disturbance, another resentful one steals in and clips off his moustaches, which were as important to his life-illusion as Wolf Solent's stick to his. Thus weakened, Sylvanus, like Samson, is led into captivity; he has to face society in the role of public nuisance, and, more seriously, corrupter of young girls; and he is confined in an asylum.

But however society may act against it, it is clear that the kind of love of which Sylvanus is a prophet is present *all over* Weymouth. Every character shares in it, and every character is rewarded with some kind of vision.

On Weymouth Sands, on August Bank Holiday, on his lonely forty-seventh birthday, walks Magnus Muir, the stolid Latin tutor, who even in the act of mentally undressing and possibly raping his beloved, is yet paralysed by the purity of his ideal. Spread over an entire chapter, Magnus's vision is perhaps the greatest sustained achievement in all Powys's work, marvellously objectifying in the panorama of the beach, the conflict in the Latin tutor's mind, so steeped in Homer and in classical history, so wrapped in a vague "Saturnian" allusiveness, yet invaded, as it repeatedly is, by the "brazen, goatish, rammish cry" of the present, of Mr. Punch, with his alarming: "Judy! Judy! Judy! Judy!"

These sands have been the scene of much of Magnus's (and Powys's) childhood, and

> That difference . . . between the *dry* sand and the *wet* sand, which had remained in the memory of Magnus as a condensation of the divergent experiences of his life, heightened the way everything looked from the esplanade till it attained the symbolism of drama. . . .
>
>   There, above, on the *dry* sand, there were forever limning and dis-limning themselves groups and conclaves of a rich, mellow Rabelaisian mortality, eating, drinking, love-making, philosophis-

ing, full of racy quips, scandalous jibes, and every sort of earthy, care-forgetting ribaldry.

Yet below was the wet sand, of the children,

> imprinted by the "printless" feet, light, immortal, bare, of what might easily have been the purer spirits of an eternal classical childhood, happy and free, in some divine limbo of unassailable play-time.

It is Magnus's ability to discover some deeper meaning that redeems the pathos of his experience. We are referred at one point to the words from *Faust*:

> "Alles vergangliche
> Ist nur ein gleichnis."
> "All appearance is but a symbol."

A little later, Magnus sees Sylvanus preaching on the beach to "a pair of the most uninteresting young women he had ever seen" (Sylvanus will be arrested that very day); and Magnus seats himself on the stern of a boat,

> not without noticing the boat's name, which was Calypso. Like a magic touch, through all his worries and obsessions, this classical word swept the mind of the teacher to the far-off realms he loved, and in a flash between that glittering bay, flecked with darting gulls, airy yachts, gaily loaded rowing-boats, and the vaporous cloud feathers of that halcyon sky, the tall figure of Sylvanus struck him as the eternal recurrence of some undying "gleichnis."
> . . . Magnus took not the smallest notice of what the man was saying, but he felt peaceful and happy as he sat on the Calypso's stern. All the fussiness, all the fretting life-worry of his usual expression left his face. The lines of his mouth grew formidable, almost majestic, his nostrils quivered like those of a proud horse.
> "Water and Sand," he thought, "are what I want. The inanimate, not flesh and blood. I am *really* happier at this minute, than I am with Curly!"

Thus Magnus wanders along the beach, imagining himself for a moment as Teiresias among the "sad troops of the enfeebled Dead," or seeing in others the likeness of Belisarius, or of Marcus Aurelius and Faustina, and yet rising again and again, above any failure with Curly, to illumination:

> It sometimes happens that a contemplative person, whose head is full of contrary thought-currents, receives, in a quick, unexpected revelation, a view of the world as it exists when many separate, far-off moments of insight, that have caught our landscape under a large and reconciling light, melt and fuse themselves together.

Maiden Castle marks the uncomfortable transition from the novels written with the premise of "modern life" as a framework to those in which archetypal emotions are presented within an historical setting. Against the banal domestic scene of modern Dorchester are set a procession of characters with bizarre archetypal names, names that breed an unreality and disturbance of their own. The central character we have to accept by the name he gives himself, Dud No-man, a reference to his own impotence, as well as to the uncertainty of his fathering. Dud eventually discovers his father (though it does not cure his ailment) in a local man, named Uryen Quirm. Next door to the Quirms live the Platonist Teucer Wye and his daughter Thuella.

Between Dud No-man and Thuella Wye, he a writer, she a painter, he impotent, she lesbian, takes place the most uncompromised of all Powys's sexual encounters, an extended, "purely cerebral" love-making, above a "scummy pond."

> The ungodly pleasure the girl was giving him began actually to take the shape of this wavering edge between greenness and blackness; and this congruity went so deep that the satisfaction of his mental desire seemed to him then like a delirious worm feeding upon the vegetation-roots of the world, a worm rising up from that black water—that was the primal gulf of space—to feed forever upon celestial duck-weed!

These pages are, however, no more than a fleeting episode in a book whose characters for the most part supply a merciless critique of the Powysian techniques for living, of which Dud No-man is a particularly pathetic representative. Dud conceives himself as "a good, quiet man, working at (his) book, going on (his) walks, enjoying (his) sensations, being kind to the girl (he) rescued." The reader is alerted to the presence in Dorchester of many old men and babies, "absolutely harmless and absolutely selfish." Dud is at one point set on by all the main characters and is told that minds like his are "inward-turned" and "maggotty, like cheeses." His cyclic experience is all too transparent: "It's round and round with you, isn't it?" And when, having lost his girl, Dud still works his usual trick of finding her in the landscape-sensations of one of his walks, he has to realise that;

> It meant nothing to her that there was in this a proof of the intensity of his feeling, a proof of its etherealized sensuality, of its all-pervasiveness and absorbing diffusion.

Dud's father, Uryen, who believes himself to be a reincarnation of Brân, the Crow, the Welsh equivalent of Cronos or Saturn, and Maiden Castle to be the ruin of some lost Saturnian city, lives by an even more precarious method. He attempts to use as *his* method of "breaking through," the power of *another person's* yearning for yet another (in this case, the yearning of Thuella for Dud's girl). *Faust* is again recalled as "frustrated love" is identified with the "key" Mephistopheles gives Faust to reach "the Mothers." The ending is as bleak as in any of Powys's works, with Uryen dead, and Dud alone, as the two girls run off together to America.

In growing old (and perhaps in moving to Wales), the focus of Powys's imaginative energy gradually passed from a condition of yearning, within our world, to the projection of a substantial "Saturnian" reality, excluding our world altogether. *Porius* for instance, is conceived largely in terms of those "patches of grass and green moss and yellow stone-crop," on that Cambridge wall; and the action of the book unfolds in vague dream-like tableaux of "rich magic and romance." The archetypal dreams of mankind are, in the final works, reenacted in a vision of the distant past, which is clearly intended also to suggest a vision of the future.

Both the central figures of the historical romances are Saturnian heroes. Owen Glendower, making his rebellion as the last king of the ancient Welsh, and Merlin (in *Porius*), counsellor to Arthur, as the last Emperor of the Romano-Britons, both are fighting for an age which is already past, for a cause which is already lost. In the last chapter of *Porius*, Merline is concretely shown to be Cronos himself, in some Eternal Recurrence, "forever plotting a second Age of Gold."

These later Saturnian quests take place in a world where there is no longer much doubt or modesty about Saturnian values. Both Merlin and Owen are able to escape, even after apparent failure, into some kind of inner, or other, dimension; and it is somehow felt in this Saturnian Wales, that failure in the outer world is almost an achievement.

> Over your body . . . our people will pass to their triumph; but it will be a triumph in the House of Saturn, not in the House of Mars.

Wales itself is identified with this sly Saturnian victory:

> Its past is its future, for it lives by memories and in advance it recedes. The greatest of its heroes have no graves, for they will come again. Indeed they have not died; they have only disappeared.

Wales is said to live by a "Mythology of escape":

> Other races love and hate, conquer and are conquered. This race avoids and evades, pursues and is pursued. Its soul is forever making a double flight. It flies into a circuitous *Inward*. It retreats into a circuitous *Outward*.

But in both these books, the absence of a concrete, social context, of the matrix provided in each of the earlier books by the microcosms of small West Country towns, makes for a slackening of tension. This everyday reality had provided a kind of critical chorus against which Powys's philosophic voice could be measured. Without such criticism, Saturnian values begin to be too obviously delusory.

In *Porius*, for instance, Prince Porius appears very much in the line of introverted and sexually indecisive heroes; but we are told that he has within him giant's blood. One of the climaxes of the book is Porius's sudden encounter with the two last aboriginal giants of Wales, a beautiful giantess and her father. In the subsequent scenes, all Porius's indecisiveness is forgotten, he behaves like a hero; it is made explicit that in finding a giantess he has found his true dimension. Are we then to reach this meaning back, through Dud No-man, to Wolf Solent: that if only they had found something large enough they would have become fully potent and responsible beings? The reader who has followed this survey thus far will see that it cannot be so; the Saturnian stance, as practised in any real context, cannot allow of any such satisfaction. Nothing but "the Whole" will serve, and no giantess will be large enough.

Despite occasional suggestions of "oracular wisdom" in some of the later books, Powys is really presenting only a method for living, not a system of values. As Christie explains to Wolf:

> "I regard each philosophy, not as the 'truth,' but just as a particular country, in which I can go about."

It was possible for Powys to regard himself as a philosopher, and yet to take as his central tenet the avoidance of any focused commitment to belief, because he viewed both Plato and Nietzsche as fellow-travellers in uncertainty. Dud observes of Plato:

> "I take him as an absolute sceptic, so uncertain about everything that he could afford to turn God and Immortality into poetry, and the Soul and Love into fairy-tales."

While Powys in a letter summarises Nietzsche's stance:

> There is no God. There is Nothing. Therefore fight!

Plato and Nietzsche thus provided a kind of tradition for Powys. They work within essentially literary forms, constructing philosophic myths around the figures of Socrates and Zarathustra, in order to project their own particular philosophic visions. Both combine a romantic idealism with a profound irony; and they both convey a cyclic experience in which "pain and pleasure grow on the same tree," so that experience goes "beyond good and evil." Socrates is proclaimed the wisest of men by Apollo's oracle, only because he knows that he does not know. Plato and Nietzsche are both, above all, intent on exhorting the reader to a particular method for living, the Socratic, or the Zarathustran, and the question of any ultimate meaning is bypassed, or else simply overlaid with words that form themselves into a world, or a rhythm, an artistic equivalence to experience.

I have used the word "romance" throughout this survey, because Powys's fiction does not really respond to most of the expectations a reader might bring to a novel. The books that were always most in Powys's mind were what are sometimes called "Worldbooks," works which attempt to convey a total picture of life; for example: Cervantes's *Don Quixote*; Rabelais's *Gargantua*; *The Anatomy of Melancholy*; *Tristram Shandy*; Wordsworth's *The Prelude*; Nietzsche's *Zarathustra*; Ibsen's *Peer Gynt*; Goethe's *Faust*. Each of these books defines its own eccentric form and expectations.

If Powys deserves to join that company, it is because one discovers in his works a particular apprehension of life, that is not to be found elsewhere, and yet seems so universal in its application that once seen, it has to be included. He is one of those fortunate artists who find themselves in possession of an authentic originality, that is, of access to a dimension that had always been present in experience, but that was waiting to be isolated and embodied.

Powys's achievement is to have projected his method for living as a genuine alternative. The quest for which a Saturnian is striving leaves on either side many other great paths, and has all the limitations of his temperament. Yet, like Prince Porius at the end of that book, Powys could say at the end of his life, "There are many gods; and I have served a great one." The loose ends of the romances are linked by that unifying presence, who in *A Glastonbury Romance* is called "Cybele," and is elsewhere "Saturn." Powys's most grateful readers will always be those people "whose heart she alone can fill." It is Saturn's traditionally contrasting potentialities that are ingredients of Powys's vision: his tenderness matched by such a shrewdness of human observation as to be indiscreet and almost malevolent, his unusually concrete descriptions overlaid with the sense of an unfinished and an unpredictable creation, his pathos so shot through with humour—and all these elements as contributing to, and included within, the vast spiritual cycle that has to be accomplished by those born beneath Saturn's enormous orbit.

This cycle does not include everything. Only by vision, never by reason, can the Saturnian hope to gain a totality of meaning. At the end of each of Powys's romances the archetypal world has been broken and the "real" world has been accepted; but accepted essentially in the golden reconciling light of the archetypes, and with their lost beauty as the ultimate to which he must hope to penetrate again.

Ford Madox Ford: *Parade's End*

Arthur Mizener

The problem faced in *Parade's End* was to put the characters Ford so vividly imagined together in a fiction that would be an image not only of his own private experience but of the public life of his society, which he believed had declined disastrously. In *It Was the Nightingale* he gives an account of how he came to write *Parade's End* as he did; it may represent all he consciously grasped of the process. Sir Edward Elgar, the composer of "Land of Hope and Glory" and a neighbor of Ford's in Bedham, stops on the road past Coopers Cottage and asks Ford if they have not met at Henry James's. "Nothing in the world was further from my thoughts than writing about the late war. But I suppose the idea was somewhere in my own subconsciousness. . . . I wondered how the common friend of myself and Sir Edward would have treated that intractable subject . . . and for the rest of the day and for several days more I lost myself in working out an imaginary war-novel on the lines of 'What Maisie Knew.' "

In fact, Ford seems to have started, not with a generalization about the war and a theory of narration, but with his vision of himself as an idealistic young man of great talent and unostentatious social superiority. The experiences of this young man that most deeply concerned him were his commitment to the Tory political doctrines that shall govern the world when Arthur is come again; the frustrated moral, social, and aesthetic activities they had led him into; the decision of this Tory self to serve his country and the war experience that followed it; and the emotional complications that resulted from his falling out of love with Violet Hunt and in love with Stella Bowen.

In technique he began where he had left off in *The Marsden Case* and *No Enemy*. Like *The Marsden Case*, *Some Do Not* . . . uses a modified chron-

From *The Saddest Story: A Biography of Ford Madox Ford*. © 1971 by Arthur Mizener. The World Publishing Company, 1971.

ological arrangement of events reduced to a relatively few scenes by a process of selection not unlike that of the well-made play. *Some Do Not . . .* consists of three acts. The first act takes place in and around Rye; the time is late June, 1912. This act takes us from the moment when we discover Christopher and Macmaster on the train to Rye until the moment when Christopher and Valentine's all-night ride ends with General Campion's running into them outside Mountby. The second act takes place in the dining room of Christopher and Sylvia's flat in Grays Inn; the time is late August, 1917. This act takes us through the early part of a single afternoon. The third act takes place on the street between Grays Inn and the War Office, in and about the War Office, and back at the flat. The time is continuous with that of the previous act and we are taken through the remainder of that afternoon and night.

Each of these acts is divided into scenes. For example, the first act begins with the scene in the train. It is followed by a scene at Lobscheid, where Sylvia Tietjens has just joined her mother and Father Consett. The third scene occurs at the inn where Christopher and Macmaster are staying; the fourth at the Duckemins', where they breakfast; the fifth on the path to the Wannops', and at luncheon there. The final scene begins near the finish of Christopher and Valentine's long ride to and from Plimsoll and ends with the accident. The other two acts are similarly divided into dramatically concentrated scenes.

But Ford's allusions to *What Maisie Knew* in both *No Enemy* and in his description of how he came to write *Parade's End* are important. For him, as for James, ultimate reality is not some event in time and space; it is the conception of that event in a consciousness. What distinguishes Ford's well-made play from a stageable fiction—as it distinguishes *What Maisie Knew* from a theatrical experiment like *Covering End*—is the extent to which the action is presented to us through a consciousness, much of the time at two removes—that is to say, through the consciousness of a character whose consciousness is described by the novel's narrator. Like James, Ford never frees his characters' minds entirely from the control of the narrator; both when he is writing as the omniscient narrator and when he is following the movement of a character's consciousness, he writes as a third person. This third person is not—except very occasionally in *Some Do Not . . .*— objective and impersonal; he is vividly present to us as a personality, as an ironic, judging mind. It is Ford's desire to let us hear his voice that makes him summarize the thoughts of his characters in the third person rather than present them to us directly. By this means he is able to show us the events as a character perceives them and at the same time to show us the narrator's judgment of the characters' thoughts and feelings.

As *Parade's End* progressed, Ford became more interested in dramatizing the perceiving consciousness, as he had in "The Water Mill" chapter in *No Enemy*. He focused more sharply on the way the conscious mind keeps several trains of thought going at once and on the extent to which the governing impulses of men come from the unconscious. Both tendencies are illustrated at the start of *Some Do Not . . ..* Vincent Macmaster sits in the train to Rye prepared to relish the "sensuous current of his prose" in his monograph on Rossetti. He knows Christopher Tietjens, sitting opposite him, does not admire Rossetti, though he does not know why. Nor does he suspect that the prose he is about to savor and the attitude it represents illustrate all that is wrong with the society that Macmaster, with his poor-Scot ambitiousness, is so anxious to make a success in. "Gabriel Charles Dante Rossetti, the subject of this little monograph, must be accorded the name of one who has profoundly influenced the outward aspects, the human contacts, and all those things that go to make up the life of our higher civilization as we live it to-day," Macmaster's monograph begins. It is all too true.

Macmaster starts to read. As he does so, a second part of his mind starts to consider why he has written this monograph: it will "consolidate his position" in his department and in society, allow him to set up an elegant establishment and to furnish it with a "tall, graceful, dark, loose-gowned, passionate yet circumspect, oval-featured, deliberative, gracious" woman. The thought triggers his recurrent fear of his starved nature's occasional uncontrollable impulses to go bald-headed after "big-bosomed, scarlet-cheeked" girls of a quite different kind. So far, he thinks, Christopher has saved him from the consequences of these impulses. Yet, ironically, Tietjens himself has fallen into the trap set for him by a woman pregnant by another man and desperate for a husband.

During all this time the first part of Macmaster's mind continues to be occupied—though without the relish he had anticipated (his feelings are being preempted by this second train of thought)—with his monograph. The thought of how Sylvia had trapped Christopher brings in its train a recollection of the scene that had occurred that morning when Christopher had received a letter from Sylvia announcing that she was returning to him after spending four months with a lover named Perowne. This part of his mind then forces him painfully to rehearse that scene, until he comes to the moment when Christopher said sardonically of the child he loves but is not convinced is his that Sylvia "gives me the benefit of the agreeable doubt." Wincing at the memory, Macmaster looks up from his monograph and notices that Christopher has gone gray. "Suddenly—and as if in a sort of unconscious losing of his head—Macmaster remarked: 'You can't say the man wasn't a poet!' The remark had been, as it were, torn from him."

This is an illustration of how the unconscious mind seeks to shift the conscious mind from one train of thought to another when the first has become unendurable. Rossetti's spiritualized sensuality fits Macmaster's unconscious desire to make his own sensuality acceptable to his conscious self by finding for it an object not big-bosomed and red-cheeked but tall and graceful, passionate yet circumspect—to whom he can quote Rossetti's

Since when we stand side by side
Only hands may meet,
Better half this weary world
Lay between us, sweet!

His insistence that Rossetti is a fine poet gives all this away. "I can't," Tietjens says contemptuously, "say [that is not poetry] . . . I don't read poetry except Byron. But it's a filthy picture." Ironically, Macmaster's subconscious has not even allowed him time to recognize that, in thus avoiding his own pain at the contemplation of Tietjens's suffering over Sylvia's conduct, he is likely to have added to that suffering. It does not give him time to consider how Christopher, brooding over his answer to Sylvia's letter, will be affected by an insistence on the magnificence of what Christopher calls Rossetti's attempt "to justify fornication" by a pretense of spirituality.

Macmaster is not a very sophisticated man, and he is scarcely aware of how he has been victimized by his subconscious mind. Ford's intelligent characters understand the power of their under selves. When Christopher reviews the scene that had occurred that morning, he remembers that Macmaster, seeing his expression as he reads Sylvia's letter, had given him brandy. "He seemed [that morning] to have no feelings about the matter"; at the same time he was aware that, subconsciously, he was feeling a great deal and he watched himself carefully for signs of what it was; he noted that only the brandy kept him from shivering uncontrollably.

Valentine, next to Christopher the novel's most sophisticated intelligence, is equally alert for the signs of what her unconscious self is up to.

> She heard herself saying, almost with a sob, so that she was evidently in a state of emotion:
> "Look here! I disapprove of this whole thing. . . ."
> At Miss Wanostrocht's perturbed expression she said to herself:
> "What on earth am I saying all this for? You'd think I was trying to cut loose from this school! Am I?"

She is, unconsciously; for unconsciously she has already decided to seek Christopher out at Grays Inn and to commit herself to him for life. But consciously she does not find out about that decision till some time later. When she finally does join Christopher at Grays Inn, her conscious mind and her unconscious feelings fall into conflict again. "This man," her conscious mind asserts indignantly, ". . . had once proposed love to her and then had gone away without a word and . . . had never so much as sent her a picture-postcard! Gauche! Haughty! Was there any other word for him? There could not be. Then she ought to feel humiliated. But she did not. . . . Joy radiated from his homespuns when you walked beside him. It welled out; it enveloped you. . . . Like the warmth from an electric heater, only that did not make you want to cry and say your prayers — the haughty oaf."

The determining responses of Ford's characters almost always take place in this way, below the level of consciousness, so that their conscious conception of themselves is always more or less at odds with the intentions of their subconscious selves. The result is a psychic conflict that goes on continually in Christopher and Valentine and Sylvia and even, occasionally, in minor characters like Vincent Macmaster and General Campion, who, while he sits writing his letter to the Secretary of State for War "with increasing satisfaction," finds that "a mind that he was not using said: 'What the devil am I going to do with that fellow?' Or: 'How the devil is that girl's name to be kept out of this mess?'"

This conflict between conscious and unconscious selves in *Parade's End* is, as was the similar but much simpler conflict in *The Good Soldier*, a genuine one. Ford does not suggest that one part of the consciousness is good, the other bad. The conscious self is the responsible, social self, and as a Tory Ford felt that this self must dominate the personality. "It is proper," as Christopher says, "that one's individual feelings should be sacrificed to the necessities of a collective entity."

> He said:
> "But it wouldn't be playing the game!"
> A long time afterwards he said:
> "Damn all principles!" And then:
> "But one has to keep on going. . . . Principles are like a skeleton map of a country—you know whether you are going east or north.

But when the socially determined habits of the conscious self begin to frustrate the unconscious feelings completely, as they do when society, failing to live up to its principles, ceases to provide occasions for the genuine satisfaction of these feelings (but only occasions for the meretricious satisfaction of them that Macmaster and Mrs. Duchemin will settle for), then a psychological crisis occurs in the society's best and most responsible people. The only salvation for such people—and the only way to preserve the essential principles of the society that has bred them—is for them to become "Tory radicals," to adopt a new mode of life, a new set of social conventions that will allow them to continue to live by those principles and yet satisfy the demands of their unconscious selves. After asserting that it is proper to sacrifice individual feelings to the collective entity, Christopher adds: "But not if that entity is betrayed from above."

The focus of our attention in *Parade's End* is on the slow, tortured process by which Christopher becomes consciously aware that the conventional life of Edwardian society no longer embodies the principles that it professes and that he has tried with such heroic literalness to live by. Then he recognizes that if these principles are to be preserved—if, indeed, he himself is to survive as a sane man—he will have to stop living as an Edwardian Younger Son, the role for which his society had cast him. "Love, ambition, the desire for wealth. They were things he had never known of as existing—as capable of existing within him. He had been the Younger Son . . . a sort of eternal Second-in-Command." He sees, to his surprise and (to Ford) comic dismay, that his unconscious self had decided to change all that long before his conscious self recognized the fact. The first hint his conscious self gets is the discovery that he wants to command the battalion, that he is ambitious. Then he discovers that he, for whom it had been a part of his duty as a member of the ruling class to lend money to anyone who asked for it, resents Colonel Partridge's request for a loan of £250 (it is a nice irony that Colonel Partridge—or at least Colonel Partridge's executors—are among the few who ever repay a debt to Christopher). Finally he recognizes that he intends to give up his public position in the government in London and go into the antique business in the country, to leave his luxurious social life with his wife, Sylvia, and live in chaste and frugal "sin" with Valentine Wannop. His old Edwardian self is, at first, shocked by these decisions. "Reprehensible! . . . He snorted! If you don't obey the rules of your club you get hoofed out, and that's that! If you retire from the post of Second-in-Command of Groby, you don't have to . . . oh, attend battalion parades! . . . Reprehensible! He said." Then his newly conscious self speaks. "For God's sake *let* us be reprehensible! And have done with it!"

The crisis of Christopher's consciousness that leads to this discovery illustrates the fully developed form of Ford's way of dealing with his characters. Christopher has been thinking of the Germans across no man's land, "confoundedly irritated to think of the mess they have made of his nice clean trenches." Then his mind makes an odd jump:

> The beastly Huns! They stood between him and Valentine Wannop. If they would go home he could be sitting talking to her for whole afternoons. . . .
>
> That in effect was love. It struck him as astonishing. The word was so little in his vocabulary. . . . He had been the Younger Son. . . .
>
> Now: what the Hell was he? A sort of Hamlet of the Trenches? No, by God he was not. . . . He was perfectly ready for action. Ready to command a battalion. He was presumably a lover. They did things like commanding battalions. And worse!
>
> He ought to write her a letter. What in the world would she think of this gentleman who had once made improper proposals to her; balked; said "So long!" or perhaps not even "So long!" And then walked off. With never a letter! Not even a picture postcard! For two years! A sort of a Hamlet all right! Or a swine!
>
> Well, then, he ought to write her a letter. He ought to say: "This is to tell you that I propose to live with you as soon as this show is over. You will be prepared immediately on cessation of active hostilities to put yourself at my disposal; Please. Signed, Xtopher Tietjens, Acting O.C. 9th Glams." A proper military communication.

Christopher's consciousness is being dramatized as interior dialogue rather than interior monologue, and over it hovers the ironic consciousness of the author, whose amused voice we can hear in phrases like "A proper military communication." This interior dialogue shows us the way Christopher's mind struggles, against its own habitual commitments, through a series of emotionally linked perceptions rising from his subconscious, toward an understanding of his own unconscious nature. It discovers with astonishment ("It struck him as astonishing") that it is in love ("That in effect was love"), that it is ambitious ("He was perfectly ready for action"), and that it is determined to act on these feelings ("He was presumably a lover. They did things like command battalions. And worse! He ought to write her a letter").

But it was not until Ford wrote *A Man Could Stand Up*— that he worked out all the possibilities of this kind of interior dialogue and the opportunities it opened up for a new kind of narrative structure. *Some Do Not . . .* works less within the consciousness of a character than any of the other novels in *Parade's End* and, when it does, more simply. Its structure is scenic, and the scenes are usually treated dramatically. When Ford does choose to present the action through the consciousness of a character, he picks whatever character suits the immediate occasion, and he moves from the consciousness of one character to that of another without hesitation.

No More Parades is a different matter. The rapidity with which Ford developed his new method of narration is indicated by the fact that he wrote a concluding scene for *Some Do Not . . .* and then suppressed it so that he could use the material in the interior dialogue of *No More Parades*. *No More Parades* takes place almost entirely in the minds of Christopher and Sylvia, and we learn a great deal about the states of their minds as they live through the experiences of the novel, though these states of mind are still, much of the time, described rather than represented ("Heavy depression settled down more heavily upon him," etc.). Only at moments of great tension does Ford dramatize their consciousnesses fully. Thus when Sylvia's desire for Christopher and her hatred of him reach a climax during the air raid, and the slightly drunken, well-meaning Cowley reminds her that Christopher had not slept the night before,

> There occurred to her irreverent mind a sentence of one of the Duchess of Marlborough's letters to Queen Anne. The duchess had visited the general during one of his campaigns in Flanders. "My Lord," she wrote, "did me the honour three times in his boots!" . . . The sort of thing she would remember [being, as she sardonically recognizes, what she is and being, at the moment, mad to be possessed by Christopher] . . . She would—she *would*— have tried it on the sergeant-major, just to see Tietjens' face, for the sergeant-major would not have understood. . . . And who cared if he did! . . . He was bibulously skirting round the same idea. . . .
>
> But the tumult increased to an incredible volume. . . . She screamed blasphemies that she was hardly aware of knowing. She

had to scream against the noise; she was no more responsible for the blasphemy than if she had lost her identity under an anesthetic. . . . She was one of this crowd!

Ford dramatizes in the same way the moment Christopher's conscious mind loses control during his interview with General Campion.

> Panic came over Tietjens. He knew it would be his last panic of that interview. No brain could stand more. Fragments of scenes of fighting, voices, names, went before his eyes and ears.

For two pages they do so. Then:

> He exclaimed to himself: "By heavens! Is this epilepsy?" He prayed: "Blessed saints, get me spared that!" He exclaimed: "No, it isn't! . . . I've complete control of my mind. My uppermost mind."

Ford's almost complete commitment to interior dialogue in *No More Parades* changes radically the organization of the narrative. The novel still has the tripartite structure of *Some Do Not . . .* and consists of fairly sharply defined scenes of either present or recollected action, and the present action is still chronological. Being continuously inside the mind of a character, however, allows Ford to use the time shift extensively, to rearrange the order of events by having the character "remember" scenes that occur at different times. Chapter 3 of part 1, for example, consists entirely of Christopher's interior dialogue at the end of the evening during which he has learned of Sylvia's presence in Rouen. This meditation, with its neat device of Christopher's putting his past relations with Sylvia in order by writing them down in the flat, impersonal style of a military report, makes it possible for us to reconstruct the history of those relations, including the episode Ford originally described in the suppressed scene of *Some Do Not . . .* (Sylvia also recalls this episode, in part 2). But the major purpose of Christopher's meditation is to arrange the events of this history in nonchronological pattern that will show us the feelings they arouse in Christopher, the entanglement of those feelings with his anxieties about his job at the base, and the way these feelings together gradually change—as it were, before our eyes—his conception of himself and of the possibilities of his life. This major purpose is clear enough if we trace the pattern Ford has imposed on Christopher's meditation.

> The one thing that stood out sharply in Tietjens' mind [it begins] when at last, with a stiff glass of rum punch, his officer's pocketbook complete with pencil . . . he sat in his flea-bag with six army blankets over him—the one thing that stood out as sharply as Staff tabs was that that ass Levin was rather pathetic. . . . On the frozen hillside, he . . . had grabbed at Tietjens' elbow, while he brought out breathlessly puzzled sentences. . . .
> There resulted a singular mosaic of extraordinary, bright-col-

oured and melodramatic statements, for Levin . . . brought out monstrosities of news about Sylvia's activities, without any sequence. . . .

And as Tietjens, seated on his hams, his knees up, pulled the soft woolliness of his flea-bag under his chin . . . it seemed to him that this affair was like coming back after two months and trying to get the hang of battalion orders. . . .

So, on that black hillside . . . what stuck out for Tietjens was that . . . the mysterious "rows" to which in his fear Levin had been continually referring had been successive letters from Sylvia to the harried general [Campion]. . . . Tietjens set himself coolly to recapitulate every aspect of his separation from his wife. . . .

The doctor's batman, from the other end of the hut, said:

"Poor _____ O Nine Morgan [whose death haunted Christopher]! . . ." in a sing-song mocking voice. . . . They might talk till half-past three.

But that was troublesome to a gentleman seeking to recapture what exactly were his relations with his wife.

Before the doctor's batman had interrupted him by speaking startlingly of O Nine Morgan, Tietjens had got as far as what follows with his recapitulation: The lady, Mrs. Tietjens. . . .

He took a sip from the glass of rum and water. . . . He had determined not to touch his grog. But his throat had gone completely dry. . . . Why should his throat be dry? . . . And why was he in this extraordinary state? . . . It was because the idea had suddenly occurred to him that his parting from his wife set him free for his girl. . . . The idea had till then never entered his head.

He said to himself: We must go methodically into this! . . .

"Better put it into writing," he said.

Well then. He clutched at his pocket-book and wrote in large pencilled characters:

"When I married Miss Satterthwaite. . . ."

He exclaimed:

"God, what a sweat I am in! . . ." . . .

It was no good going on writing. He was no writer, and this writing gave no sort of psychological pointers.

And his mind wanders off on half-a-dozen pages of brooding about his situation that do give him—and even more, us —psychological pointers.

In part 2 of *No More Parades*, which takes place in Sylvia's mind, this kind of rearrangement of the events is carried much further. The present time of part 2 begins exactly where the present time of part 1 ends, with Christopher riding down into Rouen to reserve a room for the night at the hotel; at the beginning of part 2 Sylvia, sitting in the hotel lounge with Perowne, sees Christopher come into the hotel. The presence of Perowne sends Sylvia off on a prolonged recollection of her affair with him five years before in a small French town. The scene ends in the grim comedy of her outrage at the thought that Christopher may have a girl—probably Valentine Wannop—in *this* French town, Rouen. The present time of the action—we are still in Sylvia's mind—then jumps to that evening as Sylvia sits at dinner with Christopher and Sergeant-Major Cowley. During its course Sylvia's mind drifts off into a recollection of the previous afternoon, when everyone had been at Lady Sachse's for tea, and from there into a mental debate with Father Consett in heaven.

When Christopher returns from taking a telephone call, she hands him the letters she has kept back from him all these months; one of them, which she has opened and read, is from Mark Tietjens; as Christopher reads it, she rereads it in her memory. What we have here, then, is Sylvia's recollection of Mark's sardonic description of Sylvia's efforts to persuade Mark to withhold an income Christopher has in fact refused to take from Mark. Mark had felt Christopher should take the income but had not been able to make him; Sylvia thought Christopher had taken it and wanted Mark to take it back. As Sylvia recalls Mark's letter, we hear Mark's own words about Sylvia (and Valentine) and at the same time listen to Sylvia's response to them. "Hearing" the letter repeat itself in her memory, we contemplate with her Christopher reading it to himself and—knowing well Christopher's feelings about the money, about Sylvia, and about Valentine—we imagine his response to it. Thus three minds, all intimately familiar to us, are brought before us, vivid with their own styles and voices, in response to the same matter. Part 2 ends with Sylvia and Tietjens dancing to a phonograph; they will go up to Sylvia's bedroom shortly to discuss their situation.

Part 3 begins in Christopher's mind when he awakens the next morning in his tent as General Campion and Levin enter. After a brief visit to his headquarters and a talk with Levin, Christopher is cross-examined by Campion about what had occurred the night before when he was in Sylvia's room. In this way the violent activities of the night are conveyed to us; we learn Campion's decision to send Christopher into the front lines; and we watch Christopher's mind as it comes close to breaking down. Part 3 ends with Campion's inspection of Christopher's cook-house.

By staying within the minds of his two major characters, Ford is able to limit both the time and the place of the novel's action. It takes place entirely at the base and in the hotel at Rouen. Part 1 covers part of one evening, Christopher's meditation in bed afterward, and about an hour just after noon the next day. Part 2 covers the succeeding hour or so and the time between dinner and bedtime that evening. Part 3 covers a few hours the next morning. All the rest of the events are presented in scenes— sometimes very fully developed scenes—that are remembered by Christopher or Sylvia. This concentration of presentation allows Ford to focus on the meaningful moments of the story and to bring in the rest of the events at the points in the narration where meaning rather than chronology requires them to occur; it is the meaning of a recollected scene that leads the character to remember it at the moment he does, and the way he remembers it is saturated with the meaning that made him recall it. The skeletal structure of the narrative in *No More Parades* is chronological; its three interior dialogues deal with periods that follow one another in time. But Ford arranges the events remembered in these dialogues in an order that dramatizes their meaning. A good illustration is the way Sylvia recollects, in the middle of her dinner with Christopher and Cowley, the tea that afternoon at Lady Sachse's, where Christopher handled the difficult old French duchess so perfectly that Sylvia, enraged by this successful display of tactful authority, told General Campion that Christopher was a socialist whose secret desire was to model himself on our Lord.

In *A Man Could Stand Up*—Ford completed the development of interior dialogue as a mean of representing the consciousness at war with itself. He needed to, because in this novel both Christopher and Valentine reach the climax of the long struggles by which their unconscious selves free them from Edwardian commitments and they make new ones. Ford also carried to a new extreme the rearrangement of the events in the narrative to emphasize meaning rather than chronology. *A Man Could Stand Up*— begins in the mind of Valentine Wannop at approximately eleven o'clock of November 11, 1918, Armistice Day. Valentine is at the telephone in the girls' school where she works, listening to Edith Ethel Duchemin, now Lady Macmaster, who is telling her (in the mad hope that Valentine will persuade Christopher to cancel Macmaster's debt to him) that Christopher is back in London and needs help. We stay within Valentine's mind until she has finally admitted to herself that the enlightened late-Victorian standards of her parents, which she has been trying to live by, do not work in the postwar world and have to be discarded, and has faced what she has been trying not to recognize consciously ever since she and Christopher parted in August, 1917, at the end of *Some Do Not . . .*—namely, that she is helplessly in love with Christopher. Having thus discarded the unworkable idea of life she has been struggling to realize and having faced the truth about herself, she determines to seek out Christopher and commit herself to him.

Part 2 begins "months and months before" in Christopher's mind—to be precise, six months before, at dawn of a relatively quiet morning in April, 1918, during the great battle in which Ludendorff so nearly defeated the Allies. During this morning we watch Christopher reach his decision to give up trying to be the Tory Younger Son, the role he had with such uncompromising idealism and such agony of effort been trying to live. He will cease to do what he has heretofore considered his duty, his job in the Imperial Department of Statistics (which wants him to betray the principles it stands for by faking statistics); he will give up his gentlemanly loyalty to Sylvia (who wishes he would beat her); and he will retire to George Herbert's country, join his life with Valentine Wannop's, and make a living selling antiques. Though part 2 of *A Man Could Stand Up*—has no chronological relation with part 1, it parallels it very closely in meaning. In it

Christopher goes through the same process of self-discovery that Valentine had gone through in part 1, and reaches the same conclusion about Edwardian society that Valentine had.

Part 3 begins as Valentine, following up the decision she had reached in part 1, arrives at Grays Inn and meets Christopher. Throughout the next few hours we are alternately in the minds of Valentine and Christopher as, almost wholly without words of their own, they approach complete understanding. They are much assisted in the process by another telephone call. As Edith Ethel Duchemin had, at the novel's start, put Valentine onto Christopher by her telephone call, so now Mrs. Wannop, bent on preventing Valentine and Christopher's becoming lovers if she can do so without betraying her principles, inadvertently reveals to Christopher on the telephone that Valentine had come to Grays Inn prepared to be his mistress.

Last Post carries the story on chronologically until sometime between 1926 and 1929 (Christopher is somewhere between forty and forty-three years old). Its present time covers only a few hours and it takes place entirely at Christopher and Valentine's cottage. It has almost no action; Sylvia decides to free Christopher to marry Valentine, and Christopher returns from Groby, where the Great Tree has been cut down, in time to stand with a fragment of the tree in his hand at Mark's bedside as Mark dies. Apart from brief moments when we are in the minds of Cramp, the gardener, and Christopher's son, Mark, the narrative composes into a pattern of interior dialogues: Mark, Marie Léonie, Mark, Marie Léonie; Sylvia, Valentine; Mark. Ford's emphasis is on the minds and characters of Mark and Marie Léonie, and his purpose is to conclude *Parade's End* by counterpointing the relation of Mark and Marie Léonie and the relation of Valentine and Christopher, with whom their thoughts are naturally enough much preoccupied, as his purpose in *Some Do Not . . .* at the start of *Parade's End* had been to counterpoint the relation of Macmaster and Mrs. Duchemin with that of Valentine and Christopher. Only, in *Last Post* he works mainly in the minds of Mark and Marie Léonie instead of—as he had in *Some Do Not . . .*—mainly in the minds of Christopher and Valentine.

Putting the bulk of the narration in the minds of Mark and Marie Léonie makes them the novels' most prominent characters. Both are vividly realized, and the result is striking so far as Mark is concerned, for Mark is a Christopher Tietjens without the impulse to sainthood and with a Yorkshire stubbornness so great that he would rather die with the Edwardian world than change his mode of life, as Christopher does, in order to survive into the new world. Because of this parallel, the character that is elaborated in Mark's long interior dialogues illuminates Christopher's character. The device of working within Mark's mind is, in short, successful.

But that is not true of Marie Léonie; her interior dialogue defines amusingly the French point of view which, throughout *Parade's End*, has been contrasted with the English; Marie Léonie serves the public purpose of *Parade's End* very well. In a sense, perhaps, she also serves its private purpose. Nobody could be more shrewdly practical in her conduct, more firmly bourgeois in her taste, more thoroughly and domestically marital than Marie Léonie, despite the fact that Mark picked her out of a musical-comedy chorus and has kept her as his mistress for years. Her meditation gives the maximum dramatic emphasis to the contrasting motives and attitudes of Valentine and Christopher, about whom she thinks with tolerant disapproval, in conducting their irregular union. The difficulty about Marie Léonie as a point of view is that she is not involved in the central action of *Parade's End*, not intimately linked—either logically or by the previous novels in the series—with the main characters. Ford exercised all his ingenuity to justify his abrupt introduction of her, but there is no getting around the fact that, in using her, he multiplied entities unnecessarily and shifted attention from the real center of the action; though it is easy to understand why, with his lifelong passion for the French, Ford found her irresistible.

Ford later came to dislike *Last Post* and to believe he ought to have ended *Parade's End* with *A Man Could Stand Up*—. Of this opinion the most important thing to be said is that he did not. *Last Post* cannot now be made to disappear. Ford's main objection to *Last Post* must certainly have been that it does precisely what he said in his dedication it was intended to—that is, "explain what became of Tietjens" and the people connected with him. By doing so it put the final emphasis of the series on what happened rather than on what it meant, and everything about *Parade's End* shows that what mattered most to Ford was what his story meant, not what happened in it. The arbitrary introduction of Marie Léonie may well have enforced this point for him and left him feeling that the first three novels constituted a neatly rounded-off "Affair" that begins with Valentine and Christopher as earnest Edwardians and ends with them as committed moderns about to set forth on a new life: "On an elephant. A dear, meal-sack elephant. She was setting out on." Here is that sonata form Ford had long ago described to Wells as the ideal form for a fiction. Yet even the sonata form allows for a coda, so that *Last Post* does not really break the pattern of the series; nor does it vary in technique from the other novels of the series any more than they vary from one another.

If it is possible to argue that *A Man Could Stand Up*—completes the series by leaving Valentine and Christopher on the threshold of the new, postwar world, it is also possible to argue that in *Last Post*, as Shakespeare's shepherd says to his son, 'thou met'st with things dying, I with things new-born." In *Last Post* the stubborn embodiment of the Edwardian ethos, Mark Tietjens, "chooses" to die rather than to change, while Christopher and Valentine, who have adjusted to this new world in order to preserve the essential principles they have shared with Mark, are about to see themselves newborn in the child Valentine is carrying. Perhaps the Ford who had separated from Stella thought the pastoral life of the Small Producer at Bedham with Stella and Julie was a weak manifestation of the new life of the changed soul. But the Ford who wrote *Last Post* before these changes in his circumstances would have thought exactly the opposite. Moreover, there is something to be said for this display of the hidden, honorable, frugal life ("frugal" is a key word in *Last Post*) at the end of the series, as a balance against the costly parade of Edwardian life, now drained of all meaning, with which the series had started: in *Last Post* only Sylvia can still think of living the old, luxurious, Edwardian life any longer, and even she does so with a kind of desperate weariness ("if you rid yourself of the distinction . . . of Groby Great Tree just to wound a man to the heart . . . you may as well take India").

Writing for Silence:
Dorothy Richardson and the Novel

Stephen Heath

Writing in 1923 with his usual forcefulness, D. H. Lawrence stigmatised the contemporary serious novel: "dying in a very long-drawn-out fourteen-volume death agony, and absorbedly, childishly interested in the phenomenon. 'Did I feel a twinge in my little toe, or didn't I?' asks every character of Mr Joyce or of Miss Richardson or M. Proust." The novel is sick with introspection, moribund with an interminable subjectivity: "It is self-consciousness picked into such fine bits that the bits are most of them invisible, and you have to go by smell. Through thousands and thousands of pages Mr Joyce and Miss Richardson tear themselves to pieces, strip their smallest emotions to the finest threads."

Dorothy Richardson, Proust, Joyce. The three names, the three works, were often brought together and in many ways inevitably and rightly so. The first chapter of the first of the *Pilgrimage* novels, *Pointed Roofs*, was drafted by Richardson in 1913, the same year that the initial volume of *A la recherche du temps perdu* was published in Paris and that Joyce in Trieste was making progress on *A Portrait of the Artist as a Young Man*. Like theirs, Richardson's work was to last a lifetime, life taken up in a permanent act of writing; and while there is no record that they had any knowledge of hers, Richardson read their work and gave thought to it (reviewing *Finnegans Wake*, for example, as soon as it appeared). In her "Foreword" to the 1938 collected edition of *Pilgrimage*, Richardson is careful to make reference to both Proust and Joyce but then also, it should be noted, to try to suggest something of her own individuality. For the bringing together of the three names could serve too easily to obliterate, leaving Richardson's work as a kind of subsidiary instance in a general discussion of Proust, Joyce, and the modern novel. *Pilgrimage* should be part of such a general discussion but has also its specific concerns and problems and qualities

From *Teaching the Text*. © 1983 by Stephen Heath. Routledge & Kegan Paul Ltd., 1983.

which can serve to raise certain critical questions about the modern novel; Richardson can be linked to Proust and Joyce but is not simply a cipher of the imagination of the writer we might derive from them, their myth. Her life and her work, after all, involve many contexts: she was a governess and an intimate friend of H. G. Wells; she wrote regularly in the same film magazine, *Close Up*, to which H. D. contributed her "Projector" poems; she reviewed on psychoanalysis and many other things for *Dental Record*, which she was asked to edit, and was approached by Brecht as to the possibility of becoming his translator; she was close at times to left-wing political groups and was in many senses and with many nuances a feminist, "strong, un-doctrinaire, feminine socialism," in the words of the novelist John Cowper Powys, friend and admirer; she was. . . .

But that exactly is the matter of her work: identity, one's self, its definition or not, like and book together as pilgrimage. And, of course, this is to come back to Proust and Joyce, with whose writing Richardson's intersects in its own specificity. I want briefly in the space of this [essay] to sketch out something of that specificity and so to provide an introduction to *Pilgrimage* as significant modern novel.

Freud in 1908 spoke of "the inclination of the modern writer to split up his ego by self-observation into many part egos." *Pilgrimage* is full of that inclination, informed by the necessity for self-observation. Its project is given in the title: a journey through a life in writing, a moving over questions and *the* question of identity. "Which self?" says Miriam, the central figure of the book, suddenly returning from other worlds to the conversational world around her and to its particular expectation of herself. What does it mean to say "I am?" "I suppose I'm a new woman"; "I'm a Tory-Anarchist"; "I'm a free-lover"; I am. . . . Carried along in conversation, held in the gaze of others, caught up in the public realms of work and friendship and life, taken over by her own desires for attachment, Richardson's heroine can reflect and assume identities a myriad of part egos, "I am's." Hence the name: *miriam*.

Yet there is everywhere, too, a deeper aspect of the "miriamness," the feeling of the misfit, the place not me. Miriam knows and continually learns this, has it confirmed by any occasion: a dinner party "had, in bringing together three of her worlds, shown her more clearly than she had known it before, that there was no place for her in any of them." Concomitant with which is then the experience, falling into silence, of something different, persistent and elsewhere, another reality: during the interval at a concert "her consciousness fell silent and empty. To be filled, as the moments flowed through this motionless centre, only by an awareness of the interval between the two parts of the concert as a loop in time, one of those occasions that bring with peculiar vividness the sense of identity, persistent, unchanging, personal identity, and return, in memory, inexhaustible." She too returns "inexhaustible," a difference of self which is increasingly the point of her desire, what she wants: "she *would* reach that central peace; go farther and farther into the heart of her being and be there, as if alone, tranquilly, until fully possessed by that something within her that was more than herself."

Thus the pilgrimage, the writing, "the strange journey down and down to the centre of being." Thus *Pilgrimage*, written in "scattered chapters," as Richardson put it in her subsequent "Foreword," a continuous publication from *Pointed Roofs* in 1915 to *Dimple Hill* in 1938 and then begun again with sections of *March Moonlight* appearing in 1946 in *Life and Letters*— thirteen book-chapters of an inevitably interminable project, a perpetual work on oneself. Which is Lawrence's objection, the long-drawn-out self-consciousness; what a more recent critic, Miriam Allott, calls "an alarming diffuseness and an uncritical subjectivity." Richardson herself took up such complaints in a question she formulated in one of her film pieces: "But must we not, today, emerge from our small individual existences and from narcissistic contemplation thereof?'; and answered with a stress on the importance of "mirroring the customary and resorting its essential quality." Film and writing have different possibilities, but restoring the essential, finding that in life, is the overall aim and ambition. What is "narcissism" for the critics is necessary journey for writer and reader, oneself coming into being.

A sure way of missing the essential is the novel with its smooth version of reality and all its illusions of identity. Take Wells. In 1909 he deals precisely with the "new woman" in the person of Ann Veronica, eponymous heroine of the resultant novel. From the initial crisis of resistance against her father's authority through to the final reunion with him after she has taken her full independence, Wells takes Ann Veronica out into the world and into a stand for freedom that leaves the constraints of the novel intact. Ann Veronica's career could shock in respect of the social conventions of the novel—Macmillan, Wells's habitual publisher, thought it "would be exceedingly distasteful to the public which buys books published by our firm" and refused it—but the conventional perspectives of the novel were still firmly there: "the best love story I have ever done" was just that, a story with all the fictions of character, description, and so on, with all the usual order of meaning. Ann Veronica is put in her novelistic place, rounded off into the required image, seen, supported, and summed up, identified as the new woman and tied back into the love story, the old vision repeated and updated in the terms of the novel with its usual ending: " 'Oh, my dear!' she cried, and suddenly flung herself kneeling into her husband's arms. . . . 'Blood of my heart!' whispered Capes, holding her close to him. 'I know. I understand.' " For woman today, as Ann Veronica has to demonstrate, "wants to be legally and economically free, so as not to be subject to the wrong man; but only God, who made the world, can alter things to prevent her being slave to the right one."

Wells is written into *Pilgrimage* as Hypo G. Wilson, introduced in *The Tunnel* in 1919 and a crucial presence in the novel thereafter. Ironically, and indicatively enough, the attempted seduction of Ann Veronica in Wells's novel by Ramage, a businessman neighbour of her father, is rewritten by Richardson in *Dawn's Left Hand* as Hypo's attempted seduction of Miriam. The same scenes recur—the evening at a performance of Wagner, the restaurant dinner in a private room—but now with the woman no longer an object of exchange, held for the reader in a novelistic adventure. Ramifying through the multiple drifts of Miriam's mind, the writing glimpses the seduction, its scenes, almost as a quotation from a novel, from *Ann Veronica* and all the others, part of the material of the book and the life but curiously strange and distant, falling short of any truth. Much of this gap between the idea of the novel and the reality of Richardson's writing is epitomised in her title: *Pilgrimage* as opposed to *Ann Veronica*. Wells believes in the novel, cut and dried, can finish it off with the name of his character, described, narrated, fixed; Richardson can only say the writing, the pilgrimage-journey that is this unending book in which Miriam is dispersed in a flow of thoughts and memories and bits and pieces of incident and impression and atmosphere and that can never be cast up into a "character." There are indeed parallels to be remembered here with the work of Proust and Joyce, equally at odds in their own ways with the idea of the novel: the "I" of *A la recherche* is not brought down to the usual novelistic fictions of a name, is only twice—and doubtfully—picked out as "Marcel," while in *Finnegans Wake* "Joyce" is continually present through a series of transformations, a kind of running signature, but never settled into any final appearance.

As might be expected, it is Hypo Wilson who suggests to Miriam that the novel is important, meeting with her fascinated resistance: "The torment of *all* novels is what is left out. The moment you are aware of it, there is torment in them. Bang, bang, bang, on they go, these men's books, like an L.C.C. tram." Novels are everywhere in life, spreading their fictions, giving us a role: " 'But perhaps he doesn't want to,' said Miriam, suddenly feeling that she was playing a familiar part in a novel and wanting to feel quite sure she was reading her role aright"; "A haunting familiar sense of unreality possessed her. Once more she was art of a novel; it was right, true like a book"; " 'Pray don't worry about the pace of my millinery, Mr Leyton.' That was quite good, like a society novel"; "Alma's social tone, deliberately clear and level. It made a little scene, the beginning of a novel." The novel is important and irrelevant, turning you into its terms, and then again, after all, "Perhaps novels are important."

Thus Miriam, envisaging the possibility of writing, its necessity. But Hypo, with his "hideous, irritating, meaningless word *novvle*," offers available places, recognised slots, "setting out the contents of the cruet as if they were pieces in a game." " 'Women ought to be good novelists. But they write best about their own experiences. Love-affairs and so forth. . . . Try a novel of ideas. . . . Be a feminine George Eliot. Try your hand.' " Much earlier in Miriam's life in the book, another male acquaintance had told her to write: " 'Have you ever thought of committing your ideas to paper? There's a book called *The Confessions of a Woman*. It had a great sale and its composition occupied the authoress for only six weeks. You could write it in your holidays.' " Now Hypo has it all sorted out, the professional writer offering a professional career in the novel: " '*Middles. Criticism*, which you'd do as other women do fancy-work. *Infant.* NOVEL.' " Miriam, however, is elsewhere: "But her interest had disappeared so completely that she went off in search of it."

Writing is a necessity and a problem, the pilgrimage and the difficulty of its novel. When Miriam finally begins to write, she produces a mass of hurriedly written pages that lose everything she is writing for. "These tracts of narrative were somehow false, a sort of throwing of dust that still would be dust even if its grains could be transformed to gold; question-begging, skating along surfaces to a superficial finality, gratuitously, in no matter what tone of voice, offered as a conclusion." What is needed is "to be rid of realism," as Virginia Woolf put it in a review of *The Tunnel*; or, as Richardson herself suggests in her "Foreword," to achieve the presence of a new "independently assertive reality":

> the present writer, proposing at this moment to write a novel and looking round for a contemporary pattern, was faced with the choice between following one of her regiments and attempting to produce a feminine equivalent of the current masculine realism. Choosing the latter alternative, she presently set aside, at the bidding of a dissatisfaction that revealed its nature without supplying any suggestion as to the removal of its cause, a considerable mass of manuscript. Aware, as she wrote, of the gradual falling away of the preoccupations that for a while had dictated the briskly moving script, and of the substitution, for these inspiring preoccupations, of a stranger in the form of contemplated reality having for the first time in her experience its own say, and apparently justifying those who acclaim writing as the surest means of discovering the truth about one's own thoughts and beliefs, she had been at the same time increasingly tormented, not only by the failure, of this now so independently assertive reality, adequately to appear within the text, but by its revelation, whencesoever focused, of a hundred faces, any one of which, the moment it was entrapped within the close mesh of direct statement, summoned its fellows to disqualify it.

The passage, typically complex, is an exact version of Miriam's situation with her tracts of narrative. Richardson in the 1938 "Foreword" looks back to initial attempts at writing in 1911 or before and is echoed by Miriam in *Dimple Hill*, also published in 1938, in about 1908 in the chronology of *Pilgrimage*; Miriam coming back at this point towards the close of *Pilgrimage* to the *Confessions of a Woman* advice she received at its beginning:

> It was Bob, driving so long ago a little nail into her mind when he said, "Write the confessions of a modern woman," meaning a sensational chronicle with an eye, several eyes, upon the interest

of sympathetic readers like himself—"Woman, life's heroine, the dear, exasperating creature"—who really likes to see how life looks from the other side, the women's side, who put me on the wrong track and created all those lifeless pages. Following them up, everything would be left out that is always there, preceding and accompanying and surviving the drama of human relationships; the reality from which people move away as soon as they closely approach and expect each other to be all in all.

What is at stake is writing. The book records the necessity for the book that this book is; Miriam's pilgrimage to be undertaken is this *Pilgrimage* written through the recreation of a life which is indeed already the pilgrimage for Miriam and which she must now learn in writing, "discovering the truth about one's own thoughts and beliefs." Miriam and Dorothy run into each other, "the form of contemplated reality have for the first time . . . its own say"; and the point is not that Miriam Henderson and Dorothy Richardson with their rhyming, chiming names are one and the same; it is that there is no *one*, only the myriad, the flow that only by a fiction—the old idea of the novel—can be stopped in some simple unity, some given identity. Writing is the knowledge of this: "to write is to forsake life," perhaps, but to write is also to know life, to *realise*, to say "I am" with the difference of the essential. The result is neither novel nor autobiography but an original record, a kind of "writing life" in which Richardson creates herself simultaneously with Miriam, becomes like Proust in *A la recherche* a text to be read in its single multiplicity—"cette lecture . . . un acte de création où nul ne peut nous suppléer," "notre seul livre," "la vie enfin découverte et éclaircie, la seule vie par conséquent réellement vécue."

May Sinclair, writing in 1918, found an expression for Richardson's new realism, one that was to know considerable success: "stream of consciousness." The feel of a streaming reality is certainly strong in *Pilgrimage*. For Miriam walking through the streets of London over "flags of pavement flowing," "Life streamed up from the close dense stone. With every footstep she felt she could fly." Everything interlocks in movement: the "sense of the sufficiency of life at first hand"—the shape of paving-stones, the clarity of light after rain, the set of a room—permeates the writing and is also that "quality of the atmosphere" into which Miriam is always dropping away from her public presence, and atmosphere and life at first hand are in turn the fact of response, of the flow of thoughts and memories and speculations, endless *reflections* in and out of mind, revolving lights (to take up the title of one of the book-chapters): "she found herself gliding into communion with surrounding things, shapes gleaming in the twilight, the intense thrilling beauty of the deep, lessening colours." What one wants is then not so much to recapture time lost, though the past is always present in the here and now of self-experience, "a bright moving patchwork," but rather to create the silence of oneself, to be separate, constant in movement: "There was no thought in the silence, no past or future, nothing but the strange thing for which there were no words, something that was always there as if by appointment waiting for one to get through to it away from everything in life." Dropping into "a trance of oblivion," Miriam can be herself, outside the life around her—the identities, the parts, all the novel; yet the trance is also the flow, the streaming of consciousness in and out of things and people and places, all the moments and intensities of life in which, from which alone oneself can be read.

One can say, one wants so much to say, "I am myself": divine instants of the "I" single, unique, mine; " 'It's me, *me*; this is *me* being alive,' she murmured with a feeling under her like the sudden drop of a lift." The strong baritone voice of a woman sings "Ai-me-moi!" and Miriam later remembers "that it had brought her a moment when the flower-filled drawing-room had seemed to be lit, from within herself, a sudden light that had kept her very still and made the bowls of roses blaze with deepening colours. In her mind she had seen garden beyond garden of roses, sunlit, brighter and brighter, and had made a rapturous prayer." Beyond the prayer, the pilgrimage. How is one ultimately to say "I am myself" if not in writing, the record-realisation of the unique, of "the original contents of [a] mind"?

Hence the project of the book, stream of consciousness as self-creation, not the novel but writing, not the surface but the underlying movement, a kind of elliptical concatenation of pauses in what for the novel would be reality, a story in elsewheres and silences.

"Only of course there are so many kinds of silence. But the test of absolutely everything in life is the quality of the in-between silences." Thus Miriam to Hypo, deciding no longer to be beguiled into surface and conformity: "Somehow make him aware of the reality that fell, all the time, in the surrounding silence, outside his shapes and classifications." For him that silence is merely a void, an emptiness from which to be rescued, to come back into the security of talking, conversation. For Miriam and the book, constant theme and demonstration, all conversation is "a lie"; talk goes on, smoothly renewing the surface, filling up the troubling silences: "Their talk had gone on. It was certain that always they would talk. Archipelagos of talk, avoiding anything that could endanger continuous urbanity." Under the conversational reality is another reality, forgotten and disquieting and essential:

> There are two layers of truth. The truths laid bare by common sense in swift decisive conversations, founded on apparent facts, are incomplete. They shape the surface, and make things go kaleidoscoping on, recognizable, in a sort of general busy prosperous agreement; but at every turn, with every application of the common-sense civilized decisions, enormous things are left behind, unsuspected, forced underground, but never dying, slow things with slow, slow fruit. . . . The surface shape is powerful, every one is in it, that is where free will breaks down, in the moving on

and being spirited away for another spell from the underlying things, but in every one, alone, often unconsciously, is something, a real inside personality that is turned away from the surface. In front of every one, away from the bridges and catchwords, is an invisible plank, that will bear. Always. Forgotten. Nearly all smiles are smiled from the bridges . . . Nearly all deaths are murders or suicides.

The surface is made up of bridges and catchwords, speech which "does nothing but destroy," sets things "in a mould"—a whole world of inevitable misrepresentation: "nothing can ever be communicated"; "even in the most favourable circumstances, people could hardly communicate with each other at all." And this is more than criticism of some particular social use of language, it is language itself which is the object of a radical distrust. Language classifies, fixes, defines, producing a common ground of meaning that misses individuality, uniqueness, real meaning: "language is the only way of expressing anything and it dims everything." What language does is to make statements, but statements have nothing to do with the movement of my thoughts and experiences, all the impressions of life: "Anything that can be put into propositions is suspect. The only thing that isn't suspect is individuality." To put it another way, language is technical, a kind of dull jargon which because of its necessary generality is always wrong, never fits the particular case: "Every word. In telling things, technical terms must be used; which never quite apply." So that one is writing in the end for silence: caught in language, "the only way of expressing anything," aware of its hopelessness, "it dims everything," and then committed nevertheless to seize out of it some essential expression, to make space for the individual, to give "the original contents of [a] mind": writing then as the project of that, falling into the silences.

At one point during the seduction, Hypo calls Miriam "pretty":

"You *are* a pretty creature, Miriam. I wish you could see yourself."

With the eyes of Amabel, and with her own eyes opened by Amabel, she saw the long honey-coloured ropes of hair framing the face that Amabel found beautiful in its "Flemish Madonna" type, falling across her shoulders and along her body where the last foot of their length, red-gold, gleamed marvellously against the rose-tinted velvety gleaming of her flesh. Saw the lines and curves of her limbs, their balance and harmony. Impersonally beautiful and inspiring. To him each detail was "pretty," and the whole an object of desire.

"Pretty" is his *observation*; he can only see, has only a linguistic vision of things. Thus the relationship between Miriam and the Amabel mentioned in the passage is picked up at once by his "intelligent eye, blinkered in advance with unsound generalizations about 'these intense, over-personal feminine friendships.' " But for Miriam and the reader the relationship with Amabel is never exactly defined; or rather, it is exactly defined precisely in as much as it is not dropped into any generalisation, is removed from any summary definition. Seeing through the experience of Amabel, "her own eyes opened by Amabel," Miriam—and the reader with her—sees differently, away from "the clumsy masculine machinery of observation."

The distrust of language goes along then with an opposition between women and men, and that opposition finds indeed political and social articulation in the book. The writing often engages through Miriam militant positions and offers a violent reaction to men and their world, to their impossible repression: "They despise women and they want to go on living—to reproduce—themselves. None of their achievements, no "civilization," no art, no science can redeem that. There is no pardon possible for man. The only answer to them is suicide; all women ought to agree to commit suicide." Elsewhere it marks through her a distance from militancy: the experience of the suffragette demonstrations is recorded through Amabel's participation as mediated by Miriam's removed and doubtful consciousness. Hers is an "intermittent feminism," intermittent because the commitment is to individuality, the unique complex of oneself, and because of an extreme version of the essential untouchability of women, their radical separation, something that feminists —"an insult to womanhood"—fail to grasp: "Those women's rights people are the worst of all. Because they think women have been 'subject' in the past. Women never have been subject. Never can be. . . . Disabilities, imposed by law, are a stupid insult to women, but have never touched them as individuals."

The opposition between women and men, their difference, is thus crucial, and crucial with regard to language and meaning. Everywhere one has "this muddle of men and women with nothing in common"; throughout Miriam is confirmed in "her certainty that between men and women there can be no direct communication." Indeed, they speak different languages. "She may understand his. Hers he will never speak nor understand. In pity, or from other motives, she must therefore, stammeringly, speak his. He listens and is flattered and thinks he has her mental measure when he has not touched even the fringe of her consciousness." Miriam moves her friend Michael to uneasy anger by her insistence that women "*can't* be represented by men. Because by every word they use men and women mean different things."

Women must speak in their own language, but the opposition between women and men is accompanied by the distrust anyway of language: there is no communication between the sexes, but there is no communication in language either, "nothing can ever be communicated." Is language then irredeemably male? Men and language deal in statements; men and their books, sums of language, close things up, finish off: "Clever phrases that make you see things by a deliberate arrangement, leave an impression that is false to life. But men do see life in this way, disposing of things and rushing on with their talk; they think like that, all their thoughts false to life; everything neatly described in single phrases that are not true. Starting with a false statement, they go on piling up their books." To learn this language—but is there any other?—is to fit with men, quoting the surface as " 'clever' women" do: "To write books, knowing all about style, would be to become like a man."

In a famous passage of her review of *Revolving Lights*, Virginia Woolf spoke of Richardson's invention of a woman's sentence:

> She has invented, or, if she has not invented, developed and applied to her own uses, a sentence which we might call the psychological sentence of the feminine gender. It is of a more elastic fibre than the old, capable of stretching to the extreme, of suspending the frailest particles, of enveloping the vaguest shapes. Other writers of the opposite sex have used sentences of this description and stretched them to the extreme. But there is a difference. Miss Richardson has fashioned her sentence consciously, in order that it may descend to the depths and investigate the crannies of Miriam Henderson's consciousness. It is a woman's sentence, but only in the sense that it is used to describe a woman's mind by a writer who is neither proud nor afraid of anything that she may discover in the psychology of her sex.

It is a passage that is worth holding on to in all its nuances and turns: a woman's sentence, but not because it is in its very form some essential expression of the woman writer, since men can write such sentences too; a woman's sentence because it is used to explore a woman's mind; but then again too because it is rooted in "the psychology of her sex," because there *is* the difference, some feel of an essence that allows its identification nevertheless as "the psychological sentence of the feminine gender." On the one hand for Richardson, "Everybody is a special category"; on the other, but at the same time, as it were, women share a common silence, a common elsewhereness to assertion and position, what Richardson calls in an article on "Leadership in Marriage" their " 'shapeless' shapeliness."

Men's writing is a refusal of this, and a relief from it: "It is because these men *write* so well that it is a relief, from looking and enduring the clamour of the way things state themselves from several points of view simultaneously, to read their large superficial statements. Light seems to come. . . . But the after reflection is gloom, a poisoning gloom over everything." Reality is multifarious, a mesh of diffuse and diverging intensities beyond statement or position. What is needed is a sentence, a writing, that can suspend the frailest particles, stretch to the extreme, envelop the vaguest shapes. And this is a sentence of the feminine gender, for women are multifarious, essentially beyond statements, positions ("women can hold all opinions at once, or any, or none"). What Sinclair calls "stream of consciousness" in Richardson is thus a critique of the idea of the novel, a perception of reality, and a psychology of women.

The "female psyche" is one of the great concerns of the early decades of the twentieth century when Richardson is living and writing, a concern contemporary with the powerful developments of women's struggles to change their condition and definition: on the one hand, it is part of those struggles, raising questions of the reality of women's experience and of new representations; on the other, it is a reaction to them, attempting to make up the old fictions of identity, confirm the place of "the woman." It is in this context that the issue of *The Adelphi* to which Richardson contributes an article "About Punctuation" will also contain a piece on "The Ugliness of Women" ("I believe that in every woman born there is a seed of terrible, unmentionable evil"), or that D. H. Lawrence in the 1920s will be writing popular newspaper features with titles such as "The Real Trouble About Women" and "Women Don't Change" ("women are women"). Psychoanalysis is important here too, serving largely to set out the terms of debate with its new conception of sexuality and its particular methods for exploring and understanding the psychical apparatus. Richardson herself was fully aware of this: one of her good friends, Barbara Low, was a psychoanalyst and the author of *Psycho-Analysis: A Brief Account of the Freudian Theory*, which she reviewed in 1920 for *Dental Record*; another close friend, Winifred Bryher, was analysed by Hanns Sachs and the latter wrote on psychoanalysis and film for *Close Up*. Barbara Low, moreover, enthused over Lawrence's *The Rainbow*, read in manuscript, when she first met Richardson in 1915; Richardson then sent *Pointed Roofs* to Lawrence's publisher, Duckworth, where the reader, Edward Garnett, judged it "feminine impressionism" and recommended its acceptance. These intellectual and literary interconnections thus bring us back to the novel, itself massively caught up in the concern with woman and her representation: Wells's *Ann Veronica* is one kind of example, Joyce's *Ulysses* another, with its final "female monologue" as Molly-Penelope lies musing in bed praised by Jung, no less, as "a string of veritable psychological peaches."

Richardson's work is near to all this (we should note, just to continue the interconnections, that sections from *Interim* were published alongside episodes from *Ulysses* in *The Little Review* in 1919–20 which also ran articles comparing Richardson and Joyce). When John Cowper Powys talks of Richardson bringing to light "a complete continent, a submerged Lost Atlantis of feminine susceptibility," there is no great distance from Jung's praise of Molly's monologue, Arnold Bennett's for Joyce's supreme understanding of "feminine psychology." And this is not simply a male image, not simply a determined misreading. Richardson herself uses phrases of this kind and can refer to Jung's work to do so, defining "the unique gift of the feminine psyche" and discussing "the essential characteristic of the womanly woman." The " 'shapeless' shapeliness" mentioned earlier is another such identification of woman, and *Pilgrimage* anyway, as was seen, is everywhere involved in questions of the nature of women and men, their difference and separation. *Pilgrimage* is not the *Confessions of a Woman* Miriam is advised to write, but at the same time it has something nevertheless of a reality of that title; "a lifetime might be well spent in annotating the male novelists,

filling out the vast oblivions in them" and that is at once part of the dissatisfaction with the novel and Hypo's contents-of-the-cruet slots but also
a part of the project of Richardson's novel, part of how it reads. Resistance
is the risk of essence, the opposition turns on an alternative representation
that is always potentially another definition, another given place.

The same Virginia Woolf who commended Richardson's invention of
"the psychological sentence of the feminine gender" also believed that "It
is fatal for anyone who writes to think of their sex" and that the act of
writing is androgynous, the writer male and female together. Powys said
something the same about Richardson specifically: "all authentic human
genius is, in some degree, bi-sexual. . . . she is the first *consciously to turn
the two elements upon each other* in a reciprocal fury of psychological interpretation." These notions of androgyny and bisexuality, however, are still
bound up with thinking of sex, male plus female, female plus male; are
still locked into assumptions—ideas, positions, representations—of the
one and the other. An aspect of the fatality is then precisely the difficulty
of distinguishing the alternative from the accepted representation and of
avoiding the mere repetition, but now as value, of the place already as-
signed as limitation: men are on the side of language and classification and
statement; women are elsewhere, but this is an old story of the illogical,
emotional woman; women have a shapeless shapeliness, and this too has
been heard before, men make shapes, stand out erect, women flow, like
ALP in the closing pages of *Finnegans Wake*. Joyce famously leaves the Molly
chapter of *Ulysses* unpunctuated, eight long unstopped sentences until the
final "Yes.": "Do you notice how women when they write disregard stops
and capital letters?", Richardson agrees: "Feminine prose, as Charles Dickens and James Joyce have delightfully shown themselves to be aware,
should properly be unpunctuated, moving from point to point without
formal obstructions." But why should this be if not by reference to the
representation of women as "the woman," "the feminine," as unformed,
fluid, inconsistent?

In her essay "About Punctuation," also referred to in the 1938
"Foreword," just after the remark on feminine prose quoted above, Richardson makes a different emphasis: "in the slow, attentive reading demanded by unpunctuated texts, the faculty of hearing has its chance, is
enhanced until the text *speaks* itself." Punctuation as we know it is developed concomitantly with print, with the *book*, moving from a foundation
in the encounter of voice and language to a logic of truth and its subject
(punctuating for "the better understanding of the sense" as opposed to
"for the ease of breath" is not a common conception in English, for example,
until the beginning of the eighteenth century, when it goes along with the
general desire to "fix" the language as a stable instrument for a free exchange between speaking subjects grounded in universal reason, common
sense). Without punctuation there is no single point of view; without punctuation the text speaks itself: multiple possibilities all at once, no one subject, no standard communication (early in *Pilgrimage* Miriam is offended by

the word "standard," as in "standard book": "It suggested fixed agreement about the things people ought to know and that she felt sure must be wrong, and not only wrong but 'common' . . . standard readers."). What Richardson is emphasising is again the question of identity and the fictions of its stability, its representation, in which the novel, books, talk, language itself all participate, with which they are complicit. So *Pilgrimage* is nonstandard (compare *Ann Veronica*): no endings (the last of the book's chapters stops on a question, none of them comes to any conclusion), no go-ahead narrative timing (the chapters are more and more unparaphrasable, resistant to any summary), ellipses and fragments, long intricately claused and variformly punctuated sentences, "an astonishing variety of patterns."

This it is that is simultaneously referred, and by Richardson herself, to "the feminine," and we can perhaps grasp why it should be that modern writing in the novel runs into such a reference. Language itself is neither male nor female, but nor is it simply neutral: it exists only in use, which is to say in specific orders of discourse, and these bring with them, among other things, specific representations of their speaking subject. The stabilisation of language in respect of "communication," "free exchange," "instrument" for the transmission of a general knowledge, a unity of "thoughts," is the institution of a subject position that eradicates all contradictions of class and sexual differences: indifferent, a function of the general knowledge, the subject is male; women are relegated to any excess of language, any disturbance of the norm—female illogicality, diffuseness, and so on. The novel, on the basis of this stable language and increasingly invested in as a crucial social mechanism, makes sense in the area of subjectivity, deals with the problems of the relations between the social and the individual, *represents*. Part of that representation importantly is the maintenance of the identity of the woman, stories, explorations, definitions that repeat and renew her place as a condition of the smooth operation of the whole system. "Bang, bang, bang," Miriam's words to Hypo, novels issue statements, set out the terms of the available reality.

To challenge that is then quickly to write "feminine," in contradiction, differently, to the established forms and fictions; Molly and ALP are inevitably the end of Joyce's two great texts as modern writing. Yet here, in this, the challenge works and jams; the given identities are called into question and are ever-present; opposition takes its stand on the old position. "Male" and "female," their identification, "the man" and "the woman," are after all the guarantee of stability, the very standard: the one and the other, different, unknown, the submerged continent, the formless, and so on and on. The moment the writing goes "feminine," uses that as its point of displacement, it turns from the Wells novel but can also say the same thing. The chorus of over-eager male praise for Joyce's achievement at the end of *Ulysses* is indicative and right—Joyce has (re-)produced "the woman" (and so the identity of "the man" with her).

The interest and power of Richardson's work is that it intersects with this modern writing in the novel—is itself a major example —and provides a radical edge to what effectively becomes the stock reference to "the feminine," "the woman," breaks that *image*. *Pilgrimage* is full of a psyche and a psychology, common terms, to which at the same time in its writing it never gives a final hold. Reviewing *Clear Horizon* for *Scrutiny* in 1935, Q. D. Leavis wrote of Richardson that "her pre-occupations date already as being those of a period when woman—as distinct from individual women—was a matter for defiant assertion." But this is quite wrong: woman was a concern and Richardson was concerned in the debates, and without condescension or dismissiveness, aware of their political importance; yet her essential value was always the individual, the intensity of a particular life, a unique reality ("independently assertive"). "We all have different sets of realities," says Miriam to Hypo, who replies inevitably "That, believe me, is impossible." Writing her life, Miriam's life, Richardson is involved in and against that impossibility, a process of self-discovery. Individuality, the fact of *my* experience, is not outside but through language, existing forms, social modes; essence is a production in and with all the matter of reality, has a history in history: Richardson makes out a complex historical consciousness —personal, social, and political necessarily all interwoven and traced into one another. What is important, the resistance, is to break the fixity of representations, their given identities, where one is "called upon" to be; and the crux of that fixity, the hold of the system, is the very proposition of "one"—as though *I* were some figure from a novel, like Ann Veronica, and not a Miriam, a myriad of moments and intensities and inflections—and with it "the man"/"the woman," the basic assumption of oneness, one and other, the difference on which identity can turn—so that to resist fixity, where I am called upon as *one*, is also and immediately to call into question the representation of sexual difference, fighting strongly through life and book against the oppression it sustains and writing for the individual.

What Lawrence dismissed as childish absorption is here, in fact, a kind of utopia of individuality, offered to the reader as such, as that experience. To write is to forsake life and to project the terms of its reality. "Contemplation is adventure into discovery; reality": writing is the form of contemplation, the fundamental silence. "Fully to recognize, one must be alone": writer and reader together, caught up in a movement, in the dispersion of writing, out of place, as on "neutral territory, where one can forget one is there, and be everywhere." *Pilgrimage*—writing for silence.

The Originality of E. M. Forster

Daniel R. Schwarz

Although his novels superficially resemble Victorian novels, it is not too much to say that E. M. Forster permanently changed the English novel. Perhaps his not having written novels for the last four decades of his life has inhibited recognition of the seminal role Forster played in the transformation of the Victorian novel into what we know as the modern novel. For example, Lionel Stevenson barely mentions E. M. Forster's contribution, and Walter Allen asserts that Forster cannot "be regarded as a pioneer" and places him "in the older English tradition which, beginning with Fielding, ends, we normally assume, with Meredith." In this essay, I shall make rather more substantial claims for Forster's originality as an artist than are usually made.

Forster's originality is based on four major achievements: first, in the guise of writing objective novels, he wrote personal, subjective ones. He used the conventional omniscient narrator in novels that have a large expressive component. For Forster's novels, like those of the other great modern British novelists —Joyce, Lawrence, Woolf, and Conrad—are the history of his soul, metaphors of the self. His novels not only dramatize his characters' search for values but structurally are quests for values, quests that reflect his own doubt and uncertainty.

Second, he conceived of the structure of a novel as a continuous process by which values are presented, tested, preserved, or discarded rather than as the conclusion of a series that clarifies and reorders everything that precedes. Thus, his final scene is merely one in a series of events that happens to be the last that the reader will experience. Consequently, the issues raised in the novel remain unresolved, and the future direction of the surviving characters often is open to speculation.

Third, in his novels, Forster challenged not only the artistic and the-

From *Modern Fiction Studies* 29, no. 4 (Winter 1983). © 1984 by Purdue Research Foundation.

matic conventions of the novel of manners but the traditions of manners and morals on which British life and fiction depended. His novels tested accepted Victorian shibboleths about proper and decorous behavior, about the importance of reason as necessary to control unruly passions and instincts, and about the relationships among social classes. His characters do not discover a place within the community but remain outside of it. When his characters acknowledge their sexuality in the face of conventions, they are not, as in prior novels, punished for it. The plots establish the validity of instinct, passion, and inner life.

Fourth, he expanded the novel's range beyond drawing rooms, which provide the setting for so much of the English novel. In his effort to reach for poetry and passion, he expanded the novel geographically (India, Italy), sociologically (Leonard Bast; the schisms that divide classes, races, and religions), and cosmologically (the mysterious Marabar Caves and the Hindu perspective in *Passage to India*).

II

The debt of the Victorian novel to the eighteenth-century novel includes a debt to neoclassical—what we think of as Aristotelian—assumptions about the central role of plot in a novel's form. But Forster is not an Aristotelian. He thinks of plot as a series of circumstances, often arbitrarily selected and arranged, that enables the author to explore the characters' personal lives and values. In a Forster novel, plot is important, but no more than voice or setting and less than the moral and emotional life of the characters. Forster's plots, in fact, mime the quest of his principal characters to escape social entrapment by expressing feelings and passions and by creating personal ties. It is characteristic of Forster that the ending is another in a series of episodes in which man's limitations are exposed rather than an apocalyptic episode that resolves prior social and moral problems. In *Aspects* he wrote rather critically: "Nearly all novels are feeble at the end. This is because the plot requires to be wound up." But Forster ended his novels without resolving them in order to imply that life was a continuous process that could not be summarized arbitrarily by a climactic incident (other than death) at the end of a narrative.

Like the other major British modernists—Conrad, Lawrence, Joyce, and Woolf—he understood human character as a continually changing flux of experience rather than as fixed and static, as in the traditional novel of manners, and sought to dramatize states of mind at crucial moments. The essence of a Forster novel is contained in crystallizing moments that give the flux meaning. He believed, however, that within the flux of each person's experience were crucial symbolic moments, watersheds of experience, when, as he puts it in *Aspects of the Novel*, "life in time" gives way to "life by values," and the significance of a character's life reveals itself. But these moments, akin to Joyce's epiphanies, are often not complete in themselves or clearly understood by the character who experiences them, even though the narrator and reader understand them. In part, his novels are a concatenation of these significant moments in the lives of his major characters.

For Forster, fiction provided the only possible principle of order in the face of major historical forces that seemed to have deprived man of his significance—the Industrial Revolution, imperialism, urbanization, and the intensifying organization and systemization of English life. He is interested in these historical phenomena insofar as they affect the quality of man's feelings, imagination, and personal relationships. Flux is both an inevitable part of life with which we must come to terms and an enemy that we must combat. It makes anachronistic the social solutions of the past. And Forster thought that the kind of novel that a conservative, hierarchical society produced is also anachronistic. In the face of the instability of personal relations, of class structure, and of accepted standards of social behavior, the novel of manners, in which the author relies upon his audience to recognize violations of decorum and propriety, begins to break down. In Lawrence, Joyce, and Woolf, as well as in Forster, characters are judged on whether they are true to their best impulses rather than on how they function in the community.

Forster's novels enact his quest for the inner life as well as his attempt to rescue himself from the curse of modernism. In a sense, Forster's novels are elegiac and nostalgic. Like Eliot, Joyce, Conrad, and Lawrence, he juxtaposes the present and the past, in part to define the present, in part out of nostalgia for the past. The urbanization of England undermined the sense of continuity that had prevailed in England since Elizabethan times, a continuity that even the Revolution of 1640 did not disrupt entirely. The continuity derived from land passed down through generations, from the rhythms of rural culture, from the monarchial succession, from the strong sense of English family, and from the relatively stable roles played by the clergy, aristocracy, and Parliament.

Forster's novels, like Hardy's and Lawrence's, seek to create, nostalgically, an English pastoral, a mythology with tales of English heroes that would invigorate the culture and the language. Like Lawrence, Conrad, and Hardy, Forster stands with the Coleridgeans against the Utilitarians. Thus, rural life—the myth of the English countryside—is a source of values. In *Howards End*, he writes, "In these English farms, if anywhere, one might see life steadily and see it whole, group in one version its transitoriness and its eternal youth, connect—connect without bitterness until all men are brothers." Like Arnold's, Forster's goal was "to see life steadily and see it whole." Forster is, above all, a humanist who does not believe that a God directs human destiny. And as for Arnold, Art was a surrogate for religion. With its carefully constructed patterns and symbolic scenes, the artificial order of the novel was, for Forster, an alternative to disbelief.

Beginning with Hardy and Conrad, major British writers frequently examine the events of the narrative in the context of vast historical perspectives. Lawrence, Conrad, Joyce (and, of course, Yeats and Eliot) also dramatize the present through the lens of the past. Frazer's *The Golden*

Bough (1890) extended the range of the past beyond Biblical times and beyond even historical time; later, Jung's emphasis on archetypes stresses that all cultures share common anthropological experience and psychological traits. And Forster wishes to show that, despite differences in breeding, customs, and values, a common heritage united mankind. Crucial aspects of Forster's values rest in what he calls "the inner life" and the "unseen," which resist language. By the "inner life" he means passions and feelings, those aspects of life in which man may experience poetry and romance. For Forster, the "unseen" means not the traditional Christian God but a world beyond things, a world that can be reached by passions, imagination, intelligence, and affection. Like Conrad, Lawrence, and Joyce, Forster sees the need to revivify family ties and personal relationships that form the basis of both ancient cultures and British civilization. Forster wants the novel to move beyond local, nominalistic insight and toward universal truths. As he puts it in *Aspects of the Novel*, he wants his fiction to "[reach] back . . . to join up with all the other people far back."

Whereas Victorian novelists usually wrote of how man lived in the community and examined the values for which man lived, their successors, including Forster, wrote about themselves. Influenced by impressionism and postimpressionism, which stressed the uniqueness of each man's perception, as well as by the dissolution of moral and political certainties in the 1890–1910 period, Forster wrote fiction that expressed his private feelings, the idiosyncracies of his personality, and the anxieties and frustrations of his psyche. Like Conrad, Lawrence, Joyce, and Woolf, he wished to create the order in art that the world lacked; like them, he wished to create himself in his art and to export that created self back into his life; like them, writing fiction became his means of defining himself. Forster reveals his psyche and values on every page, yet he is a far less prominent presence than Conrad, Lawrence, Joyce, or Woolf. Forster's own spiritual quest determines the form of his novels. Rather than establishing a fixed standard of values by which he measures his characters, his technically omniscient voice undergoes a quest for values.

Forster's aesthetic values cannot be separated from his moral ones. With their elegant phrasing, tact, balance, and sensibility, Forster's novels enact his values. They are the objective correlative for the keen sensibility, the personal relationships, the delicate discriminations of feeling that he sought. Within the sustained creative activity, the artist discovers unity and coherence in his own life, and the completed work of art provides unity and coherence for others. Forster sought to move beyond the subjective and to create an impersonal art out of his own experiences and feelings. But he never quite succeeded in getting outside of himself, and it may be that his novels are more exciting because of this. Although Forster grew as a novelist and gradually enlarged his scope, he never suppressed his own doubts and anxieties simply to create an objective vision for himself and his reader.

In *Aspects* he expressed his admiration for Hardy: "The work of Hardy is my home." This has been taken to mean Forster is an heir to the Victorian novel, but Forster, like Lawrence, realized that Hardy was one of the great innovators in the English novel. Hardy taught Forster, particularly in *Jude the Obscure*, that the author did not have to separate the omniscient narrator from the protagonist's perspective. Like Hardy, he uses an omniscient voice that often becomes an empathetic spokesman for major characters. Like Hardy, he creates an alternative to the benevolent cosmos that dominated English fiction prior to Hardy. Like Hardy, Forster gave up writing novels in the middle of his career. Forster not only was influenced by Hardy's skeptical world view and his sense of story but by his stress on various kinds of sexual exploitation. Forster transfers Hardy's sexual themes primarily to the upper middle class. *Howards End* is a kind of retelling of *Tess of the D'Urbervilles*, with both Jackie and Helen playing variations of Tess's role with Wilcox; Wilcox's son, Paul, is version of Alex; and Leonard is a parody of Angel. Forster is criticizing the hypocrisy and insanity of sexual morality that allows Henry Wilcox, twice a seducer, to condemn Helen Schlegel's sexual peccadillo.

Forster's view of man is somewhere between Hardy's pessimism and Lawrence's optimism; he doubts man's capacities but believes that man will muddle through and that the artist provides a model for the potential of the individual imagination to create meaning and of the individual heart to respond, on occasion, in a humane way. Forster shares with other great modernists the belief that language could create meaning, could exorcise chaos when all else fails. Forster is often a polite version of Lawrence, of whom he wrote admiringly in *Aspects*. Like Lawrence, he saw himself in the tradition of the English Romantics, who sought to combine the visionary and realistic mode, the prophetic and the personal. Both frequently sound an elegaic and nostalgic note. Both regretted that man was no longer in harmony with nature and that the Industrial Revolution had deprived man of his individuality. Forster anticipates Lawrence in dramatizing what industrialism and commercialism had taken from the modern world. Doesn't Wilcox suggest Gerald Crich? The former thinks that the force of his will can reshape the world to his own image and is "broken" when circumstances, in the form of a manslaughter charge against his son, move beyond his control.

III

The originality of the individual novels is the central focus of this essay. Such an approach may not do justice to the density and complexity of the novels, but discussing how Forster's novels differ from their predecessors not only enables us to appreciate Forster's uniqueness as an artist but places the relationship between Forster's values and techniques into a new perspective. Because Forster's two masterpieces, *Howards End* and *Passage to India*, are also his most innovative novels, I shall stress these works. But, because the implicit and explicit argument is that Forster's novels are collectively strikingly original in concept, theme, and execution, I shall discuss the entire canon.

In *Where Angels Fear to Tread* (1905), Forster begins the process of turning the English novel of manners upside down. He recognizes the role of sexual passion in human behavior and eschews moral judgment about such passions. Lilia Herriton and Caroline Abbott are attracted and aroused by the primitive energy of Gino, the young Italian son of a dentist, who, by English standards, lacks culture and civilization.

Where Angels Fear to Tread also introduces Forster's characteristic theme of a conflict between two cultures. Forster believes that place shapes character. Here it is Italy versus England, as epitomized by Mrs. Herriton and even more by the next generation in the person of her daughter Harriet, is depicted as sexually repressed, emotionally sterile, and impotent in personal relations. Philip, the self-conscious, disengaged man who has difficulty feeling and suffers from a kind of anomie, introduces a new character into English fiction. By contrast, Italy retains passion, poetry, sexuality and thus offers the possibility of "intimacy" and "perfect friendship." Gino represents an older tradition of instinctive life that survives in spite of civilization's conventions and restraints. Certainly Caroline and Philip are changed by their days at Monteriano. The passions of Lilia, Gino, and finally Caroline overwhelm the traditions that would restrain them. The novel shows that feelings and passions are the essences of being alive.

Until *Passage to India* and *Howards End*, Forster's voice rarely has the certainty of the authoritative, omniscient voice of Victorian fiction. Thus, the reader of a Forster novel must be especially attentive to irony and to the psychological nuances of character. Part of Forster's modernity is his expectation that the reader will discover relationships and significance. Forster's reticence, the sparsity of his analysis in comparison to contemporaries such as Bennett or Galsworthy, is part of his technique; as illustration, let us look at the climax of *Where Angels Fear to Tread*:

> She said plainly "That I love him." Then she broke down. Her
> body was shaken with sobs, and lest there should be any doubt
> she cried between the sobs for Gino! Gino! Gino!
>   He heard himself remark "Rather! I love him too!"

Her hysterical surrender to sexual passion and his latent homosexuality introduce something new into English fiction. Forster's range of sexual emotions goes a step further than Hardy's, even in *Jude the Obscure*. Forster's poised balance and irony reveal the limitations of characters who do not quite know themselves. No sooner does Philip move away from the aesthetic view of life than he lapses when his love is unrequited. After his declaration he becomes inhibited by his learning, his snobbery, his self-irony, and his lifelong subservience to his mother.

Forster's novels open up possibilities but do not resolve them. In his first novel, he emphasizes that the structure is a process by which characters search for values. Caroline's return alone to England is a kind of defeat.

Unlike Lilia, Caroline does seem to compromise with her passion. Given her strength of character and her ability to influence Gino, would she have failed with him had she declared her passion? Although Forster has shown us that Gino quickly has fallen into the stereotypical Italian marriage, Caroline has a depth that Lilia lacks and that Gino acknowledges. Yet Caroline has also readily submitted to convention and perhaps let the presence of Philip and Harriet check her passion. At that close, Forster leaves the reader to ponder whether not only Philip but even the more open Caroline will revert to their Sawston personalities. As Caroline and Philip go to nurse Harriet, we wonder whether either of them is open to experience.

Philip looks upon life as spectacle. He is a voyeur of the passions. His aesthetic view of life objectifies an impulse Forster both despised and feared that he possessed. Forster felt that moral engagement was the essence of art and life. When Philip finally declares his passion, Caroline Abbott's response exposes his limitations (although, to be fair to Philip, she does not realize that he is changing): "You're without passion; you look on life as a spectacle: you don't enter it; you only find it funny or beautiful." Philip's aestheticism may be part of Forster's efforts to imply obliquely his character's latent homosexuality and to define a male figure who is ambivalent about heterosexual passion (we might recall *Maurice*, where Clive's aesthetic sense and reading of *The Symposium* place Maurice and Clive's love beyond carnal intercourse).

Thus, can we not tentatively conclude that Forster's presence becomes part of the novel's imagined world? The incompleteness of heterosexual relationships, in part, represents the emotional reticence of the homosexual Forster to dramatize sexual fulfillment. The potentially fulfilling heterosexual relationship is necessarily discarded in *Where Angels Fear to Tread* when Philip cannot reach the obvious decision to rescue himself and Caroline. And this is part of a pattern in Forster's work. In *The Longest Journey*, Gerald, an appropriate mate for Agnes, dies, and Maud and Rickie never connect. *Howards End* shows marriage and heterosexual relationships as a series of missed opportunities. As we shall see, only the ending of *A Room* shows that conventions might be rejected. And, because Lucy and young Emerson seem to have turned their back on England, their triumph is purely personal and offers little hope for England.

In *The Longest Journey* (1907), Forster is unable to separate himself from Rickie. If the reader knows Forster's biography and other works, the reader understands the tension within the text, a tension heightened at crucial times within Rickie's narrative. Rickie's problem as a character is that he cannot maintain his iconoclasm and independence. An author himself, Rickie is unable to separate himself from the roles that society demands. Here, as in all Forster's novels, social conventions stifle the imagination, blunt the feelings, inhibit the passions, and ignore the demands of the inner life. Rickie diminishes as a character until he is subsumed into the role he despises. He becomes another Pembroke, his wife's philistine brother. Symbolically, Ansell and Stephen Wonham may be, as Stone contends, the "intellectual and physical halves of Rickie's estranged soul, the Apollonian and the Dionysian," and of Forster's also, but they become more substantive characters in the novel's imagined world. Unlike Rickie, who cannot sustain his identity, they maintain their authentic selves.

One of Forster's principal themes is how conventional sexual morals restrict the development of the inner life and stifle the possibilities of growth and fulfillment. In a way, *The Longest Journey* is a whimsical retelling of *Jude the Obscure*. Forster places Rickie in the role of Jude, a man whose aspirations are continually adjusted downward in a world beyond his control, and places Agnes in the peculiar role of an Arabella who poses as a Sue. Of course the real salvation for Rickie rests in implicit sexual connection with Stewart Ansell (a male Sue) and Rickie's bastard brother Stephen (a male Arabella). When Stewart holds on to Rickie's ankle in the meadow the day he is captured by Agnes (I think captured is exactly how we are supposed to regard her conquest in the dell), the homosexual relationship with Stewart represents the road not taken, the better path. The form of the novel rejects not only conventional marriage but the formal resolution of life in marriage that characterizes the novel of manners; perhaps, in one sense, the epithet "the longest journey" ironically applies to conventional marriage and the genre that testifies to its efficacy.

In the final section, after saving Stephen's life, Rickie ironically tries to recreate Stephen in his image as Herbert has done for him. The ending reaches for prophecy but unfortunately achieves bathos and fustian when Forster writes, "Though he could not phrase it, [Stephen] believed that he guided the future of our race, and that, century after century, his thoughts and his passions would triumph in England." Nothing that precedes justifies Stephen's naive faith in himself, and his erratic character hardly bodes well for the future of England or for himself.

Passion, instinct, and spontaneity surge through *A Room With A View* (1908) and challenge the formalism of Victorian manners dramatized within the novel. This formalism represses and controls the passion and energy that threaten it. It does so by imposition of stereotyped roles and conventional relationships — Charlotte, not only as guide for Lucy in Florence but as protector of her purity; Cecil, as the potential husband for Lucy, the supposedly submissive young virgin. Although we can trace Lucy Honeychurch back to George Eliot, she represents a continuation of another stage in the evolution of a new character in English fiction, the independent, self-possessed, sexually mature and responsive woman. Her soul becomes a room with a view because she discovers passions. Sexuality becomes respectable in an upper-middle-class woman.

English upper-middle-class conventions obtrude to shape Lucy's experience while she is taking the obligatory grand tour. But Florence arouses her need for something more. Lucy gradually develops in her personal life the passion and the imagination that she had projected into her music. She discovers her authentic self and becomes not a product of social artifice shaped by conventions but a creative intelligence. By contrast, Cecil, like

Philip, understands beauty but does not respond to people. He has allowed society to create his character; he lives in a world of forms and phrases. Lucy welcomes George's passionate kisses, but she disdains Cecil's formal kisses after their engagement, an engagement that represents a vestige of the claustrophobic tradition that Forster indicts.

In Forster's novels, accident and coincidence are the ways that the not-I world intrudes into the hubristic illusions of proud, narrow-minded, selfish people who think they can control the cosmos in which they live. The Emersons represent to Mrs. Honeychurch and the Vyses forces they would like to purge from their complacent Sawston world, but the Emersons' reappearance and persistence flout that wish. But Forster's poised and assured ironic detachment creates a continuing substantive alternative to Sawston values. For example, Forster uses the traditional picnic of the novel of manners, a picnic that would be an expected part of an Austen novel, to show the emptiness of Victorian social conventions and their irrelevance to personal relationships. Mr. Eager's aesthetic arrangement of the expedition is undermined by human passions, culminating in George's kiss. The polite traveller's phrase, "a room with a view," expands into the concepts of living more passionately, seeing more clearly, and breaking out of social restraints.

Typically in Forster, the novel proposes a number of apparent endings, which later events reveal as merely resting places in the narrative's evolving process. Thus, after Lucy breaks her engagement with Cecil, which is her necessary Everlasting Nay on the path to the Everlasting Yea, Forster writes of her temporarily abandoning her quest for self-fulfillment in terms that suggest the nemesis that everyone must avoid.

> She gave up trying to understand herself, and joined the vast armies of the benighted, who follow neither the heart nor the brain, and march to their destiny by catch words. The armies are full of pleasant and pious folk. But they have yielded to the only enemy that matters—the enemy within. They have sinned against passion and truth.

Gradually, the violence in the Piazza Signoria, the two impulsive and impassioned kisses of George Emerson, the spontaneity of the elder Emerson, and the ladies encountering George, Freddie, and Mr. Beebe in the nude anticipate the denouement. The reappearance of the Emersons represents the passionate self that Lucy repressed when she agreed to marry Cecil and the libidinous energy that Windy Corner and Mrs. Honeychurch have tried to ignore.

Howards End (1910) turns the novel of manners upside down and dramatizes that in the modern world there is a separation between culture, tradition, and courtesy and, on the other hand, wealth. Indeed *Howards End*, like *The Rainbow*, is conceived in terms of a dualism between the forces of light and of darkness: the Schlegels and the Wilcoxes, manners and money, Love and Truth, things as they are and things as they ought to be, personal life and the world of commerce and industry, imagination and reason, the surface life and the inner life. In this book, Forster goes beyond the novel of manners to examine the relation of public life to private values. England becomes a character, and its health is a central subject. Forster shows the impossibility of the Schlegels' desire "that public life should mirror whatever is good in the life within." The Schlegel sisters are unable to stop the advance of materialism, mediocrity, and the empirical intellect that responds only to facts. In the character of Leonard Bast, Forster uncharacteristically reaches down into the lower middle class to show how the energy and pretension of the new urban class are synonymous with that of London; we cannot but think of Eliot's line, "I had not thought death had undone so many." The Schlegels want to create Leonard into one of their sort, but they pathetically fail.

Like *Nostromo*, *Women in Love*, and *The Magic Mountain*, *Howards End* is a vision of a world in disintegration. As it moves from house to house, *Howards End*, like *Women in Love*, gradually discards or discredits major aspects of English civilization: the manorial and feudal life style at Oniton, indicted in part because of its absentee landlord who is disinterested in the property or life among the people in the environs; the recently built Ducie Street house with its utilitarian plan and overfurnished look and its location too close to stables; Swanage, representing suburbia, soon to become the "most important town of all, and ugliest of the three" with which it forms a cluster; and Wickham Place about to the swept under by the "gray tides of London." As in *The Waste Land* and *The Secret Agent*, London is as much a condition of mind as a place. And that condition of mind expresses Forster's anxiety. London has become an impersonal juggernaut, stalking the beleaguered outposts of civilization, like Wickham Place. In *Howards End*, Forster elegizes a world that he has lost.

Margaret is Forster's surrogate. Her credo of balance and proportion as a last resort is not only central to the moral values of the novel but defines Forster's concept of the form of the novel. Margaret keeps alive the potential for inner life and personal response. At the outset, she has a "profound vivacity, a continual and sincere response to all that she encountered in her path through life." Like Margaret, Forster felt "that those who prepare for all the emergencies of life beforehand may equip themselves at the expense of joy." For a time she seems to be shrinking under the pressure of Wilcox's moral obtuseness, but she survives because of her openness to experience and her ability to respond in personal terms.

Yet Margaret, finally, has her limitations. Her inner life is in danger of becoming, like Mrs. Wilcox's, virtually her whole life. Margaret moves to Mrs. Wilcox's position within the novel. Both have renounced not only their social roles but their social selves. Forster understands that this reliance upon spirituality can result in indifference not only to the concept of community as a social and political entity but even to friends. (He pursues this in *Passage to India* in the characters of Godbole and Mrs. Moore). Forster's voice oscillates between striving for an inclusive humanistic perspective and settling for a more iconoclastic voice that emphathizes with Margaret's complacency, nostalgia, and snobbery. Forster does not always view with irony Margaret's categorizing and supercilious sensibility or realize that her aesthetic, voyeuristic view of life (not unlike Philip Herriton's) results in her frequent indifference to other people.

The ending implies the possibility of establishing an enclave of affection and sensitivity but the enclave exists with even less hope of renewing itself than had the earlier enclave at Wickham Place. Not only does the fecundity of the crude Charles Wilcox threaten that precarious enclave: but Helen's child, in whom the novel's promise rests, is, after all, partly a Bast. Mr. Wilcox is an invalid; Margaret cannot love children, and the novel ends with the senior Wilcox's revelation of his keeping Margaret in the dark about his first wife's wish that Margaret be heir to Howards End. What adult relationships other than the ties between Margaret and Helen survive? Industralization and progress continue to extend their range, and the Schlegels' "triumph" is something of a defeat for the values in which they believe. But the collapse of the Wilcox family will not deter the forces that are changing England. Henry epitomizes commercial, social, and sexual values pervasive in England. Helen's response to Beethoven defines not only her "panic and emptiness" but also that of England. Finally, the title *Howards End* becomes a pun on death and destruction, a pun that reverberates throughout the novel.

Writing in 1960 in the "Terminal Note" to *Maurice*, Forster remarked:

> A happy ending was imperative. I shouldn't have bothered to write otherwise. I was determined that in fiction anyway two men should fall in love and remain in it for the ever and ever that fiction allows, and in this sense Maurice and Alex still roam the greenwood.

In this homosexual novel that Forster did not publish for nearly six decades (1913; published 1970), Forster's ending is not idyllic but inconclusive. How much of a victory is it if these single men are forced by convention to become "outlaws"? Are we not left with the impression that future Maurices will experience his confusion and loneliness and will seek advice from intolerant and incredulous doctors and well-meaning but often ineffectual hypnotists? Isn't the "disgusting and dishonourable old age" of the person who propositions Maurice on the train a real possibility for a man who himself was, in a parallel scene, once tempted to make similar advances to a man? Forster shows that because the homosexual is denied love and must repress his needs, he desperately seeks love in any way he can. (Of course the fundamental irony is that, had these been heterosexual scenes, there would have been barely cause for remark. In one scene, a man would have stifled an unfortunate impulse for an adolescent girl; and in the other he would have resisted the advances of a lewd woman). If Maurice did not have financial means, his course of action would have been far more difficult.

Indeed, Forster presents his penultimate ending as another in a series of catastrophes for the increasingly isolated and alienated title character. After Clive turns from Maurice, the latter's life is a sequence of disasters. The plot has dramatized the hopelessness and loneliness of a homosexual in England. Maurice alternates between, on the one hand, guilt and disgust (when he accepts and internalizes society's image of the homosexual) and, on the other, the acknowledging of the legitimacy of his own needs. After Alex, the Lawrentian gamekeeper with whom he experiences full physical love, at first rejects his idea that they go off together, Maurice despairs that "love had failed." Given what has preceded and the dramatic intensity of the crucial episodes in the novel, it is this penultimate ending, rather than the fairy tale of the last paragraphs, that reflects Forster's emotional engagement and artistic energy.

IV

We best understand the originality of *Passage to India* (1924), a seemingly traditional novel, if we compare it briefly with an Austen novel. *Passage to India* is a modern version of the novels of manners. It is based on Forster's desire to show that it is no longer possible to write an Austen novel without sacrificing artistic integrity.

Forster not only shows how the tradition of manners fails when it leaves the insularity of an English village but hints at its obsolescence. The English and Indians are in an imperialistic relationship where members of both the conquering and the conquered nation are corrupted and diminished because a relatively small number of representatives of one nation keeps the entire population of another in a subservient position. (But we should note that this relationship echoes a less rigorous but nonetheless stifling class system that Forster has presented in his prior novels.) Heaslop's comment, "We're not out here for the purpose of behaving pleasantly!" shows how the credo of Austen's England has been abandoned. Foster implies that the politics of imperialism and the social confusion, where the European finds "humanity grading and drifting beyond the educated vision," undermine intense personal relations and the standards on which they depend. What, for example, do these standards have to do with the nonverbal, handsome untouchable who turns the fan at the trial?

Austen, like many of her contemporaries, believed that characters in novels like people in real life could approach ideals of self-understanding and self-control. But Forster's fiction testifies that contemporary man lives in a world that has lost its grace, dignity, and humanity, and that loss is accentuated in India, which restlessly strives to find its identity while under the control of the British. Adela's poignant and ironic complaint underlines Forster's nostalgia for a time when personal relationships flourished among an aristocracy that had leisure for them: "What is the use of personal relationships when everyone brings less and less to them?"

Because the omniscient narrator expresses Forster's quest for values, he is a different kind of figure from the omniscient narrator of Victorian or eighteenth-century fiction. Whereas Austen's values within the novel's imagined world are static, Forster's evolve. Unlike Austen, he tests and sympathizes with a variety of value systems. Whereas Austen *knows* from the outset the standards by which Emma falls short and tells us in the opening pages, Forster tentatively adopts, seriatim, the perspective of Fielding, Mrs. Moore, and Godbole as he searches not only for the way to solve the Anglo-Indian problem but for his own values. Although Austen's focus is on the moral development of her characters, Forster's is on making sense of his imagined world. His omniscient narrator seeks to understand what he presents. Forster dramatizes the transformation of the narrator as new circumstances come into the narrative. It is as if learning that evil is as much in the human psyche as in the Caves shows him that Austen's England is irrelevant to India. The tale becomes a *passage* to enlightenment for Forster's surrogate and, ultimately, for us. That he has changed his values becomes part of the rhetoric and urges the reader to change his attitudes to India and to reconsider his values.

At first Forster embraces the code of Fielding, a code that would not at first glance be out of place in an Austen novel: "The world, he believed, is a globe of men who are trying to reach one another and can best do so by the help of goodwill plus culture and intelligence—a creed ill suited to Chandrapore, but he had come out too late to lose it." Forster admires his self-control, decency, and fundamental courage (what he called "pluck" in the essay "What I Believe"). After Forster's voice adopts the values of Fielding, he steps back and reexamines them when he realizes that Fielding lacks the emotional range of Aziz. The self-styled "holy man minus the holiness" is the spirit of Bloomsbury, the epitome of liberal England, and the heir to the tradition of manners and morals, represented in Austen by Knightley: "I believe in teaching people to be individuals, and to understand other individuals. It's the only thing I do believe in."

Even though his book is a room with a view of India and provides what he believes is a necessary education for the English, Forster is redefining the equation of travel with learning and moral growth that is an essential premise of much eighteenth- and nineteenth-century fiction and travel literature from *Moll Flanders* and *Tom Jones* to *Jane Eyre* and *Great Expectations*. The equation is a version of the Protestant myth of self-improvement through experience and hard work. We think of Fielding's self-image as a traveler, and we realize that the concept of traveling as an experience of learning but not necessarily of growth or or self-development is central in *Passage to India*. Fielding's education is not of the kind that makes prior fictional characters more integrated and responsive people. Bathetically, he returns to England, marries, and becomes part of officialdom, ironically proving his own contention that "any man can travel light until he has a wife or children."

Unlike Highbury, India is more than a background for events in an imagined world. The difference between Austen's Highbury and Forster's

India is the difference between Constable's eighteenth-century landscapes, depicting a scene such as Salisbury Cathedral as it might have looked at some ideal moment, and the landscapes of postimpressionists such as Cézanne and Van Gogh, which express the emotions of the painter more than they depict the actual physical scene. Thus, the Caves are a metaphor for the nonverbal world that precedes and will survive mankind. Like Hardy's Egdon Heath, they are immune to and indifferent to man's life. As Forster describes them, we feel both an imaginative effort and a personal agony unlike anything in Austen. It is as if they resist human description, even though Forster tells us they are "readily described": "Nothing, nothing attaches to them and their reputation—for they have one—does not depend upon human speech." But, of course, they depend upon oral and written language to extend their reputation; even the inadequacy of the language illustrates the mind's limitations as it confronts the unknown. He sees the irony of showing that the human mind, when seeking the ultimate comparison, uses personification to contain and to try to comprehend the caves:

> Fist and fingers thrust above the advancing soil—here at last is their skin, finer than any covering acquired by the animals, smoother than windless water, more voluptuous than love. The radiance increases, the flames touch one another, kiss, expire. The cave is dark again, like all the caves.

Yet paradoxically, Forster's perspective places human events in a geological context and reduces their proportion. For him, India is not a fiction, a metaphor for British imperialism, but an essential and troubling reality that gives significance to the world he occupies.

Even before the trial, Forster begins to separate himself from Fielding, to reveal that Fielding's truth is only a partial truth and that he lacks imagination, spirituality, and passion. The crucial moment occurs when Fielding sees the Caves from a distance. He fails to apprehend the beauty or significance of the Caves and questions his life and values. "He felt he ought to have been working at something else the whole time—he didn't know at what, never would know, never could know, and that was why he felt sad."

This moment is a paradigmatic episode that shows how Forster turns the novel of manners upside down by exposing the limitations of his erstwhile surrogate Fielding. Could we imagine Knightley in a moment of self-doubt, alone in a moral desert bereft of value? Finally, Fielding has no tradition of manners on which to rely; nor does he believe in a benevolent cosmos. Fielding is exposed and contained in a fiction in which, by tradition, he should be the hero. He has spoken for the novel's values as Forster's surrogate. He has risked career and physical well-being in the interest of truth and fairness. Yet this is not enough.

In prior novels, Forster wrote for the most part of the plague of moral relativism and materialism, plagues that could be defined and, perhaps, partially controlled if not rectified. After the trial the voice indicates that

Fielding's Western values are only one of several sets of values with which man may equip himself. In the last part of "Caves" and in the "Temple," Forster questions not only Fielding's values but the values to which he had dedicated his prior novels —the primacy of personal relationships and the necessity of understanding one another, values epitomized by the famous epigraph to *Howards End*, "Only Connect."

Yet, finally, in *Passage to India* humanism triumphs if in a reduced and more modest version. As Godbole and Mrs. Moore are tested and ultimately discarded as prophets, the voice again becomes the spokesman for the values of humanism—moderation, tolerance, tact, integrity, respect for others. His own language presents the unity and balance that life within the story lacks. Despite Mrs. Moore's insight, a schism between her vision and her behavior undermines her pretensions as a prophetic character. Mrs. Moore's selfish desertion of Aziz shows how she has put aside relations with people in her quest for spiritual self-realization. Whatever the excuse, she commits what for Forster is the heresy of deserting her friend. Seen from the standards of traditional values, her self-immersion represents a serious failure of the moral fabric that binds one man to another.

A fundamental paradox of the novel is that Forster's own prose has difficulty aligning itself with mystery and spiritual values, and Forster knows this. Yet the celebratory and static religious ritual with which "Temple" opens is an effort to move beyond the concatenation of events on which traditional Western narrative is based. Within that episode, the narrator (Forster's surrogate) adopts a double perspective: the external perspective of a secular skeptic, whose view, like Fielding's, is predicated on interest in other cultures and a desire to understand somethng different; and the inner vision of someone who experiences a spiritual revelation— Godbole. Godbole is a prophetic figure, but his failings also undermine the thrust of his ideas. He is no help to Aziz when he is falsely accused; later he allows Aziz to believe Fielding had married Adela, a belief that leads Aziz to foolish and humiliating behavior because he, as a Brahman, "had never been known to tell anyone anything." Godbole's Olympian perspective resembles one aspect of the narrator, the one that takes a historical and geographical view of the action. But the long view seems irrelevant to the manners and passions of individual human beings. "When evil occurs," says Godbole, "it expresses the whole of the universe. Similarly when good occurs. . . . Good and evil are different, as their names imply. But, in my humble opinion, they are both of them aspects of my Lord." And just as the English mind's rationalism and control his limits, so does Godbole's ascetic spirituality and ability to thrust himself out of himself; for he cannot mediate upon the stone.

If Forster adopts Lawrence's bardic voice and prophetic vision, he faces with Conrad the problem of how to cope with a purposeless, amoral, indifferent universe. He views Godbole's spiritualism as another of mankind's working arrangements. The Hindu celebration is an outlet for human and even animal passions and instincts; to perform the Rajah's holy journey after he dies, the Hindus simply (and to Western eyes bathetically) make an effigy of the Rajah. If, at first, the novel seems to reject Fielding's liberal humanism, it gradually shows that the alternatives are no better. Religion as a living force has its limits, as illustrated by Godbole's human failures. Like Mrs. Moore, he has subtracted himself from human community in his search for something more. Thus, Fielding's humanism may have a qualified triumph, after all, when we realize the futility of being "one with the universe" and its cost, as exemplified by Mrs. Moore's and Godbole's indifference to other people.

Mrs. Moore's son, Ralph, is the Western correlative to the Untouchable Indian who turns the fan in the courtroom. Yet his simple vocabulary, his depth of feeling, and his intuitive understanding of the elaborate Hindu rituals comment upon the verbosity of the Moslems and the complicated motives of the English. Although he "appear[s] to be almost an imbecile," he instinctively understands Aziz's hostility; by telling Aziz that his mother, Mrs. Moore, loved him, he is the catalyst for Aziz's temporary reconciliation with Fielding. And he anticipates Forster's final verdict—"not yet"— on the possibility of lasting reconciliation. That wisdom becomes the province of the unwitting in Ralph—as it has in the Emersons, Stephen, and Gino — is an aspect of Forster's rebellion against utilitarianism, progress, and moral education.

V

Forster's originality has to be seen in the context of the other major writers of the period—Conrad, Joyce, Lawrence, and Woolf. In Victorian fiction, characters are defined by their relationship within a community. In modern British fiction the characters are defined by alienation from that community. They are, like their creators, iconoclasts detesting the community that has created them. The major character's quest for self-understanding is the essence of the English novel from 1890 to 1925, but the focus is on the desperation of that quest, not the attainment of the goal. That quest reflects the author's own uncertainty, frustration, and anxiety. The stress on asserting private values, restoring family relationships, and developing personal relationships that matter is another characteristic of the novel of the period; it is an alternative to the Victorian novel's faith that community life can provide a social and moral fabric for each individual. The traditional novel's omniscient narrator depends for its effects upon the incongruity between what the narrator says and what the character thinks. But when the narrator's values are not stable and consistent, that irony breaks down and we feel the author as a formal presence within the text. Like his contemporaries Conrad, Lawrence, and Joyce, Forster believed that human truth must inevitably be partial, a matter of perspective.

Writing in 1925, Virginia Woolf insisted in "Mr. Bennett and Mrs. Brown" that the Georgian writers needed to abandon the "tools" and "conventions" of their Edwardian predecessors because the latter "have laid an enormous stress on the fabric of things": "At the present moment we are suffering, not from decay, but from having no code of manners which writers and readers accept as a prelude to the more exciting intercourse of friendship. . . . Grammar is violated, syntax disintegrated." Forster does not violate grammar and syntax. Forster's style has more in common with Austen, Fielding, and Dickens than with the comparatively pedestrian journalistic prose of Bennett, Wells, and Galsworthy and the experiments with diction and syntax of Joyce and Lawrence. He shows how polished, precise use of literate discourse can both render the inner life—feelings, passions, subconscious needs—and, particularly in his last two novels, create the prophetic note that he sought. Forster's conversational prose, his leisurely pace, his self-confidence, his lucid, unpretentious diction and poised syntax imply the humanistic values he espoused. Although Conrad, Lawrence, Joyce, and Woolf sought new forms and syntax, Forster shows that the English language and its novel genre already had the resources to examine the life of instincts and passions.

James Joyce's *Ulysses*:
The Complete Masculine Aesthetic

Judith Spector

That James Joyce employed a masculine aesthetic ought to come as no surprise to the discerning reader. Yet many such readers perceive this only intuitively, muttering apologetic half-truths about the "language" of Molly's monologue being "right out of a fantasy from *Playboy*," or attempting to make some similarly vague, and often erroneous, justification for what is, essentially, a correct opinion.

In fact, however, the basis of the masculine orientation of Joyce's art is not unlike that of other artists whose aesthetics are undeniably "masculine." D. H. Lawrence is an obvious example of such a writer; the incidence of aesthetic elements common to both Joyce and Lawrence is abundant. The principal difference between the two writers is that where Lawrence is tentative or covert about certain sexual components of his aesthetic, Joyce is definite and overt. In the sense that Joyce delineates articulately and openly the same principles which Lawrence applies less lucidly, Joyce represents the complete masculine aesthetic, completely accessible to any reader who possesses the requisite perseverence to exercise his or her scrutiny.

THE WOMB OF THE IMAGINATION: FROM WORD TO ART

Richard Ellmann writes:

> *A Portrait of the Artist as a Young Man* is in fact the gestation of a soul, and in the metaphor Joyce found his new principle of order. The book begins with Stephen's father and, just before the ending, it depicts the hero's severance from his mother. From the start, the soul is surrounded by liquids, urine, slime, seawater, amniotic

From *CLA Journal* 28, no. 3 (March 1985). © 1984 by College Language Association.

tides, "drops of water" (as Joyce says at the end of the first chapter) "falling softly in the brimming bowl."

"The hero's severance from his mother" in this description of *A Portrait* is part of an aesthetic, common to both Joyce and Lawrence, which involves the rejection of the mother as the comprehensive explanation of the artist's origin. The process of his separation from the mother, and, ultimately, his self-creation is as typical of Paul in *Sons and Lovers* as it is of Stephen in *A Portrait*. Exploring the similarity further, Stephen's wonderfully pompous pronouncement (upon writing a villanelle and identifying the process of inspiration), "O! In the virgin womb of the imagination the word was made flesh," reminds us of its opposite in Lawrence, who declared that the flesh was made word in artistic creation. Joyce is able to work the other way round (from word to flesh) by means of the employment of a mental womb. More explicitly "feminine" than anything Lawrence would wish to acknowledge as part of himself, Joyce seems to regard the presence of such a female component merely as a deluxe addition to an already satisfactory male model of a human being. In Stephen's case, he establishes the virginity of the womb as well, thus completing his own parody of an immaculate conception. Even, or perhaps especially, in jest (and Joyce's jests are seldom without a serious implication), Joyce indicates his rebellion against Catholicism and declares the superiority of art as a religious/spiritual/sexual endeavor. Lawrence's artist was in reaction against his mother; Joyce's artist is in reaction against mother church as well.

Joyce's emphasis on the body and its natural functions partially replaces a Catholicism which would have made art impossible by regarding physical processes and perceptions as obscene. Thus, though Stephen hastens to confess his "sins of impurity" to "our Mother Mary," he eventually rebels against both church and familial mother in an artistic revolt whose guiding impetus is the impulse to sex and life rather than filial devotion and piety. Both of Stephen's "mothers" become further identified in that Stephen's natural mother wants him to be religious for her sake. Stephen tells Cranly.

> "She wishes me to make my easter duty."
> "—And will you?"
> "—I will not," Stephen said.
> "—Why not?" Cranly said.
> "—I will not serve," answered Stephen.

This last remark, which Cranly points out "was made before," echoes Lucifer's defiant declaration to God, "Non Serviam." Lucifer fell, as the son of Dedalus will fall (in the latter case, however, into the sea of life to be reborn). Stephen explains to Cranly,

> I will not serve that in which I no longer believe whether it call itself my home, my fatherland or my church: and I will try to express myself in some mode of life or art as freely as I can and

as wholly as I can, using for my defence the only arms I allow myself to use—silence, exile, and cunning.

Stephen's final entries in his diary read,

Welcome, O life! I go to encounter for the millionth time the reality of experience and to forge in the smithy of my soul the uncreated conscience of my race.

27 *April*: Old father, old artificer, stand me now and ever in good stead.

We are to understand that Stephen is going to begin his voluntary exile. He abandons his mother, and his Virgin Mother in the Church, and appeals to a father. Dedalus is a mythical father for him, suggested (in appropriate literary context) by his name. And, as we shall see in *Ulysses*, since he thinks it possible for the writer to be his own father, we again are encountering (as we did with Lawrence) the idea that the artist creates himself. The only mothers the artist will accept from now on are earth mothers, and those ambivalently, as we will see in Joyce's treatment of Molly in *Ulysses*.

Lest we have any doubts on the matter of mortal mothers, the mortality of Stephen's mother is established at the very beginning of *Ulysses*, which opens with Stephen having returned to Ireland and "fallen" after his mother's death. He is again a disembodied spirit (the gestation of an artist's body will occur in *Ulysses*, as *A Portrait* developed his soul), his only "mother" the sea. The matter of Mrs. Dedalus's demise and the motherhood of the sea are topics taken up (however irreverently) by Buck Mulligan. He lectures Stephen on his failure as a son:

"—You could have knelt down, damn it, Kinch, when your dying mother asked you," Buck Mulligan said. "I'm hyperborean as much as you. But to think of your mother begging you with her last breath to kneel down and pray for her. And you refused. There is something sinister in you. . . ."

Stephen has refused his mother's dying request. Having been released in this manner from his mother (i.e., through her death and his unwillingness to serve her), Stephen has followed his "Greek" fictional fate as the son of Dedalus (the hapless Icarus we presume), and, appropriately, Mulligan informs him,

"—God," he said quietly. "Isn't the sea what Algy calls it: a grey sweet mother? The snotgreen sea. The scrotumtightening sea. *Epi oinopa ponton*. Ah, Dedalus, the Greeks. I must teach you. You must read them in the original. *Thalatta! Thalatta!* She is our great sweet mother. Come and look."

The sea at this point is another indicator of Stephen's once again embryonic state. He has not created himself yet. As [Stuart] Gilbert has pointed out, in Joyce's scheme of the novel the first chapter has no representative organ of the body. *Ulysses*, on one level, is the sage of the creation of an entire body, and organs are added in each chapter. The metaphor of the creation of the artist becomes incorporated into the form of the book, together with the reverence for the body which is a reaction against religion and a celebration of life and art. Stephen has not made the word flesh yet; he hasn't become embodied as an artist, and will not, until he becomes a son and discovers the principle of mental fatherhood.

Since the concept of fatherhood is central to the novel, we must first deal with the matter of the "mental womb." Such a fictional organ, the product of "sexual analogy," does not render the possessor female. Only men have mental wombs. For Joyce, mental creativity is peculiar to men alone, and for some reasons which Lawrence espoused (i.e., it is the nature of the male to create with his mind). If women have physical wombs, men must have mental counterparts. Joyce creates a comprehensive dialectic between two worlds—the physical and the mental. For everything that exists in the physical world, a counterpart must exist in the mental world. This principle produces mental androgyny—for men only, of course. (The astute thinker will at once realize that since women have physical wombs, they cannot also have mental ones. Theoretically, women might have mental penises; but for the purpose of producing works of art, only mental wombs are of value.) Men have the sole rights to mental creativity because women (as Joyce supposes) have the rights to physical creativity. Therefore, although a great part of Joyce's "system" both in *A Portrait* and *Ulysses* is the emulative imitation of the (female) physical process of human gestation and production of a human being, yet he doubted that a mere woman could be the author of such a philosophic system (all the more, since her production of persons was obviously physical).

Joyce believed in the reality of his mental womb and wrote a letter to Nora in which he discussed one of his "children." In this letter, he mentioned a letter which he had written to George Roberts after Roberts had refused to publish *Dubliners*:

> Sitting at the table, thinking of the book I have written, the child
> I have carried for years and years in the womb of imagination as
> you carried in your womb the children you love, and of how I had
> fed it day after day out of my brain and memory, [I] wrote him
> the enclosed letter.

Unlike Lawrence, Joyce was pleased to think of himself as a "womanly man." Nevertheless, he needed a female to inspire and help him (once he admitted, "Throughout my life women have been my most active helpers"), and to supply the physical (real) counterpart to his own mental (fictional) female components. Woman is a physical model from which the male artist may build his own mental superstructures. Joyce perpetuated the theory of himself as a "womanly man" because, ostensibly, he had a masculine name, James, and a feminine one, Joyce. In addition, he actually believed that certain characteristics, such as an abhorrence of violence, were "feminine," and felt that the artist should be able to declare, like Stephen, "Personally, I detest action," avoiding physical battles, the better to engage in mental confrontations ("He provokes my intelligence," declares Stephen to a bully. Bloom and Stephen are both pacific men (they are, respectively, a life-artist and an art-artist, as we shall see). [A "life-artist" is one who creates his life as if it were his own work of art. An "art-artist" actually produces works of art.] Richard Ellmann writes of Joyce's portrayal of the two characters that Joyce sympathized "with Bloom and Stephen in their resistance in terms of mind rather than body." Mental processes become the polarized opposites of physical ones, as men are the opposites of women. Joyce can only be "like" a woman mentally; physically he is her opposite. Passivity is a mental attitude, and it is also the absence of physical action. The presence of physical action would constitute aggression and would fall into the category of "masculine" behavior. Quite simply, Joyce is a man who considers himself capable of thinking like a man and like a woman. (We have already seen that women cannot do this—creatively. When Bella Cohen becomes Bello, she becomes sadistic and aggressive, not intellectual, incisive, or artistic.)

Joyce's self-conferred ability confuses some critics, especially in relation to the problem of creativity. Richard Ellmann, for example, writes that for Joyce the

> creator is not male but female; Joyce goes on to borrow an image of Flaubert by calling him a "god," but he is really a goddess. Within his womb creatures comes to life. No male intercession is necessary even; as Stephen says, "In the virgin womb of the imagination the word was made flesh."

Joyce knew perfectly well what he was doing in describing the creator as a god. (Joyce was not one to use words carelessly.) We have already seen in relation to Lawrence how the standard Christian concept of a patriarchal god supplies the model for a male creator. This is also true for Joyce, but, as we might expect, it is more complex as a result of his intimate knowledge of Catholicism and his desire to rearrange its tenets.

The gist of his theoretical model rests on two simple and parallel beliefs: the artist creates himself, and the Father is consubstantial with the Son. All of this creation takes place in the mental world. As Stephen says,

> Fatherhood, in the sense of conscious begetting, is unknown to man. It is a mystical estate, an apostolic succession, from only begetter to only begotten. On that mystery and not on the madonna which the cunning Italian intellect flung to the mob of Europe the church is founded and founded irremovably because founded, like the world, macro- and microcosm, upon the void. . . . Paternity may be a legal fiction.
>
> (*Ulysses*)

But then, the artist deals in fiction, and so is perfectly within his milieu as the father of himself and of his art. Stephen plays with the idea, putting it into an artistic context:

> "As we, or mother Dana, weave and unweave our bodies," Stephen said, "from day to day, their molecules shuttled to and fro, so does the artist weave and unweave his image. And as the mole on my right breast is where it is when I was born, though all my body has been woven of new stuff time after time, so through the ghost of the unquiet father the image of the unliving son looks forth. In the intense instant of imagination, when the mind, Shelley says, is a fading coal, that which I was is that which I am and that which in possibility I may come to be. So in the future, the sister of the past, I may see myself as I sit here not but by reflection from that which then I shall be."
>
> (*Ulysses*)

Stephen is still expounding upon his Shakespeare theory here, and it is meant to be a little confusing. He is a Charybdis of sorts, running on at the mouth with his theories of art and form and Hamlet and Shakespeare. But he is also explaining the manner in which the artist creates himself. (The identity is preserved by memory: "But I, entelechy, form of forms, am I by memory because under everchanging forms" [*Ulysses*].)

The whole issue of paternity and selfhood and the selfhood and the creation of the artist (note that true artists can therefore ony be males, however androgynous mentally) is further complicated by the issue of ghosts. Father, Son, and Holy Ghost constitute the Trinity. Therefore the ghost is consubstantial with the son and the father. (A ghost is also a memory, as the preceding quote points out.) There are a numerous ghosts (both fathers and sons) in *Ulysses*. The fictional past in literature provides one ghostly echo. Ulysses himself, the Greek father and son Daedalus and Icarus, and, of course, Shakespeare and his dead son Hamnet are present. These ghosts are part of the characters in *Ulysses*, part of their literary molecules. In *Ulysses* present, Bloom's father committed suicide, and appears in Bloom's fantasy as a ghost. Bloom's own son, Rudy, died shortly after he was born. Bloom is looking for a son, Stephen for a father (so that he can be a son and therefore the father of himself).

It is a ridiculous notion. But it is also artistically viable as a masculine aesthetic. According to Joyce's statement of his aesthetic through Stephen in *A Portrait*, the artist should ultimately recede from his own creation after he had created it until he is a ghost and a god (father). The work of art (the son) is consubstantial with him because it is his creation and exists through his perceptions. The ego of the artist expands to identify with all he perceives of life, as Stephen's world must admit Bloom, a representative everyman, and Molly, an everywoman. They (life) admit him as a "son" so that he may become a "father." Stephen, in *A Portrait*, explains:

The simplest epical form is seen emerging out of lyrical literature when the artist prolongs and broods upon himself as the centre of an epical event and this form progresses till the centre of emotional gravity is equidistant from the artist himself and from others. The narrative is no longer purely personal. The personality of the artist passes into the narration itself, flowing round and round the persons and the action like a vital sea. This progress you will see easily in that old English ballad *Turpin Hero* which begins in the first person and ends in the third person. The dramatic form is reached when the vitality which has flowed and eddied round each person fills every person with such vital force that he or she assumes a proper and intangible esthetic life. The personality of the artist, at first a cry or cadence or a mood and then a fluid and lambent narrative, finally refines itself out of existence, impersonalises itself, so to speak. The esthetic image in the dramatic form is life purified in and reprojected from the human imagination. The mystery of esthetic like that of material creation is accomplished. The artist, like the God of the creation, remains within or beyond or above his handiwork, invisible, refined out of existence, indifferent, paring his fingernails.

Joyce has outlined here in detail the process of mental conception and creation of art. It is an act which occurs in the mind of a god, self-created and created by the things which he creates (it is the production of art which makes him a god). One very valid question is whether Joyce's characters ever really assume "a proper and intangible esthetic life." A feminist critic might easily charge that Molly is more a reflection of Joyce's image of woman than a reflection of a woman. His portrayal of Molly may indicate that the artist (self-created and created by his creation) is not as successful at imparting life to others as he is in achieving autoeroticism (self-created and created by his creation).

But, to return to the aesthetic of fatherhood which Stephen presents in the library chapter, we note that the "method" of the chapter is "dialectic." We know that any actual "answer" to the problem of how art is created will come as a result of the clash between entities which are distorted in order to be successfully polarized. So if the theory in *A Portrait* has the artist standing completely apart from his work of art, paring his fingernails (a comic touch), while the one in *Ulysses* has Shakespeare writing about his own family life (also a comic touch), we know by now that both processes are valid parts of a never-to-be-achieved synthesis. It does not matter that Stephen does not believe his own theory about Shakespeare; his theory is a thesis, part of a larger process of dialectic.

Sexual dialectic in particular is cited as central to the process of creation. The following conversation between John Eglinton and Stephen is revealing:

"A shrew," John Eglinton said shrewdly, "is not a useful portal of discovery, one should imagine. What useful discovery did Socrates learn from Xanthippe?"

"Dialectic," Stephen answered, "and from his mother how to bring thoughts into the world."

"Dialectic" and "how to bring thoughts into the world" are precisely the two things which the male artist gains from woman (according to the masculine aesthetic which both Joyce and Lawrence employ). In Joyce's aesthetic scheme, however, the male artist, himself an echo of the divine model, does all of his mental creation himself—without the direct participation of woman as a medium, as in Lawrence's scheme. Women, having taught the artist the fundamentals of physical parturition, leave him to bring forth thoughts by himself. This absence of women leads to jokes near the end of the chapter about masculine sexual self-sufficiency, based on the artist's mental self-sufficiency.

When John Eglinton declares, "After God Shakespeare has created most," Stephen responds "—Man delights him not nor woman, neither." What delights the creator who has created everything (like the artist who expands his perceptions to include everything and everyone) is, of course, only himself. Stephen refers back to God:

> The playwright who wrote the folio of this world and wrote it badly (He gave us light first and the sun two days later), the lord of things as they are whom the most Roman of catholics call *dio boia*, hangman god, is doubtless all in all in all of us, ostler and butcher, and would be bawd and cuckold too but that in the economy of heaven, foretold by Hamlet, there are no more marriages, glorified man, an androgynous angel, being a wife unto himself.

Stephen's statement is reminiscent of Tom Brangwen's wedding speech in *The Rainbow*. It is intentionally funny; but it is serious, too. Unlike Tom's "angels," the angels here are not really inclusive of male and female components. They are, rather, men who are so much in love with themselves (and their mental creations) and whose egos are so expansive, that they no longer need anyone else.

Buck Mulligan immediately picks up on the theory of self-sufficiency and its implications; his response is "Eureka!" He follows his exclamation with a rhyme which ends, *"Being afraid to marry on earth, They masturbated for all they were worth,"* and presents a plan for a play:

Everyman His own Wife
or
A Honeymoon in the Hand
(a national immorality in three orgasms)
by
Ballocky Mulligan

Bluntly expressed, the male artist is a mental masturbator. Joyce imparts a certain amount of humor to the fact, and he delegates Mulligan to make the announcement. But he is perfectly in earnest, as is Lawrence, whose belief was that sex was woman's prime motivity and that man's was to create a world out of himself. Joyce tells us the same thing in a funnier, more conscious way. What he is saying is that male sexuality is cerebral, that man's central impulse is intellectualy creative (as opposed to woman's physically creative drive). Mulligan makes the idea humorous by transposing the idea of a love affair within one man's mind (the creator brooding upon himself to bring forth life) to a love affair with the body also — masturbation. Mulligan is not the only character Joyce employs to illustrate this aspect of the artist. Bloom is a more earnest example.

In a letter to Stanislaus in 1906, Joyce refers to the male's "extraordinary cerebral sexualism and bodily fervour (from which women are normally free)." Bloom, as a life-artist ("There's a touch of the artist about old Bloom" [*Ulysses*]), typifies the mental state of "cerebral sexualism." He has had only incomplete sexual intercourse with Molly for nearly eleven years, if we are to believe his account:

> There remained a period of 10 years, 5 months and 18 days during
> which carnal intercourse had been incomplete, without ejaculation
> of semen within the female organ.

The artist is not involved in the process of sexuality activity for physical procreation. (That is for women.) Molly is present in Bloom's mind as a central sexual reference point in the world he creates in and from his mind. It is terribly funny (or perhaps just terrible, according to one's taste) to see Bloom as an artist figure and to understand that such a person is necessarily a voyeur (as with Gerty MacDowelll, *Ulysses*). The artist looks at what inspires him (Gerty's undergarments in this case) from a discreet distance, and interacts with it by developing a response and experience totally within himself (i.e., Bloom's masturbation).

It is true that Gerty participates in the action, thinking that Bloom is a dark stranger with personal sorrows (he is in mourning) whose life she will take under her own tender care:

> The very heart of the girlwoman went out to him, her dream-
> husband, because she knew on the instant it was him. If he had
> suffered, more sinned against than sinning, or even, even, if he
> had been himself a sinner, a wicked man, she cared not. Even if
> he was a protestant or methodist she could convert him easily if
> he truly loved her. There were wounds that wanted healing with
> heartbalm. She was a womanly woman not like other flighty girls,
> unfeminine, he had known, those cyclists showing off what they
> hadn't got and she just yearned to know all, to forgive all if she
> could make him forget the memory of the past. Then mayhap he
> would embrace her gently, like a real man, crushing her soft body
> to him, and love her, his ownest girlie, for herself alone.

It is "herself alone" of whom Gerty is thinking, true to Joyce's formula that "A woman's love is always material and egoistic." Gerty is a bad life-artist. She distorts the world she sees, thinking things of Bloom that are not so, according to what she wishes him to be to her. Bloom, however, sees Gerty accurately, even to realizing that she waved her hand to the others on the beach to put the scent of her perfume in the air (by means of a piece of wadding which he could not possibly have seen). Bloom's own onanism is justified, because he bases it on scientifically verifiable perceptions and intellectually accurate inferences.

Stephen's theory of Shakespeare works as a metaphor. Art is an experience the artist has with himself. That is one reason why *Ulysses*, for example, or, even more obviously, *Finnegans Wake*, is so difficult to read. The reader is asked to watch the mental exhibitionism, itself a mental masturbation of an artist who claims to take in everything about the events of a day in Dublin. That is asking a lot, and there are moments when this reader, at least, begrudges Joyce the effort. In addition, his attitude toward women and his use of the muse for the selfish aggrandizement of his ego are not sufficiently counterbalanced by the "good temper" with which Mary Ellmann credits him (in contrast with Hemingway).

Joyce's model of androgyny is based on the assumption that some characteristics (such as passivity, for example) are innately female. By appropriating a few of these characteristics, he fancies himself a "womanly man," a complete person. But an androgyny which denies woman the same completeness and which is based on the assumption that men and women are different mentally because of their physical characteristics is not true androgyny. It is merely the spectacle provided by the masculine aesthetic, of a man who, complete with mental womb, thinks he has everything.

The Backbone of James Joyce's
Finnegans Wake: Narrative,
Digression, and Deconstruction

Derek Attridge

In order, no doubt, to minimize the risk of putting the most notoriously unreadable book ever published into a paperback edition, Faber and Faber attempt to woo hesitating purchasers of *Finnegans Wake* with a quotation on the back cover from Anthony Burgess (that most readable of novelists), which assures us that in this book "the puzzle element is less important than the thrust of the narrative and the shadowy majesty of the characters." The temptation to imagine Burgess-style recommendations of other un-derpurchased items on the literary shelves is irresistible —the lapidary clarity of *The Four Zoas*? the stark single-mindedness of *The Ring and the Book*? the breathless pace of *Clarissa*?—but I am drawing attention to this prominently displayed piece of wishful thinking as an emblem of the immense need felt by readers and publishers of literary texts (especially long ones) for the firm center which narrative and character provide, and as the tip of an iceberg of academic labor which has taken as its goal the production—which it usually sees as the "discovery"—of such a center in *Finnegans Wake*.

The same Anthony Burgess has also sought to aid the reading public, and Faber's sales, by producing a *Shorter Finnegans Wake*; and it is instructive to watch him about his business, filleting out the backbone of the text (to use his own metaphor) and serving it up without the flesh. After a ritual protest—"*Finnegans Wake* is one of the few books of the world that totally resist cutting"—he proceeds to sharpen his instruments by way of a brisk introduction entitled "What It's All About"; and what it's all about, we quickly learn, is the dream of a Dublin publican called Mr. Porter after a hard Saturday night in the bar, interrupted by a spell of wakefulness which occurs towards the end of the book. Unfortunately for the reader who may be sustained through several hundred dense pages by Burgess's promise

From *Genre* 17, no. 4 (Winter 1984). © 1985 by The University of Oklahoma.

of clear daylight at the end, it turns out, when Mr. Porter wakes up, that the author has also been asleep, and remains so to the final word. This separation between the publican's dream and the author's dream of the publican's waking moments is, however, far from straightforward, for ("surprisingly," as Burgess concedes) in the middle of the publican's dream, book II, chapter 3, we come upon him in his bar, dealing with customers on a busy evening—the source, we must assume, of Burgess's conviction (and that of many others) that the dream which is supposed to occupy most of the book is the dream of a publican after a busy night in the bar, a night of "rumbustious carousal," as Burgess calls it in another summary of what he sees as the book's central narrative. And sure enough, we are told that when, within the dream, the landlord is left alone in his bar, he collapses in a drunken stupor and begins to dream. The structure would seem to be an instance of what Derrida calls "invagination": enclosed by the book, the chapter also encloses it. What follows, however, is not *Finnegans Wake* (how could it be, since we're on page 383 of *Finnegans Wake*?); it is a version of the story of Tristan and Isolde, colored by the familiar narrative perspective of the four old men. Nevertheless, we are invited by Burgess to imagine as we read this chapter that it is being dreamed by the publican asleep on the floor of his bar, that sleep being itself part of his dream, and that the next three chapters are also dreams which he dreams he is dreaming, having dreamt that he was woken up and gone to bed. When, after these dreams, he finds himself in bed again, we're assured— though it's not clear why he shouldn't once more be dreaming that he's in bed—that he is really awake. Awake, that is, in James Joyce's dream.

The strain produced by this project of separating distinct dream levels is evident enough—not only in Burgess, whom I am singling out because of the breadth of his influence, but in all those who have made the attempt. It is motivated, of course, by a desire to provide the reader with a firm sense of *where* he or she is at any given point, an explanation always ready to hand for the oddness of the writing, a secure path through the threatening tangle of the text; but many readers might find that the task of imagining that what they are reading is an account of a dream (or a dream of a dream, or a dream of a dream of a dream) multiplies rather than reduces their difficulties. The reader searching for a principle on which to distinguish what is central from what is digressive is not given much assistance; after all, dreams aren't generally characterized by a clear separation between a central core and a digressive envelope—and that very distinction must present itself as problematic to anyone who has been impressed by *The Interpretation of Dreams* and recent readings of it (as Burgess clearly hasn't been). It's not that such accounts can be proved to be wrong, or serve no purpose; what is important is that they can't be proved to be right, and can work only up to a point.

On what principle, then, is the text reduced by more than half its length in *A Shorter Finnegans Wake*, to reveal what Burgess breezily terms "the gist of the book"? The gist seems to exclude a large number of passages that many readers would regard either as particularly delightful, or particularly accessible, or particularly significant (or both, or all three). The point, however, is not that Burgess has or has not made a good job in his selection, but that any selection is necessarily an arbitrary one, at least as far as the intrinsic structure of the text is concerned. The "narrative" and "characters" which Burgess produces for the *Wake* are created as much by his brief interpolated summaries as by the passages he reprints—perhaps more so. And the "backbone" he offers is a matter of moral as well as structural fiber, produced by the injection of evaluative attitudes into the connecting tissue, whence they seep into the text; thus the passage describing the sexual union of HCE and ALP in book III, chapter 4—whose final delightful sentence reads, "While the queenbee he staggerhorned blesses her bliss for to feel her funny-man's functions Tag"—is encapsulated in Burgessese as "To bed it is then, for a quick and joyless tumble."

The story thus constructed by Burgess out of the materials provided by the *Wake* (and by previous commentators on the *Wake*) is determined by his preconceptions as to what constitutes an acceptable narrative and his predilections as to moral commentary—which are by no means idiosyncratic, but representative of a whole class of critics, who are in turn representative of a wider class of readers. (It is also clear that the practical demands of reprinting the text—maintaining the same page format wherever possible, while allowing room for Burgess's summaries—must have dictated many of the choices, providing what is perhaps a more interesting principle of selection, which allows the material contingencies of language as writing, and as print, to have their say.) To insist, as Burgess does, that there must be a central core in *Finnegans Wake* is to adopt Shaun's mistrust of Shem's writing on the grounds of its dispersal of meaning through ruses and plagiarism; or as the text has it, echoing the deceived Issac: "The gist is the gist of Shaum but the hand is the hand of Sameas." All we can be given (and this is in fact what Burgess gives us) is a *sampling* of the text, because all we can ever do with a text like this is to sample it.

One reason for this is that narrative in the *Wake*—of which there is a great deal—is not a linear extension from start to finish (everyone knows the start and finish in this book are not so easily defined, anyway): it is woven through the text in a complex web, existing in varied and overlapping forms at every level, from the whole book to selections to chapters to paragraphs to sentences and even to individual words. The longer the span, however, the more rarified the narrative, and the more limited its satisfactions *as* narrative. Thus there is a perceptible movement from the fall of darkness at the end of book I, through the evening activities in much of book II and suggestions of night in book III, to the intimations of dawn at the start of book IV; but this is "plot" of the most tenuous sort, and it is forgotten for much of the time in the richness and intricacy of the detail which fills it out. Who, in actually enjoying the manifold delights of the so-called "watches of Shaun," is conscious for any length of time of a nocturnal setting for these foliating dialogues, speeches, and cross-questionings? But if we take a subsidiary narrative unit such as the story of Buckley's shooting (or non-shooting) of the Russian General, or HCE's misdemeanor (or attributed misdemeanor) involving two girls and three soldiers in the park, we find them repeatedly recurring in constantly varied forms, at every conceivable level of discourse (and they are also, of course, versions of each other). The two-page account of the Battle of Waterloo in the "museyroom" passage is a complex development of the same narrative nucleus that appears in the single phrase "nicies and priers," the game *"Fickleyes and Futilears,"* and the "mamafesta" title *"Them Lads made a Trion of Battlewatschers and They Totties a Doeit of Deers."* It occurs at slightly greater length in the nursery rhyme, "This liggy piggy wanted to go to the jampot. And this leggy peggy spelt pea. And these lucky puckers played at pooping tooletom," and in the inculpatory exculpation offered by the long sentence in book I, chapter 2, which is worth quoting for its characteristically indirect presentation of the story's outlines:

> Slander, let it lie its flattest, has never been able to convict our good and great and no ordinary South Earwicker, that homogenius man, as a pious author called him, of any graver impropriety than that, advanced by some woodwards or regarders, who did not dare deny, the shomers, that they had, chin Ted, chin Tam, chin-chin Taffyd, that day consumed their soul of the corn, of having behaved with ongentilmensky immodus opposite a pair of dainty maidservants in the swoolth of the rushy hollow whither, or so the two gown and pinners pleaded, dame nature in all innocency had spontaneously and about the same hour of the eventide sent them both but whose published combinations of silkinlaine testimonies are, where not dubiously pure, visibly divergent, as wapt from wept, on minor points touching the intimate nature of this, a first offence in vert or venison which was admittedly an incautious but, at its wildest, a partial exposure with such attenuating circumstances (garthen gaddeth green hwere sokeman brideth girling) as an abnormal Saint Swithin's summer and, (Jesses Rosasharon!) a ripe occasion to provoke it.

Similarly, *How Buckley Shot the Russian General* appears frequently in versions of that summary title, but is extended to seventeen densely packed pages in the dialogue of Butt and Taff, enfolding many other smaller-scale narratives within it.

This treatment of narrative shatters the illusion that sustains many readings of novels (and many quite sophisticated critical analyses and elaborate theoretical systems): that there is a sharp distinction between a set of preexisting events and individuals and a secondary verbal represention of them—a distinction that promotes to a central position those aspects of the text which disguise its textual and linguistic status, and gives to the whole a teleological structure determined by the question "What happened next?" *Finnegans Wake* inverts and complicates this distinction: events, people, places, times are clearly *constructed* by the text (or, more accurately, by the reader in the encounter with the text), and attention is focused on the process of linguistic fabrication itself. The question we ask here is "What is happening in the text at this point?", and the *post hoc ergo propter hoc* logic (or failure of logic) that powers narrative continuity is broken. At the same time, *Finnegans Wake* could be said to glory in the *secondariness* of language, its never-ending and ever-failing attempt to point to something beyond itself. The desire to interpret language, including fictional texts, as references to a "real world" can't simply be annulled; on the contrary, the tempting, teasing, thwarting, consoling, and occasional illusory satisfaction of that urge is the generative source of the *Wake's* textual pleasures. Reading is not so simple an activity that one has to choose between enjoying the evident unknowability of the events in Phoenix Park and scrutinizing accounts of them for signs of "what *really* happened."

It is not only centralized narrative that disappears in *Finnegans Wake*; the mass of interlaced material makes it impossible to draw out *any* single thread as central—whether plot, time-sequence, character, symbolic structure, mythic framework, voice, attitude, dogma, or any other of the threads that serve in the conventional novel. There are far too many dissolves and montages, shifts and leaps, condensed phrases and multiple allusions, for a consistent center to emerge. Joyce's use of sigla and initials as labels to stick on to huge accumulations of verbal material (containing their own inner contradictions) has very little to do with traditional concepts of "character" and "narrative"—and even these very broad categories merge (∧ and ⊏ becoming ⟋⊏), multiply (⊣ becoming ⊣⊢), or contain one another (as △ contains ∧ and ⋒ contains ⊏). Place, time, tone, imagery, symbolic suggestiveness, moral judgment, all slide and propagate in this way, resisting, by means of the full exploitation of language's own alogicality, the erection of logically consistent patterns. This resistance, it should be noted, does not take the form of *refusing* such patterns, but proffering them in such abundance that none can stand as central or even consistent with the others. The title offers no passport to the book's inner chambers (though it tends, surprisingly, to be rather neglected by those seeking a "center"), and the text is shorn of all other traditional metatextual guideposts. *Finnegans Wake* is a book without a center; which is to say that it is a book without digressions, without anything that can be skipped, taken in at a glance, or read rapidly to get the gist. (Even what *looks* like supplementary material—such as marginal notes and footnotes, or long lists of names—can't be read as such.) Which is also to say that *everything* in it is capable of being skipped, since there is no life-giving heart which might be injured. If, as Burgess says, *Finnegans Wake* totally resists cutting, this is because it does not resist it at all.

What I want to ask is if Joyce's last work is best seen, for all these reasons, and in spite of the recuperative labors of Burgess and others, as a digression from the central tradition of the novel. First, however, we need to examine the distinction between "center" and "digression" itself, as it has been understood, and continues to be understood, in that tradition.

II

As we read a novel (and I am using that term without any attempt at precision), we are continuously classifying the words we read according to the degree to which they appear progressive or digressive with regard to the movement of the narrative. Although we do this unconsciously, it influences the rhythm and tempo of our reading, the degree of our concentration at any given point, the selective operation of our short-term memory, and the formation of mental constructs relating to already-held schemata of "character," "plot," "theme," and so on; and this constant monitoring of the internal relations of the text, crucial to our ability to make it cohere, also produces formal pleasures, analagous to those provided by a musical texture of digressions and returns in harmony, melody, rhythm, and timbre. What enables digression to operate in this way is that it carries with it the notion of subordination, unimportance, and ultimately dispensability: digressions in a novel are appendages—in some sense "unnatural" ones—which could be lopped off with only minor damage to the main body.

But any rigorous account of digression will quickly counter this view with an insistence that dispensability is only a (necessary) illusion. Classical and Renaissance definitions of *digressio* or *parechasis* as a rhetorical device in oratory stress the contribution it makes to the main argument; Thomas Wilson, for example, states in his *Arte of Rhetorique* that by digression "we swerve sometimes from the matter, upon just considerations, making the same to serve for our purpose, as well as if we had kept to the matter still." The Romantic conception of organic form (of which the Hegelian dialectic may be considered a version) stresses both the importance of internal digressive movements and the contribution they make to a complex unity— as in Coleridge's description of the serpent-like motion exhibited by the reader of an organically unified poem: "at every step he pauses and half recedes, and from the retrogressive movement collects the force which again carries him onward." And structuralist attempts to formulate the codes whereby we read narrative texts, the codes that have grown up with the novel and which constitute it as a readable object, emphasize that nothing in the literary text can evade the superefficient machinery of recuperation, which operates on the simple principle that everything which is there has meaning. Roland Barthes gives a forceful statement of this principle in his survey of the structural analysis of narrative:

> A narrative is never made up of anything other than functions: in
> differing degrees, everything in it signifies. This is not a matter of
> art (on the part of the narrator), but of structure; in the realm of

discourse, what is noted is by definition noteworthy. Even were a detail to appear irretrievably insignificant, resistant to all functionality, it would nonetheless end up with precisely the meaning of absurdity or uselessness: everything has a meaning, or nothing has. To put it another way, one could say that art is without noise (as that term is employed in information theory): art is a system which is pure, no unit ever goes wasted, however long, however loose, however tenuous may be the thread connecting it to one of the levels of the story.

According to this structuralist version of organicism, a digression which obstinately refuses to respond to all the recuperative strategies at the reader's command, a digression which cannot be read as supplementary information, symbolic parallel, illustrative exemplum, will still offer itself as *digression*, as a model of the digressiveness of the mind or the world, as a demonstration of the impossibility, or the undesirability, of total and continuous relevance.

The functioning of digression as a structural principle is clearly dependent on its double nature: at once necessary and dispensable, part of the novel and excluded from it, inside and outside at the same time. Its capacity to operate without threatening the unity of the text depends on its subordination as an irrelevancy, yet to subordinate it as irrelevant is to incapacitate it. What, then, are the forces that push disgression in these two opposed directions, holding it within the text as an integral element, and expelling it as an unnecessary addition? We can begin by looking at the former, the ways in which digression operates in the service of textual *cohesion*, and in order to do so it will be useful to make a preliminary distinction between what might be called "flagrant" digression, which is openly announced as such, and passages of a more uncertain character, which we can term "equivocal" digression, where the reader postpones firm classification until further evidence is in. (These two kinds of digression are of course always merging into one another, and different readers and readings will produce different categorizations of the same passage, but this need not prevent us from discussing the strategies of interpretation and textual unification they each invite when they appear in relatively clear manifestations.)

Equivocal digression fails to announce openly its own relation to the rest of the text, and, by keeping alive the possibility that it may be more progressive than at first appears to be the case, induces in the reader an alertness to potential links which acts as a powerful binding force, and imbues the digression with all the interest of an enigma. What seems digressive at the time can, of course, be revealed in retrospect to be progressive, like some of the apparently trivial incidents in *A la recherche du temps perdu* which blossom later into major constituents of the narrator's experience (and equally, what seems part of the central narrative at the time can turn out to have been a false trail, as often happens in detective fiction). The possibility that any digression may be redeemed, or revealed as a *felix culpa*, operates at all levels to keep the reader engaged, encouraging the constant reinterpretation of earlier material and constant speculation about future directions. When an apparent digression is later retrieved, the resultant sense of an organic wholeness, and an all-embracing authorial Providence, is of a much higher order than could be produced without digressions. And the conclusion of a novel can function most fully *as* a conclusion when it retrospectively finds a place and a justification for all the wanderings that had seemed to defer and endanger it.

Flagrant digression, by contrast, announces itself unmistakably as such, and the reader is left in no doubt as to its digressive status: it clearly departs from the main business in hand, and may make use of a conventional introductory phrase as it does so ("Here we shall pause a little. . . ," etc.). Far from fracturing the text irredeemably, however, this kind of digression can have the effect of a strong guarantee of centeredness: to experience a passage as unmistakably digressive is to be reassured that what one took to be central *is* central, since it is so easy to know when one has strayed from it. It is also to be reassured in one's position as masterful and secure reader: in a digression which presents itself as digression, *one knows exactly where one is* (even though, or perhaps because, one is where one should not be). In its very resistance to recuperation, flagrant digression enhances the recuperability of the progressive narrative: straining to make the digressive material "natural," we reinforce the easy and largely unconscious naturalization of the rest. To categorize an unassimilable section of the text as digression is to save the unity of the whole by means of a gesture of controlled separation; what we cannot file directly in the drawer marked "Center" we file in another drawer marked "Digression"—and both drawers sit snugly in the same cabinet. The notion of "digression," therefore, implies and enforces a notion of "centrality"; and as long as the digression continues to be experienced as such, it is entirely at the service of the center which defines its digressiveness.

Some of the terms allied to "digression," such as "diversion" and "excursion" (or "excursus"), suggest, in their double signification of "detour" and "pleasant recreation," another function; digression's suspension of seriousness, its delight in its own irresponsibility, emphasizes the seriousness of what it has left behind, operating like the licensed holiday that guarantees strict sobriety on all working days. (Occasionally, the relationship is reversed, and the comic character of the whole is assured by the sombreness of the digression, as in the Man of the Hill's story in *Tom Jones* or the supernatural tales in *Pickwick Papers*.) Again, by virtue of its subordinate status, digression serves the whole of which it is both part and not part.

Crucial to digression is its *temporary* nature. It always swerves back, and the return, the classical *reditus ad propositum*, is a moment of satisfaction and reassurance: we were right to retain confidence in the order and wholeness of the text, and in our own secure position as readers, and we taste the sweet pleasure of relevance in a way that would have been impossible without the digressive move. Barthes's description of "suspense" is equally applicable to the suspension achieved by digression: "a game with structure, designed to endanger and glorify it, constituting a veritable 'thrilling' of intelligibility" ("Structural Analysis of Narratives"). If a text that has swerved away does not in due course swerve back, the firm structure of center and digression collapses, and the reader is left groping without secure bearings. Thus the second part of Blanchot's *L'arrêt de mort* (in its revised form) makes no overt reference back to the first part, and some of the nesting stories in Buñuel's film *Le fantôme de la liberté* never return to their enclosing narratives; and one might even cite *The Taming of the Shrew*, in which the entertainment of the title starts as a diversion and ends as the play itself. In cases like these, our strategies of recuperation are stretched, our masterful position threatened: the narrative spins away out of our control. (Though we may devise tactics whereby we can regain contol, like those theater directors who resurrect a final scene from an inferior "Shrew" play to provide a secure closing frame for Shakespeare's text.)

Over a larger domain, digression is fundamental to all narrative design, in the wandering that constitutes the movement between the state at the beginning and the state at the end. Instead of taking the direct route from A to B, the narrative delays, dilates, and digresses (in both its events and the discourse that produces them) before it reaches B—which often turns out to have more of A in it than one would have predicted from the errant paths traversed in between. The end is experienced as a conclusion only because of the wanderings in the middle, but the wanderings are acceptable only because they eventually lead to the conclusion. Classical sonata form in music offers a parallel, the development section moving away from the material of the exposition in such a way as to promote both surprise and satisfaction at the return of this material in the recapitulation, at once the same and different.

In these ways, digression is retained securely within the text of the novel as a significant contributor to its cohesion, its readability, its status as a model for an ordered, teleological, interpretable world, understood and controlled by self-knowing subjects. Yet we have seen that it can only function in this way if it is kept firmly in a subordinate position: all its strength as a support for the text's unity—and for the assumptions about art, and about human experience and knowledge, that this unity serves— depends on this fact. But what is it that gurantees its subordination? What is it that advertises the digression *as* digression in the fullest sense—as diversion, interlude, excursion, supplement? (The mere presence of a conventional introductory phrase is obviously not sufficient.) What is it, in other words, that pushes the digression towards the *edge* of the text, and in so doing enables it to return towards the center?

The distinction between narrative center and digressive periphery in the "traditional" novel appears to be a simple one between that which "advances the plot" and that which does not; but this may be described more precisely as a distinction between sections of the text which appear in the guise of mere reflection of a preexisting series of events, carrying the writing along with them by the force of their causal logic and teleological motion, and sections which bring to the fore the writing itself, dallying and delaying, freezing the stream of events and revealing them to be secondary to the text that produces them. In the central narrative, language is experienced as a transparent medium through which the world is clearly observed, and the events recounted are enjoyed directly for their own intrinsic interest. In the digression, the window grows opaque, and we focus on its texture and design. The commonest kind of digression interpolates a commentator or narrator, who is revealed as having the power to stop the flow of events (or to speed them up), to linger over this or that detail of character, to track backwards and forwards in time, to move entirely away from the plot, to introduce commentary, moralization, or subsidiary narrative—and in so doing to expose events, characters, time, and everything which is "interrupted" by the digression as already produced by the writing of the text (the same writing that produces the digressing commentator, of course, though this is usually disguised by the text). A narrating voice of this kind is not necessary for digressive effects to be felt, however: as soon as the stable ratio between the chronology of the events and the chronology of the discourse relating them— or more generally between words and matter—is broken, the constructedness of those events begins to obtrude, and writing, not the world, is felt to be in charge. The pastness of events is replaced by the presentness of narrating: a present that is already past when we read it, and was never present to itself. The digression may, in spite of itself, attempt to substantiate the referential illusion by apologizing for its intrusion upon a real scene, or it may, on the contrary, revel in the breaking of that illusion, as in some of the initial chapters of *Tom Jones*, or, more spectacularly, in the digressiveness of some of Beckett's highly unreliable narrators. In digressions, the language —no longer yoked by the pretence that it is referring to a pre-linguistic set of existents — can be given its head, deriving its energy from its own properties and proclivities. These include its capacity for intertextual allusion, for polysemy, for irony, for recursiveness, for patterning, all the byproducts of its existence as a system of differences realized in the materiality of print and sound. The central narrative, on the other hand, is at its purest, is least subject to being suspected of digressiveness, when these properties are repressed or masked, and language appears to obliterate itself in the act of referring and reporting.

What we are considering, then, is an opposition in which one member is defined as subordinate, and is regarded as valuable insofar as it *is* subordinate; but in which the dominant member retains its dominance only by the systematic exclusion of those properties which characterize the subordinated opposite. This pattern will bring to mind the similar pattern exhibited by many of the oppositions that have been discussed in deconstructive readings—literal and rhetorical, serious and nonserious, speech and writing, nature and culture, proper and improper, to name only a few—and in which the subordinate member has been shown to be generalizable in such a way as to constitute a class of which the dominant member is merely a subspecies. So, for example, the properties of writing which result in its subordination to speech have been shown by Derrida to characterize all language (and all events which are capable of iteration)—indeed, to *constitute* language as language. The gesture of subordination and exclusion—which Derrida calls "the philosophical movement par excellence"—is designed to perpetuate, among other things, assumptions about the relation of language to its speaker, its referent, and its interpreter: assumptions of direct communication between subjects fully present to themselves of truths grounded firmly in a world independent of language and consciousness. And we find the opposition between central narrative and digression displaying this familiar logic. The properties which result in the subordination of digression are the very properties which constitute the entire text as a text: the properties of writing itself—its independence from origins, goals, referents, its ceaseless production of meaning, its material patterns and rhythms. The center is able to function as a center (and to uphold a conception of language as transparent communication) only by excluding those properties, by branding them as digressive and supplementary. To restore these properties to the entire text by a deconstructive reversal is to see the narrative as only one kind of writing among many, a form in which the material and diacritical character of language operates as forcefully and fruitfully as anywhere else; it is to see the world of plot and characters as vivid and shifting designs painted on the surface of the window. It is also, of course, to view the secondariness of digression in a new light: not as the inherently subordinate status of a part of the text, guaranteeing the prime importance of the narrative and the organic unity of the whole, but as the product of only one of many ways of reading—among them (notwithstanding the long history of organic theories of form, including the structuralist variety) the possibility of letting some features or parts count for nothing, of treating the text as fragmentary, divided, or unstable. We may even come to feel that this is the *only* way in which texts can be read, and that an "organically unified" reading is achieved by just such a process of exclusion, a process repressed by the reader and by the tradition, and visible only in its effects.

This leads to an account of reading which, in its allowance for heterogeneity as between readers and readings, and its acceptance of sampling and skipping, is probably a more accurate description of what actually happens in the encounter with a text than idealized versions of total interpretation and hermeneutic rigor. But it remains true that to displace narrative from its dominant position is to read against the pressure of current conventions and habits, and, given the primacy and power of narrative in our culture, it could probably only be achieved partially and fitfully. There are, however, a few works which appear to cooperate more fully with a reading of this kind, and which in fact make the conventional gesture of exclusion impossible: works in which the "digressions" are so long, or so brilliant, that they insist on a status equal, or even superior, to that of the central narrative. Examples come readily to mind: in Swift's *Tale of a Tub* the tale itself occupies about a quarter of the text; in *Tristram Shandy* Sterne weaves a web of digressions which prevent the ostensible auto-biography from getting properly underway (we might note in passing here that Swift and Sterne are two of the most frequently cited authors in *Finnegans Wake*); the digressions in Byron's *Don Juan* are as memorable as the story of its anti-hero; Melville's accounts of whaling in *Moby-Dick* vie for attention with the story of Ahab's quest for the White Whale. In such texts, all the strategic systems for the recuperation of digression fail, since they all rely on its having a subordinate status; the hierarchical opposition between progressive and digressive, it might be argued, is deconstructed by the text itself. The result is that the reader is weaned from dependence on the illusion that novels are reports on the real world, and is encouraged to enjoy the writing as writing, in all its uncertainty, prolixity, contradictoriness, and materiality.

It is important to note, however, that with these texts the conservative reader need not relinquish a position of secure mastery: once apprised of the reversal of priority between narrative center and digressive material, he or she can read for something *other* than the narrative, while still enjoying the returns to the story, however exiguous, when they occur. The "reality-effect" of the narrative sections may even be enhanced by the presence elsewhere of an obtrusive narrator, caught up in language's proliferations precisely—such a reader might say—because it is not being employed in its proper task of representing the world. What occurs is a split between two oppositions that are normally conflated: the progressive/digressive opposition and the dominant/subordinate opposition, and a reversal of the homology between them, so that it becomes possible to read the digressive sections as dominant and the progressive ones as subordinate: the story of Peter, Martin, and Jack, the early events of Tristram's life, the adventures of Don Juan, the hunt for the White Whale, all remain structurally "central," but that centrality no longer guarantees preeminence. One still knows *where one is* in reading the text, and one enjoys the comic or ironic effects of the reversal that has been achieved. The episodes that constitute the plot become episodes inserted into a continuous non-narrative sequence, and it is possible to read the text for its digressive material, skipping the narrative entirely; thus *A Tale of a Tub* is represented in the Nonesuch edition of Swift's works by its digressions alone. What is lost in *this* kind of filleting, of course, is precisely the *digressive* quality of the digressions, their disruption of the generic conventions that arbitrate between dominant and subordinate in the text.

Texts which make it impossible to read in terms of a structure of center and digression (with priority of one of these over the other) are very rare, perhaps nonexistent: we have seen that even *Finnegans Wake* has not escaped such readings. But what all these unconventional texts (and the history of their interpretation) show more clearly than orthodox novels is the degree to which such structures are *produced*, not given. Anthony Burgess's backbone belongs less to *Finnegans Wake* than to himself. Even with conventional texts it is always possible for the reader—not as an absolutely free subject, but as the focus of a set of forces operating at a specific time and place—to privilege some feature other than narrative, to read Shakespeare for the patriotic sentiments, George Eliot for the moral wisdom, Joyce for the sexual explicitness. And editors have never been slow in bringing our selections in accordance with contemporary preoccupations or their own preferences; *A Shorter Finnegans Wake* stands within a long and flourishing tradition. If, however, structures of priority are produced and not intrinsic, they are necessarily unstable, dependent on readings and not on the text itself. Moreover, such oppositions (like the oppositions between structure and event, or cause and effect) have an *inherent* instability: to classify something as "digression" is to imply that the center from which it digresses is already firmly in place, yet to classify something as "center" is to imply that a digressive periphery is already in place. If either is experienced as "given," it is given not by the text itself, but by the conventions that govern its reading, conventions which themselves derived from a body of texts that includes the one to which they are being applied. The progressive and the digressive, in every literary text, from the simplest tale to *Finnegans Wake*, depend on each other, invade each other, exchange with each other, in the neverending production of reading, and readings.

III

I come now to the third and final part of this essay, the part which you are no doubt assuming will reveal whether part I was a digressive prelude on *Finnegans Wake* in a essay on digression, or part II a digression on digressions in a essay on *Finnegans Wake*. Fortunately, the logic of my argument frees me of any obligation to settle the question, and I can leave it to my readers to produce their own structures of center and digression.

The question I left unanswered at the end of part I—in true Shandean style—was whether *Finnegans Wake* should be seen as a digression (a flagrant digression, no doubt) from the central path of the novel as a tradition and a genre. There can be no doubt that this is how it *has* been treated, in obedience to the law I have already described, whereby the classification of something as "digression" helps to reinforce the centrality and importance of everything else. It is obvious, too, that the grounds on which this exclusion has been effected are the ones we have just been considering: *Finnegans Wake* is a digression because it fails to conform to the expectation that novels reflect a preexisting reality, foregrounding instead the properties of language—its instability and shiftiness, its material patterns and coincidences, its intertextual slidings, its freedom from limiting sources or goals, its independence from its referents, even its refusal to be bound by a single language-system. The literary tradition (which now embraces most of

Joyce's earlier writing) *needs* limit-texts against which to define itself: its sanctification of the novel's "central" concern with "the real world" or "humane values" or "common sense" is strengthened by the gesture with which it excludes *Finnegans Wake* for what it calls its "artificiality," its "shallowness," its "inaccessibility." Literary criticism rests on the givenness of the distinction between the serious and the nonserious; it can accommodate the *comic* within the serious, but in order to protect its founding exclusion it has to banish *Finnegans Wake* to the realms of the nonserious, as a mere diversion or excursion. And we can see clearly here how the distinction with which we have been concerned within the individual novel is also produced at the level of the canon by the ideologically-determined needs of those who make it. (The attempt to situate *Finnegans Wake* within the tradition of the novel, and to give it the required seriousness, by producing a backbone for it—narrative or moral/thematic—serves, of course, the same ends; indeed, a double gesture is frequently to be observed, whereby it is both excluded as a radical text and saved in the form of a grossly reduced and attenuated simulacrum.) What is being fended off by this process of marginalization is the worrying possibility that *Finnegans Wake* may be not an aberration of the literary, but an unusually thorough-going *exemplification* of the literary, of the very conditions of existence of *Middlemarch* or *Sons and Lovers* as literary texts —namely, the impossibility of ever being limited by originating intention, or external reference, or constraining context. That is to say, to the extent that literary texts can be read as *being* so limited, they perhaps fail to be literary, or at least to be read as literary, offering themselves instead as if they were reports, arguments, confessions, sermons, etc. (These other kinds of utterance are not exempt from the instabilities inherent in writing, of course, but those instabilities function in different ways.)

Does this argument hold? Can we —not as a matter of theory, but in practice—reverse the priority in the opposition between the progressive mainstream and the digressive aberration as it operates in the canon, by placing *Finnegans Wake* at the center and reading all other novels in its light, instead of the other way round? Since, as I've already stressed, no reader is free in an absolute sense, but is subject to the historically-specific constraints within which he or she is constituted as a reader, this must depend on whether or not we still experience those needs which have marginalized this text since it first appeared, our ability to read in this or that manner being determined to a large extent by the goals which we hope (consciously or unconsciously) to achieve, and the picture of the world we sustain or strengthen by doing so. Initially, such a reversal would have been impossible: Joyce's last book presented too great a challenge to the presuppositions of its readers to register as anything but an anomaly, and the efforts of those who supported it and proselytized on its behalf (no doubt often more because of their faith in Joyce than in full recognition of what the new work had to offer) were largely directed towards minimizing its threat to the assumptions that upheld the existing canon. But do we still need to be protected from that challenge, after the shifts and explosions in our conception of literary texts in the last twenty years—shifts in which Joyce's writing, and *Finnegans Wake* in particular, have themselves played a significant part? To many who have read Bakhtin, Barthes, Kristeva, Derrida, de Man, Heath, and Gasché (these names can stand for many more), *Finnegans Wake* may offer itself as the central text in the Western literary tradition. Thus David Lodge has written recently, apropos of Bakhtin's studies of the novel: "The later episodes of *Ulysses*, and the whole enterprise of *Finnegans Wake* appear not as eccentric digressions from the great tradition of the novel, sidestrains of a maindrain, but the most complete fulfillment of the expressive potential of the novel that has yet been achieved."

Let us imagine a reader who has succeeded, as Lodge believes Bakhtin did, in achieving in practice a reversal of this kind. What are the effects of this intellectual metathesis? To begin with, the face of the novel as a genre is radically altered: those features we are used to placing at the heart of our dealings with the text become peripheral, as open to question as the portmanteau words of *Finnegans Wake* have been felt to be. Plot, character, moral argument, teleological structure, chronological continuity, symbolism, emotional coherence, depiction of place, observance of lexical rules, authorial presence, linearity, identifiable voices, monolingualism, metaphorical figuration: all these, and more, are relativized, seen as options with certain effects and certain drawbacks, available to be used, ignored, played with, and joined with others in innumerable combinations. The tradition of the novel is made to appear an extraordinarily monochrome affair, so limited are the possibilities that have been exploited, so limiting is the set of conventions within which writers have doggedly confined themselves. And no individual piece of fiction remains untouched: to take one's bearings from the experience of reading *Finnegans Wake* is to induce a kind of close attention to the language of the novel hardly encouraged by the search for psychological subtlety or moral significance, or by the rush to a "represented" world of character and event. At the same time, the reversal frees the reader from the remorseless demands of "organic form," with its injunction—formulated so well by Barthes—that nothing shall be counted as waste or noise (an injunction that not even *Finnegans Wake* has escaped: witness Campbell and Robinson's *cri de coeur*: "There are no nonsense syllables in Joyce!" [*Skeleton Key*, authors' italics]). All texts can only be sampled, all readings are partial, and every reading is different from every other one: a linear reading, for instance, is only one possibility among many. (Strictly speaking, it is not even that, since reading, we realize, always moves in several directions at once.)

To treat *Finnegans Wake* as paradigmatic, as the backbone of the literary corpus, is also to undo the opposition between narrative center and digressive periphery in every novel we read: one can, after all, keep reducing the most complex novel until one reaches a sentence at the level of "How Buckley Shot the Russian General" (and perhaps further), and at no particular stage is it possible to say that the "center," as an irreducible given, has been reached. Moreover, *all* novels are seen to be woven of narratives at every level—even in the most orthodox fictions, single phrases can encapsulate plots (whether culturally conventional or repeated from elsewhere in the text)—and the separation of "events" and "narration," "story" and "discourse," becomes impossible everywhere. The primacy and productivity of language is seen to operate as much in the telling of a convincing story as in the ruminations of a narrator or the interpolations of an arranger. The boundaries of the canon are breached, too: texts which have been excluded because of their failure to conform to the norms of "unity," or "seriousness," or "realism," established for, and by, the main tradition, become readable—and, more important, enjoyable, since we are not talking about a theoretical shift in modes of describing and categorizing literature, but a real shift in perception.

By the same token, *Finnegans Wake* itself becomes readable in its own terms, not those of a naturalistic and humanistic tradition: as a text whose lack of center, and equal lack of digression, is as radical as it is productive. Every sentence in the *Wake* could be taken as the key to the entire work, or could just as well be totally ignored; and the pleasure, which so many readers experience, of tracing through the text a motif or an allusion—to find it coiling through a chapter, secreted within a word, scattered over a page, providing coherence in an otherwise chaotic passage, linking two sentences across a hundred pages, materializing when least expected, providing an absurd yet welcome note of familiarity in the midst of strangeness—need suffer no diminution from the awareness that a multitude of other motifs and allusions wait to provide similar pleasures in equal abundance. A sentence like the defense of Earwicker quoted earlier can be savored for the local delights of its textual detail without being blunted by the overriding teleological demands of narrative: as, among many other things, a game with misplaced literary clichés on the model of the "Eumaeus" episode of *Ulysses* ("Slander, let it lie its flattest . . . ," "admittedly an incautious, but at its wildest, a partial exposure . . ."); a dissolving of the boundaries between word and word and between language and language—or, more accurately, a demonstration that such boundaries are always already dissolved ("ongentilmensky immodus," "silkinlaine testimonies"); an energizing of legal language by erotic displacements ("published combinations . . . visibly divergent"); an invocation of past codes and prohibitions—and the desires that break them—through the historical sedimentation of language itself (forest laws in "woodwards and regarders," "vert or venisoin"; the Old Testament in "garthen gaddeth green"—"gad" is "snake" in Pan-Slavonic—and "Jesses Rosasharon"; medieval property and marriage agreements in "hwere sokeman brideth girling"); and a teasing out of interconnected references to clothing ("s*woo*lth," "gown and pinners," "combinations," "silkinlaine," "wapt from wept"), writing ("pious author," "*shomer*" and "homogenius," "published . . . testimonies"), vegetation ("woodwards," "corn," "rushy," "nature," "vert," "garthen," "gaddeth"—to "gad" being to "straggle," "green," "ripe"), and the childish sexual delights of urination/exhibitionism/voyeurism ("regarders," "shomers"—Hebrew for "watchmen," "rushy hollow," "dubiously pure," "partial exposure"). Syntactically, the sentence reads like a token of the infinite productivity of grammatical rules emphasized by Chomsky, here operating in the service of the interminable need to make excuses; and phonologically, it is a rhythmic texture of sounds and stresses exploiting the patterns of nursery rhyme and popular idiom ("good and great," "chin Ted, chin Tam, chinchin Taffyd," "wapt from wept," "vert or venison," "garthen gaddeth green"). And what our project of centering *Finnegans Wake* is designed to show is that such enjoyment of writing's proliferating energies extends to *all* texts: any work of literature can be seen to possess these qualities to some degree, to partake of the modes of textuality which have been variously described in terms of *écriture*, genotext, *signifiance*, heteroglossia, dissemination, rhetoricity, performativity, *scriptibilité*.

But would such a reversal of center and digression represent, at the level of the literary canon, the same operation that *Finnegans Wake* itself performs upon the distinction between progressive and digressive at the level of the text, the deconstructive operation sketched in part II? Would it not be more like the inversion carried out by *A Tale of a Tub* or *Don Juan*, a reversal of priority that leaves intact the opposition itself, as well as the assumption that this opposition is wholly given? If a crucial effect of the *Wake*'s dissolution of the distinction between center and periphery is to reveal the *constructedness*, and hence the radical instability, of any such distinction, shifts at the level of the canon must be seen as equally produced, and not as inherent properties we have discovered after years of misapprehension. When I stated earlier that the *Wake* would, after a reversal of its existing relation to the tradition of the novel, be readable "in its own terms," I meant—and could only have meant—"in the new terms made possible by that reversal." But that reversal is always itself reversible; as I suggested earlier, we would take little pleasure in Joyce's texts if we were to abandon entirely (supposing we could do so) the multitude of reading habits that enable us to transform writing, however provisionally and hypothetically, from a structure of differential signifiers to a field of interacting signifieds (and perhaps even objects and events "in the real world"). *Finnegans Wake* can no more be *intrinsically* central to the body of texts constituting the English novel than it can be intrinsically at the edge — or *Middlemarch*, say, intrinsically at the center; the structure is more like that impossible figure of Derrida's "invagination," where the inside is at the same time the outside. Which, after all, is the center of the fish on our plate: the backbone we fillet out or the flesh we eat? As long as we need centers and digressions —and presumably we always shall—we will find them; the lesson of the *Wake* is that we don't stop finding them, and building on them, when we know that they are our own productions.

In order to learn this lesson from the *Wake*, we have, in some sense, to know it already—otherwise we will approach the book as a marginal text, offering no lesson at all, saved for the literary tradition only by the efforts of its filleting commentators. The project of deconstructing center and digression in the tradition of the novel depends on the realization that we are free to choose centers and digressions (in defiance of the traditional view of canon formation as the reflex of the texts' intrinsic values), and the simultaneous recognition that we are bound in our choice by all the texts we have read (including the one we are reading). If this appears to be a proposition that refuses to yield to logic, that cannot be understood in any single way, that implicates and undoes both its utterer and its hearer—then it is faithful to the text which has been the occasion for enunciating it. Like the end of *Finnegans Wake*, my closing words do not constitute a conclusion, redeeming the digressive route by which it has been reached, but an invitation to the reader (an unnecessary one, no doubt) not to stop here.

James Joyce, Paratactitian

David Hayman

In March 1923, early in the development of *Finnegans Wake*, but late in his own, Joyce scrawled on top of two paragraphs from the second version of his "Tristan and Isolde" parody the words "Hypotaxis" and "Parataxis." In the first, Isolde's thoughts, written in free indirect discourse and imitating the roll of the Byronic ocean, may be said to characterize if not caricature the rolling or flowing rhetoric of Joyce's female persona:

> The sea looked awfully pretty at that twilight hour so lovely with such wellmannered waves. It was just too gorgeous [a] sensation he being exactly the right man in the right place and the weather conditions could not possibly have been improved on. Her role was to roll on the darkblue ocean roll that rolled on round the round roll Robert Roly rolled round. She gazed while from an altitude of 1 yard 11½ inches his deepsea peepers gazed O gazed O dazedcrazedgazed into her darkblue rolling ocean orbs.

True to the *OED* definition of hypotaxis, these lines "are subordinate in construction." That is, by their relentlessly dependent ordering, they convey a sense of the hierarchical interdependence of the grammatical components. Since the word "hypotaxis" did not find its way into the text, Joyce was clearly making the point for himself when he labeled this overblown example.

In contrast to Isolde's effusion, Tristan's paragraph in direct address is a hash of philosophical jargon which the reader must order and decipher:

> —Isolde, O Isolde, whentheeuponthus I oculise my most inmost
> Ego most vaguely senses the deprofundity of multimathematical

From *Contemporary Literature* 26, no. 2 (Summer 1985). © 1985 by the Board of Regents of the University of Wisconsin System.

immaterialities whereby in the pancosmic urge the Allimmanence of That Which Is Itself exteriorates on this here our plane of disunited solid liquid and gaseous bodies in pearl-white passion-panting intuitions of reunited Selfhood in the higherdimensional Selflessness.

This is not a textbook instance of parataxis, of, according to the *OED*, "the placing of propositions or clauses one after another without indicating by connecting words the relation (of co-ordination or subordination) between them." Even though there is some slippage between certain phrases, it is not subordination or coordination that is lacking. Joyce may have been alluding to the tortuous syntax and logic that combine to subvert comprehension or the clash of polysyllables and neologisms so appropriate to the Germanic context of his prime source, Wagner's opera. If we put aside the question of Joyce's awareness in this instance and concentrate on the larger implications of the term for his work, we find that he invented (or perhaps, after Rabelais and Sterne, reinvented) for the modern novel the use of parataxis as a structural and formal principle.

The first and in some ways the most remarkable example of Joycean parataxis occurs in the opening of *A Portrait of the Artist as a Young Man* where Stephen's experience of infancy is telescoped into two pages of stacked epiphanies, moments which have apparently marked his memory and which, as Hugh Kenner was the first to show us, find formal echoes in the book as a whole. The passage is relentlessly random in appearance, so much so that none of the discontinuity that follows can shock the reader. The paradoxical pendant to this record of infant awareness presented in free indirect style, its postleptic prelude as well, is the diary with which the book closes. Together, they mark the birth of awareness and rebirth into maturity perceived—deceptively—as a flight into artisthood.

At first glance, the opening pages seem to contain little more than a list of stimuli/responses, events that might be qualified, to use Gérard Genette's terminology, as "iterative" (that is, repeated an unspecified number of times). A closer look shows that these are one-time occurences ("singulative"). Taken together, they constitute a rational development through time from the earliest memories to the most recent, from the infant's awareness to that of a preschool boy. Clearly, there have been large temporal leaps as there will be throughout the text, where something resembling Bergsonian duration is an article of faith. In fact, this brief text illustrates with astonishing precision the "portrait" Joyce described in his earliest effort in the *bildungsroman* form as the "curve of an emotion." Joyce is making a distinction between a "life" and a "portrait." The emphasis is on the signifying, shaping, and reflecting functions of small moments as opposed to "events" in a continuum, and in this Joyce is in the tradition founded by Flaubert. But in order to make the "curve" accessible, he deliberately reversed or at least extended the conventions of narrative, emphasizing points of intersection, moments when life reveals its central impulses. Thus he enabled the reader sensitive to paratactic gaps to plot the graph of Stephen's development without being lost in minutiae.

The bold announcement at the very outset of the novel is more than a bravado act. It establishes a principle of statement by means of ellipses, of accentuated absences, advertising precisely those spaces that are so conveniently plastered over in rigorously hypotactic texts and thus proclaiming the reader's presence as producer and the reading as a production. By making his initial paratactic presentation a mixed performance, a sequence or pseudo-list of varied activities presented in a variety of discourses, Joyce sets the decorum of the novel and facilitates the much-discussed transitionless shifts in style, form, and subject matter.

The concluding diary, a coda in which the text is brutally accelerated, has been and remains a puzzle for critics. In the process of *A Portrait's* development and Stephen's, the text has become increasingly hypotactic. Chapters 4 and 5 are broken into large and continuous sequences and in chapter 5, the context has been expanded to include the university world while the focus is on Stephen in terms of that heterogeneous but compact intellectual community. Though the seams of this highly schematic chapter are still evident, the peripatetic panels are clearly interrelated in the mind of the reader who watches Stephen as he simultaneously elaborates his moral position and rejects those of his friends and family. Furthermore, by the time we reach chapter 5, the experience of the variousness of this text has inured us to the larger paratactic developments. But even in a context that naturalizes such juxtapositions, the diary's radical microparataxis unmoors the reader accustomed to a less random and fragmentary presentation and unfamiliar with the (seemingly) informal thought of the protagonist. Paradoxically, this sequence is even more of a catalogue of responses than the book's temporally unmarked opening. We recall that the latter covers an extended period of time while relying on discrete internal markers. In the diary overt temporal markers establish a very brief span for entries anchored in no immediate context. The reader experiences disembodied thought which must be fleshed out by knowledge of a Dublin context, which is in its turn elaborated upon by passages scattered throughout the diary. Thus, we learn more about the situation of Cranly and EC here than we have in the body of the chapter, though the relationship between the passages is often far from evident and the external development must be reconstituted from these meager shards. In yet another sense, just as the opening may be read as predictive, the diary functions as a fast-action recapitulation of the book, moving backward instead of forward to attain the degree of innocence suggested by the closing prayer to the absent spiritual father, last in a line of (inadequate) supportive figures, first in a new line.

The role of parataxis in the intervening pages should not be forgotten, but there is space here for only a brief treatment of this pervasive and carefully modulated tactic. At the beginning of chapter 1 we find paragraphs exhibiting a variety of conjunctions:

The wide playgrounds were swarming with boys. All were shouting and the prefects urged them on with strong cries. The evening air was pale and chilly and after every charge and thud of the footballers the greasy leather orb flew like a heavy bird through the grey light. He kept on the fringe of his line, out of sight of his prefect, out of the reach of the rude feet, feigning to run now and then. He felt his body small and weak amid the throng of players and his eyes were weak and watery. Rody Kickham was not like that: he would be captain of the third line all the fellows said.

Rody Kickham was a decent fellow but Nasty Roche was a stink. Rody Kickham had greaves in his number and a hamper in the refectory. Nasty Roche had big hands. He called the Friday pudding dog-in-the-blanket. And one day he had asked:

—What is your name? . . .

He crept about from point to point on the fringe of his line, making little runs now and then.

Here we find juxtaposed a seemingly objective vision of the playing field, the actions of a small participant, his voiced reactions, and a deftly captured interlude in modified flashback. Most striking is the use of associative procedures to bridge gaps not only in the boy's thought processes but also in the larger structure. This may be an extreme example, but we find similar effects throughout the chapter. On a broader scale we may point to the abrupt changes in scene, capped by the shift from the infirmary context through a dream sequence to the famous Christmas dinner. The latter seems radical because it is so resolutely hypotactic and hence so shockingly out of phase with what surrounds it. But though, in a larger sense, it is just another random-seeming contribution to our portrait, the dinner functions as a pause or release from the difficult work of accommodation demanded by the associative development.

Held together by the overarching theme of sexual maturation, chapter 2 covers a shorter but more crowded time span. Perhaps as a result, the segments juxtaposed by parataxis tend to be shorter while, internally, each tends towards hypotaxis. The series of three major epiphanies each beginning with the words, "He was sitting . . .," provides us with an instance of well-marked parataxis. Here briefer units are juxtaposed to project an intense emotional development within an indeterminate temporality in terms of disparate actions in a related key or mood. We may also cite the far more nuanced technique used to convey Stephen's reaction to the festive evening at school, projecting a melancholy, almost hallucinatory atmosphere by juxtaposing items chosen for their undecidable condition. The building lit up to suggest Noah's ark, the little boy disguised as a girl, the friend who is also a rival and enemy, all contribute to our sense of Stephen's own ambiguous relations to his sex and maturity. Though the form is predominantly hypotactic, an effect of parataxis is achieved by the refusal to subordinate, to create a hierarchical awareness in the text.

Parataxis is less noteworthy in chapter 3, which features a disturbingly well-organized theological argument. Still, Stephen's paratactic thought fills the interstices, providing the radical juxtapositions that give the final epiphanic sequence its bite. Chapter 4, with its simple three-part structure, and chapter 5 are both largely hypotactic. In short, the *Portrait* uses parataxis strategically to measure and record Stephen's development from a more or less indiscriminate receptor to a polished and self-contained potential creator. It follows from Joyce's ironic practice that the hypotactic phase is at least partly illusory, a mask for inner confusion, and that the paratactic mode can house several of the more conventionally hypotactic passages, though in each case the dominant mode is decisive.

Joyce's method was not to repeat but to extend or even reverse himself. Thus, the disrupted surfaces of *Portrait* are a foreshadowing but not the pattern for *Ulysses*. If the *cas limit* of parataxis in *Portrait* is the opening, in *Ulysses* stylistic outrage reaches its apogee, not in the obviously fragmented "Wandering Rocks" or the coolly encyclopedic "Ithaca," but in the hiliarious and disconcerting musical spoof of "Sirens" which opens with pure paratactic dislocation. Most striking is the overture with its arrangement in verse of phrases and sentences drawing their elements from the chronological develoment of the chapter to come:

> Bronze by gold heard the hoofirons, steelyringing.
> Imperthn thnthnthn.
> Chips, picking chips off rocky thumbnail, chips.
> Horrid! And gold flushed more.
> A husky fifenote blew.
> Blew. Blue bloom is on the.
> Gold pinnacled hair.
> A jumping rose on satiny breast of satin, rose of Castille.
> Trilling, trillling: Idolores.

The conjunctions, sharp, rapid and unmotivated though they seem, are in most cases smoothed over by what turn out to be irrational grammatical adjustments. Sentence after sentence proves on inspection to be the result of a forced juxtaposition of unrelated or at least disparate elements. Thus the first line brings together the two barmaids, whose metallic hair chimes with the sound of the viceregal procession passing by in the street. The procession is then joined to the sound of the boots' shuffling. Nothing is quite what it seems to be and at first glance the whole sequence invites but resists all attempts to rationalize it, sending the reader scurrying for hints of the familiar, for casual rhymes and rhythms before opening into a chapter where the discourse is characterized by deliberate obfuscation.

In an important sense, this chapter culminates one paratactic and formal tendency while initiating or bringing into focus a radically different one. On the one hand, we have the diurnal system of associative bundles that dominates the stream of consciousness and interior monologue chapters of the book's first half as well as its distinctive and seemingly objective narrative voice. On the other hand, there are the larger stylistic units generated by an increasingly intrusive but seemingly undifferentiated presence I have called the arranger. This presence is felt as a kind of narrative static— hence a parataxis—as early as "Eolus." But by "Sirens" it has become powerful enough to invade the narrative voice before it takes over the narrative asides of "Cyclops." At this point the reader must face and accommodate him or herself to a new sort of antinarrative, one that seemingly reverses the norms of the book's first half. In fact, the middle of the book marks what could be called the junction of the modernist and late-modernist slopes of contemporary fiction.

The role of parataxis in the stream of consciousness chapters should be obvious since the stream is generated by random associations justified within the larger narrative frame by the synthesizing propensity of the reader's mind. We may assume that all the necessary bricks are there, but we are obliged to located and asemble them. In practice the effects are various, as evidenced by this passage from "Telemachus":

> —A quart, Stephen, said.
> He watched her pour into the measure and thence into the jug rich white milk, not hers. Old shrunken paps. She poured again a measureful and a tilly. Old and secret she had entered from a morning world, maybe a messenger. She praised the goodness of the milk, pouring it out. Crouching by a patient cow at daybreak in the lush field, a witch on her toadstool, her wrinkled fingers quick at the squirting dugs. They lowed about he whom they knew, dewsilky cattle. Silk of the kine and poor old woman, names given her in old times. A wandering crone, lowly form of an immortal serving her conqueror and her gay betrayer, their common cuckquean, a messenger from the secret morning. To serve or to upbraid, whether he could not tell: but scorned to beg her favour.
> —It is indeed, ma'am, Buck Mulligan said, pouring milk into their cups.

We note first the ambiguous slippage between third-person narration and first-person reflection, an ambiguity that may be a sign of stream of consciousness, as in the phrase "not hers." Then there is the unmarked statement, "Old shrunken paps," which we ascribe to Stephen, whose associations can be established with some ease. In the fourth sentence-unit we read, "Old and secret she had entered from a morning world, maybe a messenger." This begins the process of translating the established "realistic" image into the figural mode, a procedure natural to Stephen, given his symbol-making propensity. June 16 is most certainly a day when he has trouble dealing with what he himself calls the "here and now."

The symbol-making is itself paratactic behavior since it creates sharp, seemingly unmotivated juxtapositions that frequently draw their support from the mythic underpatterns of the book as well as the baroque currents of Stephen's mind. Here the figural irruptions are in conflict. The purported messenger of the morning is not brilliant and airy but "hidden and secret," a "witch on her toadstool," alternately good and evil, powerless and powerful. Also paratactic is the alternation of narrative-voice description with Stephen's *style indirect libre*. The former is objective if syntactically eccentric. The latter is heightened by descriptive details appropriate to Loyolan "composition of place": moments in the text when the protagonist imaginatively generates a context for action he has not seen. Generally, when this occurs in the early chapters, the text becomes more hypotactic. But even here we note breaks in the discourse: "To serve or to upbraid, whether he could not tell: but scorned to beg her favour." The whole paragraph may be said to jar with its context, the condescending treatment of the milk woman by breakfasting youths. It is in contrast too with the next descriptive/monologue interlude:

> —Are you a medical student, sir? the old woman asked.
> —I am, ma'am, Buck Mulligan answered.
> —Look at that now, she said.
> Stephen listened in scornful silence. She bows her old head to a voice that speaks to her loudly, her bonesetter, her medicineman; me she slights. To the voice that will shrive and oil for the grave all there is of her but her woman's unclean loins, of man's flesh made not in God's likeness, the serpent's prey. And to the loud voice that now bids her be silent with wondering unsteady eyes.
> —Do you understand what he says? Stephen asked her.

After a brief phrase in the narrator's voice, we plunge into Stephen's stream of consciousness, which is harsh and stilted, marked by the use of the present tense, and designed to provide the directions needed to bridge thought and dialogue, to convey the sense of the words obscured by its presence. This is a dramatic illustration of Joyce's paratactic method in the early chapters, of its force, and of the demands it makes on the reader's attention. To understand and justify the words, "and to the loud voice," we must ignore the punctuation that marks a break in Stephen's thought pattern as he returns from his revery to the action that surrounds him, an action to which he has been half attending while his jealous musings stood in our light. If we do ignore the punctuation and think of "to the voice" as following "Stephen listened," we are apt to receive another paratactic jolt. For this is a broken sequence, to which the last element belongs syntactically but not logically. It is as though the language has written itself, shaped by the inertia dictated by the incomplete series. Other passages and other early chapters contain more radical and complex examples. "Proteus," in a context full of sudden associational jumps, accommodates a variety of narrative units that jar incessantly, keeping the nervous reader in perilous balance on Stephen's mental tightrope.

Styles invariably change with each chapter and transitions are always abrupt. In addition, between the Stephen and Bloom chapters there is a radical shift in tone and reader contact, a new sensual empathy generated by an increase in affective language. But the real surprises—"Eolus" apart—begin with "Scylla and Charybdis." There, in addition to the usual clash within Stephen's mind and of that mind with the elliptically presented and complex social context, we experience frequent irruption of arranger-generated textual incidents. One of the latter opens the chapter: "Urbane, to comfort them, the quaker librarian purred." As we adjust to the syntactical peculiarities of this sentence, we are struck by the originality of the new voice that will interact throughout the chapter with the conventional narrative presence, seemingly reflecting Stephen's reactions, but never marked as Stephen's. In fact "Scylla" constitutes the moment when arbitrary arrangement is best joined to the dominant narrative mode of the opening chapters. The combination results in all manner of effects that interrupt the narrative flow, delightful but intrusive, and obfuscating, impediments to "coherence" that contribute eventually to the unity of the book as a whole.

After "Scylla" with its paratactic profusion, "Wandering Rocks" seems pleasantly predictable. Narrative vignettes, temporal contexts, are randomly juxtaposed. Actions occurring in disparate Dublin spaces are joined paratactically to convey a sense of the larger environment. Time seems to have been stroboscopically frozen by means of intrusive references to parallel actions. Yet the vignettes themselves vary only slightly in their mode of presentation, which tends to be hypotactic. As if to provide a transition into the total parataxis of "Sirens," the chapter concludes with a comic list describing the motions and reactions of all of the characters, though scrupulously omitting all mention of Stephen, Bloom, and Molly. This catalogue is in itself a fine illustration of our principle. For, though it can be read as a simple list, it has obvious temporal and spatial coordinates and functions as a recapitulation—while recording the progress of the viceregal cavalcade—just as the overture to "Sirens" provides a structural preview both of that chapter's action and of its verbal high jinks. Both passages illustrate a central trait of parataxis, its role as a context that mediates between the spatiality of being there and the temporality of getting there, Stephen's famous *"nebeneinander"* and *nacheinander."*

Parataxis touches every detail of presentation in "Sirens," a chapter whose avowed fugal form lends itself to fragmentation. Not only is the motif-listing pseudo-narration of the overture disorienting; for the unwary, there is entrapment in false readings, the result of taking juxtapositions too literally. Several critics have assumed without warrant that allusions to Bloom on pages 259–60 [of the 1961 Random House edition of *Ulysses*] reflect the attitudes of the barmaids. But Bloom is a presence only because of the puckish arranger/narrator's voice that introduces him with the query, "And Bloom?," and follows his progress toward the Ormond Hotel. Entrapment is everywhere a function of juxtaposition in this chapter, where the action takes place simultaneously in several different locations. Take this passage that coincides with the singing of a patriotic song:

> Tap. Tap.
>
> Thrill now. Pity they feel. To wipe away a tear for martyrs that want to, dying to, die. For all things dying, want to, dying to, die. For all things dying, for all things born. Poor Mrs. Purefoy. Hope she's over. Because their wombs.
>
> A liquid of womb of woman eyeball gazed under a fence of lashes, calmly, hearing. See real beauty of the eye when she not speaks. On yonder river. At each slow satiny heaving bosom's wave (her heaving embon) red rose rose slowly sank red rose. Heartbeats: her breath: breath that is life. And all the tiny tiny fernfoils trembled of maidenhair.

Bloom and the barmaids are listening to Ben Dollard's song. The passage records their reactions mingled with references to the words of the song, the maidenhair shreds of tobacco, and the "tap tap" of the blind piano tuner's stick as he returns to retrieve his tuning fork. The latter is of course not audible to Bloom any more than is the obsessive jingle of Blazes Boylan's jaunty cart on its way to Molly Bloom. Apart from the obvious parataxis of Bloom's stream of consciousness and the introduction of intrusive references, a practice already evident in "Wandering Rocks," we note the technique borrowed from "Scylla and Charybdis" of permitting reflection to flow into description. In this case, Bloom's reference to "their wombs" generates the false transition or mock hypotaxis of the "liquid of womb of woman eyeball," a reference perhaps to the barmaid's unproductivity. The same device is repeated below after the radical break for thought between "gazed" and its object, "yonder river," which refers both to the river Liffey outside the door of the hotel and to a phrase from the song Dollard is singing, "The Croppy Boy." It is the river that elicits the image of wave motion in the following sentence, with its ambiguous syntax. Indeed, at every turn we find a new impediment, a fresh refusal of hypotaxis, a further demand on the reader's ingenuity and perseverance, an assertion of textual independence.

The microparataxis of the earlier chapter is muted in the book's second half upon the virtual disappearance of the narrating persona. But it is replaced by an insistent macroparataxis. Indeed, the collision of forms in "Cyclops" introduces a formal discontinuity unmatched in serious literature. On the surface, this chapter is farcical, filled with disruption and irreverence that derive from the narrative voice and combine with the seemingly gratuitous use of parodic asides. Together they turn a humdrum incident into slapstick, Bloom into a bumbling if vaguely admirable clown, the context into a community of outcasts. In the process they oblige the reader to restore balance and revalidate the Bloom we have known.

The paratactic impact of the asides need not be emphasized. Each comic intrusion interrupts the rush of narrative with a fresh and irrelevant bit of verbal horseplay, distracting the reader, diminishing Bloom's predicament, and contributing to the pantomimelike impact. It is only on close inspection of the chapter that we begin to appreciate the range and subtlety of these effects.

Perhaps the most famous and radical example of dun-ish discontinuity, a passage combining macro- and microparataxis, is the micturition sequence, a moment of blindness in the text when the narrator leaves the scene of the action, drawing us into his affective net:

> Goodbye Ireland I'm going to Gort. So I just went round to the back of the yard to pumpship and begob (hundred shillings to five) while I was letting off my (*Throwaway* twenty to) letting off my load gob says I to myself I knew he was uneasy in his (two pints off of Joe and one in Slattery's off) in his mind to get off the mark to (hundred shillings is five quid) and when they were in the (dark horse) Pisser Burke was telling me card party and letting on the child was sick (gob, must have done about a gallon) flab-byarse of a wife speaking down the tube *she's better* or *she's* (ow!) all a plan so he could vamoose with the pool if he won or (Jesus, full up I was) trading without a licence (ow!) Ireland my nation says he (hoik! phthook!) never be up to those bloody (there's the last of it) Jerusalem (ah!) cuckoos.

These lines are paratactic in ways not manifested by the stream of consciousness, in that the parenthetical asides represent an antidiscourse, perhaps muttered under the speaker's breath. As the critical controversy around the incident would suggest, this is by no means a simple question, but we might see the presentational tactic as a radical link between the system of the narrative proper and that of the structural asides. In short, it constitutes a moment of undecidability between structural parataxis and hypotaxis as well as an instance of maximum rhetorical disorder preceding the entrance of the living symbols of order led by Martin Cunningham, whose presence motivates the violently comic conclusion.

With its mock-Homeric opening, its focus on the underdeveloped psyche of a Dublin virgin, its account of a temperance service in a nearby church, and its belated and mock-melodramatic introduction of the Bloom-ish perspective, "Nausicaa" provides us with a radical change of pace, an apparent exercise in strict hypotaxis. Its retreat from cruel reality into a sentimental narcosis is reinforced by the preponderance of run-on sentences:

> Still the blue eyes were glistening with hot tears that would well up so she kissed away the hurtness and shook her hand at Master Jacky the culprit and said if she was near him she wouldn't be far from him, her eyes dancing in admonition.

Not only are subordination and coordination observed, but punctuation, which might slow the pace, is suppressed. Contributing to the effect of "feminine" gush are the clichés that function as emotional counters and vebal gestures for the "ladylike."

When we return to the by-now conventional parataxis of Bloom's meditations, we note that his thought has been infected by the flow to which the narrative contributes. Significantly, Bloom's segment is preceded by the exceptionally paratactic evocation of the shared sexual climax, a textual coupling of male and female tendencies:

> And then a rocket sprang and bang shot blind and O! then the Roman candle burst and it was like a sigh of O! and everyone cried O! O! in raptures and it gushed out of it a stream of rain gold hair threads and they shed and ah! they were all greeny dewy stars falling with golden, O so lively! O soft, sweet, soft!

The chapter concludes with another mimetic sequence as Bloom slips into sleep. Three grammatically paratactic paragraphs are interspersed with sets of three italicized cuckoo calls, comments on Bloom's marital status. Here the disruption is modified by the systematic use and rhythmic arrangement of the tripling, a form of completion and order.

The same rhythmic principle dominates the opening of "Oxen of the Sun" with its invocations of the sun/son in three paratactic and seemingly meaningless paragraphs, each of which repeats the same words three times. Thus we enter a chapter whose styles are designed to convey the growth of the fetus as a parallel to the development of English prose, while underscoring the disconnected and random conversation of the roisterers belowstairs. Predictably, this chapter raises a fresh set of problems. If the clash of prose styles would seem to be paratactic, the styles themselves are mainly hypotactic, though subject to intrusion by other voices. Further, as the chapter progresses, there is less contrast among the styles and fewer demands are made on the reader's patience, wit, and ingenuity. We have been lulled in fact into a sentimental/ironic torpor by the time of the infant's birth. Then, to the accompaniment of a bolt of lightning and the rumble of thunder, the whole crew rushes off for a pub-closing drink propelled by a storm of words unprecedented in this book and predictive of certain passages of *Finnegans Wake*:

> Query. Who's astanding this here do? Proud possessor of damnall. Declare misery. Bet to the ropes. Me nantee saltee. Not a red at me this week gone. Yours? Mead of our fathers for the *Übermensch*. Dittoh. Five number ones. You, sir? Ginger cordial. Chase me, the cabby's caudle. Stimulate the caloric. Winding of his ticker. Stopped short never to go again when the old. Absinthe for me, savvy? *Caramba!* Have an eggnog or a prairie oyster. Enemy? Avuncular's got my timepiece. Ten to. Obligated awful. Don't mention it. Got a pectoral trauma, eh, Dix? Pos fact.

The force of this finale, an early example of what Philippe Sollers calls a *polylogue exterieur,* is sufficient to alter the balance between order and chaos preparing us for the intrusive and all-encompassing disruption of "Circe."

How complete is the formal discontinuity of what appears to be the most farcical and chaotic chapter in *Ulysses*? Here the tangled skein of micro- and macrostructural and thematic considerations becomes more vexing. Several forces are operative. The text is cast in dramatic form with elaborate stage directions describing actions that subtly blend possible and impossible behavior. Even though it has been foreshadowed by the headlines in "Eolus," the asides in "Cyclops," and the interacting narrative strands elsewhere, the procedure marks an important moment in the development of the arranging presence. The demands upon the author were great. Somehow the realistic context had to be made credible, no matter how blurred its outlines. At the same time much of the dramatic impact had to be conveyed by the hallucinated stage directions. Furthermore, by virtue of their questionable relationship to reality, the latter had to be extremely clear. The result is, superficially, like the presentation of an oneiric vision in a painting by Dali where photo-realism before-the-fact is applied to the outrageous distortion of the recognizable. But the stage directions do more than describe, they impose attitudes and visions and record emotions, as when Stephen whirls in dance (an extreme instance of microparatactics).

Paradoxically, Joyce's project eliminated or minimized macrostructural *and* microstructural parataxis on the stylistic level. At the same time, the chapter is organized on principles that extend the associative parataxis of the stream of consciousness chapters. For example, the hallucinatory interludes grow directly out of cues from the real or dramatic context. Thus Zoey's "Go on. Make a stump speech out of it" elicits the lordmayoral fantasy. But it is the lesser associational paratactics of the evolving reveries that give the chapter its chaotic impact, the multiplication of seemingly unmotivated details. In any given instance the leap from topic to topic can seem great:

([Bello] *explodes in a loud phlegmy laugh.*) We'll manure you, Mr Flower! (*He pipes scoffingly.*) Byby, Poldy! Byby, Papli!

BLOOM

(*Clasps his head.*) My will power! Memory! I have sinned! I have suff . . .
(*He weeps tearlessly.*)

BELLO

(*Sneers.*) Crybabby! Crocodile tears!

(*Bloom, broken, closely veiled for the sacrifice, sobs, his face to the earth. The passing bell is heard. Darkshawled figures of the circumcised, in sackcloth and ashes, stand by the wailing wall. M. Shulomowitz, Joseph Goldwater, Moses Herzog, Harris Rosenberg, M. Moisel, J. Citron, Minnie Watchman, o. Mastiansky, the reverend*

Leopold Abramovitz, Chazen. With swaying arms they wail in pneuma over the recreant Bloom.)

THE CIRCUMCISED

(In a dark guttural chant as they cast dead sea fruit upon him, no flowers.) Shema Israel Adonai Elohenu Adonai Echad.

VOICES

(Sighing.) So he's gone. Ah, yes. Yes, indeed. Bloom? Never heard of him. No? Queer kind of chap. There's the window. That so? Ah, yes.

(From the suttee pyre the flame of gum camphire ascends. The pall of incense smoke screens and disperses. Out of her oakframe a nymph with hair unbound, lightly clad in tea-brown art colours, descends from her grotto and passing under interlacing yews, stands over Bloom.)

THE YEWS

(Their leaves whispering.) Sister. Our sister. Ssh.

THE NYMPH

(Softly.) Mortal! *(Kindly.)* Nay, dost not weepest!

BLOOM

(Crawls jellily forward under the boughs, streaked by sunlight, with dignity.) This position. I felt it was expected of me. Force of habit.

THE NYMPH

Mortal! You found me in evil company, highkickers, coster picnicmakers, pugilists, popular generals, immoral panto boys in flesh tights and the nifty shimmy dancers, La Aurora and Karini, musical act, the hit of the century.

Here Bloom moves from his preoccupation with debasement to a confrontation with guilt in the shape of the nymph on his bedroom wall. Each stage of that motion is marked by a new vision justified by some prior allusion which feeds, as does everything in "Circe," on thoughts and episodes from earlier in the day. In reaction to Bello's assault on his pride, his/her appeal to Bloom's love for Molly (for whom he is Poldy) and Milly (for whom he is Papli), Bloom casts himself in the role of Christ, repeating the interpretation of I. H. S. from "Lotus Eaters." His false tears call forth an appropriate response from anomalous mourning Jews, who, in a passage reminiscent of "Calypso," "cast dead sea fruit upon him." From the same chapter but from a different tradition comes the sacrificed widow (the nymph rather than Molly). At this point, as often happens, nature seems to intervene: the yews are given voice while Bloom enters a new landscape, resuming his previous position, crawling to her "with dignity." The nymph's speeches illustrate another paratactic dimension: the comic catalogue of items from *Titbits* pass for conversation. All of this and much more derive from earlier chapters and hence from the reader's memory. But even if that (textual) memory is precise and complete, the effect of this sequence of stop-action allusions is rigorously paratactic. Hard put to rationalize each shift in attitude and focus, we are obliged to leap and stumble over the craggy (subconscious) logic.

In contrast to "Circe," the long-winded meandering "Eumeus" with its endlessly qualified sentences is, on the surface of it, an exercise in excessive hypotactics. The style is uniform; there are virtually no surprises, little or no action, and many cliché-ridden, circumlocutory sentences like the following, which, to quote Joyce on Proust, the "reader ends before him."

> Skin-the-Goat, assuming he was he, evidently with an axe to grind, was airing his grievances in a forcible-feeble philippic anent the natural resources of Ireland or something of that sort which he described in his lengthy dissertation as the richest country bar none on the face of God's earth, far and away superior to England, with coal in large quantities, six million pounds worth of pork exported every year, ten millions between butter and eggs and all the riches drained out of it by England levying taxes on the poor people that paid through the nose always, and gobbling up the best meat in the market and a lot more surplus steam in the same vein.

But even in such grammatically rigorous hypotaxis as this, we note a disguised parataxis, a tendency to list and accumulate disparate elements. "Eumeus" may well be read as an exercise in mock hypotaxis.

"Eumeus" forms a couplet with the much maligned and overtly paratactic "Ithaca." Not only is the catechistic form obviously and deliberately discontinuous, a catalogue moving toward the condition of a development, but the questions and responses themselves frequently turn into catalogues that threaten to drown themselves and the narrative in detail. It is consistent with Joyce's method that the fragmentation and some of the humor appropriate to farce should be dampened along with the potentially moving moment when Stephen and Bloom finally "meet." The evocation of water falling from the tap, an instance of dry frozen motion for the reader, is only one example among many. In the end, the almost fanatical scrupulosity of the tongue-in-cheek disjunct narration leads to Bloom's submersion in "Penelope."

Moving from the apparent confusion of the overdocumented "Ithaca," we ourselves succumb to the charms of continuously recumbent flesh/prose. Molly's monologue, by virtue of its internal rhythms and lack of punctuation, is the ideal counterstatement to scientistic disjunction even though, in terms of its content, "Penelope" has been read as morally disruptive. Still, the tonality and the lack of punctuation conceal a marked associative parataxis in Molly's utterance and gloss over the confusions it can cause. Take the following brief example, to which I have added punctuation and italics:

> Yes, when I lit the lamp. Because he must have come 3 or 4 times with that tremendous big red brute of a thing he has. I thought the vein or whatever the dickens they call it was going to burst, though his nose is not so big, after I took off all my things with the blinds down after my hours dressing and perfuming and combing *it.* . . . He must have eaten oysters, I think, a few dozen.

Our punctuation is problematic, but so is Molly's discourse. Not only does the word "it" break a parallel construction, but there are only two sentences, one of which should probably be put between parentheses since it interrupts a description of Boylan's erection. Other problems, impediments to grammaticality, make for a halting, rather than a fluid, reading. The temporal development is in question, as is the pronominal reference, and some readers may be confused by the association of "nose" with penis size. One of the strongest paradoxes is the smoothness with which this covertly discontinuous chapter carries out its attack on the reader's sensibilities, sowing confusion while giving the impression of clarity. Joyce has once again managed to reverse conventions, and the book that begins by a chapter exposing serious matter to levity, raising high the sun, has this rosy moon for a postscript and a prelude.

Our analysis of *Ulysses* shows the careful modulation of parataxis and the modification both of the means by which it is achieved and the ends it serves. Although within the chapter-structure, we can point to strong parataxis in chapters falling between "Scylla and Charybdis" and "Oxen of the Sun," and although we find the most radical example in "Sirens," we note paratactic qualities in just about every chapter and may see discontinuity on all levels of presentation. On the other hand, even the most disruptive passage will be foiled in some way against continuous formulations. Even the most obvious imbalance will in some way be righted by this text. I would suggest that the reader's role is in many ways controlled precisely by the built-in need for proportion and balance on the structural as well as the thematic and narrative levels. That is, parataxis contributes to the dynamics of reading by continuously reasserting disequilibrium to counter the equilibrating impulse at work within our minds and latent in the formulation of the text itself. It is an important, a revolutionary part of the system of the text, one whose intricacies we have only begun to explore. We need not be surprised, therefore, that it is also the most controversial aspect of *Ulysses*, the one that, without their knowing it, has led many critics to dismiss all or part of Joyce's masterwork.

Rhetorically, *Finnegans Wake* may be the most paratactic of Joyce's books. This is in large measure due to a new component, vertical rhetoric or the discourse generated in the reader's acting imagination by a consideration of the word play. In passage after passage we find a stacking of contradictory as well as complementary meanings. Even though the juxtapositions and superpositions are not simultaneously available to each reader or on each reading, even though they are capable of rationalization, such concatenations are found to have an impact of disjunction. Beyond the vertical rhetoric, the verbal texture itself introduces radical ungrammaticalities that, though often smoothed over by the overriding rhetorical flow and the textual rhythm, are bound to stop the reader intent on even partial comprehension of the passage.

In the following random sampling we find devices that illustrate Joyce's practice:

a. "The hilariohoot of Pegger's Windup cumjustled as neatly with the tristitone of the Wet Pinter's as were they *isce et ille* equals of opposites, evolved by a onesame power of nature or of spirit, *iste*, as the sole condition and means of its himundher manifestation and polarised for reunion by the symphysis of their antiphathies."

b. "If juness she saved! Ah ho! And if yulone he pouved! The olold stoliolum! From quiqui quinet to michemiche chelet and a jambebatiste to a brulobrulo!"

c. "Yet is it, this ale of man, for him, our hubuljoynted, just a tug and a fistful as for Culsen, the Patagoreyan, chieftain of chokanchuckers and his moyety joyant, under the foamer dispensation when he pullupped the turfeycork by the greats of gobble out of Lougk Neagk."

Though each of these passages could yield pages and pages of exegesis, we must be content with some highlights. Item *a*, from chapter 4 of book I, tells of Shaun the post's testimony concerning the encounter in Phoenix park that occasioned the fall of the all-father HCE. The seeming nonsense syllables begin with "hilariohoot," which can initially be read as an expression of enthusiastic joy or a "shout of hilarity." But we may wonder whose joy: the witness's, the audience's, the utterance's, or all three? "Windup" and "Pegger" combine to suggest conclusion and throw (see American slang). But a pegger is a drunkard and there is also the expression "getting the wind up." The pun "cumjustled" suggests "contrasted" and "compared" but contains "jostled" and might even be translated as "with (*cum*) justice led," suggesting a circular motion or a joining of opposites. When we note that "tristitone" suggests not only sadness (*triste*) but also the name Tristan, we return to "hilariohoot" to find the unfunny Christian saint Hilarius and perhaps even Flaubert's devilish Hilarion from *La Tentation de St. Antoine*. It should be clear that the sentence derives its vertical parataxis in part from the references but mainly from the click effect elicited by the strange vocables within a fairly conventional utterance.

Example *b*, from the account of the ALP letter given in book I, chapter 5, illustrates a more apparent discontinuity. Each element is simply juxtaposed to its neighbor and the last sentence seems finally to degenerate into a list of punned-upon names of the languages in which the letter is "told." But the passage goes further, slamming us against reefs of words like "juness" (female June, Juno or more emphatically *jeunesse*), which is followed by an alpha/omega utterance and contrasted to the male "yulone" (Yuletide, suggesting June/January or age vs. youth; July; you alone). By the time we reach "pouved" which combines proved with *pouvoir*, we know we must return to the unsatisfactory "saved" to salvage *savoir*. The resulting old saw is less interesting than the process by which it was exposed, the oscillation that enables us to reinforce rhetorical balance. Discontinuity bordering on parataxis is both a constant and a variable, resulting in our awareness of a constantly changing texture, one of the delights of the "book of Doublends Jined."

The third passage, *c*, occurs in book II, chapter 3 as part of the description of the pubkeeper HCE behind his bar, drawing drinks for the thirsty clients. In it he is transmuted into a giant emanation from the misty past of sacrificial strangulations (see the famous Bog People), of Patagonian chieftains, and of fabulous disasters like the emptying of Lough Neagh. It also contains an evocation of phallic might (and masturbation). The "ale of man," besides suggesting the Isle of Man, refers to an evolving last supper sacrifice. Note the duplicity of "moyety joyant," which evokes both a mighty giant who is half (*moitié*) enjoying himself (or perhaps his mighty *moitié* phallus) and his wife or his joining/pleasing half. These and other vertical components, along with the usual ungrammaticalities and miming words ("pullupped"), are complemented by a system of pauses that tends to set off each unit as a problem sequence in itself, adding to the effect of complexity and disjunction. Typically, Wakean sentences are stuffed with asides, qualifications, amplifications, and other rhetorical gestures that elsewhere could serve to clarify but here tend to enrich texture and complicate our responses to the languageness of words rendered substantial.

In reading these passages we have followed the process by which one can read the *Wake* as a whole: glossing the passage; relying on rhythms, grammatical echoes, and sound similarities; probing unusual spellings and juxtapositions in search of answers to questions they inevitably raise. Progress was marked by correlating families of references and supplying meanings for nonsense traits. Ultimately, whole structures that parallel/extend and often undermine existing ones will have to be erected. Throughout, it has been the *excedant* that dictated reader behavior, since we are all conditioned to account for every seme and justify every phoneme. Inevitably something remains unresolved after any "final" reading, some quirk of spelling like "Hobos" without the apostrophe.

On the microtextual level this combination of horizontal and vertical parataxis could be qualified as *super*paratactic. Whereas in conventional parataxis coordination and subordination are left to the reader, here everything is done to maintain gaps in the discourse, to prolong the reading process.

Given the revolutionary nature of his microparataxis, it is no surprise that Joyce was quite conservative in his use of macroparataxis. The *Wake* with its seventeen chapters and four books is stylistically every bit as various as the eighteen chapters of *Ulysses*, but the shifts in style seem less emphatic and more clearly motivated—if not at first then certainly after a few read-ings —by considerations of plot, theme, and logical development. With our noses so close to the page in an effort to accommodate the texture of puns, we are not apt to take into account the shifts in style on a first reading, and we overlook for a long time the transitions that seem to motivate them. Thus, on the one hand, the richness can be ignored, while on the other, the macroparataxis can seem more radical than it actually is. Such paradoxes are natural, given the text's language and its rejection of narrative conven-tions. Still, those familiar with the book know that the logic of Joyce's structure and arrangement is more rigorous and straightforward than ever in this book, however associative it may at times be.

The first half of book I, as a record of what happens after the fall (from grace, from a ladder, from a wall or into night, into barbarism, into urban life), follows the curve of readjustment, from accommodation through jus-tification to enshrinement of the past. The second half (chapters 5 – 8) turns from the male to the female principle and concentrates on the fallen hero's progeny. It begins with an account of the discovery of a DOCUMENT or Letter written by a survivor to celebrate and defend the vanished past/hero/god (book I, chapter 5). From this discovery and out of the vast web spun by priests/historians/scholars comes the codified celebration or catechism (book I, chapter 6), which is followed by decline. Book I, chapter 7 contains an extremely uncomplimentary portrait of the "debased" writer of the word. It amounts to a rejection of the past and leads to its flushing out in book I, chapter 8. Joyce uses the stage-Irish voices of the gossiping washers at the Ford of the Hurdles to air publicly the past's dirty linen, reconstructing the history of civilization and the geography of the Dublin area through the myths of ALP and her relationships with men and family. To elaborate this account of book I's chapter structure, the reader must ignore, sublimate, or justify logical and stylistic gaps encountered during the all-important first reading.

Though there are apt to be many abrupt changes in topic in almost any chapter of book I, only chapters 1 and 6, the overture and the reca-pitulation, are structurally paratactic. Significantly, Joyce added them late, in 1926, after the book's outline was firm. The opening chapter, a joyous romp with drunken death, is patterned after the music hall ditty, "Fin-negan's Wake." It contains several arbitrary-seeming vignettes like the "museyroom" account of the battle of "Waterloose" and the tale of how the Prankquean stole the children of Jarl van Hoother. Here, as elsewhere, the transitional paragraphs have an independent life that obscures the logic of juxtaposition. For example, though we move logically enough from the museum where we hear an account of comic carnage to the field of battle itself, how did that field, on which the scavenging bird picks at the gory remains, get to be outside the structure we have just left ("Mind your boots goan out")? It is perhaps logical for that vision to usher in the historical annals of Dublin and for these to be followed by the tale of the past. But it takes a large leap of faith to accept the dramatized version of the encounter between two prehistoric tribesmen. Typically, this meeting, which takes place on the mound of the dead hero, also puts us on another time plane. In short, the chapter's progress, while not rigorously paratactic, since the changes are carefully motivated, is so busy and full of unexpected panto-mimelike scene changes and abrupt changes in style that the reader is hard pressed to organize the experience.

In book III, chapters 3 and 4 are markedly paratactic, balancing the strong narrative hypotaxis of the first two chapters. Combining qualities of the inquest, the séance, and the psychoanalytic session, chapter 3 summons voices from a recumbent Yaun in an effort to get to the bottom of the human situation by raising the all-father HCE. Here again, though the frame situation is simple and coherent, the reader is obliged to rationalize the conjunctions. Perhaps chapter 4 is the most engaging paratactic unit. Despite the careful use of transitions, the interlaced strands of action in various forms and voices convey discontinuity. The chapter as a whole discloses with considerable success the mazy consciousness of a half-wakened world by mingling cinematic, "realistic," mythic, sociological, allegorical, and voyeuristic sequences. Its impact is one of comic/cosmic disorientation. But the reader is also reassured by the approach of the workaday world of today, as the Porters approach the bed of their crying son or have intercourse under the eyes of one or more of their children. The slim strand of plot generates exceptional suspense, emerging as it does from the nocturnal flood of perverse language, Joyce's sea of words. This is so even though the realistic fabric is paratactic, though it has only limited and questionable authority in this text of many turns, and despite the fact that it abuts the historical fantasia of the ricorso in book IV.

The latter is among the more straightforwardly segmented chapters, a unit designed to house three of the earliest segments of the *Wake*. Structurally, it recalls book I, chapter 1. Here too the styles are various and the transitions set the stage without precisely preparing us for the manner of what follows. As a result, though the chapter is relatively easy to read, though conjunctions lighten the texture, and though the logic of the development is accessible, the impact is paratactic, as befits a unit bringing together a variety of thematic concerns. Book IV concludes with ALP, her "manifesto" letter, and her address to the errant city man whom she is leaving to join the cold sea. Both passages, by virtue of their run-on styles, produced a strong hypotactic effect that is undermined by the frequent use of grammatical parataxis, as witness the following brief extract with its staccato rhythms:

> And I'll be your aural eyeness. But we vain. Plain fancies. It's in
> the castles air. My currant bread's full of sillymottocraft. Aloof is

anoof. We can take or leave. He's reading his ruffs. You'll know
our way from there surely. Flura's way.

Such rhetoric not only undercuts the illusion of seamless flow, but it also
underscores the balance of hypotactics/paratactics that Joyce established for
his last book.

Clearly, order and control must be stronger than discontinuity and
disorder if the *Wake* is to be accessible to the reader. But in the service of
the dream context with its encyclopedic range, parataxis that is itself extremely various contributes to the production of seemingly endless variation
and complexity. This is, of course, but one aspect of the dynamics of the
Wake. But Joyce's practice illustrates another property of aesthetic compen-
sation: namely that several different components of the work—words, sentences, vertical and horizontal readings, formal rhythms, chapters and
segments of chapters — contribute not only to a single end but to a number
of conflicting ends which in turn may collaborate in the creation of a coherent and satisfying, if vibrant and elusive, "meaning."

It would appear that Joyce began by innovating a paratactic approach
to the problematics of the literary portrait but soon discovered in parataxis
a device for liberating novelistic discourse from the tyranny of the continuum. The unfilled gaps in the stream of consciousness passages of *Ulysses*
convey, with the reader's willing collaboration, the fullness of the human
experience on the individual level while the larger formal leaps enable and
reinforce the universalizing impulse and fill out the baroque surface. Finally,
the conscientious use of varieties of hypotaxis to balance the apparent
disorder guarantees the orderly reception of this portrait of a day in the
life of mankind. Thus parataxis-balanced-by-hypotaxis enabled Joyce to
introduce and control an encyclopedic range of devices in the service of a
unified but heterogeneous vision. It remained for *Finnegans Wake*, through
the fragmentation of language on the level of the word, to generate the
universal and meaning-filled dream vision. Here the procedure was to
explore the manifold ways of distorting and freeing rhetoric; making maximum but rational use of vertical parataxis, the *Wake* conveys not only the
fullness of the human and cosmic moment but also its innate contradictions
and endless ironies. If Joyce's practice, his passion for balance, led him to
smooth over the *Wake*'s macroparatactics, the dominance of the liberating
impulse did not escape his readers or the writers who followed him any
more than did his mastery of parataxis in the service of the profoundly
comic high seriousness that marked the crest of the modernist impulse and
pointed beyond.

Wyndham Lewis the Writer:
A Preoccupation with the Real

Terence Hegarty

All appearances indicate that a full-scale reappraisal of Wyndham Lewis is imminent. It is so long overdue that a rough new portrait, at least, is essential; even diligent readers of twentieth-century literature often have no clear idea of who he was or what he did. Yet the uniqueness of his work, and its high level of literary craftsmanship, appealed to many writers and critics from Yeats and Wells to Stephen Spender and Marshall McLuhan.

In 1914 *Blast* No. 1 shook the foundations of literary London. As editor of this aggressive publication—which beneath a patina of *épater le bourgeois* self-indulgence spearheaded a genuine revolution in writing and ushered in the era of "modernism"—Lewis enjoyed a brief fame. But 1914 was not a good year to establish a reputation, and, despite Rebecca West's perceptive review of his novel *Tarr* in 1918, it was not until the late twenties that Lewis again became prominent, this time as a critic. A string of controversial books, beginning in 1926 with *The Art of Being Ruled*, launched a major attack on the new world of behaviorism and dehumanizing technology, its assumptions and paradigms. This body of work, even when it slips into straight political journalism, still has a special value for us today. But Lewis crowned this second period of public recognition with another shocker, a book that outdid *Blast* in calculated offensiveness. When the 700-page satire *The Apes of God* appeared in 1930, an outcry arose from the art-world moguls and pretenders it exposed so direfully. For connoisseurs of savage humor with a highly polished surface, like Swift at his best, *The Apes of God* will always be a classic.

By 1939 Lewis had made many powerful enemies. His repeated insistence, growing in shrillness as the decade progressed, that Hitler would not be *solely* responsible for precipitating the coming war did not increase his popularity, and the misconception that he espoused Nazism became

From *The Massachusetts Review* 23, no. 2 (Summer 1982). © 1980 by *The Massachusetts Review, Inc.*

widespread. "That lonely old volcano of the right," Auden called Lewis at this time, meaning no harm with his homely epithet. But others, more powerful than Auden, found it easy under the circumstances to build a climate of opinion that expelled Lewis to the outer darkness of intellectual life.

This situation was complicated when the right-wing reaction of the early fifties "rediscovered" Lewis and hosted his third and last apotheosis. By now Lewis was old, blind, and ill, giving all his energy to his last great books, *Self Condemned* (1954), *Malign Fiesta* (1955), and *Monstre Gai* (1955). The two last-mentioned books complete his trilogy *The Human Age*, a fantasy about "the politics of heaven" that stands as his most challenging work, shot through with light serene and garish by turns, full of vivid realizations of abstract ideas, and with plenty of humor both high and low. The trilogy remains virtually untouched by literary criticism, although the first volume (*The Childermass*, 1928) was highly praised by Yeats, who saw in it a partial verification of some of his own theories of history and the occult.

Lewis died in 1957, at 75 years of age. His life's work as a writer had just been analyzed with supercilious distaste in *Wyndham Lewis: A Portrait of the Artist as the Enemy* by Geoffrey Wagner, a "standard work" whose severity prevented the usual process of an increase in fame following death, and which has probably withheld more readers from Lewis than anything written before or since. Beneath a veneer of scholarly impartiality, Wagner's procrustean fitting of Lewis into a mold of right-wing extremism (Sorel, Maurras, etc.) is one of the more impressive *tours de force* in literary scholarship. For twenty years students have turned to Wagner's book for guidance and been innocently persuaded by its high readability and its smooth appearance of exhaustive, last-word scholarship. Thus has Lewis become anathematized for another generation.

But steps are being taken at last to revitalize Lewis's reputation. Hugh Kenner's popular *The Pound Era* (1971), though maddeningly diffuse, gives Lewis a high place in the modernist canon, and more recently C. H. Sisson, Bernard Lafourcade, and others have published more incisive essays. A definitive bibliography of Lewis' work, and a few useful one-volume selections of his writing, have appeared. My aim in this essay is to show, not so much his universal value, as his specific relevance to our time. For this purpose I will first trace some of his political ideas to their roots in his attitudes towards technology and the kind of slavery engendered by its over-development, and then I will illustrate the related process of social degradation as he depicts it in his novel *The Revenge for Love* (1937)—considered by many to be his masterpiece. Finally I will briefly indicate the salient qualities of his literary work in general that recommend him to the roster of great twentieth-century writers.

II

Before considering Lewis at all, it is necessary to overcome, at least provisionally, the obstacle thrown in the way by his supposed "fascism." A half-hour spent with his book "in praise of Hitler"—as *Hitler* (1931) is usually described for the benefit of those who will never see a copy of it in a bookstore or a library—will reveal that it is no such thing, but a piece of journalism on the Nazi party in its early stages, before its true colors were apparent and when it was a subject of interest and debate. Lewis went on to deride Hitler and the Nazis in *The Old Gang and the New Gang* (1933), and to condemn them in *The Hitler Cult* (1939) and *Anglosaxony* (1942), but to no avail—the die had been cast in 1931, while Mayfair and Bloomsbury still smarted from the savage barbs of *The Apes of God*. The stigma persists to this day.

It is undeniably true, however, that there are aspects of Lewis's work which would appeal to the political conscience of an intelligent conservative. Lewis was consistently preoccupied with the vanishing individual, and at times even used the words "socialism" or "communism" to identify the trend. But he continued to investigate the bald words until they meant something limited and concrete, specifically connected with the social malaise under discussion; and along the way he lost the interest of many a political partisan in a questioning of every assumption, right and left. A reading of his work—especially if it is scattered and unguided—will almost certainly raise ideological inconsistencies. But a conscientious, open-minded reader will recognize the genuine radicalism of Lewis's thought, and travel with him to deeper political levels than the propagandistic commonplaces of opposing ideologies.

For the most part, Lewis was not interested in prescriptions for changing the world. He would have been satisfied to take out the *very* bad and leave the rest alone. But he knew in the twenties that a small plutocracy in Europe and America, armed with an expanding and man-eating technology, had already accumulated enough power to plan history in advance, and he perceived with a sharper eye than most that this situation was drastically diluting the quality of life. He saw that life would soon be altogether miserable for any individual whose talents and interests were not channeled towards what was directly useful to the shortsighted goals of the ruling congeries. As an artist who survived by his work he began to feel encumbered by economic realities, and he started writing about *why* he felt this way. He never wanted to talk politics; but, "one must talk politics or one must keep one's mouth shut."

I am hoping that we in the eighties are ready to appreciate the astonishingly precise critique that emerged— a critique of what democracy had become by the thirties. Subsequent developments have shown that most of Lewis's insights about the interrelations of modern technology, politics, and art were profoundly accurate. Fifty years ago he picked out the raw pattern that has grown into today's society, although he insisted that he wrote merely from observation of his own time and circumstances. In volume after volume he isolated and discussed the inchoate elements of the emerging social order—the triumph of behavioral psychology and its potential for mass hypnotism via advertising, the philosophical implications of time-physics, the social impact of feminism and what we now call gay rights, the liberal reaction to the colonizing "empire-builder" mentality and the condescension towards the oppressed that ensued (it was Lewis who first classified Uncle Tommism, for instance, when in his 1929 book *Paleface* he criticized Sherwood Anderson's *Triumph of the Egg*, singling out the character Bildad as "the kind dusky Uncle Tom with the Dickens tear in the corner of his pathetic rolling benevolent black eye"), the role of newsreels and radio in shaping public taste and opinion, the lowest-common-denominator effect in mass-market art and entertainment, the growing tyranny of the ever-more-alienating machine . . . Above all he noted a mass sympathy with the kind of individual who does not act but is acted upon, a personage he gave (in 1934) Hemingway the dubious credit of fixing in literature as a new type of hero. As the ultimate *gestalt* created by all of these cultural elements he saw a new kind of slavery in the making—the slave system we now live under: a slavery to the machine, but engineered by human agents in the light of behavioral theory and research. For the vast majority under this system it is impossible to survive without wasting at least two-thirds of one's available time in some pursuit devoid of personal satisfaction.

Lewis's social analysis does not end with this insistence on a commonsense recognition of the nature of political power in our time. As early as 1926 he also isolated a phenomenon he was later to name "the rot." If an entire society is chained increasingly to the place of business, so that "the gentler things of life are at an end," then inevitably a decay of all standards sets in. Soon it becomes impossible to believe that life was ever any different. Such a society is controlled with ease, both its buying power and its values. Lewis foresaw that after World War No. 2 (he used this term to refer to the coming war all through the thirties) the institution of government would be practically vestigial, not much more than a symbol to maintain an illusory national coherence and a front to shield the real channels of power. Its main reality would lie in a steadily decreasing accountability.

And as institutional accountability decreases, individuals will necessarily be made to feel responsible for nearly everything. Lewis saw newspapers, radio, and movie newsreels doing this in the thirties, and today we see it still, only on a much vaster scale. It infects our whole lives, not least in the places where most of us spend the most productive of our waking hours. Management consultants have "proven" that business profits rise when employees are convinced that their non-company-related behavior (on company time) is "self-destructive."

> The fault, dear Brutus, is not in our stars,
> But in ourselves that we are underlings.

Disseminated and distorted via mass media and personnel policies, Cassius's simple pragmatism encourages needless, constrained responsibility to accumulate like a deadly sediment—exactly as it did in Brutus—in each distinct, unheroic compartment of the lonely crowd. The pressure is intense. If we are in the more susceptible majority, we rummage around in our psyches till we think we find the offending nexus. One by one, privately, we succumb. We rejoice as, link by link, we expel it. But what is it we expel? Wyndham Lewis has not been the only one to answer: *the self.*

Human unhappiness, from the smallest personal pang to the grossest social evil, is in fact very often caused by *somebody else.* Whatever happens to you, it is of the utmost importance to realize that *it is not necessarily your fault.* Unless you know otherwise, a persistence in assuming all the enforced responsibility life today thrusts upon you will steal your soul more effectively than any medieval demon. If you lose track of this simple truth you are doomed to be cancelled out by "progress," a victim sacrificed to that "time" that some poet said "threatens to empty us too, to make of us echoing shells that rattle in the wind."

The *All Quiet on the Western Front* philosophy—which can be adequately paraphrased as: "Isn't the human race abominable? Isn't it horrifying that we lose control of ourselves in this way?"—is not only erroneous in its placement of responsibility, but it is also reprehensible in that it clears the path for *more* violence ("Here we go again, God help us") and contradicts its ostensible pacifism. It turns the anguish of "Why can't we stop this?" into a despairing rhetorical question. Referring to the futility of the wanton bloodletting it examines, it only stresses the alleged inevitability of human self-destruction. In the enormous popular success of Remarque's book in 1929–30, Lewis quite rightly recognized one of the earliest signs that the way was being paved for another big war.

As those two decades between the wars—the first very jolly, the second extremely grim—recede into the past, the standard historian's view of the period becomes less and less satisfactory. Lewis's best polemics fill the holes roundly, without fanaticism, and with a passionate clarity that is not without a delicious Juvenalian humor aimed with consummate precision. For Lewis's volcanic, irresistible prose is his most immediately attractive quality. It is the intensity (of vocabulary, of inexorable logic, of precise imagery and analogy) with which he charges his espousal of civilized values and priorities, and his carefully-gathered evidence that these values and priorities are being insidiously undermined, that raises his criticism head and shoulders above the work of his colleagues in the literary school that consciously struggles for the survival and continuity of "Western civilization" (a moribund term, but kept serviceable by the iron lung of academe). Where Pound rants and "loses his center fighting the world," where Eliot stresses (rightly, but to the exclusion of important related elements) the decay of spiritual values, Lewis gives us the living goods.

III

A particularly sharp political journalist of the twenties and thirties—this is certainly one of the things Lewis was. But he was much else besides, perhaps too much. Because we tend to be skeptical about the limits of one person's possible achievement, Lewis's unbelievable energy and versatility have always been obstacles to a valid estimation of his work.

By training and profession—and in the forefront of his own consciousness—Lewis was a painter. He was the prime mover of the 1912–14 art movement known as Vorticism, often regarded as the London counterpart of the Cubism of Paris. Professionally and personally he was associated with Epstein, Gaudier-Brzeska, Augustus John, William Rothenstein, McKnight Kauffer, Henry Moore, and other London artists of his day; and many younger English painters, such as Bacon and Nicolson, have acknowledged his seminal role in the development of modern British art.

Lewis wrote that his first writings represented "the crystallization of what I had to keep out of my consciousness while painting"; and his earliest writing was in the mode in which he was to excel as a writer—fiction. His first stories appeared in 1909 in Ford Madox Hueffer's legendary *English Review*, and his first published novel, *Tarr*, was serialized in Harriet Weaver's *Egoist* in 1916–17, on the heels of the serialization of Joyce's *Portrait*. Thereafter he produced somewhere between ten and fifteen volumes of fiction, the number varying insofar as a few semi-fictional and semi-dramatic works are included. He also published about a dozen uncollected stories in magazines, and left behind a mountain of unpublished fictional fragments.

His very first novel—a lighthearted thriller, written around 1908–10, which he discarded at the time, calling it a "miserable pot-boiler"—has just recently (1977) been published for the first time. It is called *Mrs. Dukes' Million*, and it is a delight from beginning to end. It is the best kind of light reading because it gives us the best of two worlds: it spoofs its genre so unobtrusively that the suspense is every bit as captivating as the hilarity. It is fast-moving, witty, and well-plotted. It may be a bit "gentle-readerish" for aficionados of today's cynical spy thrillers, but it is not overly literary and I can't imagine any reader who would not enjoy it. And I must admit that it is a serviceable introduction to Lewis also: not just because it is his first book, but because it has many odd hints of the unmistakable Lewis style and a lot of the charmingly "wicked" personality revealed in his later satires. It gently accustoms the attentive reader to some of the extravagance of characterization that marks *The Apes of God* and its descendants.

But to get the full weight of Lewis's creative mind in a deftly constructed synthesis of all his lines of thought—including his politics and their rationale—we are fortunate to have a new reprint of his great novel *The Revenge for Love* (1937). Dealing with a left-wing London art circle at the time of the turbulence in Spain immediately prior to the Civil War, it tells the tragic story of Victor Stamp and Margot Savage as they are manipulated to violent death by communist terrorists in a Pyrenees gun-running operation. It was written in 1935, but its publication was delayed for nearly two years. When it finally appeared in May 1937, Madrid had been under siege for six months and the bombing of Durango and Guernica (by

German planes) was front-page news. Under the emotion-ridden circumstances that prevailed, many of Lewis's more cold-blooded insights—such as the political value of "atrocity propaganda"—were met with revulsion and contempt. But it is not "the communists" that Lewis is indicting in *The Revenge for Love*, but the cheapening of human life that comes with devotion to a violent revolutionary cause, especially when that cause is abetted by the easy availability of weapons.

The violent climax of *The Revenge for Love*—described with merciless cinematic detail—is approached by several major roads. There is the central political counterpoint, in which "the capitalist will sell you bombs to blow up other capitalists," where he who sets out to destroy capitalism inevitably becomes an even bigger and more corrupt capitalist himself, and in which human beings are callously and indiscriminately used for ill-defined ends. There is the range of sexual attitudes, determined largely by affluence and the still omnipresent English class structure, that colors and blurs the political cause, leading people to commit themselves to impossible ideals beyond their comprehension. And above all there is the utter confusion of the real and the unreal—a miasma that engulfs everything, from the wealthy sham-socialists who are blissfully ignorant of the grosser elements of revolutionary technique (but who provide the real money to buy real guns), to the highly profitable "fake factory" that employs Victor to paint Van Gogh self-portraits. And the exciting "chase scene" at the end, just like in a million movies, is experienced by Margot as the most unreal thing of all—but it ends in very real, and utterly unnecessary, death.

Lewis is by no means a sexist writer, but he does have distinct views about the political uses of feminism. In *The Art of Being Ruled* (1926), he suggests that an important economic function of feminism, as political exploitation, is "the releasing of the hordes of idle women . . . for industrial purposes." ("Idle" not in Lewis's eyes, but in the eyes of those who wish to exploit human beings for their own ends.) In the day-to-day arena of ordinary life, this aspect of "women's liberation"—by which most women, like most men, spend their time doing other people's work rather than their own—removes the last bit of real freedom possessed by any persons of low or moderate means. In this way sexual attitudes, which are to some extent socially conditioned in the first place, in turn complicate the motives that guide political activism, often victimizing the innocent and vindicating the guilty.

Margot adores Victor in a passionate but traditional way; the only reason she lives is to preserve and protect him. "Victor is my racket," she warns the gun-running organizer when she begins to suspect her man is being set up as a scapegoat. But her interference in the real world of guns and cars plays its part in destroying both Victor and herself. Contrasted with Margot, Lewis gives us Gillian Phipps—university-educated, exceptionally good-looking, upper class, liberated, an avowed communist, wife to a successful painter. Gillian likes to tease the determined adulterer Jack Cruze with feminist propaganda, but she is completely taken in by the communist propaganda of Percy Hardcaster, "a man of good party-brains" who falls temporarily for her aggressive charms. Embittered by the loss of a leg because of an aborted prison escape in Spain, Harcaster is indiscreet enough to confide some professional secrets to Gillian. Their conversation turns into an argument; she is horrified by the blatant lies involved in his Machiavellian techniques, and disappointed that he is not the proletarian hero she had believed him to be. When he realizes he has lost his sexual advantage he reminds her angrily of her class, making it clear that *real* communists like him will, as soon as they can afford it, dispense with her kind just as readily as they will with the capitalist establishment. "Take my advice and stop kissing ideas," he tells her. "Keep your kisses for your boyfriends like Jack Cruze." Gillian follows this last suggestion, and she is able to take leave of her husband in these words:

> "It is we so-called 'intellectuals' of the upper classes, who are the only real communists. Don't you see? When a workman becomes a Communist he only does so for what he can *get*! He regards it just as *another job*. . . . He brings with him all his working class cynicism, all his underdog cowardice and disbelief in everything and everybody. All his tinpot calculations regarding his precious *value*. . . . As a Communist he has mixed with his Communism the animal characteristics of his class. All that cheap sentiment and moral squalor."

This is for Gillian the real world, brought home to her by exposure to Hardcaster's real world. And her awakening to her own shallow (but real) values is only reinforced by her husband's answer: "If you felt like that about the general run of men, then Communism would be the most *unreal* thing it is possible to conveive."

"You've learnt something through kissing the workman that could be learnt in no other way!" is one of Hardcaster's last bitter remarks to Gillian. But he himself learns that he, as a *real* communist, is not immune to the damage caused by these *unreal* communists who finance his cause. Leaving Gillian's on his crutches he actually suffers a violent beating at the hands of Jack Cruze, with her complicity. Hardcaster is the ultimate focus of the novel, the man whose conscience is fundamentally altered by the death of Victor and Margot. His intrigue with Gillian—with its brutal aftermath—is a major component of his tragic education. At the end of the novel he is once more in a Spanish jail, caught while trying to prevent the catastrophe he foresaw too late. Here he hears a "strained and hollow voice"—an echo of the dead Margot's—"singling him out as a man who led people into mortal danger, people who were dear beyond expression to the possessor of the passionate, the artificial, the unreal, yet penetrating voice, and crying to him now to give back, she implored him, the young man, Absolom, whose life he had had in his keeping, and who had somehow, unaccountably, been lost, out of the world and out of Time!"

Earlier, Margot's thoughts at a gathering of salon-revolutionaries had intimated, by their naiveté, the nature of the later tragedy. "They could not really bear you down," she had thought, looking at this "dangerous crowd of shadows." "They could only browbeat you like a gramophone, or impose on you like the projections on the screen of the cinema." And even as she experiences the catastrophe itself, she thinks of the "fatality that came into play the moment it was machines, not men, that mattered." It is of course a machine—their own speeding car—that kills her and Victor. But Hardcaster knows the whole story.

The nature of the real in a society dominated by remote technology, and by the kind of political power that uncontrolled applied scientific development leads to, is Lewis's central concern in a great deal of his writing. This is naturally a painter's preoccupation, a point of view to be expected from a visual and spatial artist who makes objects to look at and feel, things to keep around you because you know they themselves won't change, only continue to illuminate your changing. For Lewis, objects in space resist change and continually strive to maintain a fixed being, to *become real*. (In this there is more than a little of Berkeley, the philosopher who demonstrated that nothing exists which is not perceived.) Machines collide head on with this view, because by their very nature they cannot keep still. In *Time and Western Man* (1927) Lewis argues with great force that the machine has lent an awesome unreality, a time-disease that can't be pinned down, to the age which it has come to dominate. He sees a universe of unreality proceeding like clockwork towards the utter enslavement of humanity, and infers from his knowledge and experience of history that it is far from accidental. "Everywhere a starving of the healthy organism, and the gorging of the sick, so as to put a premium on the second-rate . . . to put in the place of the real the unreal," he complains in his partial autobiography *Blasting and Bombardiering* (1937). In *The Art of Being Ruled* (1926) he had written:

> Whenever we get a good thing, its shadow comes with it, its *ape* and familiar. . . . Almost anything that can be praised or advocated has been put to some disgusting use. There is no principle, however immaculate, that has not its compromising manipulator. All that must be borne in mind, and the shadow and the reality, the "real thing" and the imitation, brought forward to some extent together.

In the half century since these words were written there have been many principles and many manipulators. And the marriage of technology and advertising has gone so far as to create an imitation world of imitation qualities, especially via television.

> Between the desire
> And the spasm
> Between the potency
> And the existence
> Between the essence
> And the descent
> Falls the Shadow

It is this "Shadow" (from Eliot's *Hollow Men*) that Lewis peoples in his fiction. It is *life*, of course, but life stripped of satisfaction. It is a world of fake stimuli with no possibility of genuine response. It is the turgid atmosphere of "media blitz," foreshadowed with precision long before the burgeoning of "mass communications."

IV

On the ordinary narrative level of detail and progression, Lewis's fictional technique is varied but always powerful, his language compressed and taut with energy. Characters emerge organically out of the initial setting he creates for them. After only a brief acquaintance his prose is instantly recognizable, even though he used several different voices, distinct styles connected with each of his major types of literary achievement. His earliest stories (written 1902–17, and represented in the 1927 collection *The Wild Body*) focus, through the distorting lens of a "humorous" narrator, the more brutal elements of primitive peasant life, mostly in Brittany. The ambitious fictional technique is masterfully controlled, and the rich prose throbs with a somber coloring that is similar in feeling to Rouault's paintings of similar subjects. This style culminates—with a significant shift in location to bohemian Paris—in his novel *Tarr*. As editor and prime contributor to both issues of *Blast* (1914 and 1915), he experimented with a violently bristling prose; this is Lewis at his most mannered and demanding, but it represents the birth and early development of his potent, vigorous polemical voice. An utter reversal of style follows immediately in a brilliant group of war stories—more precisely, stories of soldiers during World War I—unfortunately never collected by Lewis and hard to find today; although several predate his direct experience in the trenches, these very moving tales are superlative war literature, written in a clear, calm, hard prose reminiscent of the nineteenth-century French masters. With *The Apes of God* (1930), Lewis's biggest book, evolved throughout the twenties, he developed a merciless, triumphant method of fictional satire that no other twentieth-century writer comes close to in scope or intensity. His "straight" novels (he used the term himself), the best of which are *The Revenge for Love* (1937), *The Vulgar Streak* (1941), and *Self Condemned* (1954), allow character and plot to dominate; with the emphasis on content, Lewis employs a brisk and pithy prose that does not draw attention to itself. And in his richly textured fantasy trilogy *The Human Age*, begun in the twenties and finished shortly before his death (actually he had projected a fourth volume), his technique is complex, suggestive, and experimental, well-suited to the time and space shifts in which the spirit-characters move. Each of these six major classes of writing represents a full-scale literary achievement on its own terms.

Other bodies of literary work that can be enumerated include his vast polemical and journalistic potpourri, adding up to more than fifteen volumes; five or six books of literary and art criticism; and two entertaining autobiographies. There are also a few odd hybrids, of these and other genres, that defy classification. *The Letters of Wyndham Lewis* (1963), an extensive and revealing lifelong selection of correspondence, beautifully edited by W. K. Rose, deserves mention also.

Recently (1979) a book appeared called *Wyndham Lewis*: *Collected Poems and Plays*, edited by Alan Munton. This is an onerous title, for Lewis did not pursue either of these particular genres with any lasting seriousness. Munton's volume gathers a few short works that are, however, among Lewis's most interesting pieces. As well as a few early lyrics and a highly professional one-act play, the book reprints *One-Way Song* (1933), a witty satire in peculiarly original heroic couplets, and *The Enemy of the Stars* in both its versions (1914 and 1932), an elaborate allegorical "play" with an abundance of narrative and descriptive stage directions. *Collected Poems and Plays* is an admirable publication in that all of its contents have been among the hardest to find among Lewis's writings, but I suspect it will be of greater interest to a reader already familiar with Lewis than to someone approaching him for the first time.

That Lewis's multifaceted and enormously valuable contribution should have been slighted by the mainstream of literary criticism for over twenty years is more than unfortunate. Now, however, we have reached a time when the transparency and irrelevance of labeling Lewis should be self-evident. Moreover, it should now be clear that it is precisely this kind of false generalization that Lewis attacked most strenuously—the urge that would substitute a label, a composite, an image, a cipher for the real thing. As a new wave of video technology, this time with two-way capability, settles quietly in our living rooms, his is a voice that will clarify the choices we will have to make, individually and as a society. And of all the voices that can do this for us, his is the most attractive, because it contains the fewest imponderables. Lewis does not, like T. S. Eliot, refer us ultimately to the mysteries of faith. In marked contrast to Pound, he immersed himself in the thirties morass of intellectual extremes and emerged unscathed, but every bit as voluble. And only very rarely—and then with exceptional justification and pointedness—does he give vent to the disgust we often find in Yeats and others. Lewis speaks with astonishing objectivity. And his unique sense of humor is never far away. In the last analysis it is his favorite Parisian drinking partner James Joyce that he seems to resemble most as a literary artist, although at first glance their *oeuvres* seem as different as night and day. But on closer inspection the difference resolves into the *touch*; the temperaments, the ultimate concerns are surprisingly similar; an intense love of life and its pleasures and rewards, respect and compassion for all that live in peace, rage at those who destroy and manipulate. Both are writers of prodigious substance and skill, and their complementary styles only serve to enhance each other. And even though Joyce was wounded at first by the other's disapproval of his time-dependent technique, years later he admitted that the only person who had ever cavilled at *Ulysses* with any real discernment was Wyndham Lewis.

Virginia Woolf

Michael Rosenthal

It is only recently that Virginia Woolf emerged from the limbo of polite esteem in which she has generally been held into the forefront of the contemporary cultural and literary scene. Having languished for decades in the shadow of her august fellow modernists like Joyce, Lawrence, and Conrad, Woolf appears at last to have secured for herself the stamp of the authentic classic that had previously managed to elude her. The obligatory if slightly stale respect invariably accorded her by readers has now given way to a passionate, searching interest in every aspect of her life. The torrent of Newsletters, Quarterlies, Miscellanies, English Institute Conferences, and Modern Language Association Sessions, among other forms of tribute, attest to her arrival. Virginia Woolf is a very hot literary property indeed.

The impulses behind this adulation are worth exploring, particularly as they tell us a good deal more about our world than they do about Woolf. To begin with, it is clear that the rediscovery of Woolf is part of the larger phenomenon of the canonization of Bloomsbury which has been in process for the past seven or eight years. If we want a specific date for its beginnings, we could point to the publication of Holroyd's biography of Lytton Strachey in 1967. It is a marvelous irony of social history that Virginia Woolf's Bloomsbury associations, which for years had damned her in the earnest eyes of the Leavises and others, now constitute one of her strongest sources of appeal. For reasons that are less literary than cultural, the cloud of moral opprobrium shrouding Bloomsbury's work and activities has lifted, revealing not a horrid group of jejune inverts but an emancipated, highly civilized group of friends leading productive lives free from the taint of pieties and conventions. No longer viewed as a sign of degeneracy, their legendary polymorphous perversity is taken as an admirable example of a highly desirable freewheeling personal and sexual style. Exemplary indeed,

---

From *Partisan Review* 43, no. 4 (1976). © 1976 by Partisan Review, Inc.

not cautionary, as Nigel Nicolson's best-selling portrait of the unusual relationship between his parents indicates. At a time when all instances of traditional sexual stereotyping are being exposed, Bloomsbury's precocious versatility is thought to have much to teach us.

The current public enthusiasm for Bloomsbury has been nourished by the scholarly mills which have been producing biographies and volumes of letters and journals with regularity. More remarkable than the sheer number of these is the commercial success they achieve. People await the newest revelations about the personal intrigues with much the same eagerness as Dickens's readers anticipated each new installment by the master. All things bearing the Bloomsbury label have demonstrable value as collector's items, so that even the office boy at the Hogarth Press, as well as the Woolfs' maid, have been enticed to come forth with their reminiscences of what that fabled world was like. It is probably fair to say that the renewed interest in Woolf on the part of the general reader is more a function of her position as "high priestess" of the chic, provocative Bloomsbury way of life than of any developing awareness of the inherent merit of her fiction.

If sheer titillation accounts for much of the public's attention, the gradual realization that Virginia Woolf was, in fact, a woman writer (or at least not a man, the androgynous theory having its own advocates) has also played a substantial role. The polemical grinder of the feminist movement has greedily devoured Woolf, spewing her forth as the appropriately committed feminist whose preoccupation with the cause is somehow the key to her fiction. Such a view of Woolf is not particularly useful. It is of course true that she was very much concerned with the economic and social plight of women and deeply sensitive to the psychic crippling inflicted on them by a male dominated world. *Orlando*, *A Room of One's Own*, *Three Guineas*, and assorted essays eloquently testify to her involvement in these issues, as well as to the deft way she can expose the absurdities of our culture. But as a novelist Woolf does not inveigh against the horrors of masculine constraint; to focus on her fiction through any sort of politicized feminist lens is seriously to distort it. Woolf herself deplored novels that preach, and hers are conspicuously free from the proselytizing that frequently occupied her when she was not at her desk struggling with her fiction. This is not to argue that Woolf was not conscious of the assumptions of an environment which held, for example, that Virginia's brothers, but not Virginia, should go to university; it is simply to protest against the reductionist view that Woolf's novels primarily speak in any essential way to feminist preoccupations. Woolf, in fact, hated the word "feminist" altogether—"What more fitting than to destroy an old word, a vicious and corrupt word that has done much harm in its day and is now obsolete? The word 'feminist' is the word indicated."—finding it divisive and inimical to the overall unity of civilized people she so desired.

The feminist claim on Woolf has lately been joined by the androgynist, which sees Woolf's novels as endorsing the splendors of the androgynous mind as a palliative to all our ills. Taking as a seminar passage Woolf's discussion in *A Room of One's Own* of the healthy adult mind being able to transcend any narrow sexual role, the hunters of androgyny doggedly chase the metaphor through all of Woolf's fiction, hacking out new patterns of meaning as they go. But metaphors are better left in peace to illuminate the specific contexts in which they appear. The illustrative use of androgyny to represent the kind of wide-ranging, nondogmatic, resonant intelligence Woolf finds admirable cannot be generalized into establishing Woolf's "androgynous vision." To discover that Woolf believes that men and women should share a complex view of reality, one as free as possible from the parochialisms of any single sex, is not to discover anything very new about her work.

If Woolf is to survive as other than a precious oddity of the modernist movement, it will be neither as a member of a coterie, a radical feminist, nor a prophetic androgynist. Sexual ideologies and exotic ambiences aside, Woolf's fiction must be able to meet the reservation still shared by many and most recently expressed by Elizabeth Hardwick in *Seduction and Betrayal*: acknowledging the richness of Woolf's language and the glow of her genius, Hardwick goes on to say, "yet in a sense, her novels aren't interesting." Whatever else novels are, they should at least be interesting, and it is a fact that hers have not always been thought so. Woolf was herself aware that her work posed more than the usual difficulties for readers. Her diary notes with sympathy (and some irritation) the puzzled efforts of critics to comprehend what she is doing. The problems are real, and a passage from *Between the Acts*, her last novel, suggests what they are: "Did the plot matter? She shifted and looked over her right shoulder. The plot was only there to beget emotion. . . . Don't bother about the plot: the plot's nothing." Isa's reflection on the meaning of Miss La Trobe's pageant at once describes Woolf's own art and points out the greatest obstacle to its appreciation. For plot is indeed nothing in Woolf's fiction and character, Isa might have gone on to say—or at least character as traditionally conceived—not much more. Novelists who dispense with both of these staples are going to have difficult times, and Woolf has received her share of critical abuse for writing novels in which, it is argued, nothing happens.

Not, of course, that she is the sole practitioner of the twentieth-century novel to have abandoned established notions of plot and character; the modern novel clearly developed through precisely such liberties, but in many ways her work is the most radical. For despite the formal breakthroughs made by Conrad, Ford, Lawrence, Joyce, and others, their work still exhibits a basic narrative interest (perhaps *Finnegans Wake*, a fictional cosmos unto itself, could be considered an exception) which is almost entirely lacking in Woolf's. However complicated the point of view and richly patterned the symbolic structure, their novels essentially remain part of a storytelling tradition from which Woolf dissociated herself. We are impelled through *Ulysses* less by its dazzling virtuosity than its abiding concern for Leopold and Stephen and what befalls them, just as we are absorbed in the destinies of Paul Morel or Decoud or Lord Jim or Benjy or even Winnie Verloc as they go about their muddled business. Although they do so in a variety of innovative ways, the great modern novels of the twentieth century implicate the reader in the lives of their characters as they confront experience, and in the problems of choice and self-definition that confrontation engenders. "Yes — oh dear yes," E.M. Forster writes in *Aspects of the Novel* with bemused resignation, "the novel tells a story." Subtilized and internalized though it is, the primitive energy of the story animates most of modern fiction.

Woolf's novels, however, contain no substantial narrative impulse. In a very real sense it is true she does write novels in which nothing happens. It would be impossible, for example, to speak in any serious way about the sustained "action" of *The Waves* or *Between the Acts*, or even of a more manageable novel like *To the Lighthouse*. Her work contains little humor, passion, or particular dramatic or even ideological tension. Demanding everything and making few concessions to readers, it seems to many hermetically sealed in its austerity and fragility from the vital currents of life. Woolf recognized, of course, that in writing novels that lacked any strong narrative thread she was cutting herself off from one of the enduring appeals of fiction, but she had no difficulty making this choice.

As an artist Woolf was obsessed with what we can call formal rather than thematic concerns, with finding ways of embodying, as she says in her diary, "the exact shapes my brain holds." That Woolf was absorbed primarily in creating shapes is what makes her such an utterly original voice in modern literature. It is also what makes her such a difficult writer to talk about, for her work does not readily lend itself to critical analysis of character or theme or philosophy. The difficulties are not simply ours: certainly Woolf's own language fails when she tries to formulate for herself her fictional intentions. Reflecting in her diary on Arnold Bennett's criticism that *Jacob's Room* doesn't have characters that survive, Woolf agrees that she hasn't "that 'reality' gift. I insubstantiate willfully to some extent, distrusting reality—its cheapness. But to get further. Have I the power of conveying the true reality." If distinctions between 'reality' and 'true reality' are seldom satisfying, this at least has the virtue of suggesting what one should *not* expect from a Woolf novel. Other attempts to state positively what she wants her fiction to achieve are no more successful:

> That is one of the experiences I have had here in some Augusts; and got there to a consciousness of what I call 'reality': a thing I see before me, something abstract but residing in the downs or sky . . . in which I shall rest and continue to exist. Reality I call it. And I fancy sometimes this is the most necessary thing to me; that which I seek. But who knows — once one takes a pen and writes? . . . Now perhaps this is my gift: this perhaps is what distinguishes me from other people. I think it may be rare to have so acute a sense of something like that—but again, who knows? I would like to express it too.

The reality Woolf wants her fiction to express cannot easily be formulated apart from the particular way it inheres in each novel. It is not a substantive vision of the sort J. Hillis Miller, in his *Poets of Reality*, finds in Conrad's fiction, whose "aim is to make the truth of life, something different from any impression or quality, momentarily visible. Not colors or light but the darkness behind them is the true reality." Woolf's reality has nothing to do with stripping away illusion or penetrating surface phenomena to unearth the grim darkness beneath, but resides in a form which makes comprehensible the way the various impressions and colors and darkness together constitute the texture of human life. It is something which is communicated emotionally rather than intellectually: "When we speak of form," Woolf writes, "we mean that certain emotions have been placed in the right relations to each other; then that the novelist is able to dispose these emotions and make them tell by methods which he inherits, bends to his purpose, models anew or even invents for himself." Endlessly evolving new techniques to dispose these emotions, Woolf succeeds in making out of the chaos and disharmony she found in the world marvelously coherent shapes.

The center of a Woolf novel, then, does not reside in any of those several themes frequently singled out for critical investigation—the workings of consciousness, the perception of time, the quality of personal relationships—but in her effort to orchestrate these in such a way as to make us feel how together they constitute part of the experience of living. The quest is always for the form that will embody Woolf's sense of what that experience is. From *Jacob's Room* to *Between the Acts*, every one of Woolf's novels originated not with any notion of theme or character but with some notion of the form the novel might take. As she indicates in her diary, *Jacob's Room* developed out of three short pieces she was working on even as she was struggling through the end of her second novel, *Night and Day*:

> I'm a great deal happier . . . today than I was yesterday having this afternoon arrived at some idea of a new form for a new novel. Suppose one thing should open out of another—as in an unwritten novel—only not for 10 pages but 200 or so — doesn't that give the looseness and lightness I want. . . . Conceive (?) "Mark on the Wall," "K.G.," ["Kew Gardens"] and "Unwritten Novel" taking hands and dancing in unity. What the unity shall be I have yet to discover; the theme is a blank to me; but I see immense possibilities in the form I hit upon more or less by chance two weeks ago.

Similarly, her first intuitions about *The Waves* were purely formal ones:

> Why not invent a new kind of play; as for instance:
> Woman thinks . . .
> He does.
> Organ plays.
> She writes.
> They say.

She sings.
Nights speaks.
They miss.
I think it must be something on this line—though I can't now see why. Away from facts; free; yet concentrated; prose yet poetry; a novel and a play.

Or consider her early sense of *Between the Acts*:

Will another novel ever swim up? If so, how? The only hint I have towards it is that it's to be dialogue: and poetry; and prose all quite distinct. No more long closely written books . . .
It came over me suddenly last night as I was reading . . . that I saw the form of a new novel. It's to be first the statement of the theme; then the restatement; and so on: repeating the same story: singing out this and then that, until the central idea is stated.

Before there is theme there is already a vision of form, and even after the substance of the novel has been thought out the commitment is always to the design.

Such a commitment does not make her, as many have claimed, a theoretician of the novel. Intuitions about form affect her in much the same way as a fresh image will stimulate a poet's creative process. Neither an abstract nor purely intellectual fascination, formal considerations provide Woolf with the emotional and imaginative impetus into each new book. Her absorption with formal matters makes the thematic content of her novels relatively unimportant to her fictional inspiration, and it is a fact that such content does not alter radically over the course of her lifetime. Although intended somewhat flippantly, her diary note that *To the Lighthouse* contains "all the usual things I try to put in—life, death, etc."—is very much to the point and might well have been written about any of her works. What distinguishes them is less the things themselves than the different patterns they achieve in each novel, the relationship she fashions between them. The impulse behind every work is always to find a new method for rendering her sense of experience: once a form has been fully worked out, Woolf moves on to a different attempt. Each experiment, she writes in her diary, is "a shot at my vision—if it's not a catch, it's a cast in the right direction"—and represents a shot she will not repeat a second time. A London day in the life of Clarissa Dalloway, the passage of ten years on an island in the Hebrides, the makeshift, harried performance of Miss La Trobe's pageant— each constitutes a unique version of Woolf's remarkably steady perception of the world. The extraordinary structural diversity of *Jacob's Room, Mrs. Dalloway, To the Lighthouse, The Waves, The Years*, and *Between the Acts* paradoxically attests to the underlying singleness of purpose Woolf held to throughout her career.

Woolf's own quest as an artist—to create shapes that will make lasting sense of the fluidity of life—is reflected within her novels by people who are engaged in the same kind of search. Insofar as it is possible to generalize about the meaning of the human activity in Woolf's fictional world, we can say that the characters in her novels constantly try, through widely different means, to establish for themselves from the chaos around them a coherent grasp of their world. What Woolf attempts to accomplish through her fiction, Lily Briscoe attempts with her painting, Bernard with his novel, Miss La Trobe with her pageant. And although these are the specific aesthetic endeavors which most closely approximate Woolf's own, the instinct to bring things together is not limited to painters and writers. Certainly it is the animating principle behind the soliloquies of all the voices in *The Waves*, not just Bernard's, and is what impels that superficially least creative of souls, Clarissa Dalloway, to give her parties. Most memorably, of course, it is Mrs. Ramsay's particular genius, possessing as she does the ability to "choose out the elements of things and piece them together and so, giving them a wholeness not theirs in life, make of some scene, or meeting of people (all now gone and separate), one of those globed compacted things over which thought lingers and love plays."

The workings of the creative imagination shaping different visions of order, then, is the single great theme which appears in Woolf's fiction. The importance of that imagination in her work comes directly out of the overwhelming sense of human isolation in which every novel is steeped. Whether it is Jacob searching for himself, or Septimus and Rezia unable to talk to each other, or Giles and Isa struggling in their tempestuous marriage, or even Mrs. Ramsay, giving of herself to exhaustion, the people in Woolf's fiction invariably feel cut off, not only from other human beings but from the world around them as well. The fact of isolation and the possibility of fleeting transcendence and communion—these are the two poles of Woolf's fictional universe. Rooted in one, characters can earn, through their own arduous efforts, brief contact with the other. Scratching out its monotonous "Unity-Dispersity . . . Un . . . dis," the gramophone of *Between the Acts* actually lays out the psychic contours of all of Woolf's mature work. "Scraps, orts, and fragments," as Miss La Trobe's pageant insists, the isolated selves in Virginia Woolf's world grapple not only with their own inadequacies and fears but with the uncertainty of personal relationships, the intractableness of language, the fact of death to achieve their completed visions. The battle is difficult—filled with the same kind of loneliness and pain Woolf experienced in her own life as she fought her way through the demons of madness and despair that constantly assailed her to the lucid forms of her fiction—and the successes transient; but there is nothing else. Whatever the suffering involved, all the novels from *Mrs. Dalloway* on manage to end on a final note of affirmation: a party is given, a lighthouse reached, a pageant produced. Such accomplishments, however trivial they might appear, suggest the basic commitment to living made by the fiction. As Lily Briscoe understands after she has finished her painting, it does not matter in the least whether the canvas is ultimately destroyed or rolled up in some dusty attic. In Woolf's universe to be able to say, "I have had my vision," is the consummate human achievement, and Lily's words, which close *To the Lighthouse*, speak not only to her particular feat in completing her canvas but to the successes of the other protagonists as well and finally, of course, to Woolf herself.

They could not be reasonably applied, however, to Woolf's first two novels, *The Voyage Out* (1915) and *Night and Day* (1919). If D. S. Savage is perhaps unduly harsh in finding *Night and Day* to be the dullest novel in the English language, it is nevertheless true that her first two books are not particularly distinguished. Lacking any kind of formal originality, both are lamentably tedious, dragging on far longer than they should in a thoroughly pedestrian manner.

Although Terence Hewet's notion in *The Voyage Out* that he would like to write a "novel about silence," about "the things people don't say," seems to anticipate Woolf's later development, neither of these initial efforts suggests the unique things to come. What they do make clear is how uncongenial the realistic—or what Woolf might call the Edwardian—method of fiction was to her genius. For Woolf, conventional techniques could produce only conventional fiction. It was not until the publication of *Jacob's Room* in 1922 that she felt, as she notes in her diary, that she had finally learned "how to begin (at 40) to say something in my own voice." Irrevocably turning away with *Jacob's Room* from the established tradition within which *The Voyage Out* and *Night and Day* were written, Woolf devotes the next nineteen years of her life to exploring the different possibilities of that newly discovered voice.

Jacob's Room is the first of her novels which tries to dispense with what Woolf calls the "appalling narrative business of the realist: getting on from lunch to dinner." Her well-known rejection of the realist method—enunciated most emphatically in two essays, "Mr. Bennett and Mrs. Brown" and "Modern Fiction"—claims that in its attention to the superficial and mundane, realism fails to catch the vital experience of living itself. Trotting out her favorite trio of Edwardian villains—Wells, Bennett, and Galsworthy—in both essays, Woolf demonstrates how they frittered away their talent "making the trivial and the transitory appear the true and enduring." In a word, they are *materialists*, devoting themselves with varying degrees of success to the pursuit of the unimportant. Opposed to these are writers who, like Joyce, are spiritual, who understand that life is a far more curious and fluid affair than the stolid materialists would have us believe. The mind does not function according to rigidly defined patterns, Woolf declares, but rather receives "an incessant shower of innumerable atoms," so that if a writer were not constrained by convention and forced to follow prescribed directions, "if he could base his work upon his own feeling . . . there would be no plot, no comedy, no tragedy, no love interest or catastrophe in the accepted style, and perhaps not a single button sewn on as the Bond Street tailors would have it." Neither unique to Woolf nor by any means a theoretical principle she holds to in her own criticism, such an argument is primarily an intensely personal assertion of what her own fiction will be.

Implicitly, we cannot help but feel it is also a way of absolving herself from continuing to labor in the direction that the rather dismal *Night and Day* and *The Voyage Out* suggest she could manage very happily.

Employing techniques of point of view and organization in *Jacob's Room* that she had tentatively experimented with in "Mark on the Wall," "Kew Gardens," and "Unwritten Novel," Woolf attempts to embrace the "unknown and uncircumscribed spirit" of life by avoiding much of the prosaic connective tissue necessary to most narrative fiction. There is nothing particularly startling (there never is in Woolf) about the subject of the novel: *Jacob's Room* is about Jacob Flanders, vaguely modeled after Virginia's brother, Thoby, whose life we follow from infancy through his years at Cambridge, his abortive love affairs, his travel in Greece, his work, and finally to his death in World War I. But of course the story, such as it is, does not absorb Woolf's energies any more than it does ours. The interest of the novel lies in the way Woolf presents the story of Jacob, in her efforts to find a form that would adequately express her vision of reality without falling prey to what she considers the deadness and waste of the realist method.

Although strictly chronological, moving from childhood to death, the chronology of *Jacob's Room* has nothing to do with the linear chronology, for example, of *The Old Wives' Tale*. For rather than giving us a story moving smoothly and continuously through time, Woolf presents us with a series of discrete moments, one following another, with little concern for the links between them. The chapters, though proceeding in a chronological way to record Jacob's development, exist primarily as separate entities, each focusing on specific events in Jacob's life or in the life of his friends. And what is true of the succession of the chapters is true also of the organization with the chapters themselves. Transitions are generally suppressed as the narrator jumps from character to character and from incident to incident without hesitation. The basic unit of organization is the isolated moment, and each chapter consists of a number of these, dealing with Jacob, or his acquaintances, or even passing strangers who make one brief appearance and then leave the novel entirely. Time moves forward in this novel, but in an extremely discontinuous, jerky manner.

The jaggedness of the narrative is deliberate, not a thwarted effort to write a smoothly flowing lyric novel. It represents Woolf's first attempt at creating a form which would in itself reflect the nature of life as she understood it. The form of *Jacob's Room* is clearly designed to parallel the "form" of living: a fragmented, discontinuous world demands a fragmented, discontinous novel. A world in which people experience time as a succession of distinct moments strung together must be embodied in a fictional world similarly constructed. Such a notion of form is, of course, painfully rudimentary; just how rudimentary can be seen by considering the kinds of rich, complex forms Woolf goes on to evoke in *The Waves* and *Between the Acts* to deal with essentially the same kind of world *Jacob's Room* is treating. Although managing for the most part to avoid the realist dead end Woolf abhorred, *Jacob's Room* nevertheless fails to achieve an aesthetically satisfying shape. Discontinuity is not in itself a particularly useful structural principle for a novel, and the different techniques Woolf borrows from her experimental short pieces are not able to provide an extended fiction with the compelling form necessary to her successful work. The novel's episodic organization does not add up to a structure that can find in the discontinuities significant patterns that imprint themselves on the imagination. If the novel succeeds in documenting the isolation and the fragmentariness of existence, at the same time it does not embrace them in an affecting, substantial form. An important new direction which helped Woolf to break free from the confines within which she had been working, *Jacob's Room* is finally a sterile form, one not capable of the resonance of her mature work.

But Woolf learned her lessons well and her next effort, *Mrs. Dalloway*, achieves a formal coherence and power altogether absent from *Jacob's Room*. In place of the flaccid chronological organization covering all of Jacob's life, *Mrs. Dalloway* effectively focuses on the events of one day in the lives of Clarissa Dalloway and Septimus Smith. Digging "caves and tunnels" beneath her characters, Woolf creates a densely structured texture in which a June day in London is constantly informed by pressures and vestiges of the past. The novel is complexly organized both spatially and temporally. Physical meetings of characters in the street—and finally in Clarissa's home—merge with a web of intersecting memories and reveries to create a form that succeeds brilliantly in conveying Woolf's sense of the isolation, ironies, and ecstasies of life. Implacably tolling out the passage of time throughout the book, Big Ben punctuates the reflection of individual characters with its unyielding insistence on the passage of time. In addition to the mundane purpose of announcing a shift of narrative focus from one character to another, the gonging serves to emphasize the restricted framework of a single day which Woolf's imagination exploited continually during her career for her best work. It is significant that Woolf's four most distinguished novels—*Mrs. Dalloway, To the Lighthouse, The Waves,* and *Between the Acts*—essentially take place, either metaphorically or actually, within a twenty-four hour period. *Mrs. Dalloway* and *Between the Acts*, of course, do so explicitly. Although ten years elapse between part one and three of *To the Lighthouse*, the novel imagistically follows the movement of an entire day from the late afternoon of the first part, through the dark night of the second, to the early morning which opens the third section. And the nine poetic interludes of *The Waves*, describing the progression of the sun across the sky, clearly set the different dramatic soliloquies within the natural rhythm of a single day. However varied in form they are, the fact that all four play variations on the basic structure of a day indicates the degree to which Woolf's imagination flourished within the security of strict limitations. When she deserts those confines, as the difficulties of *Jacob's Room* and *The Years* reveal, her work loses considerably in power.

Woolf's feelings about *Mrs. Dalloway*, as expressed in her diary while she was still completing the novel in 1924—"if this book proves anything, it proves that I can only write along those lines [of *Jacob's Room*] and shall never desert them, but explore further and further and shall, heaven be praised, never bore myself an instant"—were prophetic about the course all of her fiction was to follow. The process of formal exploration, haltingly begun in *Jacob's Room*, continues until her death in 1941. It is an open-ended search, each new novel struggling with formal problems totally alien to everything preceding it. For too long it has been a criticial commonplace to see *The Waves* as the teleological fulfillment of Woolf's genius. Such a view not only leaves critics hard pressed to explain what came after—*The Years* and *Between the Acts*—it seriously distorts the nature of what came before. For Woolf's novels do not follow a linear path, the discoveries of one leading to the production of the next, but rather constitute a series of discrete forays in altogether different directions into unknown territory. *The Waves* no more represents a culmination of her work than does *Orlando* or *To the Lighthouse*. Perhaps the most misguided enterprise on which she embarked was *The Years*, but even this was a failure of an experimental sort, not, as frequently thought, a renunciation of experiment. Moving from the sustained internality of *The Waves* to the strict "externality" of *The Years*, from the novel of vision to the novel of fact, was as daring an innovation for Woolf as was the extraordinary conception of *The Waves* itself. What matters in each novel is that Woolf was able to force herself "to break every mould and find a fresh form of being, that is of expression, for everything I feel or think." Just as *The Waves* is an entirely different book from *Orlando*, published three years earlier, so with *The Years*, Woolf comments in her diary, "I am breaking the mould made by *The Waves*."

Common to all her novels is the attempt to create a texture for them of the sort Lily Briscoe seeks for her painting: "Beautiful and bright it should be on the surface, feathery and evanescent, one colour melting into another like the colours on a butterfly's wings; but beneath the fabric must be clamped together with bolts of iron. It was to be a thing you could ruffle with your breath; and a thing you could not dislodge with a team of horses." The centrality of such a conception for Woolf is also suggested, in language strikingly similar to Lily's, by a 1925 diary entry. Musing on the greatness of Proust, Woolf praises him for qualities she unmistakably wanted to achieve in her own work: "The thing about Proust is his combination of the utmost sensibility with the utmost tenacity. He searches out those butterfly shades to the last grain. He is a tough as catgut and as evanescent as a butterfly's bloom."

The delicacy of her sensibility, of course, is granted her even by her most vehement detractors; indeed, it is frequently used as a reason for dismissing her as a serious artist, on the grounds that her exquisiteness (the epithet most generally attached to her) leads only to sterile exercises in preciosity. In fact, highly patterned and sensitive though the surface of her novels is, there is nothing exquisite in the least about her fiction. From the bewildered Mrs. Flanders, standing dumbly in Jacob's room after his death, holding out his shoes, to the curtain rising at the end of *Between the*

Acts on the confrontation between Isa and Giles, her work deals with enduring human concerns without solace of illusion or sentimentality. Woolf looks unflinchingly at a work that offers very little in the way of easy gratification. Death and the anguish of isolation are the inescapable pressures felt in every book; it is always in the fact of these that her characters attempt to fashion their precarious visions of order, and their fleeting successes never obscure our sense of the difficulty of the battle or the knowledge that the dangers remain. In affirming the possibility of order, she never falsifies the chaos threatening it. "Nothing was ever one thing," *To the Lighthouse* insists, and James's discovery as he nears the lighthouse that is not just the "silvery, misty-looking tower" that gleamed at him when he was a child, but also something stark, solid, and forbidding is precisely the kind of complex view Woolf holds to throughout her life.

Despite her tough-mindedness and complexity, it is still not clear that Woolf will ever quite luxuriate in the unquestioned eminence accorded a Conrad or a Joyce or a Faulkner. As long as the cult of Bloomsbury worship flourishes, of course, Woolf's reputation will continue to grow. But even Bloomsbury's mythic stature will one day erode and we will once again have to confront an enigmatic writer whose novels lack the narrative interest and overt social and psychological concerns of the other great twentieth-century writers. Such a confrontation will always be difficult for a large number of readers. Woolf's uncompromising effort to convey "the exact shapes my brain holds" is an enterprise whose basically subjective character has frequently been thought to ensure its ultimate insignificance. As I have tried to indicate, however, the explicitly personal nature of her attempt is neither precious nor self-indulgent. Developing out of Woolf's urgent need to get to the heart of the reality she felt was somehow available to her, the novels are at the same time informed by a strict artistic integrity which prevents them from degenerating into the narrowly private. In rendering that vision of reality, Woolf provides us with a rich variety of compelling shapes that speak in immediate ways to all of us. What Woolf needs is a criticism which, eschewing the temptations of the modish and the topical, will explore the different ways these potent shapes function. Only then will she have earned that satisfaction she briefly grants Miss La Trobe: "Hadn't she, for twenty-five minutes, made them see? A vision imparted was relief from agony . . . for one moment . . . one moment."

Virginia Woolf's *A Room of One's Own*: Reading Absence

Nelly Furman

"She had the oddest sense of being herself invisible; unseen; unknown"
—Mrs. Dalloway

On the eve of the publication of *A Room of One's Own*, Virginia Woolf wrote in her diary, "I am afraid it will not be taken seriously." Widely read as a feminist tract, it has not been studied as a literary text, and yet it is not without aesthetic value. Even E. M. Forster grants her feminist pamphlet artistic importance:

> Finally, there are the feminist books—*A Room of One's Own* and *Three Guineas*—and several short essays, etc., some of them significant. It is as a novelist that she will be judged. But the rest of her work must be remembered, partly because (as William Plomer has pointed out) she is sometimes more of a novelist in it than in her novels.

Herbert Mardner, who specifically concerned himself with feminism and art in Virginia Woolf, alludes to a deep relationship between the political and the aesthetic in her works:

> The tracts fade into fiction, the fiction echoes the tract; and the continuity is so pronounced that it seems necessary to read every book by Virginia Woolf in the context of her work as a whole. Her attitude as a feminist was intimately bound up with her attitude as an artist.

He is, however, unable to unite her feminist discourse with an aesthetic praxis, for in his study, the political elements remain strictly within the realm of subject matter. Yet, as Mark Goldman has argued, the interrelation between form and thought, particularly for Virginia Woolf, is the indispensable condition of any literary activity:

From *Women's Language and Style*. © 1978 by E. L. Epstein. L & S Books, 1978.

If her account of the critical (and creative) process is true, there is
no possibility, she would maintain, of establishing the classic dichotomy of form and content. Only the imperfect works, she insists, allow us to separate the two.

Seated on the banks of a river, meditating on the topic of women and
fiction, the narrator of *A Room of One's Own* compares her activity to that
of a fisherman, since, "the sudden conglomeration of an idea at the end
of one's line" is like "the sudden tug at the end of a rod." Ideas are like
fish: when caught, they create excitement around them, if thought to be
unimportant, they are simply discarded, and if suddenly disturbed, they
may disappear. But, just like fish, their form is inseparable from their being,
as Woolf mentions elsewhere, "Nothing exists needlessly, the fish themselves seem to have been shaped deliberately and slipped into the world
only to be themselves. They neither work nor weep. In their shape is their
reason."

A Room of One's Own could be described as a short text which examines
available books on or by women, the cultural values at work in them, the
epistemology at the core of their very existence. It investigates the topic of
women and fiction, and in the process asserts itself as both a theoretical
discourse and a fiction, an explicit statement and a literary endeavor ("I
propose, making use of all the liberties and licences of a novelist, to tell
you the story of the two days that preceded my coming here". Thus, one
way of reading *A Room of One's Own* seriously is to look for embodiment
of its ideological content with its artistic expression.

One could talk also about *A Room of One's Own* as a book about reading:
the narrator admits her penchant for it, "I like reading books in the bulk";
she tells us. In addition, four of the six chapters pertain to just that activity.
Virginia Woolf herself addresses the question of the art of reading in many
instances, particularly in her essays. Within the limits of this paper, we
have chosen to apply what we construe as the narrator's reading method
to her own text. It is this mechanism which will serve as our interpretative
metaphor in our attempt to elucidate the interpenetration of form and
content in *A Room of One's Own*.

In pursuit of truth, the narrator of *A Room of One's Own* enters the
British Museum in order to consult, as she tells us, "the learned and un-
prejudiced, who have removed themselves above the strife of tongue and
the confusion of body." A few pages later, she comes to the not too surprising conclusion that

> it seemed pure waste of time to consult all these gentlemen who
> specialize in woman and her effect on whatever it may be—politics,
> children, wages, morality,—numerous and learned as they are.
> One might as well leave their books unopened.

On the contrary, for, although she did not write down any "nuggets" of
truth, she did discover, by drawing the portrait of Professor Von X, that

the professor was writing in anger. In other words, she discovered the presence of an emotion and the presence of a man. The presence of the emotion makes her shift her attention away from what the professor was saying to focus on the man himself: "When I read what he wrote about women," she tells us, "I thought not of what he was saying, but of himself." This shift in perspective allows her to explain the professor's anger in terms of a man's role in society. For men, like women, are locked into their functions in society and while women have served as looking-glasses, men have had to pursue the paths of glory. Behind this system of roles lies the inescapable presence of the patriarchal order, and the pervading power of social and cultural prejudice. To be learned is only to be learned in the values of the system itself. In a patriarchal society, only patriarchal values are recognized, noticed, and recorded. Historians, for example, who supposedly collect facts, leave to posterity nothing more than the inventory of the constituent factors and important moments of a patriarchal society, while the events related to *herstory* remain unrecorded, the shelves empty. Like the professor, the historian does not deal with facts, or truth, but simply with preconceptions.

Thematically, a dichotomy begins to emerge: on the one hand, the world of the apparent, the visible, the recorded, the verbal, and on the other, a world marked by empty shelves, a vacant space, unnoticed, invisible, and silent. The interesting discovery the narrator made that morning in the British Museum was that of a spatial signifier, a glaring absence, which she is determined to make us notice. For by making absence conspicuous, she delineates a space within the patriarchal system of values. By positing an absence, she simultaneously suggests an existence. She gives this rather clear example: "Though we say we know nothing about Shakespeare's mind, even as we say that, we are saying something about Shakespeare's state of mind."

As a cultural artifact, literature reflects the values of society, for even the realm of the imaginary is shaped by the system from which it springs. Like history, the novel has only proposed the visible, the apparent, the vocal:

> And since a novel has this correspondence to real life, its values are to some extent those of real life. But it is obvious that the values of women differ very often from the values which have been made by the other sex; naturally, this is so, yet it is the masculine values that prevail.

Most often in literature, woman is a cultural fabrication, a representation at odds with her historical status:

> Imaginatively she is of the highest importance; practically she is completely insignificant. She pervades poetry from cover to cover; she is all but absent from history. She dominates the lives of kings and conquerors in fiction; in fact she was the slave of any boy

whose parents forced a ring upon her finger. Some of the most inspired words, some of the most profound thoughts in literature fall from her lips; in real life she could hardly spell, and was the property of her husband.

As the narrator reminds us, women's activities,—housekeeping, child-rearing—have hardly left a trace: "Nothing remains of it all. All has vanished. No biography or history has a word to say about it. And the novels, without meaning to, inevitably lie." Biological make-up may account for dissimilar views of reality, for a woman's experience of the world is commonly unlike that of a man. The narrator posits an epistemological difference between the sexes and calls for the expression of its distinctiveness. "The book has somehow to be adapted to the body." The integrity of a woman's *Weltansicht* might find a place in the realm of fiction so dominated by patriarchal values. For practical reasons—need for time and privacy—a woman's book, such as *A Room of One's Own*, might be shorter and more concentrated. But more importantly, it could reflect woman's cultural and historical status, that is to say, her conspicuous absence. Thus, one way of conveying woman's intrinsic experience in a patriarchal society could be through a thematics of absence. In a short essay, "Professions for Women," Virginia Woolf recounts the difficulties she encountered as a woman novelist. While she was able to overcome some, she felt that she had not always succeeded in expressing herself with unrestricted candor on the subject of her body: "telling the truth about my own experiences as a body, I do not think I solved." It is our contention, however, that by creating a spatial, womblike vacuity in her text, Virginia Woolf conveys something of woman's bodily interiority.

The fictitious Judith Shakespeare symbolizes woman's ambiguous status, her simultaneous inclusion and exclusion in relation to the patriarchal order. She appears twice in Virginia Woolf's text. The first time, she is presented as a young woman whose actions we observe, whose thoughts we share. We learn that now and then she picked up a book, scribbled a few lines, was almost married against her will, was severely beaten by her father, fled home and went to London to try to act, did not succeed, became pregnant and killed herself. Judith Shakespeare appears here as a traditional heroine, a fictional character made of fictional flesh and blood: a conventionally realistic literary presence. What distinguishes her from her male counterpart is that, because of cultural obstacles, she fails where he may overcome.

When, at the end of *A Room of One's Own*, Virginia Woolf tells us that she prefers to put her concluding remarks in the form of a fiction, she evokes once again Judith Shakespeare:

I told you in the course of this paper that Shakespeare had a sister; but do not look for her in Sir Sidney Lee's life of the poet. She died young—alas, she never wrote a word. She lies buried where the omnibuses now stop, opposite the Elephant and Castle. Now my belief is that this poet lives. She lives in you and in me, and in many other women who are not here tonight, for they are washing up the dishes and putting the children to bed. But she lives; for great poets do not die; they are continuing *presences*; they need only the opportunity to walk among us in the flesh. This opportunity, as I think, it is now coming within your power to give her. For my belief is that if we live another century or so — I am talking of the common lives which we live as individuals — and have five hundred a year each of us and rooms of our own; if we have the habit of freedom and the courage to write exactly what we think; if we escape a little from the common sitting-room and see human beings not always in their relation to each other but in relation to reality; and the sky, too, and the trees or whatever it may be in themselves; if we look past Milton's bogey, for no human being should shut out the view; if we face the fact, for it is a fact, that there is no arm to cling to, but that we go alone and that our relation is to the world of reality and not only the world of men and women, then the opportunity will come and the dead poet who was Shakespeare's sister will put on the body which she has so often laid down.

Here Judith Shakespeare is no longer described as a traditional heroine, a fictional presence. Contrary to her first appearance, her second portrayal is that of a feminine figure, for it reflects and expresses her historical existence. In death as in life she is an absence; defined by negative phrases she appears as a non-being. The use of the word "presences" (our italics) to mean, not as could be expected, the materiality of bodies, but rather the potential for such a materialization, calls attention to Woolf's play on the absence/presence dichotomy. Judith Shakespeare is no longer an impressive presence: she is a powerfully effective absence which may someday "put on the body which she has so often laid down."

Even in death, Judith Shakespeare remains invisible, anonymous, for her tomb is only indicated by an omnibus stop, strategically placed at a crossroad. The omnibus stop, as a spatial signifier, functions like the empty library shelves; it marks the point of juncture of two systems and partakes in both. The tombstone reveals society's attitude towards death, its desire to indicate materially a passing away, to replace the vacancy occasioned by death with a visible sign. This tombstone, however, is somewhat different; it does not bear the name of the departed one, for women are anonymous beings: "Anonymity runs in their blood," and women, contrary to men, "will pass a tombstone or a sign post without feeling an irresistible desire to cut their names on it." Following the example of her narrator who noted the inexistent empty shelves in a library filled with books, Virginia Woolf invites her readers to perceive unmarked spaces, to interpret blanks, to read absence.

Examples of Virginia Woolf's skillful use of "absence" abound. Conspicuously placed at the end of the Oxbridge episode, the section about the Manx cat prepares the passage into Fernham, the transition from a world of presence to a world of absence. The sight of the tailless cat suddenly changes the narrator's perception of the scene around her and leads her to recognize "what a difference a tail makes." One could note that it is a missing ash-tray which brings the narrator to the window and makes her notice the cat without a tail, while the cigarette, which brought the narrator to the window in order to flick the ashes, itself disappears from the text. The sight of the Manx cat makes her realize that something else is missing and that the amorous cooing between the sexes has ceased. As the narrator enters the woman's college, we are made aware that it is a place defined by absence. For not only does Fernham lack the traditions and wealth of Oxbridge, but whereas in Oxbridge the narrator faced the forbidding presence of beadles, in the gardens of Fernham she only perceives the fleeting visions of phantoms "half guessed, half seen," the very traces of absence. When she returns late at night to her inn and poetically evokes the aura of the night, the last sentence of the chapter refers to an absence; "Even the door of the hotel sprang open at the touch of an invisible hand—not a boots was sitting up to light me to bed, it was so late."

Just as, when talking about the alternations of work and rest, one should interpret "rest not as doing nothing but as doing something but something that is different," similarly absence is not to be defined simply as non-presence but as something different. For Virginia Woolf, the concept of absence and its related semantic notions—invisibility, silence, inaudibility, etc.—become the distinctive feature of woman's otherness, the locus of a woman's experience in a patriarchal society. Some women, Virginia Woolf reminds us, have been able to convey their genuinely personal woman's view. Jane Austen, for example, by steadfastly keeping to her drawing room, forced the integrity of her world and the specificity of her discourse onto man's literary tradition. The fictitious Mary Carmichael not only brings to the fore a hitherto unexplored network of relationships, such as "Chloe liked Olivia," but she almost succeeds in breaking the man-made sentence and narrative sequence. As for Virginia Woolf herself, she makes the expression of absence the signifying characteristic of her integrity as a woman novelist.

If a woman's reality in a patriarchal society is that of an invisible, inaudible, and ineffable signifier, then she cannot simultaneously be a conscious, transcendental subject. While Mr. A's book, discussed at the end of *A Room of One's Own*, has a capital "I" whose obliterating presence covers the page, in Virginia Woolf's political aesthetics, her book can only attest to the disappearance of the psychological subject. While the men can be defined by the outstanding actions they have performed which have led them to carve their names in the book of history, women are defined neither by their actions, nor their names but by their functions as daughters, wives, mothers, and breeders of the human race. The self, displaced from its purpose as originator or source, becomes the locus of a system of conventions, a network of social functions, a process we have observed in the narrator's reduction of Professor Von X's individual self to that of an element of the social system. The rejection of the notion of subject is intrinsically linked to Virginia Woolf's elaboration of a feminist aesthetic. It is, therefore, no mere gesture of authorial vanity which makes Virginia Woolf hide the narrator behind the multiple *personae* of the three Marys: "Here then was I (call me Mary Beton, Mary Seton, Mary Carmichael or by any name you please—it is not a matter of any importance," but rather the writer's understanding that the use of the pronoun "I" to stand for a pluralized *persona* can be construed as an indication of a loss of psychological content. "I," says the narrator on the second page of *A Room of One's Own*, is "only a convenient term for somebody who has no real being."

Nor is it surprising to find the pronoun "her" absent from the title of *A Room of One's Own*, where it is replaced by the indefinite "one" whose specificity and integrity are imparted by the adjective "own." If, as we have suggested, Virginia Woolf's book attempts to inscribe a feminist aesthetic within the patriarchal order, then, it simultaneously participates in both systems. On the one hand, understood as meaning, "to own a room," the title reflects a belief in a material reality and a patriarchal economy through the ownership of property. Such an interpretation conveys only the argumentative substance, the intellectual content of the book. On the other hand, if the title is also seen as meaning, "an interior space belonging to an unidentified yet specific person," the shape of the text is being accentuated. As Ellen Raskin's cover design for the American edition suggests, with its London street scene at the bottom and its window at the top, the room of the title is the book itself. Although in its materiality an artifact of patriarchal culture, Virginia Woolf's book calls attention to the empty shelves in the library while at the same time occupying one of the bare areas with its own hollowness, thus becoming itself a spatial signifier. Or, to use an economic metaphor, the text (the room/the womb) is both the locus of production and the product.

In the process of encouraging other women to write and remain true to themselves ("It is much more important to be oneself than anything else.") Woolf produces a book whose subject matter, i.e. women and fiction, and whose form expresses and exemplifies her own personal concerns as a woman-writer. By calling for more books by women on library shelves, Virginia Woolf challenges patriarchal supremacy in the realm of cultural artifacts. In as much as women have been culturally invisible, the purpose of this action is to establish a balance in the representation of the two sexes. In this respect, the sight of the taxicab with its one male passenger and one female passenger can be read as a spatial metaphor for the library shelves. This brings us to the question of androgyny. Whereas Nancy Bazin, in her book, *Virginia Woolf and the Androgynous Vision*, confines the question of androgyny to the realm of the psychological, our study situates it within the perspective of a politics of form. Woolf's indiscernible intermingling of such conventional literary *genres* as the essay and fiction could be seen as a rejection of the male-female polarization of *gender*. The essay belongs to the world of Oxbridge, to the Fellows and the Scholars, a world from which the narrator is partly excluded, while in Fernham she is in the realm of the "fair name of fiction." In her short essay, "The Art of Fiction," Woolf calls fiction "a lady" and refers to it with the pronouns "she" and "her". The interplay of *genre* and *gender*, of form and content, makes *A Room of One's Own* an "androgynous" text.

    A Room of One's Own explodes, in a self-conscious manner, all the rules of argumentation and literary convention. Virginia Woolf's seemingly rambling and digressive lecture does not, as Ralph Samuelson suggests, lack firmness and consistency: rather, it proposes a different, and tightly woven political discourse which complements an epistemology of presence with a thematics and aesthetics of absence. *A Room of One's Own* can be interpreted as a spatial signifier which demands recognition of a different system of values while simultaneously evoking it as Otherness.

Voices: Reading Virginia Woolf

Ian Gregor

We are the words; we are the music; we are the thing itself.
    —VIRGINIA WOOLF, "A Sketch of the Past"

In "The Ideal, Built-In, Nonexistent Reader" Wright Morris has remarked: "In the fullness of time the writer senses the emergence of another reader. If he can trust his impressions, the book he has written has within its pages its own sought-for reader. This reader is a seamless part of the novel, a palpable yet invisible part of the fiction. . . . The voice [the writer] then hears is not his own, nor is it the voice of 'truth' or some cunning of his ego; it is itself part and parcel of the fiction's intent to be as fully achieved as the writer can make it." The intimacy and dynamic nature of this bond between writer and reader in the novels of Virginia Woolf and the consequent creation of a voice which emerges in the process of writing itself describe my present concern. I wish to consider the presence of the novelist within her fiction, and the kind of influence that presence has on shaping the reader's response.

Let us begin by looking at a scene which "acts out" my general argument. The closing pages of the first part of *To the Lighthouse* are among the best Virginia Woolf ever wrote. She seems effortlessly in command of her technique, the effect so fluently created that with the barest of touches she can establish a relationship between surface and depth, which has about it the inevitability we associate with great art. The scene forms the climax in the author's re-creation of a day spent in the summer house of the Ramsay family, a day which, in mood and atmosphere, echoes the summer days spent by the Stephen family some thirty years earlier. The day is at an end; Mr. and Mrs. Ramsay find themselves alone for the first time. Mr. Ramsay is reading Scott's *The Antiquary*:

> Don't interrupt me, he seemed to be saying, don't say anything; just sit there. And he went on reading. His lips twitched. It filled

From *The Sewanee Review* 88, no. 4 (October–December 1980). © 1980 by Ian Gregor.

him. It fortified him. He clean forgot all the little rubs and digs of the evening. . . . This man's strength and sanity, his feeling for straighforward simple things, these fishermen, the poor old crazed creature in Mucklebackit's cottage made him feel so vigorous, so relieved of something that he felt roused and triumphant and could not choke back his tears. Raising the book a little to hide his face he let them fall and shook his head from side to side and forgot himself completely . . . forgot his own bothers and failures completely in poor Steenie's drowning and Mucklebackit's sorrow (that was Scott at his best) and the astonishing delight and feeling of vigour that it gave him.

   Well, let them improve upon that, he thought as he finished the chapter.

For Mr. Ramsay the novel has ordered, extended, and given definition to human experience. The feelings aroused by Steenie's drowning and Mucklebackit's sorrow have been so perfectly conveyed that Mr. Ramsay feels compassion turning to exhilaration; his absorption in Scott's world has filled him with a renewed vigor and confidence, and he closes the book in triumph.

Mrs. Ramsay is also reading, but her text, Shakespeare's sonnet 82, provokes her into a very different kind of response:

> Mrs Ramsay raised her head and like a person in a light sleep seemed to say that if he wanted her to wake she would, she really would, but otherwise, might she go on sleeping, just a little longer, just a little longer? She was climbing up those branches, this way and that, laying hands on one flower and then another.
>
>   Nor praise the deep vermilion in the rose,
>
> she read, and so reading she was ascending, she felt, on to the top, on to the summit. How satisfying! How restful! All the odds and ends of the day stuck to this magnet; her mind felt swept, felt clean. And then there it was, suddenly entire shaped in her hands, beautiful and reasonable, clear and complete, the essence sucked out of life and held rounded here—the sonnet.

Mr. Ramsay finds in the novel feelings independent of his own. Mrs. Ramsay absorbs the poem in such a way that its feelings become hers. For him reading is a pursuit, a line to be followed ("he felt he had been arguing with somebody"); his response seeks expression in physical gesture, his lips twitch, he slaps his thigh. For her reading is an incantation: musing upon the lines, repeating them quietly to herself, she is lulled into self-forgetfulness. If there is a physical gesture, it is simply that of her hands cupping the shape of the sonnet, "the essence sucked out of life."

   Through these contrasting reading experiences—experiences prompted not so much by what is read as by how it reads—Woolf introduces the scene in which she attempts to explore the relationship between the Ramsays as explicitly as she can. It is to be our last view of them together.

Their relationship resists compromise—characterized on his side by a need for recognition and action, on hers, by sympathy and withdrawal. Above all else the relationship expresses itself more eloquently in silence than in words, a silence which Mr. Ramsay continually longs to break but cannot, and which his wife gratefully accepts. When they talk, the dialogue is sparse, commonplace, intermittent:

> "They're engaged . . . Paul and Minta."
> "So I guessed."
> "How nice it would be to marry a man with a wash-leather bag for his watch."
> "You won't finish that stocking tonight."
> "No . . . I shan't finish it."

Behind these bare exchanges exists the powerful ebb and flow of feeling released by their reading, which is now transmuted into a feeling for each other. While reading, they are intensely aware of each other's presence, and it is this keen mutual awareness that finally renders verbal communication unnecessary. "As she looked at him she began to smile, for though she had not said a word, he knew, of course he knew, that she loved him. . . . She had not said it, but he knew it. And she looked at him smiling. For she had triumphed again."

As we come to that final short sentence we pause and ask: Who says it? Whose voice do we hear? "For she had triumphed again": the sentence seems to detach itself gently from the narrative as if it could be "spoken" variously, by the Ramsays, each in turn, by the author about them, by the reader about the author. In fact we can hear all those "voices" within it. This lapping and overlapping of tones and this fluent modulation between them come to constitute "the voice" of the book. It is not a voice which has a separate existence from the voices within it; the voice of an implied author is as much a cadence within that voice as the speech of any character would be.

In the process of his writing the author seeks, and hopes to find, a voice. And, like the human voice itself, his writing voice has within its register its own plurality of intonations: it alters continually in pitch, pace, and tone. But behind this whole range of effects lies a common authorial purpose, an undeviating aim, to find "the sought-for reader." As Wright Morris remarks, the writer "is creating, as the work progresses, what he needs to know." And what he needs to know is what he *cannot* know when he begins to write—that is, that his monologue will become a dialogue, even if, in Arnold's phrase, it is to be "the dialogue of the mind with itself."

II

Writing on Conrad, with *Chance* in mind, Henry James praised "the glory of the gaps." James was thinking of Conrad's complex use of narrators, and though the phrase has a distinct felicity in relation to Woolf, it could hardly be used to describe a more opposite effect. In Conrad the gap is something precisely calculated: narrator, author, and reader are made to feel their overlapping roles; the gap is integral to the geometry of the fiction.

With Woolf it is far otherwise. The gap is the point at which the fiction threatens to dissolve, where we hear most clearly the novel trying to maintain its own affirming impulse against mounting internal tension. Voices acquire a new urgency, questions tend to break free from the controlling context, silences seem unscripted. Such a situation occurs dramatically toward the end of the fiction section in part 3 of *To the Lighthouse.*

To appreciate the significance of the scene it is useful to recall briefly how the novel has been building up in its earlier parts. The novel is deeply autobiographical in impulse. Its genesis is described in Woolf's diary entry for May 1925: "I'm now all on the strain with desire to stop journalism and get on to *To the Lighthouse.* This is going to be fairly short; to have father's character done complete in it; and mother's; and St. Ives; and childhood; and all the usual things I try to put in, life, death etc." The first section, "The Window," superbly re-creates the past—the Ramsay house party evoking the atmosphere Woolf remembered the Stephen family as enjoying thirty years earlier. But for Virginia Woolf such a description is precisely that—a re-creation. In the second and third parts of the novel she has to go on to ask: Does it amount to more than that? What is the relationship between past experience and present recollection?

The problems posed by the writing of this novel have something in common with those posed by the writing of *Sons and Lovers.* There is the same intent absorption in reliving the past—Vanessa was to say she found Mrs. Ramsay "an amazing portrait of mother . . . the rising of the dead almost painful"—but there is the equally intent recognition that the writing of the novel *has* enabled the ghost of the past to be laid. "Look, we have come through" demands a place in novels whose deepest imaginative energies have been provoked by an intent absorption in the re-creation of a life that has ended. Paul Morel has to turn, finally, "to the humming, glowing town, quickly," and Lily Briscoe is moved to say, as she lays down her brush, "Yes. . . . I have had my vision." But these resolutions are not arrived at without considerable difficulty—a difficulty exposed in the passage at the end of the fifth section in part 3.

Lily has been musing on her failure to complete her picture; even if she were to succeed, she foresees its fate: "It would be hung in the attics . . .; it would be rolled up and flung under a sofa. . . . Her eyes were full of a hot liquid (she did not think of tears at first)." She recalls Mrs. Ramsay and her death; she sees old Mr. Carmichael standing beside her on the lawn:

> For one moment she felt that if they both got up, here, now on
> the lawn, and demanded an explanation, why was [life] so short,
> why was it so inexplicable, said it with violence, as two fully

equipped human beings from whom nothing should be hid might speak, then beauty would roll itself up; the space would fill; those empty flourishes would form into shape; if they shouted loud enough Mrs Ramsay would return. "Mrs Ramsay!" she said aloud, "Mrs Ramsay!" The tears ran down her face.

Lily's questions, in all their stark severity, seem dangerously on loan from the author; and the reader hearing them and feeling the pathos that suffuses them senses that it is not merely Lily who has nowhere to turn, but the writer herself. "The space would fill"—the hope seems in excess of the expectation.

Then, without warning, a remarkable thing happens. A new section begins, consisting of a single sentence:

[Macalister's boy took one of the fish and cut a square out of its side to bait his hook with. The mutilated body (it was alive still) was thrown back into the sea.]

The seventh section begins at precisely the point where the fifth ended: " 'Mrs Ramsay!' Lily cried, 'Mrs Ramsay!' " Virginia Woolf has created a deliberate gap in the text, into which she has inserted a sentence which has no apparent place in the narrative—indeed which she draws attention to by enclosing it in brackets. "Macalister's boy" is completely "outside" Lily's musings, but for the reader he transforms them. As the reader negotiates the gap in the narrative, there is a sudden reminder of other more tragic stories. "As flies to wanton boys . . .": Macalister's boy is not exactly to be numbered among them, but the baiting of his hook, the mutilated fish, reminds us that Lily's questions reverberate in a world of tragic literature.

Paradoxically, if Lily's musings are given the impersonality of this larger context, she herself is contracted into being once more "a character" in a particular situation, brought within the confines of a particular narrative. "No one had seen her step off her strip of board into the waters of annihilation. She remained a skimpy old maid, holding a paint-brush on the lawn." No one, that is, except the reader. Without feeling that Lily's pain has been eased, her questions resolved, the reader senses in the onward movement between these paragraphs that her creator's poise has been reestablished; like us she can see Lily again, "a skimpy old maid, holding a paint-brush."

In this incident in part 3 of *To the Lighthouse* we can see how markedly different Woolf's "gap" is from anything in Conrad. In Conrad the gap concentrates our attention on the density, on the rich folds of the narrative; in Woolf it makes us feel its transparency. But, different as the gap may be in the two novelists, it serves a common function. Through such gaps the texts define their meaning. In Woolf's case the incision occurs at a moment when, for both writer and reader, the novel is becoming dangerously becalmed and self-absorbed. It releases into the novel a fresh access of imaginative power: Lily's painting, Woolf's novel, however much they may have in common, obtain a new distinctness. When Lily says of her painting, as the novel ends, "It is finished," we feel congruence rather than equivalence. The picture, we could say, has been framed by the novel. I am not sure whether this "framing" has been successful; but if it is not, it is because the novel has taken Woolf to a point where fresh considerations about time and the role of the artist are now beginning to weigh with her, and *To the Lighthouse* can no longer accommodate them.

Matters are taken up differently in *The Waves*. Encouraged by her ability to introduce the artist into her fiction and to hold introspection at bay, Woolf now feels sufficiently emboldened to introduce the writer directly; no longer content with analogies, the relation between masses, and their significance, she is able to talk freely about writing itself. With Bernard, who plays a central role, the making—or the unmaking—of the fiction becomes a dominant theme; but on this occasion the skepticism and the gaps in the narrative are to be found, *not* at specific moments as they are in *To the Lighthouse*, but rather as shadows thrown by the shape of the novel as a whole.

When Virginia Woolf was beginning to think about *The Waves*, she wrote an essay on De Quincey under the title "Impassioned Prose." This essay illuminates our reading of the novel. Describing the world of De Quincey's *Autobiographical Sketches*, she writes:

> All these scenes have something of the soundlessness and the lustre of dreams. They swim up to the surface, they sink down again into the depths. They have, into the bargain, the strange power of growing in our minds, so that it is always a surprise to come upon them again and see what, in the interval, our minds have done to alter and expand [them]. . . . But draw a little apart, see people in groups, as outlines, and they become at once memorable and full of beauty. Then it is not the actual sight or sound itself that matters, but the *reverberations that it makes as it travels through our minds*. These are often to be found far away, strangely transformed; but it is only by gathering up and putting together these echoes and fragments that we arrive at the true nature of our experience. So thinking, [De Quincey] altered slightly the ordinary relationships. He shifted the values of familiar things. [Italics mine.].

What is striking in this passage is the intense relationship it describes between scenes which have "the lustre of dreams" and scenes which have "the strange power of growing in our minds." What Woolf seems to be creating here is an imagined world as an echo-chamber, within the reader's own mind. This passage from the De Quincey essay points to the extraordinary intimacy of the relationship between writer and reader in *The Waves*. By an effect which is retroactive, we can say that it is by considering how we *read The Waves* that we will understand better why it is written in the way it is, even though it is a way which brings with it genuine difficulties.

We can begin by observing that what Bernard, Louis, Rhoda, and the rest "say" (it is the most frequently repeated word in the novel) is precisely what they do not "say." Nor is it quite what they *would* say if they could— the supremely articulate utterance of a man called Bernard, a woman called Susan, etc. That is to give too individual a categorization to the "characters," whereas Woolf is anxious that such differentiation should be muted; we should feel them as presences in a discourse which transcends them.

The Waves has the effect of a book written inside out. Most novels, whether they proceed to tell their tale directly or by hints and guesses, are concerned to give the reader the sense that this is "how it was"; we feel this whether we are with Lockwood being introduced to Heathcliff or, in different circumstances, with Strether being introduced to Madame de Vionnet. But with *The Waves* we feel ourselves present at something which is *already* "a reading" of "how it was." We seem simultaneously to be addressed and ignored; we are both within and without the discourse; detachment and a sense of extraordinary intimacy are barely distinguishable elements in our experience.

Another way of putting this would be to say that *The Waves* does not so much speak *to* the reader as it speaks *for* him. This distinctive combination of intimacy and formality, a striking feature of the rhetorical effect made by *The Waves*, finds an analogue in the rhetoric of liturgical prayer, which combines those seemingly contrary effects as part of its nature. Precisely because *The Waves* involves the reader so intimately, our attitudes toward it can shift violently. At times we experience only its formality; we are irritatingly aware only of "words, words, words, my lord," of characters simplistically conceived, of a world without a context. At other times the novel speaks to us so immediately, so directly, that the words seem virtually to withdraw themselves from our attention; and we are aware only of voices giving shape to a sequence of moods, so finely, so precisely, that, as with Mrs. Ramsay reading the poem, the voice seems to create the very mood in which we ourselves are reading the novel. We recall the remark in Woolf's memoir "A Sketch of the Past" about the experience which precipitates her into writing: "We are the words; we are the music; we are the thing itself."

Such is the nature of *The Waves* that it becomes extremely difficult to do justice to these shifting effects. Either we tend to overconceptualize, and our stress is on the firmness of the novel's structure, or we overemphathize, and our stress falls on its texture, on "the prose poem," etc. But if what I have said about the shifting effect is persuasive, then it follows that to look for some kind of account which offers a better "balance" will be misguided, because such an account is too preoccupied with finding a "theme" and insufficiently concerned with the effect made by theme in the actual process of reading.

For instance, what can we say about our reaction to those interchapters? The intention would seem to be to create a world irretrievably other than that of "the voices" in the main text. Nature is to be shown as neither benign nor malignant, but simply as "other"; to project our own feelings into it, and find in the movement of the sun from dawn to evening a sardonic comment on the human condition, is sentimental. And this sense of otherness Woolf seeks to dramatize by carefully marking off the interchapters and altering the typography. But for all that, in my reading experience, the structural purpose of the interchapters is stubbornly in conflict with the effect they make.

The aim is to create a neutral voice, something to set against the human and the sentient. It is the kind of effect that Eliot sought, and so effectively achieved, in the time passages in *Four Quartets*. "Go, go, go, said the bird: human kind / Cannot bear very much reality": that notion of "saying" is so recessive that we are not disconcerted by a bird's capacity for aphorism. But the interchapters in *The Waves* are so densely textured that, far from being remotely impersonal, they come across as intensely "composed" and self-regarding, confident candidates for inclusion in an anthology of modern English prose.

These then are some of the difficulties, but our experience of Bernard is not one of them. Here Woolf does seem genuinely successful, in a way that she was not in her treatment of Lily in *To the Lighthouse*. Lily has no real dramatic role in the first part of the novel to prepare us for a role which she is to play in the final part; Bernard, as the writer, is continuously engaged with the questions which the novel itself is to pose in its final pages. Bernard is at once an integral part of the narrative and yet separated from it: he offers us reflections which belong to him as a character and reflections on the text in which that character has a part to play. *The Waves* dramatizes Bernard; it is also the novel Bernard is writing.

Recalling Woolf's remarks in her essay on De Quincey on the desirability of seeing people "as outlines," we read this in *The Waves*:

> "I see Louis, stone-carved, sculpturesque; Neville, scissor-cutting, exact; Susan with eyes like lumps of crystal; Jinny dancing like a flame . . .; and Rhoda the nymph of the fountain always wet. These are fantastic pictures—these are figments, these visions of friends in absence, grotesque, dropsical, vanishing at the first touch of the toe of a real boot. *Yet they drum me alive*." (Italics mine.)

For Bernard the "characters" are framed as pictures: they can be condensed into a metaphor, reduced to a gesture and a pose. But these pictures and poses "vanishing at the first touch of the toe of a real boot" have, nevertheless, the power to drum him alive. And so too it is with the reader. It is precisely the over-all *rhythm* of the work, establishing dynamic continuities, that creates the effect—sharpening our senses, defining our mood, and above all uttering the barely utterable. It is rhythm that makes *say* not only the most repeated but the most important word in the novel, the point of intersection between writer and reader, a word which belongs to them both.

This effect is not altered by any feelings we may have about the "pessimism" of the work, about whether or not Bernard's exhilaration in the closing paragraph is justified or not. That kind of discussion belongs to another level of response. What I am contending for is that, overriding the formal themes of the novel, the style creates, in its verve, its range, and its endless resourcefulness, a voice which has its own value; and where that voice cannot be maintained, we have the pauses and the silences that provide the characteristic punctuation for a Woolf novel.

A small incident occurs early in the novel which persists like a watermark in all its pages. When they are children Bernard and Susan trespass on a large estate, and when they look over the wall they see a house where "the lady sits between the two long windows, writing," and where "the gardeners sweep the lawn with giant brooms." The lady writing, the gardeners sweeping: it is a domestic variant of the dialectical rhythm which the whole novel sets up, elaborating first one, then the other; but as we read we are never allowed to forget for a moment the gap that separates them. As the novel proceeds, the scene gathers force so that it comes as no surprise when the episode takes its place in Bernard's closing summary. "Down below, through the depths of the leaves, the gardeners swept the lawn with great brooms. The lady sat writing. . . . I thought, 'I cannot interfere with a single stroke of those brooms. They sweep and they sweep. Nor with the fixity of that woman writing.' It is strange that one cannot stop gardeners sweeping nor dislodge a woman. There they have remained all my life."

And for Bernard they will to the end—but for the reader that dialectic will be assumed into something rich and strange. When he first sees the lady and the gardeners, Bernard jumps up and cries out to Susan, "Let's explore . . ."; and it is *that* voice which reverberates throughout the whole work. Bernard is complementing the work of the novelist: he is, in Wright Morris's words, "creating, as the work progresses, what he needs to know."

The dialectical themes are unquestionably there, and the antinomies of its expression have become a commonplace of Woolf discussion—fact and vision, male and female, continuity and the flux; but irradiating that dialectic is the *voice* of its utterance, buoyant, ceaselessly exploratory.

III

I have been arguing for attention to be paid in Woolf's novels to elements which override such considerations as arise directly from the substance of her novels, especially their overt themes. What has been neglected is not the constituent elements of her novels—these, in terms of themes and techniques, have received exhaustive, not to say exhausting, attention—but rather the way in which these novels have their being in the world of our reading experience, what is the nature of our encounter with them, what light they throw on the way we read fiction in general.

I want to sound the distinctive note of a Woolf novel by recalling passages from novelists of an earlier period. I introduce these comparisons with a remark she herself made in the essay "How It Strikes a Contemporary": Scott and Wordsworth "know the relations of human beings towards each other and towards the universe. Neither of them probably has a word to say about the matter outright, but everything depends on it. . . To believe that your impressions hold good for others is to be released from the cramp and confinement of personality." Woolf's point is historical; mine is aesthetic. My passages are chosen not for a chronological purpose but because they hint at the connection between the pattern of expectations an author both assumes and creates in his narrative and the way we read him. My first passage comes from Jane Austen's *Persuasion*:

> Anne's object was, not to be in the way of any body, and where the narrow paths across the fields made many separations necessary, to keep with her brother and sister. Her *pleasure* in the walk must arise from the exercise and the day, from the view of the last smiles of the year upon the tawny leaves and withered hedges, and from repeating to herself some few of the thousand poetical descriptions extant of autumn, that season of peculiar and inexhaustible influence on the mind of taste and tenderness, that season which has drawn from every poet, worthy of being read, some attempt at description, or some lines of feeling. She occupied her mind as much as possible in such like musings and quotations; but it was not possible, that when within reach of Captain Wentworth's conversation with either of the Miss Musgroves, she should not try to hear it; yet she caught little very remarkable. It was mere lively chat,—such as any young persons, on an intimate footing, might fall into. He was more engaged with Louisa than with Henrietta. Louisa certainly put more forward for his notice than her sister. The distinction appeared to increase, and there was one speech of Louisa's which struck her. After one of the many praises of the day, which were continually bursting forth, Captain Wentworth added,
> "What glorious weather for the Admiral and my sister!"

When we read "Anne's object was, not to be in the way of any body," we know the governing ironies to be perfectly judged: there is a criticism of Anne certainly, but it is suffused with affectionate understanding. Jane Austen is as assured of the constant self of Anne Elliot as she is of the constant nature of the world she contemplates. There is a perfect reciprocity between what is said and what is not said, because Jane Austen can in this instance rely completely on a reader who will assume the same reciprocity between man and nature. The nature of her irony is perfectly at home within those continuities.

My second illustration is taken from a very different novelist, writing in a very different mood. It is Hardy describing Boldwood's reaction to Bathsheba's valentine in *Far from the Madding Crowd*:

> Over the west hung the wasting moon, now dull and greenish-yellow, like tarnished brass.
>
> Boldwood was listlessly noting how the frost had hardened and glazed the surface of the snow, till it shone in the red eastern light with the polish of marble; how, in some portions of the slope, withered grass-bents, encased in icicles, bristled through the smooth wan coverlet in the twisted and curved shapes of old Venetian glass; and how the footprints of a few birds, which had hopped over the snow whilst it lay in the state of a soft fleece, were now frozen to a short permanency.

What was pique in Anne Elliot becomes in Boldwood an obsessive overwhelming jealousy. But, in common with her, he projects his mood onto a universe of things, and elegantly, as with a polished mirror, his reflection is given back to him. However listless Boldwood may be in his noting, Hardy is certainly not, as he moves brilliantly and precisely through his description—the glazed surface, the grass encased in icicles, the wan coverlet. Again the "saying" creates exactly what is hidden, what is *not* said about Boldwood's consuming frustrated passion. Hardy, in common with Jane Austen—however different his mood—has no doubt about an epistemology which finds a reciprocal bond between man and nature, a constant self in a constant world. And that bond, that constancy, affects our own relationship with the text. The continuum is pervasively dramatized by the very process of reading: it lies in the anticipations aroused, the interplay of cause and effect, the confidence that a resolution will be found. The chapter divisions are the staging posts in an onward progress. *Persuasion* and *Far from the Madding Crowd* could hardly be more different as novels, but their authors both assume that their readers will complete their scripts, and that if they choose to leave things unsaid, the area of unspoken comment is defined as exactly as if it had been written down. Both novelists eloquently embody the attitude that "their beliefs . . . will hold good for others.

My third illustration is from Virginia Woolf's *Between the Acts*:

> Miss La Trobe leant against the tree, paralyzed. Her power had left her. Beads of perspiration broke on her forehead. Illusion had failed. "This is death," she murmured, "death."
>
> Then suddenly, as the illusion petered out, the cows took up the burden. One had lost her calf. In the very nick of time she lifted her great moon-eyed head and bellowed. All the great moon-eyed heads laid themselves back. From cow after cow came the same yearning bellow. The whole world was filled with dumb yearning. It was the primeval voice sounding loud in the ear of

the present moment. Then the whole herd caught the infection. Lashing their tails, blobbed like pokers, they tossed their heads high, plunged and bellowed, as if Eros had planted his darts in their flanks and goaded them to fury. The cows annihilated the gap; bridged the distance; filled the emptiness and continued the emotion.

Miss La Trobe waved her hand ecstatically at the cows.

"Thank Heaven!" she exclaimed.

Suddenly the cows stopped; lowered their heads, and began browsing. Simultaneously the audience lowered their heads and read their programmes.

"Illusion had failed": we are taken back to Lily Briscoe's despair about her painting, to Bernard's skepticism about making up stories. But then the cows take up the burden, and the mood of the scene is transformed. Here is a playful treatment of Woolf's most serious and abiding theme. The absence of reciprocity between man and nature, the discontinuities, lend themselves as readily to the comic as to the tragic. But the comic is not edged with bitterness; in *Between the Acts* it is exuberant, self-delighting.

Characteristically the passage turns on reversals. No longer is Nature imaged as an echo-chamber for the human mood. "The cows annihilated the gap; bridged the distance; filled the emptiness and continued the emotion." It is a delightful parody of the "romantic" situation, and in a splendid line Nature's help is gratefully acknowledged. "Miss La Trobe waved her hand ecstatically at the cows." But such a shift entails a shift in how we read. In moving from a narrative designed to give us a sense of "how it was," to one more disposed to give us a sense of "how it is," we no longer feel the momentum of the onward drive. The reader is persuaded to be hospitable to postponement, to defer conclusions. And so if we read of Miss La Trobe moving rapidly from one intensity of feeling to another, we are encouraged not so much to reflect on the revelation of her "mercurial" character as to see in those intensities opportunities for the novelist to give us a heightened apprehension of human feeling. Such an apprehension is intimately bound in a fresh consciousness of the text itself, its continuities and disjunctions miming the themes it conveys.

For Woolf our fictions no longer contain their own title deeds; the author can no longer assume that what is not written will be endorsed by the reader. The novelist must dramatize his own skepticism about his created world, and the gaps and silences that punctuate his text will bear witness to that necessity.

Virginia Woolf, unlike Jane Austen and Hardy, makes not so much a contract with as a promise to the reader. She will create a mood which carries an assurance beyond her formal intention. *Trust me*, she seems to say. If we try to characterize that mood, we are made to reflect that in each Woolf novel there is a dominant voice, with its own inflections, its own nuances, its own register of feeling. The voice alters from novel to novel, but it gives them, perhaps more than anything else, their identity. It is not a voice which is shared with any particular character (though it can, on occasion, come close to being so); it is not coterminous with the narrative and the themes it weaves; it is not within the mind of the reader. We recall Bernard's words about the characters in *The Waves*—so thin as to be little more than "outlines," but "they drum me alive." We think of that animating rhythm, its energy and power, and of the writer needing to find "the sought-for reader." Needing, because it is the condition which enables the fiction to be achieved, needing, because, as *The Writer's Diary* makes abundantly clear, Woolf seeks to be the ideal reader of that fiction—if she were not obliged to write it. Like the characters in *The Waves* for Bernard, the reader may be no more than an outline for Woolf, but he drums her alive and she finds a writing voice, not her own, but, as Wright Morris remarked, a voice which is "part and parcel of the fiction's intent to be as fully achieved as the writer can make it"—the voice, in other words, of the created book.

The Intimate World
of Ivy Compton-Burnett

Frederick R. Karl

Miss Ivy Compton-Burnett is a family chronicler whose late-Victorian home-bodies become possessive, sadistic mothers, destructive, self-willed fathers, and persecuted children who try to murder their parents. For her, family life is a jungle in which no holds are barred; tooth and nail are preferable to persuasion, and verbal wit helps one gain what rightfully belongs to another. Only the fittest survive throughout the in-fighting; the battle goes to the strong-willed and the deceptive. The weak and honest lose their fortunes as well as their self-possession, while the winner cheats with all the resources available to him.

Her large Victorian families, with their intertwining relationships of numerous cousins, aunts (fewer uncles), and grandparents, are predatory as sharks, their teeth out, their fins, so to speak, always in someone else's pocket. Everyone —usually a small army of relatives—is dependent on one or two others, and the latter are systematically bled until they have little left to give. Then they can be abandoned, although some spark of vestigial feeling usually keeps the family together. Perhaps it is not feeling that finally unifies, but the law of the jungle.

The morality of Miss Compton-Burnett's work involves material values—how does one sustain himself in what amounts to a predatory jungle? The family is not a reservoir of sympathy and feeling but a miniature of the larger world in which self-interest is the sole motivation. A person survives in the family group through conniving and competing. Frequently, the forces are divided: the children on one side, the parents or adults on the other. Neither side is restricted to gentleman's weapons. Nagging is raised to an art, and each side dogs the other, looking for an advantage,

From *The Contemporary English Novel*. © 1962 by Frederick R. Karl. Farrar, Straus & Giroux, 1962.

trying to thrust in a verbal dagger. For in the destruction of the other person, whether actual or figurative, the individual gains his own life.

In nearly all of Miss Compton-Burnett's novels the stories take place before the turn of the century, a period wherein the family was still strong enough to be central in a character's life. Her large family groups, like so many armies fighting off the enemy and then breaking down into civil war, allow ready-made relationships. There are few friends of the family involved in these struggles, and when they do appear they are peripheral. The friends for the children are their own brothers and sisters, but even here cruelty is not precluded. Siblings, however, are rarely as cruel to each other as their parents are to them: they have less to gain. Parents work out their guilt, insufficiencies, vanity, and frustrations through the vicarious torture of their children, and the latter are fully aware of what is happening. They react with their only weapons: conspiracy and deception, for they too must survive.

Thus, in *Bullivant and the Lambs* (published in England as *Manservant and Maidservant*, 1947), Horace Lamb's two children (age twelve and eleven) allow him to approach a bridge that they know is washed out; they are aware that he is walking toward his death, and yet they hesitate to warn him until it might be too late. Horace has reformed himself from what he was—a tyrant in the home—but the boys agree that no father at all is preferable to what Horace formerly was, and he might regress at any time. Their decision is simply one to insure survival; the former Horace, with his nagging criticism and his inability to let anyone else breathe, was suffocating them.

The situation in *Bullivant and the Lambs*, in which the father tries to restrain his instincts and feelings, is less insidious than in several of the other novels. For Horace's actions are at least in the open: everyone sees him for what he is. Far more dangerous is the person who hides behind a mask and gains his ends without revealing what he actually is, or one who disguises his trail by revealing just enough to keep his real motives hidden. That type of person treads a path of destruction and, in Miss Compton-Burnett's world, will find himself rewarded. In *Elders and Betters* (1944), a key novel in Miss Compton-Burnett's charting of late Victorian manners and morals, Anna Donne destroys her aunt's original will and becomes sole heir in the new will, which her aunt did not want to stand. Then she proceeds to lie her way to success, driving to suicide a second aunt who had expected the money, getting engaged to her cousin, whom she can now support, and acquiring everything that money, no matter how ill-gained, can buy in the way of happiness.

In this world, money can indeed buy happiness, for social morality is attached to self-gain, both material and psychological. There are no real heroes: one is a hero or heroine only in his own eyes. One survives in fact by becoming, through vanity, his own hero, and then trying to impose his role upon everyone. There is no salvation, no repentance (there are few visible crimes), no chance for redemption. As Miss Compton-Burnett suggests in *A Family and a Fortune* (1939), to sacrifice oneself may seem fine for others, but it is horrible for oneself.

Miss Compton-Burnett has of course taken the Victorian family novel and turned it inside out, revealing the dirt behind the romantic exterior. Although her subject matter seems close to that of the mid-Victorian novelists, unlike many of them she recognizes that below normal social behavior lies a swamp of discontent, mixed motives, and deception.

In *Mother and Son* (1955), Rosebery Hume is so closely attached to his mother that no other satisfactory relationship is possible for him, and after her death he throws himself indiscriminately at every available female, only to find that his sole company for life will be children two generations his junior. In *Brothers and Sisters* (1929), Christian and Sophia Stace have become the parents of three children, although they are half brother and sister. In *Darkness and Day* (1951), the reader first believes that Edmund and Bridget Lovat, now long married, are father and daughter, only to discover that they are merely half brother and sister. In *The Present and the Past* (1953), Cassius Clare attempts to become the center of family activity by a false attempt at suicide; when he does die, everyone thinks it is another false suicide attempt and ignores him. In *Two Worlds and Their Ways* (1949), each member of the family has something to hide: the two children have cheated at school; Sir Roderick Shelley has fathered a son who works in the house as a servant; Maria, Sir Roderick's wife, has almost "destroyed" her children trying to make them shine in their father's eyes.

In nearly every one of the novels, there is movement toward a revelation that will, inevitably, make the characters aware of what they are and what the situation is. The revelation takes the form of a recognition scene (many critics have thus compared Miss Compton-Burnett's novels with Greek tragedy), but the recognition itself does not appear to change the characters. In Greek tragedy, the recognition was the climax of the rising action, entailing a meeting between the protagonist's past and future—for what he has been will now determine what he will be. After the recognition scene, the character passes into a decline that is in some ways the equivalent of Christian contrition, except that there is ultimately no salvation. His exile is from his self; he must pay for the rest of his life for something he was unable to control.

This, obviously, is not the pattern in Ivy Compton-Burnett's novels. True, she shares with the Greek tragedian his awareness of the importance of the recognition scene, but she has reworked the materials of the tragic vision so that further comparison is valueless. Frequently, the revelation amuses the reader more than it changes the character. Instead of facing the revelation, the character merely tries to hush up the news and live with it. The incestuous pair in *Brothers and Sisters* are treated comically, as they are in *Darkness and Day*. First, we are led to believe that Edmund and Bridget Lovat are father and daughter, but later we find they are half brother and sister—and thus their marriage should not seem outrageous. If only Oedipus and Jocasta had been siblings! Meanwhile, their incest has become a source of common gossip among the children and servants. No one, however, is particularly upset, for incest serves as well as anything else to gossip about.

Furthermore, in Miss Compton-Burnett's world there is no repentance, no Christian charity which will reward the good person, no Christian revenge which will punish the bad. There are no amenities whatsoever. If one has been incestuous, it is discreet to keep the news to oneself and continue living. If the news does get out, then one hopes that the other fellow has done something even worse so that incest will not disturb him. If one has had illegitimate children in the past, then he usually finds that his husband or wife has committed a similar folly, and the two indiscretions cancel each other. If one loves his brother's wife or fiancée, he finds that another woman can be provided for the brother, perhaps a maid or governess.

Governesses in Miss Compton-Burnett's world are extremely expendable; the supply appears inexhaustible, and they are usually available for whatever the household requires of them. While they teach the younger children, generally an older child (one about fifty, the product of a previous marriage) is measuring their suitability for marriage. The governess, frequently, becomes a competitor with the mother for the affection of the children, and in this scheme the father is excluded, unless he himself makes a play for the governess. When he does, he finds his older son in competition. One need not be a hypocrite to survive in Miss Compton-Burnett's world; cruelty and expedience are sufficient.

The lack of repentance and salvation makes possible the comic play of the novels. If the amenities are meaningless, the law of the jungle must prevail. And all this against the background of a Christian society! The surface of behavior is impeccable, but beneath lie arrogance, vanity, jealousy, and excessive pride—all the characteristics of normal people. Miss Compton-Burnett's characters are always themselves. And just as no force from within can change them (only circumstances change, they remain the same), so no force from the outside can alter them. They are fixed by their characters and doomed, to some extent, by their heritage. They resist progress with the fierceness of people who recognize that change means death, although not to change is also a kind of death. Their death throes, however, are often comic.

The chief weight of this amoral world falls on the children. They are the beneficiaries of the muddle that adults make of their lives; but rather than learn from their sad experiences, these children perpetuate similar lives in their own children. The cycle of infamy is endless. For someone to have learned from his experience would be for him to deny what he is. His individuality consists of denying that his children's claim on life might be superior to his own; the struggle between the two, consequently, becomes one of life and death, with the children hanging on through desperation.

Lest the reader feel sorry for these children, Miss Compton-Burnett has made them monsters who speak and understand in an adult way. Unlike the Victorian children who had to be seen but not heard, Miss Compton-Burnett's children are constantly uttering witticisms to dissipate their parents' evil. In a society in which even the family becomes an institution supporting injustice, the children must conspire with each other to float above the backwash of their parents' past. Like Dickens's long-suffering youngsters, they too must endure the absurdity of their elders, but they have weapons and armor that Dickens could not have conceived. By hiding beneath couches or in doorways, they become aware of everything; and, with the servants, provide a chorus-like comment upon their parents. Their revenge comes from understanding exactly what is happening to them, and at a suitable time they torture the adults by withholding affection and love. Precisely as their elders use love to gain what they want, so the children themselves form alignments and use love, withdrawn or extended, as an offensive weapon in their struggle for survival.

In a tragic or semi-tragic novel, the child must become the victim of adult duplicity in the comic novel, however, the adult becomes the child's victim. And yet the weapons of each side in Miss Compton-Burnett's novels are so fierce and the moves so predatory that comedy gains a new dimension. This is comedy based on torture, cruelty, and selfishness, in which no one can afford to relent because to survive he must continue being what he is. Graham Greene's dialogue between man and God, with the ensuing conflicts, becomes in Ivy Compton-Burnett's hands the everyday conflicts between the generations, between parents and children, between grandparents and their children, between aunts and nephews and nieces.

The construction of Ivy Compton-Burnett's novels is essentially the same in the seventeen she has published from 1911 (*Dolores* is juvenilia) to 1959, with *A Heritage and Its History*. The departures from a common structure are fewer than the adherences: Miss Compton-Burnett has marked her originality not only in the conversational idiom but in the form of her novels. The reader is first introduced to a family, usually one with numerous children. The father may be senile or else in vigorous middle age, and there is often a disparity between the ages of the younger children and the older one(s)—an age gap of twenty years is not uncommon. Thus, the older children, in their twenties and thirties, form one band, while the younger ones, usually around ten or eleven, form a second. The two bands often join in order to fight the parents, but frequently their problems differ in degree (not kind—they are all persecuted by the parents) so that there cannot be full agreement on a course of action.

The elders themselves are not united; an old relative —father, aunt, or uncle —will ally himself with one of the parents to form a conflicting band. The patriarch or matriarch is often in his eighties, and during his lifetime he casts gloom over the entire house; even those who do not hate him wait for his death. He knows, however, that he is useless and employs his great age as a way of obtaining sympathy and deference. An old person is indeed a scarecrow upon a stick, but nevertheless a voluble one—being unwanted does not hush him. His isolation, in fact, seems to act as goad for further intrusion in what does not concern him. Although no one has love for the elder statesman, there is, nevertheless, a primitive connection that has nothing to do with love—what savages must feel for their elders who have attained an untouchable situation within the tribal hierarchy.

Within this family, there may be an alien member who belongs to a second family, and this latter group is then presented in similar terms. These two interrelated families, with perhaps a third, or with fragments of other families (brothers and sisters, aunts and nieces, mothers and sons), constitute Miss Compton-Burnett's "society." There is no other "group" in her novels: outside the family lies a shadowy substance, the great world, which has no bearing on that primal relationship. One achieves something, or is destroyed, not because of the world but because of the family; and a son or daughter reels from family to family seeking a haven. The rebel does not run off to London to find solace in material success; such things do not exist. The family is his all: it dominates, circumvents, encloses, frustrates, and provides one with mates (so many cousins marry in these novels that the hundreds of characters in the seventeen books must somehow all be related as second and third cousins). In *Elders and Betters*, for example, there is such extensive intermarrying contemplated among cousins that congratulations are in order for the first person to marry outside the family, and he weds the governess's niece.

It is this tightness of family structure—the family both gives sustenance and destroys what it maintains—which causes the claustrophobic quality of Miss Compton-Burnett's novels. With the family blocking its members on every side, the latter are repeatedly thrown back into the cauldron, which burns with a heat that must nullify everyone within its confines. What a hideous revenge society has planned for itself: its sole unifying unit is a group that tortures its members for pleasure and gain. What a vision of the world: a vast network of relatives who do the work of the devil; and there is no escape. Without families, they would have to work, or give up their education, or search for a mate, or stand on their own feet. And since no one desires such pursuits, he inevitably falls back on the family, which provides all these essentials in exchange for sucking dry his soul and spirit.

Miss Compton-Burnett's method of narration is perfectly coordinated with the subject matter. By bringing two or three families together as the whole of society, she makes their interplay the sum of all essential forces in the world, until nothing else seems to matter. Her conversational method creates, as it were, an external stream of consciousness, in which the characters overtly voice what the traditional novelist usually explains about them. Consequently, in a literal way, we see what they are—there is nothing to hide, for the very nature of their communication forces complete disclosure of their thoughts. Only infrequently do the characters enter into a conspiracy to withhold information. More often, the characters reveal everything they know, and their disclosures suggest the limits of their cruelty.

This aspect of the method is effective, for its very freakishness becomes a way of complementing the eccentricity of Miss Compton-Burnett's characters. The stream of consciousness has been transformed into a spray of epigrams. The conversational method that Henry Green was seeking in his last two novels, *Nothing* and *Doting*, has been a staple of Miss Compton-Burnett's work for thirty years. Most novelists assume that their characters will hide certain things about themselves, since they are ashamed of their iniquity. For Ivy Compton-Burnett, however, iniquity is not a marginal characteristic of a chosen few but the substance of the whole world. To feel shame indicates a commitment to a morality of good and evil, but to be unaware of shame is to show allegiance to an amoral world in which a generous action is repaid not by kindness but by retribution, in which a sympathetic word is offered—for a gain, in which the old must survive by fighting their children for their rights.

The method suggests, then, that if a character has a thought of any kind, he will shape it into words. And even more, into an epigram. The conversational idiom, however, does result in emotionally flaccid people, although this consequence does not disturb the author. Her characters are not emotional beings under any circumstances; they react with reason, and reason is their only god. For the reader, nevertheless, there is a curious sameness of character and narrative, perhaps because we tend to remember literary creations by their emotions. In these novels, however, no survivor grieves for the deceased, no one is horrified to see what his children have turned into, no one questions that a mother has the right to destroy her son(s), no one is particularly upset to discover incest or infidelity. The emotions are so well controlled that the most startling revelation will not elicit surprise. Life itself seems frozen.

The conversational idiom of the characters helps establish their complacency. Their epigrams are rapier thrusts cleaned of all sweat and all effort—the thrust is cool and straight to the mark, as though they had spent their lives polishing their marksmanship for precisely this situation. Even the children are untouched by the grossest of deceptions. In *Daughters and Sons*, for example, the daughter of John Ponsonby, a popular novelist, accepts unquestioningly that her father's writing career is finished, and that he must be protected from this knowledge. Accordingly, she turns her own novel over to a publisher, receives a large sum of money, and then pretends that the money has been sent her father by an admirer. Mr. Ponsonby inadvertently thinks the money comes from the family governess and marries her, setting off a whole series of misunderstandings. Yet, Frances, the novelist-daughter, calmly accepts that her father is written-out and that she must sacrifice herself for him. An ancient ritual is carried out in modern dress.

This very lack of emotion or surprise creates a good part of the horror—a kind of intellectual sport—which an Ivy Compton-Burnett novel generates. The glitter of the conversation helps form a tight wall around the characters, as the novelist herself has built precisely such a wall around her society. The epigrams convey an exclusive quality, as though these are special people who cannot react or speak in any other way. In *Two Worlds and Their Ways*, these sallies occur on every page. For example:

> "Is your family musical, Mr. Spode?" said Juliet, with no sug-
> gestion of a change of subject.
> "My mother is one of those people, who do not know one note
> from another. That means that they do not concern themselves
> with notes. I do not know about my father. He died when I was
> born."
> "What?" said more than one voice.
> "It appears to have been the case. There is a primitive people,
> whose men take to their beds, when their wives have children. It
> seems that my father followed that course, and never rose again."
> "So your mother is a widow?" said Mr. Bigwell.
> "That is one of the consequences."
> "We must remember that Mrs. Cassidy is present."
> "I did remember it. I was trying to cause her some amusement."
> "Thank you so much," said Juliet. "You have quite taken my
> thoughts off our disgrace."

This is a special language, one that is sheathed and unsheathed like a sword or dagger, a language that, so to speak, lies in wait for its victim, scores a light hit, and then moves away preparatory to another strike. Consequently, because the children in these novels can survive only by answering back, their conversational abilities are phenomenal. They speak like adults, indeed like special adults—like Henry James and La Fontaine. Their use of language stylizes them, gives them the brittleness and ner-vousness one expects of children whose parents "use" them. They rebel without illusions, conspire without shame, and survive without love. And while they fail to gain our sympathy, they do win our amazement.

Despite the virtues of the conversational method—its literalness, its sharp definition of issues, its penetration into the thoughts of the charac-ters—despite these, its deficiencies are apparent. Miss Compton-Burnett's characters all seem cut from the same mold; the children all have the same awareness of evil, and the parents and grandparents all demonstrate the same predatory expedience. When a mother in one novel says, "My good, dear children," or something similar, she is preparing to sacrifice them at the first need, and the mother in the next novel is little different. A widower makes a "wife" of his eldest daughter, and a widow makes a "husband" of her eldest son. To gain a life, one must crush a life. A flat sameness is evident both in character development and plot, and it precludes Miss Compton-Burnett's being a creator of memorable characters.

Another factor, and one that drives to the heart of the creative process itself, is the lack of motivation in her characters. Here the novelist allows the surface to be definitive: either the character explains himself or he does not. There is no "background filler" to provide the explanatory material which the character himself is unaware of. Part of the unreality of the conception is that the character maintains almost total awareness of himself: what he is, how he got that way, what direction he is to take. There are no uncertainties. The author assumes that the background of the elders was the same as that of the children, and that the cycle perpetuates itself.

An almost total reliance on dialogue further weakens characterization by making people float, as it were, on the rhythms of their speech. Miss Compton-Burnett's characters seem to have no substance except what their words give them. They are little more than mouthpieces, wits, talking heads, disembodied streams of words. And yet strikingly, despite the brilliant flow of words, there are no characters who are expert in their work. Her writers are second-rate, her professionals marginal and uninvolved in their work, her "intellectuals" uninterested in pursuing ideas. Every ideal is in decline.

There is of course little doubt that Miss Compton-Burnett is indebted to the fiction of Henry James, she is interested in late-Victorian attitudes, and, again like him, she is concerned with revealing the hypocrisy that the age has disguised as hearty materialism. Both have placed limitations on the range of the novel so that they could probe in depth, and both have emphasized characters whose lives are built on sand or based on misconceived relationships that are no longer viable.

Miss Compton-Burnett's restrictions on the range of her novels seem an epitome of the contemporary English novel, which has forsaken adventurous forms and broad content for the small, intensive work. Often like the Greek tragedian in her attempt to convey the doom that waits for the successful man, she is unlike him in her inability to project individual ills upon the social framework. The "sickness" of her characters is theirs alone, a condition of their lives, and there is no other life. Perhaps this is her main point. Despite her fierce brightness, the inner world of her typical characters is as moribund as that of a Beckett bum; for both, love, hope, faith, and desire are meaningless values in a world that only language can define.

Of the seventeen novels in Ivy Compton-Burnett's canon, the two that have gained the widest popularity, *Bullivant and the Lambs* (1947) and *Two Worlds and Their Ways* (1949), best illustrate her values and the kind of world she is involved in. They, along with three others, *Brothers and Sisters* (1929), *Elders and Betters* (1944), and *Mother and Son* (1955), demonstrate the author's main themes: the stifling of the child by the parent, the nature of successful deception, and the great secret which slowly and silently destroys.

Bullivant, as his truculent name suggests, is a bull of a servant in the house of the Lambs, who, however, contain a fierceness of their own. One expects them to be Lambs, but Horace is anything but that: a domineering, self-centered, egotistical man who has nagged and terrorized his children until they plot his death to insure their own survival. Bullivant and the servants in the kitchen serve as a sub-plot countering the life and death struggle between Horace and his children. They act as chorus, gaining all information as soon as the reader himself knows it. In this way, *Bullivant and the Lambs* recalls Henry Green's *Loving*, which had appeared two years earlier (in 1945). The servant has his masters cowed: the initial description indicates the relationship:

> Bullivant was a larger man than his masters, and had an air of being on a considerable scale in every sense. He had pendulous cheeks, heavy eyelids that followed their direction, solid, thick hands whose movements were deft and swift and precise, a nose that hardly differentiated itself from its surroundings, and a deeply folded neck and chin with no definite line between them. His small, steady, hazel eyes were fixed on his assistant, and he wore an air of resigned and almost humorous deprecation, that suggested a tendency to catch his masters' glance.

In small, the theme of the novel is here. The relation between masters and a servant as feared as Bullivant—in Dickens, the servant has an eye, here he has a glance—can be nothing but comic. Servants, like their masters, are interested in power: Bullivant's power is over the Lambs, while Horace's is directed toward his children. Horace's use of power, however, is more brutal, because it takes advantage of ties based on trust. The servant's future depends on the fear he can build around his demands, but the child's depends on the love and sympathy he can obtain. Horace offers neither love nor sympathy: he demands obedience.

The result is that the five children, whose ages run from thirteen to seven, have set up a war camp of their own, and find solace in the kitchen with the servants. There they escape Horace's dictum—reminiscent of Meredith's Sir Austin Feverel's—that " 'Civilised life consists in suppressing our instincts.' " Horace imposes on them the burden of being adults while they are still children; he denies that they should want anything—Christmas stockings, for instance—which he is unwilling to provide.

The children, however, reject both the wisdom and the man, and Horace gradually becomes a stranger in his home, doubly so when he recognizes that his wife, Charlotte, intends to run off with his cousin—both, evidently, feel about him the way the children do. After a severe illness, Horace reforms. He becomes the opposite of what he was: sympathetic, yielding, flexible in his wishes, and discreet in his demands. He becomes a model father and husband, and wins back to some extent both his chldren and his wife. Residual fear, nevertheless, remains: he may return to what he was, and after the respite, that would be more than the family could bear. So the boys reason when they think Horace is walking toward his death—" 'It would be better for him to die, if it was the only thing to prevent that.' " When Horace returns, as if from the dead, he questions his boys sadly, and they answer:

> "We are afraid of you. You know we are," said Marcus [age 11].
> "Your being different for a little while has not altered all that went

before. Nothing can alter it. You did not let us have anything; you would not let us be ourselves. If it had not been for Mother, we would rather have been dead. It was feeling like that so often, that made us think dying an ordinary thing."

Kafka's own appeal to his father was not more bitter. The words of the boy come with the force of a judge's reprimand to a criminal awaiting sentence. Horace answers that he will be careful, that he will not stumble back into what he was, but also that he will always remember their capacity for evil. Nevertheless, he sadly perceives their act was little more than self-defense. If the children recognize that their parents want to suck them of life, they have the moral right to retaliate in kind. Murder itself becomes a relative thing, and at times one must murder (it must, however, be matricide or parricide) to maintain life. Both Horace and his sons have been initiated into the real world in which fear has transformed a possibly loving relationship into one of hate and desire for revenge. Unlike Kafka, Miss Compton-Burnett's "sons" do not write letters to their father: they plot his death.

As a counterpoint to this theme of parent-children brutality, there is the presence of the third power group in the Lamb household, the servants. Ever-aware and ever-hovering, the servants maintain their independent existence despite the presence of tyranny in the house. Bullivant burns with his own type of dominance, but there is within him a sense of proportion, something almost akin to kindness. In his dealings with Miss Buchanan—a storekeeper whose great secret is her inability to read—Bullivant displays tact and discretion, the very qualities that Horace Lamb failed to show toward his children. The two halves of the book work as complements: Bullivant, despite his bull-like independence, is able to demonstrate kindness toward those who are helpless, while Horace Lamb attacks his children because of their helplessness. The "moral" of the book is that Horace must learn the lesson that Bullivant has known all along; the penalty for refusing to learn it is to be re-condemned to death by his children.

In *Two Worlds and Their Ways*, which appeared two years later, the attitude is similar: the two worlds of the title are primarily those of the children and the adults. Also, there are the two worlds of the differing generations, the former and the present, and the two worlds of Sir Roderick Shelley's two wives, the first now long dead and the second, Maria, who wishes to best her in Sir Roderick's eyes. Maria's ambition is that her two children, Clemence and Sefton, should surpass their half brother, Oliver, Sir Roderick's child by his first wife, Mary (the similarity of the wives' names is not fortuitous—the two maintain a constant rivalry).

Since the childrens' own wishes are not represented in this intrafamiliar competition, they feel that whatever they do is permissible. There is no moral question involved, for if one is to obey his elders, then he must not scruple over base action in order to fulfill what is expected of him. Therefore, when Maria requires a high standard of the children, they feel obliged not to disappoint her, for her disappointment may return to them in the form of subtle changes of attitude: withheld love, declining affection, diminishing interest—all of those intangible areas of which the parent thinks the child is unaware.

The children, who had been protected by being educated at home, are sent away to boarding schools run by Sir Roderick's two sisters. Once at school, each child is thrown against older children, who add to their sense of inadequacy and act as goads to their need for success. The competitive children at school, no more monstrous than children at any school, maintain their high places through systematic cheating and gain congratulations for accomplishments that were expected of them. In their own eyes, they are doing no more than they are supposed to do.

Their experiences are the same; both are caught cheating, both are disgraced at school, and both return home at vacation guilt-stricken, humiliated, and ashamed, waiting for the knowledge of their actions to reach their parents. What makes it unbearable is that the owners of the schools are their aunts, and they must live with the very people whom they have cheated. The shadow of their guilt is present in their homes, present in every aspect of their lives. Truth is no longer of any consequence. Their childhood, their youthful aspirations, their own quest after personal goals— all these aspects of their individuality have been lost. They were expected to compete unnaturally, and now they find themselves awaiting punishment for having fulfilled their mother's expectations. The basic immorality is clear: the parent tries to gain personal status by bending his children to his will instead of letting them follow their own course.

What makes this a comic and not a tragic novel is the fact that the children themselves treat their cheating as normal behavior. Furthermore, the comedy gains momentum when the parents and the aunts accept the cheating as unfortunate but not serious, and they gossip about it as if it will have little bearing on their lives. In addition to their relative insouciance in this matter, the parents reveal striking things about themselves—Sir Roderick has fathered an illegitimate son who works as a manservant in the home, and Maria has deceived everyone about earrings she had sold to gain money. These revelations place the parents on the same level with the children; nearly everyone in the household turns out to have been a cheat.

The burden that Sir Roderick and Maria have placed on the children is humorously dismissed by Oliver, Sir Roderick's son by his first wife:

> Children are always reproached for doing what we do ourselves.
> What else could they be reproached for? They must have some
> bringing up, and that consists of reproach. A term as a school-
> master shows you that. And without it they would yield too much
> to their instincts.

And the children themselves ponder the situation, ruing that they ever went to school:

Of course it is a pity. No one is in any doubt. Now we think Mother is odd and shabby; and Father is simple; and Miss Petticoat [their governess] is on the level of matrons; and none of them is different from what they were. And they see us as children who would get things by cheating, if they could. They do not think of us in the same way. And that is hardly an enrichment of our family life.

All this chaos has resulted from sending the two children away to school. In the home they might have survived without difficulty, for there nothing was expected of them; as soon, however, as they were sent out into the world, for which they were entirely unprepared, they compromised their aspirations, although not tragically. As much as Ibsen, Miss Compton-Burnett accepts that the sins of the parents are visited upon the children, even though, like Molière, she has turned melodramatic tragedy into the stuff of "serious farce."

The basic conflict is worked out, then, in terms of the two worlds. The home has provided the children with no resources for living outside it, and as soon as they must manage alone, they capitulate to the worst part of their natures. They struggle to survive at the lowest level of their instincts; by cheating, lying, and deceiving, they have assumed the values of the world. When we view this novel against the background of Miss Compton-Burnett's others, we can see its trenchant humor: the home itself in most of her novels destroys, but even at its worst it provides a framework for behavior. Her characters, children as well as adults, are trapped. In the home, they remain semi-developed, immature, clinging, and protected, but at least alive; outside, where the wicked world awaits them with an entirely different set of values, they can hope for no solace whatsoever. The conflict cannot easily be resolved: the children can stay at home where the parents determine all courses of action and crush all spirit, or go out into the world where in different terms virtually the same occurs. To be caught between the two worlds, as Clemence and Sefton are, suggests humor, but of the grim sort that characterizes all of Miss Compton-Burnett's novels.

As her characters soon discover, life is destructive no matter how it is conceived; this is the one central truth that runs through Ivy Compton-Burnett's work, from her first mature work, *Pastors and Masters* (1925), to her most recent, *A Heritage and Its History* (1959). In her first novel, we meet several people of little or no accomplishment who think themselves extraordinary figures of great personal achievement. Their basic hypocrisy is immediately established, and in their way they are humorous monsters, deceiving themselves as to what they are and deceiving, or trying to deceive, everyone they meet, including each other. This is the chief pattern which runs through her chronicle of late-Victorian England, a chronicle that catches much of the worst that people can say and do. And yet behind their monstrous motivation and evil intentions, there is an energy that enables them to survive and to maintain the kind of strength that most characters in fiction no longer have. Miss Compton-Burnett's characters avoid nothing in order to assert themselves, and while they lack self-knowledge of a profound sort, they do know enough about life to recognize that to relent is to give themselves over to other equally monstrous people. They fight for what they are and for what they want with a tenacity that marks them as people for whom nothing has come cheaply. In their struggles, they revert to primitive passions, and for a novelist to bring back the primitive in a late-Victorian character indicates a special talent for the comic.

Accident and Purpose: "Bad Form" in D. H. Lawrence's Fiction

Robert Kiely

Though D. H. Lawrence is accepted as one of the major English writers of the twentieth century, he is still regarded, except by his most loyal defenders, as an author for whom we must make apologies. There is wisdom and profound insight, but there are also ideas that are naive and illiberal. There are deft economies of detail and powerfully realized characterizations, but there are also tedious pages of repetitious exposition. Most of Lawrence's admirers have learned to excuse the unattractive ideas and language as lapses in the work of an unruly genius. Some of his detractors have argued that the faults are not incidental but rather symptoms of an essentially crude mentality.

Lawrence probably would have preferred the latter judgment to the former, since he was not one for half measures or polite evasions. Though he was not always a consistent thinker, he admired integrity. He wanted "wholeness," and though he did not readily accept conventional explanations, he believed in a universal coherence of things and thought that it was the business of human beings to discover the connections within themselves and with others. Despite his well-known dislike of Freud, he too thought that "slips of the tongue" and sporadic departures from ordinary behavior were meaningful expressions of the whole personality.

Certainly, Lawrence without the lapses would not be Lawrence. His sins against "good form" and "straight thinking," however we may explain them, are, unless we reedit his books, part of his literary legacy. In exploring his own fictional characters, he himself hardly overlooks or deemphasizes the rough spots. On the contrary, much of what we admire in him is his ability to reveal precisely those thoughts, actions, and traits often discounted by other writers as significant indicators of character.

My question is not "How can we forgive this gifted eccentric?" but

From *D. H. Lawrence: A Centenary Consideration.* © 1985 by Cornell University Press.

rather "How was what he did a necessary part of what he was trying to do?" Lawrence warns his readers to trust the tale, not the teller. But in exercising discretion with regard to the intentional fallacy, critics have not always been fair to Lawrence. What is self-conscious in Joyce and Eliot, for example, is usually treated as the ultimate in sophisticated modernism. These are writers who knew what they wanted to do and did it. The image of Lawrence as spontaneous to the point of carelessness has too often overshadowed his own typically modern tendency to reflect on the nature of his art.

Of course, Lawrence's manner of writing criticism no less than his manner of writing fiction has created this image. Lawrence has not simply been the victim of obtuse critics. To a large extent, he is the author of his own reputation. Joyce never fails to remind us of the discipline—classical and Ignatian—of his vocation as an artist. Lawrence, on the contrary, pictures himself as a sloppy, loud-mouthed intruder, not a literary man himself, certainly not restrained or careful about what he says, one who enjoys smashing things and shocking people.

Sometimes in his critical writing, Lawrence sounds as though he were opposed to all received forms of art and literature. "The moment man became aware of himself he made a picture of himself, and began to live from the picture. . . . If we could once get into our heads . . . that we are *not* the picture, and the picture is not what we are, then we might lay a new hold on life. For the picture is really the death, and certainly the neurosis, of us all." Elsewhere he refers to art as a "tomb" inside which mankind is trapped like a corpse. The great need is to "break the present great picture." Such talk conjures up images of hammers smashing pianos, of a new breed of "artists" able to express themselves only through their hatred of the inherited picture.

But Lawrence was not that kind of artist. Despite his anger and rebelliousness, his books represent much less of an assault on the tradition than those of contemporaries such as Stein, Pound, or Joyce. Furthermore, he was not really that kind of critic either. As one reads on in his essays, the source of his irritation becomes more clearly and narrowly defined. In a suggestive essay on Thomas Mann, Lawrence makes it plain that he mistrusts not art but a certain conception of form.

Form, as he finds it in Mann, is "like logic," impersonal, abstract, definite, and externally imposed. In recalling *Death in Venice*, Lawrence considers the morbidity of the theme in perfect keeping with the too carefully schematized narrative, the neatly placed symbols, the unswerving logic of the protagonist's motivation. These strict patternings have a death hold on art, according to Lawrence, not simply because they impose severe limits on its range but because they represent a spiritual malaise. "This craving for form is the outcome, not of artistic conscience, but of a certain attitude to life." He compares Mann with Pope and Flaubert, resorting to aesthetic absolutes because of their distaste for physical life, seeking invented perfections as alternatives to a life that fills them with loathing.

The picture that Lawrence wishes to smash is not only one of Victorian prudery and sentimentality but the more modern and to him even more deadly one of world-weary despair and self-hatred. He was never so naive as to believe that an artist could proceed without design, but he thought that when design became an end in itself, inflexible and absolute, it undermined the highest purpose of art and cast a shadow over life. In his discussion of the principles of Law and Love in the essay on Thomas Hardy, he expresses his belief that art, like morality, must continually seek a balance between stability and motion, order and change. He singles out Shelley's "To a Skylark" as a successful representation of "conflict contained within a reconciliation," in which the poet creates a vital tension between the bird as creature and pure spirit.

There is no doubt that Lawrence's views of organic form and the fluidity of symbolic language owe much to the ideas and practices of the English Romantic poets. But he was much more than a Romantic willing to deal more frankly with "up-to-date" subject matter. His versions of the "conflict" between order and change have an intensity, an urgency touched by Shelley and Blake but stressed and sustained in a fashion unique to him and his century. For Lawrence, as for many of his contemporaries, life seemed peculiarly threatened by the attitudes and events of the early twentieth century. His use of terms such as "adventurer" or "explorer" to describe the modern artist sound overblown, but he did believe that the situation was desperate enough to require risks. Moving into unknown territories seemed infinitely better than staying where you were.

Despite the vigor with which he stated his critical opinions, Lawrence, like Eliot and Joyce, believed that the work of art must exist and must be considered separately from the personality and prejudices of the artist. He reserves some of his highest critical praise for Cézanne and, in doing so, moves beyond the Romantics and locates himself in the modern world: "Cézanne's apples are a real attempt to let the apple exist in its own separate entity, without transfusing it with personal emotion. Cézanne's great effort was, as it were, to shove the apple away from him, and let it live of itself."

Lawrence's characterization of Cézanne's artistic effort sounds so much like noninterference that it raises questions about the motivation of the artist or writer. Why paint or write at all if the best that can be done is to let things "live of themselves?" The simplest way to do that, it would seem, is to leave the apples to their own devices, to let nature alone. But though Lawrence admired Cézanne's attempt to withhold "personal emotion" from the objects of his art, he did not equate this attitude with a relinquishing of contact. The best art for Lawrence and what he seemed to want to attain in his own writing was a relationship with the natural world that was unpossessive, balancing intimacy with the familiar and reverence for that which is unalterably separate.

Like many of his modernist contemporaries, Lawrence frequently reveals his preoccupation with art in his creative work. But unlike James, Eliot, Woolf, Pound, and Joyce, he rarely seems at his best when doing so.

For the more he seems bent on naturalizing art, on eliminating personal emotion and setting nature free, the more he seems to intrude and destroy the balance. Few readers can fail to notice the disparity between Lawrence's "natural" artistry and his fevered attempts to persuade us that he can remove all artifice from art and batter it back into the earth. His successful books rarely resemble the notions about art or works of art described in them. Paul Morel's comments about his painting ("as if I'd painted the shimmering protoplasm in the leaves . . . and not the stiffness of the shape") may be "pure" Lawrence, but they are not especially accurate reflections of the structure or quality of *Sons and Lovers*, which Virginia Woolf, among many others, praised for its craftsmanship and clarity of form.

In two fascinating but highly flawed novels—*The Lost Girl* and *Aaron's Rod*—promising narratives go disastrously out of control when Lawrence allows his preoccupation with the naturalization of art to become an obsession. *The Lost Girl* begins as an imitation of Arnold Bennett, a brilliant imitation full of an energy unique to Lawrence. The stifling atmosphere of a Midlands town and the frustrations of the young heroine are vividly realized until various troupes of visiting performers appear on the stage of the local theater and provide Lawrence with the opportunity to assail his heroine and reader with the hypnotic attractions of art and sexuality all rolled up into one confusing "whole." One of the heroine's first awakenings comes when she sees a tattooed Japanese appear on stage: "She wished she could jump across the distance. Particularly with the Jap, who was almost quite naked, but clothed with the most exquisite tattooing. Never would she forget the eagle that flew with terrible spread wings between his shoulders, or the strange mazy pattern that netted the roundness of his buttocks."

As an isolated instance of inhibition thawed by the exposure to flesh "clothed" by a design, this is pardonable. But the tattooed "Jap" is only a preamble. Another troupe appears from the continent ready to dress up as American Indians and dance about the stage. When the heroine falls in love with a handsome Italian, the entire course of her life and the novel changes. Significantly, it is when she first sees him in costume, his face "wonderfully and terribly painted," that she is deeply and irreversibly moved. Along with his obvious relish in the encounter between a kind of bohemian primitivism and the stuffy inhabitants of the Midlands English town, Lawrence has a more complicated interest in the situation he has created. He is intrigued by the notion of the imprinted skin, the flesh as canvas or page. The foreignness of the imprinted figures betrays a touch of Edwardian decadence, but it also suggests the possibility of a nonverbal language, of powerful systems of communication not dependent on a common vocabulary.

The difficulty we have in taking Lawrence's tattooed man and masquerade Indians seriously stems not, as is often assumed, from their inherent "vulgarity." Shakespeare and Dickens made powerful use of amateur theatricals; circuses and clowns have often been employed as effective symbols of art and artists. However, in *The Lost Girl*, it is not only the heroine but the author who seems to wish to "jump across the distance" between art and nature. It is partly because the players in *Hamlet* make so little claim to credibility that they astonish us and the king with the "truth" of their performance. As Lawrence's perspective converges more and more completely with that of his heroine and she becomes more and more submerged in the attractions of the imprinted male body, the narrative swerves out of control. By trying to force a union of design and flesh, Lawrence succeeds in reminding us of their disparity. We resist the equation and can only watch with morbid curiosity as author and heroine pursue the decorated physique in search of a code but instead become lost in a muddle.

Aaron's Rod provides another illustration of Lawrence's impulse to naturalize art. It too is an odd combination of promising starts and unresolved muddles. The piccolo of the musician hero is so often likened to a flower or branch of a tree that the reader is prevented from inventing associations that a freer, less insistent use of metaphor invites. The phallic identification is even more dominant. When Aaron plays his flute for a woman with whom he has an affair, the music is described as a "pure male voice"; when the affair comes to an end, his flute is broken, his sense of purpose gone. Lawrence chooses not to make clear whether Aaron's failure is musical or sexual because he seems to want the reader to see them as the same, or at least as so closely meshed as to be inseparable. Once again, we rebel at the forced connection. The narrative collapses under the weight of abstract theories, which Lawrence always said were the death of art.

It is tempting merely to ridicule or apologize for these and similar "lapses" in Lawrence's fiction. But it is worth remembering that the failures in these books are not deviations from some main Lawrentian current; they are parts of that current. In both *The Lost Girl* and *Aaron's Rod*, Lawrence is trying to rescue art from the moral and formal confines of the middle class. The seamy theatrics of the one and the pagan pipe of the other, whether or not convincing, are consistent with Lawrence's refusal to see art as polite and mildly uplifting entertainment. He always believed, as writers of his generation had good reason to believe, that respectability and creativity were inimical. But Lawrence's social fervor was never distinct from his urgent sense of individual need. Above all else, he wanted an art that could reestablish contact between human beings, their own nature, and that of the living world.

Even in his most successful fiction, Lawrence never gave up the desire to "jump across the distance" between the self, isolated by experience, intelligence, and conscience, and the completeness of unreflective nature. The most memorable chapters in *Women in Love*, for example, bring powerful intensity to individual efforts to conquer isolation through natural contact: Gerald breaking the horse; Hermione attacking Birkin with a paperweight; Gudrun dancing before the bullocks; Ursula and Birkin coming together in the fields; Gerald and Birkin wrestling; Birkin dashing stones at the moon's reflection. Though there are survivors, the drowning of the newlyweds and Gerald's death in the snow seem inevitable consequences of relationships with nature that are unrelentingly aggressive and competitive. The wish for harmony appears to be confused with the will to dominate. That, of course, is a major theme of the novel, as it is of all of Lawrence's work. But, as has often been noted, this is not only Lawrence's main theme but also one of his problems as a writer. He too often "jumps across the distance" and wrestles his subject to the death.

Yet there is another crucially important side to Lawrence, as much a hallmark of his genius as his notorious and passionate intensity. There is a Lawrence that lets the gaps between man and nature be, an ironical, humorous, relaxed though never resigned Lawrence, who *does not insist on anything*. Nowhere is this side more effectively in evidence than in *Women in Love*. For among the vividly memorable chapters are others, quieter, less graphic, a bit rambling, without which the novel could not stand and which the reader cannot afford to forget.

Three such chapters—"Shortlands," "Sketch-Book," and "A Chair"—contain structural and thematic elements in common, which at the same time link them to the other chapters of the novel and set them apart from them. Most significantly in this book of large problems and strong wills, each of these chapter dramatizes a small "mistake," a trivial accident surrounded by implications of psychological intention. Equally surprising, given the potent and rather solemn symbolism of the "strong" chapters, is the fact that each of these chapters introduces an ordinary object—a hat, a sketch, a chair—momentarily made meaningful by the characters and then abruptly released from imposed significance. Each chapter also introduces a familiar activity—a wedding reception, sketching, buying furniture—the conventional course of which is interrupted, challenged, defamiliarized. In each there is a character or several characters who seem out of place but who nonetheless have a magnetic attraction for one of the main characters. The dialogue, even more than is usual in Lawrence, tends to the philosophical and beyond, to a kind of parody of philosophical inquiry in which all questions seem to be asked as if for the first time. None of these chapters concludes with an air of finality. On the contrary, the situations and dialogues they introduce invariably drift into irresolution.

In chapter 2, "Shortlands," the wedding reception of a conventionally happy and well-matched young couple serves as the context for unpremeditated and socially uncategorizable "pairings." Birkin, the outsider, feels unaccountably attracted by old Mrs. Crich, a stranger in her own house, and by her stolid son, Gerald:

> Suddenly Mrs. Crich came noiselessly into the room, peering about with her strong, clear face. She was still wearing her hat. . . .
>   "What is it, mother?" said Gerald.
>   "Nothing, nothing!" she answered vaguely. And she went straight towards Birkin. . . .

"How do you do, Mr. Birkin," she said in her low voice, that seemed to take no count of her guests. . . . "I don't know half the people here."

"And you don't like strangers?" laughed Birkin. "I myself can never see why one should take account of people, just because they happen to be in the room . . .: why *should* I know they are there?"

"Why indeed, why indeed!" said Mrs. Crich, in her low tense voice. "Except that they *are* there. I don't know people whom I find in the house. The children introduce them to me. . . . I am no further. What has Mr. So-and-so to do with his own name?— and what have I to do with either him or his name?"

She looked up at Birkin. She startled him. He was flattered. . . . He noticed . . . how her hair looped in slack, slovenly strands over her rather beautiful ears, which were not quite clean. Neither was her neck perfectly clean. Even in that he seemed to belong to her, rather than to the rest of the company, though . . . he was always well washed . . . he and the elderly, estranged woman were conferring together like traitors.

When Birkin suggests that most other people do not exist, Mrs. Crich punctures his airy assertion:

"But we don't imagine them," she said sharply.

"There's nothing to imagine, that's why they don't exist."

"Well," she said, "I would hardly go as far as that. There they are, whether they exist or no. It doesn't rest with me to decide on their existence. I only know that I can't be expected to take count of them all."

On the way to the dining room, one of the Crich daughters suggests, with some embarrassment, that her mother, as hostess in her own house, should remove her hat. Whether the guests have noticed the social impropriety is not mentioned, but within a few moments Lawrence introduces an exchange in which the word "hat" accumulates and sheds meaning. Gerald begins in earnest:

"If I go and take a man's hat from off his head, that hat becomes a symbol of that man's liberty. . . ."

Hermione was nonplussed. . . . "But that way of arguing by imaginary instances is not supposed to be genuine, is it? A man does *not* come and take my hat from off my head, does he?"

"Only because the law prevents him," said Gerald.

"Not only," said Birkin. "Ninety-nine men out of a hundred don't want my hat."

"That's a matter of opinion," said Gerald.

"Or the hat," laughed the bridegroom.

When pressed about what she would do if someone did try to take her hat, Hermione shifts the mood abruptly. "Probably I should kill him." Trying to return to a lighter, more bantering tone, Birkin calls Gerald's nationalism "old hat" and the conversation is broken off by the call for toasts:

> Birkin, thinking about race or national death, watched his glass being filled with champagne. . . . Feeling a sudden thirst at the sight of the fresh wine, Birkin drank up his glass. A queer little tension in the room roused him. He felt a sharp constraint.
>
> "Did I do it by accident, or on purpose?" he asked himself. And he decided that, according to the vulgar phrase, he had done it "accidentally on purpose."

The chapter concludes with an "inconsequential" dialogue between Birkin and Gerald. As with Birkin and Mrs. Crich, there is an undercurrent of attraction that neither understands. And there is an unmistakable irony in the fact that, for the world that celebrates weddings and worries about when to put on and take off hats, such attractions have no significance. Indeed, they might as well not exist.

The entire chapter, a bit slack and meandering on first reading, seems to resemble those chapters in long Victorian novels that accomplish certain necessary business but are not otherwise interesting or important. Particular characters and situations are brought to the reader's attention, background information is provided, and a credible time lapse is provided between the more dramatic moments. On closer reading, however, the chapter is not at all loose in construction, nor does it function largely as filler for the plot. Indeed, the main narrative line of the novel could survive very well without it. Nor is this chapter merely a relief from some of the intensities of the novel as a whole. Rather it is an alternative to them and a comment on them. The best-laid human plans—whether for weddings or novels—are subjected to odd quirks of chance; encounters with no future, debates without bearings, words adrift between high symbolism and commonplace literality. The chapter itself seems to be the author's purposeful "accident," the exposure of his own masterly design to contradictory elements.

What the characters discuss and enact refers as much to the creative process as it does to the various human relationships that are the subject of the novel. The debates about true existence—whether of the people in the room or of British rights—mean, for the artist, as for Mrs. Crich, whether or not one "takes account" of them. The writer brings into existence what he notices, and he notices, according to the logic of this chapter, not always what makes a "good story" or satisfying moral but what attracts him. The social or ethical justification for the attraction may or may not be clear, but for Lawrence, to ignore it is to let the work of art die. Yet in "taking account" of certain things, it is inevitable that the artist will risk making "too much" of them, like the characters who force too much weight on the poor old hat until it collapses and reasserts its *insignificance*. The author who would be honest and produce a vital work of art must move with a particular kind of alertness. He must exercise his judgment and will in conceiving a plan and, at the same time, must remain sufficiently passive to be open to the unexpected interventions that seem to threaten the plan but in fact keep it alive.

Chapter 10, "Sketch-Book," opens with a sensual description of the unmistakably phallic waterplants being painted by Gudrun. There is at first no indication of irony in these descriptions, no indication that Lawrence is up to anything other than his characteristic form of sexual symbolism. Suddenly a rowboat with two figures in it appears on the lake. It is Gerald and Hermione, who are composing another kind of picture; he in white, she with a Japanese parasol look, at a distance, like the figures in a Romantic idyll. But as the gap between Gudrun and the boat narrows, the hazy illusion is pierced by the emotions of each character reacting with unexpected violence to a seemingly trivial meeting. At first, Hermione insists on approaching Gudrun because it seems daring to show an interest in someone of her class. Gerald has no interest in her, and Gudrun is annoyed by the interruption, "for she always hated to have her unfinished work exposed."

However, when Hermione insists, Gudrun hands her sketch over to be inspected. The real "event" that occurs during this forced encounter between the two women is a wordless but powerful current of attraction between Gudrun and Gerald. Gudrun's phallic imagination is transferred from the water plants to Gerald. When the boat begins to drift, "he lifted the oar to bring it back. And the exquisite pleasure of slowly arresting the boat, in the heavy-soft wave, was complete as a swoon." The paragraph in which this attraction occurs begins with Gudrun's point of view ("Gudrun was aware of his body"), but "the exquisite pleasure" is a mutual one. It forms a link of communication in which Hermione has no part. Her awareness of exclusion infuriates her and when Gerald asks to see the sketch, there is an "accident":

> A little shock, a storm of revulsion against him, shook Hermione unconsciously. She released the book when he had not properly got it, and it tumbled against the side of the boat and bounced into the water.
>
> "There!" sang Hermione, with a strange ring of malevolent victory. "I'm so sorry, so awfully sorry. Can't you get it, Gerald?"

As Gerald reaches into the water to retrieve the book, he realizes that "his position is ridiculous." Indeed, the entire episode hovers between heavy sensuality and ludicrous slapstick. It is important to say that the wavering mood is not the result of narrative ineptitude but appears to be very much part of the pattern of the purposeful accident by which the solemnity and coherence of the primary narrative design are temporarily broken. As in the wedding reception, the social niceties appear particularly thin in comparision with the strong undertones of feeling. As Hermione continues to repeat her apologies, words seem less and less capable of reflecting the truth of the situation. Yet even this assumption is broken when Gudrun speaks out: " 'I assure you,' said Gudrun, with cutting distinctness, 'the drawings are quite as good as ever they were, for my purpose. I want them only for reference.' "

Hermione, who exerts her will in trying to convert art as well as sexual emotion into social categories, is defeated by Gudrun's notion of her art as personal and "referential." Hermione's purposeful "accident," her little joke at the expense of Gudrun, plays right to an aesthetic attitude that she cannot understand. The unfinished sketch "spoiled" by water is also an emblem of art immersed in nature (concrete reality untransformed by the ordering imagination) and not, according to some views, the worse for it. If the drifts and currents of nature are not permitted now and then to "spoil" the perfect plan of the artist, the result will be neat but, in Lawrence's terminology, "decadent," without life. As Gerald rows away absentmindedly, watching Gudrun with her wet sketchbook, the boat drifts off course and Hermione is more furious than ever.

As with the hat in the discussion at the wedding reception, Lawrence uses the sketchbook for a variety of purposes, including as an occasion to reflect on the process of symbol making. Whereas the debate in "Shortlands" is a satire on inflated political rhetoric, Gudrun's view of her sketchbook comes close to Lawrence's theories of art. He does not undermine these theories with mockery but illustrates aspects of them and gives them life. In order to function effectively in a symbolic pattern, objects must be allowed their own reality. This seems Lawrence's meaning when he says that Cézanne "shoves the apple away from him." For Lawrence, the artist does not "convert" reality to his own purposes without recognizing the tenuousness of that process in the face of the intractability and waywardness of things. Symbols may fly as long as matter is not deprived of gravity.

As in chapter 10, "Sketch-Book," an object with symbolic possibilities is the central figure of chapter 26, "A Chair." Ursula and Birkin are browsing in an open market when they come upon a patched-up antique chair of elegant proportions. The classically harmonious design, associated with Jane Austen's England, pleases the couple, and there is no indication from the narrative that Lawrence does not share their admiration for its "fine delicacy." Impulsively, the couple buys the chair, and almost immediately it becomes in their eyes something more than the well-designed "arm-chair of simple wood" that had first attracted their attention.

The chair becomes a representative object, a sign of the past, of materialism, of the accumulation of ideas and things that point to a "settling down" that Birkin particularly wishes to resist. They decide that they have made a "mistake" in buying the chair. But like the earlier "accidents," this one has its purpose. As Birkin tries to explain his desire to leave certain aspects of his life unsettled, he resorts to an artistic analogy: "You have to be like Rodin, Michelangelo, and leave a piece of raw rock unfinished to your figure. You must leave your surroundings sketchy, unfinished, so that you are never contained, never confined, never dominated from the outside."

The analogy brings the reader back to the chair, whose perfect finish is "spoiled" by a poor attempt to repair a break: " 'It was once,' said Birkin, 'gilded—and it had a cane seat. Somebody has nailed this wooden seat in. . . . It is the fine unity of the lines that is so attractive. . . . But of course the wooden seat is wrong. . . . I like it though.' "

In the context of Birkin's philosophy and his reference to Rodin and Michelangelo, the chair assumes another kind of significance. Its attraction resides partly in its broken symmetry, since its perfect lines appear to have an effect similar to the careful plans of a neatly arranged life. Both have their attractions, but completeness, their most apparent virtue, is a trap. The claim to perfect harmony is confining to the spirit and is, for Lawrence, a false representation of reality. The greatest artistic masterpieces pay homage to nature by acknowledging their own defects. Of course, as Lawrence realized, the "defect" itself can quickly be imitated until it too is absorbed into conventional notions of harmony. Nothing is more mannered than poor copies of Rodin, Michelangelo and, for that matter, Lawrence. The artist's "purposeful accident" is as much a part of his peculiar genius as his most graceful and self-contained designs.

Though the impulsive act itself cannot be undone, Lawrence manages to keep its significance alive without attaching it neatly to a linear chain of events in his plot. One of his major objections to Hardy was his habit of stringing fatal consequences onto chance events. Such carefully determined pessimism, he felt, was as untrue to life as its sentimental opposite. In the introduction to *Women in Love*, he wrote: "Fate dictated from outside, from theory or circumstance, is a false fate." Lawrence believed that individuals could change the direction of their lives, that accidents could be meaningful without being fatal.

It is interesting that a writer who studied Hardy with such care and obviously learned much from him does not often choose to introduce nature into his fiction by means of the external "acts of God." There are mining accidents in *Sons and Lovers* and floods in *The Rainbow*, but when lightning strikes a Lawrence character, it is much more likely to strike from within. Obsessive, violent, or ecstatic passions well up inside his characters, causing unexpected behavior. When external nature seems to duplicate their internal state, the effect is not really that of the pathetic fallacy, a cosmic echo, but rather a blurring of the boundaries between the individual and the world.

Every internal tremor does not signal an earthquake, however. The impulsive actions of Lawrence's characters *may* be bursting with serious consequences; then again, they may not. An even greater departure from Hardy is represented by those moments in Lawrence when a chance encounter or "fatal" mistake is raised to high symbolic potential and is then abruptly deflated.

Ursula and Birkin decide to give the chair to a young couple whom they do not know but have observed browsing at the market. Their attitude toward the couple is at first a mixture of pity and condescension; they are lower class, and the woman, not yet a wife, is pregnant. Suddenly, to her surprise, Ursula finds herself attracted to the young man. He disarms her by stripping the chair of any special meaning and treating it as a chair, which Birkin cannot do: " 'Ave a sit in it, you'll wish you'd kept it,' said the young man. Ursula promptly sat down in the middle of the marketplace. 'Awfully comfortable,' she said. 'But rather hard. You try it.' "

The mild flirtation leads nowhere. Ursula does not run off with the young man, and Birkin hardly notices the undercurrent. But the chair has been returned to its unsymbolic state, and Ursula's character is shown to have its own built-in resistance to finality. The chapter concludes, foreshadowing the end of the novel, with a discussion between Ursula and Birkin about his seeming need for Gerald's love. On this subject, even Birkin has no answers. "His face was full of real perplexity. . . . 'It's the problem I can't solve.' "

The recurrence of certain patterns in these three chapters suggests a strong impulse in Lawrence's narrative imagination. While disrupting some structures, he is building and reinforcing others. He does not obliterate familiar forms. Each of these episodes, like most of those in his fiction, contains easily recognizable elements of social and literary convention. But he does open up familiar forms, exposes them to uncertainty, removes their "finish," and thereby brings them closer to reality as he conceives of it. For Lawrence, reality was not chaotic, but neither was it in any of its aspects completely knowable. Thus, the most honest artist had to allow room for the "unplanned" in his plan.

To try to overcome this contradiction by means of sheer rhetorical willpower is, as in the examples from *The Lost Girl* and *Aaron's Rod*, to destroy both the conventional coherences and the liberating effect of natural spontaneity. The problem with Lawrence's weaker fiction is not mere sloppiness but a forced, strident, insistent sloppiness. The "purposeful accident" becomes a long disaster, the justification for which too often takes on the duration and tone of a crusade. The "accidents" in *Women in Love*, by contrast, are beautifully poised between playfulness and high seriousness, as they are between literal objectivity and symbolism. The "quiet" chapters are unfinished in the sense that they end with inconclusive encounters or dialogues and because throughout they dramatize an endless dialectic on the definitions of art and reality.

Lawrence does not force a union between the two in *Women in Love* without at the same time showing his awareness of the irony or danger of doing so. The hat, the sketch-book, and the chair are never allowed to "take leave of themselves" once and for all, as Aaron's rod does. Though he does not acknowledge clear boundaries between art and reality, Lawrence does in *Women in Love* treat them as different from each other. The thing and the thing perceived (and named) are not the same. Yet he does not accept the kind of distinction that he attributes to Flaubert and Mann: that art is mostly will, and nature random chance. Lawrence believed that nature has design, whether or not mankind can understand it, and that, in allowing "accident" to enter in, the writer can create an art that imitates a design larger, deeper, than he himself or any of his characters can fully know.

There is no doubt that Lawrence could pursue spontaneity with a zeal so deliberate as to scare the quarry. But it is worth noting that he could also laugh at the chase, showing, despite Eliot, that he had a sense of humor and that he was not working in the dark. Lawrence's apparent alternation between loosening and tightening of control throughout *Women in Love*, the rhythm he establishes between the symbolic, sharply visual, emotionally intense chapters and those of a more meandering, discursive, humorous character, produces a symphonic variety of near discords working always toward unexpected resolutions.

The meeting with Loerke and Leitner in the Alps near the novel's end is not an accident in the sense that has been discussed thus far. But it is an odd, unexpected, seemingly gratuitous introduction of at least one important character so late in the narrative as to appear an afterthought. The malicious, implike Loerke seems an excuse for Lawrence to enter into a satiric diatribe against a conception of art particularly distasteful to him. In the midst of the agonizing relationship of Gerald and Gudrun and the forced gaiety of the Alpine holiday, Lawrence's timing and focus at first seem questionable. Why such long discussions of art with an obsessive German throughout a fatal idyll of lovers?

In the first place, the subject of art in both the "quiet" and the more dramatic chapters is never completely absent from the narrative. Furthermore, in one form or another, Lawrence never ceases trying to search out ways in which art and love intersect. That is one of the major subjects of the novel. His characters, like Birkin and Ursula, either find a way to balance between design and passion, purpose and accident, or, like Gudrun and Gerald, they find themselves engaged in a struggle to the death. In Loerke, small, dark, cerebral, and dogmatic, Lawrence creates a Wagnerian emanation of Gerald's will, the will to order, dominate, annihilate. In his fair, "well-built," handsome young companion, Leitner, who dances with Gudrun, he creates the sensuous, unformed, potentially lovable Gerald who had appealed from the first to Birkin.

Gerald's unintegrated self is shown in the Loerke-Leitner projection to be a menacing, absurd grotesque. Yet Gudrun had once characterized one side of Gerald in terms that bear a striking resemblance to certain classical definitions of the artist, especially the narrative artist: "He had the faculty of making order out of confusion. Only let him grip hold of a situation, and he would bring to pass an inevitable conclusion." In Loerke, Lawrence shows a perverse and dehumanized version of this mentality stripped of class and sexual glamor. What Gerald comes to represent in social, political, and sexual terms, Loerke defends in art.

When Ursula is repelled by the "stiffness" of his sculpture of a horse, Loerke lashes out in a summary of everything that Lawrence hated about the theories of certain of his contemporaries:

> It is a work of art, it is a picture of nothing, of absolutely nothing. It has nothing to do with anything but itself, it has no relation with the everyday world of this and other, there is no connection between them, absolutely none, they are two different and distinct planes of existence, and to translate one into the other is worse than foolish, it is a darkening of all counsel, a making confusion everywhere.

It is the keeping of the "accidents" of feeling, intuition, and awe separate from the serious "purposes" of art, business, politics, and human relationships that Lawrence saw as among the central tragedies of his time. And it is precisely a "translation" from one plane to another, a "darkening of all counsel," a "making confusion everywhere" that he attempted as a remedy. When he tried to turn the process into a dogma, he killed it. But the "purposeful accidents" in *Women in Love* are among the many examples of extraordinary poise, wit, and suppleness with which he managed to keep this daring and impossible program alive.

It is tempting to reverse Gudrun's description of Gerald to characterize Lawrence's image of himself as an artist: "He had the faculty of making confusion out of order. Only let him grip hold of a situation, and he would disrupt the inevitable conclusion." But readers of Lawrence will not be fully satisfied with this picture, for without the ordering genius, the disruptive demon has nothing to do. As the narrative of *Women in Love* persistently implies, Birkin needs Gerald as badly as Gerald needs Birkin.

Women in Love:
D. H. Lawrence's Judgment Book

Maria DiBattista

It was Frieda Lawrence who wanted the sequel to *The Rainbow* entitled *Dies Irae*, the Days of Wrath, the Final Days. Lawrence preferred the less apocalyptically charged *Women in Love*. Frieda's suggestion preserved for Lawrence's proposed "double" novel the grace of symmetry: Genesis and Apocalypse, the total history of Creation recapitulated and reinterpreted in modern times. *The Rainbow* was a novel chronicling the creation of the first woman in "the Essential Days"; *Women in Love* actually concerns the destiny of the last men in the final days: the death of Gerald Crich, the Nietzschean captain of industry; and the eclipse, whether temporary or terminal, of Rupert Birkin, the artist as social prophet and sage.

As a novelist and polemicist of the final days, Lawrence always insists, as he does in "Fantasia of the Unconscious," that he is merely "trying to stammer out the first terms of a forgotten knowledge." For him, the first terms are always the primary principles of a metaphysic that is both comprehended and lived: "Men live and see according to some gradually developing and gradually withering vision. This vision exists also as a dynamic idea or metaphysics — exists first as such. Then it is unfolded into life and art. Our vision, our belief, our metaphysic is wearing woefully thin, and the art is wearing absolutely threadbare. We have no future; neither for our hopes nor our aims nor our art." In Lawrence's view, the dependency of art on a metaphysic, its secondariness before the larger forms of an authentic cosmology, is compensated by art's transparency as the expressive medium for an unknown time, what Lawrence calls the "next future," an odd and apparently redundant locution that testifies to the Lawrentian belief that the future is what succeeds the present yet remains unconditioned by it. The present always contains the possibility of a "renewed chaos" from which emerges "the strangeness and rainbow-change of ever-

From *D. H. Lawrence: A Centenary Consideration*. © 1985 by Cornell University Press.

renewed creative civilisations." As a symbolic object, the rainbow recommends itself as a model of historical development because it possesses both the aura of natural phenomena—hence its familiar and reassuring presence in the world's landscapes—and the strangeness of a numinous object invested with the prestige and power of the sacred, a promissory sign of the eternal word keeping faith with the world of time.

However, the "earth's new architecture" announced in *The Rainbow*'s final transformative vision of "a world built up in a living fabric of Truth, fitting to the over-arching heaven" is only experienced through the visionary ecstasies of the redeemed female. The New Eve always precedes the newly awakened Adam into a paradise of fulfilled desire; the Old Adam, that typological and typical Lawrentian hero, dies belatedly, if at all. Men in *The Rainbow*, as in *Women in Love*, are the preservers of the past; they are the lovers of the Gothic "which always asserted the broken desire of mankind," abjuring the spectacle of "Absolute Beauty." Most of Lawrence's men are the artists of the elegiac for whom "a temple is never perfectly a temple, till it was ruined." For such men, the sublime is ineluctably connected with the sites of the ruined past.

The Rainbow thus adumbrates the sexual dialectic that informs the struggle for imaginative mastery in its successor fiction. But unlike Lawrence's generational novel, *Women in Love* places its human subjects against a backdrop largely absent from *The Rainbow*, the "great retrogression" of mankind into a "process of active corruption." Lawrence insists on distinguishing between the degenerate metaphysic that precipitates the historical decline of the West and his own resurgent sexual symbolism that issues from this renewed chaos born of decay. From the opening chapter of *The Rainbow* through the last major polemic of his career, *Apocalypse*, Lawrence argues, both as a predicate of his metaphysic and as a structure of his fiction that, "when there is a touch of true symbolism, it is not of the nature of a ruin or a remains embedded in the present structure, it is rather an archaic reminiscence" [*Apocalypse*]. Finally, it is Lawrence's generic memory that determines the forgotten knowledge his novels seek to revive and communicate. And it is his controversial genius that traces all inherited symbolic codes to their origin in sexual difference.

II

The first terms of a forgotten knowledge are summarily recalled in the Foreword to *Women in Love*, where Lawrence announces the absolute equality of desire and destiny as coefficients in the balanced equation of creation. The business of the novelist is to express the true fate: "The creative, spontaneous soul sends forth its promptings of desire and aspiration in us. These promptings are our true fate, which is our business to fulfil. A fate dictated from outside, from theory or from circumstance, is a false fate." In his "Study of Thomas Hardy," Lawrence had complained that the novels of the great metaphysical realists Hardy and Tolstoy projected a false rather than a true image of fate by confusing the individual's war against society with the individual's struggle with God. The novels of classical realism are predicated on a false judgment and a fatal imagining of necessity "where transgression against the social code is made to bring destruction, as though the social code worked our irrevocable fate." Exhaustive criticism of Hardy's characters, Lawrence maintained, "would fill the Judgment book," a final accounting of life novelistically rendered. Unable to liberate themselves from "the greater idea of self-preservation, which is formulated in the State, in the whole modelling of the community," Hardy's heroes and heroines are doomed to perish in the wilderness: "This is the tragedy of Hardy, always the same: the tragedy of those who, more or less pioneers, have died in the wilderness, whither they had escaped for free action, after having left the walled security, and the comparative imprisonment, of the established convention."

Hardy's walled city is the novelistic space defined by the false fate dictated by theory (religious or biological determinism), or by circumstance (society in its practical and moral forms). The wilderness is the precarious open that designates the creative prodigalities of the eternal origin whose spontaneous activities always impress us as "the waste enormity of Nature." But waste, Blakean excess, is the principle that rules in nature and authorizes what Lawrence insists is the "greater morality" of unfathomed Nature. In the true Judgment Book, *Women in Love*, unfathomed Nature becomes the backdrop of the lesser morality play enacted in that walled city, the novel of manners (with its central plot—the double love stories of Birkin and Ursula, Gerald and Gudrun). It would take, as Lawrence well knew, a radical revisioning of novelistic convention to release his characters from the established representations of life. But to reform generic conventions is, of course, to subject novelistic characters to yet another set of conventions (however "natural" their unfolding) and therefore, potentially, to a false fate.

Lawrence ignores the paradox at the novel's beginning, but it reappears to exact its full metaphysical payment at the novel's ending. The opening chapter, "Sisters," echoes, with characteristic Lawrentian self-overcoming, *The Rainbow*'s familial and generational interest in a female destiny. Yet this apparent continuity disguises a real disjunction between the initial and final segments of the double novel. In *Women in Love*'s original opening, the canceled prologue, the state of the male soul, the sexual torments of Rupert Birkin, was symptomatic of modernist dis-ease. Birkin's obsession was with the male body, "whilst he studied the women as *sisters*, knowing their meaning and intents" (emphasis added): "It was the men's physique which held the passion and mystery to him. The women he seemed to be kin to, he looked for the soul in them." Birkin's erotic longings merely duplicate, under the sign of sexual difference, the very soul/body dualism that his sexual ideal would abolish: "to love completely, in one and the same act: both body and soul at once." Women will appear in *Women in Love* as sisters, but they are no longer represented as Birkin's spiritual kin.

If writers shed sicknesses in books, as Lawrence claimed, it is Lawrence's own soulfulness that *Women in Love* exorcises. The novel consciously disavows the knowledge of the female soul acquired in the writing of *The Rainbow*. It restores to women their mystery and freedom as novelistic subjects whose meaning and intents cannot, as the prologue mistakenly implied, be foreknown.

The passional mystery of female desire is renewed in the opening discussion between Gudrun and Ursula about their marriage "prospects." To marry or not to marry—that is the question that conventionally defines the choices open to novelistic heroines. But never has the dilemma been formulated in such pained alternatives: Gudrun ironically insisting that marriage, whatever the desire or the fitness of the individuals, is "bound to be an experience of some sort," and Ursula, in her first display of apocalyptic thinking, suggesting that marriage is "more likely the end of experience."

The marriage question is not just linked to the modernist crisis of disassociation and anomie but precipitates it. Nietzsche asserts in that gnomic book, *Twilight of the Idols*, that "modern" marriage and its supporting mythology of Romantic love bear witness to the decadence in the modern's "valuating instinct," a spiritual decline so pronounced that the modern "*instinctively prefer[s]* that which leads to dissolution, that which hastens the end." The objection to modern marriage lies not in marriage but in modernity, which has lost the beneficial instincts out "of which institutions grow, out of which the *future* grows": "The rationale of marriage lay in its indissolubility in principle: it thereby acquired an accent which could *make itself heard* against the accidents of feeling, passion, and the moment." For Lawrence, who like Nietzsche desires a permanent marriage not susceptible to the vagaries of passion, feeling, or the moment, marriage is also the final test of the instinct for life, the modern riddle whose solution would unveil the mystery of being. Marriage, he claimed, is the great puzzle of modern times, its sphinx riddle. "Solve it or be torn to pieces" is the decree.

Failure to solve the riddle of marriage entails the ritual penalty known as *sparagmos*, the dismemberment of the sacred body, without the ritualistic consolations and controls of ancient Dionysian rites. Modern attitudes toward marriage inevitably fragment the unitary fullness of being into subjective particles, novelistic (Jamesian) "points of view" instead of comprehensive cosmologies. It is at this point that Ursula and Gudrun begin taking "last stands" before they need to do so, a symptom of their fall into the fragmented world of modernity. " 'When it comes to the point, one isn't even tempted— oh, if I were tempted, I'd marry like a shot.—I'm only tempted *not* to.' The faces of both sisters suddenly lit up with amusement. 'Isn't it an amazing thing,' cried Gudrun, 'how strong the temptation is, not to!' They both laughed, looking at each other. In their hearts they were frightened."

The exchange of secret looks, "whilst each sister vaguely considered her fate," communicates more than the malaise of diminished desire; it introduces into the novel's emergent sexual dialectic a primary female negativity before any external forces of prohibition or interdiction are called into play. This negativity, registered in the sisters' denial of their own possible future, is essentially temporal; it signals a collapse of the time needed for the self's unfolding into the compacted and airless space of irony (Gudrun) or anomie (Ursula). Both responses measure the distance separating female desire from the established familial system of filiation and alliance. This distance between desire and the concrete forms of marriage Lawrence's novel must either traverse or abolish entirely.

"Sisters" centers on the radical isolation of the modern woman, alienated from marriage and its central affirmations: the principle of existential security—the promise of indissolubility—and the principle of temporal security, the insured destiny of future generations. The next chapter of *Women in Love*, "Shortlands" (the manor of the Crich dynasty), considers the same problem, but from the perspective of the male will. Lawrence dramatizes in the career of Gerald Crich the peculiarly modern tragedy of the anarchic Dionysian spirit trying to express itself in the Apollonian (degraded) forms of industrial production. Gerald reminds Ursula "of Dionysus, because his hair was really yellow, his figure so full and laughing"; this reminder anticipates the male fate he must reenact: the modern god dying in the Nordic rite of ice annihilation. At issue in Gerald's destiny is the very meaning of "purpose" in the modern world, an issue addressed in the Lawrentian critique of work, the activity by which man, directed by the spontaneous aspirations of his creative soul, both reclaims his past and organizes his future.

Man works, writes Lawrence in his "Study of Thomas Hardy," because the source of his life is overfull and thus "presses for utterance." "Weltschmerz and other unlocalized pains" signify the pressures within man to "produce" himself. Work therefore constitutes both an inherent passion, a craving "to produce, to create, to be as God," and a faulty mimesis, for in craving to be as God, man can only repeat and reproduce "the movement life made in its initial passage, the movement life still makes, and will continue to make, as a habit, the movement already made so unthinkably often that rather than a movement it has become a state, a condition of all life; it has become matter, or the force of gravity, or cohesion, or heat, or light. These old, old habits of life man rejoices to rediscover in all their detail."

Work entails a conscious reminiscence of those generative movements that have congealed into immemorial "habits" that constitute the given, known conditions of nature: matter, gravity, cohesion, heat, light. The purpose of work is thus present in its basic form as *repetition*, "the repetition of some one of those rediscovered movements, the enacting of some part imitated from life, the attaining of a similar result as life attained." The motive of labor should be consonant with the meaning of work: "to bring all life into the human consciousness."

The mystic harmony between knowledge and life that obtains in the truly creative work is never realized in *Women in Love*. Lawrence's philosophy of work, derived from his reading of Hardy, finds expression only in its demonic opposite: the mechanical philosophy justifying the "life-work" of Gerald Crich. Lawrence, in a rare moment of conventional psychologizing, exposes the grounds of Gerald's savage materialism, tracing it to an early repression of his authentic desire for the epic existence of Homeric days: "During his childhood and his boyhood he had wanted a sort of savagedom. The days of Homer were his ideal, when a man was chief of an army of heroes, or spent his years in wonderful Odyssey." Gerald's drive to impose his will on the material universe is analyzed as a corrupt form of quixotic idealism. His idealizing compulsion, unlike Quixote's inventive madness, seeks to subjugate the world with "the sword of mechanical necessity" rather than with the broadsword of romance. But like all mad constructionists, Gerald elaborates a system of life that is internally consistent but weakly founded, predicated as it is on two faulty acts of translation—Gerald's mistaking the mystic word "harmony" for the practical word "organization" and his grotesque mistranslation of the godhead into pure mechanism: "He found his eternal and his infinite in the pure machine-principle of perfect coordination into one pure, complex infinitely repeated motion, like the spinning of a wheel: but a productive spinning, as the revolving of the universe may be called a productive spinning, a productive repetition through eternity, to infinity. And this is the God-motion, this productive repetition ad infinitum. And Gerald was the God of the machine, Deus ex Machina."

Not just the echo of Blake's Satanic Mills but the entire antirationalist tradition empowers Lawrence's parody of the materialist analytics that makes the godhead immanent in the world's material motions. Lawrence appropriates Blake's critique in his own polemical diagnosis of the "pure orders" valorized by rationalist metaphysics, the ideology whose historical products—the Krupp Mills, German militarism, and "the sick Man of Europe"—are fabled in the family chronicle of the Crich dynasty, from its sick and dying patriarch, Thomas Crich, to its Bismarckian savior, Gerald Crich. In fact, this historical dimension of the novel is so obvious that, like the Great War, its informing presence can, as Lawrence said, merely be taken for granted.

III

I began my treatment of *Women in Love* with mention of its initial chapters, "Sisters" and "Shortlands," because these early installments recapitulate the old novelistic themes that the unfolding narrative will seek to work through until they are either transmuted into something "new" or are dispersed by the energy of Lawrence's own apocalyptic imaginings. I have perhaps reductively identified these old themes as marriage and work, the private and public destinies apportioned to novelistic character. The novel's visionary plot to inaugurate a genuinely free, unpredictable course of narrative development actually commences with the third chapter, "Class-Room." "Class-Room" initiates the novel's real effort at a new beginning, a radical departure from the moribund traditions of realist fiction.

The formal attempt to purge the novel of its sentimental and sickly conventions is thematized in the personal drama enacted in "Class-Room": Birkin's attempt to dissassociate himself from Hermione, both as a lover and as a demonic double who mimics his ideas on spontaneous animal joy. Hermione is a Cassandra, but unlike the ancient prophetess whose knowledge is authentic and whose words are discredited, the modern Cassandra is a spectral presence whose agonies result not from the ironic reception of her predictions but from the ironic distance between her speech and the knowledge she would communicate. Her ecstatic language is derided as the "worst and last form of intellectualism," her transports as the convulsions of a will that can only experience the "animalistic" nature of the body as a mental abstraction. Hermione is not only a Cassandra but the Lady of Shalott, another cursed female visionary whose will-bound imagination condemns her to a mirror world of shadows that will never materialize: "You've got that mirror, your own fixed will, your immortal understanding, your own tight conscious world, and there is nothing beyond it."

Birkin's struggle with Hermione, whose rhetoric shadows Birkin's in the vampirish form of unconscious parody and conscious mockery, and who reflects his fear of self-mirroring, is thus part of the larger struggle the novel seeks to portray: the "struggle for verbal consciousness," as Lawrence identifies it in his Foreword. Only the verbalizing "instinct" possesses the eruptive force needed to reclaim the past and to project a future in one totalizing movement. The ceaseless promptings of desire *must* find their way into language where they can be materialized into living forms, or else they will languish in the mind. Lawrence's famous manifesto on novelistic character insists on replacing "the old forms and sentimentalities" of novelistic discourse with this new *materializing* language:

> You mustn't look in my novel for the old stable ego of the character. There is another ego according to whose action the individual is unrecognizable, and passes through, as it were, allotropic states which it needs a deeper sense than any we've been used to exercise, to discover are states of the same single radically-unchanged element. (Like as diamond and coal are the same pure single element of carbon. The ordinary novel would trace the history of the diamond—but I say "diamond, what! This is carbon." And my diamond might be coal or soot, and my theme is carbon.)

To chronicle this allotropic development, in which the elemental ego passes through the successive stages of its potentiality, Lawrence appropriates an archaic language that posited the existence of multiple states, the language of totemism. Totemism is the atavistic language by which the constituent elements that collectively compose the given themes of any culture find their living expression. Totemism provides a serviceable no-menclature for an otherwise "unrecognizable" and therefore potentially *unrespresentable* Lawrentian ego because, as Birkin implies in the chapter entitled "Totem," totemic objects convey the complete truth of a "state" without vitiating or compromising it under the morally static signs of an-alytic language.

Lawrence, of course, read widely in the burgeoning anthropological literature (Frazer, Weston, Tylor, Harrison) that helped inspire the pan-cultural myths of modernist works such as *Ulysses* and *The Waste Land* or *Totem and Taboo* (1913). His particular interest in totemism may have derived from totemism's privileged position in the anthropological descriptions of primitive cultures. According to [J. G.] Frazer's *Totemism and Exogamy*, religion itself emerged out of the disruption and decay of totemism; and totemism survives as an elemental remainder and reminder of older social forms in the "later phase of religious evolution." Totemism's capacity to survive as an "archaic reminiscence" of the collective mind thus accounts for its pancultural *and* panhistorical vitality. As Frazer observes, "There is nothing in the institution itself incompatible with the pastoral, agricultural, even the commercial and industrial modes of life, since in point of fact it remains to this day in vogue among hunters, fishers, farmers, traders, weavers, leather-makers, and stone-masons, not to mention the less rep-utable professions of quackery, fortune-telling, and robbery."

The real appeal of totemism for Lawrence, whatever its diversionary interest as a patron institution for quacks and fortune tellers, is that it constitutes a system of relationships—animalistic, spiritual, and social—that honors the law of difference, primarily through the stabilizing insti-tution of exogamy. Lawrence's criticism of the modern democratic "isms" (Fabianism, liberalism, socialism, and communism) is that each system advocates a social state based on the utopian goal of material and spiritual equality. Speaking through the bitter declamations of Birkin, Lawrence maintains that social life must reflect and foster the original and originating purpose of life: differentiation. "We are all abstractly or mathematically equal, if you like. Every man has hunger and thirst, two eyes, one nose and two legs. We're all the same in point of number. But spiritually, there is pure difference and neither equality nor inequality counts. It is upon these two bits of knowledge that you must found a state. . . . One man isn't any better than another, not because they are equal, but because they are intrinsically *other*, that there is no term of comparison." Equality is a theoretical construct abstracted out of the data of material necessity; hence Birkin banishes it to the realm of number, wherein its truth and utility, if any, are to be found. In the essay "Democracy," Lawrence converts the primal fact of Otherness into the first term of his "metaphysics of presence." "Our life, our being depends upon the incalculable issue from the central Mystery into indefinable *presence*. This sounds in itself an abstraction. But not so. It is rather the perfect absence of abstraction. The central Mystery is no generalized abstraction. It is each man's primal original soul or self, within him."

The metaphysics of presence demands a language purified of any false "term of comparison" if it is to preserve the inviolability of its "central Mystery." Yet how is the absolute law of otherness to be fulfilled (or even monitored) in the verbal and social contacts of individuals and to retain its ontological status as "the undefinable"? This problem Birkin himself encounters in a rather playful dialectical conversation with Ursula about the "nature" of daisies.

> "They are nice flowers," he said, her emotional tones putting a constraint on him.
> "You know that a daisy is a company of florets, a concourse, become individual. Don't the botanists put it highest in the line of development? I believe they do."
> "The compositae, yes, I think so," said Ursula, who was never very sure of anything. Things she knew perfectly well, at one moment, seemed to become doubtful the next.
> "Explain it so, then," he said. "The daisy is a perfect little democracy, so it's the highest of flowers, hence its charm."
> "No," she cried, "no—never. It isn't democratic."
> "No," he admitted. "It's the golden mob of the proletariat, surrounded by a showy white fence of the idle rich."
> "How hateful—your hateful social orders!" she cried.
> "Quite! It's a daisy—we'll leave it alone."

The ease with Birkin can postulate the terms of comparison between democracy and the composite structure of the daisy, the facility with which he can transform the daisy into an emblem of the class divisions segregating the proletariat from the idle rich testify to the seductiveness of analogical language. Resisting the temptations of false resemblance is part of the struggle for verbal consciousness that the novel recounts. Birkin must forebear seeking explanations in the concave mirror of false analogy; therein lies the significance of his deferential act in the presence of the daisy: "It's a daisy—we'll leave it alone." The verbal gesture is slight, even comic, but Birkin honors the uniqueness of the daisy as the absolute *other*.

Lawrence's rhetoric of difference found inspiration in the naturalistic language of totemism. Totemism establishes a classificatory system of relationships predicated on the imaginary brotherhood of resemblances in difference. Totemic langauge externalizes the "primal, original soul within"; it signifies the living realities issuing from the depths of the central mystery and posits their organic relationships. The authority of this totemic identity justifies Lawrence's banishment of the old "stable ego" hypostasized in the novelistic cult of "personality" and the "great Mind" from which it descends.

> You can't have life two ways. Either everything is created from the mind, downwards; or else everything proceeds from the creative quick, outwards into exfoliation and blossom. Either a great Mind floats in space: God, the Anima Mundi, the Oversoul, draw-

ing with a pair of compasses and making everything to scale, even emotions and self-conscious effusions; or else creation proceeds from the forever inscrutable quicks of living beings, men, women, animals, plants. The actual living quick itself is alone the creative reality.

["Democracy"]

The struggle for verbal consciousness is waged in the unspoken battle raging between Birkin, the metaphysician of presence, who celebrates the inscrutable quick of living beings, and Gudrun, that formidable apostle of Mind for whom the world is a spectacle of descending creations, life defined (and degenerating) downward, abstracted, "preconcluded." Committed to the notion of personality, she regards the human being "as a complete figure, like a character in a book, or a subject in a picture, or a marionette in a theatre, a finished creation." When she sees Gerald for the first time, the novel, adopting her mode of perception, lapses into the language typical of "old" narrative habits of representation. Gerald is described in terms of externals, "a fair, sun-tanned type, rather above middle height, well-made, and almost exaggeratedly well-dressed": "But about him also was the strange, guarded look, the unconscious glisten, as if he did not belong to the same creation as the people about him."

Gudrun can only express the unconscious glisten that identifies Gerald as *another*, not the *same* creation as the fixed and finished characters about him, by invoking his totemic reality: " 'His totem is the wolf,' she repeated to herself. 'His mother is an old, unbroken wolf.' And then she experienced a keen paroxysm, a transport, as if she had made some incredible discovery, known to nobody else on earth." Gudrun's "powerful apprehension" of Gerald's essence is not the result of conscious metaphor making, that is, metaphor making as an exercise of the will intent on connecting the known with the unknown. "His totem is the wolf" is rather a kind of double metaphor, the first part, totem, assimilating even as it traverses the second part, wolf. Totemistically, Gerald is that doubly unknown and undefinable reality, wolf manifest. Wolf is the ancestral and universal reality struggling to express itself through him. The totemic depths of Gerald's individuality are brought to the narrative surface through a process of charged language that does not bother to discriminate between generative forces and their individual manifestations. Lawrence's language here is designed to radicalize metaphor and all other "terms of comparison" by eliminating the mediating middle term in the vital transfer of meaning from the depths to the surfaces. He wants his language to destroy or incapacitate that part of the verbal consciousness, best represented in the "mind" of Gudrun, which habitually employs language to encircle, complete, and define (fix) the real.

Thus language determines novelistic destiny in *Women in Love*. The novel's climactic moment of reckoning may be seen in the great chapter "Gudrun in the Pompadour," which stages the secular spectacle of the Logos "harrowing hell," Birkin's excoriation of the decadent Halliday crowd with his prophetic "letter" proclaiming the unalterable law that will prevail in *Dies Irae*: "the Flux of corruption . . . , the reducing back of the created body of life." The episode's dramatic power issues from the charged interplay between the novel's two competing "artists," the absent Birkin (present by virtue of his jeremiad on modernism) and Gudrun, the fashioner of miniatures, the respecter of the old virtues and corrupt privileges of the dead letter "I," and Birkin's only real rival in *Women in Love*.

Gudrun incarnates "a desire for the reduction process in oneself" that Birkin identifies as the sign of modern decadence. Her art represents "the process of active corruption" that results in Baudelairian "fleurs du mal," those (literary) flowers of evil that hauntingly contrast with Birkin's pristine daisies. When Gudrun overhears the Halliday party ridiculing Birkin's "genuine letter," she goes over to their table, retrieves the letter, and walks out of the Pompadour "in her measured fashion." In the ethos of a traditional novel, Gudrun's act is praiseworthy, a dignified defense of a friend's right to privacy, the decorous rescue of a private letter from mocking public scrutiny. But Gudrun is defending values that Lawrence cannot and will not endorse: the value of privacy and family loyalty, the affiliative ties that defined the obligations and prescribed the roles of an "older," stable ego. Her act is justly recorded in the language of the narrative commentary as a misdeed. Gudrun rescues the letter at the expense of its spirit, and the novel, after her dramatic act of retrieval and repossession, reverts to the literalism of "realistic" description in narrating her triumphant exit:

> From Halliday's table came half articulate cries, then somebody booed, then all the far end of the place began booing after Gudrun's retreating form. She was fashionably dressed in blackish-green and silver, her hat was brilliant green, like the sheen on an insect, but the brim was soft dark green, a falling edge with fine silver, her coat was dark green, brillantly glossy, with a high collar of grey fur, and great fur cuffs, the edge of her dress showed silver and black velvet, her stockings and shoes were silver grey. She moved with slow, fashionable indifference to the door.

Gudrun's movements are tracked in this pure description of surfaces, a narrative gesture on Lawrence's part that is at best supererogatory and at worst damning. Gudrun moves within the colorful modalities of self-display, while the real existential issue for Birkin is nakedness. Birkin argues with Gerald and Ursula about the dispensability of clothes; he wrestles naked with Gerald in "Gladiatorial"; and he and Ursula ritually disrobe in "Excurse" to experience the "unrevealed nudity" of the mystic body of reality. Gudrun in the Pompadour acts out the old ethics—and psychology—of self-presentation; Birkin yearns for a kind of psychic nakedness in the reality of human encounters. Gudrun defines and defends the rhetoric of finality, the aesthetic of the finished and polished creation. Birkin attempts to stammer out the words of a new rhetoric of futurity in the last facts of nakedness. The novel as it nears its conclusion represents a battle between these two rhetorics, a struggle between Gudrun and Birkin, not just for mastery over the novelistic spaces they occupy, but over the soul of the last modern hero—Gerald Crich. Their competition generates a system of warring metaphysics (neither fully articulated nor fully sufficient), and the aesthetics appropriate to each: Birkin, the voyager into the unknown, the Hardyean "pioneer" who journeys into the fruitful wastes seeking his destiny in what he calls "mystic marriage"; Gudrun, the "Glucksritter," riding the unstable currents of fashion, the Eternal Feminine pursuing her own degradation as the whore of Fortune, whose vehicle is the wheel of mechanical transformation.

IV

Birkin's salvationist reimagining of the creative life is nowhere as dramatically figured as in "Moony," Lawrence's most controlled and condensed narrative meditation on modern love purged of its Meredithian "sickly cant." "Moony" describes Birkin's obsessive disfigurement of the image of the moon reflected in the surfaces of a pond. This lunar reflection is not for him a natural icon for the order of mutability but a demonized image of Cybele, the "accursed Syria Dea" of Asiatic mother cults. In an effort to discharge the powers of darkness gathering force within him, Birkin throws stone after stone into the motionless pond, turning it into "a battlefield of broken lights and shadows," a field of "white fragments" that mirrors his own obsession with those disintegrative processes that may portend, for all their negativity, a positive struggle to emerge from the womb of creation. Yet the moon's image remains unviolated—Nature sees to it that the "scattered fragments" course their way back to the still center: "He saw the moon regathering itself insidiously, saw the heart of the rose intertwining vigorously and blindly, calling back the scattered fragments, winning home the fragments, in a pulse and in effort of return." Sparagmos to *nostos*: the winning home of fragments—that, of course, is the desired homecoming at the thematic and mythic heart of modern narratives from Joyce's *Ulysses* to Beckett's grimly ironic, vagrant fictions of disintegration. Winning home is the telos of modern art—to repair, no matter how tempting the urge to fall "back in panic," the "ragged rose," Dante's rose of the World. Winning home is what Birkin sees as "the remaining way" open to those weary of contemplating the modern mysteries of dissolution: "There was another way, the way of freedom. There was the paradisal entry into pure, single being, the individual soul taking precedence over love and desire for union, stronger than any pangs of emotion, a lovely state of free proud-singleness, which accepted the obligation of the permanent connection with others, and with the others, submits to the yoke and leash of love, but never forfeits its own proud individual singleness, even while it loves and yields." Birkin, however, remains unsure whether his vision of free proud singleness is "only an idea, or . . . the interpretation of a profound yearning." Love must be experienced as a "travelling together," a mobile nostos, an exploratory way, never a final destination. Lawrence's novel never abandons its desire to see the elemental ego find its own way into the unknown, its true fate.

The "love" story of Birkin and Ursula embedded in and illuminating the dark heart of *Women in Love* represents Lawrence's attempt to render the great, perhaps the last, epic adventure of modernity—the exploration of the as yet unknown. This love story generically attains its consummatory moment of winning home, its paradisal entry into a new world, in the chapter peripatetically entitled "Excurse," in which Birkin proposes to Ursula the terms of his star marriage, terms she will come to accept as the liberating fatality of love. The chapter opens with Birkin's decision to renounce the tutelage of Luck as a vulgar minister of destiny; he refuses to accept that life is "a series of accidents—like a picaresque novel." "Excurse" thus becomes one of Lawrence's most successful fictional representations of a "generic" self-overcoming. The picaresque, the narrative of human destiny imaged forth as a series of accidents originating in the contingencies of history, social caste, and economic conditions, is invoked only to be revoked as a fictional legacy that validates a "false fate." In "Excurse" the promise of *The Rainbow* is realized: Ursula's "new knowledge of eternity in the flux of time" is fulfilled in her *internally* apprehended knowledge of "the inevitability and beauty of fate, fate which one asks for, which one accepts in full" and in "this star-equilibrium which alone is freedom."

Yet despite her revelatory vision of a self-generated fate, the true "fate which one asks for," not the untoward destiny one struggles against, like a picaresque heroine, Ursula does not always accede to the conditions of her newfound freedom in star-equilibrium. The reason is partly that Lawrence prefers to leave his characters in uncertainty and partly that Ursula remains for Lawrence totemically bound to her essence as Magna Mater, the Great Mother who insists on pressing for a reactionary and limited kind of love, love as ecstatic fusion. Like all of Lawrence's early heroines, from Mrs. Morel to Anna "Victrix" Brangwen, Ursula has a predilection for a consuming romance whose central episode is the idyll of a sexual paradise regained. Generically, romance is the narrative form that seeks to cancel out the differences separating love and its objects. For Lawrence, it is *the* female form of imaginative desire, born out of the female will to absorb the "Other" in the all-comprehending womb. The Great Mother would reclaim all individualized life into the undifferentiated Source, drawing all articulated meanings and distinctions into herself. For Ursula, who might be won over by love's (and Birkin's) excursionary nature, intercourse is still initially and perhaps finally the act of homecoming, the winning home of the errant male.

Birkin's suspicions that the Magna Mater's lust for "unspeakable intimacies" lurks behind every female's urge to "mate" leave him dissatisfied with mystic marriage as the controlling metaphor for his transvaluing vision of life. Because marriage is disposed, by the sheer force of institutional inertia and by the reactionary demands of the "feminine" will to enforce

a unity where none should exist, Birkin advocates the complementary revolutionary relation of *Blutbrüderschaft*. The truly subversive content of
Women in Love, its well-conceived threat to the conventional attitudes toward human relationships propagated by the "bourgeois" novel, is in expanding the idea of spiritual mating to encompass a male-to-male relation,
a broader and less interested relation than the "égoïsme à deux" or "hunting
in couples" that characterizes modern marriages.

Birkin's rite of "bloodbrotherhood" is authorized both by his personal
desire for a male relationship and by the more utilitarian need to populate
the "new world" of his visions with as yet undefined human constellations
in supposed star-equilibrium. But beneath Birkin's ideological justification
for such a male rite as a "new utterance" issuing out of life's creative
mysteries, there abides the epic striving condensed and displaced in the
obsessions of Birkin's *Salvator Mundi* complex: his classical yearning for the
"Gladiatorial" *virtus* embodied in the Homeric figure of Gerald Crich. Of
course Gerald has ostensibly betrayed his heroic nature by dedicating himself to the "established world" and its decadent, moribund orders "in which
he did not livingly believe." Conventional marriage would prove "the seal
of his condemnation": it would condemn him to the underworld "like a
soul damned but living forever in damnation." Birkin's offer of Blutbrüderschaft is the redemptive alliance that Gerald considers in the chapter
"Marriage or Not": "If he pledged himself with the man he would later be
able to pledge himself with the woman: not merely in legal marriage, but
in absolute, mystic marriage." But Gerald declines Rupert's offer, whether
because of "unborn, absent volition or of atrophy" Birkin declines to speculate and Lawrence refuses to say.

Of course Birkin's revolutionary offer to rescue Gerald from his im-
pending doom is exposed as an illusory choice in the novel's depiction of
the Final Days. For Gerald has already made his choice in the previous
chapter, prophetically entitled "Death and Love." The death of his father
brings Gerald to a crisis state in which, poised on the edge of the grave,
the image of the perilous void, he "must take direction." Crisis, as Frank
Kermode reminds us, citing the pun of St. John, comprises a moment both
of judgment and of separation. For Gerald the moment of crisis resolves
itself in a decision to separate himself from the "one center" authorized
and inhabited by his father—"the unseen, raw grave": "No, he had nothing
to stay here for." He then forms his "dangerous resolve"—to go to Gudrun,
"persistently, like a wind, straight forwards, as if to his fate." But this
resolution issues in a false "separation" of love and death. Even as Gerald
enters Gudrun's bedroom seeking comfort in love's restorative rites, he
tracks in the cold clay of the grave. Death and love become dialectically
wedded, composing the signs that dictate Gerald's true fate. Whatever
Birkin might do to oppose it, Gerald is set on an irreversible course of self-
destruction. In a letter to John Middleton Murry, Lawrence describes the
limits of his own revolutionary vision of the millennium when the world
will be repopulated with the new men and women of his imaginings: "I

think that one day—before so very long—we shall come together again, this time on a living earth, not in the world of destructive going apart. I believe we shall do things together, and be happy. But we can't dictate the terms, nor the times. It has to come to pass in us. Yet one has the hope, that is the reality."

The *Götterdämmerung* finale of the novel confirms Lawrence's intuition that neither the terms nor the times ordained for the world's "destructive going apart" can be dictated by the human will— either the regenerate will of the prophet, or the corrupt will of the insane "ecstatics," like Gudrun and Loerke, who herald the dawn of "the obscene beyond." Birkin's vision thus acquires an ambiguous status in the novel's already tortuous eschatology—it expresses the hope for, not the imminence of, a new creative order. This hope diminishes as the novel relentlessly moves toward its last days, whose end terms are dominated not by Birkin's visionary excursions but by the sick "love story" of Gudrun and Gerald.

The destinies of Gerald and Gudrun constitute, as Lawrence once wrote of Dostoevsky's novels, "great parables . . . but false art." Their love story represents, that is, the dead life and the moribund forms of older (tragic) narratives whose formal integrity conformed to a deterministic notion of historical causality. This formalism appears in an early exchange between Gudrun and Gerald: "You have struck the first blow," Gerald reminds Gudrun, to which she responds with "confident assurance," "And I shall strike the last." That Gudrun's threat sounds like a prediction is a sign of her (and the reader's) confidence in the symmetry intrinsic to the resolutions of the classical novel. Lawrence's own analysis of Dostoevsky's "parables" helps illuminate his unwilling incorporation of this "false" yet inevitable formalism into the last stages of *Women in Love*. Writing again to Murry, who was working on a study of Dostoevsky, Lawrence observes: "The Christian ecstasy leads to imbecility (the Idiot). The sensual ecstasy leads to universal murder: for mind, the acme of sensual ecstasy lies in *devouring* the other, even in the pleasures of love, it is a devouring, like a tiger drinking blood (Rogozhin). But the full sensual ecstasy is never reached except by Rogozhin in murdering Nastasya. It is nipped in the last stages by the *will*, the social will."

This Dostoevskian insight shadows Lawrence's representation of Thomas Crich's sentimental Christianity and Gudrun's demonic sensuality. Christian ecstasy, which Thomas Crich seeks through his self-abnegating charities and his sentimental, "democratic" politics, leads to his final imbecility and the slow stupor of lingering death. Sensual ecstasy is the special lust of Gudrun, whose face betrays the insane will of the "demoniacal ecstatic" and whose love affair with Gerald, like her nostalgic fascination with the underworld of his mines, grows out of her desire to experience the "perfect voluptuous finality." Her affair with Gerald must end with her triumph in "the last stages" and, as the Dostoevskian parable instructs, in sensually gratifying murder.

Lawrence's unwilling but not inadvertent accommodation of Dostoevsky's spiritual determinism *as the only possible* resolution to his visionary narrative is also reflected in the larger structural configurations of the novel. *Women in Love* begins with an unstable triangle —Hermione, Ursula, and Birkin—that Birkin attempts to replace with the transforming relationships comprehended in mystic marriage. But as the novel moves toward the Continent and into its *Götterdämmerung* phase, the generic imperative to observe certain novelistic symmetries begins to reassert itself. The novel's initial sexual triangle reappears in the parodic and demonic trinity of Loerke, Gudrun, and Gerald. Moreover, the novel also regresses to a formalist rigidity in echoing Birkin's vision of male love in Loerke's relation to Leitner, an alliance that demystifies Birkin's mystic sense of *Blutbrüderschaft* in the perversions of "ecstatic" and exploitive homosexuality.

To discredit the determinism that is overwhelming his narrative, Lawrence has Gudrun mock the conventional explanation that the violence called forth in the final stages of her battle with Gerald is due to the tensions and jealousies traditionally associated with the "eternal" love triangle: " 'A pretty little sample of the eternal triangle!' And she turned ironically away, because she knew that the fight had been between Gerald and herself and that the presence of the third party was a mere contingency—an inevitable contingency perhaps, but a contingency none the less. But let them have it as an example of the eternal triangle, the trinity of hate. It would be simpler for them." Gudrun's scathing dismissal of the idea that her triangular entanglements with Gerald and Loerke compose a trinity of hate, a demonic variation on the eternal triangle, is based on a quibble about the meaning and importance of "contingencies." But what does she, or even Lawrence, mean by the self-contradictory assertion that Loerke's presence operates as an "inevitable" contingency? How can a contingency be both accidental and forseeable, dependent on chance yet necessary as both a primary and secondary cause? What is important to Gudrun's self-interpretation is not her claim that her battle with Gerald represents a singular death struggle between two insane wills; rather, what emerges as significant and triumphant is Gudrun's power of dismissive irony, her tonal mastery over the reality of the last facts, the violent ends of *Dies Irae*.

In *Women in Love*, Gudrun's vision, the ironical vision of love and death, overwhelms the imaginations of the artist of life, Rupert Birkin. Birkin tries to inaugurate a reign of freedom, the new time of the transcendent individual who lives in close contact with the inexhaustible life source. Gudrun, with Loerke, her demonic consort, inaugurates the totalitarian regime of terror, the nightmare of history and historicism, the coming era of real social hatred. Gudrun's is a peculiarly "modern" madness, not the classical and even pathos-ridden madness of Hermione, who is partially redeemed by her mythic affinity with Cassandra. In her prophetic but unredeeming imagination, Gudrun confronts and then *becomes* the specter that haunts the modern mind, the specter of mechanical causation.

Perhaps she was healthy. Perhaps it was only her unabatable health that left her so exposed to the truth. If she were sickly she would have her illusions, imaginations. As it was, there was no escape. She must always see and know and never escape. She could never escape. There she was, placed before the clock-face of life. . . . She was watching the fingers twitch across the eternal, mechanical, monotonous clock-face of time. She never really lived, she only watched. Indeed, she was like a little, twelve-hour clock, vis-à-vis with the enormous clock of eternity—there she was, like Dignity and Impudence, or Impudence and Dignity.

Gudrun identifies with the eternal repetition of the clock face as the internal principle of her existence, thus alienating herself from the nurturing and restorative cycles of natural time: hence "her unripening nights, her unfruitful slumbers." She is the mad prophetess who presides over the apocalyptic Terrors that proclaim the end of the world as a ceaseless duration. *Dies Irae* for Gudrun take the form of a perpetual *chronos*, to paraphrase Kermode's formulation of the modernist's "intemporal agony," chronos without kairos, without a transforming, all-reversing and all-renewing eruption of creative mystery into the remorseless chronicity of linear, clock-face time. Gudrun can neither envision nor hope for deliverance. She can only persist in fashioning the totalitarian, apocalyptic fantasies she plays out with Loerke, the "final craftsman" of "the last series of subtleties," who "did not deceive himself in the last issue":

As for the future, that they never mentioned except one laughed out some mocking dream of the destruction of the world by a ridiculous catastrophe of man's invention: a man invented such a perfect explosive that it blew the earth in two, and the two halves set off in different directions through space, to the dismay of the inhabitants: or else the people of the world divided into two halves, and each half decided *it* was the perfect and right, the other half was wrong and must be destroyed; so another end of the world.

Gudrun and Loerke translate the central rite of modernity—sparagmos—into global and genocidal terms: the earth torn in two, mankind's destructive dream of exterminating the ideologically corrupt other. As the final form in their last series of subtleties, Loerke and Gudrun construct this mad parody that inverts Plato's myth of the origin of sexual love in Zeus's punitive division of the original hermaphroditic body into halves, who thereafter seek to reunite through love. Time becomes a clock face onto which they project their false "Dignity" and their true "Impudence" as artists of the obscene whose ecstatic vision of the End finds its consummation in universal murder.

Gudrun's myth of finality is registered in the cold, life-betraying voice of irony: "Everything turned to irony with her: the last flavour of everything was ironical." Kierkegaard claimed that irony was "in the strictest sense a mastered moment" and saw in the birth of ironic consciousness "the absolute beginning of the personal life." For Kierkegaard, irony is the baptism of human beginning; for Lawrence irony is the last rites of the living-dead.

That the creative moment could in any way be limited to and defined by the needs and desires, the dignities—and impudence—of the personal life is repugnant to his metaphysical and rhetorical doctrines of impersonality. For Lawrence language should adhere and inhere in the reality it denominates, in the new utterances it struggles to deliver over to verbal consciousness. Irony, the conscious displacement of meaning from its vehicles of expression, irony as the deliberate estrangement of essence and phenomena, is the last betrayal of the creative Source.

Gerald's death vindicates Gudrun's status as the ironical artist who has mastered the creative moments immanent in the "time" of Nature. It is Gudrun who regards Gerald's death as an inevitable contingency attending the Final Days, a necessary but "barren tragedy" without meaning or significance, but hers is the view of cold irony. It is at this point that Birkin returns to the novel that he has abandoned (and that has abandoned him) to contest Gudrun's ironical reading of Gerald's death. He mourns the fallen hero and retreats, not behind the frigid dignities of irony, but into the enclosed and emotionally charged spaces of elegy: "I didn't want it to be like this." Ursula, to her horror, hears the accent of nostalgia in Birkin's valedictory lament and cannot help thinking of the Kaiser's "Ich habe es nicht gewollt." In exposing the historical retreat implicit in Birkin's elegiac meditations, Ursula argues for the "realities" honored in the resolutions of the classical novel and in so doing interprets Birkin's grief as a perversion, a refusal to accept the fate decreed by those impersonal forces that constitute the Real.

> "You can't have two kinds of love. Why should you!"
> "It seems as if I can't," he said. "Yet I wanted it."
> "You can't have it, because it's wrong, impossible," she said.
> "I don't believe that," he answered.

Women in Love thus represents and advances the modernist crisis of separation and judgment. Its *Götterdämmerung* finale envisions the last symmetries in the form of an impasse and an argument. Birkin's perverse insistence that his desire to "save" Gerald was not a false, nor even a barren, hope, but a living expression of his heart's desire, his true fate, is contrasted with Gudrun's grim, ironical view of necessity. His quarrel with Gudrun over the meaning of history is perhaps less threaetening to his metaphysic than his argument with Ursula over the visionary possibility of *Blutbrüderschaft*, men wedded in purpose and in love. Both the historical impasse and the emotional argument remain unresolved, their outcome temporarily suspended by a narrative moratorium dictated by Birkin's grief and Lawrence's own need to reimagine the presence of the creative mystery that will "carry on the embodiment of creation" even if mankind is exterminated—or annihilates itself. The novel opens itself up to the future only by insisting on a kind of blank space in time, empty yet still capable of being filled with new utterances, "miraculous unborn species."

In an essay on modern painting, Lawrence pictured Cézanne's struggle with the visual clichés that composed the tainted inheritance, the corrupted legacy of pictorial form. His analysis illuminates and corresponds to Lawrence's own transvaluing critique of novelistic conventions. "In other pictures he seems to be saying: Landscape is not like this and not like this and not like this and not . . . etc.—and every *not* is a little blank space in the canvas, defined by the remains of an assertion. Sometimes Cézanne builds up a landscape essentially out of omissions. He puts fringes on the complicated vacuum of the cliché, so to speak, and offers us that. It is interesting in a repudiative fashion but it is not the new thing." *Women in Love*, despite its efforts to imagine and realize a "new thing," comes to rest on the fringe of the complicated vacuum of novelistic cliché. Birkin's belief that life need "not," is "not" like this and this—contains the remains of an assertion, but it is hard to determine whether his refusal to submit to Ursula's pragmatic and historical view of the limits of human desire is anything more than mental repudiation. *Women in Love* begins but cannot conclude Lawrence's own struggle with the memory of classical narrative, which trusted, not naively, but livingly, in a final day of historical reckoning. *Women in Love* is the Judgment Book that publishes the decrees of a Providence that Lawrence could neither ignore nor accept.

Joyce Cary: The Abstract Real

Hazard Adams

I begin with consideration of one of Cary's words that frequently enters discussions of Cary at an early stage, often in a confusing and sometimes in a confused way. For Cary, "real" is usually a noun. It contains persons, places, things, ideas that have gotten to the stage of expression, and ideas still on the way. It is very, very large—too large to be of much use as a critical term or a philosophical term. The "real" is also very powerful, in the sense that it is always *here*, something for human power to confront. One is likely to understand it in the way that one comes to grasp the ubiquity of fate in Hardy or the enveloping fog in Dickens's *Bleak House*. Except that it is rarely mentioned by name in the novels; it is present only in its many separate unique instances. In Cary's nonfiction, by contrast, it is the product of Cary's speculation, something built up as an abstraction. Yet as an abstraction it has a dubious life of its own, and it is voracious, enveloping other words almost as fast as Cary offers them to it. It is not something sought but never found; that would be "being," a term Cary employs a few times, but not with the enthusiasm that he expends to make "real" a noun. The stubborn "nounness" of "real"—there are "reals" in Cary, like Blake's spaces—strikes me as a deliberate form of emphasis which, even in the writing of Cary that comes closest to philosophy, seems to be trying to make abstractions into particulars. "Every class is individual," Blake held against Reynolds in his annotations to the third discourse, and Cary, who read Blake carefully, probably agreed. I believe he regarded his major abstraction as a giant form grown from experiences of particular othernesses. He would have liked it to have the force of a thing. Jack Wolkenfeld (*Joyce Cary, The Developing Style*) is correct to remark that "Cary . . . denies the existence of abstractions except for the strange, the often

From *Joyce Cary's Trilogies: Pursuit of the Particular Real*. © 1983 by the Board of Regents of the State of Florida. The University Presses of Florida, 1983.

dangerous and contradictory existence they have in real people in real situations." In *Power in Men* Cary writes, "Tradition, patriotism, the ideas of national honour have immense power; so also do ideas common to humanity—brotherhood, equality; but they are real only in the acts of individual men," and "what is certain in the average is merely probability in the individual." Cary has not too much respect for probability. The whole of his approach might well be summed up in a remark he makes in *Power in Men*, where, with respect to a matter he is discussing, he says, "Abstractly this difference is trifling; in practice it is real and profound."

Before he was finished the noun "real" was crammed full of all that is available to intuition. There is something left on the other side of it called "being," but "being" strikes one here as an afterthought, while in a philosopher's work one knows that if it is mentioned it is central even in its absence. "Being" appears in *Art and Reality* to be the product of an obeisance to philosophy itself and to a momentary desire for metaphysical neatness. As far as I can see, it has no status at all in the novels, whereas all that fills up the noun "real" is very, very present there, and is quite enough.

If one needs a large critical frame to put around the novels, the "real" is it, but it is more a proscenium arch than a frame, because one looks through it. From a distance necessary to get a general impression through the arch, the design one sees is quite large and only a design. Early Cary criticism, and much of the late, has seen the "real" of the speculative prose in the novels, not so often the "reals" that make it up. This has been quite all right and perhaps even necessary. This [essay] does almost the same thing, but it also insists that as we get farther away into an abstract notion of the "real," that particular "reals" of the novels tend to get lost. Criticism must return to them. Blake had his heroic figure Los going around making "spaces" as a contrary to abstract Newtonian space, because particular experience is lost in that space.

Sometimes in the speculative writing—that is, chiefly *Power in Men*, *Art and Reality*, and some of the essays—Cary appears to be speaking of a metaphysical real or an epistemological objectivity, but he is not a philosopher, though clearly he enjoyed speculation. Although he engages philosophical notions in these works—Kant's thing-in-itself and categorical imperative, Croce's intuition—one soon realizes that his interest is that of a novelist in experience, and the "real" is *really* whatever any character comes up against, including that character's own selfhood, the intransigent and the unpredictable in the world.

Behind the "real" there is, as I have mentioned, "being." This is absolute truth, which we cannot know. Although Cary rejects the Kantian thing-in-itself, he allows it in through the back door in a remark in *Art and Reality*: "immediately life takes place in the subconscious, before it is known to reflection; and its sources, the active nature of being itself, are completely beyond the human imagination." This tends to make Cary's "real" an attribute of "being," which is an absence, but in his trilogies one doesn't find this "being" as an absence. It is ignored. Rather, one discovers a reversal, because the "real" is so fundamentally present in the forms of all that opposes the individual human will that there is no room for it except as an attribute of "real." Unless it is God. But God, too, becomes for Cary a presence.

Let me ask again, what is this "real" of Cary's speculative writing? One other mention of "being" is necessary. He speaks of "matter" as "certain fixed characteristics of being"; it presents us with a "whole framework of reality" (*Art and Reality*). This "real" is physical law, which we defy at our peril. But though the "real" contains physical law, it is much more. Cary says simply that it is the world as it is, the world in its own quality. It is the world independent of the perceiver, but Cary does not intend this to mean that he defines it in terms of Locke's primary qualities of experience, though it would include those qualities, did they exist outside of Locke's fictive construction. Cary does not engage that venerable question of the subject and the object, though he uses both terms. Indeed, he calls the "real" the objective world, but it is not a world objective merely because measurable, though it includes this aspect of things and physical laws. As Jack Wolkenfeld points out, Cary objects to Hegel because he feels that Hegel doesn't take into account a physical reality that "affects the needs and feelings of men." Cary's "real" always involves an individual, but is not there by virtue only of the individual. It is at the same time always a particular here and now, not simply *for* an individual but involving the individual. Further, the individual belongs to this "real," while yet he is apart from it. This is the first and most important of a series of five paradoxes which I shall attempt to isolate and by means of which I hope we can understand the trilogies from the abstracted distance the paradoxes create.

Cary describes the "real" in a number of ways. The "real" is dynamic, a temporal process; yet it has within it fixed characteristics. There is, for example, a "universal real" of feelings, which I take to mean an unchanging human nature. There is a "universal moral real" that accompanies the consistencies of physical fact (laws) and of human feelings. Mainly, though, Cary fills up the "real" with attributes: freedom, liberty, power, family love and responsibility, the good, ambition, loss, bitterness, danger, cruelty, anxiety, injustice, disease, evil. The "real" includes the "facts." The above are "facts" that Cary specifically identifies with the "real." Another fact is that of human "machinery," which is the individual's own physical being. It can be a part of the real as *other*, part of a real placed over against one's freedom. It can also be the vehicle of freedom. A subparadox here is Cary's insistence that "liberty cannot exist without determinism or determinism without liberty," that "the freedom of man absolutely depends on the determinism of matter for its own exercise." The alternative is chaos as chaos.

Events constitute the real. They are the "actual." Cary sometimes calls things in novels "actual," that is, particular; but mainly the "actual" is what makes up society, the sum of events at any time. Events, simply as events, are a chaos full of chance and injustice. There is a lot of determinism in events because of physical laws and human machinery (but that does not make them less a chaos in sum). Ideas as events are only partly determined. Cary invokes the idea of human freedom here, always pushing back against the real as determined events. One notices that the real itself is insufficiently formed, despite its laws, at least for the human imagination, which sets out to do something with it, rather than merely to react passively to it. . . .

But there is a problem here, because this pushing back against the real, which is freedom itself in Cary, sometimes looks very much like possession—not quite demonic possession, but almost—and thus free only from the rational. It is perhaps captured by a sort of instinct. One sometimes wonders how close Cary's notion of freedom comes to the quality that Plato worried about in poets and rhapsodes.

The second of Cary's paradoxes is that even a determined event is unique. The basic real is a machine or a bundle of laws, but it is also a "living whole," being infused with the products of a freedom acting over against it. Though the sun rises daily according to physical law, and each day as mechanism is the same, as event it is unique. This uniqueness is the result of the free individual's involvement with the real.

The fundamental relation of individual and real is grounded in "intuition." Cary quarrels with Croce over the nature of intuition, and that quarrel I discuss [elsewhere]. Here I want only to show how Cary uses the term and draws from it a third paradox. Intuition, as Cary uses the word in *Art and Reality*, seems to be feeling working directly upon events at a pre-verbal or pre-symbolic level. Intuition is the power of an individual (as separate from the real) to reconnect with the real. In one's effort to express an intuition . . . one achieves sympathy with other minds and things which constitute part of the real. Intuitions are ways of "checking" our abstract notions of the real against reality itself.

This emphasis on "checking" against the real is one reason Cary rejects Croce's argument:

> I have to admit that for all Croce's brilliant argument, I think his theory fails to meet the facts. I suspect also that it has been disastrous to artists who have attempted to believe that all intuition is expression, all expression art. For if intuition is expression, how does the artist know anything but his expression? He is cut off from reality by his own act.
>
> (*Selected Essays*, ed. A.G. Joseph [London: Michael Joseph, 1976])

In all of this, feeling plays a role that dominates reason and method. It is the "ultimate motive power of man's action." So one can see that Cary does not think of contact with the "real" merely in the language of verification according to science, though he does not reject such methods. But it is clear that feeling is a means of checking one's fictive constructs (scientific or mythical) by correspondence to the real. The paradox, our third, is that intuition is the first step by which we proceed to make the fictions that require checking by feeling, which is intuition's ground. The reason for this paradox, which is of a circular nature, is that for Cary there is a gap between intuition and expression. Expression culminates in the symbol, which involves a certain coherence while at the same time it runs the risk of losing correspondence achieved in the intuition. Expression seems to be intuition thematized via technique, producing the symbol.

The symbol is a sign by means of which we fix and communicate the real of intuition. At least we try to. The gap between intuition and expression via these signs causes a certain loss of the intuition or, perhaps, a distorting elaboration, whether aesthetic or conceptual. This expressed symbol is what constitutes the social or cultural world in which we live, the humanly created social structure at any given time, which is combined with the "real," but in fact becomes part of the real that the individual in his freedom faces. But it is always *in process* like Blake's London, eternally building and decaying. Thus we live in part in a dream of the future, a remembrance of the past. Dreams of the future can go wrong, of course, and remembrance can be sentimental. All these are the risks of symbolic constructions that are essentially "as if," including scientific constructions:

> [W]hat scientists do is to dissect the living body of the world and examine one cell or organ *as if* it could work alone and by itself. And the *as if* is achieved by an effort of the imagination, representing to the scientist's mind, a situation which does not or could not exist.

The fourth paradox is that suggested by the notion of a "total environment," partly "real," partly symbolic, based on an "as if," that can go wrong and needs to be checked by intuition against the "real," but also, wrong as it may be, can become part of the real by the persistence of its wrongness in society. This becomes a total "real," inasmuch as the individual comes up against the symbolic beliefs of others, no matter how fanciful. A total "real" at any given time can be infused with varying degrees of good and evil. Because there is a "universal moral real" available to intuition, we can know such worlds directly in their goodness and evil and act upon that intuition to create a new symbolic order. One can then claim that nature affects the symbolic, which has to come up against it, and the symbolic can affect the real by its simple presence in nature. This is not exactly the way Oscar Wilde had it in *"The Decay of Lying"* when he said that nature imitates art as much as art imitates nature, but it is close. Cary will have little to do with the idea of imitation, while Wilde was still trying to demolish it.

Finally, there is something we call "meaning," which is a characteristic of life, though meaning often seems to dissolve in the chaos of event. "Trollope found in life what we all find, a mass of detail without meaning, of useless cruelty, stupid evil, blind fate, fools doing accidental good, and well-meaning saints doing immense evil." For this reason Cary declares that "to copy life would be to produce nonsense" (*Selected Essays*). Meaning is a product of art, which Cary defines very broadly as any submission of intuition to expression and the symbol. The fifth paradox is that meaning is clearly meant to be a return to the "real," a deepening of our sense of it, in a coherent shape that in its coherence nevertheless maintains a correspondence by means of feeling: "The reader is often aware of learning more about the world from a book than he gets from actual experience, not only because in the book he is prepared to find significance in events that mean nothing in life, but because those events in the book are related to each other in a coherent valuation which sets them in ordered relation of importance, and this can reveal to him in what had seemed the mere confusion of his daily affairs new orders of meaning" [*Art and Reality*]. Cary sees as very difficult this effort to return to the real via the expression of a symbolic structure. We, too, see it as difficult as we try to follow his arguments in the speculative writing. With all the obstacles, how can we possibly ever return to the "real"? No one, let alone Cary in his novels, says it is easy!

Moreover, this problem is intensified by Cary's concern with the necessity of communication among individuals via the feeling:

1. "Only art can convey both the fact and the feeling about the fact, for it works in the medium of common sympathies" (*Art and Reality*).
2. "The symbol, in short, like the concept . . . is also the enemy of the intuition" (*Art and Reality*).
3. "Wittgenstein has said that everyone has his own world. I should rather say that men are together in feeling, in sympathy, but alone in mind" (*Selected Essays*).

Clearly it is art, in Cary's very broad sense of all symbolic expression, that is supposed to be the vehicle of sympathetic identification. But may not art, by Cary's own argument, or part of it at least, be creating as many difficulties for communion as it overcomes, as many false "as ifs" as true ones? Is not the artist dissatisfied with the "real," clashing with it and even, therefore, with those to whom he is supposed to be communicating? Cary's novels, at least, seem to answer "yes" to these questions without giving up the possibility of a fortunate success, and so there is darkness beneath Cary's optimism. He fears for what man may do with his imagination.

The five paradoxes I have mentioned are not all explicitly stated as paradoxes by Cary, but a study of the vocabulary he employs—being, matter, the real, the actual, facts, events, intuition, expression, symbol, art, meaning—leads us to them when we attempt to bring an abstract order to his speculative thought. But this thought is hardly rigorous in its use of these words. They come and go, enlarge and contract. Past a certain point one is imposing a conceptual neatness at a higher level that is not present at the lower where Cary is working. Furthermore, one senses that even

Cary's lower level is not the level on which he is really thinking, that he is thinking in specific events that expand into the abstract quasi-metaphysical vocabulary with which I have been coping. Even here the words seem more like creatures in a fiction, strange Blakean creatures with powers of sudden expansion and contraction in a hierarchical world. One might at this point think of one of Gulley Jimson's ideas for a painting—a presentation of God as a huge human form with people moving about and fighting in his stomach, causing a cosmic gastric disturbance. One senses, too, that Cary's speculative vocabulary is evolved as meaning from his novels or the experience of making them. They seem like abstractions from intransigent living forms with which he had to cope. His *Art and Reality* seems to draw its power from certain spots of time that engender, in the course of speculation on them, the more abstract vocabulary. The two are, in fact, intermeshed; but one senses the priority of the particular events.

> I remember one of my children, as a baby of about fourteen months, sitting in its pram watching a newspaper on the grass close by. There was a breeze along the ground and the newspaper was moving. Sometimes the top page swelled up and fluttered; sometimes two or three pages were moved and seemed to struggle together; sometimes the whole paper rose up on one side and flapped awkwardly for a few feet before tumbling down again. The child did not know that this object was a newspaper moved by the wind. It was watching with intense absorbed curiosity a creature entirely new to its experience, and through the child's eyes I had a pure intuition of the newspaper as object, as an individual thing at a specific moment.

This precedes a charming description of a young child's drawing of a swan that I discuss [elsewhere].

Cary returns to events like this frequently in his writing as if, indeed, they were a special sort of Wordsworthian remembrance—intellectual food. They are, to employ Eliseo Vivas's term, "insistences." They are ground for abstraction into *existences* or meanings. One of these remembrances of an old brokenhearted French painter appears in *The Horse's Mouth* and is thought upon abstractly in *Art and Reality* and elsewhere. In some writers one might think of these things as illustrations, but with Cary they are sources. The process in this is revealed when Cary recalls the source of one of his own stories in an event that occurred on a sightseeing tour around Manhattan Island. What Cary made of this he goes on to describe in some detail, but this description is itself of an activity, and the generalizations about creativity emerge *from* it. This is about as complete a contrast to the philosophical analysis of intuition and expression in Croce's *Aesthetic* as it can be, and it is not surprising that Cary says of Croce's theory: "But this is not at all the way it seems to an artist or a writer!" For Cary, previous philosophers and artists are part of a reality one comes up against. I don't mean by this to adopt Harold Bloom's ingenious theory of misprision or creative swerve, though one can say, I think, that there is a good bit of individualistic interpretation of others in Cary's writing, but not for the psychological reasons Bloom would proffer.

One part of the real that Cary read very seriously was William Blake, and his inspiration by Blake is a matter of personal record, as an unpublished letter to the Blake Society, written in 1956, indicates:

> I have been a devotee of Blake since my nonage. I still possess the two volumes of the Ellis edition which I used at College, heavily annotated. He is for me the only philosopher, the only great poet, who had a real understanding of the nature of the world as seen by an artist, that is to say, the world of the individual, unique person, the unique thing. The world, of course, is as much a unity as a collection of individualities, that is the fundamental problem for all systematic philosophers, as it is for religion. And for Blake its unity is that of a character, a harmony of particulars.
>
> What every artist needs is both a general idea of the world and a strong sense of the individual, whether in person or thing, and Blake, of all artist-poets, had both in the highest intensity. No one conveys more sharply the unique quality of the particular thing or event, no one is more consistently aware of the world character in which all particulars have universal significance and all events relate to final causes. No one more completely despised on one hand the worm's eye view of the materialist, and on the other, more successfully escaped the dazzled myopia of the idealist philosopher or transcendental poet confounding the limitless novelty of concrete living existence in some empty abstraction called spirit or the absolute, destitute of form or significant action. For him the thinghood of reality was as immediate as its energetic soul, its person; he knew them both in their eternal and pungent quality.

This is an adulatory letter and there is no reason to think Cary did not mean every word of it. In the thirteenth chapter of *The Horse's Mouth*, Gulley Jimson recalls an important moment early in his career when he "took Blake's Job drawings out of somebody's bookshelf and peeped into them and shut them up again. Like a chap who's fallen down the cellar steps and knocked his skull in and opens a window too quick, on something too big." Apparently, Cary himself put Blake away for a time. His early, privately printed and embarrassingly bad *Verse* (1908) shows some influence of Blake's youthful *Poetical Sketches* (both books seem to have been suppressed by their authors), but the many years between *Verse* and publication of *The Horse's Mouth* do not reveal an obvious Blakean influence. For Jimson, Blake's influence emerged as he moved from his "lyric" to his "epic" phase, following Blake's own pattern of development. For Cary, Blake's influence emerged as he moved from the African novels to the more spacious trilogies, where he developed his themes most fully.

Still, it is possible to go at the very considerable connection to Blake in the wrong way and give it the wrong emphasis. For example, to call Hickson in *The Horse's Mouth* "Bromion and Theotormon, both patron of the arts and defender of order," as Fred Stockholder does, seems abstract and unproductive, merely grinding Cary exceedingly rough. Cary and Blake do not agree in all things, as for example the relation of soul and body, Cary's mind and machine. In any case, it would be far too abstract to treat all of Cary's novels as strictly Blakean. In the two trilogies, outside of *The Horse's Mouth*, Blake is mentioned but once. Sara Monday in *Herself Surprised* does so, but only because Jimson speaks of him frequently. Sara's sense of Blake is rather dim, and when she does refer to him, she feels she must identify him to us as "a poet about a hundred years ago" whom Jimson was always reading. Even in *The House's Mouth*, Blake's role can be made too literal and less playful than it is. Both "The Mental Traveller" and *Milton* have been considered bases for the structure of *The Horse's Mouth*, and Cary's own working notes have a lot about Blake in them. There is among them even an elaborate scribbled chart which purports to organize events of *The Horse's Mouth* in parallel columns according to the cyclical process of "The Mental Traveller." I cannot decipher every word of the chart, but I can read most of it—enough to see that the chart didn't work out for Cary except in an exceedingly rudimentary way as an early plan for his novel. Its relevance is limited for the most part to chapter 13. Indeed, several of his notes on Blake, like many of the notes for his heavily revised novels, are speculations and ideas not actually carried out in the text as we have it and often not even in earlier drafts. Cary once made a list of nicknames Jimson might use for Blake, but only one is finally employed: "Blake. The prophetic. The crackerjack. Old Hammer and Tongs. Los. Old Rampant. Old Randipole. Old trouble the waters. Old shoot the moon. Old Billyache. Old catch 'em alive. Old Adam. The two eyed stance. Old middlestump." And a good thing, too.

At an early stage he considered a possibility that is too mechanical and that he doesn't use:"? if one could find 300 linked quotations from Blake to run through the book, with argument and the pictures, Gulley investigating. He has the book, Blake in his pocket, but some pages missing. He uses it as a sorter." He writes elsewhere: "Quotations must be organized and follow train of feeling independent of the scene, i.e., the train of pictures." There is even ground to think that the well-known chapter 13, which is constituted by Jimson's history of his artistic development, with parts of "The Mental Traveller" as commentary, is something of a mistake. We know it was a late interpolation in the text. I shall return to this matter [elsewhere]; here it is important to get clear in what ways Cary did respond to Blake, whose image has loomed large in Cary scholarship. . . .

For Cary, as we have seen, there is a crisis of the "real." The "real" is *there* in Cary in a way different from the presence of the real in Blake. It is not true, as some seem to think, that Blake fails to recognize the existence of a separate real. The question is what *status* he gives to it. He gives it very little, because what is supremely important to him is the creation out of it of an ever-new culture, society, and the moral real. A Blake devotee may balk here, remembering that Blake always employed the world "moral" in a derogatory sense. Blake's notion of morality is not based on an "abstract real" of moral law, but on a radically Protestant notion of individual inspiration, enthusiasm, and responsibility through love. Blake is so radically Protestant that, as Jimson says of his friend Mr. Plant, he is "against all churches, especially the Protestant"; the activity implied here is the shaping of the world of matter into cultural form. The figure in Blake's long poems who thinks that the world of matter shapes man becomes Satan, while those who recognize a world to be shaped become identified with Jesus.

Jesus acted not according to law but according to imagination. In Blake, the ultimate real is the ethical world made from what is given to man, and that given, Blake diminishes in authority; it is only a potentiality for ethical action. Blake's four degrees of vision are levels of humanly shaped reality. The lowest is externality as Lockean primary material and Newtonian Law—single vision. Its moral parallel is the law of an external, hidden, avenging sky-god. This vision is real, in a sense, but its existence is a sign of moral and imaginative passivity, which creates only the abstract. One has to rise up to a higher level of vision in order to apprehend anything truly solid to the senses, for matter is abstract and ephemeral. Solidity is the work of imagination. When one begins to do this, one comes into the realm of *relationships* (of natural objects and animals) and finally into a human society. Relationships of love are imaginative and moral, the highest form of the real.

Blake seems to posit for man a radical freedom for the imagination. He is an optimist and prophesies (that is to say, imagines) a free, classless culture. It is true that he speaks of the "stubborn structure of the language," which would appear to be an obstacle to creation; but for him this is a recalcitrance holding immense possibilities—a thereness for use and making. Words are potentially human forms, by which Blake means, among other things, that they make and contain their meanings rather than signify difference. This optimism about language, so foreign to so many today, is only one aspect of his enthusiasm, which is connected closely with the tradition of religious "enthusiasm" in his age. Of course, the word "religious" is a negative word in Blake, connected as it is with organization into churches and the abstract moral law, but certainly the ground of Blake's whole vision lies in great part in enthusiasm, a religious movement that emphasized feeling over law and has been defined by Walter E. Houghton as a "standard of judgment which may be called moral optimism" (*The Victorian Frame of Mind*).

Cary describes himself as an optimist for man. He said on several occasions that he thought the opportunities for progress were immense. At the same time, Helen Gardner was certainly right to observe that the Cary she knew had a tragic aspect beneath a gallant exterior. He himself recalls in one of his last essays that as a young liberal he "overlooked the enormous power of evil working incessantly to destroy happiness and peace anywhere in the world." And he speculated about the future ironically:

> It is quite certain that in twenty-five years the present day [1956] will seem even more remote than 1900 does now. For the revolution of the free mind goes faster as that mind invents new tools. We live, literally, in the creation, and every year there are more creative imaginations at work. And more, much more, for them to feed on. The world grows more tense, more dangerous, but also infinitely richer in experience. There is no more happiness, perhaps less, but very much more intensity of living, more occupation for the mind and the senses.

(*Selected Essays*)

By any Blakean standard, Cary is a pessimist, though an exuberant one. This is not to claim that Blake was a sentimental, blinded optimist, only that the pressures Cary speaks of were not as significant for Blake, perhaps not as severe in Blake's time. Cary, himself, admired Blake's toughness and tended to imagine him in the modern context of tension he describes:

> Point of Blake is his depth and adequacy—close to the ground. His acceptance of *evil as real*. Through creation, generation to regeneration. The stoic English view but he enters into freedom and individuality through experience.

Cary is probably the only person ever to connect Blake and stoicism. Surely he clothes Blake in something more characteristic of himself, if Helen Gardner is right. Further, Blake always treated the world "evil" as error to be overcome in visionary creativity at a higher level. For Cary it is ineradicably present in the "real," which is always there and always a stumbling block. It is there, regardless of man. What culture achieves is as much in spite of it as with it. This accounts for Cary's choosing Blake's pessimistic vision of the cyclical world, "The Mental Traveller," to use in *The Horse's Mouth* and why it seems so universally illustrative of his world.

Blake's poem can be regarded as a vision of what Cary might have called the "abstract real." In tone and stance it is exceedingly distant, a quality it shares with several of the other poems from the so-called Pickering Manuscript but does not share with the rest of Blake's work. What Gulley Jimson tries to do with Blake's only diagrammatic poem is to individualize it radically and to offer an interpretation (if that is what I may call it) that stresses its variety of individual application. There is exuberance in this, but like most of Jimson's talk it is a sort of whistling in the dark. In the light of it, it seems possible to imagine Jimson as a projection of the last Blakean, who in a supreme effort turns Blake's enthusiasm into a discipline of self-protection and getting on.

Cary, on the other hand, whistles in the dark to a different tune. Jimson whistles to try to maintain his own creative powers in action. He has enough difficulty doing that without taking on the problems of the rest of society. He is well aware of them, as I believe the titles of his epic paintings make clear; but for the sake of his activity and sanity he deliberately ignores them or builds ironic attitudes toward them, treating them as part of the inevitable intransigence of the "real."

Cary takes a larger view. It is larger even than the view Jimson deliberately suppresses in order to function as a type of artist. It is larger in the sense that Cary can encompass Jimson's attitude in a view of the relation of individual to real that covers a greater range—from optimism to a vision of the darkness. It is this moral encompassment, not the so-called indeterminacy of his world, that characterizes Cary's work in the two trilogies and offers an identification with Blake while at the same time asserting its own modernity.

The Whodunit as Riddle:
Block Elements in Agatha Christie

Eliot A. Singer

> To my utter amazement and, I must admit, somewhat to my dis-
> gust, Poirot began suddenly to shake with laughter. He shook and
> he shook. Something was evidently causing him the most exquisite
> mirth.
>
> "What the devil are you laughing at?" I said sharply.
>
> "Oh! Oh! Oh!" gasped Poirot. "It is nothing. It is that I think
> of a riddle I hear the other day. I will tell it to you. What is it that
> has two legs, feathers, and barks like a dog?"
>
> "A chicken, of course," I said wearily. "I knew that in the
> nursery."
>
> "You are too well informed, Hastings. You should say, 'I do
> not know.' And then me, I say, 'A chicken,' and then you say,
> 'But a chicken does not bark like a dog,' and I say, 'Ah! I just put
> that in to make it more difficult.' Supposing, Hastings, that there
> we have the explanation. . . ."
>
> [*Thirteen at Dinner*]

In calling attention to a shared enigmatic quality, the analogy *whodunit* to
riddle is such a commonplace that it is almost more a synonym than a cliché.
Yet analogy is never a substitute for analysis, and the very obviousness of
this equation has seemed to mask the extent to which the riddle can provide
real clues to the structure of the whodunit. Many traditional speech genres
present distillations of fundamental literary devices. In more complex literary constructions, even in a popular culture form like the mystery, the
combination of such devices often covers up the simplicity of the devices
themselves. Thus, by carefully considering the construction of folkloric
forms, it often becomes possible to uncover devices that are essential to

From *Western Folklore* 43, no. 3 (July 1984). © 1984 by the California Folklore Society.

literature but concealed in it. This essay suggests that by taking seriously the notion of the whodunit as riddle, that is by applying those devices utilized in riddling strategies to this type of mystery, it becomes both possible and necessary to reconsider the basic nature of whodunit construction.

Riddling is a form of social interaction that involves an asymmetric power relationship. The poser of the enigma maintains the right to impose a predetermined solution. Alternative solutions, even if cleverer than that of the poser, are automatically rejected as incorrect. Likewise, in the whodunit, the writer is the authoritative source. The murderer is whomever the author, not the reader, chooses it to be. But this asymmetry is not institutionalized; it is a product of choice within the social interaction itself. The hearer or reader also retains a degree of power, albeit of a higher logical type. He or she may interrupt, walk away, throw a book into the fire, ruin the author's livelihood by refusing to buy another, or hypothetically, even murder the perpetrator for a particularly annoying solution. The poser of the enigma is omnipotent at the whim of the posee, and that whim lasts only so long as the solutions are satisfying. The aesthetics of the mystery is that of rationality rather than of morality or sentiment; as Roger Caillois has said, "What the reader demands is that [someone] with believable human motives pull off a crime that seems to defy reason but that reason can eventually uncover." Thus, a satisfactory solution to a mystery, must be acceptable as *rationally* superior to those alternatives that the reader has conceived.

The dominant conception among both critics and other readers is that reading a whodunit is an almost pure hermeneutic exercise in which bits of conflicting information are given the reader to enable him or her to arrive at a solution through systematic analysis. (This is why the genre is a favored paradigm for much recent reader-centered literary theory.) In [Frank] Kermode's words, "The narrative is ideally required to provide, by various enigmatic clues, all the evidence concerning the true character of [the murder] that the investigator and the reader require to reconstruct [it]." The reader and the story detective, then, are expected to follow the same hermeneutic procedure, sorting through true and false clues and eschewing "red herrings" in order to discover a coherent pattern.

Riddle scholars often refer to solutions as being "arbitrary," and as any experienced reader can attest, in reading a whodunit, it is almost always possible to conceive of several rational solutions that account for at least the most crucial disparate clues. Most whodunits suggest numerous incorrect solutions in the course of the telling, and while these are rejected because of incongruous elements, it takes little imagination to bypass these incongruities. As parodies like the film *Sleuth* imply by giving and then dismissing alternative solutions without even bothering to falsify them, in many whodunits the reason why a subsequent solution takes precedence over an earlier one has to do with its temporal placement, not its superior logic; the final solution is merely the last one. Such solutions are indeed arbitrary. But whodunits whose murderers are arbitrary choices no better than the reader's suspects do not provide satisfactory reading experiences, and their authors cannot expect to achieve consistent popularity unless, like Dorothy Sayers or Peter Dickinson, their writing is satisfying for reasons other than the mystery.

Of all the authors of the true whodunit, Agatha Christie, as is evidenced by her popularity in volume and over time, has had the greatest success in satisfying her readership. The key to this success lies in the nonarbitrariness of most of her solutions. Contrary to the common practice of whodunit writers, which, as Haycraft points out, goes back to Poe, Agatha Christie's murderers are not "*the least likely*." Nor are they taken at random from the list of suspects. Rather, more often than not, they are *the most likely*—husbands, wives, lovers, relatives, or others with clear-cut motives of gain or vengeance —that is, murderers much like those in real life. As Miss Marple explains in *The Moving Finger*, "Most crimes, you see, are so absurdly simple . . . Quite sane and straightforward—and quite understandable —in an unpleasant way of course."

Given the straightforwardness of her murders, why then are Agatha Christie's whodunits so difficult to solve? The answer lies in the reader's mistaken presumption that the mystery is complex and that the texts are hermeneutically structured to enable a reader to imitate the detective or alter-ego in sorting through clues to discover a pattern. Agatha Christie's hermeneutic, however, is a negating one, one that takes a relatively simple murder and through the reading process controverts the reader's reason. To quote again that source of wisdom, Miss Marple, "The greatest thing in these cases is to keep an absolutely open mind." What Dame Agatha consciously and insidiously does is *close the reader's mind*. The clues themselves, then, become insignificant, and the solution lies not in untangling their pattern, but in discovering the mechanism by which the reader's mind is closed.

A riddle is enigmatic because there is an obstruction between the image it presents and the referent the riddlee is supposed to guess. In riddling scholarship this obstruction, following [Robert] Petsch, is usually called *the block element*. Roger Abrahams has elaborated upon this concept by delineating four different, though not always distinct, block elements (or riddling strategies): *too little information, too much information, contradiction*, and *false gestalt*. A close examination of the construction of Agatha Christie's whodunits shows that, at one time or another, she makes use of each of these block elements to detour the reader from the solution.

While most Agatha Christie mysteries utilize a multiplicity of riddling strategies, it is usually possible to single out one block element as dominant. The 1939 Hercule Poirot novel, *Sad Cypress*, for instance, is unsolvable because there is *too little information*. In this story a poisoning takes place in the presence of two women, one of whom, as the reader learns at the outset, is on trial for murder, and hence may be presumed innocent (despite *Witness for the Prosecution*). The other woman, Nurse Hopkins, not only has the opportunity to commit the murder, but having "misplaced" the precise poison used, has the means as well. Moreover, she is seen urging the murdered girl to make a will leaving everything (which turns out to be a considerable legacy, not a pittance) to her aunt in Australia. The block occurs because Nurse Hopkins has no apparent motive. There is too little information to connect Nurse Hopkins to the inheritance since the only hint the reader receives is an aside that the unseen aunt is a nurse. The crucial fact, that Nurse Hopkins and the Australian aunt are one and the same, is revealed only in a Perry Mason style ending.

For a satisfying reading experience, as [S. S.] Van Dine insists, "The reader must have an equal opportunity with the detective for solving the mystery. All clues must be plainly stated and described." And since a reader cannot reason out a solution for which there is too little information, but can only guess at it, this mystery riddling strategy is the least fair. It is one, however, to which Christie rarely resorts, and in *Sad Cypress* even the slightest hint would make it trivial to arrive at the solution. (For other writers, Conan Doyle, for instance, giving too little information is essential—Holmes is forever sending off telegrams or utilizing arcane knowledge.)

A more reasonable block element is the opposite one, *too much information*. There is a sense in which all "red herrings" are too much information, extraneous facts that lead the reader astray. With writers like Chandler and Hammett, as [F. R.] Jameson points out, entire subplots filled with gangland murders are too much information, which is irrelevant to the enigma of the central murder. Agatha Christie, too, uses many "red herrings"—the embezzling lawyer in *Death on the Nile*, or the imposter archaeologist in *Murder at the Vicarage* are examples—but they are usually introduced late in the text, and are easily identifiable by the attentive reader. Sometimes, however, too much information becomes the dominant strategy for misleading the reader. In *Funerals Are Fatal*, for example, Aunt Cora, who is known for her tendency to state awkward and embarrassing truths, blurts out at her brother's funeral, "But he was murdered wasn't he?" When she in turn is murdered, the police and reader alike assume that her death is a result of knowledge about that of her brother. This awkward "truth," however, turns out to be extraneous information; the brother, in fact, had died an innocent death, and the murderer of Aunt Cora is the only person it could be, her companion and legatee, Miss Gilchrist, who had impersonated the victim in order to produce the misdirecting clue.

An even more elaborate use of *two much information* is *The A.B.C. Murders*. In this novel there are three murders for which the only apparent connection is that the victims' first and last initials coincide with the first letter of the town where the murders take place in alphabetical order. This coincidence, along with other clues such as the presence of the British train time table known as the ABC, insists that an alphabetical pattern be deciphered. The block element is that there is no pattern, or, rather, that the pattern is the murderer's artifice. The real victim is the third one, Sir Carmichael Clarke of Churston (the only wealthy victim), and the murderer is simply his avaricious brother, Frank, who committed the other murders to establish a false pattern to throw the police, and of course the reader, off the scent. A similar block element is used in *A Pocket Full of Rye* in which the elaborate pattern coinciding with the nursery rhyme is the fabrication of the murderer, the black sheep son of the victim.

Perhaps even more basic to the whodunit than the "red herring" is the block element *contradiction*. Locked rooms, ironclad alibis, falsified times of death, letters from the already dead, and other contradictory clues of time, place, and manner usually must be explained away before a murder can be deciphered. But such empirical contradictions, favorites of writers as diverse as Poe, Conan Doyle, and John Dickson Carr, should not bother the experienced reader, and are usually only used by Christie as secondary devices. (One exception is *Murder in Mesopotamia* where the principle block involves figuring out how "Dr. Lerdner could murder his wife from the roof without leaving it," a murder which is easily accomplished by the dropping of a heavy quern attached to a rope.)

More subtle are contradictions in character, murderous stratagems that seem implausible because they require more physical strength or more intelligence than a given character would seem to possess. In *The Hollow*, for instance, the philandering murdered husband's wife is found standing over the body with a gun in her hand, but is easily cleared since this gun turns out not to be the murder weapon. The contradiction occurs because to throw initial suspicion on oneself in order to be eliminated as a suspect is a stratagem that requires more imagination and intelligence than the wife, "poor Gerda," who is consistently portrayed as a simpleton, would seem to possess. But she is not so simple as all that, as the attentive reader should remember from when early in the book she muses, "It was amusing to know more than they thought you knew. To be able to do a thing, but not let anyone know that you could do it."

An even better illustration of contradiction occurs in one of Christie's classics, *And Then There Were None*. In this book one fact totally contradicts all others, rendering any solution impossible. All of the suspects are dead, and the last to die could not have committed suicide. The reader, of course, assumes that the dead must remain dead, so when Justice Hargrave (the notorious "hanging judge" and the only character not guilty of the death of an innocent, except perhaps in his official capacity, and therefore the most obvious suspect of these execution-style killings) becomes the sixth victim, he is immediately presumed innocent. But the reader learns of his death through the statement of Dr. Armstrong, "He's been shot." As Agatha Christie insists time and again, information and interpretation provided by characters is often accidentally or deliberately false. The reader, however, is usually too little wary of prevarication. One can recognize that Dame Agatha in her last pronouncement is speaking to the reader as well as to Hastings when Poirot says, "But perhaps, after all, you have suspected the truth? Perhaps when you read this, you already know. But somehow I do not think so . . . No, you are too trusting . . . You have too beautiful a nature." That which is the product of a character's discourse is not necessarily true, and so the once and future murdered Justice Hargrave may reasonably rise from the dead to stalk his final victims.

[Viktor] Sklovskij, in an early Russian formalist study, has pointed to the false gestalt as a general analogy for the whodunit. "These mysteries at first present false solutions," he writes, as in the Russian folk riddle, " 'It hangs dangling. Everybody grabs for it.' The solution: 'A towel.' " This analogy is, however, a little broad, and the notion of false gestalt is better limited to those texts that allow not only for alternative solutions, but for general misconceptions. (It should be noted that, while for the riddle false gestalt involves instantaneous recognition of a solution, usually an obscene one, which turns out to be false, for the whodunit this block element is not distinct but is a result of too much information or of a contradiction that leads the reader into forming a false picture of the whole circumstances of the murder, not just of its details.) One such false gestalt occurs in *The Body in the Library* where the reader assumes that the body is who it is supposed to be. This gestalt is reconstituted only when the witness who identifies the body is shown to be an accomplice. Another false gestalt that Christie induces is a misconception as to victim. In *Peril at End House* the reader assumes that, unlike Hastings who tends to jump to conclusions, Poirot is infallible, and therefore, he or she follows the detective in believing that quiet Maggie Buckley has been mistakenly done in instead of her lively cousin, Nick, whose potential assassination Poirot has cleverly deduced. In *The Mirror Cracked*, when a harmless busybody, Mrs. Badcock, is killed by an overdose, Dame Agatha hits the reader over the head with an epigraph from Tennyson, "the mirror crack'd from side to side; 'The doom has come upon me' cried the lady of Shallot," repeated, in slightly altered form, by a reliable witness to describe the actress Marina Gregg's reaction upon learning that the busybody is the probable cause of her unhappy infertility. Yet characters and readers alike are led astray because the rest of the novel provokes the false gestalt that the murder is a mistake, that the intended victim is the jaded actress, herself, for whose death there would be many possible suspects. In both cases the reader, like Poirot, fails to consider "K," "a person who should have been included in the original list, but who was overlooked." One need only remember that corpses are usually not those of mistaken victims to realize that it is the assumed targets, Nick Buckley and Marina Gregg, who are actually the guilty parties. (*The Caribbean Murders*, in which there really is a mistaken murder, albeit late in the book, is, I believe, one of Christie's failures.)

Most scholars accept any of these four block elements as legitimate riddling devices appropriate to the "true riddle." Much less accepted are those riddles that play with the riddle form itself, what are usually called, somewhat disdainfully, *"riddle parodies."* In riddle parodies what prevents the riddlee from guessing the answer is certain assumptions about the nature of riddling. These may be termed *generic blockers*. All genres set up certain norms and expectations—in riddling, that the question is an enig-

matic one, and that the information provided is valid—which help inform
the listener's or reader's interpretation. The generic norms and expectations
for the riddle and the whodunit are quite different, so while the four basic
block elements for the riddle are directly applicable to the whodunit, this
is not the case for the generic blockers. One can certainly conceive of mysteries that use the riddle parody device of having no enigma to confuse
the reader, in which, as in the riddle in the epigraph, misleading information is given not by a character (in such cases the strategy is simply *too
much information* or *false gestalt*) but by the author, or in which, as in many
"neck-riddles," the solution is wholly idiosyncratic (carrying "too little information" to the extreme). Such mysteries would, however, involve radical
transformations in form, changes in the generic dominant of the sort I have
elsewhere termed "breaking genre." Certain post-modern novelists (e.g.,
Sorrentino, Berger, Feiffer, Brautigan), playing with the mystery form, have
indeed broken genre, transforming the dominant from "Who done it?" to
more existential mysteries such as "Who am I?" or "What is fiction?" But
the whodunit as a more complex form also has a multitude of less fundamental norms and expectations not present in the riddle, and these may
be used to create generic blockers without calling into question the very
nature of the form.

Various attempts have been made to codify the mystery. Van Dine's
famous set of twenty rules proclaims, among other things, "The detective
himself, or one of the official investigators, should never turn out to be the
culprit . . . there may be but one culprit . . . the culprit must turn out to
be a person who has played a more or less prominent part in the story . . .
[and] the method of the murder, and the means of detecting it, must be
rational and scientific." Members of the British "Detective Club" must
swear

> That your detective shall well and truly detect the crimes presented
> to them, using the wits it may please you to bestow upon them
> and not placing reliance on nor making use of Divine Revelation,
> Feminine Intuition, Mumbo-Jumbo, Jiggery-Pokery, Coincidence
> or the Act of God . . . To observe a seemly moderation in the use
> of Gangs, Conspiracies, Death-Rays, Ghosts, Hypnotism, Trap-
> Doors, Chinamen, Super-Criminals, and Lunatics, and utterly and
> for ever to foreswear Mysterious Poisons unknown to Science.

But such codifications invariably confuse expectations with norms. It is
absolutely essential to the whodunit that there be an apparent crime (usually a murder), that someone seek to solve that crime, and that the reader
not learn of the solution until the final epiphany. All other conventions,
while presenting a certain aesthetic and insisting upon fairness to the
reader, are merely expectations.

Agatha Christie's genius lies most of all in her ability to prey upon the
reader's tendency to confuse expectations with norms to invent generic
blockers for her mysteries. For this skill, she was reviled by some of her

contemporaries: Van Dine dismissed one of her devices as "bald trickery, on the par with offering some one a bright penny for a five-dollar gold piece," and [Raymond] Chandler said that another was "guaranteed to knock the keenest mind for a loop. Only a half wit could guess it." But, as Dorothy Sayers argued, "I fancy . . . this opinion merely represents a natural resentment at having been ingeniously bamboozled. All the necessary data are given. The reader ought to be able to guess the criminal, if he is sharp enough, and nobody can ask for more than this. It is, after all, the reader's job to keep his wits about him, and, like the perfect detective, to suspect *everybody*." Certainly readers do not seem to feel cheated by Agatha Christie's whodunits with generic blockers, which include some of her most famous and bestselling works. While she could probably not get away with eschewing the interdiction against fantastic solutions (rationality is too central to the whodunit) or with overuse of the same generic blocker (after a while the reader's expectations would change), she has clearly shown that highly satisfying mysteries can be constructed by testing the limits of generic expectations.

As [I. I.] Revzin has pointed out, the solutions to whodunits involve the equation of other *dramatis personae* with the murderer, but what he fails to note is that certain dramatis personae, the conventional roles of Holmes, Watson, and Lestrade, are expected to be immune from this equation. Christie has systematically broken this expectation. Her most famous case is, of course, *The Murder of Roger Ackroyd*. Here the murderer, again the most obvious, is Dr. Sheppard, who, unfortunately for the reader, is also the narrator. Christie is eminently fair, here, in that she makes it clear that the role of narrator is of Dr. Sheppard's own choosing, that he is not a particular friend of Hercule Poirot. But the generic block is so powerful that this mystery is almost impossible for any reader to solve. In *A Holiday for Murder*, it is the investigating policeman, Superintendent Sugden, who commits the murder. Again the narrative discourse provides ample clues — Sugden is introduced before the murder takes place, coincidentally arrives on the scene as the body is being discovered, and is around altogether too much for someone in the Lestrade role — but the generic block prevents him from being suspected. In *Curtain* even Poirot becomes a murderer. As he insists in a letter to Hastings, the solution should be obvious, given the execution-style of the killing ("the mark of Cain" made by a bullet in the center of the forehead), the presence of lesser details such as that only Poirot was shorter than the victim, and especially the fact that Poirot had already demonstrated that the victim was an unconvictable murderer. And *Curtain* is, after all, a posthumous book. But who could be more above suspicion than the hero of most of Dame Agatha's greatest works.

Christie also systematically breaks other generic expectations. In several books she uses Van Dine's *only one culprit* rule as a generic blocker. In *Death on the Nile*, for instance, three murders are committed, and everyone has an inviolate alibi for at least one of them. The solution would be obvious in real life: the primary victim's husband, Simon Doyle, and his apparently estranged lover, Jacqueline de Bellefort, are conspirators attempting to inherit a rich wife's wealth. But whodunit conventions so frown upon accomplices that Christie's use of them is surprising and effective. *Murder on the Calais Coach* (better known as *Murder on the Orient Express*) takes this generic blocker even further. The wounds on the body seem to have been made by a dozen different people, and all of the passengers on the train have fabricated their identities to cover up connections to the victim. As in so many whodunits, everyone looks guilty. What makes this novel so original and unsolvable is that everyone *is* guilty.

Another generic blocker is the expectation that *characters who are suspected* by the police are automatically innocent. In Christie's first novel, *The Mysterious Affair at Styles*, the victim's husband Alfred Inglethorp is under the heavy suspicion of the police until Poirot, with great show and effort, uncovers an alibi, which because of its scandalous nature, the suspect is apparently unwilling to use. Since, conventionally, the detective and not the police must be correct, the reader is induced to check the husband off the list of real suspects. But by using a readily discoverable alibi to clear the husband earlier rather than later in the text, Poirot is then free to demonstrate an alternative solution with Inglethorp as the murderer. In the more mature *Murder at the Vicarage*, Lawrence Redding, the victim's wife's lover, actually is arrested. He is, however, quickly cleared on evidence supplied by none other than Miss Marple. But since his innocence is established early in the book, it then becomes possible for Christie to reestablish him as the murderer at the end.

Probably the most basic whodunit expectation is that *the murder must be committed by the murderer*. But in *Curtain*, as is appropriate for Christie's terminal Poirot mystery, even this expectation is broken. Stephen Norton does not murder anyone; yet as a catalyst he is *the murderer*. Dame Agatha gives the reader no less a clue than *Othello*, but the whodunit genre is not Shakespearean drama, so recognition of this Iago's culpability is firmly blocked.

Most texts withhold key bits of information necessary to their interpretation. In *Tom Jones*, for instance, the revelation of the crucial identity of Tom's mother is saved for the end (and there are similar lesser revelations throughout.) *Finnegans Wake* is so hermetic that the words themselves must be deciphered. But it is in the whodunit that what Barthes calls the "hermeneutic code" becomes dominant; the pleasure of the text lies principally in its enigma, and in "the expectation and desire for its solution."

Nevertheless, while all whodunits may be dominated by the hermeneutic code, not all entail the same hermeneutic process. "Classic detective stories rely on a simple pattern of interpretation, treating sensory data (clues) as signs for hidden facts about events in the past and hidden truths about characters' personalities." Holmes's "method," for instance, "is a practical semiotics: his goal is to consider data of all kinds of potential signifiers and to link them, however disparate and incoherent they seem, to a coherent set of signifieds, that is to turn them into signs of a hidden *order* behind the manifest confusion, of the *solution* to the mystery, of the *truth*." The conventional wisdom is that the whodunit reader, like the detective, starts with a blank slate, and then receives a series of clues, each of which must be deciphered and properly arranged on the slate until a complete pattern can be formed. The process of pattern formation is gradual, and the reading, like the playing of the board game *Clue*, is progressive; presumably, the further along the narrative and the more clues available, the more complete the pattern.

Such a progressive hermeneutic structure most resembles a puzzle, and the author an encoding cryptographer. But, as [Julian] Symons argues, "The deception in . . . Christie stories is much more like the conjurer's sleight of hand. She shows us the ace of spades face up. Then she turns it over, but we still know where it is, so how has it been transformed into the five of diamonds?" Or more accurately, we assume that the card will no longer be the ace of spades, and yet it is. Following a progressive series of Agatha Christie's clues only leads to total confusion: the significance of each is very obscure, and it is impossible to decide which signifiers may, in fact, have empty signifieds. The reader is no nearer the solution and indeed is often further from it, just before the epiphany than at the beginning of the book; the only characters who have really been eliminated as suspects are the dead, and even these not absolutely. (My own experience has been that I have been most successful in guessing the murderer before the first murder occurs, or by choosing from a list of the "cast of characters" before even starting to read.) When it comes, the revelation is sudden and surprising. And it is not built up to by a series of clues; it is systematically obstructed.

When most critics use the terms "puzzle" and "riddle" interchangeably as synonyms for the whodunit, they are missing a crucial structural difference. Puzzles are really solved through the accumulation of clues. Riddles can almost never be solved deductively; the key to their hermeneutic structure is the block element. It is the block element that Agatha Christie has elevated to the prominent hermeneutic device for the whodunit. While she is not the only mystery writer who structures her plots around the block element (nor is it invariably present in her books), she certainly has made the most systematic and best use of it. One text or another of hers has incorporated all of the available kinds of blockers, and even when she has repeated herself, as is inevitable given the paucity of riddling strategies and her prolific output, there is a sufficient freshness to minimize the sense of *déjà-vu*. And by fooling the reader into overlooking the most obvious suspects, rather than by selecting some clues and ignoring others in choosing an arbitrary murderer, Agatha Christie, almost uniquely, has consistently been able to produce whodunits whose final solutions are the most reasonable and, therefore, the most satisfying.

Aldous Huxley
and the Two Nothings

A. E. Dyson

"Classified, like a museum specimen, and lectured about, I felt most dismally posthumous." This is Aldous Huxley, reminding us that donnish acclaim is not necessarily the summit of a writer's ambition. And if one feels that academic criticism has been less than fair to him, to think in terms of amendment might be over-solemn. He has had a wide success after all, among readers who delight in intelligence as an end as well as a means: and Time will bring the Ph.D. thesis along with the worm.

But it remains odd that the universities have paid so little attention to an outstandingly intelligent writer: odd, and perhaps symptomatic of the mistrust with which intelligence is often viewed in Britain, especially by those who possess it. Not that this is the whole story, by any means. "Sincerity in Art" Huxley has more than once said, "is mainly a matter of talent"; the writer who specialises in such truths can be assured of a good many enemies. He is, moreover, an example of the type of writer, more congenial to the French than to the English, who has understood and condemned his own puritanism without in any great measure escaping from it.

My main concern in what follows will be with his irony, which links him with Swift not only in certain specific ways, such as its capacity for disgust and its nearness to tragedy, but also in its continuing relevance as an interpreter of life. "Add to one touch of nature one touch of irony," he writes, "and you have a comment on life more profound, in spite of its casualness, its seeming levity, than the most eloquent ramblings of the oracles." When such a comment is offered on Gibbon or Voltaire, we are disposed to agree; as a comment on Huxley himself, it runs into hesitations and doubts. Is he not, perhaps, too detached to be a major ironist, or too cynical? When his irony is given full play, are we not reminded of a surgeon

From *The Critical Quarterly* 3, no. 4 (Winter 1961). © 1961 by *The Critical Quarterly*.

with outstanding gifts of diagnosis, whose patients nonetheless always die? The knife cuts sharp and true, but there is no property of healing in it; or possibly the malignancy goes too deep. I shall argue later that Huxley specialises in ironic traps from which there seems to be no way out; that he has a genius for locking us in Doubting Castle and demonstrating that all the keys have been lost. At times, one even feels that his offer to the reader is a simple choice between two Nothings—the Nothing of Mrs. Viveash's boredom in *Antic Hay*, and the Nothing of Mr. Propter's God in *After Many a Summer*. I shall be returning to this suggestion several times, but it is as well to remember that Swift also can spring traps of a notoriously effective kind; *Brave New World* has more in common with book IV of *Gulliver* than a few tricks of style. If we look at Huxley's irony not in one work but over a period of years, the notion that he is chiefly a negative writer becomes increasingly hard to sustain. What I want to do here is to look in turn at five of the novels, which between them span the twenty years between the two world wars.

II

Huxley's first novel, *Crome Yellow*, is in the satiric line of Peacock. It is full of fun, as we too easily forget after putting it down. But while some episodes are simply amusing, others already hint at a profoundly disturbing astringency. The hero's torments as an intellectual endlessly wounded by self-knowledge are a clear pointer towards much that is to come.

Antic Hay, published in 1923 and the first to concern us here, is an altogether more important work. As in *Crome Yellow* we meet a group of characters in whom intelligence is an unfailing source of disquiet. But the range is now wider, and Huxley's irony too subtle for simple analysis. He plays on our own capacity for uneasy self-knowledge with horrifying sureness of touch. More than any ironist I can think of, he evokes fear in his readers as an integral part of his technique. And in *Antic Hay* he explores, as he has often done since, the degree to which honest intelligence can lead to cynicism, self-loathing, mental paralysis rather than to knowledge, self-control and committal. For some critics, this is enough in itself to damn him. They see in it a sort of diabolical gravitation, a foil at best for Lawrence's opposite pull of the intelligence towards moral maturity. To take this view, however, may well be to risk confusing art with morality. It overlooks the manner in which Huxley himself places negative attitudes, in his depiction of Coleman for instance. And it overlooks the difficulties which even Lawrence sometimes had in preserving his vision unspotted from the world. I shall return to this matter later, but wish simply to assert at this stage that the insistence upon degradation and disgust in Huxley's work is not fundamentally due to masochism—though this enters into it— but to his utterly ruthless and uncompromising honesty. What needs to be said, perhaps, is that the puritan tradition, of which we hear a good deal these days, has always included men of Huxley's temperament as well as men of Lawrence's. If moral earnestness, fierce energy, strong committal are one side of puritanism, then revulsion from the body, savage denunciation, bitter irony are no less certainly the other. Huxley's puritanism, I would say, is of Swift's type, which increases rather than diminishes in fierceness as it senses its own impotence to alter anything. It is the puritanism which is compelled to approach the best, if at all, by way of the worst; so that if the worst proves too strong for it, the very energy on which it lives can turn to destruction. To accuse Huxley of frivolousness for not seeing eye to eye with Lawrence is just about as sensible as accusing an Agnostic of frivolousness for not professing to believe in God. The difference between the two men is to be thought of in terms of temperament rather than of integrity. Both disturb us in their different ways because they have too much honesty, not because they have too little.

Antic Hay, moreover, is nearer to the centre of twentieth-century literature than any single novel of Lawrence's one could name; its pessimism is nearer to T. S. Eliot, James Joyce, Scott Fitzgerald, Franz Kafka than is often supposed. In this sense, Huxley can be seen as another reporter of the Waste Land; one in whom contemplation of the twentieth century produces a curiously un-English blend of laughter and despair. *Antic Hay* is his first important creative response to the type of society and situation that was later to be satirised equally amusingly, with greater urbanity but far less concern, by Evelyn Waugh.

But Huxley does not write only as a judge, nor does he suggest that any easy solutions exist for the evils and weaknesses that he sees. If the tribulations of the smart set seem well-merited as they progress through self-indulgence to infinite boredom, we are also shown that introspection and self-doubt can afflict any thinking man, irrespective of his degree of moral guilt. When Huxley shows how anything can be grist to this particular mill, from the remnants of a Christian conscience to the newest of Freudian insights, his irony is not only a defensive misanthrophy, but a glimpse into the traditional hell of ultimate despair. In portraying the unsuccessful painter Old Lypiatt, he undermines creative energy itself, by putting its aspirations and pretensions into the mouth of a failure. And in casting doubts on the holiness of the heart's affections, he attacks the very citadel of romanticism; if hopes of self-fulfilment are made to seem as idle as hopes of Heaven, where is the romantic to turn? "Poor Old Lypiatt" . . . the very formula is a secret nightmare for scores of would-be creative young men, as Huxley very well knows. Nor does he stop here, since Lypiatt has to peel off layer after layer of self-deception as one might peel an onion, until the nothingness at the centre of his life can no longer be doubted or escaped.

Now what is the point of a ruthless honesty like this? A Christian writer might conduct similar operations, as C. S. Lewis does in *The Screwtape Letters*, but as a prelude to grace. In Huxley, there is no *deus ex machina* in the wings, only the erosion of dignity and purpose as one illusion after another is exposed. "Everyone's a walking farce and a walking tragedy at the same time," he comments, poor consolation indeed for what has been lost. But we should not overlook the discriminations of cynicism which are already part of the satiric texture; if Coleman's cynicism is a sickness of the soul, Huxley's own cynicism is often the reverse side of the soul's passionate longing for health. For *Antic Hay* opens by drawing attention to a dislocation which is at the heart of Huxley's own ironic vision. There are two Gods, one emotional, the other logical, and these two are not One. His hero Gumbril, who is both acutely aware of this dislocation, and afflicted with the characteristic torments of the young, withdraws into a fantasy world of his own devising. He compounds from elements aesthetic, messianic, and erotic a fanciful self-idealisation, which later impinges on his real life through his farcical charade as the Complete Man. All of this, we might agree, is good adolescent psychology, without being startlingly new. But it is something more as well; there is an intensity of perception which makes the word 'adolescent' more of a hindrance to the critic than a help. Gumbril is surrounded by other characters who in various ways correspond to his most cynical apprehensions. In Coleman, who verbalises and luxuriates in filth as a connoisseur might in beauty, Huxley shows us the last degradation to which accepted cynicism can lead. This purest variant of hell is a fore-shadowing of Spandrell in *Point Counterpoint*, Staithes in *Eyeless in Gaza*, Dr. Obispo in *After Many a Summer*—a whole sequence of cynics who remind us that though the data for pessimism are such that no honest man can afford to deny them, the acceptance of pessimism can be no less than the cancer of the soul. Confronted with such characters we are able neither to reject them easily, since so much of what they say is true, nor in any sense to accept the on their own terms. What Huxley is concerned to show, I imagine, is that 'honesty' is a criterion which must be applied at least as much to the manner in which a man holds his views as to the nature of the views themselves. His most evil characters have among their literary ancestors Iago and Bosola, both very honest men in their way.

When we turn from Coleman to Mrs. Viveash, as she walks "her private knife-edge between her personal abysses," it is to encounter another classic type of damnation. " 'But I don't like anyone,' cried Mrs. Viveash with terrible vehemence." Cynicism has produced in her not violence, but the annihilating prospect of immeasurable boredom. Her eyes, we are told, "had a formidable capacity for looking and expressing nothing . . . as though she were worshipping almighty and omnipresent Nil." She too is a prototype for important characters in the later novels—for Lucy Tanta-mount in *Point Counterpoint* who is a more terrifying variant, and for Helen in *Eyeless in Gaza*, who is an altogether more rounded and moving one.

On the other side of the picture, we find Gumbril Senior, the first of yet another well-defined and increasingly influential sequence of Huxley characters—Rachel Quarles in *Point Counterpoint*, Miller in *Eyeless in Gaza*, Mr. Propter in *After Many a Summer*. Old Gumbril shares with the other people in the novel their sense of futility, but not their propensity to despair. The body might be unredeemable, but there remains a realm of serene disengagement for the soul. What we have to do, he thinks, is to reject "the wretched human scale" which is "the scale of the sickly body, not of the mind." His offer, as I have already hinted, is the possibility of exchanging for Mrs. Viveash's Nil, which is the nothingness of the body, that other great Nil, which is the nothingness of the soul.

And this, as we can see looking back, is the true pointer to Huxley's own development as a novelist; the choice which in almost every novel he will return to, with greater or lesser realism as the case might be. But in the years immediately following *Antic Hay*, he was diverted by the influence of D. H. Lawrence into another type of exploration, which reaches its culmination five years later in *Point Counterpoint*. "Man is one," wrote Lawrence, "body and soul; and his parts are not at war with one another." Huxley's sympathetic attempt to come to terms with this view, and his eventual failure to do so, are among the most interesting features of his development. By the early thirties he had reverted to the view of *Antic Hay*, which could be fairly summarized by turning the sentence I have just quoted from Lawrence inside out. In moving as close to Lawrence as he does in *Point Counterpoint*, however, he proves beyond doubt his seriousness as a man and a novelist. He provides too an important critique of Lawrence himself, and one which it is time, perhaps, that we started to take note of again.

III

"If you only knew how dreadful love seems to somebody who doesn't love, what a violation, what an outrage." This now familiar torment is Walter's, at the beginning of *Point Counterpoint*, and he goes on to reflect as follows:

> Perhaps we're brought up too wholesomely and asceptically, he thought. An education that results in one's feeling sick in the company of one's fellow-men, one's brothers — can it be good? He would have liked to love them. But love does not flourish in an atmosphere that nauseates the lover with an uncontrolled disgust.

The carry-over from *Antic Hay* is clear enough, but Huxley is ready now to extend his canvas. As the title implies there is to be a greater variety of characters than before, indeed something of a representative survey. They are likened to the instruments of an orchestra, all of which, however, play their own tunes "equally right and equally wrong; and none of them will listen to the others."

Among the characters who can be considered in any way happy John Bidlake is of immediate interest to a reader coming from *Antic Hay*. He is a painter who unlike Old Lypiatt really does have great talent, so that his *obiter dicta* on art are preserved from irony. He is also a lighthearted sensualist, practising sex while Rampion preaches about it, with less damage to his partners than readers of the early Huxley might expect. At the other end of the scale, Rachel Quarles finds happiness in renunciation of the flesh, and in the mystic way of negation. Somewhere between the two

Lord Edward also achieves the happiness which comes of disengagement, in his case through the abstractions of science. Another character who finds a kind of happiness is the Fascist leader, Webley; though his pride is the sort which proverbially goes before a fall ("He wants to be treated as though he were his own colossal statue, erected by an admiring and grateful nation"), it is the authentic pride of the prophet—fiercely dynamic for all its arrogance, and undeterred by self-doubt up to the actual moment of death.

All of these characters have some measure of contentment with their lot, but the limits within which this happiness exists are sharply defined. Rachel Quarles and Lord Edward win serenity at the expense of human concern. Though the one is a mystic, the other a scientist, both cultivate a degree of detachment which cannot easily be distinguished from indifference. Webley's limited success as a leader rests on the dubious foundation of fascist theory bolstered up by violence; when he is murdered, it seems little more than poetic justice. Even Bidlake's zest and good humour fail to survive the tumour in his stomach, or to see him through with dignity to the grave.

And what then are we to make of Mark Rampion—whose happiness seems better based than that of the others, and his energy a remarkable triumph, for once, of body and spirit working together? Rampion, one need hardly add, is closely modelled on Lawrence, and his wife Mary on Frieda. The chapter where his first meeting with Mary is described brings to mind Mellors's meeting with Lady Chatterley, as well as Lawrence's personal history. But almost at once, we are struck by something very odd about his place in this novel. Alone among the characters, with the possible and decidedly ironic exception of Webley, he seems not just one instrument singing his own tune, but the very theme the whole orchestra might exist to develop. The pivotal question in this novel, and indeed in Huxley's whole career as a novelist, turns out to be simply this: is Rampion big enough to contain the whole novel, or is he not? As it turns out, he is not; mainly, one senses, because Huxley's emotional prejudice in his favour cannot finally overcome the weight of creative intuition that works against him. We are not convinced in the end that Rampion is talking about realities; and this is because Huxley himself is unconvinced, despite the very best will in the world.

Nor is this any great reason for surprise. Lawrence's attraction to him is at least in part the attraction of opposites. As we hear Rampion expounding Lawrence's ideas in Huxley's prose, there is an unmistakable falsity of tone: everything is familiar, but it is like a lecture on Lawrence rather than the man himself. And alone among Huxley's characters, except for the mystically inclined, Rampion is insulated against the prevailing atmosphere of irony. In a book written by an author to whom irony is something of an instinct, and never more so than when the body is being extolled, this insulation seems doubly artificial. Not that we doubt the sincerity of Huxley's admiration for Rampion. "He can smell people's souls," says Mary Rampion, making just the claim for her husband that

Lawrence would most have wished. And just for a chapter or so it looks as though Rampion might really swing the whole novel, with its galaxy of bored and wicked people and its disastrous events, into the ambience of his personal vision. The magic is strong enough, at any rate, to hold Huxley's normal vision in balance against something very like its opposite; we can understand how he came, under the spell of it, to write on Lawrence one of the brilliantly seminal critical essays of our time. But in the end, Rampion's dynamic decency doesn't win the day. He vanishes from the novel before its climax, and when the irony of point-counterpoint reasserts itself, it is grimmer and nearer to tragedy than before. Rampion hasn't explained, for all his good sense, the complexities of sexual depravity which Lucy Tantamount, Walter, and Burlap in their different ways exemplify. He has analysed but not saved Spandrell, whose nihilism plays a terrifying part in the novel's climax. Above all, he has been unable to exorcise certain *facts*, which haunt Huxley's imagination in all that he writes. There is the cancer which kills Bidlake, for instance ("Deplorable," writes Philip, "to see an Olympian reduced by a little tumour in his stomach to the state of subhumanness"). There is the murder of Webley—the joint outcome of Illidge's social grudges and Spandrell's unmotivated, unassuageable hatred of life. There is the meningitis which kills Philip's young son, with its mindless cruelty, its terrible cat-and-mouse game with its prey.

The novel returns, then, through its vision of the worst that can happen, to Huxley's usual sense of life; that matter is evil, the body a torment and a trap. Philip Quarles, writing about Rampion in his diary, says "The chief difference between us, alas, is that his opinions are lived and mine, in the main, merely thought." This glib and partial antithesis between "thinking" and "living" has been taken up by some critics, as though it were also the major difference between Huxley himself as a writer, and Lawrence. I have already tried to establish how superficial any such notion would be. Huxley rejects Lawrence in the long run for the same reason that he rejects incarnational religion. Attractive though the redemption of the flesh is as a belief, plausible as it can on occasion be made to sound, it doesn't *feel* convincing to him in the end. This may be his tragedy, no doubt, or it may be a simple difference in temperament that goes deeper than any theorising can plumb. But we cannot doubt that Huxley is as honest in his own way as Lawrence was, equally sensitive and intelligent in his search for truth though the report that he comes back with is darker. His true affinity, as I have already hinted, is with Swift; with the vision of Lilliputian man, incurably small, and Yahoo man, incurably dirty. One of the most perceptive remarks ever made about Swift is Huxley's, and it applies with equal, if not greater force to himself. Swift, he wrote, "could never forgive man for being a vertebrate mammal as well as an immortal soul."

What we come back to is the need to distinguish in *Point Counterpoint* between cynicism of Spandrell's type, which is the cancer of the soul, and pessimism which might look very cynical, but is the simple refusal of Huxley's personal honesty to abdicate. It is Elinor Quarles who makes, towards the end of the novel, the fullest statement of its main theme: "But the very possession of a body is a cynical comment on the soul and all its ways. It is a piece of cynicism, however, which the soul must accept, whether it likes it or not."

"To be with Lawrence," Huxley wrote elsewhere, "was a kind of adventure, a voyage of discovery into newness and otherness. For being himself of a different order, he inhabited a different universe from that of common men—a brighter and intenser world, of which, while he spoke, he would make you free." Rampion is Huxley's generous salute, as a novelist, to this spell, but the clause "while he spoke" cannot be overlooked. After *Point Counterpoint* Huxley moves off again in his own direction, no longer expecting that the war between flesh and spirit will ever be ended. He intensifies instead his search for man the Houyhnhnm—for the mental abstraction, disguised maybe as an animal, who will offer the spirit an escape from the evils it can no longer hope to cure.

IV

Brave New World, written in 1932, is the best known of Huxley's novels, and inside its conventions very possibly his best. The theme is an old one; where is happiness to be found? Like many previous explorers, including Dr. Johnson in *Rasselas,* the answer Huxley appears to offer is "nowhere." "At the time the book was written," he commented in 1946, "this idea, that human beings are given free will in order to choose between insanity on the one hand and lunacy on the other, was one that I found amusing and regarded as quite possibly true." The novel is similar in structure to book IV of *Gulliver,* particularly in that the direction the irony seems to be taking is devastatingly reversed half-way through, and everything thrown in the melting-pot again. We are presented at first with a world set in the future; a seeming utopia of a nonmoral kind, which turns out to be the creation of applied science harnessed to a totalitarian state. Babies are made and conditioned in test-tubes, luxuries abound; sex has been dissociated at long last from procreation, and freed to compete on equal terms with the other amusements. Dirt and squalor have been done away with, since in a promiscuous society hygiene and cleanliness are everywhere a *sine-qua-non*. Most sources of tension have disappeared with the taboos that engendered them, but if life still threatens to become disquieting, a "holiday in eternity" can always be obtained with the drug *suma*: "Christianity without tears," as Huxley calls it.

The presentation of this Brave New World is shot through with irony, as we should expect. In doing away with pain the scientists have also made an end of greatness. "Civilisation has absolutely no need of nobility and heroism," says the Controller, "these things are symptoms of political inefficiency." They have also abolished freedom, since the conditioning of babies for happiness has necessarily curtailed their power of choice, and as the Controller also says, what is happiness but "liking what one *has* to do?" Other casualties of the utopian society include liberalism, democracy, Shakespeare, and God. There used to be such things, but they were all found conducive to pain, guilt, and an unstable society. The individual has absolutely ceased to matter, since if some accident overtakes him, he can readily be replaced from a test-tube. Only the State is unique, and therefore uniquely entitled to preserve itself.

The main ironic points here are clear enough. Reversing his grand-father's belief that science is the generous friend of man, Huxley sees it as his last and deadliest enemy. And anticipating such nightmares as Orwell's *1984* and David Karp's *One*, he foresees the process of conditioning by which a totalitarian regime might abolish the human race as we have hith-erto come to know it. He makes the further ironic point that sexual pro-miscuity, though superficially making for happiness, is to any sensitive soul the very negation of it. As we know from his essays, he agreed with Lawrence in thinking that free love is as dangerous, or very nearly so, as "that melancholy sexual perversion known as continence." "Too much liberty is as life-destroying as too much restraint," he says, and again, "Nothing is more dreadful than a cold, unimpassioned indulgence." In the Brave New World of the future any sexual relationship that lasts long enough to suggest emotional attachment is opposed, and 'mother' has become a supremely dirty word.

The trap in the novel is sprung when Huxley turns to the other side of the picture: to Bernard, whose conditioning in the test-tube went wrong, so that his spirit yearns for things other than he has; and to the Savage, who continues the old way of life in an artificially preserved Mexican set-tlement until he is disastrously brought face to face with the new. Bernard, who strives towards just the standards by which the new society is tried and found wanting, turns out to be a typical early Huxley hero. His phallic self-consciousness leads to disgust rather than to liberation; and sexuality, when it ceases to be trivial, reverts to being a torment. As to the Mexican settlement (was its location chosen, one wonders, out of fading deference to Lawrence?), it turns out to be every bit as dirty, degraded, and neurotic as the London of *Antic Hay*. When the Savage is brought face to face with the new utopia, his response is so morbid that we feel it to be almost justified after all. His obsession with Shakespeare proves to be fully as dangerous as the creators of the Brave New World would have anticipated. When he can no longer dramatise himself as Ferdinand he casts himself instead as Othello, the whole force of outraged idealism turning into hatred and violence. His obsession with Jesus shows itself to be if anything even worse. In his hatred of amoral pleasures he cries out to be hurt; pain will both prove his manhood, and expiate his guilt. But his disillusionment with Lenina/Miranda is at least as much a satire on himself as on her. When his search for pain turns into action, it can be seen as the cruelty of the puritan temperament having its fling.

In the powerful scene between the Savage and the Controller, both talk the same language, but from opposite camps. The Savage can think of the stable society of "nice tame animals" only as an outrage; the Controller claims that it is the best of all possible worlds without pretending that the best is especially good. In his 1946 Introduction, Huxley says that were he rewriting the book he would include a further alternative for the human species. Between lunacy and insanity, there would now be something more positive than a vacuum. The passage is of such key interest that I should like to quote it in full.

> If I were now to rewrite the book, I would offer the savage a third alternative. Between the utopian and the primitive horns of his dilemma would lie the possibility of sanity—a possibility already actualised, to some extent, in a community of exiles and refugees from the Brave New World, living within the borders of the Reservation. In this community economics would be decentralist and Henry-Georgian, politics Kropotkinesque and co-operative. Science and technology would be used as though, like the Sabbath, they had been made for man, not (as at present and still more so in the Brave New World) as though man were to be adapted and enslaved to them. Religion would be the conscious and intelligent pursuit of man's Final End, and unitive knowledge of the immanent Tao or Logos, the transcendent Godhead or Brahman. And the prevailing philosophy of life would be a kind of Higher Utilitarianism, in which the Greatest Happiness principle would be secondary to the Final End principle—the first question to be asked and answered in every contingency of life being: "How will this thought or action contribute to, or interfere with, the achievement, by me and the greatest number of other individuals, of man's Final End?"

The relevance of this to Huxley's later work is beyond question; but in 1932 he chose to leave humanity poised between two types of madness. In 1961, would his intentions in rewriting have changed again? More than most of our writers, with the supremely honourable exception of Bertrand Russell, he has remained flexible amid the rapid vicissitudes of twentieth-century history. The rewriting of philosophies and with them such novels as may be influenced by philosophies has become a major pressure on honest writers today as never before. One wonders what changes Lawrence might have been disposed to make in his world, had he lived on into the atomic age.

V

Eyeless in Gaza, published in 1936, might have been Huxley's greatest novel, but unhappily it is badly flawed. The characters all talk too much, holding up the narrative for chapters on end. The hero sprawls through the novel, in essays and jottings more shapeless than one would have thought possible.

The obviously controversial thing about *Eyeless in Gaza* is its bold experiment with time. Like *Tristram Shandy* it abandons a chronological sequence in favour of a flashback technique of great complexity. The main events span a period of more than thirty years. Each chapter is headed with the date on which its events take place, and the chapters are interspersed in what appears to be a random fashion.

Now what does Huxley hope to gain by this method? Mainly, I would say, psychological suspense. For much of the time we are wondering *why* the characters are as they are, and the author deliberately holds back key events until we have been able, from their behaviour, almost to deduce what has happened in the past. The extremely important episode surrounding Anthony's relationship with Brian at the time of his death is kept until near the end, when it comes almost with the shock of recognition. Several times Huxley is enabled by his freedom with time to supply vital clues to his characters at moments when these are most useful to our total understanding of them. And we are less disposed to commit ourselves to hasty judgment when certain vital clues from the past are still likely to be revealed. There is, too, something curiously and usefully disturbing about the rapid transitions between (say) Mary Amberley's youthful brilliance, and her squalid degradation in middle age.

The technical experiment is strikingly successful, then, in some ways, but there are losses to balance the gains. Perhaps a novelist can justify the strains put upon us when he tampers with the time sequence only if he has other excellencies of an unusual kind. Sterne can capture our attention with his characters, who are so marvelously vivid and idiosyncratic that the order in which things happen to them hardly matters. James Joyce can hold us, in *Ulysses* if not in *Finnegans Wake*, with his splendid manipulation of theme and symbol. And Virginia Woolf unfailingly captivates with her style; in which other writer is the tension between an aristocratic tone and a deeply troubled consciousness so poignant, or the gift for writing prose with the intensity of poetry so finely achieved? Huxley, who has none of these virtues to the same degree, is left too nakedly depending on ideas to sustain our interest. Even his visual sense is not good; in *The Doors of Perception* he has harsh things to say of writers who too readily assimilate what is felt to what is thought, perhaps recognising this as a major weakness in himself.

A further disadvantage in the technique is that it distorts certain moments in the past by making them more statically important to the characters than they normally would be. Mr. C. B. Cox has made a similar point [elsewhere] about Virginia Woolf, and it seems to apply with equal if not greater force to *Eyeless in Gaza*. The importance to Hugh, for instance, of the moment in school when he is caught masturbating by some of his schoolfellows, suggests nothing so much as arrested development. The criticism one has to make on this score is twofold. On the one hand, we are shown Hugh's schoolfellows actually recalling this episode, much later in their lives, and behind his back. In other words, Hugh's fears that it will make him permanently ridiculous are not, Huxley would seem to suggest, groundless. But surely in fact they would be—for who cares whether a man has been found masturbating in his schooldays or not? This may seem a minor point, but its implications are rather larger than they appear to be. The great American novelist Scott Fitzgerald makes one of the characters in *Tender is the Night* say this: "Most people . . . think other people's opinions of them swing through great arcs of approval or disapproval." Fitzgerald, with his unerring sense of social realities, places this fear for what it is. In Huxley, such fears are regarded as normal; indeed, the reader himself is frequently played upon through such potential neuroses in himself.

The second point that must be made is that moments from the past have this static importance not only for Hugh, who is of a recognisably neurotic temperament, but for Anthony and Helen as well. And when the normal time sequence is departed from, perhaps to some degree this is unavoidable. The different episodes become almost like a series of framed photographs; we compare them with one another with heightened feelings of nostalgia or irony, but the sense of cause and effect is curiously weakened.

Even more than *Point Counterpoint* this novel is punctuated by scenes of violence and disgust, which shape as well as symbolise its central crises. There is Helen's revulsion as a child from the feel of butcher's kidneys, and her disgust and self-disgust when a pet cat dies. There is Brian's violent and terrible death by falling; the amputation of Staithes's leg (after an intolerable delay while Miller discourses on Buddhism); the murder of Ekki by the Nazis. Above all, there is the notorious scene early in the book when Anthony's lovemaking on the roof is cut short by the arrival of a very dead and very messy dog (a misfortune that Mellors himself mightn't have survived, as Huxley could even have reflected when conceiving it). The scene demonstrates the hypersensitivity to suffering of both Helen and Anthony; it also marks a turning point in their relationship, since Anthony comes to realise that he loves Helen as well as desires her at the very time that Helen is deterred fron any further physical intimacy with him. As a symbol of human brutality it is as fierce as anything in Hardy; and I think we feel it is a valid symbol and not merely contrived, since Huxley's revulsion from the natural world is so clearly adequate to it.

Certain of the characters from the early novels reappear, but to be treated with greater realism, so that one is able to feel for them more. Staithes is in the line of Coleman and Spandrell, a Thersites-like commentator bent on "forcing humans to be fully *verbally* conscious of their own disgustingness." His description of the making of scent from the excrements of a pole-cat is Swiftian in intensity, yet he is by no means a puppet, since we are permitted to see more clearly than in earlier novels the vulnerability behind his restless arrogance. When he allows his wounded leg to rot away, the desire for pain reminds us of the Savage in *Brave New World*. When he is eventually anaesthetised and the ghastly amputation is taking place, his face in repose has the untroubled innocence of a child.

Helen, too, reminds us of earlier characters — of Mrs. Viveash and Lucy Tantamount, though she is more real than the one, and altogether more human than the other. Caught in her "ordinary hell of emptiness, and drought, and discontent" she has nothing but her own torments to offer to those who are closest to her. Yet the intimacy with which Huxley draws her is remarkable; for once he seems to be exposing himself more than his readers in doing so. And the fact that her affair with Ekki brings her temporarily to life and hope, as though Fate had prepared a crowning savagery for her rebellious and over-sensitive nature, brings her nearer to tragic status than Huxley's characters usually come.

Anthony, who is an extended portrait of the familiar self-wounding, self-consuming intellectual, is also curiously sympathetic—if only because he has more to be tormented about, more real cause for guilt, than his earlier prototypes. In spite of his long, shapeless essays, and his endless spiritual exhibitionism, we are able to feel concern as well as interest in his predicament. The tragedy of Brian's death, for which he is morally responsible, has aggravated (as we later learn) his search for safety at all costs. His cynicism, his sexual promiscuity, his intellectual evasiveness are all part of this quest for peace and quiet. When he is forced back into the vulnerable world of emotional relationships again—first by his love for Helen, later by his long-deferred committal to a cause —it is with feelings of the deepest disquiet. Even so, the Cause which eventually attracts him has more to do with mysticism, with the ultimate escape from committal, than with any clear-cut social dynamic. And this, we cannot help remembering, is in 1935.

The picture of Mrs. Foxe as a woman in whom genuine charm and religious principle turn, unperceived by herself and under the pressure of almost incestuous possessiveness, into cruelty, is remarkably good of its kind. She is perhaps the one character of Huxley's who might have been created by George Eliot. In the ill-fated relationship between Brian and Joan, Huxley explores with compassion as well as irony yet another classic trap in the no-man's-land between love and sex. Brian is the victim equally of Mrs. Foxe, who uses prudery in the service of possessiveness; and of Mary Amberley and Anthony, who allow free love to become an excuse for betrayal. The puritanism of Brian's mother, the licentiousness and treachery of his best friend, alike conspire to bring about his death. The passages leading up to this are among the finest things Huxley has achieved as a novelist. But in carrying his art to this new level of psychological realism, he demonstrates how far he now is from any belief in earthly happiness, at least for the great majority of human beings as they actually are. The plight of Helen is such that neither dancing (in which she for a moment "lost her identity, and became something larger than herself") nor art, nor sexual ecstasy can offer more than momentary respite from the unbearable loathing of self-knowledge. "Tortured by pleasure, tortured by pain," she reflects, "at the mercy of one's skin and mucus, at the mercy of those thin threads of nerves" . . . this is the reality about life, if one is honest. Miller alone among the characters has a genuine hope, which is to escape from this cycle altogether into the untroubled serenity of Nirvana. Again the two Nothings hang in delicate balance, for all the added psychological realism that has been achieved.

VI

The last novel I want to mention, very briefly, is *After Many a Summer*, which brings the wheel full circle. The theme, as the title discloses to those who know their Tennyson, is cruel immortality; the horror of prolonging the life of the body without at the same time arresting its decay. (Here, book III of *Gulliver*, as well as the inevitable book IV, springs to mind.) Though in parts very amusing, the novel is wrecked by Mr. Propter, whose exposition of God as a "nothingness capable of free power" sprawls monstrously over half of it. Its theme is nowhere more amusingly stated than in the comments of its ill-starred heroine when she sees two baboons copulating ("Virginia clapped her hands with pleasure. 'Aren't they cute!' she cried, 'Aren't they human!' "). Dr. Obispo's disgust as he examines Mr. Stoyte, the would-be immortal, and reflects on "the whisperings and crepitations inside the warm smelly barrel before him," brings us on to equally familiar ground. The last scene of the novel, a supremely cynical apotheosis of the human beast, is for once comparable, in its sheer audacity, with the denouements of Evelyn Waugh. But an amusing last chapter does not make a major success; *After Many a Summer* has neither the psychological interest of *Eyeless in Gaza*, nor the consistent interest as fable of *Brave New World*. What it does provide is the purest expression yet of Huxley's constant dichotomy between flesh and spirit. The human animal becomes simply Yahoo, the human soul simply Houyhnhnm; the one loathsome, the other a devitalised abstraction at best. The Buddhism which Mr. Propter discourses upon as a "liberation from personality" may strike one as a greater threat to the individual than the machinations of the scientist in *Brave New World*. Even the small degree of committal suggested to Anthony by Miller's mysticism in *Eyeless in Gaza* has disappeared again, since the idealism of the reformer is just as vain, in Mr. Propter's view, as the fornication of the rake. Huxley returns, then, to the total disbelief in worthwhile committal which characterised his early work. And even if the spirit's Nothing is now a shade more emphasised than the body's, a liberal critic will no doubt feel that *here* is the tendency in Huxley that he has to resist.

VII

From here, I can perhaps summarise the case against Huxley, as it is sometimes presented. In moving on to the phase represented by *After Many a*

Summer and his more recent work, is he not offering an impossible dilemma? Instead of *suma*, which came in for ironic treatment in 1933, we are presented with mescaline, of which we are expected to approve. Instead of the Nothing of Mrs. Viveash's boredom, we have the Nothingness of Mr. Propter's God: a very dubious exchange we might think, in that Mrs. Viveash is at least conscious that her Nothing is an emptiness, whereas Mr. Propter thinks that his Nothing is everything there is. After the traps have all closed, and the circle of humiliation and suffering is complete, are we not left more or less where we started, having gained from intelligence only a very full insight into its own futility?

The force of this criticism is inescapable, and any answer to it must perhaps be of a personal kind. I began by asserting that Huxley has understood and condemned his own puritanism, even though he has never managed to escape from it. Though the events in his novels seem sometimes almost to justify the Colemans and Spandrells, Huxley never fails to discern in them the very sickness of the soul. His own irony, I have argued, is born in the ruthlessness of honesty; if he sets out to shock us, it is as a challenge to new thought, new directions, not to apathy and despair. "Those who are shocked by truth," he says himself, "are not only stupid, but morally reprehensible as well." How then does he differ from his own most despairing characters? Not, perhaps, by offering a Cause we can be devoted to, or by proposing answers to the various problems with which he deals; but by continuing to trust to honesty and intelligence as goods-in-themselves, however dark their data and their situation; by remaining lively, alert, even exuberant whatever the story that he has to tell. I had occasion when writing on Swift to draw attention to an important ambivalence which inheres in the irony of this kind: though its content may sometimes deny the possibility of civilised values, its style actually embodies such values as it goes along. Huxley's exuberance, moreover, is inseparable from his restless curiosity, his constant readiness to change his opinions, or develop them, or reaffirm them as the twentieth century unrolls its own surprises and ironies to our gaze. Whereas the Colemans and the Spandrells luxuriate in negation, Huxley himself never ceases to fight against it. In his essays, he frequently makes as strong a stand for the liberal decencies as Lawrence himself. The two recently published collections remind us that he is not only one of the most intelligent and readable of our writers —an endless source of delight to everyone who enjoys ideas—but also one of the most ruthless opponents of cant, prudery, hypocrisy that we have had. On art and music he writes with especial authority, since he is not only a connoisseur, but one whose range extends equally to all the arts, and coexists with creative talents of the most flexible kind. About art, he is never cynical, though it has always been something of a mystery to him: how can a race so squalid as ours perceive or create so much beauty? He has always, too, been fascinated by the various ways in which art hints at immortality—through the static endurance of its form, so much longer-lived than the men who create it; through its suggestion that beauty is, after all, an absolute, upon which windows can sometimes be opened. In *The Doors of Perception* and *Heaven and Hell*, the part which art has played in forming his religious mysticism becomes clearer than it has ever been before. These two long essays are, I need hardly add, among the most exciting of his writings yet. They are far more plausible than most of the reviewers have suggested, and by no means a further installment of Mr. Propter, as readers of *After Many a Summer* will naturally fear.

In closing, there is one further point which I think should certainly be made. Huxley is often spoken of these days as negative, and resented for a number of reasons, about some of which I have tried to speak. But I think myself that we are faced with a much more terrifying type of cynicism, which is perhaps in the very bones and marrow of the atomic age. Too often these days even liberal writers adopt a tone of portmanteau know-ingness—a tone in which protest is automatically made to sound naive, and moral earnestness the prerogative of the crank. Huxley himself, for all his ironic intelligence, is a writer who still believes that irony and intelligence matter. Whatever the abysses opened up in his novels, he continues to seek for the truth, in a direction which has a respectable history whether we subscribe to it ourselves or not. And confronted with the brutal or the stupid, he is willing to offer a face-to-face challenge, as were Shaw, Russell, Orwell in their time. Today, we need voices that will be angered by injustices but remain urbane and civilised as well as uncompromising in their anger. Huxley is preeminently a writer that university students should be reading, however their teachers may hold aloof.

L. P. Hartley's *The Go-Between:*
Neo-Victorian or New Novel?

Neil McEwan

The Go-Between was published the same year as Alain Robbe-Grillet's *Les Gommes*: 1953. It might seem that here are two extremes in the standard critical contrast between English conservatism and French experiment in the novel in the 1950s. The years 1953–54 saw the appearance of Amis, Murdoch, and Golding working in the mode of fiction which has seemed so conventional by contrast with the new developments in France. Hartley was neither young nor new in 1953. He was fifty-eight and had published what many consider his finest achievement, the trilogy of novels known as *Eustace and Hilda*, in the 1940s. He is often regarded as a disciple of Henry James, even of Hawthorne: here, it might be thought, is the arch neo-Victorian. But now that the originality of the *nouveau roman* (no longer so new) can be regarded with a degree of scepticism, and the innovatory character of English fiction recognised, it is interesting to discover, in what is maybe the most widely admired "conventional" novel of the last thirty years, a parallel with the "new novel" in France.

Criticism in England has praised Hartley in conventional terms. Some critics, as we shall see, have praised his oblique rendering of twentieth-century horrors, reflected in quiet, domestic scenes. He has been regarded as the most expert of the "novelists of childhood." Penguin Books, who have reissued paperback editions of *The Go-Between* constantly throughout the 1960s and 1970s, make this claim for it, and their blurb implies a comfortably traditional method, quoting Sir John Betjeman: "of all the novels L. P. Hartley has written I think *The Go-Between* is the best . . . it is in what is to me the best tradition of fiction." He is recommended also as a religious or mystical writer, influenced by Emily Brontë, able to create a sense of spiritual realities. His *Times* obituary (December 14, 1972) saw him in all

From *The Survival of the Novel: British Fiction in the Later Twentieth Century*. © 1981 by Neil McEwan. The Macmillan Press Ltd., 1981.

these ways and as an artistic, Jamesian, social historian, recapturing better than anyone country-house life at the turn of the century.

This reflects the way Hartley saw himself. His book of criticism, *The Novelist's Responsibility* (1967), looks back to Jane Austen, Emily Brontë, Hawthorne, and James rather than to the modernists—Proust, Mann, Joyce, Kafka, Musil—whom the French new novelists regarded as their predecessors, in so far as they had any. As a reviewer of fiction since the 1920s, on the other hand, Hartley was fully aware of the achievements of modernism. He had a professional understanding of the situation of the novel in the twentieth century. Perhaps his familiarity with excesses and absurdities in writers of the thirties and forties who tried to shock their readers into "a new consciousness of reality" made him inclined to pose as a traditionalist with a soothing respect for the least adventurous Common Reader. Neither *Possibilities* nor *The Situation of the Novel* mentions *The Go-Between*, perhaps because it was found too lightweight. The following account of the novel looks at it as a work of technical interest, relevant to the present period of fiction, whose traditional appearance is something of a pose.

A summary of the story can be made fairly straightforwardly (which is not the case with any "new novel"). Indeed, a brief account of the setting and characters might seem like a parody of Betjeman's idea of "the best tradition of fiction." If Lawrence Durrell had attempted a burlesque of what Pursewarden's hawk-featured publishers with binoculars were looking out for to supply to their public, he might have tried something like this. An old gentleman is remembering his boyhood visit to a country house: an intrigue develops against a background of bathing parties and picnics, an approaching ball and a cricket match. The marriageable heiress, Marian, is undecided between gallant and gentle Lord Trimingham, recently disfigured in the Boer War, and the virile but socially "unknowable" local farmer, Ted Burgess. The boy, acting innocently as go-between, arranges her trysts with Burgess. Tension mounts until, in the catastrophe, the lovers are discovered coupling on an outhouse floor. Ted commits suicide; Trimingham marries Marian; Leo's emotional life is arrested by the shock; it is only now, fifty years later, that he begins to remember and understand.

Such an account falsifies, because of the central and pervasive interest of the narrative technique. Yet a summary shows that Hartley was using a very conventional type of story and deliberately evoking an earlier tradition of fiction as if to emphasise that nothing new was to be looked for at that level of interest. It is in the relationship between the conspicuously modernist craftsmanship and the stock, commonplace scenes and characters of the novel that Hartley might be considered as a novelist in the sense defined by Michel Butor in the essay of 1955, "Le Roman comme recherche":

> Although a true story can always in the last resort be supported by outside evidence, the novel must itself create what it tells us about. That is why it is *the* phenomenological domain, the place

above all in which to study how reality appears, or can appear; it is why the novel is the laboratory of narrative.

[*Alors que le récit viridique a toujours l'appui, la ressource d'une évidence extérieure, le roman doit suffire à susciter ce dont il nous entretient. C'est pourquoi il est le domaine phénoménologique par excellence, le lieu par excellence ou étudier de quelle façon la réalité nous apparaît ou peut nous apparaître; c'est pourquoi le roman est le laboratoire du récit.*]

Thinking on these lines, one sees that Iris Murdoch's proposal that modern novels be considered under the two heads of "crystalline" and "journalistic" suggests a way to link *The Go-Between* with the *nouveau roman*:

Indeed it [the crystalline novel] *is* Romanticism in a later phase. The pure, clean, self-contained "symbol" . . . is the analogue of the lonely self-contained individual. It is what is left of the other-worldliness of Romanticism when the "messy" humanitarian and revolutionary elements have spent their force. The temptation of art, a temptation to which every work of art yields except the greatest ones, is to console. The modern writer, frightened of technology and (in England) abandoned by philosophy and (in France) presented with simplified dramatic theories, attempts to console us by myths or by stories.

["Against Dryness"]

Hartley's Christianity and his Herbert Spencerian liberalism failed to provide him with much philosophical support, as is clear from *The Novelist's Responsibility*, and he was certainly dismayed by twentieth-century conditions in general. He readily comes to seem "crystalline" in disposition. Iris Murdoch does admit that the better modern novelists are of this kind.

Viewing his work in relation to this concept would have the merit of rescuing him to some extent from the labels of Jamesian and Hawthornean. Being post-Symbolist and post-Romantic, he can be seen as the contemporary of Butor and Robbe-Grillet. In the case of *The Go-Between*, symbolism is exactly analogous to the "lonely self-contained individual" in the appeal it has for the narrator whose lonely and self-contained nature, and need for consolation, are the reason the story is told. For him, as for the figures behind the dreamlike constructions of Robbe-Grillet and Butor, narrative has a therapeutic role. Of course this idea can, like most of the principles behind the *nouveau roman*, be found in earlier literature too. Many narrators in past fiction are consoling themselves by telling stories. *The Go-Between* does, certainly, invite symbolic interpretation in the manner of the older (pre-Sartrean) symbolist novel; a somewhat remorseless symbol-mindedness is something that the older Leo has in common with the younger self he "resurrects," who is conceived in relation to symbols. But this, like everything else in the novel, is subordinated to the method whereby the narrator re-creates his past through the imaginative working of memory, and here, in the Proustian aspect of the book, a comparison with French fiction of the 1950s is revealing. The first sentence of *The Go-Between* is an epigram that has become famous: "The past is a foreign country: they do things differently there." That line might serve as a gloss on Michel Butor's linking of Paris and Rome in *La Modification* (1957). Such a parallel helps to set his work in the decade where it belongs.

The "crystalline" novel is unlike the nineteenth-century novel, Iris Murdoch says, in portraying the human condition "without characters in the nineteenth-century sense." In the larger meaning of the word "symbolism"—"the sum of the relationships of what the novel describes to the reality we experience," in Michel Butor's definition—Leo's self-discovery through narrative is a process that contains a rich display of old habits of fiction, but then so in their own way do the novels of Michel Butor. "Characters in the nineteenth-century sense" are an old habit which the new novel claimed to have abandoned, although, as various English critics have pointed out, the reader characterises the anonymous figures in these novels, especially on a second reading. As for *The Go-Between*, its stereotyped characters appear as "archetypal figures" to Anne Mulkeen in her 1974 study of Hartley, *Wild Thyme, Winter Lightning*. She describes "strange configurations in *The Go-Between* where the heat, the deadly nightshade, the winning and losing of the cricket match, and the 'distant war' (the Boer War) are connected with the central triangle of characters, where there are 'strange parallels' between nature and man and history," where "Marian, Ted and Hugh are archetypal figures" and the novelist's problem is how to combine the child's spiritual vision and the knowledge of evil in man. Blake and Emily Brontë, from whose lyrics Hartley took his epigraphs for *The Shrimp and the Anemone* and *The Go-Between*, are the best guides to this kind of understanding of his achievement, which was touched on by the *Times*'s obituary: "As in *Eustace and Hilda* Hartley delineates in *The Go-Between* the small things of life, the small pleasures and the small miseries with such affectionate precision that one trusts implicitly the vision of the darker things that he sees as lying below, but only just below, the surface of the ordinary." The Brontë epigraph to *The Go-Between* evokes the poignancy of childhood:

> But, child of dust, the fragrant flowers,
> The bright blue sky and velvet sod
> Were strange conductors to the bowers
> Thy daring footsteps must have trod.

These lines are from an 1837 lyric, "I saw thee, child, one summer's day," which ends "And childhood's flower must waste its bloom / Beneath the shadow of the tomb." The novel does create brilliantly a sense of the small pleasures and miseries of a child's life, and evokes with a formidable delicacy and elusiveness of touch the presence of darker things. In Leo's watching the monstrous growth induced by the heat on the belladonna, his catching Ted at cricket, his chatting with Lord Trimingham about war, we are given a sense of "configurations" involving nature, chance, and evil. The sexual drama and the destruction of the boy's trust in life are linked especially with the pervasive reminders of "the distant war." "Trying to sneak past in dead ground," Hugh calls after Leo; Hugh with "his whole face . . . lopsided" from his scar and Leo's boyish dartings about in the gardens merge for a moment with the Boer War Hugh has just come back from. The way the narrator has the two world wars in mind justifies Anne Mulkeen's comment that he is "the type of Briton stunned, shattered, discouraged by the impact and horror of war."

War, in the present century, has made it more urgent, Iris Murdoch says, for the novelist to try to come to terms with basic human problems of good and evil. But the crystalline novelist tends to take refuge in fantasy, to "operate . . . with small myths, toys, crystals" and not "to grapple with reality" or, if at all, only to console. "Le Roman comme recherche" demanded that the novelist portray the human condition, and "present reality." But in France the sense of overwhelming evil in contemporary reality has just as often unnerved the novelist, as it did Nathalie Sarraute: "*Quelle histoire inventée pourrait rivaliser avec . . . les récits des camps de concentration . . .?*" Hartley does take refuge from the horrors of modern existence in fictions which deal artfully with private sorrows. Yet his ability to reflect the conflicts of his age has been recognised by the British critics Walter Allen and W. W. Robson.

Robson sees in *Eustace and Hilda* "a more profound study than *Lord of the Flies* of the 'impulse to dominate' which has nearly wrecked our world already and may one day succeed in doing so entirely." Walter Allen has also emphasised Hartley's power to use a limited social world, and one viewed through the medium of childhood, to explore indirectly the twentieth-century experience of evil on a scale beyond the scope of direct treatment in literature. In *Tradition and Dream* he writes: "Yet though his world is a small one, and apparently demure, the smallness and the demureness are deceptive, for his world can uncannily reflect the violence and the conflicts from which it is seemingly isolated." The opening scene of the *Eustace and Hilda* trilogy has become famous for the image it provides of the helplessness of moral scruple before the natural impulses in marine creatures, and in people too. Eustace, aged nine, peers into a rock pool where an anemone is devouring a shrimp. He ponders each creature's case and the irreconcilable conflict of interests. He calls in Hilda, his elder sister, whose "ruthless" moral sense grasps "an evil principle at the back of the anemone affair." Her intervention is too late to save the shrimp, and the anemone is disembowelled. Hartley develops gradually, in the course of the novel, the ironic relevance of this incident to the relationship of Eustace and Hilda and to the destructive nature of human dependence as a fact of life.

Hartley may be considered as a novelist of our insecure era, without it being taken for granted that he is either a talented survival from an earlier period, as even his admirers imply, or merely a maker of beautiful "toys."

The Go-Between is often regarded this way: as a fine, old-fashioned artefact. It is steeped in Hartley's awareness of novels of the past, but is written nevertheless with a sense of the situation of the novel, in Europe as well as in England, in the age of Robbe-Grillet and Butor.

The narrator of *The Go-Between* is engaged in a peculiarly drastic type of self-appraisal. He is occupied throughout the novel in remembering the events of fifty years ago when, on his thirteenth birthday, he suffered a trauma from which he has never recovered: we share his gradual rediscovery of his earlier self. Although the voice which addresses us is intelligently and pleasingly modulated, the Leo Colston who has existed until now—subject to the block which made him forget what happened in 1900—is as oddly removed from normal life as a Beckett protagonist.

"All dried up inside" is Marian's impression of him in the Epilogue: the desiccation is Beckettian—no religious beliefs, no friends, no emotional life, no sexual desire, no music, no war-time risks or peace-time pleasures, no creative work, no introspection has until now disturbed Leo's commitment to bibliography (and kindred war-work) for half a century. Bibliography is a fine profession and involves disciplines doubtless beyond the capacity of Murphy and Malone. But its routine and factual character is what attracts Leo: it offers him an escape from life: "another world came to my aid—the world of facts. I accumulated facts: facts which existed independently of me, facts which my private wishes could not add to or subtract from. Soon I came to regard these facts as truths . . ." (Epilogue). Trapped by routine and obsessed with collecting data, Leo resembles researchers in Robbe-Grillet and Butor. The contribution his skill with facts makes to the narrative is a point in common with their self-analyses, although he is an "active" conventional narrator.

In view of the relative openness to interpretation of the "passive" narrative method in the *nouveau roman*, comparison may seem superficial. Leo's retreat from life can be explained conventionally, as it is by Anne Mulkeen. But it is a sexual trauma with Oedipal connotations that has stunned Leo and its connection with a death (Ted's) for which Leo feels guilty provides a theme in common with *Les Gommes* and *Passage de Milan*. Leo is less likely to remind us of the brokenhearted and broken-down characters of Victorian fiction because we aren't shown whatever crabbed external symptoms he may have developed; internal discourse was a mode with which French fiction experimented in the 1950s—often with disabled, implausible figures—and this is the mode of *The Go-Between*. Hartley's being so readable need not oblige us to see him as merely readable, in the derogatory sense propagated by Roland Barthes in the 1960s when promoting the "new novel" as a "writerly" or "open" type of literature. Barthes has since revised his views, attacking . . . a "new conformism of the unreadable." Robbe-Grillet, who used to ignore the existence of English precedents to his own original schemes (as did Barthes), now admits that the Anglo-Saxon tradition in fiction has always been more flexible than the French. Barthes's tendency has been to contrast extremes: Philippe Sollers and

Alexandre Dumas. The narrative method of *The Go-Between* can be seen as "open" and experimental in ways of its own.

It has been a novel often set for examinations, and students frequently object that they don't believe that the shock Leo suffers from the scene in the outhouse would have a permanently disabling psychological effect. Hartley intended to stretch credulity and to stress the damage done to Leo for dramatic and for moral reasons. Harold Pinter has described how he first read the novel, having been commissioned to do the screenplay for Joseph Losey's film-version, and was struck by the contrast between the two Leos. A dialogue takes place in the Prologue between these discordant selves: there is an allegorical aspect to it, youth eager and old age disappointed; but the incongruity of the *dédoublements* (or doublings) of the *nouveau roman* is present too, and one might well be reminded of the keen sense in modern French writers of how identity is subject to time.

The relativity in the portrayal of the two Leos is as rigorous as it would be in a French novel influenced by Saussure. Apart from the fragmentary diary entries, the younger Leo is brought into being by the memories of Leo at sixty-five. But there is hardly a sentence of his narrative in which the older Leo is not occupied in thinking about his earlier self. What we encounter, in fact, is a third version of him, since he is bringing himself back to life in the course of explaining himself to us, reestablishing touch with a vitality that was arrested fifty years ago.

First-person narrative has always raised theoretical doubts for readers who let their minds dwell on the method; Henry James had many reservations about it. One can argue that the gentlemanly tone of Pip's narrative throughout *Great Expectations* undermines the novel's satire on the concept of gentleman, which is perhaps why conservative reviewers of 1860 were so unalarmed by what modern critics see as a radically critical and even subversive work. But *The Go-Between* emphasises the curious relationship between the hero and the narrator: each is in a sense the author of the other. Hartley does not allow it to disturb our enjoyment of the story or the human interest, but he sharpens our awareness of the technique and of what is absurd in the powers of a novelist. "If my twelve-year-old self, of whom I had grown rather fond, thinking about him, were to reproach me: 'Why have you grown up such a dull dog . . .?' " muses Leo in the Prologue. "Interiority" is a coinage used of various post-Joycean developments in fiction; interiority here allows a constant comic interplay between two stylistic registers, the small boy's and the bibliographer's: on going downstairs, "I went bumping down the cataract. I was a Red Indian this morning . . ." (chapter 5); or on sliding down a straw-stack: "I omitted a necessary and practical precaution always taken, and without loss of face, by experienced straw-stack sliders . . ." (chapter 7). The tastes of the boy of twelve are recorded in the prim, precise tone of the old man: "It was true that I hadn't seen the garden properly. Frankly I preferred the rubbish-heap, for there I had a sense of adventure which was absent from the garden" (chapter 23).

In *Great Expectations*, we take for granted touches of whimsy in the narrator's account of his own childish mind and behaviour. But the older Leo is so absorbed in rediscovering his lost vivacity, and at the same time so bizarrely remote from it, that the two sets of style and taste coexist in his narrative, and an interest in seventeenth-century art and literature is imposed on a relish for haystacks and rubbish-heaps, and scholarly diction is mixed with schoolboy slang. The counterpointing of personas is so systematic that an effect of *dédoublement* arises, in the interaction of raw immediacy and mellow irony, as if events were being relived with a double consciousness.

In a similar way, the reader's attention is drawn to the organisation of time in the novel. The date 1900 has an almost structuralist prominence, because of the diary, and because of Leo's obsession with the turn of the century, and with round numbers generally. Two centuries and two epochs are opposed by the stressing of the year, and so are two contrasted eras in Leo's life, before and after his thirteenth birthday in 1900. A second time-scheme involves the nineteen days of the visit to Brandham Hall, between the ninth and the twenty-seventh of July. The contrast between the long-range view of two centuries and the boy's minute ordering of time into segments during his stay is a conspicuously diagrammatic feature of the novel's design, and helps make the reader more conscious of the problems of time in fiction.

A good incidental feature of Hartley's understanding of childhood is Leo's power to lose himself in the present event while fascinated by the measurement of time. We have a vivid impression of the expanse of his day, with tracts of time between the fixed hours for meals, and how the days merged together in experience: three days, in chapter 9, are made to seem, in the reading, like a phase of life, although every detail can be placed in time. The diary (a typical *nouveau roman* device, incidentally) helps with this and so does Leo's daily recording of temperatures. His trips as go-between require timing. The events of the last afternoon are measured by the clock. One is struck by the significance of time during these nineteen days which stand out from the vague passage of the subsequent fifty years. The cricket-match provides examples of the novelist's control, evoking cricket's delays and suspense, or a moment of stillness, out of play: "the ball lay at Mrs. Maudsley's feet looking strangely small and harmless"; and of cricket's suddenness too—Leo catches Ted in a moment that ends the game. In a rash moment, a week later, Ted is to shoot himself. *Les Gommes* takes place within the timespan of a gunshot. Clocks and calendars obsess the "new novel" because their writers are intrigued by the illusion of fictional time and by the gap between time as we know it and time as we measure it. Hartley intimates a similar awareness, without fuss.

John Barth's "Life Story" in *Lost in the Funhouse* (1968) includes some ingenious grumbling about the troubles of being a technician of the novel: "Another story about a writer writing a story! Another regressus in infinitum! Who doesn't prefer art that at least overtly imitates something other than its own processes? That doesn't proclaim 'Don't forget I'm an artifice!'? That takes for granted its mimetic nature instead of asserting it in order (not so slyly after all) to deny it, or vice versa?" Given this kind of awareness of "fabulation" in fiction it is increasingly impossible to write with the straightforwardness John Barth is making fun of. Hartley's work does not proclaim its own artifice, but insinuates it discretely.

While the conventions of first-person narration in Dickens or Conrad allowed prodigious efforts of recall, Leo reconstructs his past with the aid of certain figurative devices for which, as Peter Bien has pointed out [*L. P. Hartley*], "symbol" is an inadequate term. The young Leo, inspired by the zodiac, obviously was inclined to find meaning in everything around him: to select and order his experience. The old Leo remembers him this way, with the help of the deadly nightshade, the heat, the green of his clothes and his bicycle, the Boers, unlucky thirteen, the fateful catch at cricket. The narrator finds in them a relevance to events which enables him to assemble a story. He does so with a studied care which is typical of him, although the result seems implausible to some readers. The cricket-match is less a sporting event than a ritual display of relationships between the teams and among the players. At best, the fusion of memory and meaning is perfect, as when Leo finds an image of Ted's social exclusion and vulnerability in his first appearance at the swimming pool, "not a weed marred the surface, only one thing broke it: the intruder's bobbing head" (chapter 4); or remembers the effect of grotesque distortion created by the fully raised seat of the bicycle ready for Marian to ride it at his birthday party. At other times, as with the many omens of Ted's end there is a sense of strain and improbability.

But readers who complain that the novel's proliferation of signs is overdone or "contrived" are reading within the convention of a first-person narrator's total recall of just what happened. A less conventional response seems called for, which admits the selective, interpretive nature of memory, and sees Leo's contriving of his own story as an aspect of his attempt of self-recovery. The strong Victorian convention of the "confessional" mode keeps us from confusing Pip or Jane Eyre with novelists, but Leo reshapes his memories with a writer's awareness; to use an educated character as a first-person narrator today makes that almost inevitable, as Fowles's *Daniel Martin*, where narrator becomes novelist, shows. Leo appears at times like a novelist *manqué* who has at last discovered the story he can write.

We are familiar in modern fiction with unreliable, corrupt, unstable, and even insane narrators. Leo might be described as an urbane neurotic. Hartley has, like most novelists, fended off suggestions that he was influenced by Freud, and critics have, as usual, offered accounts of his work in Freudian terms nonetheless. Leo's mixture of withdrawal from "the world of the emotions" and curiosity about it, in the course of his reconstituting of himself through memory, is reminiscent of Michel Butor's more consciously Freudian concern with his characters' mental blocks, probing of the past, and quest for reassurance through ordering material. But Hartley is too conscious of the mystery in what is unique in his character's experience for Freud to be helpful in explaining his work, and that is where he is really unlike the "new novelists."

Alain Robbe-Grillet's wish to abolish humanism is connected with his hope of disconnecting the type of novel he inaugurated from literature of the past. Hartley's mildly mystical Christian humanism is deeply attached to the past of English literature and especially to certain nineteenth-century authors: Emily Brontë, Henry James. He was, moreover, personally tied to the world of the country-house —already archaic when he was young in the purity which he pictures in *The Go-Between*—by a feeling which few modern French intellectuals would appreciate. "That famous cloudless summer of 1914 extends backwards a long way into a world more civil, more confident, more humanely articulate than any we have known since," writes George Steiner [in *In Bluebeard's Castle*] and these words convey the mood of calm conjured up in *The Go-Between*. Steiner is writing about a "myth of the past"; the popularity of Hartley's novel may be due partly to the strength of the myth. The phrase "a country house in 1900," is evocative, and mythic, indeed, in Roland Barthes's meaning of the term. Hartley was susceptible to nostalgic imagery, and the Barthes who published *Mythologies* (1954–56, 1957) not long after *The Go-Between* would no doubt have denounced him for indulging bourgeois fantasies, though the later Barthes might well have been more broadminded, less doctrinaire. Like that of all effective novelists, Hartley's work makes creative use of his private mythology; like most intelligent writers, he is aware of it. He is as conscious as Robbe-Grillet or Steiner or Barthes of how we mirror ourselves in versions of the past, and his writing shows an intuitive sympathy of how most of us do so.

The half-century span that Hartley uses allows him, by encompassing everything within the narrator's memory, to evade the problem of point of view which John Fowles exploits so well when he looks back over a century. Memory and a "mythic" view of the past go naturally together, as Steiner points out. The tranquil country scenes and stable social order which form the background to the characters' lives, the rich harvest and calm, cricketing peasantry illustrate what Steiner means by "myths of the past that rule us." Fowles's narrator would be quick to point out the misery—as he does the home circumstances of the servant girl Millie in *The French Lieutenant's Woman*—behind idyllic country appearances. This façade is only one aspect, in *The Go-Between*, of what John Bayley calls "pastoral."

Hartley's setting is pastoral in the sense of common usage. John Bayley's concept is much wider, including whatever is "framed," "characteristic" or "proffered": characters determined by their roles are pastoral, in his sense, in a way relevant to *The Go-Between*. "A coalminer, or a retired colonel in Camberley, are seen as pastoral in their functions and their characters —the fact that they may not feel like or be aware of themselves as a coalminer or a colonel cannot be considered": Bayley is discussing realism in Tolstoy (in *Tolstoy and the Novel*, part 3, section 10) but his discussion (as throughout his book) ranges over literature and critical ideas: Conrad's *Nostromo* is pastoral because the state of "Costaguana holds and determines the characters": *The Shadow Line* is not, because the sea for Conrad "is not a pastoral setting but the natural instructive setting of felt and experienced life" (part 3, section 10). This distinction and the illustrations which John Bayley draws from life are illuminating: we adopt a pastoral mode when we buy a new suit or get a new job. They help to illumine the working of Leo's double-vision—and its results. The scenes and characters of the novel are conveyed to us through one determining frame formed by Leo's memory and, within that, through another formed by the idealising mind of his twelve-year-old self. After the first few days of his visit (and the gift of a new suit), Leo remembers he was carried away in his imagination by the generosity shown to him:

> The expenditure had been godlike; it belonged to another, ampler phase of being than the one I was accustomed to. My mind could not grasp it but my imagination could make play with it, for unlike the mind, which could dismiss what it did not understand, my imagination loved to contemplate the incomprehensible and try to express my sense of it by an analogy. And I had one ready made. From those resplendent beings, golden with sovereigns (and, I suspected, guineas) arriving, staying, leaving apparently unaffected by any restrictions of work or family ties, citizens of the world who made the world their playground, who had it in their power (for I did not forget that) to make me miserable with a laugh and happy with a smile —from them it was but a short step to the hardly more august and legendary figures of the zodiac.
>
> (chapter 4)

This severance of the young Leo from reality is what makes him vulnerable. The Marian and Trimingham whom the go-between sees are like creatures in daydreams. Leo likes Trimingham because he is a ninth viscount; he hardly conceives of a "Hugh" apart from that status: he is impressed and pleased by Trimingham's friendliness —he would have expected, he says, that a lord would be haughty. At the same level of understanding, Leo registers Marian's character: she is "a beauty": " 'My sister is very beautiful,' Marcus said to me one day. He announced it quite impersonally, as who should say 'Two and two make four', and I received it in the same spirit. It was a fact, like other facts, something to be learned" (chapter 2). Of course Marian becomes personally important to Leo after her initiative over the new suit, but she remains within the function implied for him by her beauty; he wants her to marry Trimingham because that seems fitting. As for Ted Burgess, his function determines Leo's dealings with him too. When Burgess first discovers Leo on his haystack, he mistakes him for a village boy and threatens him with "the biggest thrashing you've ever had in your life." But "oddly enough this didn't put me against him: I thought it was exactly what an angry farmer ought to say: in a way I should have been disappointed if he had spoken less harshly" (chapter 5). Despite a mixture of real feelings about Ted, including envy, affection, and resentment, Leo never quite grasps that Ted exists separately from the image of an "angry farmer."

The adult Leo who recalls this idealizing vision he once possessed has the detachment, the moral sense, and the feeling of grievance to convey the bewildered desires of Trimingham, Ted Burgess, and Marian. All three are types, who think of themselves as such. It is as a working farmer and not a gentleman, as village not Hall, as a man of fields and barns not of sofas and tea-tables, that Ted is conceived as a lover: physically assured and morally uneasy: his "quick look" when Leo asks politely about his domestic arrangements, "Do you have a woman every day?": and his angry outburst, "Clear out of here quick," when pressed to tell about "spooning," imply a coarseness, a lack of humour and resilience, and of a sense of proportion; and these shortcomings belong with his farmer's role. He is convincing and memorable, but never "unframed." Trimingham's blend of simple enthusiasm over being in love with Marian and crisp authority derived from social and military rank are equally stereotyped. Ted might be an Edwardian character sketch of "The Working Farmer," Trimingham of "The Gentleman." Both seem meant to typify what was best in the older order and calmer world before 1914 which George Steiner tells us we dream about. Certainly, such a contrasted pair as Ted and Trimingham, appearing in a novel of 1900, would seem like the products of wishful thinking. But in *The Go-Between*'s scheme of reconstruction of a personal past through memory, they are appropriate; they correspond to our collective notions of what 1900 must have been like. Marian is equally decorous as a heroine: "there was a sparkle in everything she did"; vivacious, moody, wilful, scheming, she fills the heroine's role in Leo's imagination. Her own memory of her 1900 circumstances, when Leo revisits her in the Epilogue, is trite: "All those house-parties—people being paired off like animals at stud—it wasn't like that with us. We were made for each other." Her egotism remains intact. Hartley's subsequent uncertainty about the novel's moral bearing seems irrelevant because she is so true to a nature which we want to bestow on her, as the narrator does: she would have been like that!

The same characteristic, pastoral mode governs the presentation of minor figures like the footman, Henry; and extends to the picnics, the carriage outings among the lanes where the passersby stare and children scramble for coins the coachman throws them; the cricket with the village side coming up to play at the Hall. Everything is as we would have imagined. It is not unlike the effect of Robbe-Grillet's Hong Kong where the details belong to the Hong Kong which everybody knows and not to the real place, except that here it is the past which is "the foreign country."

The characters are miniatures beside the characters of the great nineteenth-century novelists. But the strength of the novel's technique is that it acknowledges their remoteness and mystery; they can be known to us only very indirectly: through the memory of the old Leo, an emotional cripple, who knew them briefly fifty years ago, when he was thirteen and living in a dream. They are, as fictional characters, as remote and touching as people whose pasts have been excavated archaeologically, and we are moved by a similar mixture of intimacy and strangeness by their deaths, when Leo sees Hugh's name on the plaque (in the Epilogue) or hears how "Marcus was killed in the first war, and Denys too. I forget which went first. Denys, I think." The vast scale on which lives were lost in the 1914 War, and, later, in the concentration camps, is, as Nathalie Sarraute said, one reason why the artistic portrayal of individual character came to seem inadequate. In the finely attuned setting of Leo's mind the assorted facts about Marcus and Trimingham convey a respect for the individual, however little known or knowable; and the destructiveness of the century is reflected in Hartley's quiet manner as effectively as in novels which deal with war direct.

The Go-Between is equally undemonstrative yet acute in registering social tensions at a distance of fifty years. *Lord of the Flies* is generally seen as a reinterpretation of Victorian "myths" in *Coral Island*. *The Go-Between* examines a newly invented situation which is intended to strike the reader as characteristically Victorian. The plot and the relationships among the characters are adapted to the way we look at Victorian society. In John Fowles's *The French Lieutenant's Woman* the desire to study and explain the mid-Victorian past is much more explicit, but not necessarily more effective than Hartley's unruffled composure which effaces any hint of its own importance. If the plan of the novel offers a simplified social model of rural England in the nineteenth century—with nobleman, merchant, yeoman, country people, and servants—we can share Leo's sense of how "natural" a "good match" between Marian and Trimingham seemed then, while remaining aware of how "social" it seems today. Trimingham's line about Ted's military promise is revealing about late Victorian assumptions: "A likely man, single—no ties—he'd make a first rate N.C.O." (chapter 18). It is Hugh's certainty that Ted couldn't go higher, combined with the lightly stressed irony in "no ties"—Hugh doesn't know about Ted's tie with Marian—that conveys how incongruous the social arrangements seem now. Such points are not laboured: not even the scene in the outhouse or the appearance of Ted's grandson as eleventh Viscount (in the Epilogue) has the air of scoring a point; but the most delicate hints can have considerable force. Leo asks Hugh his opinion of Ted. " 'Well, he's quite a decent feller'—I remembered he had said this about the Boers—'but he's a bit wild.' " The comment on the Boers came in chapter 14: " 'The Boer's not a bad feller,' said Lord Trimingham tolerantly. 'I don't dislike him personally. It's a pity we have to shoot so many of them, but there you are.' " These remarks convey the tone of the English ruling class in the nineteenth century without needing the sort of commentary the narrator of *The French Lieutenant's Woman* supplies.

In another passage, the cricket match creates metaphorically the threat of a Boer victory. When the village side, though not even properly in whites for cricket, seems to be winning:

> Further disasters followed; five wickets down for fifty-six. These Boers in their motley raiment, triumphantly throwing the ball into the air after each kill, how I disliked them! The spectators disposed along the boundary, standing, sitting, lying, or propped against trees, I imagined to be animated by a revolutionary spirit, and revelling in the downfall of their betters.
>
> [chapter 11]

Later, the social panic and hysteria following the discovery of Ted with Marian, and Ted's suicide, are emphasised as agents of Leo's personal breakdown. A cruder art would have shown them as the breakdown of a social system. *The Go-Between*'s best effects are often in what is unsaid, or allowed to remain as nuance, the basic structure being so unmistakable.

The Go-Between, a frankly contrived, mannerist novel, which applies a brilliant technique to a simple story, is perfectly suited to reflect our sense of the Victorian age. If the modern novelist feels inferior as an artist when he looks at the great nineteenth-century novels, he also believes that we *know* more and are able to see through the social façades the Victorian novel took for granted. That belief underlies the "dismantled" novels in France. Hartley preserves the elements of conventional narrative while showing his reader how selective and inadequate narrative has to be. *The Go-Between* contrives to be intriguing as an exercise in fiction and moving as a novel. We feel how well country-house life before 1914 has been captured: and the illusory nature of any account of the past. Joseph Losey used cinema techniques to evoke the security of the "more civil, more confident world" before 1914; Harold Pinter's screenplay caught the evanescent and the absurd in Hartley's art. The success of the film is the best evidence of Hartley's place as a new English novelist.

Liam O'Flaherty

John Zneimer

More than anything else, John Millington Synge saw in the Aran Islands the heightened contrast between life and death, represented most vividly in the same chant for the dead that often rises in O'Flaherty's stories:

> This grief of the keen is of no personal complaint for the death of one woman over eighty years, but seems to contain the whole passionate rage that lurks somewhere in every native of the island. In this cry of pain the inner consciousness of the people seems to lay itself bare for an instant, and to reveal the mood of beings who feel their isolation in the face of a universe that wars on them with winds and seas. They are usually silent, but in the presence of death all outward show of indifference or patience is forgotten, and they shriek with pitiable despair before the horror of the fate to which they are all doomed.

This is the mark with which O'Flaherty was stamped and on which his distinctive manner of seeing depends. Reality was life and death in awesome contrast. No philosophy could explain nor could culture weave an intricate tapestry to obscure these elemental facts. To focus on life called up inevitably a vision of death. To focus on death called up a vision of life. The intensity of the one increased the intensity of the other. O'Flaherty's art is an expression of the tension between these two poles. The novels focus on life; as the reality of life comes to heightened awareness, death, equally real, rises in proportionate measure to consume it. The short stories emerge from the vision of death in the novels, and focusing on that death calls up a vision of life.

From the beginning, O'Flaherty's true subject was the meaning of life — the fact of existence — in the face of the awful reality of death. This is the central drama in all the black soul novels and the central issue in O'Flaherty's own life. His autobiographies ultimately dwell on this issue. It becomes the central feature of his account of his visit to Russia. In relation to the awesome reality of life and death the petty social intrigues of man in society, accepting society's norms, are so inconsequential as not to warrant the artist's concern except perhaps as a background where the intensity of the central drama emphasizes the pettiness. In the black soul novels O'Flaherty reenacts in his characters his own spiritual crisis, projecting himself into them, giving them life and consciousness from his own consciousness. They are defined as they face their heightened awareness of their own existence. The violence of their actions is commensurate with the intensity of their spiritual turmoil. As they are weak, like McDara, Gilhooley, and Ferriter, they end in despair, suicide, and insanity. If they are gifted, like Fergus O'Connor, they rise to a new spiritual vision. Only if they are strong can they smash themselves against life in a grand tragic gesture, like Ramon Mor and Skerrett. Regardless of their end, their passionate intensity is everything; for above them is O'Flaherty the artist watching, describing, like Stapleton the poet or the artist in "The Child of God," absorbed in the beauty of passion, feeding on the horrors that would make weaker men cry out in terror or be overcome with sympathy. This is the role of the poet, the artist, who, as O'Flaherty says in *Land*, must be ruthless in the pursuit of his ideal, which is beauty.

Only *Famine* among the novels does not have for its real subject man's plight in a universe of frightening immensity which appears totally indifferent to his dreams or fears or aspirations. Regardless of the horror of famine and plague, these afflictions are within the scope of man's measure. They may inspire fear, but the fear is definite and the relief from fear is definite. The problem in *Famine* can be solved by food, medicine, and better government. Men can band together against this kind of fear. They have common aims against a common enemy. But there is no relief from the dread that sends a strong man like Gypo Nolan into spasms of terror. Compared with the terror of existence, the terror of famine is almost comforting in its definiteness. *Famine* is an anomaly among O'Flaherty's novels because it is not about individual men, isolated within their own consciousness, but social men measurable by social norms. Because *Famine* is about man in opposition to nature, some critics see in its peasants and natural scenery part of the same spirit as in O'Flaherty's short stories, but these critics mistake the subject matter for the real subject. The difference between *Famine* and the short stories is profound. *Famine* is a warm novel, full of human sympathy. It is a humanitarian novel containing common human values. But the short stories spring from no such sympathy. They achieve their effects through the coldness, not the warmth, of their vision. They express the beauty of the awesomeness of nature. The vision of the short stories brought to *Famine* would dwell on the beauty of the horror, as Peter O'Toole, the Child of God, drew his inspiration from the grotesque wake. Human sympathy is entirely alien to the true nature of O'Flaherty's creative genius. As Stapleton expressed it, the poet's love showers its bounty on all, without exception, the oppressor and the oppressed. All is holy. The poet is allowed no special human partiality.

Set in a world which allows human values and human sympathies, *Famine* is not the best but the most conventional of O'Flaherty's novels. For the critic who feels as Margery Latimer did when she read O'Flaherty's short stories, "a chilled, locked place in her bones" which only feeling could loosen and his stories did not, *Famine* offers affirmation, sympathy, and hope. As Benedict Kiely said, Dark Daniel is not there, but because Dark Daniel is not there, O'Flaherty's genius is not there. The world of *Famine* is a comfortable old-fashioned world, but it is not O'Flaherty's world. To prefer *Famine* over the earlier novels is to prefer the comfort of affirmation over the chill of absolute negation, although the latter is O'Flaherty's truest expression; and to link *Famine* with the short stories because both are about peasants and nature is to miss the whole informing spirit of O'Flaherty's genius.

In O'Flaherty's last novels, *Land* and *Insurrection*, the subject is the same as in his earlier novels, but the tension is lacking. In *I Went to Russia* O'Flaherty said that "they who effect a harmony between their reason and their actions lose the power to create beauty." This is exactly what has occurred in these last works. Michael O'Dwyer sees the beauty of danger, but it is a theoretical beauty derived from a theoretical danger. O'Flaherty has arrived at a rational position, an understanding, and with the understanding the negative quality of intellect disappears. Previously he could say "All things appear equally futile when examined by reason," but in the last novels reason conquers the futility. When confronted with his moment of truth, Fergus O'Connor, truly a naked soul, was at the nadir of despair. All thought merely increased his awareness of futility and intensified his despair. His new awareness which arose from this despair was not an intellectual awareness or a set of beliefs or ideals which he possessed. His moment of truth occurred in absolute negativity, when all beliefs and all hopes became equally futile and he was left with nothing. Stapleton, Madden, and Kinsella also are brought to a moment of truth, but it is their belief which sustains them. Their ideals, which they possess with their minds, are absolutely positive, and their choice is positive. Each is sustained, even unto death, by his vision of truth, which is an intellectual vision. For Fergus O'Connor, reason leads to despair. For Stapleton, reason leads to truth, for it is reason which grasps the highest truth, which has the ultimate vision of the good, the beautiful, and the true. In the last novels O'Flaherty effects the greatest harmony between the actions and reason of his characters, and in a thoroughly Platonic atmosphere they undergo their deaths like Socrates, without doubts but firm in their resolve.

In his last novels O'Flaherty has arrived at a thoroughly Platonic philosophy. The poet is the "insurgent *par excellence*," as Stapleton says, because he, like Plato's guardians, has seen the ultimate good, while conventional government and morality still live in the shadow world of deception and illusion. The types of poet, soldier, and saint are more real than the persons who fill the types. The theory of beauty and tragedy is more important than the expression of beauty and tragedy. In the last novels the question of values appears settled. The characters make no choices because when they chose their roles (which are as much destiny as choice) they made the ultimate value choice. The earlier novels, in which reason was a negative, destructive force, would have stressed the ironies of these choices, all being equally futile when viewed with reason. In the last novels the reasonable world is accepted as the true world.

But the philosophy which represents the triumphs of reason is a construction that answers the need of Fergus O'Connor and Raoul St. George, both of whom cried out desperately for authority to sustain them in a universe of apparent chaos. The earliest and the latest novels are based upon the ultimate question: What is man in the face of death and annihilation? The earlier novels approach the question subjectively, existentially, and record the struggles of men impelled toward truth foredoomed to failure because there is no objective truth. The beauty is in the intensity of the struggle, a tragic beauty, as men extend themselves to their limits in their desperation. The last novels approach the question objectively, theoretically; and reason, asserting its preeminence over life, builds in its own image a universe in which individual man and his struggles illustrate the truth of the theory.

In the earlier novels the men are individuals, stripped of all their theoretical qualities to the essence of what it means to be a man in the horror and wonder of existence. In the last novels the men are types, divested of choice, of passion, of doubt, of terror, of all the qualities of individual life. The earlier novels are suffused with the tension of uncertainty and life. The last novels are enveloped in the philanthropic calm of certainty and death. In the last novels O'Flaherty ceased being the artist whose role is to sing the beauty of life's tragedy to become the philosopher for whom life is less important than the constructions of reason. The latter role is more comfortable, but it does not yield art.

The intensely subjective and personal quality that forms the basis of his artistic vision was already fixed before O'Flaherty returned to Dublin to work among those who were the writers in Ireland's literary revival. He was a man before he was an Irishman, just as he was a man before he was a Communist. And being a man—isolated, individual, intensely conscious of his own existence as a person in a universe that his reason showed him as impersonal and indifferent—he could not choose to be an Irishman or a Communist, for he could not choose to be what he was so forcefully aware he was not. To *be* meant to be isolated and individual, faced always with absurdity and annihilation. He might cry out for belief, for authority, for a cause in which to lose himself. He might try to escape from himself by throwing himself into Irish affairs, but always his negative intellect was there, forcing him back upon himself. He could not choose to dream the Irish dream, because the dream was a quality of being, not a conscious choice.

O'Flaherty's relationship to the Irish literary revival is an index to the force that impelled that revival, for his conscious effort to be a part of the revival indicated that the revival had lost its force to absorb consciousness. The literary revival came from the Irish dream, a shared consciousness. The dream was quality of consciousness, not something apart to be accepted or rejected. Within the dream existence was not absurd and man was not isolated and individual. The dream was the meaning of existence, a faith that existence had meaning so pervasive that there could be no questioning. It existed when it could absorb men's consciousness. It ceased to exist when it could not. O'Flaherty could not choose the dream. It either possessed consciousness or it did not. When it possessed consciousness it was reality, not an alternative, not a cultivated faith, not something to be affirmed or denied. It was a reality as O'Flaherty's individual being was a reality with its awareness of absurdity and annihilation. Both realities were undeniable. That O'Flaherty had the one sense of reality and not the other, that his sense of reality was even possible, is an indication of the disintegration of the binding force of the Irish literary revival.

O'Flaherty's style is a direct consequence of the furious intensity of his manner of seeing which made anything but immediate and direct expression seem superficial and irrelevant, a self-indulgent toying with frivolities. He was impatient with [Edward] Garnett's efforts to have him cultivate a deliberate style, a "mania" as he called it, which had crippled most of the young English writers of talent. He set himself against style: "Damn it man, I have no style. I don't want any style. I refuse to have a style. I have no time for style. I think style is artificial and vulgar," he tells Garnett (April 2, 1924). He thought a writer a fool to sidetrack his creative energy in an attempt to develop a style. He meant, of course, style in the sense of a deliberate effort to write beautifully, as if the words themselves and their patterns were the artist's end. For O'Flaherty did not conceive of words alone as being certain good. He did not think of writing as in-cantation or symbolism whereby the artist evoked powers and emotions outside of himself. Nor did he think of art as that which is interposed between man and the harshness of reality. What he had to express was the momentous quality of his manner of seeing. For him the poet was not a craftsman but a seer. That which characterized the poet for Stapleton in *Insurrection* was not his way with words (O'Flaherty's poets are not nec-essarily creators) but his awareness of the true nature of things. When O'Flaherty thought of his own creative activity he could describe it only as a "creative mania" or a "fever in the bowels" which was inexplicable. Art for him was not a subtle refinement of civilization, the delicate weaving of shreds of beauty into harmonious designs. As he said in his study of Conrad, the artist is the "cold-eyed adventurer" who "peers over the brink of chaos in search of truth."

Thus in O'Flaherty's work there is little deliberate artistry where the craftsmanship itself is a part of the artistic experience. Only in *The Black Soul* does O'Flaherty deliberately try to be "poetic" and this was at the insistence of Edward Garnett, who urged him to raise the language to a poetic level. For the most part his writing is characterized by impatience and simplicity. What he has to express is not a subtle perception of the nuances of human experience where intricate shadings or techniques are needed to explore character and society. A stream of consciousness technique would emphasize the converse of what he attempted to portray, for he wished to dwell not on the irrelevancies which make up so much of the flow of experience but on the one relevancy which so overshadowed everything else in its import that it could be the only true matter for artistic expression. Beside his overwhelming awareness of existence and mortality, anything else seemed to be error or escapism.

William York Tindall described O'Flaherty's novels up to *The Martyr* as "crude," and measured by the usual standards of craftsmanship there can be no other judgment. Frank O'Connor thought that O'Flaherty's novels could be used as evidence to prove that an Irish novel was impossible. Each considers O'Flaherty's novels by the conventional criteria—plot, character, dialogue, description—or by refinements of technique to explore human consciousness. When thought of as representing human beings in society, as describing the delicate interplay between characters, as revealing any humanistic values or insights, O'Flaherty's novels do appear crude and inadequate. The characters generally are not skillfully drawn but sketched in rapidly and roughly and set into motion as soon as they are given sufficient body to support motion. The appearance of Fergus O'Connor or Francis Ferriter is of little consequence compared to O'Flaherty's main concern with these characters. The characters do not develop either within themselves or in their relationship to others. When they talk, it is to convey information about themselves or others necessary to advance the plot or to tell of their own motives. There is no wordplay, no exchange of ideas. The characters do not modify one another. For the most part their actions are described directly by the omniscient author. By every conventional norm (and the appearance of O'Flaherty's novels is entirely conventional) O'Flaherty displays no skill as a novelist.

Yet his best novels have unquestionable power, not because of the refinement of any part but from the movement of the whole. Although the technical point of view is external and omniscient, the best novels move with an inevitability that has no hint of author manipulation. They move like a storm, a cloudburst, over which the author has no control. Typically they begin like *The Assassin* ("At three o'clock in the afternoon, Michael McDara alighted from the tram-car at the corner of Findlater's Church") or *The Puritan* ("Shortly after midnight on Sunday, June 21st, Francis Ferriter left the offices of the Morning Star in O'Connell Street, Dublin, and returned to his lodgings in Lower Gardiner Street"). From some simple beginning they move swiftly and relentlessly to a furious climax, with all the violence of a storm until the storm is spent. That is the end. There is no sunlight or rainbow. The clouds gather swiftly. An occasional lightning flash shows up this or that portion of the scene, a face perhaps, a street or a room. The author describes what he sees.

O'Flaherty's novels are not about man in society but the storm in the human soul as it comes to an intensified awareness of its own existence in a universe where existence has no meaning. He is not a Renaissance artist celebrating the joy of life but more akin to the medieval, following the advice of Fra Lippo Lippi's superiors who counseled him to "Give us no more of body than shows soul." O'Flaherty's true subject is the individual soul, becoming individual as it is separated form its role in society, focused in upon itself. The external world in the novels is not a systematic realistic drawing of society. It is what O'Flaherty sees clearly and harshly in the lightning flashes that occasionally illuminate the soul's storm. The real focus is on the soul's struggle, and to record that struggle O'Flaherty grabs out furiously at the most immediate material at hand to hurl it upon the page.

He does not seek stylistic refinement that focuses upon itself but the immediacy of the horror and the wonder of the storm. The external violence that all critics note mirrors soul states. The enormity of the soul's upheaval can be expressed only in the most violent external action. At the end of *Shame the Devil* O'Flaherty says, "I reach the spirit through the flesh." This is the essential technique of the novels. He is like Dante in that the physical represents the spiritual. But O'Flaherty's is no systematic allegorical construction. It is the immediacy and not the meaning of the storm that absorbs him. To catch that immediacy his work is rapid, impatient, raw, turbulent. The lines are dark, bold, and slashing, unfinished, like nature herself. If his novels take the form of melodrama, it is because the storm he represents is melodramatic, as William Troy defined the term, "the elaboration of human motives on a grand scale, against immense backgrounds, and to the accompaniment of enormous music." O'Flaherty's form, however, is not a courageous choice, as Troy suggested, but the inevitable result of his real subject.

To appraise O'Flaherty's novels by conventional novel standards is to assume that the novelist's subject is man in or opposed to society and to look at the man and the society as being his subject. But except for *Famine* the novels are essentially asocial. Man does not define himself in or against society's norms but against the fact of his own existence. To judge the novels by the skill with which he delineates society—characters in relation to their social roles or one another—is to miss O'Flaherty's real subject which is not concerned with any of these.

If O'Flaherty's novels are the storm, the short stories are the calm that follows the storm or, better, the eye of a hurricane, for the short stories are not happy moments that follow the stress, as if man can ultimately win peace if he can only endure. Like the novels, the subject of the short stories is the awe and wonder of existence. The stories are moments of vision that arise out of the ashes of the struggle. They represent not the frenzy of man struggling against his tragedy but the chill vision that arises when the inevitability of annihilation is accepted. The style of the short stories depends upon the nature of that acceptance, because a man as long as he is a man cannot accept that inevitability. In the short stories the man who can accept has been annihilated, merged into the awe and wonder of the experience. The short stories are suprahuman. Man appears not as man distinct from nature but as manifestation of nature, as a wave or a seabird is a manifestation of nature. The simplicity of the short stories owes to the elimination of human complexity, the tangles of reason constructed to explain what reason is futile to explain. The novels are dashed upon the page, furiously, to catch the violence of the soul's storm. The short stories appear to arise out of nature itself, beyond human control.

Regardless of his protests to Garnett, O'Flaherty does have style; but because it depends so entirely upon experience forcing itself upon the artist rather than the artist arranging experience, he is not a stylist. As an artist he is the instrument and not a creator of life: "I am no philosopher, but vessel into which life pours sweet wine or vinegar, from a hand that is indifferently careless. Wine or vinegar, I must accept it and drink it to the dregs" [*Shame the Devil*]. He does not use his genius to create. He *is used* by his genius to express. And what he expresses is the immediacy of the experience of what it means to be a man. Sometimes it is storm, sometimes calm. The style is frantic or simple in measure. O'Flaherty has not developed a style to order experience. His style is the consequence of the intensity of his manner of seeing.

The change that occurred in O'Flaherty's novels with *Famine* was accompanied by an abrupt decline in the quantity as well as the quality of his literary productivity. From 1937 to the present just three novels have been published in addition to the short-story collection of 1948, *Two Lovely Beasts*. Surveying Irish literature in 1945, [John V.] Kelleher saw that a decline in quantity was general and that the few Irish works being published scarcely constituted a literary movement. He attributed this to the rapid use of Ireland's literary resources during the height of the revival which had mined out most of the material. He thought the writers of 1945 were looking at a "diminished reality," and by "faithfully drawing a paltry truth" they got, too often and "with much effort, a paltry result." He classed O'Flaherty with [Frank] O'Connor and [Sean] O'Faolain who were trying to discover their country's history with their historical novels, but he believed that the heroes of Irish history were too small and too mortal to inspire worthwhile expression. He saw *Famine* as a part of this historical trend.

However, O'Flaherty during the peak of his creativity had not been mining Irish resources but spiritual resources. When he turned to Irish history, it was not because he could not find materials around him. The lack was within him. During the course of all the novels up to *Famine* he had but one theme—man's desperation to find meaning in an inscrutable universe. In the black soul novels he repeated an essential pattern of struggle until it was apparent that mode was exhausted. And with *Skerrett* he achieved the fullest development of the alternate mode, creating the tragic hero not possible within the black soul consciousness. E. M. Forster, of course, is the classic example of the writer who wrote what he had to say and stopped. In a way O'Flaherty was like this, but because he was not the conscious craftsman that Forster was, depending, rather on a distinctive tension for the impetus of his art, his decline in productivity was due more to the decline in tension than to a conscious awareness that his artistic resources had been used up.

Nothing seems more apparent than that spiritual torment is the essential ingredient of O'Flaherty's art. The last novels, lacking the torment, do not illustrate his real power. The struggle is gone. In the midst of battle a philosophic calm prevails. In those novels there is the reconciliation of thought and action that O'Flaherty earlier said destroyed the power to create beauty. If all the earlier novels were expressions of his own spiritual awareness and torment, they were expressions derived from his own tension between his will to believe and his intellect which destroyed all belief. The tension could not be understood and still be tension, because the understanding itself was one pole of the tension. The tension was dependent upon O'Flaherty's divided self, each self asserting its own claim. The earlier novels depended upon his division, not unity of being. He could not understand himself and still be the artist he was, because his unity of being was achieved within and not outside his art, and the unity was the expression of the tension. There was no understanding *I* who could say I am this or that. The earlier novels were Oedipus-like efforts to find identity, and like Oedipus the protagonists found their identity in the horror of the awareness of their own existence. It was as if O'Flaherty were condemned, like Sisyphus, to a continual repetition of a struggle foredoomed to failure, with the clearest awareness of identity possible only at the moment of clearest awareness of the ultimate annihilation of identity.

In 1934 O'Flaherty wrote *Shame the Devil* to tell the truth about himself. But it was also a self-analysis of searching intensity in which he looked directly at those segments of his being previously dramatized in his novels. *Shame the Devil* was a direct and deliberate quest for unity of being in which O'Flaherty explored his past and his present, saw himself as the artist and the man. He achieved a view of himself in which the subjective and objective coalesced; and whether or not this self-analysis brought his subconscious into harmony with his conscious mind, he achieved a whole view and understanding of himself, and the tension between the artist and the man yielded to this understanding. He saw the malign snake's eye, his mocking genius, as a part of himself and knew it was impossible to flee from it: "I must face it boldly and try to put it into harness." He felt that he had undergone a torment from which he emerged purified: "This is the end of my journey. I have been to hell and now I may rise again." After *Shame the Devil*, and whether because of this or because of the exhaustion of his theme, he wrote no more novels about souls in spiritual torment. If his previous novels had not, *Shame the Devil* exhausted the topic.

Yet his last two novels, though historical in setting, were not historical novels in Kelleher's sense of trying to discover his country's history. Rather, they used the occasion of historical events to draw from men a full expression of their being. In one sense O'Flaherty returned to his familiar topic—what it means to be a man—in that men are put into situations which call for a full expenditure of their spiritual resources. But the test is not the ultimate crisis of the earlier novels. It is based on understanding reason and not passion. Men do not struggle; they endure.

O'Flaherty's art is based on power due not to his careful use of words but to the passion of the artist who in a creative fury hurls the material closest at hand upon the page to catch the immediacy of his impressions. O'Flaherty was aware of this quality of his work. He told Garnett that he was not aware of exerting any judgment whatsoever at the moment of writing: "And of course that has the drawback of all instinctive writing, that it appears to be unfinished, just like a natural landscape" (July 31, 1925). He chose to cultivate the power rather than the skill, preferring the unfinished as a truer representation of his creative expression. But because the power was gone, and he lacked the skill (or he felt such use of skill was false) to achieve with finesse the effects he had previously achieved with personal fury.

O'Flaherty's essential artistic vision derived from the intensity of his awareness of his own existence in a universe that gives no meaning for existence. His subject is man as he becomes aware of himself in a universe which his reason shows him is absurd. In this sense O'Flaherty can be considered an existentialist. His awareness of the absurdity of existence, however, was not a philosophical position but a condition of his being. It was a condition from which he constantly struggled to escape, not a way of seeing he wished to promulgate. O'Flaherty is an artist, not a thinker. Man's existential plight was the subject of art, not of truth. When O'Flaherty sought truth and became a positive thinker as the last novels indicate, he ceased being an artist.

O'Flaherty's subject is existence because he is a modern writer who sees man not as a manifestation of culture, tradition, or civilization, but as a naked soul alien to the culture, tradition, and civilization that offer only deceptions to obscure from men the true and awful nature of their being. His view of the artist is that which Lionel Trilling considers the characteristically modern belief: "the man who goes down into that hell which is the historical beginning of the human soul, a beginning not outgrown but established in humanity as we know it now, preferring the reality of this hell to the bland lies of the civilization that has overlaid it."

When O'Flaherty moved out from the isolated world of the Aran Islands into the world of Western culture, the image of reality that he bore from those elemental storm-lashed rocks was not shattered, but confirmed. The Aran Islands were reality in microcosm, for the Aran Islands were to earth as earth was to universe; and individual man on the islands, confronted with awesome nature, isolated, constantly aware of life because of his proximity to death, screaming out in horror at his inevitable fate, was true man, not overlaid by a complex culture that deceived. And because O'Flaherty was a modern writer he could not be an Irish writer in the sense of belonging to Ireland, speaking for Ireland, expressing Ireland and Irish dreams. What made Ireland significant for the Irish literary revival was a distinctive culture and tradition to which the Irish writers felt they belonged. It did not deceive them but sustained them.

O'Flaherty could only look at Ireland and envy, but he could not belong; for he had seen, felt to the marrow of his being, the awful truth of his own existence. He could cry out like Kurtz, "The horror! The horror!" but he could not deny that truth when, as an artist, he forced himself again and again to peer over the brink of Chaos.

The Creative Act:
C. S. Lewis on God and Art

Janice Witherspoon Neuleib

In one of his *Letters to Malcolm* Lewis says "One of the purposes for which God instituted prayer may have been to bear witness that the course of events is not governed like a state but created like a work of art to which every being makes its contribution and (in prayer) a conscious contribution, and in which every being is both an end and a means." Lewis's God is the great artist forming the universe in a gigantic eternal pattern that "was made for the sake of all it does and is, down to the curve of every wave and the flight of every insect." Because of this interpretation of the Divine as artist, Lewis was able to deal consistently and effectively with the question of free will and predestination in his art, as well as in his nonfictional prose. It thus was possible for Lewis to deliver a religious "message" without didactic overtones because he "made" his fiction in such a way that the medium became the message.

Devout Lewis enthusiasts may perhaps object to the application of the McLuhan title to one so conscientiously old-fashioned as Lewis. No phrase, however, could pinpoint more accurately Lewis's art and his ideas. It was very important to Lewis that God be understood as existing in eternity. The concepts of past, present, and future are concepts that are accurate only for those of us who live in time. For God there is no time; there is only the gigantic picture of the whole. About the question of the afterlife and about salvation, Lewis said in one of his letters, "the Timeless God chooses the timeless soul timelessly. . . . I believe the saved soul always (timelessly) chooses Him. And the reprobate soul in like manner always rejects him. This response of rejection in fact *is* the soul. The good and bad deeds done on earth are the appearance (in Time) of its willed nature." The insistence that God is not in time is certainly not new with Lewis, but

---

From *The Longing for a Form: Essays on the Fiction of C. S. Lewis.* © 1977 by The Kent State University Press.

he did apply that concept in a practical way. At the same time, he did, of course, see that there were problems with his interpretation. God is still the artist, and the artist is in some sense responsible for his characters' blessed or cursed natures. Lewis chose to explain the "how" but admitted that he could not explain the "why." He solved the dilemma by instructing Mr. Lennox in the above quoted letter that one is "not to *worry.*"

Any reader who knows Lewis at all will want to smile at that last admonition. It is so characteristic. There is a huge problem that has been debated for centuries. Lewis gives his interpretation of the answer, admits the difficulties, and then cautions the reader that he is not to worry. Perhaps Lewis can be a carefree comforter because as artist he is able to explain the "why" that was left unanswered in his persuasive arguments.

Since Greek times artists have been defending their work with the argument that their art imitates nature and by the analogy that they themselves in some way imitate the creator. Lewis, in the latter part of his career, extended the image to make it clear that the artist offers a means of understanding the ways of God. This conviction he imbedded in his later works: the Ransom trilogy, the Chronicles of Narnia, and *Till We Have Faces.* The troublesome problems of God's will versus man's will and free will versus predestination are dealt with in these works not as philosophical questions but as artistic building blocks which strengthen the creations and make them more subtle and impressive in their structures.

Blending theology, philosophy, and art is not an easy task for any author. To combine all three with what might be called a "popular art form" might seem a less than modest undertaking, but such is exactly the task of Lewis the creator in the trilogy. In these three novels Lewis deals with the fall of man, including all the implied questions about the responsibility of God for evil and about His seemingly inevitable control over the events of men's lives.

In the first novel of the trilogy the main character Ransom is set quite literally spinning on an adventure to the planet Mars, or Malacandra. Within the first few pages, questions arise about Ransom's free will. The man hardly plans to be walking down a country road at dusk, or to be captured by two ruffian scientists who bundle him into a Wellsian space vehicle and whisk him out of earth's domain. Upon his arrival on the red planet, Ransom is running wildly from his captors when he meets the gentle Hyoi and begins to be changed by the life and attitudes of an unspoiled planet. In both aspects of the plot, events that appear to the character to be random occurrences turn out to be for the reader, who stands outside the frame of the whole, events which must lead to some preset climax— else why write a novel?

More importantly, since Ransom is a character who is to appear in the two later volumes of the trilogy as hero and saviour, those events which to him seem to be so much happenstance are central to the thread of, as Lewis would call it, "the whole show." For the reader of the entire trilogy it is important to have at all times the conviction that the characters are acting of their owns wills in a game in which the stakes really matter and in which something is to be won and lost. No one would read the trilogy if this apparent approximation of human action were not there. At the same time, there must also be the feeling that there is purpose in action. Even more importantly, we want to be assured that the artist is back there somewhere guiding the actions so that it has order as well as apparent freedom. And we want to be able to do both things without being aware that anything more is happening to us than the excitement of the story itself.

Lewis manages to incorporate our well-learned faith in the artist into the texture of his own artistic creation. When at the end of *Out of the Silent Planet* the Oyarsa says that he expects to see Ransom again and that "it is not without the wisdom of Maleldil that we have met now," the reader is willing to accept both the control of the artist and of the divine Maleldil. Both are behind the action of the story. Of course, no sensible reader is going to identify consciously the real artist with the imagined God figure, but the technique serves to suggest its own purpose. So much does this technique work its special suggestiveness that by the time one turns to the second volume of the trilogy, he or she is ready to face the perplexing question of man's apparent freedom to sin in a world which is controlled by God. No heavy discussion of Arminianism versus Calvinism is offered in *Perelandra*; rather, Lewis shows a perfect and an imperfect creature, each making significant decisions.

This portrayal of the process of salvation as it works itself out in life is the technique of *Perelandra*. The reader, having finished the novel, looks at the whole and says it must have been so, but the character within the frame of the picture sees choice and freedom. The advantage of a good creative work is that one may reread it; a second reading provides the opportunity to experience both the controlled whole and the chosen moment. A second reading offers one a chance to experience time as the Divine nature might, viewing the entire panorama as one grand scene.

Previous critical opinion has seen *Perelandra* as a statement in myth of the essential weakness of human nature, the revolt of the personal will against God's will. Certainly it is that. There is no way, however, that one could trace a dialectic on the issue through the novel. Rather it is the process of the telling that conveys the message about the human and the Divine natures. One first sees Ransom taking off for outer space again, but this time he goes of his own will, or so it appears. The coffinlike thing in which he travels is a symbol for a kind of death to his former personal existence. His new or renewed experience on the planet unfolds slowly. There are all sorts of exotic plants and creatures which cause Ransom to speculate about both philosophy and art. The bubble trees cause him to ask himself if evil is the willed repetition of experience, in defiance of obvious Divine direction. The dragon, too, makes Ransom ask whether myth as pictured in art reflects reality elsewhere in God's creation. Such speculations may serve to make the reader question previous assumptions, but I think not. What they certainly do, however, is to suggest the artistic control behind apparent reality. Ransom is able to see for the first time the flow of the universe, to appreciate the variety and breadth of possible created forms and events. In fact, for the first time, he begins to see events as created rather than experienced. The unfolding of the created event is the essence of *Perelandra*.

Joy in the God-given experience as well as in the God-given object is what the Green Lady learns early in her conversations with Ransom. Not only is she a physical creature, she is also being created spiritually and may participate in that creation. " 'I thought,' she said, 'that I was carried in the will of Him I love, but now I see that I walk with it.' " She sees that she is able to form herself to fit Maleldil's will or to defy that will if she chooses. Of course, from the reader's point of view, her decision conforms to the plot and theme of the novel as well as to Maleldil's will. There is dissonance between her apparent freedom to choose and her actual suspension within the motion of the novel's plot. That dissonance establishes the artistic consistency of *Perelandra*. Intellectually and in retrospect the discrepancy is apparent to the reader. At the moment and in the process of reading the novel, that reader is enmeshed in the implied comparison of artist and Maleldil. Lewis does not have to go out of his way to remind his reader that the Green Lady is a character in a novel. The reader knows, but he is aware only of Divine control, not, of course, of artistic. Lewis, not being a Divine creator, cannot offer her the Divine paradox, to be created, controlled, and free at once.

Neither does he offer it to Ransom, but Ransom's choices are more difficult than the Lady's. Ransom's dark night of the soul is much closer to an artist-persona struggling with the demands of the world he has created. Maleldil does not talk to him as He does to the Lady, nor does He reveal His will explicitly. Not until Ransom struggles through a dialogue half with the Divine and half with his own conscience does he see that he is destined to act a part that he would never choose. His decision is to go willingly into the created event though his every fiber rejects what he knows is to come. Lewis, the artist, describes Ransom's attitude after the moment of decision so: "The thing was going to be done. There was going to arrive, in the course of time, a moment at which he would have done it. The future act stood there, fixed and unaltered as if he had already performed it. It was a mere irrelevant detail that it happened to occupy the position we call future instead of that which we call past. . . . Predestination and freedom were apparently identical. He could no longer see any meaning in the many arguments he had heard on this subject."

Again the reader is asked to be convinced not on the basis of argued reason but on the basis of the feelings of a character. The created being sees his own relationship to the divine will as both his own decision and as a set of circumstances already stretched out on the painted canvas of eternity. He sees no conflict, nor does Lewis offer the reader an opportunity to construct one. In the next few pages Ransom meets the Un-man in battle and is able to save the green planet. By the time the issue of "What would have happened if. . ." arises, Ransom is safe with the Lady and her King and all conjecture seems unlikely, as any guess about a different past always does. The novel's end is near and all has been accomplished. Speculation only causes the pattern as it is to seem more vivid because the Divine artist, as well as the mortal artist, is given credit for the picture.

In the last book of the trilogy a woman is the focus of the struggle — not, however, in the same way as the Green Lady. The Lady was a walking myth whose submission was made believable because of her superior ability to communicate with the Creator. Jane Studdock, on the other hand, is a very modern young woman who has the Divine plan imposed upon her life in a way that she cannot ignore. She is forced to make a decision for or against Maleldil despite a desire to withdraw from cosmic conflict and live her own life. Jane is probably more appealing to many modern readers because of this desire to be a private person; she is also, therefore, the ideal character to show how no one can be indifferent to the Creator. Again, Lewis's technique is perfect. He creates a story that works on the reader in much the same way that the events in the novel work on the main character.

Jane is impressive. She is a good person who tries to be a modern scholar and to be a woman at the same time. Her self-reliance and her individuality make her the ideal heroine for the typical modern novel (assuming, of course, that there is such a thing). She is so sensible that it is impossible not to be sympathetic when she starts to have nightmares. One is also inclined to sympathize with her frustration when her friends cannot offer her any relief from the nightly intrusions into her privacy. In Jane's case, it is not as if the Divine has chosen her; it is as if the Divine has barged in and permanently settled itself in her life without asking leave at all. Lewis presents her indignation as being exactly appropriate. That is why it is such a jolt to the reader when this independent Jane comes face to face with the reborn Ransom and is immediately undone.

One must recall that, in the first two novels, Ransom was about as sensible and ordinary as Jane herself. His metamorphosis is spectacular, as Jane discovers when she walks into a room and meets a man who looks like a Greek god and who is able to change her life at a glance. The phrase used to describe this change is "her world was unmade." Even so, Jane resists the test for a while, still planning to avoid all the irrational nonsense involved in strange men and stranger dreams. Not until she meets the Fairy, a female secret police officer, does she run toward the fate that has apparently been pursuing her throughout the novel. From Jane's point of view, it seems clear that she has made the best decision and made it none too soon. If one steps outside the novel, however, it becomes apparent that there was little choice. The Divine seemed to be relentlessly pursuing the good that was in Jane. The author also seems to have created a situation for her that could move in only one direction. She is free, and yet she is trapped in a stream of events. Thus, here in the novel that is set on earth, the panorama of the created work illustrating the form and freedom of the created universe as displayed in the Ransom trilogy is completed.

Although the trilogy talks of Maleldil, he never is described or given the dimension offered to characters portrayed in the text. In the Chronicles of Narnia, however, Divinity takes on incarnate form in the person of the great lion, Aslan. Both the Divine creator and the artistic creator appear within the pages of these books, albeit the authorial intrusions of Lewis's persona are limited to such advice as the firm warning that one must never step into and close a wardrobe. Still, he does remind the reader that he is there and that he will keep a firm hand on the story. Aslan does more. He makes it clear from the beginning that he is in command of all events which occur in Narnia and that he is the chosen embodiment of his Father, sent to create life forms and events in the country of animals. Lewis, the narrator, says of Aslan, "People who have not been in Narnia sometimes think that a thing cannot be good and terrible at the same time. If the children had ever thought so, they were cured of it now" [*The Lion, the Witch and the Wardrobe*]. The great lion produces the awe due both to his lordly animal nature and to his Divine nature. In the first of the Chronicles this marvellous beast dies a terrible death in exchange for the life of a treacherous child. Not only is the description of Aslan's death powerful, it also serves to associate for the reader the great lion Aslan with the Lion of Judah.

In the sixth book, *The Magician's Nephew*, Lewis shows Aslan creating Narnia. The scene identifies the Divine act of creation with the artistic act of creation. Rather than move a magic wand or do any of a number of things a creator might do, Aslan sings the land of Narnia into existence. Through an artistic act, he creates the world of talking animals and living trees. Lewis says of Digory's response to the singing that "it was so beautiful he could hardly bear it." That one voice is soon joined by the music of the stars which he is creating and then by all the beings of the planet as it springs to life. Lewis makes the music of creation into a literal scene. All this description helps to show the artistic whole that is the world of Narnia. In fact, the last book of the Chronicles gives exactly as powerful a description of the unmaking of Narnia as the preceding description of its making. In the end, all turns cold at Aslan's command as the land is devoured and the nothingness of the void returns. Aslan's final command is that Peter shut the door on the barren darkness [*The Last Battle*]. Lewis cannot, of course, leave the portrait so; this is the world of the eternal creator with no finite limits. Thus, the final book ends with all the characters going up and into an infinite number of pictured frames of both Narnia and of England, "like an onion," says Mr. Tumnus, "except that as you continue to go in and in, each circle is larger than the last."

Lewis has given a closed picture of a world that begins and ends within the supposed time scheme of what would be only fifty years or so by earth time. By doing this, he is able to establish the sense of freedom and control that I have been illustrating. Aslan creates and rules what is very clearly an artistic unit, yet within the bounds of that unit there are seven adventure stories, all of which deal with numerous moral choices on the parts of the young adventurers. From their points of view there is certainly freedom, perhaps more than some of them would prefer. From the viewpoint of the creators, leonine and human, the characters' lives are constantly controlled. From the point of view of the reader, both are true at the same time. In these Chronicles of Narnia Lewis closed the circle of his art even more firmly than he had done in the more familiar worlds of Maleldil.

The Chronicles of Narnia completed, Lewis wrote his last work of fiction. Whereas the two earlier sets of books are future fantasy or parallel universe fantasy, *Till We Have Faces* is the modern retelling of an ancient myth. At first glance, it might seem that this novel deals very specifically with free will and leaves the question of Predestination completely untouched. If one looks carefully at the ending, however, it becomes clear that Orual's lesson is precisely the lesson about the Divine nature that only art can illustrate. At first, she curses the gods for tricking her and ruining her life by hiding from her at the most crucial moments. After many years as queen and after a challenge to the gods, she makes the amazing discovery that the evil in her life was her own doing, called on herself precisely because she refused to accept the Divine nature. Not until she sees her sister, Psyche, journey into Hell, taunted by all Orual's demands, does this unhappy queen admit her own guilt in refusing to realize the Divine control of life and to see the ultimate benevolence behind that control. In this tale Lewis is able to emphasize the importance of the creative nature of the Divine. Wisdom comes to the main character when she, the artist of her own life's story, is able to recognize the beauty in the whole story, ugly as the parts may have seemed.

So Lewis ended his career as writer of fiction, insisting that beauty was to be found in the pattern of the divine will. The corollary is that the artist can see the illustration of that will in his own creation. Though it is impossible to see the whole picture of eternity as God sees it, man can certainly see the pattern of a work of fiction as the artist presents it. If the Divine nature is incorporated into the novel, then the reader is able to see both the freedom of the characters and the control of both artist and God. This use of the most perplexing paradox thus becomes a building block for a skillfully executed work of art in which the form perfectly illustrates the theme and the artist is able to teach and delight in one purposeful act of creation.

Women and Language
in the Fiction of Elizabeth Bowen

Harriet S. Chessman

"But what story *is* true? Such a pity, I sometimes think, that there should have to be any stories. We might have been happy the way we were."

"Something has got to become of everybody, I suppose, Cousin Nettie."

"No, I don't see why. Nothing has become of me: here I am, and you can't make any more stories out of that."

(*The Heat of the Day*)

Elizabeth Bowen's fiction, like much modern fiction, compels a recognition of the danger inherent in all fiction-making. Stories are, quite simply, untrue; they capture us, as they tried to capture Cousin Nettie, in their nets. Roderick's response, in this context, that "Something has got to become of everybody, I suppose," sounds weak. Yet Nettie's resistance to stories offers a problematic alternative. Nettie asserts a state of being, an essential unchangingness, inviolable by story; but what is this state of being? How is it to be defined? Who, finally, *is* "Cousin Nettie" except as this figure enters into some relationship, and by extension into the *relation* of some story?

Like all characters, Nettie literally owes her existence entirely to her author; she inhabits a story whether she wants to or not. One could say that her author gives her asylum, within the text—the text allows a space within itself for a critique of the text's own project—but it is also true that the text contains Nettie, just as the literal asylum, Wisteria Lodge, contains her. She is kept out of the larger picture. It is Roderick who occupies more textual space. Inheriting the ancestral home of Nettie's husband, attempting to fill the gaps in family stories and the family line, Roderick occupies the

From *Twentieth Century Literature* 29, no. 1 (Spring 1983). © 1983 by Hofstra University Press.

position of a believer and a participant in story—a position which coincides directly with his own assumption of authority as head of the family. Roderick's acceptance of history, in all its senses, clearly emerges out of his happy assumption of the power to author the continuing story he has inherited.

The dialogue between these two figures becomes paradigmatic of the struggle, within Bowen's fictions, between two stances toward story and language, which find expression as two differing narrative impulses. I wish both to explore this struggle, and to determine its connection with gender, because Bowen appears to point to such a connection, and because such an inquiry raises significant questions about women writers in their relation to their own authority as storytellers. I hope to suggest that Bowen, like many women writers, reveals a profound ambivalence toward her own powers of authorship, and that his ambivalence involves a sense of her betrayal of her own gender. Women, in Bowen's vision, are inherently outsiders to discourse, unless they turn traitor and defect to the other side.

Bowen defines two primary positions for women with regard both to narrative and to language. Certain women become objects of narration, in stories told both by the primary narrators and by characters who act as narrators. Yet, as objects, these women tend to resist their forced entrance into narrative, and to desire the presence of another narrative form. Usually these figures are either silent or inarticulate, and point to a desire for a new language based on models of silent and symbiotic union—a desire which emerges in the work of many other modern women writers, especially Virginia Woolf. Other female figures, however, assume a place as author, or coauthor, of a story. These women, who become alter egos of the inarticulate female figures, have the capacity to author, through their mastery of language, these other women; yet often, as with Iseult's half-authoring of Eva in *Eva Trout*, such creation comes freighted with danger. To bring such resisters into full character could result in an end to the story as it has been written. It is precisely this fear that allows the female storytellers to gain control over their own monstrous alter egos, and to silence their attempts at resistance. The story, in any case, is not one's own. Such female "authors" are often characters themselves in other people's texts: Iseult is not only a "D. H. Lawrence reader," but a D. H. Lawrence character, and it stands to reason that her own narrative impulse might be suspect, or perhaps divided.

It is the relations between these two positions that structures Bowen's fiction. Usually, the positions are fleshed out quite clearly in the form of two primary female characters, who become representative of these two roles: storyteller and object of the story, "insider" and "outsider." The plot tends to be generated by the distance between these alter egos—the struggle which occurs as a result of their difference—and by this movement into or out of authorship.

What is at stake here is a radical schizophrenia, and one which holds particular significance for women. If it is true, as Luce Irigaray has suggested, that women have remained silent within discourse, and that to become a speaking or writing subject is by definition to become "the masculine," then an apparently unbridgeable gap exists between woman as subject and woman as object. To become a subject necessitates a loss of one's actual being, in a distortion and appropriation through language. A woman entering the symbolic becomes by the workings of this logic a masculine speaker, and in "speaking for" herself as woman, she participates in a masculine misprision and silencing.

Whether this model is "true" or not has certainly become an issue of debate, among feminist critics, but what is clear is that, regardless of its absolute truth, it makes some stunning appearances in the work of many women writers, and therefore seems to bear a significant relation to women's own experience of themselves. What emerges is the problematic of how women can produce their own stories, as subjects, without being "appropriated to and by the masculine." Bowen scatters her novels with female figures who not only resist the narratives they see around them, but who themselves have no language, and who therefore cannot generate other texts. These figures haunt her: they represent the unarticulated and inchoate femaleness which must in some sense be betrayed or at least abandoned, in the very act of entering language to tell stories.

And this femaleness, in Bowen's terms, is as silent as Irigaray would suggest. Apart from the apparent distinction between women with language and women without it, Bowen often hints at the larger silence all women share within culture. In *The Heat of the Day*, it is Stella (her name—already unoriginal—emerging, possibly, straight out of Sidney's poem) who, according to her inarticulate alter ego Louie, can "sp[eak] beautifully," yet who discovers the bonds of silence between women in the drawing room of Mount Morris. The conventions of the drawing room, both in life and in art, necessitate certain linguistic conventions: certain stories must be upheld, certain words must not be spoken. In fact, the words do not exist which might break the "deep silence" sustained by generations of "Ladies" (not "women" now). It is this bond of silence which forms the identificaiton between Stella and Louie, or Anna and Portia in *The Death of the Heart*, or Iseult and Eva in *Eva Trout*, an identification which persists in spite of the gap between two apparently different discourses. Yet it is the refusal to recognize this bond of cultural and linguistic silence which causes the alienation and withdrawal of both the female "speakers" and the primary narrators.

Through silence, Nettie resists the story she had been built into: the story of the wife contained on her husband's estate, held within the four walls of his house. In another version of such resistance, Louie Lewis, in the same novel, struggles directly against language itself. Louie longs for a return to a state of being which requires no language; as she says, " 'At home where I used always to be there never used to be any necessity *to* say; neither was there with Tom, as long as they let him stop here. But look now—whatever *am* I to, now there's the necessity?' " Like most of her Bowen counterparts, Louie desires a symbiotic union with another, in which silence would become the medium of communication. Bowen defines this desire as a female one, no matter what the gender of the other figure within this union shifts to: the mother can give way to the man, but the model for this union lies in the bond of prelinguistic identification between a mother and daughter. At the end of the novel, with her own baby, she achieves such a union again.

Yet this opposing stance toward language and story comes riddled with ambivalence. Just as Nettie's retreat from story lands her in a static and nonsignificant world, a world cut off completely even from the view outside her one window, Louie's incapacity to use language forces her into a perpetual regression. She can gain no identity without the defining power of words. When confronted with people who *can* "say," she tries desperately to enter their world of language, because she recognizes words as her only key to a visible existence. Significantly, it is to Harrison, subtle and insinuating wielder of language, that Louie first attempts to speak: "her object was to feel that she, Louie, *was.* . . ." By talking she hopes to assert a "self" from which such talk can proceed.

The impossibility of articulateness, however, overwhelms her. To her friend Connie she confesses:

> "It isn't you only. It's the taking and taking up of men on the part of everyone when I have no words. Often you say the advantage I should be at if I could speak grammar; but it's not only that. Look the trouble there is when I have to only say what I *can* say, and so cannot ever say what it is really. Inside me it's like being crowded to death—and more of it all getting into me. I could more bear it if I could only say."

Louie chafes within language's bounds. Her words sit awkwardly and clash against each other, without the smooth structure of "grammar." Yet what is this structure? The very way in which "grammar" begins to disintegrate here could be said to point to the fictiveness of the structure of grammar itself. Louie opens gaps in language. She serves to alienate us too from its operations. We begin to feel, with her, the impossible gap between words and their meanings which lies at the heart of signification. The ambiguity and shiftiness of the referent intended by the word "it" in this passage suggests the arbitrariness and uncertainty of referentiality. There is a sense in which whatever the "it" refers to can never be spoken. The unarticulated world which "crowd[s]" Louie "to death" is precisely that realm of experience which can find no place in language. And once one enters language, the world one desired to make present is abandoned and perhaps betrayed.

Is it only Louie, and figures like her, then, who "cannot ever say what it is really"? Is it just that she "ha[s] no words," or is it possible that the referent, whatever it is, cannot be referred to with language and so be communicated. Louie's speech here —and it stands out partly by being far and away the longest speech that Louie ever makes, and the most abstract—

gains a resonance that goes further than Louie herself. It strikes a difficulty at the core of this book, and of most of Bowen's work. Its resonance with other speeches, by other figures who apparently occupy positions within language, begins to suggest how the boundary between those inside and those outside language or story can disintegrate into a common knowledge of language's inadequacy. Justin, a writer, states in one of Bowen's short stories, "Summer Night":

> "We can no longer express ourselves: what we say doesn't even approximate to reality; it only approximates to what's been said. I say, this war's an awful illumination; it's destroyed our dark; we have to see where we are. Immobilised, God help us, and each so far apart that we can't even try to signal each other. And our currency's worthless. . . . We've got to mint a new one. . . . I taste the dust in the street and I smell the limes in the square and I beat round inside this beastly shell of the past among images that all the more torment me as they lose any sense that they had."

Language, in Justin's view, is wholly mediated. It does not achieve a transparent union of signifier and signified, but veers instead toward a continual approximation of other signifiers. It remains self-contained and unreferential. "What's been said" stands in the way of any new saying. The writer's imagination becomes merely "this beastly shell of the past."

Yet such confessions, on the part of insiders, are rare. It is the function of the female characters outside the dominant discourse to undercut their alter egos' movement into language and story by pointing to the arbitrariness and inadequacy of these phenomena. It is precisely because of this deconstructive function that these figures are dealt with so ambivalently, by both the primary narrators and the storytelling characters: "Is she a snake or a rabbit?" as Anna says of Portia [in *The Death of the Heart*]. These figures outside discourse, in their potential manifestation as "snakes," haunt the garden that writers, among others, cherish. Resisting stories, and resisting language, they uncover the scandal at the heart of authorship itself. In Edward Said's terms, they are occupied with molestation; they expose the shaky and fictive ground that writing rests on. And they suggest, as well, what might have been left out of "writing" as it has been.

Why, then, does Bowen give them breath? And why does she place them in a position of such tension with other female characters? I would suggest that they represent Bowen's own resistance to what she conceives to be the act of fiction-making, which serves to silence and to distort an experience primarily defined as female. A longing for another language, one of transparency and truthfulness, resides just to the side of this resistance. One could say that this desire is a traditional Romantic one for an absence of mediation, and it is romantic; yet Bowen defines it further as a peculiarly female desire. Her female "outsiders" blunder into the truth, despite, or perhaps because of, their bad "grammar." Because they stand outside the confines of linguistic convention, which is predicated upon an artificial distance between what is said and what is referred to, they appear to have the freedom to speak at least some of the "truth," even if they "cannot ever say what it is really." To be able to say "what it is really" would be to take this desire for truth to a longed-for but impossible extent: this truth and this reality are precisely what language as it is now constructed cannot represent. Yet clearly these figures point the way. As Louie says: "Because *I* can't help what it sounds like; I speak the truth every time." And as the narrator observes: "Halted and voluble, this could be but a mouth that blurted rather than spoke, a mouth incontinent and at the same time artless."

The possibility for redemption, then, exists in the artlessness; yet what would the text look like that relied wholly on this lack of form? It is Bowen's own fear that allows these figures room—even rooms of their own—but doesn't allow them power, or certainly not enough power to crack the walls of convention completely, even if this were possible. These figures represent her own impulse toward a breaking of narrative form, yet her treatment of them, her containment of them, as a narrator and as an author, prevents the attempt to embody this impulse.

Bowen's own identification with these figures is represented in part by the identification other female characters experience. The alter egos of the registers (Stella in *The Heat of the Day*, in *To the North*, Anna in *The Death of the Heart*, Mrs. Kerr in *The Hotel*, or Iseult in *Eva Trout*) can also touch on the truth; such revelatory moments always occur in conjunction with a movement toward identification at some point in the text between these two female figures. Louie, in the same long speech referred to above, contrasts Stella's way of speaking with her own: "Now she tonight, she spoke beautifully: I needn't pity her—there it was, off her chest." Stella, at the moment Louie refers to her, speaks only to Louie; they have come together in a wholly accidental way—the man Harrison is the link that draws them into speech. Yet the very accidental nature of this encounter— the very improbability of it—suggests the presence of a bond between them which is hidden almost completely by the rest of the text.

The intricacy of their encounter bears examination: it becomes paradigmatic of the doubleness of the alter ego bond, for these two women experience both identification with and alienation from each other, in terms of their relation both to language in general and to the story in which they each find themselves. Louie's response to Harrison's language is what sparks the moment of dialogue between Louie and Stella: Harrison uses words to define both women. " 'What I saw you were, *and* are,' replied Harrison, 'is a pest. . . .' He looked at Stella and said: 'As for you, are you off your head? Do you think we have got all night?' " Louie reacts to this onslaught with a direct and artless cry: "No . . . how he can have the heart!" to which she adds, to Stella, "Oh, I wonder you go with him!" Louie protests Harrison's definitions, but at another level she could also be said to be protesting definition itself, for the distortion it imposes on its objects. Stella, by contrast, acts as apologist for Harrison. Opening her private dialogue with Louie, Stella says:

"You mustn't mind his manner."

"Don't you mind his manner?"

"One cannot always choose."

"I should have thought you should have had other chances," said
Louie lifelessly . . . "Though you ought not to mind me either,"
she had to add, "because I always do get upset: they say so."

"Manner" here suggests at first simply a surface mode of behavior; but its
implications reach further. It touches closely upon convention itself, at both
a social and a literary level. Harrison is "mannered": the form he participates in is both conventional and artificial. The configuration of the first
three letters —"man"—may be wholly accidental, but, in conjunction with
the masculine pronoun "his," the hint of gender here is unmistakable: this
manner emerges from a man's world, which Stella attaches herself to and
appears to accept, no matter how hard she fights it. The language she
shares in with Harrison is opaque, indirect, censored, just as the language
she exchanges with Robert, her lover, is predicated upon a silence: in the
first moment of speech between Stella and Robert, their words are unheard,
shattered by the detonation of a bomb. "What they *had* both been saying,
or been on the point of saying, neither of them ever now were to know."

The dominant discourse in *The Heat of the Day*, then, as in most Bowen
novels, becomes suspect for two primary reasons: its power of defining its
objects, and thereby misrepresenting them; and its suppression of possible
truth. A further question arises, however, as to the representability of this
"truth" at all within language as it is arranged. When Stella, inspired by
Louie's resistance to Harrison's language, attempts to identify with Louie
and speak the truth, she resorts to a further indirection. Referring obliquely
and with irony to the position Harrison has brought her to—she must
submit to an affair with him if she wishes to prolong Robert's life—Stella
states:

> "This evening was to have been a celebration, the first of many
> more evenings. It may still be the first of many more evenings,
> but what will they be worth? This is the truth," she said, looking
> round her at all the other people apprehensively staring into each
> other's faces. "He cannot bear it; let's hope he will forget it—let's
> hope that; it is the least we can do. We're all three human."

As Louie will later say, "there it was, off her chest": but what is the "it"?
An astonishing absence of referentiality here — or perhaps an evasion of
referentiality—undercuts the assertion of truth-telling. Syntactically, neither the "This" nor the "it" possess a signified object, unless the referent
is precisely that "nothing" that remains unstated within the gap between
the question and the apparent answer. The near quotation of T. S. Eliot's
"Burnt Norton" raises a further problem: is Bowen, like Stella or like Justin
in "Summer Night," referring only to other art, other words? The possibility
of a continual regression, from signifier to other signifier, gives further
support to the possibility that "what it is really," as Louie would put it,
can never be expressed.

Louie's response to this language of indirection, which Stella still participates in, marks one side of Bowen's own response. At first Louie is "overpowered" and literally paralyzed: she "heaved about on her chair as though bound by ropes to it." The language has power over her; it binds her in by its enforcement both of her silence (she does not speak during Stella's monologue) and, in a larger sense, of silence itself. Yet Louie "g[ets] herself free, st[ands] up," and asserts simply: "I ought to be getting back to where I am." The oddity of Louie's language here represents her assertion of freedom from language's ordinary bounds: in breaking its code of convention she allows us the illicit hope that another language will be able to be found. *And* another subject, for another story: "she found, with a shock, that what she now most wanted was never to speak of [Harrison] again." "[A]lready" "[a] fog of abhorrence" is "blotting out what he said." As potential storyteller, Louie substitutes, in place of Harrison, a female cast of characters: Stella without Harrison, Stella with Louie. As Anna will do at the end of *The Death of the Heart* with regard to her alter ego Portia, Louie imagines what Stella is like and gives her voice; yet what is odd is that now it is the inarticulate who imagines the articulate into existence. At the heart of the imagining is identification: Louie may feel herself "entered by what was foreign," yet this alienation is also a fusion. We are offered the possibility for a new story that will be composed of such fusions: in place of gaps, between characters or between signifiers and their significations, there will be a wholeness and a transparency. A genuine dialogue will replace a silencing monologue. Objects will not be captured and defined by words or by narrative, but will become subjects in their own right.

Yet this new language and new story remain problematic. Louie still cannot write this unwritten text. In her inspired musing on Stella, Louie sees "pictures" but no "words." The words she does come up with ("A soul astray") mark a sudden distancing from Stella as the object being defined through a rather artificial and timeworn synecdoche. Louie, like Portia or Eva Trout, avoids an assertion of power through definition as long as she stays away from language; yet how can their stories be told without the use of some language? In Louie's picturing of Stella, Stella becomes co-subject: no gap exists between subject and object. Yet Louie's "pictures" must be translated. The narrator acts as translator, but we must question the accuracy of the translation. To a large and disturbing extent, Louie's actual imaginings can never find adequate representation within language, and the possibility for a new language remains only in the realm of desire. Furthermore, the object of her imaginings eludes even her pictures, to the extent that this object occupies a realm of language inaccessible to Louie: " 'But this is not goodbye, I hope,' had been said—but what, how much, had she [Stella] meant to mean?"

Bowen's figures outside language, then, hint at possibilities for language and for story that remain unfulfilled. The power to represent and define rests with other characters, including both male characters and the

female characters who stand as alter egos to their female counterparts outside. Such representation involves betrayal. As those with language become
storytellers, they participate in the "overpowering" of inarticulate or silent
objects which all authorship—at least in part—involves.

The Death of the Heart (1938) explores this question of authorship more
directly than almost any other Bowen novel. It is no accident that one of
the central characters, St. Quentin, is a novelist; and his vocation becomes
in some sense diffused among the other characters, most of whom attempt
to construct their own stories. Anna is one of the strongest "authors," and
it is her sister-in-law Portia who becomes an unwitting and unwilling character in Anna's story.

Chapter 1 of the first book, "The World," can serve as a model for this
dynamic: in it, Anna joins with St. Quentin in talk, the object of which is,
of course, Portia. Although St. Quentin asks questions, and plays the part
of responder, Anna's talk is essentially a monologue, not a dialogue, which
gives us a clue as to the nature of her discourse: she occupies a position
more of authority than of possible collaboration. This is not "gossip" of an
educative and bond-creating kind: such gossip, as Patricia Meyer Spacks
suggests, involves the participation of two intimate subjects who explore
crucial issues through a discussion of an absent third. Anna and St. Quentin
are involved less in attempting to establish their own intimacy (St. Quentin,
in fact, "detested intimacy, which, so far, has brought him nothing but
pain"), or to discover answers together, than in what Spacks terms
"power," a third element of gossip: Anna seeks power over Portia by
defining her. And she defines with a vengeance. As Anna begins, about
the servant, Matchett:

> "You know what some servants are—how they ride one down,
> and at the same time make all sorts of allowance for temperament
> in children and animals."
> "You would call her a child?"
> "In ways, she's more like an animal. I made that room so pretty
> before she came. I had no idea how blindly she was going to live."

Further, this blind animal-like creature, according to Anna, "has made
nothing but trouble since before she was born." Anna proceeds to tell her
version of what she terms the "story" of Portia's birth, a narrative which
takes up approximately ten pages and possesses a clear bias and deliberate
shaping. Anna's storytelling becomes suspect partly through the fact that
we hear this story again, in different forms, both in chapter 6, when Matchett retells it to Portia, and in chapter 2, when we have a sudden and unusual
glimpse into Portia's own memory of her mother. Yet, no matter which
way the story is told, Anna's version holds, to the extent that Portia's birth,
and the circumstances of her birth, emerge as an unfortunate fall. Both
Matchett's and Anna's versions converge on this point, and Portia is left
imprisoned by her status within the story, as the accidental product of an
illegitimate and rather ridiculous union. Portia attempts a revision of this

ending: to Matchett she protests, "in a panic: 'But we were happy, Matchett. We had each other; he had Mother and me—Oh, don't be so angry: you make me feel it was my fault for having had to be born.' "

What is striking is that Anna is so often seconded, in her representation of Portia, by the narrator of the *The Death of the Heart*, not only in the famous "innocence" passage, but throughout the text. In comparing Anna's response to the spring to Portia's, for example, the narrator clearly sides with Anna: "This was Portia's first spring in England: very young people are true but not resounding instruments. Their senses are tuned to the earth, like the sense of animals; they feel, but without conflict or pain." One may wonder how, after a story which has described precisely Portia's "conflict" and "pain," the narrator could suddenly simplify and distance this figure in a definition so resonant with Anna's earlier definitions. The narrator displays at various points in the text an ambivalence toward this creature who becomes the object of narration. The narrator, in fact, stands in the same double relation of identification and alienation to Portia as Anna does. While the narrator assumes such authority of definition, and thus of alienation, this authority becomes questioned by the continual sense that another side to the story may remain.

Portia's desire for her own language and story, like Louie's, then, undergoes a double treatment by the author. This object of so many stories attempts to become a subject in her own right. Significantly, it is her own text—her diary—that lends to Anna's long opening narrative. Portia's diary represents the characteristic Bowenesque yearning for a language which is transparent, not opaque, which contains the "truth," as opposed to the shadows and lies of the dominant discourse. Yet the model for such a language hints at the impossibility of its actual emergence: this desire, like Louie's, originates in silence. It is the memory of the utterly silent bond of communication which existed between her mother and herself that inspires Portia's need for a true language. Portia's first recorded memory, within the novel, is of ascending the crag in Switzerland with Irene, "arm-in-arm in the dark . . . pressing each other's elbows," as if within the womb-like "tent for the mind" created by the rain they can merge into each other bodily, and form one being, just as "arm-in-arm" forms one word. Everything they do is done together, often in "turn abouts." Even their wishes are wished together, and at every point what they do or feel seems to be less spoken than understood perfectly before speech: "Untaught, they had walked arm-in-arm along city pavements, and at nights had pulled their beds close together or slept in the same bed— overcoming, as far as might be, the separation of birth."

Yet this desire for perfect communion, and for a language which could reproduce this communion, resembles Louie's "pictures": it loses in the translation. It can be imagined, but the narrative itself radically questions whether, given the nature of language, it can ever be reproduced. Portia's diary, as a private entity, may reach for a true language; yet, as St. Quentin points out, even Portia's first sentence shows "style." And "[s]tyle is the thing that's always a bit phony, and at the same time you cannot write without style. . . . And a diary, after all, is written to please oneself—therefore it's bound to be enormously written up."

St. Quentin acts as counterpoint to Portia: the novelist points out the resemblances to his own art in an art which attempts to move beyond fiction. Pure fiction, according to his scheme, is safer than her kind; his novels attempt no referentiality, and so manage to avoid the truth entirely. As he puts it: "if one didn't let oneself swallow some few lies, I don't know how one would ever carry the past." Yet even though a diary appears to reproduce "facts," and so becomes dangerous, it too can never capture them fully, and perhaps, as St. Quentin suggests, the result can be even more treacherous:

> "You're working on us, making us into something. . . . You precipitate things. I daresay," said St. Quentin kindly, "that what you write is quite silly, but all the same, you are taking a liberty. You set traps for us. You ruin our free will."
> "I write what has happened. I don't invent."
> "You put constructions on things. You are a most dangerous girl."
> "No one knows what I do."
> "Oh, but believe me, we feel it. You must see how rattled we are by now."
> "I don't know what you *were* like."
> "Neither did we: we got on quite well then."

No act of writing, St. Quentin suggests, can free itself of interpretation and distortion. Writing itself transforms what it desires to represent: it cannot present things wholly and transparently; it can only present *again*. This dialogue between St. Quentin, the novelist, and Portia Quayne, the diarist, bears a peculiar resonance which travels well beyond the situation at hand. Who is really speaking here? We are reminded that the novel in which this dialogue takes place, *The Death of the Heart*, is "working" on precisely the same characters as Portia's diary. Portia's words here, in defense of her own act of writing, could be Elizabeth Bowen's just as it is Bowen's own character, St. Quentin, who questions and accuses his author. None of us can know "what [these characters] *were* like," for Bowen's authoring of the characters, no matter what desires she originally had, has shaped them—changed them?—and other possibilities have been lost. What manifests itself here is a sense of guilt at the act of authorship itself, as well as a fear that no form of language or story can be found that isn't "distorted and distorting." "You are a most dangerous girl," Bowen could be saying, with some wryness, to herself. Portia is one of the few female characters who attempts to write, and who clearly attempts another form of writing. Her failure becomes by extension Bowen's failure, and the result is a troubled belief in the danger of attempting to write at all.

This guilt of authorship reappears with compelling force in Bowen's last completed novel, *Eva Trout, or Changing Scenes* (1968). The structure of authorship is intricate: two "authors" exist, Iseult and Eva, yet Eva has also been "authored" by Iseult, or at least half-authored. Such creation of an other—which in this book becomes defined as a female creation—is burdened with danger. It rests on the schizophrenia which I have been exploring throughout this essay: the division between the insider and the outsider, the figure who inhabits the world of language or story and the figure who remains somehow outside that world.

Eva Trout hovers between these two realms: she is both motherless and fatherless, a position which translates into linguistic terms. Like Louie or Portia, she longs for a symbiotic and silent union with another woman, a mother; her own mother died when she was three (presumably at the age when Eva left this world of pre-linguistic union), and she tries to re-create such a bond with another girl in adolescence. Significantly, this girl, Elsinore, is in a coma; "[t]his deathly yet living stillness, together, of two beings, this unapartness," which "came to be the requital of all longing," does not rely on active and separate identities. Identity, in fact, does not yet exist, for language does not exist. It is toward what appears to be a father-tongue that Iseult, Eva's second mother, pushes her. Iseult takes it upon herself to raise Eva up into language, to give her an identity within language. She asks Eva to attempt making connections and sequences out of her "cement-like" "conversational style": "try joining things together: this, then that, then the other."

Yet Iseult's very name gives us a glimpse into the nature of this father-tongue. She is above all a character herself, created in male texts. She reads not only D. H. Lawrence, but Henry James and Charles Dickens: it is in Dickens's house that she meets Eva at one point. She has also been a "teacher of English." Finally, she is allied with Eva's "guardian," Constantine, who becomes a part-author as well: he must "authorise" "any arrangement involving money" for Eva, and we are told that Eva's residence with Iseult "suited Constantine's book" as if, godlike (or emperor-like), he owns the book in which Eva's life is written. Even Iseult is on salary to him, and is dependent on his "authorisations."

It was presumably Eva's parents who named her; but it is Constantine who explains the name through his definition of Eva: "Eva's capacity for making trouble, attracting trouble, stewing trouble around her, is quite endless. She, er, begets trouble—a dreadful gift. And the more so for being inborn." The "trouble" this latter-day Eve "begets" apparently has to do with her relation to language, and, at a larger cultural level, to convention. Eva's language is "outlandish"—literally, it is from out of the land, not indigenous. She does not know how to speak English. She is named, and in the naming she is thrust into structures of language and convention extending as far back as the Bible (the first book of *Eva Trout* is entitled "Genesis"), yet she herself, because of her status outside the dominant discourse, does not participate in such naming, and, in fact, her position as outsider becomes one of a potentially freeing power. As Margaret Homans states in *Women Writers and Poetic Identity*, the Biblical "Eve, and women after her, have been dislocated from the ability to feel that they are speaking their own language." Such dislocation, as Homans suggests, can be liberating for the woman writer, as it was for Emily Dickinson, if it leads to a satanic discovery that all discourse is not literal, but fictive. A suggestion hovers throughout *Eva Trout* that perhaps, if Eva had been brought fully into language by her teacher Iseult, the result might have been strangely disruptive of the linguistic world around her, which is so clearly fictive but which relies on its unquestioned sense of its own truthfulness. Iseult fears Eva as a potential Dickinsonian author, in Homans's terms. Yet the possibility for such freely duplicitous and deconstructive language is unrealized. Eva can barely articulate her own presence, and in fact seems to become trapped in conjugations of the primary verb of presence, "To be": Eva states that what she longed for was "To be, to become—I had never been." "I was *beginning* to be." According to Eva, Iseult then "sent me back again—to be nothing. . . . I remain gone. Where am I? I do not know—I was cast out from where I believed I was." "Cast out" from the Garden, this Eve yearns only to return, and to reenter the Adamic structure of naming which had originally marked her exclusion.

Iseult's sending of Eva "back," out of language, parallels her own backing away, from the potential inherent in her own language. It is possible that it was Eva's very outlandishness that both attracted and repelled this English teacher. As Eva tries to explain later:

> "Only then, I saw that she hated me, hated the work she had feared to finish. And I who WAS that work, who had hoped so much—how should I not hate her? She saw. Twice over. She could not abide me there; I became a witness. How she had cast away everything, she had seen me see."

What is it about this "work" that Iseult fears so deeply? Her fear may be measured by her retreat: she "had cast away everything" for her entrance into marriage. Her marriage, in fact, cancels her creativity: she does only translations now. A fear of her powers of authorship seems to haunt her, not only because of the betrayal of her own self which authoring would involve, but precisely because of what she *might* author, given the chance. Eva is already half-monstrous, a "giantess." What would she wreak upon the world if she were given the tools of language, and if she were put into writing? And what new language might she come up with? Already Eva suggests a form of language which would disrupt all the old forms, and a form of story which would resist not only sequence and causality, but the ordinary conventions of probability.

Yet, as with Louie or Portia, such possibilities for a new language remain utopian and unrealized, and meanwhile no resolution between "tongues" can be found. Eva attempts first to retreat into the mother-tongue by becoming a mother herself, and authoring a silent text: with the deaf-mute Jeremy, whose origins are wholly unknown, Eva forms a "cinematographic existence, with no soundtrack"; they are "cocooned," "near as twins in the womb." Yet, largely through the agency of other characters, Eva begins to abandon this world and to enter, finally, the other, that of the dominant discourse, which is allied with her plans to marry. In an exaggerated version of Eva's own feelings of abandonment by Iseult, when Iseult left her to go "back" into silence, Jeremy experiences abandonment by Eva, as she leaves him in his silence and pushes on into the language of convention. Yet Eva never enters the train, or the marriage, which become metaphors for her acquisition of the connections and bonds language brings her into, for Jeremy murders her in the last few sentences of the novel. It is, this time, the silent self who kills the self in language; the schizophrenia is now complete. No third term remains.

Eva Trout, as Elizabeth Bowen's last fully imagined character, achieves such haunting magnitude because she embodies all that resides in a femaleness which asks to be expressed, but which can find no expression. From the perspective of those inside the language and stories that already exist, this presence appears monstrous because of its capacity to disrupt. It must be defined and bound into some narrative. Yet from the perspective of those outside, it is precisely this language which constitutes betrayal. The double perspective is retained, because it is the doubleness which is problematic. Bowen offers hints of a collapse of this barrier, but her own ambivalence toward such collapse prevents her from allowing it narrative representation, and the possibility for such representation, in any case, remains questionable. She leaves us always, however, with the desire to imagine a language and a narrative form, however utopian, that would overcome the treacherous distance she herself represents between author and object, and between those women who possess language and those who do not.

Stevie Smith

Hermione Lee

"Remember life not to cling to it," says Father Whatshisname to the lady in her cell.

> Well I don't you know, said the lady, then aware of
>   something comical
> Shot him a look that made him feel uncomfortable.

Like much of Stevie Smith's work, this poem ("The Hostage") makes a reasoned, humorous, and dignified case for welcoming Death, as Seneca and the Stoics did. But it is a useful starting point in other ways, too. The lady's unexplained dramatic situation ("You hang at dawn, they said") is one of many mysterious journeys, fatal or fortunate quests, in Stevie Smith's poems and fictions. Her characters are perpetually saying goodbye to their friends, riding away on dangerous missions, like Browning's Childe Roland, or getting lost in a blue light or a dark wood. One "lady" is swept off by her huge hat on to a "peculiar island"; others are magicked out of the real world into a Turner painting, or into the domain of a river-god or of "the lady of the Well-spring." The hostage's reasons for wanting to die, and her quizzical reception of Father W.'s well-meant Christian consolations, are quite as characteristic. Stevie Smith is childish, whimsical, fantastical, escapist; she is, equally, tough, pragmatic, satirical (especially of "the Christian solution" and of the English middle classes to whom she belongs) and intellectually rigorous. Her tone of voice, at once alarming and domesticated, combines these two sides. In the two lines from "The Hostage," the lady's flat, matter-of-fact colloquial remark, the long, chatty, narrative line, and the purposely obtrusive half-rhyme give an effect at once comical and uncomfortable. Her poems all shoot us this sort of look,

From *Stevie Smith: A Selection*. © 1983 by Hermione Lee. Faber & Faber Ltd., 1983.

and make us "aware of something comical" going on. They are about feeling funny, and they give us funny feelings.

"The Hostage" is typical, too, in being a conversation piece, in which the lady makes her confession to the priest. Seamus Heaney has called Stevie Smith "a memorable voice," meaning not only that her own reading voice affected his response to her poems, but also that they are "poems of the ear." They make us aware of a relationship between "a speaking voice, a literary voice (or style) and a style of speech shared by and typical of a certain social and cultural grouping"—that is, the educated English middle classes. An idiosyncratic speaking voice that accosts the reader, a voice of a particular class, speaking with what Heaney calls the accents of "disenchanted gentility"—as though the Ancient Mariner had taken up residence in Palmers Green—is, certainly, the most striking quality (and not just of the poems: "This is the talking voice that runs on," says the narrator of *Novel on Yellow Paper*). And all kinds of "speaking" are found in the poems: letters, confessions, prayers, songs, messenger speeches, dramatic monologues, addresses, advice-columns, conversations (some rather one-sided, like "The After-thought"), Socratic dialogues, debates, and arguments. Invocations are frequent: "Away, melancholy," "Do take Muriel out," "Honour and magnify this man of men," "Girls!," "Reader before you condemn, pause," "Crop, spirit, crop thy stony pasture!," "Farewell, dear friends," and (most of all) "Come, Death."

This talking voice sounds simple and spontaneous, but is more cunning than it seems. Stevie Smith's manner can be baffling; at times, as D. J. Enright says, one simply asks: "So what?" The zany, scatty, somewhat Thurberesque illustrations, the eccentric reading manner—she would sing her poems off-key, or recite them in a rather childish voice—the cryptic off-hand oddity of some of the shorter poems, invite dismissive words like "batty" and "fey." Her early reviews were condescending ("Miss Smith is carrying her individuality and eccentricity further than ever," *Times Literary Supplement*, April 1943; "Does Miss Smith mean herself to be taken seriously?" *Times Literary Supplement*, December 1950; "As with Ogden Nash, a small amount goes a long way toward being enough," *Poetry*, August 1958). Her reputation grew during the sixties and seventies, and since her death in 1971, Virago's reissuing of all the prose has ensured that she is taken seriously. The other tribute to her popularity, Hugh Whitemore's play (and film) *Stevie*, unfortunately laid the emphasis on the dotty spinster of Palmers Green, all funny hats and pussy cats. The suspicion that she is an overrated minor English comic writer is likely to persist; Stevie Smith is a riddler, and has concealed her own complexity. Her fictional heroines' favourite pursuit is unravelling codes and ciphers, and she likes riddle poems ("The Ambassador"), or gnomic verses which can't be understood without their illustrations ("The Rehearsal," "The Persian"). The larger riddle, however, is how her "Naive" effects are produced.

She has, to begin with, a very sophisticated and exact sense of line. This can take the form of strong hymn and ballad metres ("To the Tune of the Coventry Carol," "The Lads of the Village," "At School," "Nor We Of Her To Him") or of experiments with a range of metrical forms. She writes in hendecasyllables, in iambic pentameter ("Great Unaffected Vampires and the Moon"), in the eight-stress trochaic tetrameter of Tennyson's "Locksley Hall" ("The Airy Christ"), or in firm seven or four stress lines ("Anger's Freeing Power" has both). Some poems will infiltrate a strong regular metre into a free running line (as in the second verse of "Thoughts about the Person from Porlock"); some will change their tune by abandoning a regular metre in the last line ("To a Dead Vole," "O Happy Dogs of England").

    The long conversational line of many of the poems ("The Hostage," "The Deserter," "The After-thought" among others) is not as casual as it looks. The rhythms of speech are carefully played into the lines:

> Marriage? Out of the question. Well for instance
> It might be infectious, this malaise of mine . . .

as is the sense of physical movement:

> As Red and Honey push by,
> The old dogs,
> Gone away, gone hunting by the marsh bogs.

> I can hear Arthur roaming overhead

> He loves to roam
> Thank heavens he has plenty of space to roam in

The line-endings create suspense and surprise, or a sense of enchanted stasis, like the river-god's

> Hi yih, do not let her
> Go. There is no one on earth who does not forget her
> Now.

or Persephone's

> O do not fret me
> Mother, let me
> Stay, forget me

Eve and Mary's argument in "A Dream of Comparison" is established by such suspensions:

> "Oh to be Nothing," said Eve, "oh for a
> Cessation of consciousness . . ."

> Mary laughed: "I love Life . . .
> That's a feeling, you say? I will find
> A reason for it."

The patient's longing for oblivion in "The Doctor" is felt through the running-on of her lines:

> give me some bromide
> And then I will go away for a long time and hide
> Somewhere on the seashore where the tide
>
> Coming upon me when I am asleep shall cover
> Me.

The transformation of "The House of Over-Dew" from story to poem ("If it doesn't fall into verse I'm going to help it") shows the creation of this "casual" line, with its hiatuses and subdued climaxes.

> But, oh, when Cynthia heard that word it was the knell to all her life and love. This, she said, is the end of happy days and the beginning of calamity. *Over-Dew*, she thought, shall be the death of my love, and the death of life. For to that tune, she thought, shall come up a European war and personal defeat.
>
> (*The Holiday*)

In verse this becomes:

> But oh when Cynthia heard that word
> It was the knell
> Of all her life and love. This, she said,
> Is the end of happy days, and the beginning
> Of calamity. Over-Dew, she thought,
> Shall be the death of my love and the death of life.
> For to that tune, she thought,
> Shall come up a European war and personal defeat.

The "free" conversational line is buttressed from within by the use of internal rhymes ("The gray of this heavy day / Makes the green of the trees' leaves and the grass brighter,") alliteration ("salt silt," "reverent reveries," "fuel fed fire"), startlingly concentrated monosyllables ("Ah, croaked / The door-set crone, Sun's cloaked,") and the repetition of simple key words: "farewell," "happy," "glad," "tender," "blue." Rhyme is her most pronounced device for controlling the line, her favourite kind of joke, and one of her most cunning skills. The rhymes are often purposely unpoetical, McGonagall-ish, or Byronesque: orthodox/shut in a box, praevalebit/in a bit, lent a/magenta, hittapotamus/lost in the fuss, ill-fed/Wilfred, benison/to go on. This flat-footed comical perversity, which manages to combine despair and high spirits in a quizzical, shrugging way, frequently shades into something sinister, delicate or haunting, like the rhyme of "curlews" and "purlieus" in "The Magic Morning," of "mother" and "smother" in "Persephone," of "phantoms" and "tantrums" in "Le Majeur Ydow," or the half-rhyme of "East" and "Christ" in "The Airy Christ." The poems are full of these elegant, mournful half-rhymes:

There is an island in the lake, old brick walled,
Where the laurestina climbs and is not spoiled.

All her friends are gone
And she is alone

And they talked until nightfall,
But the difference between them was radical.

I am happy, I like the life,
Can swim for many a mile
(When I have hopped to the river)
And am for ever agile.

Her rapid changes in tone, from the maladroit and whimsical to the lyrical, from the *faux-naïf* to the artful, from the flat and gauche to the resonant, are brought about partly by that mastery of line and rhyme, and partly by an extraordinarily heterogeneous diction. Stevie Smith's poems mix Biblical archaisms with genteel suburban clichés, ornate Latinate vocabulary (she loves polysyllabic rhymes like inclement/convenient, temporization/indignation, felicity/sufficiency, consideration/realization/preoccupation) with the most matter-of-fact Anglo-Saxon bathos, (words like "glum" and "plod"), invocations to Death and the Lamb of God with silly names like Mr Over or Lady "Rogue" Singleton. Poems such as "Aubade," "A Humane Materialist . . ." "The Recluse," and "Great Unaffected Vampires and the Moon," are lush and clotted with poetic diction. More often, such languages will jostle with commonplace, reductive, colloquial idioms (see, for instance, "My Hat," "The After-thought," and "Dido's Farewell to Aeneas") which may themselves take on a peculiar suggestiveness. The not-quite-romantic wan swan "On the lake / Like a cake / Of Soap": the bodies in the cemetery made more gruesome because they "have that look of a cheese do you know sour-sweet / You can smell their feet"; the sinister perkiness of phrases in "The River God" like "contrary to rules" or "plenty of go"; the desolating use of "larking" in "Not Waving but Drowning"; the ordinary, polite beginning of "Do Take Muriel Out"; Guinevere's cosy "where are you dear?" in the strange uncosy "The Blue from Heaven": these are examples of the arresting effects of this mixture of idioms:

(I often wonder what it will be like
To have one's soul required of one
But all I can think of is the Out-Patients' Department—
"Are you Mrs Briggs, dear?"
No, I am Scorpion.)

Stevie Smith often uses the word "peculiar," and it is the best word with which to describe her effects.

Though her voice is always recognizable for its peculiarities, it is much given to doing impersonations. Occasionally these move into another "social grouping" ("Proper done out of 'er rights, she was, a b. shame,") but mostly they are middle-class characterizations, like the smug, huffy professional invalid in "The Deserter":

> And every morning the doctor comes and lances my
>   tuberculous glands.
> He says he does nothing of the sort, but I have my own
>   feelings about that,
> And what they are if you don't mind I shall continue to keep
>   under my hat.

or the malevolent suburban gossip of "Emily writes such a good letter":

> Yes, I remember Maurice very well
> Fancy getting married at his age
> *She* must be a fool.

The novels and stories, though dominated by "the talking voice that runs on," are full of people very vividly characterized by their speech. There are the fearsome upper-class children in Kensington Gardens; or (also in *The Holiday*) Clem, the malicious rich homosexual socialist whose sayings include "My little brother is a carpet-communist," or "She is a most remarkable woman, she has tired out three riding horses before breakfast," or (of the countryside) "One always comes back to the English school"; or the nagging husband in the story "Sunday at Home":

> "All I ask," sang out Ivor," is a little peace and quiet; an agreeable wife, a wife who is pleasant to my friends; one who occasionally has the room swept, the breakfast prepared, and the expensive bric-a-brac of our cultivated landlord—*dusted*. I am after all a fairly easy fellow."

Most of the fictional voices are based on Stevie Smith's friends and enemies (George Orwell, for instance, was split into two of the characters in *The Holiday*, Basil and Tengal). These impersonations were so sharply done as, on occasion, to get her into the kind of trouble that is described in "The Story of a Story."

The pleasure in satirical characterizations goes with a relish for parody, imitation, and pastiche. . . . Stevie Smith is a highly literary and referential writer, and one of the peculiarities of her style is the way she infiltrates other voices into her own. Such references range from the ostentatious and insistent to the oblique and concealed. (They range, too, from the accurate to the purposely inaccurate.) Some of her best poems are translations ("Dido's Farewell To Aeneas," "Songe D'Athalie") or free renderings ("Dear Little Sirmio"). Many of them evoke a particular manner or vocabulary, or mix up several at once: "Our Bog is Dood" and "One of Many" are extraordinary amalgams of Blake, Hardy, Lewis Carroll, and Wordsworth.

One of a generation which learned poetry by heart at school, and which knew the Bible and the classics well, Stevie Smith's mind is a "rag-bag" of quotations. In an essay on her schooldays, she gives a list of the poems she heard young, which include *The Ancient Mariner*, Tennyson's "Ulysses," some Milton, *Childe Roland to the Dark Tower Came*, and a good deal of seventeenth-century religious poetry. In her own selection of verse for children, she expresses a preference for "fiercer" poems, and includes long extracts from the Book of Job, and a great deal of Romantic poetry (Shelley's "Ozymandias" and parts of "The Masque of Anarchy," Keats's passage on Isabella's proud brothers, Byron's "beautifully *ratty* lines to Caroline Lamb," and Blake's "The Sick Rose," "Gnomic Verses," and parts of *Auguries of Innocence*). Among seventeenth-century poems she chooses Southwell's "The Burning Babe" and parts of Crashaw's "Office of the Holy Cross" (from which she often quotes). Her nineteenth-century poems show a liking for the grotesque (Tennyson's "The Kraken," Melville's "The Maldive Shark," Poe's "Annabel Lee") and the heroic (Macaulay's *Lays of Ancient Rome*). There is very little modern poetry: Yeats's "Two Songs of a Fool," Edward Thomas's "Adlestrop," Frost's "Acquainted with the Night," and some of her own.

Stevie Smith is often compared to Blake, sometimes to Edward Lear (Heaney says "she reminds you of two Lears," the suffering king and the nonsense poet), sometimes to Emily Dickinson. Her fondness for hymns, fairy stories, and nursery rhymes is evident. There are also very marked echoes of the religious poetry heard at school (Crashaw, Herbert, Phineas Fletcher) and of Victorian poets, especially Tennyson and Browning. Mixed with this strong attachment to the English traditional, there is a powerful feeling for Greek and French classical tragedy, for Virgil, Homer, Catullus, Plotinus, and Seneca, for the liturgy and the Book of Common Prayer.

Her writing is full of these voices, but their use is complex. The paradox of her art is that it is at once so allusive and so idiosyncratic. Other people's phrases become her own:

> . . . we do not wish to understand . . . it is for us somebody else's
> cup of tea that we do not even say: May it pass from us. . . .

> I regard them as a contribution to almighty Truth, magna est
>   veritas et praevalebit,
> Agreeing with that Latin writer, Great is Truth and will prevail
>   in a bit.

More than direct translation or quotation, she likes half-echoes, reminders, reworkings, travesties. A poem such as "Old Ghosts" or "A Dream of Comparison" may be sparked off by a passage from de Quincey or Milton; or a story or poem may be written out of a general feeling for another writer. In this way "Little Boy Lost" is Blakean, "The House of Over-Dew" is Tennysonian. She likes to make comically casual, fleeting allusions: "The funeral paths are hung with snow / About the graves the mourners go" calls up Housman's "About the Woodlands I will go / To see the cherry hung with snow." "Cold as no love, and wild with all negation— / Oh Death in Life, the lack of animation" invokes Tennyson's "Deep as first love, and wild with all regret: / Oh Death in life, the days that are no more." More elusively, the *tone* of a poet may be evoked. There are shades of *Childe Roland* in "the crescent moon / Performed a devil's purpose for she shewed / The earth a-heap where smooth it should have lain" and an echo of Tennyson (particularly of "The Poet's Mind" and "A Spirit Haunts the Year's Last Hours") in "My soul within the shades of night / Like a languid plant with a fungoid blight."

Some poems rework whole plays and legends ("Phèdre," Persephone," "The After-thought"), or make play with a well-known anecdote, such as Coleridge's being interrupted in the middle of writing "Kubla Khan" by a person from Porlock. In her prose she will often retell stories— Euripides' *Bacchae* or a Grimm fairy-tale in *Novel on Yellow Paper*, a life of Boethius in *The Holiday*. She parodies tones of voice: a condescending Church of England vicar, or a self-important literary man, or the blushful, hectoring Miss Hogmanimy, lecturing to schoolgirls on purity and abstinence. In *Over the Frontier* Pompey has to listen to a bad-tempered academic reading Pater's description of the Mona Lisa: "the too-ripeness, the concealed verse forms . . . the dying fall at the end of each paragraph." Stevie Smith's own voice (itself much given to mingling prose with verse) brilliantly catches the cadence of that sensitive, pulsating, closeted, Anglo-Catholic aestheticism she so fiercely dislikes.

Pompey listening furiously to Pater's dying falls consoles herself inwardly with a satirical line from Juvenal, whom she calls "a greater than Pater." Classical rigour set against narcissism, neurosis, melancholia, is the key to her work. D. J. Enright (referring to her preference for Racine because he is more "truly Greek" than Euripides) says that Stevie Smith's poetry is itself "somewhat Greek"—"severe, austere, simple, bracing, impersonal"—and goes on to describe her thumping, perverse off-rhymes, her wariness of love and Christianity, her Blakean realism, her stoicism, as "an avoidance of the romantic." But Stevie Smith's classicism is coloured by what it criticizes. Her thoughts, like her style, play with contraries: Christianity and paganism, religious fanaticism and the rational intellect, domesticity and loneliness, lassitude and energy, sentimentality and severity, power and escape, human possessiveness and animal (or natural) aloofness, illusions and disenchantment, giving up and going on, love of life and hopes of death. These are not straightforward alternatives. She is, for instance, strongly attracted to "the Christian solution" (see "How Do You See?") and has to reason herself out of its dangerous fairy-tale consolations. (Her attempt at compromise is to call herself a "neo-Platonic Christian.") Her writing is suffused with "loamish Victorian melancholy," with tears, longings for oblivion, nostalgia for childhood, quite as much as with classical severity. And her classicism is gothic and barbarous rather than Olympian and serene: she likes best the sinister terrors of Dionysus, or the story in the *Iliad* of the shades who must drink blood before they can speak, or the prayer of the Roman soldiers who devoted themselves to death in battle. Her Persephone prefers the dark underworld (as well as wanting to get away from mother). "Pompey Casmilus," the name of the heroine in *Novel on Yellow Paper* and *Over the Frontier*, refers us to the "ambassador" of the gods and the patron of poets, thieves, and merchants, and, primarily, to the god who conducted souls to the underworld.

The Holiday (which Stevie Smith thought of calling "Death and the Girl") perfectly displays this mixture of classical severity and tearful Victorian neurosis. Celia and her cousin, who takes the name "Casmilus" here, are like Persephone and Pluto, and the landscape of their holiday seems to be the landscape of the underworld. But Casmilus tells Celia that she has "a romantic feeling for Death," and at one point she floats down the Lincolnshire river like Millais's Ophelia. Her satirical fierceness about postwar England is mingled with a nervous confusion: "Everything is in fits and splinters." "The House of Over-Dew," which appears as a story in *The Holiday*, a dreadful tale of gloomy English Christianity and lost love, grafts a classical idea of fatality and stoicism on to a murky Victorian setting.

The stories Stevie Smith chooses to tell are not as simple, or as playful, as they may look. Certainly her enchanted characters prefer being lost or spellbound to being at home. Persephone likes the wintriness, the "little boy lost" would be happy without "father, mother, home" if he could find some food (but he will die of cold and hunger), the girl swept away by her hat will not be taking it off ("Go home, you see, well I wouldn't run a risk like that"), Arthur rides off into the "blue light / Of the peculiar towering cornflowers," gladly saying goodbye to Guinevere and his throne, and the morbid girl from the office who disappears into Turner's painting is happy for evermore.

But these metamorphoses are often alarming, sometimes cruel ("The Magic Morning," "The River God"), sometimes doubtful: Muriel, like Scorpion, is still waiting for Death to take her out; the frog prince has mixed feelings about becoming a "disenchanted" prince and giving up the "quiet life" of a frog. One of her more childish poems has the epigram "This is not kind," and she says of poetry that, like a classical deity, "she is very strong and never has any kindness at all." False, cosy enchantments are dangerous, like the fairy-tale of Christianity. Trusting innocents have to be educated into disenchantment and experience, like the children in "At School," or the little boy who has to learn how to write a business letter. Innocent childish characters may be "translated" into another existence (Arthur in "The Blue from Heaven") or else hung from the gallows ("One of Many") but if innocence is to survive in the real world it must compromise. The poems are full of fierce, lonely misfits who choose not to join in ("Croft," "My Heart was Full," "Scorpion," "The Hostage," "Magna est Veritas"): they prefer to play simple, as Stevie Smith's poetry does in part. These characters are waiting to be taken away: "For it was not in this world that the Christians were desirous of being either useful or desirable" she once quoted from Gibbon in a poetry reading. They are passing through this world on the way to something better.

From the eight-year-old infant Pompey in *Novel on Yellow Paper* who makes up her mind that "Death has got to come if I call him," to the aging Scorpion, who "so wishes to be gone," Stevie Smith's versions of herself all take the Senecan attitude to suicide, as a noble and encouraging possibility, should life become "more than I choose to bear." Many of her poems summon Death as a friend and servant. (Her reaction to Virginia Woolf's suicide is tellingly matter-of-fact: "just generally fed up all round I suppose" (*Me Again*). But Stevie Smith did not kill herself (she once tried to), nor was she a recluse. Though she admires the simpletons like Croft, she is scornful of characters who give up altogether or fail for lack of courage ("The Deserter," "The Weak Monk," "The Recluse," "The Failed Spirit"). The concomitant of the Senecan attitude to death is a stoicism about life (as in "Ceux qui luttent . . ." and "Away, Melancholy"). People who "manage to keep going" under pressure or in pain are to be "honoured and magnified," even if the pretence of being "jolly and ordinary" and of "feeling at home in the world" (phrases used during a poetry reading) sometimes breaks down, as in "Not Waving but Drowning." Even so, you must

> Smile, smile, and get some work to do
> Then you will be practically unconscious without positively
>   having to go.

To do any more than that is to be a hero, like Harold, even if the heroic act turns out to be futile:

> I would not say that he was wrong,
> Although he succeeded in doing nothing but die.

The argument in "A Dream of Comparison" between Mary, who loves life ("I would fight to the death for it") and Eve, who longs for consciousness to cease ("Storm back through the gates of Birth") is central to all Stevie Smith's work.

"These are all very moral poems, you know" (*Me Again*). Under cover of playing simple or looking silly (as in "Croft") she gives us firm opinions about behaviour. In some of the more didactic poems, like those about cruelty to animals, a nagging tone can creep in:

> Of all the disgraceful and abominable things
> Making animals perform for the amusement of human
>   beings is
> Utterly disgraceful and abominable.

But indignation is an essential part of her writing: she is trenchant, belligerent, acidulous, argumentative, believing with Blake that anger teaches sense. Her most passionate quarrel is with the Church: she distrusts Christianity's "sweetness and cruelty," and its system of prizes and punishments, she has a horror of religious persecution and fanaticism (see the deceptively comical "Our Bog is Dood" and "The House of Over-Dew"), a wry distaste for Jesuitical wiles, and an impatience with the modern Church's vulgar attempts to talk down and to popularize. (There is a furious poem about the alterations to the Prayer Book, and a furious review of the New English Bible in *Me Again*.) Though she writes some stirring poems of belief ("God the Eater," "The Airy Christ") her more characteristic treatment of religion is in her fine anguished poems of debate ("Was He Married?" "Thoughts about the Christian Doctrine of Eternal Hell," "How Do You See?").

Stevie Smith is a fierce critic of male privileges. Living her whole life in "a house of female habitation"—*Novel on Yellow Paper* tells the story of "daddy's" disappearance and of the Aunt's adoption of Pompey and her sister after their mother's death—she is caustic about the common forms of male chauvinism. Tyrannical husbands like Major Macroo or the "tigers" of "Bottle Green," bossy male bureaucrats and smug male writers get short shrift. Sex is fun (cenobites are as bad as dictators) but the boyfriends in the novels are always a bore in the end, and girls who can't say no are urged to be more fierce and proud. Domestic bliss (closely observed on visits to married couples) is outweighed by the pleasures of female friendship and of a gregarious independence, worth the risk of loneliness. And she writes as savagely about the cruelty *of* children as about cruelty *to* them.

Her idiosyncratic feminism is only one element in her social and political satire. Here the relationship between prose and poetry is very close: "Who Shot Eugenie?" is a version of *Over the Frontier*; the poetic treatment of war ("The Lads of the Village," "Private Means is Dead"), of the upper classes ("A Father for Fool") and of the literary establishment ("Tom Snooks the Pundit") is reworked in the fictions; and many of the political poems are put into the novels as part of the long debates on war, empire, government, power, and English society.

Her political attitudes might best be described by comparing her with the great Victorian reformist writers. Carlyle's *Sartor Resartus* and Arnold's *Culture and Anarchy* loom behind her savage moral irritation with English complacency and vulgarity, and the vigorous authority with which she defines the English virtues. She has a passion for English places—Lincolnshire, the Humber, Norfolk, the sea at Swanage, the North London suburb where she lived from the age of three, the Home Counties: "I suspect that for me Hertfordshire is the operative word" (*Over the Frontier*). She detests what she considers to be English decadence and preciousness—Pater, the Pre-Raphaelites, the Bloomsbury group, Anglo-Catholicism, upper-class inbreeding, homosexuals—as much as she dislikes the middle-class snobbery of the suburbs and the commercial vulgarity of the "women's" magazines published by the firm she worked for, Newnes and Pearson. All this Old English Toryism is best summed up by her devotion to her Dickensian aunt, with whom she lived in Palmers Green, and whose crabby eccentricities earned her the same nickname as the British Empire's, the "lion."

But though opinionated and intolerant, her arguments against tyranny and stupidity are not simplistic. Her painful quarrel with Christianity is symptomatic of how much she is torn and divided. She loves Germany, but sees early in the 1930s to what it is moving. She hates anti-Semitism, but knows what it can feel like, and that a single thought of it can "swell the mass of cruelty working up against them" (*Novel on Yellow Paper*). She defends the Empire, but knows that nothing becomes it like the relinquishing of its conquests (as in India). She has no patience with pacifism in the face of the Nazis, but knows that war brings out the darkness in people. In overthrowing cruelty one can become cruel. When Pompey puts on a uniform in *Over the Frontier* she finds barbarism, military ambition, and the fanaticism of a nationalist ideology latent in herself.

Stevie Smith's political thoughts are realist and anti-romantic. It is not revolutions which stir her, but "the time when revolutions succeed and must govern," and the pragmatic question of compromise is raised: "Can resistance pass to government and not take to itself the violence of its oppressors, the absolutism and the torture?" (*The Holiday*). There must, she supposes, always be "a loss, a falling off, a distortion," in politics as in Christianity, when "thought passes into word, idea into action, revolution into government" (*Me Again*). Nevertheless, for all her satire and grief, she is a meliorist, in the tradition of Victorian writers such as Tennyson and Carlyle. It is "touch and go," but there are signs that man may be coming out of the mountains. At least "Man aspires / To good," at least we may be approaching a time when men "love love and hate hate but do not deify them." One must be disenchanted, but hopeful:

> Away, melancholy,
> Away with it, let it go.

George Orwell's Search for a Voice

Lynette Hunter

GENRE AND RHETORIC

Orwell is considered one of the foremost commentators on literature and politics in the twentieth century and this is primarily due to the reputation of his writing style as clear, direct, and precise. In view of this it is surprising that this "clear style" lies at the centre of enormous debate and controversy which call into question his literary and political contributions. In effect he has been consistently underestimated in terms of his awareness of the complexity of literary and linguistic strategy. From the beginning he recognizes that the distinctions between form and content, subject and object, fiction and documentary, are all versions of the fundamental separation between fact and value that has dominated rationalist humanism since the seventeenth century. And for Orwell, the final question is indeed one of value and morality: his writing career is concerned with a search for a valid voice with which to persuade others and express opinion.

Questions of persuasion, morality, and value are intimately part of the study of rhetoric, and in the process of exploration Orwell drew the outlines of an understanding of rhetoric in a manner that is extraordinarily prescient of the work in this discipline that would follow over the next thirty years. Rhetoric is a blanket term for both persuasion and the study of persuasion. Broadly speaking, people tend to think of rhetoric as something that persuades them to do something they do not want to do. However, rhetoric has nothing to do with what you are being asked to do, but how you are being asked to do it. This may have negative and restrictive aspects but it may also have alternative, positive elements.

Rhetorical studies are made up of the strategy and stance of rhetoric.

From *George Orwell: The Search for a Voice*. © 1984 by Lynette Hunter. Open University Press, 1984.

Put most simply, strategy defines the techniques that can be used in persuasion. In literature, strategy provides an artificial divisiveness that separates out the components of writer, work, and reader, and allows us to define and discuss what each does. For example, we can speak of the strategy of the writer in using a first-person narrator, or the strategy of a work that moves in and out of the satiric genre. But while this can be most helpful, it can also be very restrictive and distorting of the event of reading and writing which includes writer, work, and reader in their combined activity. Stance describes this combined activity; and stance, like all activity, involves morality and at root indicates the beliefs that people have about their relationship with the external world.

Rhetorical strategy can be neither positive nor negative, in the sense of opening out or limiting a text, because its techniques have no value in themselves: for example, metaphor is not inherently generative or restrictive. However, when part of an event of reading and writing, strategy is placed in a context of value by the activity of rhetorical stance. This activity can take many directions, but in general stance may take a negative path and restrict the interaction of writer, work, and reader, or it may act positively and encourage and stimulate that interaction. Neither writer, nor work nor reader can alone define stance. A writer may want to restrict and impose a specific structure of meaning on the actvity of reading. Depending upon the strategic skill of the writer, many readers can find themselves caught within the restriction, finding only the allotted meaning. But a particularly active reader may have strategies to perceive that restriction, pierce the structure, and in leaving it behind, may go on to read the broader implications of the work. Since stance is the event in which all three combine, any definition that is arrived at is an indication of a tendency rather than a fixed solution, and a far more precise description of stance lies within the values that its activity generates.

It is necessary to outline this briefly partly because of the common limitation of rhetorical studies to tactics and occasionally to more involved stratagems which has led to the idea of rhetoric simply as a handbook of techniques. But it is also necessary because of the contemporary, widespread delusion that rhetoric can and should be avoided completely. This idea arises from the whole activity of negative rhetoric which hides its use of strategy and therefore of its stance. At the same time it insidiously attempts an imposing control, and aims toward a successful end rather than toward quality.

For the last three hundred years an epistemology that claims a neutral logic and a neutral language has been the main source for strategies of imposition, and these have concentrated on claiming access to absolute truth. A well-documented area of the history of rhetoric notes the rise during the seventeenth century of a rational, analytical logic and the idea of a univocal language, which provided the perfect breeding ground for a negative rhetoric because persuasion appeared to be completely unnecessary. The very concept of stance was not just hidden but completely wiped out, and with this loss also went any concept of active value—one is left with a static morality of fixed standards. Against this background truth becomes a commodity that can be reached if you pile up enough units of information, or facts gained by sequential rational logic. Language enables the accuracy of this activity because it is exact. The process reaches its apotheosis in post-Renaissance science, in which the dominance of fact appears to bring the external world completely within mankind's control. This was a brief flush of extraordinary confidence and while modern Western history may be read as a series of attempts to achieve this control, much of Western philosophy can be seen as an attempt to come to terms with its impossibility.

I would argue that Orwell is particularly sensitive to the limitations of this outlook and spent his writing life searching for alternatives through experiments with genre. Up until the writing of his documentaries Orwell is concerned more with strategy than with stance, but with *The Road to Wigan Pier* he shifts the focus. When this happens the dualities involved in the question of who controls and who is controlled which have dominated Western metaphysics, become transformed into the more profound issues of evaluation and belief. The divisions between subject and object, fiction and fact, novel and documentary, and the whole field of static genre became subordinate to stance. And at the same time that Orwell recognizes the ambivalent status of these divisions he realizes that the factual, rationalist basis for morality is not sufficient to human value.

First his novels, and then later his critical essays as well, present a recognition of the external materiality of language and literature. This becomes the basis for his separation between fantasy and allegory, the former denying materiality and the latter explicitly indicating it, which informs his search for valid stance. He was able to define the means and ends of fantasy, which maintains the dualisms of rationalist thought, in quite explicit terms; but allegory eludes attempts at strategic definition because its activity is specific to each event of reading and writing. Unlike many contemporary critics, who have followed the lead of J. Huizinga, Orwell not only appreciated the function but perceived and outlined the limitations and dangers of games within fantasy. Despite recent writers such as Colin Manlove noting and underlining these problems, most critics either do not perceive them or become involved in a tortuous logic in order to evade them. At the same time Orwell's inconclusiveness about allegory and its spread through the genres of utopia, satire, and nonsense, reflects a problem in current criticism which has suggested instead alternative generic words such as apologue, anatomy, and modern romance. Yet the development of an allegorical stance within his writing indicates a resolution similar to that of commentators such as Paul de Man who, in *Allegories of Reading*, begins to look at allegory in terms of stance rather than rigid genre.

Orwell's approach to fantasy and allegory as stances meant that they extended out of literature into a range of disciplines including politics and philosophy: with this approach he could speak of these disciplines both in theory and practice as analogous. But while theoretical definition was easy, it was far more difficult to pick out the practical effects. Once he began doing so he began to recognize the basis of all fantasy strategies in a rational logic that leads to limited rationalist humanism, and to perceive the vicious circle of political authoritarianism and the selfishly private individual that lies within that humanism. He became dissatisfied with nineteenth-century liberalism, which he suggested had led to twentieth-century fascism, but also with Stalinist communism which was not only the most dominant alternative in the 1930s but derived from the same rationalist grounds. In Orwell's assessment of the grounds themselves he speaks not only for his contemporaries but for many people today, and reflects their desires and frustrations in his search for a valid political and literary alternative.

It may be the profoundly radical nature of Orwell's questioning that leads to an underestimation of his work, both political and literary. Although I would not agree with his conclusions, I would agree entirely with Raymond Williams's suggestion that to describe this "paradox of Orwell we would need concepts beyond the consciousness and social structures of his period" [*Orwell*]. Too many commentators read from within the very grounds that Orwell was questioning and as a result limit their readings and find themselves in contradictory positions. The critical confusion that exists around Orwell's literary work focuses on the attempt to define it in strict generic terms. From *Down and Out in Paris and London* which is both straightforward and overwritten, to *Keep the Aspidistra Flying* which is not a novel but an argument, yet also a parody, a burlesque and a satire, to the struggle for definition in *Animal Farm* and *Nineteen Eighty-Four*, the issue of genre appears to worry critics.

The critical comments on *Animal Farm* are linked with theoretical problems in genre theory itself and with political and moral issues. There are two primary and opposed readings: the first is that it is an allegory because of point-to-point correspondence with events in the Russian revolution, and the second is that it is allegorical because of the very fact that that correspondence does not dominate it. These opinions are underwritten by contrasting assumptions that the book needs external events to make sense, or that, on the contrary, it is not just an anti-Soviet story but more generally applicable. This leads to definitions of the book as a beast fable and therefore on the one hand a restricted puzzle, but on the other dynamic. It has been called a satire and a didactic sermon as opposed to an anatomy which generates interactive readings; the animals are simply types or complex humours. The opposing definitions are parallel to readings of the story as Orwell's abandonment of political polemics as opposed to a political act in itself, and to judgments of it as both a moral story and not really moral at all.

But nearly always the possibility that Orwell is experimenting with genre, teasing out the edges so that conventional assumptions cannot be counted on, is dismissed or discounted. His skill and consciousness of writing is consistently underrated and leads to accusations of failure, of lack of logic. John Wain states that Orwell is remembered more for his ideas than his skill. [Alex] Zwerdling's *Orwell and the Left* notes the critical consensus on Orwell's "failure" as a writer and moves on to suggest that Orwell did experiment with genre. But he concludes by saying that Orwell's commitment to prose made him parasitic on existing trends "rather than transforming them." Even George Woodcock's perceptive biography *The Crystal Spirit* claims that Orwell was not interested in experiments with form.

An important source for these dismissals of Orwell's skill is that commentators come to the writing with critical expectations that lie within the framework that Orwell came to challenge. The most common expectation is that fiction and nonfiction, the novel and the documentary are always significantly divided from each other, and this prevents the reader from appreciating Orwell's own suggestion that they can be viewed fruitfully as part of a continuum. The attitude becomes especially limiting if a critic claims to believe in the value of the overlap, but criticizes Orwell for separating them. Williams claims that Orwell fails to reshape the novel because "he seems to have accepted the division between 'documentary' and 'fiction' " but in fact it is Williams who distinguishes between them saying that the 1930s distinction between the two is "evident enough." He goes on to say that Orwell got past the division in practice, but he implies that he did not do so consciously: a judgment that restricts the scope of the rest of his discussion.

Another critical expectation that contributes to the confusion is that genres are fixed. This leads many critics to condemn any development that lies outwith the accepted conventions even though they may profess to want Orwell to be reaching for a new expression. There is, for instance, the criticism of Orwell as a novelist: he does not control his material through his plots, nor can he create rounded characters as novelists should. This approach is underwritten by a tendency to take Orwell's comment that he was not a real novelist as a confession of failure rather than an indication that he was trying to achieve something rather different. When Zwerdling examines Orwell's unwillingness to transform genre, he suggests that it arises from a hesitation between subjective and objective forms that undermines the realistic genre of novel; and in the end he criticizes Orwell's writing for not being "seamless" but has no regard for the possibility that Orwell may not have been aiming at these ends, may not have wanted seamless writing. Woodcock again is more generous, and says that because Orwell is a moralist he writes fables and parables rather than novels, and even notes the allegorical play around a central topic or area of content, that each work develops. Yet he too is severely critical and asserts that Orwell was not interested in a structure for his novel-writing.

Underlying these readings are certain philosophical and critical assumptions that blind readers to alternative directions in Orwell's thought. The enormous range, diversity, and contradictory nature of the criticisms and commentaries on his philosophy, literature, and politics should indicate the richness of his work, the comprehensive grasp that Orwell himself had of the complexity of contemporary issues. But all too often critics place him within the grounds of the predominant dualism of rationalist thought, and appear reluctant to acknowledge the possibility that he was conscious of that dualism and purposively setting out to go outside it.

Although many writers provoke debate, few do so in terms of such diametric opposition with readers explicitly defining one side or the other of the dualism, as Orwell. Some critics have claimed religion and morality as the basis for his work, while other have stated firmly that he has no interest in either. Within Christian theology itself he has been claimed for both Protestant and Catholic. He has been called a rationalist and a sentimentalist, he is for science and against it; he is objective and subjective or both and hence a solipsist. Similarly, he has at times been accused of making the individual dominant and at others of making him passive, of refusing to see the conditioned nature of life and of believing in a determined pattern of institutional change.

In terms of literature, some critics say his readers are imposed upon, others that they are left without guidance. By corollary his fictions are designed either to dominate or to evade, and even his documentaries exist both to voice the subjective or to achieve objective truth. All of these divisions are used indiscriminately to present the writer as either dishonest, honest, or sincere with varying degrees of subtlety and perception as to the "criterion of truth" that underlies such judgments. Politically Orwell is for change, against change, or for neither. He is for the oppressed then for the oppressor, both of which are usually phrased in terms of the extent of his political knowledge or ignorance. This is reflected in the assessments of those who claim that he recognized the profound difficulty in changing one's class, as against those who make the romantic claim that he tried personally to be classless. But at most times opinion places him in the paradox of being both, although on rare occasions he is neither and apolitical.

The interesting point about the political criticism is not that it indicates a superficial division between "liberal humanism"—a term I dislike for its vagueness but which often appears to indicate a contemporary form of nineteenth-century *laissez-faire* liberalism—and state-centred communism, but the way that its paradoxes indicate similar divisions in each. The positive aspect of Orwell is that he is neither for the private individual nor for any oligarchical state, whether based on fixed ideology or rationalized pluralism. He suggests instead another form of collective humanism but he never fully defines it in the practical terms which he posits and discusses in the activity of his writing.

The assessments of Orwell's politics concentrate on examining his strategies and in doing so they restrict themselves to the superficial "message" of his writing. On the basis of strategy many have claimed that he fundamentally undermined the strength of the left in British politics. Reactions to *The Road to Wigan Pier* bear out this claim, not only in [Victor] Gollancz's famous introduction condemning the book for facile calls to Liberty and Equality, but also in those who complain that it provides no definite answers. Others have noted that Orwell never wanted to provide definite answers. While he recognized that strategy influenced others, it is not as important as stance. Yet stance is not "the only answer of the exile who cannot provide solutions," but the response of the constructive thinker who recognizes the limitations in all the prevailing ideologies because of their common grounds, and who tries to indicate radical alternatives to those grounds. The important aspect of Orwell's thought for both contemporary socialism and liberalism is that he perceived their common basis in humanism, and criticized their rationalist developments. Orwell is not pro-humanist but neither is he anti-humanist. What he does is to question the attempt to make humanist values fixed standards in themselves, in other words he refuses to accept any grounds as unalterable. He is not questioning their quality in action but in their common use as a means or an end.

The emphasis on stance needs a shift in attitude to politics, literature, and philosophy, by all those whose thinking derives from the dominant rationalist logic and the dualisms it generates, and depends upon the naively univocal and exact relationships between word and object that arise from it. Orwell came to recognize that words were neither equal to objects, and nor do the two maintain an adequate and defined relationship, but that language and literature are part of the materiality of the world. When readers discuss Orwell's need for a pure, clear, precise language that attempts to reflect an external world, they tend to focus on an attitude of dominance over an objective, physical world. There is the assertion that his concerns with language and politics derive from a belief in objective, discoverable truths, that solid objects are the source for truth, that the fact and observation of the documentary fiction is a more trustworthy and objective account of the world than "myth."

These judgments in turn encourage opponents to stress the reverse: the subjectivity involved in all objective statement, and the imposition of supposedly "free" fiction. Such accusations range from comments on the emotive organization of the documentaries, to studies of his supposed claim to put aside the aesthetic and speak authentically, whose purpose is to expose the claim as misleading. Like the political divisions, these conflicting critical responses result from a concentration on strategy, and too often become mutually destructive. For Orwell the external world became important for its materiality, its radical otherness and alien quality: it could never be dominated nor dominating, it made necessary the interaction of a positive stance.

Similarly, the activity of his writing was not a matter of communicating explicit messages, although throughout the contemporary debate runs an insistent emphasis on Orwell's clear, precise prose that on one level always implies that he is "easy to read," that his "message" is obvious. This assumption underlies many of the contradictory, sometimes superficial readings of his work. The catalogue of adjectives used to describe his prose reads like a thesaurus entry: its aim is said to be the expression of truth "by the concrete and the simple word," to be neutral with "cold, clear prose," "saying straight out" what he means with a clear prose style.

This leads even the most perceptive into contradiction. Woodcock starts by illustraing that Orwell's "pure and transparent" prose in fact concealed complexity. Yet he moves through the statement that in his best writing language and meaning were so close that metaphor could not intervene, to conclude that the prose was created so that reality could shine through its transparency. The implication of the statement is that we can "have" reality exactly as it is. Others have noted that the transparent "windowpane" of his writing was in effect personal rather than characterless, and Christopher Small speaks for many when he notes that the paradoxical subjectivity of the "dry, clear, almost flat tone . . . the effacement of the writer's 'own personality' nevertheless allows what he wants to say to show more clearly and, indeed to be most unmistakably his." Small proceeds to comment on the complexity of the writing, but this tone is often simply dismissed as a "talent" for "lucid prose." More problematic are the misreadings that completely invert the direction of Orwell's writing by claiming that it sought objectivity and absolute truth, and that by failing to recognize the naive implications of this stance he perverts the influence of the writing. Some critics have gone further and suggested that he consciously manipulated his audience through this appearance of neutrality. There is, for example, the comment that Orwell's "plain reportorial style coerces history, process, knowledge itself into mere events being witnessed . . . such a style is far more insidiously unfair, so much more subtly dissembling of its affiliations with power, than any avowedly political rhetoric" [Edward Said in *The New Statesman*, January 1980].

On another level the misreading becomes fused with the idea that Orwell's prose "gives" the actual human being, an event complicated by and taken up into the George Orwell and Eric Blair separation. Time and time again, Orwell's supposed autobiography is used as the primary access to his writing. The comments can be revealing but as other critics have suggested they can also mislead, sometimes producing startling critical assessments. None are more startling than some of the extraordinary judgments of *Nineteen Eighty-Four*. There is not only the commonly found assessment that Orwell's tuberculosis gave the book "the gloomy intensity of his vision and language," but also the "explanations" for its negative reading in Orwell's hypothezised homosexuality or sado-masochism. These are not so much odd as limiting, and obstruct broader, more enjoyable readings of the work.

The author is conflated with the characters of his novels, despite an awareness that this may be a rather limited way of reading. Take Gordon Comstock in *Keep the Aspidistra Flying*: he is continually identified with Orwell; he embodies his hatreds; he, like the author, oscillates between Romantic and anti-Romantic. In more general terms similar comments on the characters in his novels indicate the restrictions of this critical approach more clearly. It is said that Orwell's lack of human understanding combined with the fact that he always puts himself forward as the protagonist, leaves all the novels the same. His business was human relationships, but because he had no resources of great depth his characters are flat and undeveloped.

The confusion of Orwell with the major characters goes hand in hand with an unwillingness to make them "live"; they are merely types. George Woodcock's assessment that the characters created from within are like Orwell himself, leads him to criticize the lack of development in the others that undercuts any real "relationships." Woodcock notes elsewhere in his biography the contrast of the essays, where "We no longer feel that we are inside the author's mind," but in practice the same conflation also occurs in criticism by others of the documentaries and essays. For example, it is the accusation that Orwell is not showing the whole picture in *The Road to Wigan Pier* in comparison with his diary entries, that leads to the naive conclusion that he is "fixing" the evidence, defining the conclusions before he starts. But as Bernard Crick acutely points out in *George Orwell: A Life*, the diary "must have been worked up afterwards . . . 'The Diary' is not necessarily a more literal record of 'what actually happened' than the published book." Because it is assumed that Orwell is at one with his creations, his ability to construct skilful narrator and character interaction is underestimated, whereas in effect these provide a clear indication of his developing attitude to stance and the interaction between reader, writer, and text.

The assumption that in Orwell's plain writing style we can find an actual man giving us an explicit message, places a considerable amount of commentary within grounds that Orwell himself challenged and thus restricts their reading and evaluation. A case in point is a comment by Raymond Williams on that clear precise prose, ironically placed just after he has taken Orwell to task for, as he thinks, a belief that language does convey content directly. He moves on to state that "Orwell usually describes his feelings so accurately that surface analysis is hardly even necessary." The implication is not only that Orwell's writing is obvious, his messages easy to define, but that the text is giving us Orwell the man himself and his feelings.

Even Bernard Crick noted in 1977 that people went looking for difficulties in Orwell's writing. By 1980 he has come to emphasize the need for such explicit study, saying that the writing is indeed difficult, generating "several different Orwells. The wielder of plain prose becomes complex and enigmatic." Here the recognition that the plain prose style is neither easy nor direct is linked to the caution that we can never "have" Orwell the man. At least three separate critics took Crick to task for "laboriously" coming to obvious solutions about Orwell, and for overemphasizing and overanalyzing the problem of the division between the autobiographical person and the construction of biography. Yet the historical interpretations of Orwell vary so widely, all the while asserting so much authority, that

Crick's painstaking method was necessary to his exemplary biography and is necessary to any study that faces the same divergences.

The assumption that one can absolutely define Orwell in biographical terms is parallel to the assumption that his writing and its message or interpretation are equally clear and fixed. But the very attempt to define and fix into stasis is part of a world view that Orwell rejected. If this is not recognized then the outcome is often the suggestion that Orwell is being inconsistent, hence untrustworthy and deceitful. And the deep-rooted desire evidenced throughout the criticism to make Orwell into a truthful, honest representative of at least two generations of English political thought, turns on its head and becomes a virulent attack on his "character." These readings are not only unnecessary but self-limiting. They confine themselves to strategy rather than stance. Yet it is in the questions of belief and value that inform the writing and are approached by stance that the reader can move past party ideology toward what Orwell called politics in "the widest possible sense," which was an activity necessary to any effective ideology.

In approaching Orwell's own outlook it is helpful to recognize that Richard Hoggart's description of *The Road to Wigan Pier* as the story of an education may be seen as a suitable description for Orwell's entire writing life. All too often there is an unwillingness to accept that Orwell might learn, come to appreciate different things and change his mind, and to recognize that this apparent inconsistency overlays a fundamentally consistent belief in the need to evaluate actively, never to assume the quality of axioms and fixed standards. Because Orwell has always questioned, he has been called a revisionist as a matter of course. However he is in effect engaged in a complex rhetorical activity with both positive and negative aspects. The rejection of his ability to learn results in a tendency to impose one view of the man on all his life, one aspect of his thought or writing on the whole: and inevitably this leads to charges of contradiction and judgments of weakness.

There is also too little appreciation of Orwell's own attitude to learning: that it is not what you learn so much as how you learn, and the corollary that movement from ignorance to a position of knowledge does not mean that knowledge is then something fixed and to be imposed upon others. A fundamental part of this attitude is an appreciation of the role of stance which Orwell's writing comes to in *The Road to Wigan Pier*. As the writer recognizes that moral activity is more important than techniques in themselves, he comes to outline positive and negative directions in persuasion or expression and communication of opinion. The positive directions are ones which stimulate to discussion and then further to a full interaction, whereas negative directions restrict and control by imposition.

Orwell's search for a valid voice through experimentation with genre was a search for writing that would be able to move outside the dualisms that surrounded him. The early writing explores the relationship of this dualistic outlook to a self-enclosed deluding stance in both literature and politics that he later comes to call fantasy. *The Road to Wigan Pier* is the story of a political education in this stance, and it is the danger of the extreme political fantasy of totalitarianism that alerts Orwell to the danger of this stance in literature. The structures of *The Road to Wigan Pier* provide an admittedly rough beginning of an attempt to move out of that stance through a literary voice that does not impose opinion on others but invites discussion.

The strategies of familiarization and alienation that he uses in *The Road to Wigan Pier* are part of the luggage of the 1930s. But just as he is not long a political fellow-traveller so his literary search goes on to take a rather different route. *Homage to Catalonia* transforms the strategy into a complex writing of elusive analogy that establishes the basis for his allegorical stance: a writing that leaves the reader in little doubt as to Orwell's opinion but opens up the text to active involvement. The valid voice is not a question of simply claiming good faith, but of a mature and comprehensive outline of rhetorical stance, that recognizes the tendency to restrictive readings in the dualism of the time, and consciously moves past discussion to explore alternatives that make possible interaction with the text itself.

By the time Orwell writes *Animal Farm* he has developed his grasp of stance into a formidable presentation of the activity of reading. Through fantasy it can be read as a simple, rigidly moralistic comment on the events and consequences of the Russian revolution conveyed through animal emblems. But through allegory it can be read as a perceptive invitation to discuss the responsibility of human beings to take up their political destiny because they, in contrast to the animals, do have the ability to communicate. *Nineteen Eight-Four* may also be read either through the stance of fantasy or through that of allegory. Read as the former it appears to be a perverse, neurotic, depressing, and limited view of an extremist politics. But read as the latter, as an allegory of a political fantasy, it is not only more enjoyable but the writing enacts the possibility of a political alternative. At the moment that Orwell's life is interrupted by death, the earlier analogy is reversed and it is the literary that informs the political.

THE STANCE OF ALLEGORY

An early, undated extract from the manuscript notebook that Orwell kept during the last year of his life discusses the main problems of the twentieth-century novel by focusing on the first-person novel, which can easily become completely authoritarian and develop into the stance of fantasy literature. The similarity of the following observation on such novels with earlier comments on escape literature is significant:

> to write a novel in the first person is like dosing yourself with some stimulating but very deleterious and very habit-forming drug. The temptation to do it is very great, but at every stage of the proceedings you know perfectly well that you are doing something wrong and foolish.

Its advantages are that the use of "I" gets a writer over his initial shyness, that it allows him to arrive at the concept he started out with, and that *"anything* can be made to sound credible" because identification with the reader is easier. But the credibility is dangerous. Disadvantages of the technique arise from the limitation of the novel to that character. He will be a three-dimensional character amidst caricatures and the work "cannot be a true novel" by narrowing the range of feeling to one. Further, because the narrator is not separate from the author he cannot comment, and "even in a novel the author must occasionally comment."

Orwell says in "Why I Write" that "one can write nothing readable unless one constantly struggles to efface one's personality." By personality he refers to the desire for personal control over the external world. *Coming Up for Air* attempted to extend the form of the novel and incorporate the writer's voice, so that the reader would know the basis for the opinions in it and how its decisions were made. But the attempt did not fully succeed. The use of first-person control caused Orwell to observe in a letter to Julian Symons of May 1948,

> Of course you are right about my own character constantly intruding on that of the narrator. I am not a real novelist anyway, and that particular vice is inherent in writing a novel in the first person, which one should never do.

The novelist, especially the first-person novelist, is always in danger of imposing control without sufficient reference to his standards. The modern novel illustrates the negative characteristics of the first-person technique. Only one set of grounds for reality is accepted and any conflicting set of opinions is either evaded, suppressed, or denied. One point of view completely dominates the action, whether it be of the first-person character or of a narcissistic narrator. The result is a culmination of the nineteenth-century movement toward naturalistic realism which gets so involved with the grounds of its society that criticism of and interaction with it become impossible.

But as Orwell has noted a novel need not be naturalistic, and his increasing interest in utopian novels examines the non-naturalistic possibilities of that genre. As he commented in a broadcast programme on Butler, utopian literature has the double-sided aspects of satire and allegory. Both create alternative worlds. But the more immediate reference to actuality of satire ties it closer to naturalism, while allegory has greater scope. It is significant that he observes this alternative as one with a tradition including Swift, Butler, and Zamyatin, but only partly including Huxley who is too satirical for his liking. The genre has much in common with the nonsense literature of Lear and Carroll, and is also based on the same principle as surrealism, that of creating conceptual and visual landscapes that comment by juxtaposition on conventionally accepted interpretations of the actual world.

For Orwell, Swift is a highly individual utopian writer, inspired by an anarchic impulse close to a personal totalitarianism. He notes Swift's technique of inserting a word of praise "into a passage that ought to be purely satirical," which is "a mark of vitality in Utopia books." Inconsistency, disruption, and vitality are linked with the non-satirical elements of utopian literature. Similarly he comments on Butler that he, "like many other writers of Utopia books . . . doesn't fully make up his mind whether he is writing pure satire or whether he is making constructive suggestions." The two lived during different times, and whereas Swift's utopia was necessarily individual and private, Butler's is unsatisfactory because of his "lack of interest in politics . . . he doesn't pay much attention to the structure of society."

It is the interest in politics that makes Zamyatin's *We* more successful as a novel than Huxley's *Brave New World*, despite its weak plot and other deviations from novelistic construction. Zamyatin's work is read not as a direct political satire on Russian or other contemporary politics, but as a work dealing with more general political issues. Huxley's novel concentrates on criticizing the existence of a mechanical world by suggesting that its leaders would become so apathetic that concepts of power would disappear. Orwell dismisses the suggestion and says that it weakens the novel by failing to connect with the cause of the actual political situation that exists.

Zamyatin on the other hand specifically points to the greed for power as the central motive for the political world he creates. A letter to F. J. Warburg written just before Orwell's death clarifies the difference. *We* "debunks the super-rational, hedonistic type of Utopia" also found in *Brave New World*, yet it continues not only to satirize it, but to suggest that it is made possible by a relegation of all other factors to "diabolism and the tendency to return to an earlier form of civilization which seems to be part of totalitarianism." The extension of utopian writing past a satire of individual aspects of totalitarianism, to the presentation of a landscape illustrating the source of its conceptual limitations and the negative strategies of hence controls by imposing opinion, but allegory comments by juxtaposition of the writer's values with those of the habitual world. Evaluation and assessment is only achieved if the reader himself makes the necessary connections and interacts with the literature.

The brief comments on allegory which surface from Orwell's later criticism never become a consistent pattern of commentary in the way that his discussions of fantasy do. We learn far more about literary strategies for a positive rhetoric from his development of juxtaposed analogies in *Homage to Catalonia*, his treatment of narratorial voice in *Animal Farm*, or his complex tensions of repetition in *Nineteen Eighty-Four*. But the few comments we do find indicate his growing search in contemporary literature for strategies actively involving both reader and writer to parallel the interaction between personal and party politics. The writer is no longer concerned with telling the reader something explicit, but with creating structures within which they can both discuss but also then proceed to move beyond. Failure to recognize this, failure to take up our side of the activity, severely limits the reader's enjoyment of Orwell's work.

Animal Farm, written when the writer had rejected the form of the novel but not yet turned to utopian allegorical literature, is both satirical and allegorical. As a satire on the Russian revolution it is, as many critics have noted, not particularly illuminating. However as an allegory containing grounds not explicitly tied to historical event it is of enduring value. Similarly, *Nineteen Eighty-Four* is satire, irony, and allegory. Orwell notes that the work is not a fantasy in terms of "a thriller mixed up with a love story," but a fantasy in terms of nonsense literature that indicates "by parodying them the intellectual implications of totalitarianism." He wishes to combine the identification of naturalism with the distortion of fantasy, to provide an alternative world not in order to supplant this one but to set it up in a commenting tension with it and encourage the reader's involvement in assessment and evaluation. *Nineteen Eighty-Four* is a "Utopia in the form of a novel." As a utopia its naturalistic elements present a satire on the shifting truths of a totalitarian state, and it is in this sense that it is much criticized in a later age which is perhaps mistakenly more dismissive of the possibility of such a state. But as an allegory of the ease with which we lose ourselves to habitual convention, of the failure of the individual to renew tradition and of the withdrawal from a responsibility to discuss and communicate values, it is horrifyingly precise.

CLOSING REMARKS

[Earlier on] I suggested that many of the readings of Orwell's work restricted what he had to offer by placing him within a social, historical, and philosophical framework that he would have questioned. The dominant, rationalist mode of much contemporary thought generates a series of dualisms that arise from its separation between fact and value, and to read Orwell's work within these dualisms is unsatisfactory: not only for the practical reason that works are not as interesting or stimulating, but also because Orwell himself was trying to move beyond the separation, to combine description of the world with his personal interaction with it so that the activity of the writing would engage the reader into active evaluation.

Orwell's development of fantasy and allegory was not toward a specific solution or end for his writing, but toward ways of reading. They are based on fundamental attitudes to the external world that body forth, among other things, our beliefs about whether we impose upon the external, treat it as different, or with the absurdists, as unalterably alien. They are beliefs that express themselves in various rhetorical stances, which describe the interaction of human beings and that external world. Fantasy in Orwell's terms, as in those of many critics of fantasy writing, is a stance encouraged by rationalism. But Orwell went on to outline the negativity that arises from the all too easy breakdown of the activity of rational logic into restrictive, dualistic systems. In contrast, allegory is a stance that is helped by strategies that expose their own grounds, assess themselves and their limitations, and is most positive when it provides the opportunity for going beyond those limitations.

Just because fantasy and allegory are rhetorical stances they apply to all disciplines. They inform philosophy, politics, and art as analogous activities. It was the perception of the extreme fantasy in the politics of totalitarianism that alerted Orwell to the strategies conducive to negative stance in literature. And in searching for a valid personal voice in literature, he posits the basis for a positive stance in contemporary politics. But fundamental to stance is its immediate activity: a political event or a piece of writing may be read in a number of ways, but I would suggest that Orwell is saying that fantasy and allegory are two predominant activities in the twentieth century. The controversy surrounding him as a writer indicates that his own work was just as subject to both readings, but it is also the basis for suggesting that he did achieve the positive voice for which he was searching, that his clear transparent prose did indeed conceal a complex and enigmatic writing that stimulates discussion far beyond the limitations of the grounds of contemporary politics and art.

Running in Circles:
The Early Novels of Evelyn Waugh

Alvin B. Kernan

In Evelyn Waugh's novel *Helena*, Constantius, father of the future Roman emperor Constantine, rides with his new bride Helena, later St. Helena the discoverer of the true cross, along the rough Roman wall which separates Gaul from Germany and forms the outermost defense of the City of Rome. He explains to Helena the meaning of the wall:

> Think of it, mile upon mile, from snow to desert, a single great girdle round the civilized world; inside, peace, decency, the law, the altars of the Gods, industry, the arts, order; outside, wild beasts and savages, forest and swamp, bloody mumbo-jumbo, men like wolf-packs; and along the wall the armed might of the Empire, sleepless, holding the line. Doesn't it make you see what The City means?
>
> (chapter 3)

On one side of a guarded wall, barbarism, on the other civilization; on one side animals, on the other social man; on one side the jungle, on the other The City; on one side chaos, on the other order.

This is a particularly clear geographical form of a master image of history, society, and human nature which underlies Waugh's satiric novels. But since in Waugh's hardheaded conservative view of life the powers of destruction are ineradicable, this scene represents an ideal situation. Here the opposing forces are distinctly separated, barbarism and chaos on the outside, civilization and order on the inside, with the ceaselessly manned wall in between.

But in the postwar England of the twenties and thirties, the principal setting of Waugh's first four satiric novels, *Decline and Fall* (1928), *Vile Bodies* (1930), *Black Mischief* (1932), and *A Handful of Dust* (1934)—which I propose

From *The Plot of Satire*. © 1965 by Yale University. Yale University Press, 1965.

to treat as a unit—the walls have already been breached and the jungle powers are at work within The City. *Decline and Fall* opens with a night scene in the quadrangle of Scone College, Oxford. High up in the walls of the college sit the present-day guardians of order, education, and tradition—the Junior Dean, Mr. Sniggs, and the Domestic Bursar, Mr. Postlethwaite. Their lights are extinguished for fear that they will be seen by the rioting members of the Bollinger Club holding their annual meeting in college. From below in the darkness comes the shrill sound of "the English country families baying for broken glass," and out into the quad, dressed in bottle-green evening coats, rush the members of the Boller, "epileptic royalty from their villas of exile; uncouth peers from crumbling country seats; smooth young men of uncertain tastes from embassies and legations; illiterate lairds from wet granite hovels in the Highlands; ambitious young barristers and Conservative candidates torn from the London season and the indelicate advances of debutantes." Savagely drunk, they break up a grand piano, smash a china collection, throw a Matisse into a waterjug, have "great fun" with the manuscript of a Newdigate prize poem found in an undergraduate's room, and round off their evening, before becoming sick and passing out, by debagging and throwing into the fountain a passing student who is unfortunate enough to be wearing a tie resembling the Boller's. Above, the two dons creep to the window, peer cautiously out, and rub their hands in anticipation of the huge fines, which will provide a week of Founder's port for the senior common room. The Junior Dean, hoping for even larger fines and more port, prays for ultimate barbarism: "Oh, please God, make them attack the Chapel." Next day authority reasserts itself with all pomp and ceremony: in solemn assembly the officals of Scone fine the undergraduate members of the Bollinger Club, ensure founder's port for the High Table, and send down the young man who was debagged for indecent behavior with the awesome words, "That sort of young man does the College no good."

Nearly every scene in Waugh's satiric novels is built on the pattern of the Scone College scene. When an actual wall appears, its form and history betray its inability to hold out the forces of barbarism. The machiolated, towered, and turreted wall—with workable portcullis—around Llanabba Castle in *Decline and Fall* was built by unemployed mill workers during the cotton famine of the 1860s. The ladies of the house were upset by the thought of the men starving and went so far as to hold a charity bazaar to raise money for relief; the husband, a Lancashire millowner influenced by the Liberal economists, was equally upset by the thought of giving the men money "without due return." Sentimentality and enlightened self-interest were both neatly satisfied by putting the men to work on the wall. "A great deal of work was done very cheaply," and the Victorian taste for the romantic was satisfied by the neo-Gothic character of the construction which transformed plain Llanabba House into Llanabba Castle. The shabby, self-satisfied, and self-glorifying attitudes which caused the wall to be built were merely the leached-out remnants of older, more meaningful values such as work and responsibility toward one's workers and fellow men. Already well along the way toward barbarism themselves, these Victorian attitudes offer no real resistance to the forces of destruction, and the wall they built is overwhelmed in the next century when the house becomes a boys' school which shelters every kind of greed, ignorance, and savagery.

While actual stone walls are not always present in Waugh's scenes, the immaterial walls of culture are. The traditions, the social institutions, the ancient rites, the buildings, the manners, the morals, the logic and grammar of English, the codes of service, the aesthetic values, "all that seemingly solid, patiently built, gorgeously ornamented structure of Western life," are for Waugh the walls protecting the ordered, meaningful life from riot and savagery. These defenses of value are omnipresent in Waugh's works, and one of the major effects of his novels comes from the ceremonial fullness with which they are voiced and acted out. His statesmen, financiers, peers, and educators carry such heroic titles, fill out their robes so superbly, speak with such golden tongues, and conduct themselves with such marvelous certainty that the world seems as solid and substantial as ever. Dignified judges speak with timeless authority of the right of society to repress ruthlessly those "human vampires who prey upon the degradation of their species"; earnest, well-trained customs officials meticulously sift all incoming books to exclude any writing which might affect the moral welfare of the English people; ministers of His Britannic Majesty are sent to savage lands to protect truth and justice, and to show the more unfortunate peoples of the earth the way to civilization; the children destined to rule the nation study at ancient public schools where their minds and characters are carefully moulded; and the inquiring minds of men of science press forward to the discovery of new truths about the operations of nature.

But Waugh is a vicious ironist, and he always places us where we can look beneath the robes of the great. The judge who defends society with such sonority is condemning an innocent, powerless man and letting the real criminal go free. The careful customs officials ferret out and burn Dante with a warning delivered in official tones that, "if we can't stamp out literature in this country, we can at least stop its being brought in from the outside." The Envoy Extraordinary to Azania has forgotten how to speak all foreign languages and spends his time at the Legation, located ten miles outside the capital where the air is better, playing in the bath with rubber animals. A new master at a public school who asks what he should try to teach the boys is handed a heavy stick and told, "Oh, I shouldn't try to *teach* them anything, not just yet, anyway. Just keep them quiet." Scientific inquiry continues its onward march with such inventions as the Huxdane-Halley bomb, "for the dissemination of leprosy germs"; and the spirit of Mill and Darwin descends to the sociologist Sir Wilfred Lucas-Dockery, the warden of Blackstone Gaol, who when he hears that the hungry prisoners working in the prison bindery have been eating paste, instructs his keepers to weigh them daily to find out if they are gaining or losing weight.

Waugh has frequently been accused of being a snob and a deadly conservative, but it should be noted that he finds as much dullness and savagery in the representatives of the old order as he does in the new barbarians. He defends tradition, not the status quo; social order, not the establishment. He chronicles life among the ruins of a magnificent civilization, and here, as in the older Central American cultures where "Man had deserted his post and the jungle was creeping back to its old strongholds," the invasion has taken place and is continuing from within, not without.

But no one who lives in this world sees the irony and takes Waugh's England for anything other than the familiar, secure old Empire. The realities of this strange half-world are caught perfectly, though unknowingly of course, by the Christmas Sermon delivered in an English church of an addled minister who somehow forgets that he is no longer the chaplain of a regiment on foreign service:

> How difficult it is for us . . . to realize that this is indeed Christmas. Instead of the glowing log fire and windows tight shuttered against the drifting snow, we have only the harsh glare of an alien sun; instead of the happy circle of loved faces, of home and family, we have the uncomprehending states of the subjugated, though no doubt grateful, heathen. Instead of the placid ox and ass of Bethlehem . . . we have for companions the ravening tiger and the exotic camel, the furtive jackal and the ponderous elephant.
>
> (*A Handful of Dust*, chapter 2)

These lines describe exactly the peculiar quality of Waugh's England. It is at once the happy circle of loved faces and a strange wasteland burning under the harsh glare of an alien sun. It is peopled with all the familiar types of English comic fiction, and yet these people are ravening tigers and furtive jackals. The anarchic appetites of these animals are shown to be ineradicable human traits which at times break out into the open in cannibal feasts, jungle dances, savage riots, and great battlefields. Ordinarily this love of violence is muted, but it always throbs in the background, like the drums which continually beat in the hills just outside the city of Debra Dowa, where the Emperor Seth in *Black Mischief* attempts to create a modern state. It will appear only slightly disguised as an insane carpenter who has visions in which an Angel of the Lord commands him to smite the Philistines hip and thigh. Then it is the epileptic royalty, savage lairds, and opportunistic politicans of the Bollinger Club. Or it may take the form of the random sexual appetite of Brenda Last in *A Handful of Dust*, who abandons her family when she inexplicably becomes enamoured of the despicable John Beaver. Another time it will be the charming ruthlessness of a "howling cad" like Basil Seal, the eccentricity of "Lady ———, whose imitations of animal sounds are so lifelike that she can seldom be persuaded to converse in any other way," the brutality of a Colonel MacAdder or a General Strapper, the deviations of Miles Malpractice and Mrs. Panrast, or the far-flung operations of the efficiently run Latin American Entertainment Company, Ltd., Lady Metroland's chain of South American brothels.

But this more or less direct violence and depravity is less dangerous to civilization than emptyheaded vanity and mindless gravity, the exotic camel and the ponderous elephant. This emptiness of the mind and heart seems at first to be no more than traditional English reticence, but it is extended until great voids open up in the center of the characters and they are revealed as having no private minds, no intense feelings whatsoever. The novels are filled with automatons composed of readymade, fashionable phrases—"too sick making," "too, too bogus," "a top-hole little spot," "it doesn't tabulate"—of verbal formulas rattled off without the slightest comprehension—"If it's a choice between my moral judgment and the nationalization of banking, I prefer nationalization"; "I've always maintained that success in this world depends on knowing exactly how little each job is worth." Such characters can be fully and adequately described by such newspaper clichés as "the lovely young daughter of Lord Chasm" or "the bright young things." Their names tell us all there is to know about them: Lady Circumference and her son little Lord Tangent, the Earl of Pastmaster, Paul Pennyfeather, Lord Maltravers the Minister of Transportation, Basil Seal, Agatha Runcible.

The use of type characters is, of course, common in satire, for the satirist is never interested in deep explorations of human nature. His characters are merely personifications of the particular form of dullness he wishes to give visible shape. But what in some other satirists is an artistic device for getting dullness out into the open by disentangling it from the complexities of real character, becomes in Waugh realism of sorts. He sings the rich, the powerful, the fashionable and the fortunate; and he shows them to be as stiff, empty, and mechanical as fictive abstractions. The rare occasions when there are hints that a character is feeling or thinking come as a great surprise. Who would have thought that the butterfly Agatha Runcible in *Vile Bodies* had any mind to go mad? Or that Simon Balcairn, the aristocrat turned gossip columnist in the same novel, could have felt enough despair to require suicide? Even when a rudimentary mind or heart is established by such actions, the thoughts and emotions which emerge have a primitive, childlike quality, as if the owners were completely unused to such functions as thinking and feeling.

The all-pervasive simplicity and mindlessness is one of the principal causes of the trouble in Waugh's satiric world. What hope for the future when the full exercise of intellect in one of the leading politicians of the country, Lord Metroland, results only in such "hand-to-mouth thinking" as this? He has been told at a party that the mad antics of the younger generation result from a "radical instability" in the country. Somewhat puzzled and concerned because his sense of security is disturbed, Metroland returns to his mansion to find his drunken stepson, Peter Pastmaster, fumbling with the lock. To his greeting Peter's only answer, repeated several times, is "Oh, go to hell." Seeing a tall hat on the table by the door,

Metroland concludes that it belongs to his wife's lover, Alastair Digby-Vaine-Trumpington, and goes into the study because "it would be awkward if he met young Trumpington on the stairs." Once in his study, he surveys the familiar details: the businesslike arrangement of the furniture, the solid green safe with the brass handle, and the rows of books which seem to guarantee the continuation of order and security, *Who's Who*, the *Encyclopaedia Brittanica*, *Debrett*, *The Dictionary of National Biography*. These reassure him greatly, and after he hears Trumpington leave, he exclaims, "radical instability indeed," and goes upstairs to his beautiful, aristocratic wife, whose wealth comes from the operation of a chain of South American brothels.

Such vacuity—and Metroland is a *thinker* compared to most of Waugh's characters—justifies Waugh's unstated but insistent argument that a meaningful society can only be one which follows and defends strenuously some traditional pattern of belief and value. If people cannot reason clearly or feel deeply—and there is no indication in Waugh's novels that the majority of them ever could—then their only hope of a full and valuable life is to follow the traditions evolved during the long course of trial and error which is human history. Leave man, individual man, to decide on his own values, throw him into a relativistic world in which nothing is certain, debase the traditional ways of doing things so that no honest man can believe in them, and the result will be, as Waugh regularly shows, confusion, self-defeat, the grotesque distortion of human nature, and frantic but meaningless activity.

Someone has said that a good satirist really loves his fools. They are, after all, such perfect specimens of their kind, so unalloyed with sense or virtue, that it is impossible not to be delighted with their purity. Waugh must love his fools very much, for they are such perfect idiots that it is possible to take their actions as no more than happy bumbling, and a good many reviewers have read these satires as "hilarious tales of high society" or as "gay, comic adventures of the dazzling younger generation." That these novels are, however, savage indictments of a civilization in the last stages of its decline because the defenders have left the wall needs little argument. The consistent counterpoint of the old traditions and the new emptiness, the recurrent images of jungle chaos and animal madness, the futile activities of the characters, all these provide a bitter comment on the types of dullness Waugh chronicles so gaily.

It is, however, the arrangement of incidents and the overall pattern of events—plot—which Waugh uses most effectively to show the emptiness in the lives of his representatives of twentieth-century progress and emancipation. Like most satires, these lack a conventional story, intricately contrived and carefully followed. The sporadic attempts of two young people to get married, a picaresque ramble through English society, occasional references to the decay of a marriage, these and other such devices loosely bind the incidents together. But the books are not constructed around these story lines, for they are referred to only sporadically. When the story does appear, the situation will often have changed considerably from what it was at last appearance, but no explanation is offered of how these changes came about. The effect is of something "just happening," of a discontinuity through which some unknown and unidentifiable power is working to force matters to a disastrous conclusion.

The major portion of the satires is composed of a series of brief and apparently unrelated—by cause and effect—episodes which flash on the pages in the manner of scenes from a newsreel. A scene in a fashionable London restaurant will be followed by a meal in the African or Brazilian jungles; a business journey will be interrupted by a long, carefully reported conversation between two women—neither of whom we have ever seen before or see again—about a recent scandal at Ten Downing Street. Varied events at a boys' school will give way to a discussion of modern architecture by a Professor Otto Silenus. Even when Waugh follows for a considerable length of time the adventures of the same characters, they will move at random from watching a movie being made, to a party, to an automobile race, stopping along the way to have a number of drinks, look for a hotel room, drive through a slum in the industrial Midlands. Then the scene flickers to another setting and we are watching the ridiculous pretensions of a sister in a fashionable nursing home, listening to a gossip columnist telephone his editor, and hearing about a young boy who fell out of an airplane.

By some standards Waugh would appear to have put his novels together very badly, but he is, of course, reproducing in his arrangement of scenes and his handling of time the frenetic, disconnected movements of modern life. Only a true culture, not a disintegrating one, can have an Aristotelian plot in which one event follows inevitably from another and the whole is composed of a beginning, a middle, and an end. But randomness and disorganization are only surface effects. Each of the episodes is thematically related to the others with which it is in sequence. All show in different terms the assault of appetite and stupidity on the old beliefs and ways of life, and the consequent emptiness. The scenes are also carefully arranged to allow the events in one scene to define the events in the next: an episode of polite savagery in the jungle, or a description of an ultra-modern house built for machines to live in rather than men will border on a party scene in which fashionable men and women move with the predictability of machines or in a pattern of conditioned responses.

Satire regularly offers, not a still, quiet world, but a busy, bustling one in which crowds of men race furiously about pursuing some *ignis fatuus*. In Waugh's satires railway lines are thrown across great primitive wastes, huge business empires are in ceaseless movement searching for new markets, busy factories cover the landscape, and cars race madly about the roads. Solemn, serious politicians, educators, clergymen, financiers, and men of affairs move confidently forward on the path of change, progress, and enlightened self-interest. The disillusioned younger generation rushes restlessly about in search of pleasure and something new in life. Amiable rogues move endlessly on looking for new amusements and more profitable deals. This is, on the surface, the humming, vigorous world of the twentieth century, the era of ceaseless change and inevitable progress. But all this movement is illusory, for in Waugh's world, as in Carroll's Wonderland, "it takes all the running you can do, to keep in the same place. If you want to get somewhere else, you must run at least twice as fast as that."

What in fact happens in Waugh's novels is that all the running produces only circular movement—the second of the patterns Swift shows to result from self-delusive flights of fancy, which go "like one who travels the East into West; or like a strait line drawn by its own length into a Circle." The circle has been in the past a figure of perfection, but it has also been the figure of empty, meaningless movement, of eternal hunger which never finds satisfaction or rest:

> Here saw I people, more than elsewhere, many,
>   On one side and the other, with great howls,
>   Rolling weights forward by main-force of chest.
> They clashed together, and then at that point
>   Each one turned backward, rolling retrograde,
>   Crying, "Why keepest?" and, "Why squanderest thou?"
> Thus they returned along the lurid circle
>   On either hand unto the opposite point,
>   Shouting their shameful metre evermore.
> Then each, when he arrived there, wheeled about
>   Through his half-circle to another joust.
>   [*The Inferno*, Canto VII, 25–35]

It is in this "infernal" sense that circularity appears in Waugh. It is the pattern of aimless, self-defeating life, the natural movement of the jungle and the savage:

> Dancing was resumed, faster this time and more clearly oblivious of fatigue. In emulation of the witch doctors, the tribesmen began slashing themselves on chest and arms with their hunting knives; blood and sweat mingled in shining rivulets over their dark skins. Now and then one of them would pitch forward onto his face and lie panting or roll stiff in a nervous seizure. Women joined in the dance, making another chain, circling in the reverse way to the men. They were dazed with drink, stamping themselves into ecstasy. The two chains jostled and combined. They shuffled together interlocked.
>
>   (*Black Mischief*, chapter 7)

The English spectator at this dance draws back dazed from the heat of the fire, the monotonous sound of the drums, and the mind-obliterating circular movement of the dance; but the man of the future, the hypercivilized Professor Otto Silenus, who looks forward to the day when men will be

as functional as machines and houses as simple in design as factories, finds
the circle the only true image of life:

> It's like the big wheel at Luna Park. . . . You pay five francs and
> go into a room with tiers of seats all round, and in the centre the
> floor is made of a great disc of polished wood that revolves quickly.
> At first you sit down and watch the others. They are all trying to
> sit in the wheel, and they keep getting flung off, and that makes
> them laugh, and you laugh too . . . the nearer you can get to the
> hub of the wheel the slower it is moving and the easier it is to
> stay on. There's generally someone in the centre who stands up
> and sometimes does a sort of dance. Often he's paid by the man-
> agement, though. . . . Of course at the very centre there's a point
> completely at rest, if one could only find it. . . . Lots of people
> just enjoy scrambling on and being whisked off and scrambling
> on again. . . . Then there are others . . . who sit as far out as they
> can and hold on for dear life . . . the scrambling and excitement
> and bumps and the effort to get to the middle, and when we do
> get to the middle, it's just as if we never started. It's so odd.
>
> (*Decline and Fall*, part III, chapter 7)

The jungle dance and the wheel at Luna Park are the two extremes
which meet, primitive past and primitive future, the blood-crazed wandering of the stone-age savage and the mechanical construction of a tech-
nologically advanced civilization without humane direction. These are the
two great images of hopeless circles on which existence moves in Waugh's
world, but the circular pattern appears everywhere in more attenuated
forms. Politics is a circular game. The Right Honourable Walter Outrage
M.P. is in one week as Prime Minister and out the next, and it is an attentive
man who can tell at any given moment whether Outrage is in or out. The
bright young things in search of amusement go to an endless series of
parties—parties in hospitals, parties in hotels, masked parties, savage par-
ties, parties in stately old homes, parties in bed—but all parties turn out
to be the same party where one hears the same talk and sees the same
faces. Waugh's trick, picked up from Thackeray and Chesterton, of having
the same people with the same ridiculous names pop up again and again
in different books makes it appear that it is impossible to break out of this
circle of familiars. And when these people do pop up, they are always
doing the same old things. Lady Metroland is always suggesting to attractive young girls that if they are dissatisfied with their present situation, a
position can be found for them as an entertainer in Buenos Aires. Lord
Monomark is still surrounded by several perfect beauties and several sy-
cophants listening to him talk about his latest fad diet. Peter Pastmaster is
still drunk, Alastair Digby-Vaine-Trumpington is still drinking, and the
mysterious Toby Crutwell—sometime cat burglar, war hero, and M.P.—
has still left the party just before we arrived. *The Daily Excess* and *The Daily
Beast* are still getting the news wrong, the older generation is still worried

about the younger, Parsnip and Pimpernell are still writing left-wing poetry and issuing manifestoes, and Basil Seal is still managing to get money out of someone.

Round and round go the parts of the world, each setting up a centrifugal movement which contributes to the larger circular plot in each novel. *Decline and Fall* follows the adventures of a young innocent, Paul Pennyfeather, who is sent down from Scone College for running pantless across the quadrangle after being debagged by the Bollinger Club. In his search for a living he first takes a position as a master in a boys' school, Llanabba Castle, run as a private venture by Augustus Fagan, Ph.D. Falling in love with Margot Beste-Chetwynde, the mother of one of his students, he follows her into the fashionable world of wealthy London society. Just before they are to be married, she sends him on a business trip to Marseilles to clear up some difficulties about the transportation of several girls to her South American enterprise. Paul, completely unaware of the nature of this business, is shadowed by a League of Nations representative — an old college chum named Potts — and later arrested. Sentenced to a long term in jail, he is later rescued by Margot, who buys him out by agreeing to marry Metroland, the Home Secretary. A bogus death is arranged at a nursing home run by Dr. Fagan, and later Paul returns to Scone to resume his "education." He uses the same name, explaining that he is a cousin of the deceased Pennyfeather, and grows a moustache. As the book ends, Paul has just returned from listening to a paper on the Polish plebiscites, the subject of the paper he had listened to on the fateful evening when he was caught by the Boller. Outside there is "a confused roaring and breaking of glass." The Bollinger Club is again holding its annual meeting.

What starts as a linear progress, a picaresque journey, through the various levels of English society gradually takes the shape of a great circle, the wheel in Luna Park described by Professor Silenus. Men and women scramble frantically over its surface, dancing, cavorting, grimly seeking the center, or just spinning dizzily for the ride. But they get nowhere. As the wheel turns we see different aspects of English society—a college at Oxford, the home of a well-to-do lawyer, an employment office in London, a school in Wales, an old manor house, a fashionable weekend party in a modern house in the country, a police court, a parson's house, a prison, a nursing home, and again the college at Oxford. As each new scene turns into view it becomes but a new version of what we have already found elsewhere. These recurring forms of dullness have sometimes different, sometimes the same names. Augustus Fagan, Ph.D., first appears running a pretentious school designed simply to make money, and he ends running a shabby nursing home and arranging false death certificates to make money. Prendergast will appear as the minister who while sitting one day in his pleasant house with the chintz curtains put up by his mother suddenly is unable to understand "why God made the world at all." He is next a master at a school where he is unable to discipline the boys and cannot teach them anything because he has nothing to teach. Then he crops up as a Modern Churchman—"who draws the full salary of a beneficed clergyman and need not commit himself to any religious belief"—and the Chaplain of the prison to which Paul is sent. Here he has the same trouble with the prisoners that he had with the boys and ends, appropriately enough, as the victim of the mad carpenter who with true dissenting zeal dreams that he is commanded by the Angel of the Lord to "Kill and Spare Not." This little parable on the contemporary Church of England serves also to demonstrate the disordering effects in church, school, and prison of loss of belief. In every place, this and similar disordering powers—savagery, greed, pomposity, ignorance, and idealism so simpleminded as to be criminal—crop up in the characters of Grimes, Philbrick, Maltravers, Margot Beste-Chetwynde, and Peter Pastmaster, and their doubles; and their recurrence turns every scene into the same scene. College, school, prison, the Ritz are all the same places, governed by the same people, for the same purposes. Perhaps the only change in the novel occurs in Paul who, having died and been reborn, has lost his simpleminded beliefs about the inherent goodness of human nature and the perfectibility of man and come to share Waugh's view of the necessity of a rigidly enforced social order. Upon returning to Scone and hearing of a heretical second-century bishop who "denied the divinity of Christ, the immortality of the soul, the existence of good, the legality of marriage, and the validity of the Sacrament of Extreme Unction"—all the values denied in the giddy world through which he has passed—Paul can only reflect with satisfaction, "How right they had been to condemn him!"

Vile Bodies is a panorama of the life of the "bright young things" of the late twenties and their disapproving elders. The scenes of the novel are gathered loosely around the engagement of Adam Fenwick-Symes and Nina Blount, which is now on, now off, now on, as Adam seeks, finds, and then loses the money which would enable them to marry. As giddy as they are, their search for marriage represents the search for a traditional way of life and solid values, which in many ways all the younger people of the book restlessly seek. Money comes to represent the support offered by society and by the older generation to those who will share and perpetuate their values. Adam first tries to earn the necessary money, the emblematic support, by writing his autobiography, but officious, ignorant customs officials, acting in accordance with government policy, destroy his manuscript with the ominous words, "that's just downright dirt, and we burns that straight away, see." Adam turns then for money to the business world and is forced to sign a "very simple" contract with the publishers Rampole and Benfleet:

> No royalty on the first two thousand, then a royalty of two and a half per cent., rising to five per cent. on the tenth thousand. We retain serial, cinema, dramatic, American, Colonial and translation rights, of course. And, of course, an option on your next twelve books on the same terms. It's a very straightforward arrangement really. Doesn't leave room for any of the disputes which embitter the relations of author and publisher.
>
> (chapter 2)

Still seeking support, Adam travels down to see Colonel Blount, Nina's father and the master of Doubting Hall—usually pronounced Doubting 'All by the natives—a halfwitted but cunning old eccentric who spends all his time sleeping and eating. Lately Colonel Blount has found a passion for the "silver screen" and in hopes of getting a bit part he has financed a fantastic horse-opera version of the life of John Wesley which has been filmed at his house. When Adam asks him for money, the old man responds cheerfully with a check for a thousand pounds, signed "Charlie Chaplin."

His identity rejected with his autobiography, his hope of making a living by writing turned to economic slavery, and all possibility of support from the older generation and traditional social arrangements obliterated, Adam and Nina can only trust themselves to Fortune and its turning wheel. They begin a joyless little affair, and Fortune then arrives in the person of a drunk Major to whom Adam entrusts a thousand pounds he has just won in an idiotic bet. The money is to be placed on a horse named Indian Runner. The horse wins, but for the remainder of the book Adam and the drunk Major chase one another around trying to collect or give away 35,000 pounds, though it is never quite certain whether the Major really has the money or whether he has simply bilked Adam. Each time the fortune seems within Adam's grasp, the marriage to Nina is on; each time he loses sight of the Major, it is off. No Juliet, Nina finally marries a wealthy young boor named Ginger Littlejohn but immediately recommences the affair with Adam, even passing him off as her husband on a Christmas visit to Doubting 'All. When Adam and the Major finally do complete their transaction, it is on the enormous wasteland of the greatest battlefield in history, where the book ends; but the 35,000 devalued pounds are only worth a couple of drinks and a newspaper. Nina, still married to Ginger, is about to bear Adam's child, and all the other nincompoops of the book are carrying on in their usual way.

Most of the scenes in *Vile Bodies* deal with the varied activities of the other "bright young things," Miles Malpractice, Agatha Runcible, Archie Schwert, and Mary Mouse. They have, like Adam and Nina, committed themselves to fortune because everything else in their world is, in their language, "too, too bogus." They reel from party to party, body to body, and binge to binge, racing faster and faster after an elusive something which always escapes them. And because they have lost their bearings, they travel in endless circles. The dizzying circularity of their movements is objectified in the motor races, the great scene of the book. These dirt-track races are held in the Midlands near a grimy industrial city where a vast crowd, fascinated with speed and hoping for bloodshed, gathers to watch the "Speed Kings" go round and round. But the real Speed Kings are the bright, young people whose mad races are reported daily to the sensation-hungry readers of the press, and it is inevitable that one of them will find his way into the race. Dead drunk and mistakenly wearing a spare driver's brassard, Agatha Runcible ends up behind the wheel of the Plunkett-Bowse. After a few magnificent whirls around the course, she speeds off into the countryside until, losing control of the car, she runs head on into a market cross. She later dies in a delirium still shouting, "faster, faster."

Black Mischief is essentially the story of the arch-rogue Basil Seal and Seth, "Emperor of Azania, Chief of Chiefs of the Sakuyu, Lord of the Wanda and Tyrant of the Seas, Bachelor of the Arts of Oxford University." Azania is a thinly disguised version of Abyssinia, which Waugh visited as a reporter twice during the 1930s. The book turns around Seth's random attempts to make of Azania a model state and to impose on his savage people those modern ways of thought, institutions, and hard goods which romantic liberals at one time or another believed would bring about the reform of society and the perfection of man: paper money, birth control, boots for the imperial guards, woman suffrage, atheism, a bicameral legislature, kindness to animals, modern architecture and esperanto. The local population offers considerable resistance to such innovations—the guardsmen eat the boots—and when they do accept the new ideas, they somehow get them all wrong. They think, for example, that birth control and its apparatus—which is known as "the Emperor's juju"—will provide them with immense numbers of children, and so they march proudly in the Place Marie Stopes under the brave banner, "Through Sterility to Culture." Most readers have considered, wrongly, that *Black Mischief* is a brutal and unjustified satire on the stupidity of the black races and their comical mangling of Western ideas and institutions. Some elements of racial chauvinism can undoubtedly be found, but the main thrust of the satire is against Western liberals who believe that life can be utterly reformed, anywhere, by increased control over nature and the change of social institutions. Waugh makes this point very cleverly, and very consistently, by juxtaposing similar scenes in Africa and England, showing the same forces at work in both places, and by the cunning use of various kinds of imagery and inversions. When we see a gigantic savage with the unlikely title of the Earl of Ngumo roaring for raw camel meat in a local restaurant, do we laugh at his pretensions to the title of Earl or do we laugh at the pretensions of certain members of the English aristocracy to be something more than illiterate savages? And when an Azanian noble at a banquet for two English ladies who have come to his savage land to insure that no animals are being mistreated remarks humbly that, though the Azanians have much to learn from the white races, they too are in their "small way . . . cruel to animals" and sweeps on grandly to declaiming, "Ladies and Gentlemen we must be Modern, we must be refined in our Cruelty to Animals," where is the satire directed?

Black Mischief is not a caricature of a savage and ludicrous African kingdom but a grotesque image of Western civilization in the twentieth century. Where in Waugh's earlier books he sends his characters into only the figurative jungles of English society to encounter metaphoric snakes, tigers, and ponderous elephants, he now sends Seth and Basil Seal into an actual jungle where cannibalism becomes a reality and the barbarians file their teeth, not just their tongues and wits. The apostles of progress, the defenders of the old order, and the jungle savages of Azania are extensions of attitudes and people who appear in more usual clothes and speak in more familiar accents in the novels set in England.

Here as in England life runs in great meaningless circles. At the center deep in the Azanian jungle Basil Seal buries the murdered Emperor and Bachelor of the Arts of Oxford University who had thought to abolish savagery and darkness by fiat, technology, education, and Swedish exercises. The drums throb in the funeral ceremony, round and round goes the maddened dance until it at last distintegrates into grunting couples on the ground in the darkness. Out of the stewpot and into Basil's stomach comes the unrecognized flesh of Prudence Courteney, his mistress and the silly daughter of the even sillier English envoy to Azania, who because he believed that all the threats of trouble would "no doubt blow over," tended to his knitting, literally, and never concerned himself with politics or his official duties. Out beyond these circles there are others which look less insane only because they are more familiar. *Black Mischief* begins with a description of early Portuguese attempts to colonize Azania and the later invasion of the Arabs, and then deals with, in succession, the rise to power of a Wanda chief, Seth's progressive administration, and the establishment of a protectorate by the French and English. This latter looks like what is called progress: paved roads, neat administrative bungalows, clean water supply, lighted and policed streets. But it is in fact only another form of the old power game, and back in the jungle the drums still beat and the tribesmen still tear up the railroad irons for spearheads and rip down telegraph lines to make copper bracelets for their women. In the middle of the main thoroughfare of town a family that no government has been able to move, still squats in a wrecked car, while in the market place, the age-old racket of selling junk to the government goes on. Plus ça change, plus c'est la même chose. After his cannibal feast Basil Seal returns to the savages of London and finds them still doing the same things they were doing when he left. Azania fades from sight with the comforting music of Gilbert and Sullivan floating out over the waters which lap continuously at the sea wall,

> "Is it weakness of intellect, birdie?" I cried,
> "Or a rather tough worm in your little inside?"

A question to which Waugh's satires give the most un-Victorian answer, "Both."

A Handful of Dust gives the illusion of a developing plot. It begins with another of Waugh's havens of innocence, Hetton, a huge Victorian Gothic house which is the family home of the Lasts. Tony Last, the present owner, is an English gentleman raised in the humane tradition. He loves his home, cares for the tenantry long after it has ceased to be economical to do so, is seriously concerned with new farming methods and improving the land, loves his wife and only son, has charming manners, and goes to church every week, though he has no religious beliefs. Tony Last is, as Waugh once pointed out, a "humanist," and his old-fashioned, nineteenth-century dream of a City of Man held together by good sense and warm hearts finds its architectural expression in the grotesquely attractive Victorian-Gothic Hetton, which is, significantly, a reconstruction of an older, more beautiful Hetton Abbey. The present Hetton's heavy battlements, clock tower, armorial stained glass, huge brass and wrought iron gasolier, and pitch-pine minstrels' gallery, whatever their peculiar interest, were no more than a dream of chivalry and ancient values when they were put together in the 1860s with money earned from the cotton mills, collieries, and furnaces of Coketown. The impracticality of Hetton in the twentieth century is apparent in the impossibility of keeping it in repair, staffing it, or heating it after paying death duties and estate taxes. The naiveté of the social values it expresses in glazed brick and encaustic tile is apparent in the names given its bedrooms—Yseult, Elaine, Mordred, Gawain, Lancelot, and Guinevere—by men who read Tennyson rather than Malory.

In Waugh's world such a dream, no matter how attractive it may appear, is doomed, for it provides no defenses against the inevitable attacks of savagery and brutality. Tony Last's amusing and beautiful wife, Brenda, bored with life at Hetton, conceives an inexplicable and uncontrolled passion for a bloodless, self-centered young man, John Beaver, and leaves Hetton to plunge into the polite cruelty of London social life. Each week end she returns and looses a new group of savages on Hetton: interior decorators, spiritualists, international fancy women, young gigolos, and fashionable sponges. Each week she drains more money from Hetton to support her young man and pay for her pleasures. There is no planned malice in this, only a kind of mindless cruelty, which is echoed in nature by a highly bred and poorly trained horse who kicks Tony's only child, John Andrew, to death at a hunt.

This accident brings the marriage to an end, and Brenda demands a divorce and all the money needed to run Hetton. Tony refuses, but even after all this he cannot give up his humanistic dream of a City of Man:

> The Shining, the Many Watered, the Bright Feathered, the Aromatic Jam. He had a clear picture of it in his mind. It was Gothic in character, all vanes and pinnacles, gargoyles, battlements, groining and tracery, pavilions and terraces, a transfigured Hetton, pennons and banners floating on the sweet breeze, everything luminous and translucent; a coral citadel crowning a green hill top sown with daisies, among groves and streams; a tapestry landscape filled with heraldic and fabulous animals and symmetrical, disproportionate blossom.
>
> (chapter 5)

Led on by tales of a lost city, Tony plunges into the Brazilian jungle, still in search of his dream. But the fabled city turns out also to be an illusion, and with his guide dead, Tony wanders feverishly through the jungle to fall at last into the hands of an unquestionable madman, the illiterate half-caste Todd. Todd's father has left him a complete set of Dickens which he loves to have read to him. He holds Tony prisoner, forcing him to read again and again those sentimental stories—which, like Hetton, express the Victorian, humane vision of life—in which villains always die and intelligent little boys and pure young women after periods of trial and suffering win through at last to peace, prosperity, and the discovery of their rightful names and heritages.

The wheel has come full circle once again, with the difference that Tony is now condemned to live forever reading over and over his dream of life in a setting which makes clear that it is nothing but a dream. At the opening of *A Handful of Dust* the fiction embodied in the architecture of Hetton, Brenda's familiar face and kind voice, and the peaceful round of daily life concealed from Tony the fact that he lived not among the "happy circle of loved faces," but under "the harsh glare of an alien sun" among the "ravening tiger and the exotic camel, the furtive jackal and the ponderous elephant." At the end he can stare into the mad eyes of Mr. Todd and look at the tangled jungle and empty waste around him and see the truth. But on and on he must go, reading again and again of how all turns out well because the human heart is good and kind.

But back in England the pretense of The City continues untroubled. Brenda, after a period of difficulties, finally marries a rising young politician, Jock Grant-Menzies, whom everyone had expected her to marry before she met Tony. At Hetton, inherited by a cousin, more rooms are closed off, more servants let go, but the old dream hangs on. A noble statue of Tony is set up with the inscription, "Anthony Last of Hetton, Explorer," and the new owner turns the estate into a silver fox farm. Once again animals are penned in ingenious cages and carefully tended. Richard Last innocently hopes to restore the ancient glory of Hetton with these animals, but they, like the previous animals, cannot be relied on. More than one of the keepers has been badly bitten.

In Waugh's first novel, *Decline and Fall*, there is a remarkably fine comic description of the Annual School Sports at Llanabba Castle. The stated purpose of the meet is, of course, to encourage and test the endurance, courage, and physical skills of the young gentlemen being educated at Llanabba. The actual purpose is to impress and gratify, by allowing their sons to win, several important visiting parents. Since the parsimonious daughter of the headmaster has burned the high and low hurdles for firewood during the winter—and the spiked iron railings provided as substitutes are at length declared unsuitable—the major events of the meet are the foot races. Dr. Fagan, the headmaster, has stated firmly that he is not interested in the details of the races but in "style," and very stylish the fête is, with champagne cup, masses of flowers, a pavilion, elaborately printed programs, and the Llandudno Silver Band ceaselessly playing "Men of Harlech." But there is no track, no distance markers are set out, and no decision is made about the distance of the races. The boys chosen to race for the delight of their parents are simply lined up and told to run to a clump of trees and back again. They are to go on racing "until it is time for tea." Mr. Prendergast, the master serving as starter, is dead drunk and fires his first shot from an enormous pistol loaned by Philbrick the butler into one of the boys, little Lord Tangent. Tangent is carried off, and around and around go the boys to the encouraging shouts of "Well run, Percy!" and "Jolly good race," and the unceasing noise of the Llandudno Silver Band. One boy, young Clutterbuck the son of the local brewer, simply omits a lap by hiding behind the trees, and when at last the race is brought to a conclusion by the arrival of the most important guest and the beginning of tea, he "breasts the tape" well ahead of the others. When the win is disputed, Dr. Fagan easily settles the matter by declaring Clutterbuck the winner of the five-furlong race, "a very exacting length," while the other boys are called the winner and runners-up in the three-mile, another "exacting length." The prizes for the winners in these remarkable games are, fittingly enough, awarded by Lady Circumference.

It is, I believe, impossible to discover in Waugh's early novels any specific social arrangements or absolute set of values which he espouses and uses as a standard for measuring the failure of modern life. The pomposity of the old regime is always as ridiculous and self-defeating as the grotesque antics of the new men, and the bits of more ancient history which appear here and there suggest that in Waugh's view human beings have seldom been more gifted or capable of handling things much better than they do in the twentieth century. What Waugh seems to value is order in social and personal life—not any particular order, but order. In his description of the revolutionary government in Mexico in the 1930s, *Robbery Under Law*, Waugh remarks that he does not believe that there is any one God-given form of government, but that a government consistent in its principles and dedicated to keeping order is necessary because "the anarchic elements in society are so strong that it is a wholetime task to keep the peace." Failure to keep the peace results in those meaningless, endless circles around which the characters run in his novels. Once the boundaries, the rules, and the markers are destroyed, as they are at the Llanabba races, then the rational judgment no longer has a framework within which to locate and identify things, and the purpose of human effort is lost. Cupidity, pride, stupidity, and cunning are loosed to complete the wreckage of order and obliterate the meaning of any dimly remembered purpose. However, running round and round until the time and the arrival of the most important guest is no doubt the best possible training for boys about to enter the giddy whirl of Waugh's world, where all rules are off, all the markers gone, all races shams because there is no longer any sense of being a "creature with a defined purpose."

Reluctant Heroes:
The Novels of Graham Greene

Terry Eagleton

At the end of *The Power and the Glory*, the whisky priest dismisses the half-caste who has betrayed him into the hands of the lieutenant of police with a gesture of forgiveness. "The priest waved his hand; he bore no grudge because he expected nothing else of anything human." It is a characteristic moment in Greene, and one which demands analysis. The priest's gesture embodies a paradox: it has the quality of Christian humanity, yet that humanity is ironically dependent on an overriding sense of man's cheapness. The forgiving wave dignifies and devalues man in a single gesture: in enacting a compassionate solidarity with human corruption, it endorses, at the same time, the unchanging reality of that corruption. Yet by the same token, the sceptical disillusion which makes forgiveness automatic qualifies any suggestion of outstanding sanctity on the priest's part: it is easy to forgive creatures from whom one expects little. Greene, then, allows his whisky priest a compassionate holiness while protecting him from the dangers of pride; because the priest devalues himself, knowing the half-caste's weakness within his own body, he can be safely dignified by his author. The priest is raised above corruption without being detached from it; it is by his sense of complicity with sin that he is able partially to transcend it. Through an image of despairing forgiveness, then, Greene is able to dramatise two qualities of feeling which are everywhere deeply interrelated in his work: a pitying compassion which confirms a kind of value without thereby challenging the fact of human worthlessness, and a potentially heroic virtue which is at the same time fiercely or sceptically hostile to the notion of goodness. In both cases, it seems necessary to affirm and deny human value in the same moment.

After his fruitless interview with Father Rank in *The Heart of the Matter,*

From *Exiles and Emigrés: Studies in Modern Literature.* © 1970 by Terry Eagleton. Schocken Books, 1970.

Scobie recognises that he is incapable of conforming to what he sees as orthodox Roman Catholicism. "I know the answers as well as he does. One should look after one's own soul at whatever cost to another, and that's what I can't do, what I shall never be able to do." Scobie's attitude here is essentially Greene's: given a tragic tension between the claims of human relationship and the demands of faith, the rigours of orthodoxy must be guiltily denied in the name of the human. The irony implicit in Greene's view, however, is more subtle than this simple counterpoising. For although an individualist "soul-saving" theology is rejected, the concomitant feelings crystallised around the same phase of Roman Catholic history— the sense of relationships as negative and treacherous, corrosive of personal integrity—are uncompromisingly retained. Indeed they are extended, at times, into a version of the human world as putrid corruption which moves beyond the Catholic tradition into forms of radical Protestantism. The result is a striking paradox: Greene's protagonists turn, at the risk of damnation, from a soul-saving theology to the insidious pressures of humanity, but only in the context of a continually undermining disbelief in the final validity of such claims. Orthodox Catholicism is denied in the name of "humanism"; yet that humanism is itself critically qualified by traditionally Catholic ways of feeling. The upshot of this is a kind of deadlock: the human value of men like Scobie or the whisky priest lies in their readiness to reject an orthodoxy in which they nevertheless continue to believe; yet to acknowledge the superior truth of that orthodoxy, in the act of refusing it, is to confront the inadequacy of the sheerly human commitments they embrace.

By affirming an absolute standard, then, Greene's characters are able to retain a sceptical detachment from human values: a detachment which lends them superiority, in the final analysis, to the rationalist or liberal humanist. Yet by failing that standard in action while endorsing it in consciousness, they can reveal qualities of compassion which are again superior to the humanist's ethic by virtue of the disillusion and damnation—and so lack of self-deception—in which they are rooted. To go through the motions of human love, in a nagging awareness of its inevitable partiality, emerges as a more courageously mature and disinterested attitude than that of the humanist, who trusts naively and destructively to an ultimate value in man. By a curious irony, scepticism, *dégagement* and disbelief furnish a more positive ethic than a committed faith in the possibilities of human good. The fundamental detachment from the mess of secular complexities which permits the Christian a deeper insight than the humanist also allows him to outstrip the humanist on his own territory.

The point may be usefully illustrated by *The Heart of the Matter*. Here, as in all Greene's novels, human relationship is inherently tragic: love, pity, and innocence are lethal because they entice men out of their safely sterile *dégagements* into the corrupting complicities of passion and responsibility, into infectious and conflicting involvements which proliferate beyond control. This is the thesis which the novel is intended to illustrate, and it centres on Scobie because he alone is agonisedly conscious of the inescapable debt and damage implicit in the vulnerabilities of feeling. Because the thesis is given rather than argued, we are asked to admire Scobie's moral pragmatism: his sluggish, compassionate enactment of the motions of relationship, constantly penetrated by a desire for the peace of death, is offered as wiser than that ethic of decisive action which can belong only to the innocent, to those damagingly ignorant of the heart of the matter. Yet what is obvious in the novel is that this tragic version of life is the result, as well as the motivation, of Scobie's behavior: his well-intentioned bungling, his rejection of truth for a patching-up of immediate pain which merely delays and complicates decision, his despairing half-commitment and wry passivity, his self-disgusted inability to value himself, his complicity in allowing others to live a lie, his sentimental attraction to suffering, his disbelief in the possibility of happiness—all these are offered as *responses* to a given hopelessness, but are, just as much, the sources of that paralysis. Scobie acts as he does because he sees the human condition as irreparable, but it is at least partially true that the human condition of the novel is irreparable because he acts as he does. (It is perhaps worth mentioning that the aspect of traditional Christian ethics which Scobie finds most unpalatable—their apparently intransigent insistence on the need to take a stand in certain situations at the cost of immediate damage—is related to a belief that the alternative is likely to be the kind of mess in which Scobie finds himself.) Because human relationships are viewed as inherently unviable, moral blame attaches, not chiefly to Scobie himself, but to the "condition of life"; relationships fail "naturally," evil spreads by its own momentum, and what is then in question is not the quality of action, but the nature of intention, despite its inevitably negative effects. In this continuing concern with motive rather than effect, Greene is, ironically, very Roman Catholic in attitude. It is necessary that Scobie's efforts to redeem his situation should fail, since this validates the novel's thesis; but it is also essential that he should fail with good intentions, since this allows him a moral superiority to his situation without suggesting the possibility of a transforming morality which might effectively challenge that condition. Scobie's "anti-heroism," his failure to conform to his own absolute standard, is the source of his humanism, and thus of a moral worth greater than others—than his trivially malicious fellow-colonialists, for instance. Yet his conscious commitment to the standard he betrays both critically qualifies the humanism, lending him a perspective beyond its limits, and intensifies the price he pays for humane action in a way which renders it even more admirable. Once more, an affirmation of human goodness is accompanied with strict reservations about its validity.

Greene's "bad" Catholics, then, condemn themselves by the rigour of an absolute orthodoxy while consciously breaking its rules. Sanctity, like the damnation of Pinkie in *Brighton Rock*, consists in recognising and refusing the rules simultaneously; the two conditions are allied in this as in other respects. The characters' failure to conform to the standard is essential for humane action; their continued acceptance of it is necessary, not only if they are to be distinguished from non-Christian humanists, but if they are to experience that self-deprecating humility of failure which is, for Greene, the condition of holiness. The standard is refused in the name of the corrupting complexities of routine experience; yet precisely because that experience is still seen, from the standpoint of orthodoxy, as tangled, amorphous, and self-defeating, it provides no basis for the formulation of any alternative ethic by which a man could press through to a questioning of orthodoxy itself. Orthodoxy is submitted to the test of experience, and its inadequacies exposed: but not to the point where it might be shown up as hollow—revealed, for instance, as bad theology—for that would be to slacken the tension between orthodoxy and humanity, and so to destroy that guilty self-disgust by which the believer is rendered superior to the rationalist. The orthodox standard reveals itself in a mainly negative way: in the characters' guilty scrupulousness in offending against it. Their anxiety at being bad Catholics is one of their most notably Catholic traits.

The novels, then, have to preserve a very fine tension between their characters' conscious commitment to orthodoxy and their active rejection of its limits. Yet there is more than one occasion where the effort to sustain the tension leads them into serious ambiguity and confusion. The behaviour of the priest in *The Power and the Glory* is a case in point. If the priest is to be saintly, he must infringe the orthodoxy; yet if he is to have the self-castigating humility of holiness, he must also remain convinced of its truth. The novel does not everywhere succeed in persuading us of the logicality of this paradox. In the prison scene, for instance, when the priest is confronted with the intolerably pious complacency of the middle-aged woman beside him in the darkness, he is almost able to articulate his "unorthodoxy" into an affirmative argument which could undermine the falsity of the woman's religious respectability. He refuses, for example, to accept her dogmatic assertion that the sexual intercourse of the couple in the dark corner of the cell is mortal sin, and allows only that "We don't know. It may be." Yet although he is here on the point of formulating his superior depth of experience into a "position," his criticism of established religion must not be allowed to develop into a radical assault, for this would be to deprive him of the very standard by which he measures his own humble unworthiness, and so the means by which he achieves a kind of heroism. Yet the problem persists: if the priest is able to extend forgiving leniency to the sexual sins of others, why is he unable to do this in his own case? The priest is extraordinarily stringent with himself, but ceaselessly liberal with others; he can perceive the bad faith of respectable Catholicism and its pressing dangers to the soul, but is at the same time gripped with scruples for such things as saying mass in mudhuts without an altar stone. The ambiguity is also evident at another point: in his self-accusation of sins which we are forced to take on credence because they are nowhere shown in the novel. "The words proud, lustful, envious, cowardly, ungrateful . . . he was all these things." There is a genuine obscurity here: either the priest is accurate in his self-evaluation, in which case his apparent virtue is cast damagingly into question; or he is self-deceived, in which case the novel can impress us with his humility only at the cost of implying in him a disturbing and ultimately unaccountable lack of insight. The novel effectively refuses to choose: either possibility would harm the image of the whisky priest which it is concerned to project. One is forced to conclude that the priest's self-estimation cannot really be true, since it obstinately refuses to accommodate itself to the novel's actual presentation of him; but neither can it really be false, since the authenticity of the priest's experience depends upon our giving at least some credence to the accuracy of his judgments and the reality of his sense of failure. To deny this is to conclude that the priest's perceptive insight into the condition of others consorts mysteriously with a peculiar obtuseness in his view of himself—an obtuseness which the term "humility" is too indiscriminate to cover.

Yet "humility" is, of course, the formal explanation which the novel offers for his incongruency: the priest's overbearing sense of inadequacy as a man of God. That inadequacy, however, lies largely in infringements of an orthodoxy which he recognises as actively harmful in the case of the woman prisoner, or, later in the novel, in the bourgeois religion of the hygienically Lutheran Lehrs. It is his humility which prevents him from pressing through his sense of these falsities into anything which might approach a radical criticism: he believes that the woman prisoner needs sympathy, not correction. Yet in emphasising this humility as his virtue, the novel also covertly indulges in the priest what is really a kind of defectiveness, akin to his nervous giggling and card-tricks; it exploits the priest's inability to take himself seriously in order to ward off criticisms of the Church, while at the same time giving the priest's experience a serious value. The novel, in other words, needs to endorse the significance of its protagonist's experience, but needs to prevent him from doing the same. The humility is part of a general experience which objectively aims a radical criticism at orthodoxy, but it is simultaneously used to forestall any subjective appropriation of such criticism on the part of the priest himself—a move which might lead the novel and its hero into the camp of the revolutionary lieutenant of police. When the priest confronts the lieutenant before his death, the novel's attitude is less than candid: the priest agrees, briefly and unspecifically, with the lieutenant's attack on the established Church, but then affirms the superiority of the Christian faith:

> "What an excuse it all was, what a fake. Sell all and give to the poor—that was the lesson, wasn't it? And Senora so-and-so, the druggist's wife, would say the family wasn't really deserving of charity, and Senor This, That and the Other would say that if they starved, what else did they deserve, they were Socialist anyway, and the priest—you—would notice who had done his Easter duty and paid his Easter offering. . . ."
>
> The priest said, "You are so right." He added quickly, "Wrong too, of course."

"Well, we have ideas too," the lieutenant was saying. "No more money for saying prayers, no more money for building places to say prayers in. We'll give people food instead, teach them to read, give them books. We'll see they don't suffer."

"But if they want to suffer. . . . We have facts, too, we don't try to alter—that the world's unhappy whether you are rich or poor—unless you are a saint and there aren't many of those. It's not worth bothering too much about a little pain here."

The area of real agreement between priest and policeman—their common dislike of established religion—is quickly blurred over, and the differences sharpened. The priest's callous attitude to suffering can be made more palatable by an appeal to his experience—he, after all, has known pain, and so his last statement can be made to seem courageous rather than cruel—but it is really a kind of trick. We are persuaded, by the depth and value of the priest's experience, to accept from his mouth an attitude we would be less willing to take from the pious clerics whose way of life he has renounced; and yet the statement is the kind of platitude which belongs essentially to their world. The novel appeals to the priest's wisdom only as a way of asking us to accept the persuasions of an orthodoxy which it has been part of that wisdom to criticise. So, once more, humane values are both affirmed and heavily qualified: the whisky priest is revealed as superior to bourgeois pieties by virtue of his humane compassion, but superior to humanism by virtue of his identification with orthodox piety. A precariously narrow line must be balanced between a rejection of love, and a belief that it can be in any sense effective.

There are similar unresolved ambiguities in almost all of Greene's "Catholic" novels. Why in any case does the unheroic whisky priest stay in the country at the risk of his life? Why does Scobie stay in his African colony? Why does Sarah Miles, in *The End of the Affair*, make a vow to a God she doesn't believe in? Why does she see herself as "a bitch and a fake"? Why does Querry, in *A Burnt-Out Case*, stay overnight in the forest to comfort his injured servant Deo Gratias? At the root of all these questions lies a common problem. Each of these facts counts to the credit of the character concerned: in different ways, they are evidence of moral distinction, of a capacity for some kind of love. Yet love, in the world of Greene's novels, is an even more treacherous passion than pity: "I don't believe in anyone who says love, love, love," says Louise Scobie, in response to the self-dramatising advances of Wilson: "It means self, self, self." And this is an attitude which Greene's novels on the whole endorse. Love is a self-regarding emotion or a destructive possessiveness; it is innocent of the reality of failure, and so dangerously naive, finally indistinguishable from egoism. There is no alternative in Greene's world between the diseased compassion of a Scobie, dissolving the self's integrity into the shapelessness of a growing stain, and the callow self-assertiveness of a Wilson or the public-school bumptiousness of a Bagster. Each of the novels, then, confronts a crucial difficulty. If God's love is real, it must be in some sense incarnated in human living: Greene is sufficiently Roman Catholic to reject any non-incarnational view of divine love. Yet how is this to be shown, when human love is also seen, in an extreme Protestant mode, as merely one more deceptive form of the pride of self, one more sign of false consciousness and bad faith? In any final analysis, the issue is incapable of adequate resolution: all the novels can hope to do is to suggest the presence of charity in particular men and women while simultaneously protecting them from a pharisaic awareness of their own better feelings.

But this can be done only by convincing the protagonist of a curious lack of self-knowledge, or simply by obscuring vital evidence. The case of the priest in *The Power and the Glory* is again relevant: why does the giggling, frightened, self-doubting renegade risk death by refusing to join his fellow-clerics in their flight from the country? The question of motivation is not convincingly established:

> "That's another thing I don't understand," the lieutenant said, "why you— of all people —should have stayed when the others ran."
>
> "They didn't all run," the priest said.
>
> "But why did you stay?"
>
> "Once," the priest said, 'I asked myself that. The fact is, a man isn't presented suddenly with two courses to follow: one good and one bad. He gets caught up. The first year—well, I didn't believe there was really any cause to run. Churches have been burnt before now. You know how often. It doesn't mean much. I thought I'd stay till next month, say, and see if things were better. Then— oh, you don't know how time can slip by. . . . Do you know I suddenly realised that I was the only priest left for miles around? There was one priest in particular—he had always disapproved of me. I have a tongue, you know, and it used to wag. He said— quite rightly—that I wasn't a firm character. He escaped. It felt—you'll laugh at this—just as it did at school when a bully I had been afraid of—for years —got too old for any more teaching and was turned out. . . .
>
> "It was when he left I began to go to pieces. One thing went after another. I got careless about my duties. I began to drink. It would have been much better, I think, if I had gone too. Because pride was at work all the time. Not love of God. . . . I thought I was a fine fellow to have stayed when the others had gone. . . . I wasn't any use, but I stayed. At least, not much use. . . . It's a mistake one makes—to think just because a thing is difficult or dangerous. . . ." He made a flapping motion with his hands.

The priest has taken no definable moral decision: a man "gets caught up," and then "you don't know how time can slip by"; the vagueness of this is then concealed by a displacement of attention to the self-righteous fellow-priest who fled. That priest's flight throws the whisky priest himself into a morally favourable light, but also qualifies his courage: it was after that incident that he "began to go to pieces," and one thing led, automatically, to another. The priest then settles on pride as his motive, and in doing so once more appeals to a moral condition which, given the lack of essential evidence, the reader can neither confirm nor effectively question. Because of his pride, he "wasn't any use"; but that too explicitly demeaning comment is then instantly qualified: "At least, not much use." The priest's final comment trails off into inarticulate ambiguity: "It's a mistake one makes— to think just because a thing is difficult or dangerous." If this is to be interpreted as hinting that the priest consciously embraced those dangers, judging his action more valuable on their account, then, even if this too is merely to be dismissed as proud self-deception, it seems difficult to square its suggestion of conscious courage with the notion that he has simply been "caught up."

If the whisky priest was merely "caught up," the same can be said of Scobie. Scobie's inability actively to control his environment, to prevent the inexorable spreading of evil through the air breathed by innocents, if offered as part of the nature of things, a defeatism nurtured by the "conditions of life"; but it also allows him to be led passively into a possibly heroic posture, by the sheer logic of his unheroically fragmented situation-ethics. Scobie, too, gets "caught up," and like the whisky priest what he gets caught up in is a kind of sanctity which transcends pragmatism. It is important for the novel both to affirm the qualify of virtue—to show it as more than mere circumstantial determinism—and yet to stress at the same time the seemingly inexorable, partial, piecemeal process by which it is attained, so as to avoid any damagingly pharisaic implication that it was a course of action he ever consciously chose. A kind of self-sacrifice possible only to the morally courageous must be endorsed, but not at the cost of questioning the wisdom of a pragmatic passivity. Once again, the novel has to tread an awkwardly narrow line between conscious and confused motivations, between the objective reality of goodness and a subjective unawareness of its presence. Scobie's impotent passivity, his chronic incapacity for decisive moral action, is a criticism of his behaviour; yet it is lessened in force, not only because the mood and comment of the novel cooperate in confirming the intelligence of this stance (even the climate is made to suggest its natural inevitability: "This isn't a climate for emotion . . . anything like hate or love drives a man off his head"), but because it is precisely his passivity, his desperately pragmatic scepticism, which leads him to a courageous act and at the same time shields him from any destructive belief in its value. Because Scobie is caught up by his very pragmatism into an action which both transcends that process and yet is also its last, logical step, the novel is able to validate and criticise this ethic at the same time. He is led, by decent, "rational" behaviour, to a kind of courage which outstrips the behaviour of the decent rationalist.

A similar ambiguity is apparent in *The End of the Affair*; in this novel, however, it is built into the very structure of the work. The novel operates essentially at two distinct levels: on one level we are shown the conscious motives and actions of the characters; on a deeper level, the mysteriously obscure purposes which they are fulfilling, unknown to themselves, as the agents of God's devious love. In this way, Greene is able to provide himself with a structural framework for resolving the disparities of human self-estimation and the reality of the divine love at work within and between men. Because the action of God is now an unconscious process, insidiously and invisibly at work, the difficulties of accommodating the power of this love to corrupt human motive and behaviour are lessened; Sarah, Bendrix, Henry, Parkis and more minor characters can act consciously at one level while the true "meaning" of their behaviour is revealed only within a deeper dimension of which they are all for the most part unaware. In this way, Sarah's dramatic conversion may be squared with her previous agnosticism because it is an event for which she is really in no sense fully responsible; we are asked to believe that it is the organic culmination of that invisible process which began, unknown to herself, with her secret baptism as a child. Because Sarah is not fully responsible for her own holiness, she can be given moral value without this qualifying her own judgment on herself as "a bitch and a fake"; the two levels, divine and human, can coexist without mutual interference, and one distinct advantage of this is that Greene is thereby able to preserve his thesis that common human life is sterile and corrupt. Yet at the same time the action of grace cannot be shown as wholly deterministic and invisibly disembodied, for this would be to equate Sarah the saint with Bendrix and Smythe the rationalists. Somehow, the two levels of meaning must interact—Sarah must be shown, as a person, to have the qualities of God's love—without one level being fully reconciled to the other, since this would suggest that men were of their own efforts capable of merit—a thesis the novel wants to reject. So once more there is a problem: we can neither believe, nor disbelieve, Sarah's judgment of herself. To believe it is to dislocate too radically the action of grace and the quality of persons: to render Sarah morally equal to Bendrix. But to disbelieve it is to suggest that the love of God can issue in outstanding human value—can actively redeem, at least in a local sense, that fallenness which for Greene is "given" from the outset. The ambiguity is "resolved," as it was in *The Power and the Glory*, by the tactic of concealing essential evidence. Sarah, much more than the whisky priest, is presented to us obliquely, by virtue of the novel's structure: she is seen either from the tendentious angle of Bendrix's own tortured account, or through her own self-demeaning record in her diary. In neither case is she seen "objectively." What we *see* would suggest that her low self-estimation springs from the deceptions of humility; yet, as with the whisky priest, it is vital, if we are not to miss the tension between human cheapness and divine power, that we do not entirely dismiss it as such.

There is a parallel obscurity in the question of Sarah's vow to a God in whom, at the time, she has no conscious belief. "Why did this promise stay," she asks herself, "like an ugly vase a friend has given and one waits for a maid to break it . . .?" Sarah's own irritated bewilderment suggests an answer: it stayed because God wanted it to, against the grain of Sarah's own frustrated bitterness at the loss of Bendrix's love which was its result. Yet although responsibility for the persistence of the vow is to that extent removed from Sarah's own control, and any dangerous hint of consciously heroic love thereby avoided, it is not wholly that: for Sarah's commitment to her promise, against her own deepest instincts, *is* offered, elsewhere, as a distinguishing mark of personal sanctity. It is neither simply a question of a courageous decision which elevates her morally above others, nor simply a choice made for her by God himself: by sustaining this ambiguity, the novel refuses to choose clearly between seeing Sarah merely as the determined instrument of grace, or seeing her as a self-determining saint. Either alternative, in itself, would be detrimental to Greene's viewpoint. Thus, it is important that Sarah's death should be markedly unheroic—it results from her catching cold—yet it is also important that the cold should be caught in her efforts to avoid Bendrix, and so the temptation to betray God. Her death can neither be consciously chosen nor merely accidental: she must be protected alike from the falsities of both Christian martyrdom and sheerly human contingency. Once more, the possibility of outstanding virtue must be affirmed in the context of a radical suspicion of conscious goodness.

In a later novel, *A Burnt-Out Case*, the clash between "heroism" and "anti-heroism" becomes a dominant theme. Querry, the burnt-out architect, is cynically aware of his own worthlessness; yet his actions trigger off a conspiracy to enshrine him as a saint. The chief actions which lead us to be suspicious of his own radical self-disgust are his care of the injured African Deo Gratias, and his concern for the vulnerably innocent, maltreated Marie Rycker. Here is the incident where he follows Deo Gratias into the forest, vaguely aware that he may have met with an accident:

> His own presence here was hardly more explicable than that of Deo Gratias. The thought of his servant lying injured in the forest waiting for the call or footstep of any human being would perhaps at an earlier time have vexed him all night until he was forced into making a token gesture. But now that he cared for nothing, perhaps he was being driven only by a vestige of intellectual curiosity. What had brought Deo Gratias here out of the safety and familiarity of the leproserie? . . . What was the meaning of the sweat he had seen pouring down the man's face? . . . Interest began to move painfully in him like a nerve that had been frozen. He had lived with inertia so long that he examined his "interest" with clinical detachment.

At the end of the path into the forest, Querry finds the African injured and paralysed with fright:

> After ten minutes of struggle Querry managed to drag his limbs
> out of the water—it was all he could do. . . . The fingerless hand
> fell on Querry's arm like a hammer and held him there.
>
> There was nothing to be done but wait for the morning. . . . He
> took Deo Gratias' hand to reassure him. . . . Deo Gratias grunted
> twice, and then uttered a word. It sounded like "Pendélé."

Querry's motives for pursuing his servant are "inexplicable"; or, if a motive
is demanded, it is "perhaps" merely curiosity. Yet that curiosity, while
possibly "clinical," is itself obscurely related to what the novel sees as best
in Querry: his persistent search, despite the conscious detachment, for the
path which leads to "Pendélé," to a mysterious haven of peace. So while
his concern for Deo Gratias is at one level an intellectual interest which is
not allowed to count in his favour, the African's curious disappearance
stirs in him, at a deeper level, that yearning for an absolute reality which
renders him in some senses morally superior to those more committed
rationalists or pragmatists who discount such strivings—Dr. Colin, or the
Father Superior. The decision to seek out Deo Gratias is "inexplicable"
rather than clearly defined; and once this is taken, Querry is passively
caught up in an act of charity, led on by his own half-conscious motive to
the point where "There was nothing to be done but wait for the morning."
That "nothing to be done" qualifies any hint of compassion by suggesting
a circumstantial inevitability; yet the same comment cannot adequately
explain his taking hold of the leper's hand to comfort him. One is forced
to conclude that the novel is using here, rather less emphatically, something
of the technique of *The End of the Affair*. Like Sarah, Querry's deepest motive
is a search for God, but its very unconsciousness prevents him from being
in possession of his own experience and so running the contaminating risks
of valuing himself highly. Yet again, as in *The End of the Affair*, the meri-
torious motive cannot be allowed to remain wholly submerged: if it is to
be more than mere determinism, it must find tangible expression at some
point in the character's actual behaviour. And so the novel shows Querry
perform a charitable act without, however, revealing his attitude: the account is kept scrupulously external. In a similar way, Querry's involvement
with Marie Rycker appears to indicate in him a kind of negative humanity—
it is chiefly through Querry's eyes that her brutally egoistic husband is
exposed for what he is—yet once more the involvement which leads to
the night in the hotel and so to Querry's death simply "happens" as an
accumulation of trivial actions, a process within which no isolatable moment
of commitment occurs. The balance, as usual, is precariously preserved:
Querry's comments on the sterility of the Ryckers's marriage count to un-
derscore his cynical view of man; yet they also count, at least in a negative
sense, to reveal in him a moral sensitivity and insight. Again, Querry's
journey to the leper-hospital is a conscious renunciation of humanity; yet
he is anxious from the beginning to help with menial tasks, and the dis-

crepancy of motive is not successfully accounted for. Once more, we cannot explain the incongruency by saying that Querry is merely self-deceived, for this would be finally to invalidate a misanthropy which the novel wishes at least in part to endorse, and to slip into the camp of those who wish to make Querry a cult-hero and destroy him in the process; but on the other hand, we are meant to see, as with Scobie and the whisky priest, that the very stringency of his self-condemnation discloses a negative moral value:

> He thought: there was only one thing I could do and that is reason enough for being here. I can promise you. Marie, *toute à toi*, all of you, never again from boredom or vanity to involve another human being in my lack of love. I shall do no more harm.

This both emphasises the deceptions of human feeling, and by the same token reveals a sort of humanity in Querry. The novel is able to reconcile its affirmation and rejection of human love by suggesting that affirmative qualities must be implicit in such a rejection. In a parallel way, the book also implies that there is value present in the very unflinching honesty with which Querry confronts his own worthlessness: it is his honesty, after all, which distinguishes his own "dark night of the soul" from Rycker's. To assert this is to lend Querry dignity without questioning his low self-estimation: in this novel, Greene can reconcile his paradox of a man being at once worthless and better than he thinks by finding his best qualities in the way he faces his worthlessness. The bad Catholic is redeemed by the very intensity of his scruples: "You must have had a lot of belief once to miss it the way you do," Colin tells Querry. It is no longer a case, as it was with Scobie and the whisky priest, that Querry is especially self-deceived: it is true, as the novel shows us, that he has little or no capacity for genuine love. Nevertheless, the man who continues to seek faith has already found it: once again value lies in good intentions, however obscure to consciousness. Querry shares the pragmatic rationalism of Dr. Colin, against the pious egoism of Rycker or Father Thomas; yet his quest for an absolute value beyond the mess of human reality also lends him a certain superiority to the rationalists. He shares the Superior's lack of concern with moral theology, but also, in a way hardly evident to himself, Father Thomas's preoccupation with absolute questions; they are both, as Colin comments, "men of extremes," whereas Colin himself—the most positively admirable character in the novel—is not. Querry is thus protected from being completely identified either with materialistic rationalism or metaphysical dogmatism, with a conscious commitment to the human world or with an egoistic asceticism which rejects it. In the case of Querry, as of Scobie, Greene is able to have his pragmatic scepticism and reach beyond it at the same time.

It is worth turning at this point to *The Quiet American*. The book centres on a conflict, common to Greene's writing, between the destructive ruthlessness of innocence and principled action on the one hand, and the corrupting guilt of pragmatic humanism on the other. Pyle, the quiet

American, is strong, innocent, decisive and so dangerous; Fowler is weak, cynical, compromised and corrupted, and so both inferior and superior to Pyle's kind of virtue. Like the priest of *The Power and the Glory*, Fowler opposes decisively radical social action; he does so in the name of a desire to preserve life which, like the priest's, is based on a belief in the unchanging meanness of human nature—a belief which Pyle is unable to challenge because it is founded on Fowler's "experience," as against the rigidities of his own "ideology." (The radically ideological nature of the stance to which Fowler's experience has led him is not, of course, allowed.) It is important that Fowler's jaundiced view of the human situation should not go uncriticised—indeed, as often with Greene, it is part of the quality of that view that its exponent should be self-critical. Fowler can see that Pyle is in many ways the "better" man, and so can we; indeed, given a wholly different context, there is in the relationship of Fowler and Pyle a faint but detectable resonance of the relationship of Pinkie and Rose in *Brighton Rock*. In both cases, the role of the innocent partner is unwittingly to reveal to the other his own corruption. But Fowler's self-disgust lends credence to his condemnation of Pyle at the same time as it permits him to acknowledge his inferiority: the self-disgust springs from the same depth of "experience" from which the criticism of Pyle's murderously naive ideologising is launched. And because Fowler is empty of self-esteem, his dislike of Pyle can be seen as disinterested. In a better world, Pyle's energy and commitment would overshadow Fowler's flaccid cynicism, and to this extent Fowler is critically placed; but because Fowler's view that a better world is impossible is, despite the criticism, endorsed, Pyle can be rejected. (He is, in any case, something of a straw target, with his crew-cut and volumes of ideology; the effective humour reaped at his expense comes suspiciously easily.) The man who rates human potential highly is thus destructive; the man with a confused regard for life has a low estimation of its worth.

Yet once more Greene faces an intractable problem. If the rejection of Pyle's murderous innocence is to have validity, it must be made from a humane standpoint; yet what is being denied is in fact the view that significant human value exists. Fowler, then, must be allowed a certain humanity— enough, in fact, to let him conquer Pyle in ideological argument without convicting him of ideological views, and so of an articulate commitment to purposive action. Thus, when the two men are arguing in the watch-tower, Fowler can clinch the political discussion by commenting: "I've been here a long time. You know, it's lucky I'm not *engagé*, because there are things I might be tempted to do —because here in the East—well, I don't like Ike. I like—well, these two." "These two" are the silent Vietnamese soldiers who crouch with them in the tower; and Fowler's appeal to them is meant to undercut the "unreal" ideologising to the level of the simply human. "I'd like those two poor buggers there to be happy—that's all." He appeals to a life in which the Vietnamese peasants can simply get enough rice and avoid being shot at: "They want one day to be much the same as another."

Fowler's political position is, in fact, deeply confused. The question of how peace and enough rice are to be attained—the fact that it is, inescapably, a *political* question, and that it slides over certain additional issues, such as whether the peasants are to govern themselves or be governed by imperialist regimes—is seriously blurred. Fowler is, of course, rabidly anti-American, but to avoid the disruptions of "ideology" he must launch his satirical assault on U.S. imperialism from a nonpolitical standpoint: from a commitment to "the human" which detaches it from its inevitably political embodiments, and which moreover must avoid imbuing "the human" itself with too much value. This is the point of his suggestion that the peasants merely want enough rice and a settled routine: to imply a sympathy with the peasant which at the same time contains the judgment that he lacks the capacity to see further than his stomach. Yet there is a further, more serious ambiguity in Fowler's attitude: the conflict between his passionate anti-Americanism and his carefully nurtured cult of dispassionately objective *dégagement*. The first would indicate a humane indignation; the second implies its opposite. The problem of resolving these attitudes is lessened to some degree by the fact that Fowler's anti-Americanism is for the most part less an objection to what the Americans *do*—and so, at least by implication, a commitment to their victims—than a criticism of what they *are*, an almost physical disgust for the trivia of hairstyle and manner. Fowler's anti-Americanism is closer to a vulgar snobbery than to a shrewd analysis of the brutalities of U.S. imperialism, a fact which the novel itself seems significantly not to question. Nevertheless, Fowler's anti-American feeling draws him emotionally towards an engagement he would intellectually repudiate: if he were not *dégagé*, there are things he "might be tempted to do," morally committed courses of action he might follow. These would be "temptation," since committed action is bound to fail and destroy: one of the novel's epigraphs is Arthur Clough's comment that "I do not like being moved: for the will is excited; and action is a most dangerous thing." Yet such tempting actions might also reveal a kind of moral fibre: they would have behind them the ratifying force of Fowler's "best self," his disgust at imperialist manipulation.

The climax of the novel is Fowler's submission to temptation. Swayed by a "moment of emotion," a swift response of shocked horror at the bomb-murders with which Pyle is involved, he betrays the American to his death. Again, there is no clearly defined moment of moral decision: having decided to have Pyle silenced, he gives him various chances to escape. Yet in taking this action, Fowler is obedient to the impulse of common humanity he felt for the soldiers in the tower: his detachment is exposed as self-deception and yields to principled decision. To the extent that his action emerges from the humanism which gives him a title to reject Pyle, it is related to what is most morally valuable in him: by performing it, he transcends his sterile cynicism and betrays a feeling for life. Yet to the extent to which the act of consigning Pyle to his death reaches beyond the confusions and half-commitments of pragmatism into serious involvement, it must fall under the strictures which Fowler himself has made on Pyle. Thus Fowler's action both substantiates a humanity which is, in the last analysis, more worthy than Pyle's fanaticism, and at the same time, through Fowler's guilt at having killed a kind and honourable man, serves to ratify the wisdom of his previous detachment. Both involvement and detachment are therefore criticised; but the "moral" is not quite that detachment is desirable, but impossible. Detachment is desirable, but only to the degree that it does not sterilise the humane feelings by which criticism of others' more committed (and so more destructive) involvements can be made. The uncommitted man must be shown as both inhumanly cynical and humanly sensitive: either perspective can be selected to attack the revolutionary, but both are necessary if the attack is to rest on a version of man both inferior and superior to the revolutionary's own. And this, essentially, is what Greene's novels want to do.

II

It is possible to express the tensions we have traced within Greene's work in slightly different terms. There is a sense in which the ethics of Greene's "bad" Catholic characters differ from the ethics of pragmatic humanism only in the guilt by which the actions they lead to are accompanied. Yet the guilt is an essential element: as we have seen, it allows humanism to be both qualified and endorsed. Greene's kind of Christianity, in fact, makes remarkably little difference to the quality of human life itself: it makes its difference felt chiefly at the end of life, in the reality of death. God is peace and love, the Pendélé at the end of the path through the decayed human jungle, glimpsed in frustrating moments through its undergrowth; in *The End of the Affair*, God is the presence which emerges when human relationships have broken down. Neither Bendrix nor Fowler are Christians, and the fact has some significance: because of it, Greene can distance himself to some extent from their crude acquisitiveness. Yet what is striking is how little difference belief would really make to either man's attitudes. Fowler himself defines what faith might mean to him in a way which suggests this fact: "The job of a reporter is to expose and record. I had never in my career discovered the inexplicable. . . . I had no visions or miracles in my repertoire of memories." Christianity is seen as the "inexplicable," which makes a difference to ordinary human life chiefly by not fitting in with it—by being superadded vision and miracle. And in this sense, it need not alter the sceptical version of man which Bendrix and Fowler hold. Through these men, Greene does not simply express a view of what the world seems like without God; he expresses what the world seems like with God too. It is just that, for Sarah and Deo Gratias, there is something beyond the world which the atheist does not recognise. Greene's attitude in this respect seems, indeed, to have become increasingly pessimistic as he has developed: it is true that divine grace makes a qualitative difference to the whisky priest's behaviour in *The Power and the Glory*, and still, although less true, in the case of Scobie; but in Sarah's case, the symbols of divine love are miracles which occur after her death. She is, so to speak, most effectively present in the world after she has left it.

There is a theological basis to this way of seeing. Although Greene's novels centre again and again on the truths of passion and crucifixion, the definitive event of Christian faith—resurrection—finds no place in their economy. God is not seen as the living power which sustains and renews human relationship; He is what is found among the debris of their collapse. We can return at this point to a problem touched on earlier: the tension between Greene's extreme Protestant view of men as radically corrupt, and his more orthodox belief in a divine love which is somehow tangibly incarnated. The novels escape this dilemma by seeing God as incarnate, not in human creativity, but in human failure. Failure, for Greene, is at once what is most essentially human about man (Scobie speaks of "the loyalty we all feel to unhappiness—the sense that that is where we really belong") and yet is also what reveals him in the least heroic or impressive light. It is therefore safe to love failure, as Sarah "loves" the disfigured Smythe, because it involves one in loving, not humanity, but its negation—in loving that in man which finally points beyond him. "I am kissing pain," says Sarah when she presses her lips to Smythe's strawberry-mark, "and pain belongs to You as happiness never does." The more men are exposed as broken and corrupted failures, the more one can love them and so have one's "humanism," but the more, by the same token, they endorse an anti-humanist view of their fallenness. The more you love men, the less you value them: "Here," says Scobie, "you could love human beings nearly as God loved them, knowing the worst." When the whisky priest ponders that "it needed a god to die for the half-hearted and the corrupt," he dignifies and demeans humanity at the same time. In the light of this, the humility of Greene's characters gains an added significance: what the novels do not see is that their characters' inability to value themselves is intimately related to their inability to value others. Their attitude is the direct reverse of the traditional Christian insight that, in order to be able genuinely to love another, one must also be able to love oneself.

The whisky priest's sense of solidarity with suffering, guilt, and weakness is one instance of a pervasive belief, in almost all of Greene's novels, that it is here that God is most concretely present. It is only by the experience of suffering, guilt, weakness, and so of compassion, that the pharisaic egoisms of respectable religion, hygienic innocence, and the ethic of success can be avoided. Yet this, while radical in its attitude towards orthodoxy ("God might forgive cowardice and passion, but was it possible to forgive the habit of piety?"), is at another point deeply conservative: it leads the whisky priest to a rejection of those beliefs which would hope to remove the unhappiness where men "really belong." Once men cannot be pitied they cannot be loved, since the love was, all along, only a form of pity. Scobie wants his wife Louise to be happy, but can't love success: "He thought: it was the hysterical woman who felt the world laughing behind her back that I loved. I love failure: I can't love success. And how successful she looks, sitting there: one of the saved." The extent to which pity degrades its object (the term is apt) is realised: it occurs to Scobie that Louise is "someone of human stature with her own sense of responsibility, not simply the object of his care and kindness." He half-recognises that, precisely because his "automatic terrible pity" goes out to *any* human need, regardless of the particular persons involved, it is to that degree a kind of abstraction. Yet although the dangers of pity are seen, it is preferable, in the end, to the callow arrogance of love.

Greene's novels, then, have to accommodate their strong impulse towards a rejection of human experience itself as inherently flawed—the instinct of the police lieutenant, who wishes to "destroy everything" and begin afresh—to a tired respect for a pragmatic negotiation of ordinary life. It is worth looking finally at one of Greene's earliest novels, *Brighton Rock*, since there some of the tensions we have discussed seem least satisfactorily resolved. The evil of Pinkie, in *Brighton Rock*, lies in his uncompromisingly total rejection of ordinary human reality: of the texture of human experience itself. His evil is closely linked with his social and sexual ignorance: he embodies a kind of pure negation, an "annihilating eternity." Yet Pinkie's view of experience is time and again confirmed by the novel itself: his revolted rejection of life is underpinned by the book's mood and imagery, which remorselessly elaborate the selective sordities of Brighton to the status of an entire human condition: "The sun slid off the sea and like a cuttlefish shot into the sky with the stain of agonies and endurances." Brighton, a seedy, flashy, candy-floss world, is seen by the novel with a coldly dehumanising perception which parallels Pinkie's own responses. "Down the steps of the Cosmopolitan came a couple of expensive women with bright brass hair and ermine coats and heads close together like parrots exchanging metallic confidences . . . they flashed their pointed painted nails at each other and cackled." "Bright," "brass," "metallic," "flashed," "painted," "cackled": these are the terms in which the whole of Brighton is seen, and the verbal artifice, the over-insistent, over-written dragooning of casual detail into tendentious effect, is characteristic of the whole book. The Brighton world finds its unreal epitome in Ida Arnold, the brassily sentimental whore who intervenes to save the innocent Rose from the evil Pinkie:

> "You leave her alone," the woman said. "I know all about you."
> It was as if she were in a strange country: the typical Englishwoman abroad. She hadn't even got a phrasebook. She was as far from either of them as she was from Hell—or Heaven. Good and evil lived in the same country, spoke the same language, came together like old friends, feeling the same completion, touching hands beside the iron bedstead.

Ida enters the metaphysical world of Pinkie and Rose as a self-righteous day-tripper from the land of pragmatic humanism; for all her knowledge of "human nature" she is a vulgar and irrelevant voice in the absolutist country into which she blunders. Pinkie and Rose belong to a metaphysical élite who have transcended the seedy ethics of quotidian experience for the superior world of those "real" enough to embrace or reject divine salvation. "She!" says Pinkie of Ida. "She's just nothing"; and the novel confirms his judgment.

Pinkie, then, is damned because of his incapacity to surrender himself to life; yet we are nowhere shown that life as particularly worth surrendering to. We condemn his murders, of course, but not from any standpoint of sympathy with his brutal or broken victims. If Ida Arnold and Pinkie's underworld friends are truly representative of the human condition, then it is difficult to avoid feeling that Pinkie is damned by his author for holding a view of life which the novel validates.

At least, this would be so if it were not for Rose, Pinkie's innocent girl. Rose is the mute, living embodiment of the terrible judgment in store for Pinkie, accompanying him everywhere, inseparable from his nature; it is Rose who incarnates that capacity for loving self-abandonment which manifests Pinkie as lost. Rose is the criterion by which Pinkie is damned, yet at least two facts in the novel work against the effectiveness of this. First, Rose's goodness is entirely passive: it cannot assume the form of positive action, for positive action belongs to the self-righteously ethical world of Ida Arnold, the realm of obtusely interfering do-gooding. Action, in any case, presumes a knowledge of the world which the incorruptible Rose cannot be allowed. Rose is the only person in the world who symbolises the love which Pinkie has denied, but she is hardly "in" the world at all: she belongs to Brighton no more than Pinkie. (It is significant, incidentally, that Brighton is where Pinkie grew up: by making his home a no-home, a seaside resort for London, a town usually thought of as a place people visit rather than inhabit, the novel detaches him from any natural locality and so renders his evil less environmentally explicable.) Secondly, Rose's association with Pinkie works as much in his favour as to his disadvantage: they are linked together as the complementary polarities of good and evil, and the differences between them are less significant, for both of them, than their mutual opposition to the shabbily unheroic world of Ida Arnold. Rose recognises what Pinkie is, in a world too flashily one-dimensional to evaluate the terrifying meaning of his life; Pinkie, unlike other Greene characters, is fully aware of his own metaphysical significance, and it is a criticism of the world that it cannot see this significance. Pinkie may be "evil," but he is not "corrupt": his evil is a pure, pristine integrity, a priestly asceticism which refuses the contaminations of ordinary living. Moreover, in this early novel, the disgusted desire to shake oneself free from experience is not emphasised as naiveté or false consciousness; the incidents which reveal Pinkie's unworldly integrity of evil—his sexual clumsiness with the girl in the car-park, for instance—count at least as much against social "decadence" as against Pinkie himself. Pinkie *is* innocent, but while he is damned for it, it is also a mark of his superiority to the Ida

Arnolds of the world. His innocence is not a fault which could be corrected with time, as one could argue, perhaps, about Pyle in *The Quiet American*: it is integral to what he is, part of the essence of his evil. And to that degree it is part of his general, metaphysical superiority to the Brighton world. Pinkie cannot understand human reality, but the human reality we are shown has nothing substantial about it to be understood; Pinkie and Brighton are two negations linked in a fixed opposition. Pinkie regards human involvement as despicable weakness, and is damned for it; yet the novel's major image of such involvement is the despicable Ida.

Brighton Rock, then, has its share of the ambiguities we have seen elsewhere in Greene, but it also has its divergencies. By choosing a wholly evil figure as its focus, the book can indulge that vision of the world as putrid corruption which is a significant element of other novels without this leading to difficult tensions with a simultaneous suggestion of virtue. Virtue is affirmed elsewhere, in Rose; yet in a way which, as we have seen, connives at rather than qualifies the detailed imagery of fallenness. Again, by choosing an evil "hero" (and the term has, perhaps, some force), the novel is saved from later problems of accommodating conscious to unconscious motives. If it is of the essence of good for Greene that it should be to some degree humbly ignorant of itself, it is of the essence of evil that it should know itself for what it is: a man cannot be damned against his will.

As a consequence of this difference in the protagonist, there is a corresponding difference in the attitude towards corruption. The "good" men of Greene's later novels cannot take Pinkie's uncompromising stance towards the ordinary universe, although they are constantly attracted to some version of it; to do this would be to betray their goodness, which lies, precisely, in a solidarity with human weakness. What is interesting in *Brighton Rock*, in this respect, is the ambiguous characterisation of Ida Arnold; for Ida is both a warm, relaxed, lenient earth-mother, embracing all human weakness to her ample bosom, and yet, in her pursuit of Pinkie and Rose, a relentless avenger of wrong. The novel, in fact, has some difficulty in squaring these disparate aspects of Ida: in endowing her at once with a breezy hedonism and an adequate motivation in her remorseless quest for justice. The aesthetic weakness embodies a moral dilemma: it springs from the novel's desire to reveal ordinary life not only as corrupt, but also as crassly assertive and interfering, and so to engage it in a confrontation with metaphysics which will expose its inferiority. The attempt is unconvincing: it entails our belief in Ida as both amoral vitalist and indignant moralist. The novel, once more, is over-insistent: it is torn between an impulse to dismiss routine life as glitteringly empty, and a need to worst it in argument.

In Greene's next important novel, *The Power and the Glory*, the situation has significantly changed: corruption and self-righteousness are no longer clumsily combined within the same person, but confront each other as polarities. This is the condition we have examined throughout, with its attendant problems and ambivalences. The exploration of evil in *Brighton Rock* is in one sense a dead-end; Greene turns from it to a more subtle and shaded analysis, in which despair and virtue, value and cheapness, are intricately interwoven. One condition for doing this is the transplanting of the action outside England, to the tropics: for here a corruption which in the domestic setting of *Brighton Rock* is seen merely as flashily or brutally superficial becomes full-blooded and intense. Deaths, betrayals, and despair are now no longer confined to a criminal underworld within the "sordid" respectabilities of a seaside resort, but become the fabric of a whole way of life. And so a different attitude may be taken to the "fallen" world: whereas the official world of Brighton is merely seedy, the worlds of Africa, Latin America, and the East are seen as both seedy and extreme, decrepit and exotic. And because corruption is more exotic and intense, it can be connected with the imagery of redemption and damnation which in *Brighton Rock* was jealously confined to an élite. The half-caste of *The Power and the Glory* can be related to metaphysical conditions in a way impossible for Ida Arnold. In these situations, as we have seen, Greene is able to find in the realities of suffering and weakness a value absent in the earlier novel: by the dialectics of death and salvation, cynicism and heroism, meanness and moral worth, a compassionate engagement with those merely despised in *Brighton Rock* can be made to consort with rejection of the human world, and of the possibilities of sanctity within it, which still owes much to Pinkie's way of seeing. . . .

Greene projects a seedy and hopeless world, a pervasive corruption which is both disgusting and yet—when compared with the pieties of privileged conservatism or the dreams of revolution—solidly "real." [Greene] criticises both the formulations of radical ideology and the falsity of *dégagement*: [he remains] desperately bound to a quotidian world which is hated but which cannot be changed. Greene has available, of course, a "totalisation": . . . that of Roman Catholic orthodoxy. That orthodoxy can provide a way of transcending the pressures of routine experience, but only partially: the only way to achieve such transcendence is to remain wryly committed to the entangling morass of "fallen" human life. A totalisation exists, but it can be lived only negatively, as a revelation of human inadequacies; a salvation which transcends the world is possible, but the world is not changed by it. In all these ways, Greene the "metaphysical" novelist is more deeply influenced by the pressures and limits of a particular social world than the novels would have us believe; in feeling and attitude, he is closer to Orwell, and to a specific strain in the English novel, than to the more overtly theological writers with whom he is often compared. The "annihilating" eyes of Pinkie may embody an eternity beyond the limits of specific place and time: but the expressions which that "eternity" is given, as, indeed, with all Greene's theological values, are more deeply determined by a particular cultural standpoint than Greene is prepared to admit.

Henry Green: Surfaces and Depths

Bruce Bassoff

> *The bottom of the sea is cruel.*
> —HART CRANE, "Voyages I"

There is an interesting conflict between the views of Victor Shklovsky and Georg Lukács about the conspicuousness of artistic means in the novel. Shklovsky says of *Tristram Shandy*: "Sterne even lays bare the technique of combining separate story lines to make up the novel. In general, he accentuates the very structure of the novel. By violating the form, he forces us to attend to it, and, for him, this awareness of the form through its violation constitutes the content of the novel." Lukács, on the other hand, pointing to a gap between great epic and minor epic, says: "The subject's form-giving, structuring, delimiting act, his sovereign dominance over the created object, is the lyricism of those epic forms which are without totality." Having commented upon the self-effacing subjectivity of great epic, in which the whole life of a society is revealed, and having censured the "self-created ruins" of Sterne, Lukács discusses the function of verse in epic forms. Homer's verse is liberating because "a pre-stabilised harmony decrees that epic verse should sing of the blessedly existent totality of life; the pre-poetic process of embracing all life in a mythology had liberated existence from all trivial heaviness." In an age where immanent meaning has become a problem, only prose, with its "unfettered plasticity," can encompass the dynamics of struggle and success: "In the world of distances, all epic verse turns into lyric poetry . . . for, in verse, everything hidden becomes manifest, and the swift flight of verse makes the distance over which prose travels with its deliberate pace as it gradually approaches meaning appear naked, mocked, trampled, or merely a forgotten dream." This assessment of verse inverts Shklovsky's advocacy of laying bare one's devices; its plea for unselfconscious deliberateness underlies David Lodge's statement: "The circumstantial particularity of the novel is thus a kind of

From *Toward* Loving: *The Poetics of the Novel and the Practice of Henry Green.* © 1975 by the University of South Carolina. The University of South Carolina Press, 1975.

anti-convention. It attempts to disguise the fact that a novel is discontinuous with real life."

From Lukács's point of view some of Green's literary traits are lyrical short-circuitings of the novelist's quest for meaning. Green's books lack the elaborate and sustained metonymic achievements of Balzac and Tolstoy, whose works become metaphors for entire civilizations. His books lack what Lukács calls "philosophy," which is a symptom of and an attempt to bridge the gap between inner and outer, self and world, the empirical and the intelligible. At least his ambitions in this respect are limited, intermediate. If the question generated by the epic is "how can life become essential?"— to which Homer gave an answer before the question was formed—the questions generated by Green's books are less final and less detailed in their process of formulation. Green's gerundive and adjectival titles are disclaimers against the ambition for closure. The lack of exposition Green points to as characteristic of the novel of the future is accompanied, moreover, in Green's best novels, by poetic devices which evoke traditional humanistic problems without documenting their context. One might, as we have said, extrapolate from Lukács a wariness of Green's metaphoric short-circuiting of the cautious elaborations of prose and claim that the meanings arrived at by this method are unearned and idiosyncratic.

This quality of short-circuiting, of unearned meaning, seems to me to be more characteristic of allusive than of internal metaphors. By the former I mean metaphors which compare an item (*A*) within the work to another (*B*) outside it. By the latter I mean metaphors generated by the repetition or "rhyming" of certain motifs within the work, by which those motifs accumulate certain tones and meanings. In the latter case these metaphors will be effective only if the contexts in which the motifs appears are well realized. Otherwise, one may not be aware of the motif; or its repetition will seem abstract, algebraic, like the insertion of x in an equation. The same provisions are true regarding the validity of allusive metaphors, except that unearned allusive metaphors tend to be more seductive. The kind of metaphor I have in mind is one in which *B* has a rich cultural context which gives a false sense of meaning and profundity to *A*. An example is Edward Albee's *Zoo Story*, which, like *Who's Afraid of Virginia Woolf*, is not really about its putative theme. The play deals with a man named Jerry who, accosting another man named Peter on a park bench, proceeds to taunt and humiliate him until Jerry drives Peter to kill him. The major portion of this one-act play deals, however, with the horror of Jerry's life and specifically with sexual horror—in the form of a libidinous landlady and her dog ("malevolence with an erection"). Albee was not content, however, with writing a brief play about sexual horror but felt that he had to invest Jerry with social significance, a message-for-us-all. The facile way he does this is to make Jerry a parallel to Christ: Jerry impales himself on a knife, Peter cries "Oh my god," and Jerry says, "I came unto you . . . and you have comforted me." The stage direction "He laughs, so faintly," which occurs in place of the above ellipsis, anticipates the audience's ironic re-

action to this pretentiousness. In other words, this motif is not realized in
the play; it is only referred to.

Similarly, *Doting* contains a Saint Peter motif that provides a facile and
overly crude irony, as if Green is not certain whether we have really appreciated the absurdity of his "doting" characters. It also seems to extend
the significance of this doting to an entire civilization—an extension which
the substance of the book cannot really bear. Arthur Middleton dotes on
a young woman named Annabel Paynton; in retaliation Arthur's wife,
Diana, almost has an affair with their friend Charles Addinsell; when things
get too warm, Arthur passes Ann on to Charles, who is also unsuccessful
in seducing her; in attempting to break up Charles's relationship with Ann,
Diana introduces him to Ann's friend Claire Belain, whom he successfully
seduces. Diana and Arthur have a son, Peter, who is something of a prig.
At the end of the book, all the characters come together in a night club for
a going-back-to-school party for Peter. The book ends, "The next day they
all went on very much the same." The book is for the most part self-
consciously flat, as we can see by examining the chapter endings (which,
like poetic line ends, are salient places for rhyming). The second chapter
of the book ends:

> He snored.
> "There, sleep my darling," she murmured.

The fifth chapter of the book ends:

> "There, sleep my darling," she mumbled.
> And in a moment or two he snored.

This formula, in its mindless connection of motifs (the reversal in sequence
vitiates all but a temporal relationship), keeps our apprehension of the
action on the surface. Similar chapter endings accomplish the same arresting
of the attention at the surface. Chapter 1 ends with this sequence of
dialogue:

> "So what?" Miss Paynton demanded.
> "Nothing" the boy replied.
> "Steak's cold" Mr. Middleton grumbled.
> "Darling, Peter was so hungry" his wife explained.

Chapter 3, in which nothing of much consequence happens, ends with this
sentence-paragraph: "Soon after this he paid the bill and they left without
arranging to meet again." Most of the other chapters end with a similar
flat sentence (often consisting of compound sentence patterns or predi-
cates)—either of action or of dialogue.

The first and last chapters of the book, however, contain two elaborate
descriptions of the night club in which the Middletons hold a party for
Peter. In addition to the stylistic disharmony of these scenes, Green introduces a Saint Peter theme vis-à-vis Peter. During the book Peter is a fisherman, and Diane refers several times to the number of fish he has caught

(he ends up with twelve). The night club where they gather is called Rome, where they are to watch some wrestlers as part of the stage show. At one point "a near miracle occurred," and they are served their meals. Peter keeps returning to his "goblet" throughout the meal. He at first wets himself with ice water from the wine bottle but later avoids this baptismal act by being more careful. Peter keeps saying "Oh God" through the scene and says it for the last time when a conjuror comes on stage. This evocation of Roman decadence and of a priggish and ineffectual Simon Peter is rather a heavy joke which undermines the delicate farce of the book.

Green's internal metaphors (or the rhyming of compositional motifs) are not short-circuitings of an expository process. Despite the fact that there are few compositional motifs in *Doting* and *Nothing*, there is also little exposition. If, according to Lukács, man and his environment have become problematic in the novel, Green's reticence reflects or anticipates the further atomization of society. George Eliot's characters cannot be known in the way Achilles or Odysseus are known, but they can be investigated. Green's characters are problematic in two senses: we are very often not certain whether or not their substance is exhausted by their appearance; and if there is some residue which is not expressed by appearance, we can only approach it obliquely through uneasy intuitions. Let me illustrate these phenomena.

One of the motifs in *Party Going* is that of surfaces and depths. During Miss Fellowes's delirium she is threatened with drowning by increasingly tempestuous waters. Robin is described as "drowning in his depth" as he struggles with his feelings for Angela Crevy. After discussing the value of fellow feeling, Thomson is described as pitying himself and the girl Emily (who has given him a friendly and unexpected kiss) as they cling together "on dim whirling waters." Amabel is pictured in the bathroom after having taken a bath: Her image is clouded over by steam, and only gradually, as her body turns from pink to white, does more and more of herself begin to be reflected. The images of surfaces and depths have to do with two related problems: As stated above, are the characters in this novel so shallow that their substance is exhausted by their appearance? Is the positivist mode of the traditional novel discredited by [recent epistemological changes]? Is it not probable that the "age of suspicion" Nathalie Sarraute talks about is not restricted to literary conventions? that we distrust Balzac's psychological motivation and feel that it is at best an abstraction from a "smear of probabilities" and at worst a subsuming of individual actions under arbitrary commonplaces of human behavior? That is, the control an author exercises over our point of view makes us credulous regarding his authoritative explanations of behavior. It is this control, invested with the confidence of a strong authorial voice (Fielding's geniality, George Eliot's intelligence) that has come under fire in the modern novel. Many critics of Kafka will minimize the expository passages of *The Trial* (the parable of the gatekeeper and K.'s "realizations" at the end) to note the automatization of the subjective that is the *real* subject of the book. Camus's *The Stranger*, similarly, represents a "degree zero" of motivation. If characters are not exhausted by their appearance, their depth can only be intimated. The light of analysis in the modern novel, like the effect of light in some physics experiments, distorts the phenomena it is attempting to illuminate. One is reminded of Jacques Lacan's approach in his psychoanalytical writings, where the language of analysis becomes as dense as the language of the unconscious. Exposition becomes poetry.

The depiction of Amabel's image being clouded over by steam and reappearing as her skin turns from pink to white suggests the exhaustiveness of appearance. This phenomenon is summarized by Evelyna: "If people vary at all then it can only be in the impressions they leave on others' minds, and if their turns of phrases are similar and if their rooms are done up by the same firm and, when they are women, if they go to the same shops, what is it makes them different, Evelyna asked herself and then gave the answer: money." Regarding Amabel's inner life, one notes that she is capable of going to sleep immediately whenever she wants. Max is also exhausted by his appearance, an appearance which is not, moreover, completely reliable. All that we really know about Max is that he is rich, handsome, and idle, drinks a lot and sleeps with many women, and is not terribly careful about the way he spends his money. Part of Max's attraction, moreover, is "in his having started so well with someone even richer than himself." As it happens, however, he and the older woman with whom he is linked have never met.

After Julia tells Max about her charms and demands that he tell her about his childhood toys, Max considers it an "unlucky business" and makes up a toy doll to meet her expectations. His inner life is as follows: "When he thought, he was only conscious of uneasy feelings and he only knew that he had been what he did not even call thinking when his feelings hurt him." These feelings, moreover, seem to pertain almost exclusively to sex.

Julia is exhausted by her charms: expressions of her childish egotism and talismans against brutal reality. Like Max she is not one for words, i.e., for thought: "If she had no memory for words she could always tell what she had worn each time she met him. Turning over her clothes as they had been packed she was turning over days." Angela Crevy, the least "respectable" member of the group, is almost always referred to as "Miss Crevy" by Green. She is described as follows: "She was very pretty and dressed well, her hands were ridiculously white and her face had an expression so bland, so magnificently untouched and calm she might never had been more than amused and as though nothing had ever been more than tiresome." In the following and last sentence of the paragraph, her "young man" is described: "His expression was of intolerance." Robin's exhaustibility is subtly indicated later in the book: "Meanwhile Mr. Robin Adams, Miss Angela Crevy's young man. . . ." The redundancy of the full name, including the "Mr." and of his identification vis-à-vis Angela seems to underline the exhaustiveness of this identification. The images used to describe Angela and Robin (lilies in a pond, etc.) are subverted by "if you will" and "if you like," as if such metaphors were redundant or gratuitous.

Green underlines the shallowness of these characters by authorial comments on the identical furnishings of Max's and Amabel's apartments: "There were in London at this time more than one hundred rooms identical with these. . . . If people then who see much of each other come to do their rooms up the same, all one can say is they are like household servants in a prince's service, all in his livery." But Green combines this contextual (mimetic) phenomenon with the problem of narrative strategy by means of free, indirect speech. About Alex's reaction to Amabel's arrival, Green says: "In this way he showed how he had been taken in by Amabel, whose wish it was that she should not show haste. In this way also he showed again how impossible it is to tell what others are thinking or what, in ordinary life, brings people to do what they are doing." It is then problematic how much of the superficiality (in a nonpejorative sense) of Green's books is accounted for by the apparent superficiality of some of his characters or by his reticence toward probing human personality.

One of the essays in Robbe-Grillet's *For a New Novel* is entitled "New Novel, New Man," since Robbe-Grillet's account of the new novel is also an account of a cultural debacle—man no longer believing in a nature invested with values. Unable to assume the a priori consensus of the traditional novel, the modern novel creates its own significations as it proceeds. Robbe-Grillet's novels are novels of surfaces generated by an insistent regard. Although the novels consist of elaborate enumerations of objective details, and although Robbe-Grillet repudiates our traditional humanistic designs on the world and insists that objects must be presented in their otherness, the consciousness that views these objects is "the least neutral, the least impartial of men: *always* engaged, on the contrary, in an emotional adventure of the most obsessive kind, to the point of often distorting his vision and of producing imaginings close to delirium." This kind of intelligence, like Benjy's in the first section of *The Sound and the Fury*, makes apparently for total presentness and surface. Such an intelligence is completely without self-reflexiveness and is fully defined by its impressions. To put the problem another way, the flatness of Robbe-Grillet's books is not too far from the flatness that would result from having *Bleak House* narrated by Mr. Krook. The social and psychic dislocations characterizing *Bleak House*, and the attendant obsessive behavior, are intensified in Kafka and in the *nouveau roman*.

Lucien Goldmann accounts for the gradual dehumanization of the modern novel by pointing to the increasing reification of modern society. Though the liberal capitalist economy provided some area for individual initiative at the same time it took on a life of its own, further phases— involving the development of monopolies and especially the intervention of the state in the economy—have completed the individual's alienation from his environment, his sense that things have a life of their own. Although England, bolstered by its empirical-pragmatic traditions, has tended to maintain traditional humanistic values more stubbornly in philosophy and literature than have Continental countries, a modern novelist like Green, as Nathalie Sarraute claims, cannot accept the bad faith of traditional novelistic exposition. Nor can he abide the "innocence" of Valéry's famous normative sentence, "La marquise sortit à cinq heures." In fact *Nothing* and *Doting* may partially be parodies of this norm: "The next day they all went on very much the same." Even in England modern novelists like Joyce, Woolf, and Green seem to sense the conflict between de jure humanistic values (of individualism, for example) and the reification which makes those values impossible to fulfill, which separates man from his environment. The penultimate chapter of *Ulysses* is written in a mode not unlike the mode of *Jealousy*—things taking on the agencing power abandoned by men. In *Finnegans Wake* man confronts the otherness of his language, just as man in the modern novel confronts the otherness of his environment. But Joyce has no real progeny except Beckett. If Henry Green rejects the legislative assurance of novelists like E. M. Forster, he maintains a measure of faith in the freedom of individuals. If his novels are realized by surfaces, those surfaces imply the problematic value of depths. Despite the internal laws we have discerned [previously] in Green's books, one seldom senses that their momentum comes from the act of describing, as Ricardou discusses it in his chapter on "creative description": "Thus a novel is for us less *the writing of an adventure than the adventure of a writing*." It is noteworthy that there are numerous authorial intrusions in *Party Going* ("I" instead of "Eye"), which express a priori designs. At one point, for example, Green asks his readers' indulgence for his metaphorical descriptions, which are prefaced by "if you will" and "if you like." At another point he intrudes with an omniscient "as we shall see." The book in which he comes closest to Ricardou's creative description is *Back,* in which the name "Rose" generates an image of time-lapse photography of blooming and dying roses. It is notable that the hero and central consciousness of *Back* is suffering from war trauma, which he is obsessively reexperiencing.

We noted that Robin and Miss Fellowes drown in their depths, whereas Thomson and Emily, clinging together, are *on* "dim whirling water." For Green that dimness is a priori, to be evoked but not to be probed. His usual tactic is to realize surfaces which suggest, without quite revealing, that dimness. In his book on Green, John Russell states parenthetically that "reflections and reverberations are Green's favorite devices for robbing space of its limits." Just as linear description is the literary equivalent to (and defamiliarization of) visual perception, so the expansion and repetition of surfaces (with their accompanying pulsations of awareness) are Green's equivalents to (and defamiliarization of) the discursive probing of depths. A comparison of two passages will clarify this statement. In chapter 20 of *Middlemarch*, George Eliot gives a marvelous exposition of Dorothea's situation in Rome with her new husband. Description and interpretation are subtly modulated into each other as this account proceeds:

To those who have looked at Rome with the quickening power of a knowledge which breathes a growing soul into all historic shapes, and traces out the suppressed transitions which unite all contrasts, Rome may still be the spiritual centre and interpreter of the world. But let them conceive one more historical contrast: the gigantic broken revelations of that Imperial and Papal city thrust abruptly on the notions of a girl who had been brought up in English and Swiss Puritanism, fed on meagre Protestant histories and on art chiefly of the hand-screen sort; a girl whose ardent nature turned all her small allowance of knowledge into principles, fusing her actions into their mould, and whose quick emotions gave the most abstract things the quality of a pleasure or a pain; a girl who had lately become a wife, and from the enthusiastic acceptance of untried duty found herself plunged in tumultuous preoccupation with her personal lot.

Eliot gradually moves into the crisis in Dorothea's marriage, scrupulously examining the coordinates of her feelings. To penetrate thus into one of his characters would seem indecent to Green, who creates surfaces that suggest but do not "give away."

In the following scene from *Loving*, the description suggests the qualities latent in the characters' situation, but these qualities are held in suspension, qualified as the book goes on, without ever yielding to discursive translation:

"No," she said muffled, "no," as O'Conor's life was opened, as Kate let the sun in and Edith bent to look.

What they saw was a saddleroom which dated back to the time when there had been guests out hunting from Kinalty. It was a place from which light was almost exlcuded now by cobwebs across its two windows and into which, with the door ajar, the shafted sun lay in a lengthened arch of blazing sovereigns. Over a corn bin on which he had packed last autumn's ferns lay Paddy snoring between these windows, a web strung from one lock of hair back onto the sill above and which rose and fell as he breathed. Caught in the reflection of spring sunlight this cobweb looked to be made of gold as did those others which by working long minutes spiders had drawn from spar to spar of the fern bedding on which his head rested. It might have been almost that O'Conor's dreams were held by hairs of gold binding his head beneath a vaulted roof on which the floor of cobbles reflected an old king's molten treasure from the bog. . . .

. . . Then they were arrested by movement in the sunset of that sidewall which reflected glare from the floor in its glass.

For most of one side of this room was taken up by a vast glass-fronted cupboard in which had once been kept the bits, the halters and bridles, and the martingales. At some time O'Conor had cut away wooden partitioning at the back to make a window into this next chamber, given over nowadays to his peacocks. This was where these birds sheltered in winter, nested in spring, and where they died of natural causes at the end. As though stuffed in a dusty case they showed themselves from time to time as one after another across the heavy days they came up to look at him. Now, through a veil of light reflected over this plate glass from beneath, Edith could dimly see, not hear, a number of peacocks driven into view by some disturbance on their side and hardly to be recognized in this sovereign light. For their eyes had changed to rubies, their plumage to orange as they bowed and scraped at each other against the equal danger. Then again they were gone with a beat of wings, and in their room stood Charley Raunce, the skin of his pale face altered by refraction to red morocco leather.

　　The girls stood transfixed as if by arrows between the Irishman dead motionless asleep and the other intent and quiet behind a division. Then, dropping everything, they turned, they also fled.

I have quoted so extensively both because this is the richest scene in the book and because it is so unseamed in texture—even the brief ellipses seem rather a violation of its spell. Like the phenomenon of subliminal advertising, which immediately loses its effectiveness once we are made aware of it, the effectiveness of Green's surfaces depends on his ability to make us refrain from interpretation while the book goes on. If once we found the source of the echo in *Concluding*, the spell of the book would be lost.

　　We have discussed the use of internal metaphors in Green's novels to give intuitions of depth. In his article "A Novelist to His Readers," Green describes the related method of achieving depth by means of surfaces: "Where and how he places his characters in fiction is for the writer the context of his story. . . . The superimposing of one scene on another, or the telescoping of two scenes into one, are methods which the novelist is bound to adopt in order to obtain substance and depth." This too is a form of metaphor, one example of which in *Party Going* is the movement back and forth between the chauffeurs Thomson and Edwards "down below" in the crowd and Max and Julia in an upstairs room in the hotel. Thomson, consigned to mind Julia's luggage in the crowd of people waiting for the fog to lift, gets a friendly kiss ("it's fellow feeling, that's what I like about it") from a strange girl. In the hotel Julia, who is childishly self-absorbed, says, "Poor Thomson . . . d'you think he's all right, and what about his tea?" She immediately seeks some reassurance from Max regarding their trip. We then switch back to Thomson, who is defending the girl's action against Edward's priggish objections and is extolling the virtues of fellow feeling. Just as the good-natured generosity of that kiss contrasts with the sexual sparring that occurs among the party-goers, the fellow feeling Thomson talks about contrasts with their mutual exploitation. Green's statement about depth reminds one of the special 3-D glasses that were used years ago in the movies to resolve superimposed images into three dimensions.

　　A variation of this use of montage is the cross-purpose dialogue, employed in *Loving* by Miss Burch and Mrs. Welch, and by Miss Burch and Nanny Swift. In one scene, as Miss Burch tries to interest Mrs. Welch in the erotic goings on between Raunce and her girls, Mrs. Welch keeps talking about her "little terror," Albert, who has just killed a peacock. The phrase "there you are" is a frequent gambit in Green for avoiding discourse or for shifting the grounds of conversation. Discussing the "mad Irishman" Paddy's possible wrath over Albert's act, Mrs. Welch says:

> "As to that I've only to pluck it . . . and 'e won't ever distinguish the bird from a chicken they're that ignorant the savages. Mrs. Tennant can't miss just the one out of above two hundred. But I won't deny it give me a start."
>
> "There you are," Miss Burch said, "but listen to this. I was upstairs in the Long Gallery this morning to get on with my work when I heard a screech, why I thought one of the girls had come by some terrible accident, or had their necks broke with one of the sashcords going which are a proper deathtrap along the Passage out of the Gallery. Well what d'you think? I'll give you three guesses.'"
>
> "You heard me 'oller out very likely," Mrs. Welch replied, watching the door yet that Albert had shut behind him.

Miss Burch's concern for Raunce's social and sexual aggressiveness is juxtaposed on Mrs. Welch's tacit admiration for her nephew's aggressiveness and her desire to protect him. In another scene Miss Burch's desire to air her grievances about Raunce and about Mrs. Jack (who has been "caught" in bed with Captain Davenport) is frustrated by Nanny Swift's desire to think the best of the situation and especially of her "little girl," Mrs. Jack. The nostalgia of Mrs. Welch and Nanny Swift for past times results in a syncopation of thoughts and memories. In another scene Mrs. Tennant and Mrs. Jack talk at cross purposes—Mrs. Tennant airing her grievances about the servants and Mrs. Jack interpreting many of Mrs. Tennant's remarks as characterizing her own adultery.

Another variation of montage, already discussed [elsewhere], is the *mise en abyme*. As Ricardou points out, the main story is often contested by the *mise en abyme*—as the action in "The Fall of the House of Usher" is contested by the story which the narrator reads to Usher, or as Oedipus's endeavors are contested by the pronouncements of the oracle. In *Loving* Nanny Swift tells the children a story about six little doves that are poor and hungry and a "wicked tempting bird" who comes to the father to ask for the hand of one of the doves. While Nanny Swift tells them this story with shut eyes (just as she later shuts her eyes to what Miss Burch is trying to tell her about Mrs. Jack), the children witness the "quarrelling, murdering, and making love again" of the doves on the dovecot. The aggressive little Albert, after sardonically describing these goings on, threatens the girls by saying that he is going to bite off the head of one of the doves. "In the pub down in the country. There was a man there bit the 'eads off of mice for a pint." Nanny Burch's story is an implicit injunction for the children to remain innocent of "quarrelling, murdering, and making love again," even as they are witnessing these life processes and even as the girls are coming under the sway of the tough, proletarian Albert.

The form of *Loving*, a fairy tale with "once upon a day," a missing ring, and "they lived happily ever after," is itself a kind of adumbrated *mise en abyme* contrasting with the exigencies of living and loving that become more apparent as the book goes on. None of the princes or knights in fairy tales, however, have indigestion—a sign in Green's novels of a constitutional rejection of life—like Charlie Raunce, who suffers from dyspepsia, exacerbated by his need for Edith and his venturing out-of-doors. (Similarly, Dale, the frustrated suitor in *Living*, has severe indigestion; Charley Summers in *Back* has a block in his stomach; Richard Abbott in *Nothing* has choking fits.) Charlie's compositional "death" at the end of *Loving* is a fall into experience, like the compositional injury which Merode suffers in the "fallen world of birds" in *Concluding*. His murmured cry, "Edie," made in the tone with which Mr. Eldon cried out "Ellen" on his deathbed, is an anguished response to the plentitude of life Edith offers him. At the end Raunce and Edith do not live "happily ever after" in a kingdom purged of its dragons; they leave their castle (which, as Green tells us, is to be bombed anyway) to go to England, where a war is going on.

A similar conflict between anecdotal flatness (best exemplified in the fairy tale) and the pulsing exigencies of life takes place at the end of *Back*: "So she had asked him to marry her, and had been accepted. She had made only one condition, which was that they should have a trial trip. So it was the same night, under Mr. Mandrew's roof, that he went to her room, for the first time in what was to be a happy married life." This anecdotal, anticipative flatness is contested by the mature awareness of the last sentences: "And she knew what she had taken on. It was no more or less, really, than she had expected."

The most obvious *mise en abyme* is the story of Sophie Septimanie de Richelieu, which occurs in the middle of *Back* and both parallels and contests the experience of Charley Summers. An eighteenth-century memoir narrates that Septimanie fell in love with a young nobleman but was forced by her father to marry a dull count of better family. The young man was killed, but subsequently Septimanie met his half brother, who was also his double. After Septimanie created a scandal at court by her feelings for the young man, he was done away with, and Septimanie pined away and died. Edward Stokes comments, "This parallel, like the legendary overtones, has the effect of universalizing the novel's central situation, of making it seem, not something merely bizarre and unlikely, but an archetype of human experience." In an article on *Back* Stephen Shapiro qualifies this statement:

> The odd thing about Stokes' comment is that he neglects to specify the *content* of this archetype. Surely Stokes is not claiming that all men and women fall in love with the doubles of dead lovers and

then fail to distinguish between the living and the dead. Charley's situation is universal only on an unconscious level. The "dead" lover we all know is the repressed memory of our erotic connection to our parents. The pressure past events exert on consciousness results in a partial fusion of past and present in the person of the loved object. When Septimanie and Charley fuse the dead with the living they are symbolically enacting—in an "abnormal" way— the "normal," unconscious process of choosing to love someone who represents a compromise between present possibilities and infantile desires.

Both critics fail to see that the *mise en abyme* contests, as well as parallels, the main story. (If the archetypal dimensions of Charley's story are as clear as Shapiro thinks, why do we need a *mise en abyme*?) Shapiro makes the same mistake as A. Kingsley Weatherhead frequently makes in his book on Green: In interpreting *Back* Shapiro is insufficiently attentive to its surface, and he tends to reify some of his own figures of speech. For example, he states: "Charley's return home is ultimately to signify his rebirth. And the connection of birth with war, anxiety, death, and sex is quite provocative." Rebirth is only Shapiro's way of describing Charley's development in the novel, but Shapiro then reifies his own figure by including it in a complex of elements that really are in the novel (war, death, anxiety, and sex). By this gambit he can now call our attention to a suggestive Freudian constellation. Shapiro criticizes Stokes and Russell for not getting at the "real" meaning of the title (which Shapiro takes as meaning back to the womb), but himself conveniently ignores the surface reference of the title, which is back from the war. It is clear from Green's autobiogrpahy, *Pack My Bag*, and from John Russell's article on him, "There It Is," that the war was a devastating experience for Green. Russell states:

> So anyone familiar with his work would expect that war and fire would leave their mark on him. He was then thirty-five; first with his hands and lungs, afterward with his imagination, he had to come to grips with the fact of the whole place burning. But five more novels followed *Caught* and the three stories, and one might have supposed that in his imagination the War had receded. Without knowing him or knowing of his nightmare dreams at night, one could hardly be expected to realize how massive and lasting the effect of the War has been on him.

This fact will enable us to see how the *mise en abyme* functions in *Back*.

The contestation between the main story and the *mise en abyme* is similar to that between the courtly love ethic and the realities of war and human nature in Chaucer's *Troilus and Cressida*. Unlike the loss of love in the eighteenth-century memoir, Charley's loss of love, and his obsessive reenactment of that deprivation, is part of an overall sense of loss and dislocation he is suffering after returning from the war. Similarly, in *Caught* Richard

Roe has lost his wife, and this loss is a synecdoche for the generalized sense of loss he feels, just as the "heraldic deer" he sees are emblematic of life "before the revolution." In *Pack My Bag* Green associates war and sex:

> Another story preyed on us then, and, as I have said before, one remembers only the horrible of times like those. It was the tale of the Germans being so short of fats they boiled their own dead down with ours to make food. This lie which we took for truth gave me exactly those awed feelings I had when we talked of sex. Sex was a dread mystery. No story could be so dreadful, more full of agitated awe than sex. We felt there might almost be some connection between what the Germans were said to have done and this mysterious urgency we did not feel and which was worse than eating human fats; or so it seems now, looking back on what many call their happiest time.

In *Caught*, where roses have constant erotic associations, and where erotic longings are constantly evoked by the stress of war, the following passage telescopes the themes of war and sex: "The air caught at his wind passage as though briars and their red roses were being dragged up from his lungs." In fact, war is equated with sex when Prudence compares Pye's longing for her to a pilot's longing for his target: "War," she thinks, "is sex." At another point Richard Roe reflects that it would have been better to paint the fire engines "pink, a boudoir shade, to match that half light which was to settle, night after night, around the larger conflagration."

The equation "war is sex" translates as follows: since neither Green nor the characters in his novels have a sense of the totality of war, these novels—in Lukács's terms—have lyrical rather than epic ambitions. Green attempts to translate the stress of war into personal-lyrical terms. War is sex or war is the loss of a loved one. The characters' experience of war is relatively dissociated from its socio-historical dimensions, as it is not in Stendhal, Tolstoy, or Sartre. Under the stress of war these characters are set adrift from their familiar modes of existence and are made to come to terms with their human separateness. Problems of sex, love, death, authority, and fellowship are defamiliarized by the disjunctions war brings about. In *Caught* Richard Roe says of Pye (who has committed suicide), "But it was sex finished him off, and sex arising out of his authority."

If the *mise en abyme* in *Back* relates the "twin attachment" or "extraordinary passions" that Septimanie felt for a young man and his double, and if her passion is defeated by the intrigues of the court, the main story moves from Charley's obsessive conviction that Rose has not died, that she and others are plotting to make him think that she is dead, to Charley's realization that the two women in the book are separate: "He felt that this was the final confirmation that Rose was truly dead, that Nance was a real person." At the same time we learn that Charley has gone through a literally unspeakable experience during the war and in a prison camp. Green's strategy in this book is similar to the strategies that A. Kingsley Weatherhead notes in *Loving, Nothing,* and *Concluding,* where characters deal publicly with private desires or anxieties by translating them into figurative terms that are decorous and manageable. In *Nothing,* for example, Jane Weatherby uses her daughter Penelope as a metaphor for her own desires and fears. As soon as these are resolved, Penelope is packed off to boarding school. A similar process is at work in *Back:* " 'Oh Rose, Rose,' he [Charley] cried out in himself, not noticing he did this without having real regret, 'Oh, why did you?' He began to cry, in his self pity seeing himself again with his hands, like a monkey's, hung up on the barbed wire which had confined him within the camp." As Mrs. Grant cries out at her husband's deathbed, "Come back," Green comments, "And the culmination of all this was about to remind Summers of something in France which he knew, as he valued his reason, that he must always shut out." The only occasion on which Charley speaks directly of his experience in the prison camp, he says, "I had a mouse out there." This remark is connected metonymically with his observation with Nance of a cat and its kittens, and we recall that in Green's novels mice always have erotic associations. Mr. Mead, Charley's employer, sums up Charley's plight: "It's sex is the whole trouble. There you are. Sex." Green's point seems to be that under stress certain areas of our experience (and especially the erotic) become kinds of neuralgic indices of that stress. The time-lapse effect of blooming and withering roses in *Back,* Charley's obsession with Rose, evokes his way of reenacting and managing the trauma he has suffered in war and his generalized sense of loss. As narrative strategy, moreover, this process is Green's way of evoking the quality of Charley's experience without having to plumb it. Whatever the suggestive value of Shapiro's Freudian interpretation of *Back* in dealing with certain details, he does a disservice to the surface of Green's book by not dealing with it in its own terms. The *mise en abyme* in *Back,* like the play within the play in *Hamlet,* is a model for what the book is like in broad outline but what it is very unlike in realization.

A. Kingsley Weatherhead's book on Green is another example of a kind of interpretation that sacrifices surfaces for depths. Weatherhead says of his purpose:

> This study considers each of Green's novels and discovers some kind of order in the theme of self-creation. Characters emerge from childhood or other static situations, descend with whatever pains into the dark for the discovery of self, and break through alienation into community; or they partly proceed thus; or, faced with the opportunity, they altogether decline to. Then the order so discovered sometimes reveals in turn the significance of structures in the novels; and it offers a rationale for incident, imagery, and characters that are manifestly not of the "story" and do not contribute primarily to atmosphere.

Weatherhead attempts to see Green's novels as concrete realizations of some of the abstract problems that one finds in such thinkers as Kierke-gaard, Sartre, and Freud. In this sense his endeavor is like those of Umberto Eco, who sees literature as an "epistemological metaphor," and Lucien Goldmann, who thinks that both literature and philosophy are intelligibly related to the world view of a given social class. . . . However, the effort to delimit the informing structure of a writer's work, to trace its structural analogies with other cultural phenomena, and to place this structure in a more global structure, which explains it, is an enormous undertaking. De-spite Weatherhead's frequent perceptiveness, his sense of structure in Green's novels is faulty and warps his interpretations.

In discussing *Party Going*, Weatherhead says: "The sexual encounter is no mere animal comfort for the party as it is for Thomson, Julia's chauf-feur, who seems to regard it as an alternative to tea. It is, or may be, a significant part of the process of self-creation." He then talks of the im-proper, narcissistic sexuality offered by Amabel as opposed to the proper sexuality (involving a mutual giving and taking) offered by Julia. In this discussion Weatherhead is inattentive to the way in which the book actually works; in plumbing depths, he is inattentive to surfaces. We have pointed to the context of Thomson's sexual encounter and his notion of fellow feeling. In contrast, Julia comments to Max about the crowd below: "After all . . . one must not hear too many cries for help in this world." In contrast to Thomson's casual acceptance of a good-natured kiss, we have Green's ironically pedantic "explanation" of the motives behind Julia and Angela having kissed their "young men":

> Now both Julia and Angela had kissed their young men when these had been cross, when Mr. Adams had made off down in the station and when Max had stopped chasing Julia to sit in his chair.
>
> People, in their relations with one another, are continually doing similar things but never for similar reasons.

Angela's kiss is a form of dismissal; Julia's kiss is meant to "keep Max sweet" for the trip. Julia is no less self-absorbed than Amabel; her approach to men is simply different—child-woman instead of femme fatale. The passage Weatherhead quotes to show the mutual giving and taking that characterizes Julia's sexuality is more expressive of childish regression than of mature sexuality: "And as she hoped this party would be, if she could get a hold of Max, it would be as though she could take him back into her life from where it had started and show it to him for them to share in a much more exciting thing of their own, artichokes, pigeons and all, she thought and laughed aloud." The run-on sentence preceding this passage is, "So like when you were small and they brought children over to play with you and you wanted to play on your own then someone, as they hardly ever did, came along and took them off so you could do what you wanted." The willfulness of that sentence governs her designs on Max (whom she is going to "get a hold of").

Similarly, Weatherhead says that in *Party Going* Green chooses the metaphor of traveling to describe growth. As a matter of fact, he says that "The journey to the south of France tends to lose its real nature in accommodating itself to its archetypal function." The novel, however, is not about a journey; it is about waiting to make a journey. The only journey that takes place in the book is that of Miss Fellowes, who, after her illness, "looked as if she had been travelling." The journey to France is outside the framework of the book, and in terms of archetypes one might as well (or better) take it as a metaphor for death than for growth. Julia (who dreams of childhood) and the effete Alex are the two characters in the book (except for the delirious Miss Fellowes) who are most conscious of death. Alex thinks of himself as dead, a ghost driving through the streets; later he thinks about the different qualities of dying depending on one's social class. When Max lies about his whereabouts and says that he had to see his lawyer, Julia thinks that perhaps he had wanted to make out his will; she then sees the hall of the station as a doctor's huge waiting room, similar to what it would be like when "they were all dead and waiting at the gates." One bit of montage that the book provides is the alternating descriptions of the claustrophobic Alex and Julia climbing the stairs of the hotel and of people carrying the ill Miss Fellowes up the stairs. The point is that traveling is *not* used archetypally in the book, or at least its context confounds any clear archetypal significance. Unlike Kim's journey in Rudyard Kipling's book (where the journey does signify a process of growth and discovery) or the journey in *Outward Bound* (which univocally signifies death), the journey in *Party Going* is, first of all, present only in an anticipative sense; second, it is only one of a number of similar journeys that Max has sponsored; and third, it comprises a number of elements. The fall of the pigeon at the beginning of the book is as much a journey as the flight of sea gulls out to sea which Julia takes as a good omen.

Even Julia's omen is ambiguous. "And now she remembered those two birds which had flown under the arch she had been on when she had started, and now she forgot they were sea gulls and thought they had been doves and so was comforted." It is noteworthy that Julia remembers having seen only two birds, whereas she really saw three. Moreover, doves connote messengers of peace; gulls, scavengers. It is one of a few such substitutions in *Party Going*: The bird that falls at the beginning of the book is a "pigeon," but Miss Fellowes later refers to it as a "swallow," which can refer, with qualifying words, to birds of other families resembling swallows. It can thus refer to a variety of domestic pigeon (see the *OED* for this 1668 usage). The word "dove" was formerly applied to all the species of pigeon native to or known in Britain but is now restricted to the turtledove and its congeners (see the *OED*). Other birds which become part of this generic complex are sea gulls and geese (through metonymy, not through taxonomy). At one point Evelyn wonders whether the bird in brown paper would have been less odd if it had been a goose or another bird. The missing bird (as three sea gulls [doves] become two) can only be the bird that tumbles to death at the beginning of the book. At another point Edwards says to Thomson, "Go on if you like and pick up some bird, alive or dead, Thomson, get yourself your cup o'tea if you feel like it." Thomson replies, "Not wrapped in brown paper." The missing bird is associated with death, which is associated with a lack of fellow feeling; and it is this tacit equation that vitiates Weatherhead's interpretation of Julia's role in the book.

Weatherhead, in his search for a repressive parent figure in Green's novels, distorts the role of Miss Fellowes:

> The main business of the novel is the "departure" of young people for maturity. In a word, it concerns the death of youth, the abstract, which formerly had been presided over by the nannies and Miss Fellowes. Miss Fellowes now sees fit to watch over the death of youth and to grant it a decent burial. Her care of the pigeon figures her last proper function as a guardian of youth. But if she had finally disposed of it her usefulness would be at an end. She would be cast off, like nannies elsewhere in Green when their maturing protégés pass beyond their control. Naturally she seeks to protract her usefulness; hence she clings to the bird, clinging thereby to life itself.

But it is clearly not life "done up in brown paper" that Miss Fellowes retrieves when she begins to feel better; it is death. The pigeon is not "only a local figure in a novel of which the large figurative structure now needs consideration." It is the single most powerful compositional motif in the book—the fall of the pigeon dominates the atmosphere of this book as the echo dominates the atmosphere of *Concluding*. Miss Fellowes, as her name indicates, is a touchstone for fellow feeling in the book, and the death of the pigeon signifies the death that the lack of, or warping of, that quality entails. The sexual associations of the pigeon motif are also part of a complex that includes fellow feeling, sex, and death. Most of the party-goers at one time or another abuse Miss Fellowes; Alex asks whether anyone really cares whether she dies or not. We noted earlier that the enjambments in *Party Going* prepared us for non sequiturs and coincidences: For no apparent reason Robert blurts out her name while he is supposedly looking for Max; moreover, no sooner does he mention Miss Fellowes than he sees her at the bar. Like the Ancient Mariner, Robert compulsively tells the story of this non sequitur and coincidence to anyone who will listen, but without making much of an impression. Robert thinks that he has found "his ruined temple" (the goal of his childhood games) in Max, but he really finds it in Miss Fellowes. It is the possibility of fellow feeling, unlooked for in the moral economy of Robert's circle, that he finds so uncanny.

In his commitment to an a priori psycho-philosophical scheme, Weatherhead commits similar distortions in his interpretations of other novels. He ignores their obvious rhetorical strategies, like the metonymic linkages I pointed to in *Party Going*, where, in a sense, the central character is the absent Embassy Richard, emblematic of the futility of this party-going class.

Despite his frequent perceptiveness (especially toward Green's last novels), Weatherhead sometimes masks what it is like to read these novels by the demands of a priori ideas. These demands, in turn, are uncontrolled by the socio-historical parameters that Goldmann posits in his sociology of the novel.

Biographical Notes

John Cowper Powys (1872–1963). A collateral descendant of William Cowper and John Donne, Powys was born in Derbyshire and educated at Sherborne School and Corpus Christi College, Cambridge. He travelled to the United States as a lecturer from 1904 to 1934, spending his winters there from 1910 on, and from 1928 to 1934 dividing year-round residence between New York and California. He was a popular, expressive speaker, and his critical works, from *Visions and Revisions* (1915) to *Mortal Strife* (1942), are often said to reflect the platform style.

His career as a novelist began with the "romances" *Wood and Stone* (1915), *Wolf's Bane* and *Rodmoor* (1916), and *Ducdame* (1925). These were followed by the major novels, *Wolf Solent* (1929) and *A Glastonbury Romance* (1932). Other works include the historical novels *Owen Glendower* (1940) and *Porius: A Romance of the Dark Ages* (1951); *Homer and the Aether* (1959), an adaptation of the *Iliad*; *Odes and Other Poems* (1896), and *Poems* (1899); as well as *Weymouth Sands* (1934), *Jobber Skald* (1935), *Morwyn* (1937), *The Inmates* (1952), *Atlantis* (1954), *The Brazen Head* (1956), and *All or Nothing* (1960). The aesthetic and metaphysical theories which underlie Powys's fiction are put forth in *The Complex Vision* (1920) and the 1934 *Autobiography*.

Ford Madox Ford (1873–1939). Born Ford Hermann Hueffer in Surrey, Ford (he changed his name to Ford Madox Ford in 1919 and published before that as Ford Madox Hueffer) was educated at a private school in Folkestone and at University College in London, where he studied music. His first published works included tales for children, the novel *The Shifting of the Fire* (1892), and a book of verse, *The Questions at the Well* (1893). In collaboration with Joseph Conrad he produced *The Inheritors* (1901), *Romance* (1903), and the "rounded fragment" (Conrad's description) *The Nature of a Crime* (1909 in the *English Review*; 1924). He was editor of the *English Review* (1908–10), where he was the first publisher of the work of Lawrence and Pound, and of the *Transatlantic Review* (1924–25).

Ford's fiction first attracted serious critical attention with *The Good Soldier* (1915) and the *Parade's End* tetralogy, or "Tietjens sequence": *Some Do Not . . .* (1924), *No More Parades* (1925), *A Man Could Stand Up* (1926), and *The Last Post* (1928). Other works include several novels (notably the historical *Fifth Queen* trilogy, 1906–8), reminiscences, and criticism: *Ford Madox Brown* (1896; the pre-Raphaelite painter was Ford's maternal grandfather), *Rossetti* (1902), *The Pre-Raphaelite Brotherhood* (1907), *The Critical Attitude* (1911), *Women and Men* (1923), and *Portraits from Life* (1937). In 1922 Ford moved to France, and divided the rest of his life between Provence, Paris, and the United States, where he lectured in comparative literature at Olivet College, Michigan in 1937.

Dorothy M(iller) Richardson (1873–1957). Born in Berkshire, Richardson attended private schools there and in London until 1893, the year of her father's bankruptcy. She then worked as governess, teacher, secretary, translator, and journalist. She had published *The Quakers Past and Present* (1914) and *Gleanings from the Work of George Fox* (1914) before the appearance of her first novel, *Pointed Roofs*, in 1915. This was the first of a thirteen-volume sequence, entitled *Pilgrimage*, which has been noted almost exclusively for its introduction of the "stream of consciousness" technique (a term which Richardson disliked).

The other "chapters," as Richardson referred to the novels, are: *Backwater* (1916), *Honeycomb* (1917), *The Tunnel* (1919), *Interim* (1919), *Deadlock* (1921), *Revolving Lights* (1923), *The Trap* (1925), *Oberland* (1927), *Dawn's Left Hand* (1931), *Clear Horizon* (1935), *Dimple Hill* (1938), and *March Moonlight* (1967).

E(dward) M(organ) Forster (1879–1970). Born in London, Forster was educated at Tonbridge School and King's College, Cambridge. Forster's father died in 1880, but his education and future independence from work were financed by a legacy left him by his great aunt, Marianne Thornton, in 1887. He was occasionally employed, however, as a tutor and lecturer, and in India as secretary to the Maharajah of Dewas State Senior.

Forster's most well-known and critically respected novels are *Howards End* (1910) and *A Passage to India* (1924). Other works include the novels *Where Angels Fear to Tread* (1905), *The Longest Journey* (1907), and *A Room with a View* (1908); the short story collections *The Celestial Omnibus* (1911) and *The Eternal Moment* (1928); *Aspects of the Novel* (1927), his Clark Lectures at Cambridge; the essay collections *Abinger Harvest* (1936) and *Two Cheers for Democracy* (1951); the libretto to Benjamin Britten's *Billy Budd* (1949); and the biographies *Goldsworthy Lowes Dickinson* (1934) and *Marianne Thornton* (1956). *Maurice* (1971) and *The Life to Come* (1972) were published posthumously. Forster refused a knighthood in 1949, but became a Companion of Honour to the Queen in 1953 and received the Order of Merit in 1969.

James (Augustine Aloysius) Joyce (1882–1941). Born in Dublin, Joyce attended Clongowes Wood College, Kildare, Belvedere College, Dublin, and University College, Dublin, where he studied modern languages. After graduation and a brief period of medical studies in Paris, he worked sporadically as an English tutor and contributor of reviews to Dublin newspapers before being employed in 1905 by the Berlitz School of Languages in Trieste. *Chamber Music* (1907), a collection of short poems, was his first published book, followed by *Dubliners* in 1914. The latter was read by Ezra Pound, who arranged for the serial publication (February 1914–September 1915) of *A Portrait of the Artist as a Young Man* in *The Egoist*, under the editorial direction of T. S. Eliot and Harriet Weaver. The novel, the early drafts of which were entitled *Stephen Hero*, appeared as a volume in 1916.

The Joyce household spent the duration of the First World War in Zurich, where Joyce worked on *Ulysses*. This was serialized in the New York *The Little Review* from April 1918 to December 1920, when publication was halted by an obscenity suit. The complete novel was published in France in 1922, but copies were seized and burned upon importation into England and the United States, where the book was banned until 1933. The first complete and unexpurgated edition was published in England in 1936. *Finnegans Wake* was begun in Paris in 1923 (where the Joyce family lived from 1920 to 1939, when they returned to Switzerland) and was published in twelve installments as *Work in Progress* between 1928 and 1937, appearing in book form in 1939. *Pomes Penyeach* was published in 1927.

(Percy) Wyndham Lewis (1884–1957). Born on his father's yacht off the coast of Maine, Lewis was educated at Rugby School and the Slade School of Art. After graduation he spent some years in the prewar artistic circles of Paris, which provided the setting for his first novel, *Tarr* (1918). In the 1920s Lewis was an active member of the London avant-garde, achieving a considerable reputation as a painter of the Vorticist school. The trilogy *The Human Age* was begun with *The Childermass* in 1928, but was not completed until 1955 with the simultaneous publication of *Monstre Gai* and *Malign Fiesta*. *The Apes of God* (1930) and *The Revenge for Love* are considered his major novels.

Lewis's nonfiction works, aside from reviews and manifestos, consist of critical and political commentary (he is infamous for the 1931 *Hitler*, although he repudiated that book's somewhat bemused fascination in *The Hitler Cult, and How It Will End* in 1939), including *The Lion and the Fox* (1927), *Time and Western Man* (1927), *Men without Art* (1934), *The Mysterious Mr. Bull* (1938), *America and Cosmic Man* (1948), and *The Writer and the Absolute* (1952). Other works include the verse satire *One-Way Song* (1933), the short story collections *The Wild Body* (1927) and *Rotting Hill* (1951), the autobiographies *Blasting and Bombardiering* (1937) and *Rude Assignment* (1950), and the semi-autobiographical novel *Self-Condemned* (1954).

(Adeline) Virginia Woolf (1882–1941). Born Adeline Virginia Stephen (she changed her name upon marriage in 1912), Woolf was educated privately.

Following the death of her father in 1904, Woolf and her brothers and sister first moved to the Bloomsbury section of London. The "evenings" begun by Thoby Stephen before his death in 1906 provided the forum for the formation of what came to be known as the Bloomsbury Group. Woolf published reviews in the *Manchester Guardian* and *The Times Literary Supplement* before the appearance of her first novel, *The Voyage Out*, in 1915. In the same year Woolf began keeping her diaries, all of which have now been published. In 1917 she and her husband founded the Hogarth Press, whose first printing included Woolf's story "The Mark on the Wall." Woolf's other novels include *Night and Day* (1919), *Jacob's Room* (1922), *Mrs. Dalloway* (1925), *To the Lighthouse* (1927), *The Waves* (1931), *The Years* (1937), and *Between the Acts* (1941). Other fiction includes the short story collections *The Mark on the Wall* (1919), *Kew Gardens* (1919), *Monday or Tuesday* (1921), *A Haunted House and Other Stories* (1943); the play *Freshwater* (1935); and the "fictional biographies" *Orlando* (1928) and *Flush* (1933). Her nonfiction includes the biography *Roger Fry* (1940) and several essays: *Mr. Bennett and Mrs. Brown* (1924), *The Common Reader* (1925), *A Room of One's Own* (1929), *The Common Reader, Second Series* (1932), and *Three Guineas* (1938).

Ivy Compton-Burnett (1892–1969). Born in London and educated at Royal Holloway College, London University, Compton-Burnett published her first novel, *Dolores*, in 1911. This was not followed by another until 1925: *Pastors and Masters* established a distinctive pattern of setting, structure, and style which was followed in the remaining novels. These were *Brothers and Sisters* (1929), *Men and Wives* (1931), *More Women Than Men* (1933), *A House and Its Head* (1935), *Daughters and Sons* (1937), *A Family and a Fortune* (1939), *Parents and Children* (1941), *Elders and Betters* (1944), *Manservant and Maidservant* (1947; published in 1948 in the United States as *Bullivant and the Lambs*), *Two Worlds and Their Ways* (1949), *Darkness and Day* (1951), *The Present and the Past* (1953), *Mother and Son* (1955), *A Father and His Fate* (1957), *A Heritage and Its History* (1959), *The Mighty and Their Fall* (1961), and *A God and His Gifts* (1963). Compton-Burnett was made a Commander of the Order of the British Empire (CBE) in 1951.

D(avid) H(erbert) Lawrence (1885–1930). Born in Nottinghamshire, Lawrence was educated at Nottingham High School and Nottingham University College, where he earned a teaching certificate in 1908. Some of his poems were published in the *English Review* (1909) by Ford Madox Hueffer (later Ford Madox Ford), who also helped bring about the publication of *The White Peacock* (1911). Lawrence quit his teaching post and in 1912 published *The Trespasser* as well as completing the first draft of *Paul Morel*, later retitled *Sons and Lovers* (1913); in the same year he moved to Germany with Frieda, the wife of a former teacher and daughter of Baron von Richtofen. His expressed opposition to the First World War provoked the seizure of all copies of *The Rainbow* (1915), and, after their return to England, the formal expulsion of the Lawrences from the county of Cornwall in 1917. In 1919, they left England, never to return, and the rest of Lawrence's life was spent in almost constant travel (Italy, Sardinia, Ceylon, Australia, New Mexico, Mexico, and Europe, after 1926) in search of a climate to alleviate his always poor health.

Lawrence's other novels include *Twilight in Italy* (1916), *The Lost Girl* (1920), *Women in Love* (1921), *Kangaroo* (1923), and *Lady Chatterley's Lover* (1928; censored in England until 1961). His shorter fiction is found in *The Prussian Officer* (1914), *England, My England* (1922), *The Captain's Doll* (1923), *St. Mawr* (1925), *The Woman Who Rode Away* (1928), *The Man Who Died* (1931), *The Lovely Lady* (1932), and *The Tales of D. H. Lawrence* (1934). *The Complete Poems* and *The Complete Plays* appeared in 1964 and 1965. Lawrence's non-fiction includes several travel sketches, a school textbook, *Movements in European History* (1921; originally published under the pseudonym Lawrence H. Davison), *Psychoanalysis and the Unconscious* (1921), and *Studies in Classic American Literature* (1923).

(Arthur) Joyce (Lunel) Cary (1888–1957). Born in Londonderry, Northern Ireland, and educated at Tunbridge Wells and Clifton College, Cary attended Trinity College, Oxford, after studying art in Edinburgh and Paris (1904–9). After service in the Red Cross during the Balkan Wars and as a district magistrate and administrative officer in Nigeria, he resigned from the colonial service in 1920, returning to reside in Oxford. He had published *Verse* in 1908 under the name Arthur Cary, but adopted his mother's surname as his first name with the publication of *Aissa Saved* in 1932. This was the first of four novels set in West Africa, the others being *An American Visitor* (1933), *The African Witch* (1936), and *Mister Johnson* (1939).

Apart from the African novels, critical attention has mainly focused on Cary's two trilogies: *Herself Surprised* (1941), *To Be a Pilgrim* (1942), *The Horse's Mouth* (1944); and *Prisoner of Grace* (1952), *Except the Lord* (1953), *Not Honour More* (1955). Other novels include *Castle Corner* (1938), *Charley Is My Darling* (1940), *The House of Children* (1941), *The Moonlight* (1946), *A Fearful Joy* (1949), and *The Captive and the Free* (1959), which was edited from an unfinished manuscript. Cary's verse is found in *Marching Soldier* (1945) and *The Drunken Sailor: A Ballad-Epic* (1947), his short stories in *Spring Song* (1960). Other nonfiction work includes *The Case for African Freedom* (1941), *Britain and West Africa* (1946), *Art and Reality: Ways of the Creative Process* (1958), and *Power in Men* (1963).

Agatha Christie (1890–1976). Born Agatha May Clarissa Miller in Devonshire (she changed her name upon her first marriage in 1914), Christie was educated privately and at a Paris finishing school. Apart from several poems in *The Poetry Review*, Christie's first publication was *The Mysterious Affair at Styles* (1920). This was followed by the thriller *The Secret Adversary* in 1922, and thereafter by well over one hundred works, including novels, short story collections, plays, volumes of poetry, and an autobiography (1977). Of the mysteries some of the most popular are *The Murder of Roger Ackroyd*

(1926); *Murder on the Orient Express,* or *Murder in the Calais Coach* (1934); *Death on the Nile* (1937); *Appointment with Death* (1938); *Ten Little Niggers* (*Ten Little Indians*), or *And Then There Were None* (1939); *Witness for the Prosecution* (1948); *Three Blind Mice,* or *The Mousetrap* (1950); *Hickory, Dickory, Death* (1955); *Hercule Poirot's Early Cases* (1974); and *Curtain* (1975). Six novels were published (1930–56) under the name Mary Westmacott. Christie was named a Commander of the Order of the British Empire (CBE) in 1956 and received the Order of Dame Commander of the British Empire (DBE) in 1971, as well as receiving the title of Lady Mallowan upon her second husband's knighthood in 1968.

Aldous (Leonard) Huxley (1894–1963). Born in Surrey, Huxley was educated at Eton College and Balliol College, Oxford. A serious eye condition ended his hopes for a medical career, and after graduation in 1915 Huxley became a journalist. He published four collections of verse and one of short stories (*Limbo,* 1920) before the appearance of his first novel, *Crome Yellow,* in 1921. This was followed by the other "novels of ideas": *Antic Hay* (1923), *Those Barren Leaves* (1925), and *Point Counter Point* (1928). Four other short story collections and the novels *Brave New World* (1932) and *Eyeless in Gaza* (1936) preceded his emigration in 1938 to the United States. His later novels include *After Many a Summer* (1939), *Time Must Have a Stop* (1944), *Ape and Essence* (1948), *The Genius and the Goddess* (1955), and *Island* (1962).

Huxley's increasing preoccupation with the relationship between reality and artistic perception led to the publication of several speculative works: *The Perennial Philosophy* (1946), *Themes and Variations* (1950), *The Doors of Perception* (1954), *Adonis and Alphabet* (1956), and *Heaven and Hell* (1956). Other works of nonfiction included the historical studies *Grey Eminence* (1941) and *The Devils of Loudun* (1952); *The Art of Seeing* (1942), a description of the eye-training method which saved Huxley's sight; the travel books *Jesting Pilate* (1926) and *Beyond the Mexique Bay* (1943); and the *Collected Essays* (1959). Huxley also edited *The Letters of D. H. Lawrence* (1932).

L(eslie) P(oles) Hartley (1895–1972). Born in Cambridgeshire and educated at Harrow and Balliol College, Oxford, Hartley's first publication was a volume of short stories, *Night Fears* (1924). This was followed by the novel *Simonetta Perkins* (1925) and *The Killing Bottle* (1932), another short story collection. Widespread interest in Hartley's work was first aroused by the trilogy consisting of *The Shrimp and the Anemone* (1944), *The Sixth Heaven* (1946), and *Eustace and Hilda* (1947). These were followed by *The Boat* (1949), *My Fellow Devils* (1951), *The Go-Between* (1953), *A Perfect Woman* (1955), *The Hireling* (1957), *Facial Justice* (1960), *The Brickfield* (1964), *The Betrayal* (1966), *Poor Clare* (1968), and *The Love-adept* (1969). Hartley's short stories are also found in *The Travelling Grave* (1951), *The White Wand* (1954), and *Two for the River* (1961). A volume of critical essays, *The Novelist's Responsibility,* appeared in 1968.

Liam (William) O'Flaherty (1896–1984). Born in the Aran Islands, County

Galway, Ireland, and educated at Rockwell and Blackrock Colleges, O'Flaherty spent three months in a diocesan seminary before attending University College, Dublin. He was awarded a War degree in 1918 following his service in the Irish Guards. He spent the postwar years in extensive travel and involvement as a Republican in the Irish Civil War. His first publication, under the name William O'Flaherty, was a short story, "The Sniper," in *The New Leader*. In subsequent publications he used the Gaelic Liam instead of William.

His first novel was *Thy Neighbour's Wife* (1923), followed by *The Black Soul* and *Spring Sowing* in 1924. Other novels include *The Informer* (1925), *Mr. Gilhooley* (1926), *The Assassin* (1928), *The Puritan* (1931), *Skerrett* (1932), *The Martyr* (1933), *Famine* (1937), *Land* (1946), and *Insurrection* (1950). Other publications include short stories in English and Gaelic (most of the Gaelic stories are available in translation): *The Short Stories of Liam O'Flaherty* (1937), *Two Lovely Beasts and Other Stories* (1948), and *The Stories of Liam O'Flaherty* (1956); a play, *Darkness* (1926); and nonfiction, including *A Tourist's Guide to Ireland* (1929), *Joseph Conrad: An Appreciation* (1930), and *I Went to Russia* (1931). O'Flaherty was one of the founding members of the Irish Academy of Letters.

C(live) S(taples) Lewis (1898–1963). Born in Belfast and privately educated, Lewis was elected a scholar of University College, Oxford, in 1916, but interrupted his studies to serve in World War I. After being invalided out of the war he returned to Oxford, where he became a tutor at Magdalene College in 1925. In 1954 he moved to Cambridge, assuming a chair of Medieval and Renaissance English and becoming a Fellow of Magdalene, positions which he held until shortly before his death. Lewis's first publications were two books of verse, *Spirits in Bondage* (1919) and *Dymer* (1926), under the pseudonym Clive Hamilton. His career in fiction began with *Out of the Silent Planet* (1938), the first volume of a trilogy completed by *Perelandra* (1943) and *That Hideous Strength* (1945). Among the more popular of Lewis's fictions are *The Screwtape Letters* (1942) and the seven volumes of the "Narnia books," from *The Lion, the Witch and the Wardrobe* (1950) to *The Last Battle* (1956). Lewis's publications include several volumes of medieval, literary, and theological scholarship, as well as commentary, short stories, poetry, letters, and autobiography (*Surprised by Joy*, 1955).

Elizabeth (Dorothea Cole) Bowen (1899–1973). Born in Dublin and educated at the Downe House School, Kent, Bowen spent a brief period studying at the London Council School of Art, but withdrew to travel on the Continent. A short story collection, *Encounters*, was published in 1923. In the same year she was married and settled near Oxford, where she remained until moving to London in 1935. A second collection, *Ann Lee's and Other Stories* (1926), was followed by her first novel, *The Hotel*, in 1927. Other novels include *The Last September* (1929), *Friends and Relations* (1931), *To the North* (1932), *The House in Paris* (1935), *The Death of the Heart* (1938), *The Heat of the Day* (1949), *A World of Love* (1955), *The Little Girls* (1964), *A Day in the Dark* (1965), and *Eva Trout* (1969). Other short story collections are *Joining Charles* (1929), *The Cat Jumps* (1934), *Look at All Those Roses* (1941), and *The Demon Lover* (1945). Bowen's criticism and essays are found in *English Novelists* (1942) and *Collected Impressions* (1950). She was an associate editor of *London Magazine* and was made a Commander of the Order of the British Empire (CBE) in 1948.

Stevie Smith (1902–71). Born Florence Margaret Smith at Hull and educated at Palmers Green High School and the North London Collegiate School for Girls, Smith assumed the nickname Stevie as her *nom de plume*. After graduation she was employed as a private secretary in the publishing industry, a position which she held until retirement. Her first publication, *Novel on Yellow Paper; or, Work It Out for Yourself* (1936), takes its title from the office stationery on which it was typed. This was followed by the poetry collections *A Good Time Was Had by All* (1937) and *Tender Only to One* (1938), and the novel *Over the Frontier* (1938). Another volume of poetry, *Mother, What Is Man?* (1942) preceded the last of the novels, *The Holiday* (1949). Smith was also a visual artist whose illustrations often accompanied her verse, and a volume consisting almost exclusively of illustrations, *Some Are More Human Than Others*, appeared in 1958. Three other books of verse were published during her lifetime: *Selected Poems* (1964), *The Frog Prince* (1966), and *The Best Beast* (1969). Posthumous collections are *Scorpion and Other Poems* (1972), *Me Again* (1981), and *Stevie Smith, A Selection* (1983).

George Orwell (1903–50). Orwell is the pseudonym of Eric Arthur Blair, born in Bengal and educated at Eton College. In 1922, he joined the Indian Civil Police in Burma, returning to Europe in 1927. A period of destitution spent in Paris and England ended only when his work began to be printed in *The Adelphi* in 1930. His first book was *Down and Out in Paris and London* (1933), followed by the novel *Burmese Days* in 1934. The proceeds from these allowed Orwell to set himself up as a small country shopkeeper while he produced *A Clergyman's Daughter* (1935) and *Keep the Aspidistra Flying* (1936). A commission from The Left Book Club supported his study of unemployment in Lancashire, *The Road To Wigan Pier* (1937). In 1936 Orwell went to the Spanish Civil War, and *Homage to Catalonia* (1937) followed.

After returning to England, Orwell published the novel *Coming Up for Air* (1939), the collection of essays *Inside the Whale* (1940), and the political speculation *The Lion and the Unicorn* (1941) before achieving world fame with the 1945 publication of *Animal Farm*. *Nineteen Eighty-Four* followed in 1949. Other nonfiction includes *Critical Essays* (1946), *The English People* (1947), *Politics and the English Language* (1947), *Shooting an Elephant* (1950), *England, Your England* (1953), and *The Collected Essays, Journalism and Letters of George Orwell* (four vols., 1968).

Evelyn (Arthur St. John) Waugh (1903–66). Born in London and educated at Lancing School and Hertford College, Oxford, Waugh taught briefly in various private schools after graduating. Already having privately printed two of his own works, *The World to Come: A Poem in Three Cantos* (1916) and *PRB: An Essay on the Pre-Raphaelite Brotherhood* (1926), Waugh commercially published *Rossetti: His Life and Works* and *Decline and Fall* in 1928. The latter work was the first of the early satirical novels, followed by *Vile Bodies* (1930), *Black Mischief* (1932), *A Handful of Dust* (1934), *Mr. Loveday's Little Outing, and Other Sad Stories* (1936), *Scoop* (1938), and *Put Out More Flags* (1942). *Work Suspended* (1942) consists of two chapters to an unfinished novel.

After service in the Royal Marines and the British Military Mission to Yugoslavia, Waugh published *Brideshead Revisited* in 1945, followed by the last of the satires, *The Loved One* (1948). Major late works include the trilogy *Sword of Honour* (1965): *Men at Arms* (1952), *Officers and Gentlemen* (1955), *Unconditional Surrender* (1961); and *The Ordeal of Gilbert Pinfold* (1957). Other works include the novels *Scott-King's Modern Europe* (1947), *Helena* (1950), *Love among the Ruins: A Romance of the Near Future* (1953); the biographies *Edmund Campion* (1935) and *The Life of Ronald Knox* (1959); several travel sketches; and the autobiographical chapter *A Little Learning* (1964).

(Henry) Graham Greene (1904–   ). Born in Hertfordshire, and educated at his father's school and Balliol College, Oxford, Greene spent the years following graduation employed in journalism. He had published a book of verse, *Babbling April* in 1925, before the appearance of his first novel, *The Man Without* (1929). His book-length fictions, divided, in Greene's classification, between "novels" and "entertainments," include *Stamboul Train* (1932), *It's a Battlefield* (1934), *A Gun for Sale* or *This Gun For Hire* (1936), *Brighton Rock* (1938), *The Power and the Glory* (1940), *The Ministry of Fear* (1943), *The Heart of the Matter* (1948), *The Third Man* (1950), *The End of the Affair* (1951), *The Quiet American* (1955), *A Burnt-Out Case* (1961), *The Honorary Consul* (1973), *The Human Factor* (1978), *Doctor Fischer of Geneva or the Bomb Party* (1980), and *Monsignor Quixote* (1982). Greene's short stories are published in *The Basement Room and Other Stories* (1935), *Nineteen Stories* (1947), *Twenty-one Stories* (1954), *A Sense of Reality* (1963), and *May We Borrow Your Husband?* (1967). Other publications include plays, travel sketches, biography, essays, and autobiography. Greene was literary editor of *The Spectator* before his employment in the Foreign Office from 1941 to 1946 in London and Africa.

Henry Green (1905–73). Green is the pseudonym of Henry Vincent Yorke, born in Gloucestershire and educated at Eton and Oxford. Green's first novel, *Blindness* (1926), was published while he was at the university. After graduation he was employed as an engineer and later as managing director of his family's Birmingham engineering company. *Living* appeared in 1929, followed after a hiatus by *Party Going* (1939) and the autobiographical *Pack My Bag: A Self-Portrait* (1940). Green's other novels are *Caught* (1943), *Loving* (1945), *Back* (1946), *Concluding* (1948), *Nothing* (1950), and *Doting* (1952).

Contributors

Harold Bloom, Sterling Professor of the Humanities at Yale University, is the author of *The Anxiety of Influence*, *Poetry and Repression*, and many other volumes of literary criticism. His forthcoming study, *Freud: Transference and Authority*, attempts a full-scale reading of all of Freud's major writings. A MacArthur Prize Fellow, he is general editor of five series of literary criticism published by Chelsea House.

Timothy Hyman is an artist, graduate of the Slade School of Art; lecturer at The Working Men's College, England; and author of several papers on the works of Powys.

Arthur Mizener is Professor of Humanities at Cornell University. He is the author of *The Far Side of Paradise* (a biography of F. Scott Fitzgerald), *The Sense of Life in the Modern Novel*, *Twelve Great American Novels*, and *Scott Fitzgerald and His World*.

Stephen Heath is Fellow of Jesus College and University Lecturer on the Faculty of English, Cambridge. He is the author of *The Nouveau Roman: A Study in the Practice of Writing*, *Questions of Cinema*, and *The Sexual Fix*.

Daniel R. Schwarz is Professor of English at Cornell University. He is the author of *Disraeli's Fiction* and *Conrad: Almayer's Folly to Under Western Eyes*.

Judith Spector is Assistant Professor of English at IUPUI Columbus, an extension of Indiana University/Purdue University at Indianapolis. Her publications have appeared in *College English*, *Literature and Psychology*, and *Midwest Quarterly*.

Derek Attridge is Professor of English at the University of Strathclyde, Scotland. He is the author of *Well-Weighed Syllables: Elizabethan Verse in Classical*

Metres and *The Rhythms of English Poetry*, as well as coeditor of *Post-Structuralist Joyce: Essays from the French*.

David Hayman is Professor of Comparative Literature and Department Chairman at the University of Wisconsin, Madison. He is the author of *Joyce et Mallarmé* and *Ulysses: The Mechanics of Meaning*, as well as several other works on modern literature. He has edited *A First-Draft Version of Finnegans Wake* and two collections of essays on Joyce.

Terence Hegarty is a native of Dublin, Ireland, who now resides in Rensselaer County, New York, where he writes essays and fiction.

Michael Rosenthal teaches at Columbia University and is the author of *Virginia Woolf*.

Nelly Furman is Associate Professor in the Department of Romance Studies at Cornell University. She is coeditor of *Women and Language in Literature and Society*.

Ian Gregor is Professor of Modern English at the University of Kent. He is the author of *The Moral and the Story* and *The Great Web: The Form of Hardy's Major Fiction*. He has edited collections of essays on the Brontës, religion and anti-religion in imaginative literature, and the English novel.

Frederick R. Karl is Professor of English and Director of Graduate English at City College of New York. He has published books on Joseph Conrad, C. P. Snow, and the English novel of the eighteenth, nineteenth, and twentieth centuries.

Robert Kiely is Loker Professor of English at the University of California at Davis. He is the author of *Beyond Egotism: The Fiction of James Joyce, Virginia Woolf, and D. H. Lawrence*; *Robert Louis Stevenson and the Fiction of Adventure*; and *The Romantic Novel in England*. He is the editor of *Modernism Reconsidered*.

Maria DiBattista is Associate Professor of English at Princeton University. She is the author of *Virginia Woolf's Major Novels: Fables of Anon*, and is preparing a study of apocalyptic figures in the modern novel.

Hazard Adams is a member of the Departments of English and Comparative Literature at the University of Washington, Seattle. He is the author of *Blake and Yeats: The Contrary Vision*, *The Contexts of Poetry*, *The Interests of Criticism*, and *Philosophy of the Literary Symbolic*.

Eliot A. Singer is an instructor at the University of Pennsylvania.

A. E. Dyson is Lecturer in English at University College, Bangor. He is the author of *The Crazy Fabric: Essays in Irony*, *The Inimitable Dickens: A Reading of the Novels*, *Between Two Worlds: Aspects of Literary Forms*, and *Yeats, Eliot, and R. S. Thomas: Riding the Echo*.

Neil McEwan is the author of *Africa and the Novel*.

John Zneimer is Associate Professor of English at Indiana University Northwest.

Janice Witherspoon Neuleib is Assistant Professor of English at Illinois State University, Bloomington-Normal. She has published several articles on Lewis.

Harriet S. Chessman is Assistant Professor of English at Yale University. She is at work on a book entitled *Women, Writing, and Silence in the Twentieth-Century Novel*, which will explore the issue of female authorship and narrative authority in the works of Woolf, Stein, Nin, and Hurston.

Hermione Lee is Lecturer in English at the University of York. She is the author of *The Novels of Virginia Woolf, Philip Roth*, and *Elizabeth Bowen: An Estimation*.

Lynette Hunter has been a University Research Fellow at the Universities of Liverpool and Wales. She is the author of *G. K. Chesterton: Explorations in Allegory*.

Alvin B. Kernan is A. W. Mellon Professor of the Humanities at Princeton University. He is the author of several works, including *Modern American Theater, The Playwright as Magician*, and *The Imaginary Library*.

Terry Eagleton is Fellow and Tutor in English, Wadham College, Oxford. He is the author of *Criticism and Ideology, Marxism and Literary Criticism*, and *Literary Theory: An Introduction*, as well as studies of Shakespeare, Richardson, the Brontës, and Benjamin.

Bruce Bassoff is a member of the Department of English at the University of Colorado, Boulder. He is the author of *The Secret Sharers: Studies in Contemporary Fictions*.

Bibliography

JOHN COWPER POWYS

Brebner, John Alexander. *The Demon Within: A Study of John Cowper Powys' Novels*. New York: Barnes & Noble Books, 1973.

Cavaliero, Glen. *John Cowper Powys: Novelist*. Oxford: Clarendon Press, 1973.

Coates, C. A. *John Cowper Powys in Search of a Landscape*. London: Macmillan, 1982.

Hooker, Jeremy. *John Cowper Powys*. Cardiff: University of Wales Press, 1973.

Humfrey, Belinda, ed. *Essays on John Cowper Powys*. Cardiff: University of Wales Press, 1972.

Krissdottir, Morine. *John Cowper Powys and the Magical Quest*. London: Macdonald & Jane's, 1980.

Mathias, Roland. *The Hollowed-Out Elder Stalk: John Cowper Powys as Poet*. London: Enitharmon Press, 1979.

FORD MADOX FORD

Andreach, Robert J. *The Slain and Resurrected God: Conrad, Ford, and the Christian Myth*. New York: New York University Press, 1970.

Cassell, Richard A. *Ford Madox Ford*. New York: Macmillan, 1972.

Green, Robert. *Ford Madox Ford: Prose and Politics*. New York: Cambridge University Press, 1981.

Huntley, H. Robert. *The Alien Protagonist of Ford Madox Ford*. Chapel Hill: University of North Carolina Press, 1970.

Moser, Thomas C. *The Life in the Fiction of Ford Madox Ford*. Princeton: Princeton University Press, 1980.

Smith, Grover. *Ford Madox Ford*. New York: Columbia University Press, 1972.

407

Snitow, Ann Barr. *Ford Madox Ford and the Voice of Uncertainty*. Baton Rouge: Louisiana State University Press, 1984.

Stange, Sondra J., ed. *The Presence of Ford Madox Ford*. Philadelphia: University of Pennsylvania Press, 1981.

DOROTHY RICHARDSON

Blake, Caesar Robert. *Dorothy Richardson*. Ann Arbor: University of Michigan Press, 1960.

Hanscombe, Gillian E. *The Art of Life*: *Dorothy Richardson and the Development of Feminist Consciousness*. Boston: Peter Owen, 1982.

Rosenberg, John. *Dorothy Richardson*. New York: Alfred A. Knopf, 1973.

Staley, Thomas F. *Dorothy Richardson*. Boston: Twayne Publishers, 1976.

E. M. FORSTER

Cavaliero, Glen. *A Reading of E. M. Forster*. London: Macmillan, 1979.

Das, G. K., and John Beer, eds. *E. M. Forster*: *A Human Exploration*: *Centenary Essays*. London: Macmillan, 1979.

Gillie, Christopher. *A Preface to Forster*. New York: Longman, 1983.

Herz, Judith Scherer, and Robert K. Martin, eds. *E. M. Forster*: *Centenary Revaluations*. Toronto: University of Toronto Press, 1982.

McDowell, Frederick P. W. *E. M. Forster*. Boston: Twayne Publishers, 1982.

Page, Norman. *E. M. Forster's Posthumous Fiction*. Victoria: English Literary Studies, University of Victoria, 1977.

Rosecrance, Barbara. *Forster's Narrative Vision*. Ithaca: Cornell University Press, 1982.

Scott, P. J. M. *E. M. Forster*: *Our Permanent Contemporary*. Totowa, N. J.: Barnes & Noble Books, 1984.

JAMES JOYCE

Attridge, Derek, and Daniel Ferrer, eds. *Post-Structuralist Joyce*: *Essays from the French*. New York: Cambridge University Press, 1984.

Benstock, Bernard, ed. *The Seventh of Joyce*. Bloomington: Indiana University Press, 1982.

Brown, Richard. *James Joyce and Sexuality*. New York: Cambridge University Press, 1985.

Bushrui, Suheil Badi, and Bernard Benstock, eds. *James Joyce, an International Perspective*: *Centenary Essays in Honour of the Late Sir Desmond Cochrane*. Totowa, N. J.: Barnes & Noble Books, 1982.

Ehrlich, Howard, ed. *Light Rays*: *James Joyce and Modernism*. New York: New Horizon Press, 1984.

Epstein, E. L., ed. *A Starchamber Quiry*: *A James Joyce Centennial Volume, 1882–1982*. New York: Methuen & Co., 1982.

MacCabe, Colin, ed. *James Joyce, New Perspectives*. Bloomington: Indiana University Press, 1982.

McCormack, W. J., and Alistair Stead, eds. *James Joyce and Modern Literature*. London and Boston: Routledge & Kegan Paul, 1982.

Parrinder, Patrick. *James Joyce*. New York: Cambridge University Press, 1984.

Peterson, Richard F., Alan M. Cohn, and Edmund L. Epstein, eds. *Work in Progress*: *Joyce Centenary Essays*. Carbondale: Southern Illinois University Press, 1982.

WYNDHAM LEWIS

Bridson, D. G. *The Filibuster*: *A Study of the Political Ideas of Wyndham Lewis*. London: Cassell, 1972.

Chapman, Robert T. *Wyndham Lewis*: *Fiction and Satires*. London: Vision Press, 1973.

Dasenbrock, Reed Way. *The Literary Vorticism of Ezra Pound and Wyndham Lewis*: *Towards the Condition of Painting*. Baltimore: The Johns Hopkins University Press, 1985.

Jameson, Fredric. *Fables of Aggression*: *Wyndham Lewis, the Modernist as Fascist*. Berkeley: University of California Press, 1979.

Materer, Timothy. *Vortex*: *Pound, Eliot, and Lewis*. Ithaca: Cornell University Press, 1979.

———. *Wyndham Lewis, the Novelist*. Detroit: Wayne State University Press, 1976.

Meyers, Jeffrey, ed. *Wyndham Lewis, a Revaluation*: *New Essays*. Montreal: McGill-Queen's University Press, 1980.

Pritchard, William H. *Wyndham Lewis*. London: Routledge & Kegan Paul, 1972.

VIRGINIA WOOLF

Clements, Patricia, and Isobel Grundy, eds. *Virginia Woolf*: *New Critical Essays*. Totowa, N. J.: Barnes & Noble Books, 1983.

DiBattista, Maria. *Virginia Woolf's Major Novels*: *The Fables of Anon*. New Haven: Yale University Press, 1980.

Freedman, Ralph, ed. *Virginia Woolf*: *Revaluation and Continuity*: *A Collection of Essays*. Berkeley: University of California Press, 1980.

Ginsberg, Elaine K., and Laura Moss Gottlieb, eds. *Virginia Woolf*: *Centennial Essays*. Troy, N. Y.: Whitston, 1983.

Harper, Howard M. *Between Language and Silence*: *The Novels of Virginia Woolf*. Baton Rouge: Louisiana State University Press, 1982.

Little, Judy. *Comedy and the Woman Writer*: *Woolf, Spark, and Feminism*. Lincoln: University of Nebraska Press, 1983.

Marcus, Jane, ed. *New Feminist Essays on Virginia Woolf*. Lincoln: University of Nebraska Press, 1981.

————. *Virginia Woolf: A Feminist Slant*. Lincoln: University of Nebraska Press, 1983.

Moore, Madeline. *The Short Season between Two Silences: The Mystical and the Political in the Novels of Virginia Woolf*. Boston: Allen & Unwin, 1984.

Spilka, Mark. *Virginia Woolf's Quarrel with Grieving*. Lincoln: University of Nebraska Press, 1980.

IVY COMPTON-BURNETT

Baldanza, Frank. *Ivy Compton-Burnett*. New York: Twayne Publishers, 1964.

Dick, Kay. *Ivy and Stevie: Ivy Compton-Burnett and Stevie Smith: Conversations and Reflections*. London: Duckworth, 1971.

Grylls, R. Glynn. *I. Compton-Burnett*. Harlow, England: Longman Group, 1971.

Johnson, Pamela Hansford. *I. Compton-Burnett*. New York: Longmans, Green, 1951.

Liddell, Robert. *The Novels of I. Compton-Burnett*. London: Gollancz, 1955.

Nevius, Blake. *Ivy Compton-Burnett*. New York: Columbia University Press, 1970.

D. H. LAWRENCE

Balbert, Peter, and Phillip L. Marcus, eds. *D. H. Lawrence: A Centenary Consideration*. Ithaca: Cornell University Press, 1985.

Ben-Ephraim, Gavriel. *The Moon's Dominion: Narrative Dichotomy and Female Dominance in Lawrence's Early Novels*. Rutherford, N. J.: Fairleigh Dickinson University Press, 1981.

Clark, L. D. *The Minoan Distance: The Symbolism of Travel in D. H. Lawrence*. Tucson: University of Arizona Press, 1980.

Ebbatson, Roger. *Lawrence and the Nature Tradition: A Theme in English Fiction, 1859–1914*. Atlantic Highlands, N. J.: Humanities Press, 1980.

Gutierrez, Donald. *Lapsing Out: Embodiments of Death and Rebirth in the Last Writings of D. H. Lawrence*. Rutherford, N. J.: Fairleigh Dickinson University Press, 1980.

Harris, Janice Hubbard. *The Short Fiction of D. H. Lawrence*. New Brunswick, N. J.: Rutgers University Press, 1984.

Hobsbaum, Philip. *A Reader's Guide to D. H. Lawrence*. London: Thames & Hudson, 1981.

Holderness, Graham. *D. H. Lawrence: History, Ideology, and Fiction*. Atlantic Highlands, N. J.: Humanities Press, 1982.

Ruderman, Judith. *D. H. Lawrence and the Devouring Mother: The Search for a Patriarchal Ideal of Leadership*. Durham, N. C.: Duke University Press, 1984.

Simpson, Hilary. *D. H. Lawrence and Feminism*. London: Croom Helm, 1982.

JOYCE CARY

Adams, Hazard. *Joyce Cary's Trilogies*: *Pursuit of the Particular Real*. Tallahassee: University Presses of Florida, 1983.

Cook, Cornelia. *Joyce Cary*: *Liberal Principles*. Totowa, N. J.: Barnes & Noble Books, 1981.

Echeruo, Michael J. C. *Joyce Cary and the Dimensions of Order*. London: Macmillan, 1979.

Hall, Dennis. *Joyce Cary*: *A Reappraisal*. New York: St. Martin's, 1983.

Kanu, S. H. *A World of Everlasting Conflict*: *Joyce Cary's View of Man and Society*. Ibadan, Nigeria: Ibadan University Press, 1974.

Roby, Kinley H. *Joyce Cary*. Boston: Twayne Publishers, 1984.

AGATHA CHRISTIE

Bargainnier, Earl F. *The Gentle Art of Murder: The Detective Fiction of Agatha Christie*. Bowling Green, Ohio: Bowling Green State University Popular Press, 1980.

Barnard, Robert. *A Talent to Deceive*: *An Appreciation of Agatha Christie*. New York: Dodd, Mead, 1980.

Fitzgibbon, Russell H. *The Agatha Christie Companion*. Bowling Green, Ohio: Bowling Green State University Popular Press, 1980.

Keating, H. R. F. *Agatha Christie*: *First Lady of Crime*. New York: Holt, Rinehart & Winston, 1977.

Maida, Patricia D. *Murder She Wrote*: *A Study of Agatha Christie's Detective Fiction*. Bowling Green, Ohio: Bowling Green State University Popular Press, 1982.

ALDOUS HUXLEY

Baker, Robert S. *The Dark Historic Page*: *Social Satire and Historicism in the Novels of Aldous Huxley, 1921–39*. Madison: University of Wisconsin Press, 1982.

Ferns, C. S. *Aldous Huxley, Novelist*. London: Athlone Press, 1980.

Firchow, Peter Edgerly. *The End of Utopia*: *A Study of Aldous Huxley's Brave New World*. Lewisburg, Pa.: Bucknell University Press, 1984.

Kuehn, Robert E., ed. *Aldous Huxley*: *A Collection of Critical Essays*. Englewood Cliffs, N. J.: Prentice-Hall, 1974.

L. P. HARTLEY

Bien, Peter. *L. P. Hartley*. University Park: The Pennsylvania State University Press, 1963.

Jones, Edward Trostle. *L. P. Hartley*. Boston: Twayne Publishers, 1978.

Mulkeen, Anne. *Wild Thyme, Winter Lightning*: *The Symbolic Novels of L. P. Hartley*. Detroit: Wayne State University Press, 1974.

LIAM O'FLAHERTY

Doyle, Paul A. *Liam O'Flaherty*. New York: Twayne Publishers, 1971.

O'Brien, James H. *Liam O'Flaherty*. Lewisburg, Pa.: Bucknell University Press, 1973.

Sheeran, Patrick F. *The Novels of Liam O'Flaherty: A Study in Romantic Realism*. Dublin: Wolfhound Press, 1976.

Zneimer, John. *The Literary Vision of Liam O'Flaherty*. Syracuse, N. Y.: Syracuse University Press, 1970.

C. S. LEWIS

Aeschliman, Michael D. *The Restitution of Man: C. S. Lewis and the Case against Scientism*. Grand Rapids, Mich.: W. B. Eerdmans, 1983.

Hart, Dabney Adams. *Through the Open Door: A New Look at C. S. Lewis*. University: University of Alabama Press, 1984.

Hillegas, Mark Robert, ed. *Shadows of Imagination: The Fantasies of C. S. Lewis, J. R. R. Tolkien, and Charles Williams*. Carbondale: Southern Illinois University Press, 1979.

Schakel, Peter J., ed. *The Longing for a Form: Essays on the Fiction of C. S. Lewis*. Kent, Ohio: Kent State University Press, 1977.

Walsh, Chad. *The Literary Legacy of C. S. Lewis*. New York: Harcourt Brace Jovanovich, 1979.

ELIZABETH BOWEN

Austin, Allen E. *Elizabeth Bowen*. New York: Twayne Publishers, 1971.

Blodgett, Harriet. *Patterns of Reality: Elizabeth Bowen's Novels*. The Hague: Mouton, 1975.

Kenney, Edwin J., Jr. *Elizabeth Bowen*. Lewisburg, Pa.: Bucknell University Press, 1975.

Lee, Hermione. *Elizabeth Bowen: An Estimation*. Totowa, N. J.: Barnes & Noble Books, 1981.

STEVIE SMITH

Dick, Kay. *Ivy and Stevie: Ivy Compton-Burnett and Stevie Smith: Conversations and Reflections*. London: Duckworth, 1971.

MacGibbon, James. Preface to *Me Again: Uncollected Writings of Stevie Smith*. Edited by Jack Barbera and William McBrien. London: Virago, 1981.

Rankin, Arthur. *The Poetry of Stevie Smith, "Little Girl Lost."* Totowa, N. J.: Barnes & Noble Books, 1985.

GEORGE ORWELL

Bolton, W. F. *The Language of 1984: Orwell's English and Ours*. Oxford: Basil Blackwell, with Andre Deutsch, 1984.

Burgess, Anthony. *1985*. Boston: Little, Brown, 1978.

Hammond, J. R. *A George Orwell Companion*: *A Guide to the Novels, Documentaries, and Essays*. London: Macmillan, 1982.

Jensen, Ejner J., ed. *The Future of Nineteen Eighty-Four*. Ann Arbor: University of Michigan Press, 1984.

Kuppig, C. J., ed. *Nineteen Eighty-Four to 1984*: *A Companion to the Classic Novel of Our Times*. New York: Carroll & Graf, 1984.

Patai, Daphne. *The Orwell Mystique*: *A Study in Male Ideology*. Amherst: University of Massachusetts Press, 1984.

Smyer, Richard I. *Primal Dream and Primal Crime: Orwell's Development as a Psychological Novelist*. Columbia: University of Missouri Press, 1979.

EVELYN WAUGH

Heath, Jeffrey M. *The Picturesque Prison*: *Evelyn Waugh and His Writing*. Montreal: McGill-Queen's University Press, 1982.

Lane, Calvin W. *Evelyn Waugh*. Boston: Twayne Publishers, 1981.

Littlewood, Ian. *The Writings of Evelyn Waugh*. Oxford: Basil Blackwell, 1983.

GRAHAM GREENE

Hynes, Samuel Lynn, ed. *Graham Greene*: *A Collection of Critical Essays*. Englewood Cliffs, N. J.: Prentice-Hall, 1973.

O'Donnell, Donat. "Graham Greene: The Anatomy of Pity." In *Maria Cross*: *Imaginative Patterns in a Group of Modern Catholic Writers*. New York: Oxford University Press, 1952.

Pryce-Jones, David. *Graham Greene*. Edinburgh: Oliver & Boyd, 1973.

Spurling, John. *Graham Greene*. New York: Methuen & Co., 1983.

Veitch, Douglas W. *Lawrence, Greene, and Lowry*: *The Fictional Landscape of Mexico*. Waterloo, Ont.: Wilfrid Laurier University Press, 1978.

Wolfe, Peter. *Graham Greene: The Entertainer*. Carbondale: Southern Illinois University Press, 1972.

HENRY GREEN

Mengham, Rod. *The Idiom of the Time*: *The Writings of Henry Green*. New York: Cambridge University Press, 1982.

North, Michael. *Henry Green and the Writing of His Generation*. Charlottesville: University Presses of Virginia, 1984.

Odom, Keith C. *Henry Green*. Boston: Twayne Publishers, 1978.

Acknowledgments

"The Modus Vivendi of John Cowper Powys" by Timothy Hyman from *Essays on John Cowper Powys*, edited by Belinda Humfrey, © 1972 by The Authors and the University of Wales Press. Reprinted by permission of the author and the University of Wales Press.

"Ford Madox Ford: *Parade's End*" (originally entitled "Appendix: *Parade's End*") by Arthur Mizener from *The Saddest Story*: *A Biography of Ford Madox Ford* by Arthur Mizener, © 1971 by Arthur Mizener. Reprinted by permission.

"Writing for Silence: Dorothy Richardson and the Novel" by Stephen Heath from *Teaching the Text*, edited by Suzanne Kappeler and Norman Bryson, © 1983 by Stephen Heath. Reprinted by permission of the author and Routledge & Kegan Paul Ltd.

"The Originality of E. M. Forster" by Daniel R. Schwarz from *Modern Fiction Studies* 29, no. 4 (Winter 1983), © 1984 by Purdue Research Foundation, West Lafayette, Ind. Reprinted by permission.

"James Joyce's *Ulysses*: The Complete Masculine Aesthetic" by Judith Spector from *CLA Journal* 28, no. 3 (March 1985), 299–313, © 1984 by College Language Association. Reprinted by permission.

"The Backbone of James Joyce's *Finnegans Wake*: Narrative, Digression, and Deconstruction" (originally entitled "The Backbone of *Finnegans Wake*: Narrative, Digression, and Deconstruction") by Derek Attridge from *Genre* 17, no. 4 (Winter 1984), © 1985 by The University of Oklahoma. Reprinted by permission.

"James Joyce, Paratactitian" by David Hayman from *Contemporary Literature* 26, no. 2 (Summer 1985), © 1985 by the Board of Regents of the University of Wisconsin System. Reprinted by permission of the University of Wisconsin Press.

"Wyndham Lewis the Writer: A Preoccupation with the Real" by Terence Hegarty from *The Massachusetts Review* 23, no. 2 (Summer 1982), © 1982 by *The Massachusetts Review, Inc.* Reprinted by permission.

"Virginia Woolf" by Michael Rosenthal from *Partisan Review* 43, no. 4 (1976), © 1976 by P. R., Inc. Reprinted by permission.

"Virginia Woolf's *A Room of One's Own*: Reading Absence" (originally entitled "*A Room of One's Own*: Reading Absence") by Nelly Furman from *Women's Language and Style*, edited by Douglas Butturff and Edmund L. Epstein, © 1978 by E. L. Epstein. Reprinted by permission of the editor and L & S Books.

"Voices: Reading Virginia Woolf" by Ian Gregor from *The Sewanee Review* 88, no. 4 (October–December 1980), © 1980 by Ian Gregor and the University of the South. Reprinted by permission of the author and the editor of The *Sewanee Review*.

"The Intimate World of Ivy Compton-Burnett" by Frederick R. Karl from *The Contemporary English Novel* by Frederick R. Karl, © 1962 by Frederick R. Karl. Reprinted by permission of the author and Farrar, Straus & Giroux.

"Accident and Purpose: 'Bad Form' in D. H. Lawrence's Fiction" (originally entitled "Accident and Purpose: 'Bad Form' in Lawrence's Fiction") by Robert Kiely from *D. H. Lawrence: A Centenary Consideration*, edited by Peter Balbert and Phillip L. Marcus, © 1985 by Cornell University Press. Reprinted by permission of the publisher.

"*Women in Love*: D. H. Lawrence's Judgment Book" by Maria DiBattista from *D. H. Lawrence: A Centenary Consideration*, edited by Peter Balbert and Phillip L. Marcus, © 1985 by Cornell University Press. Reprinted by permission of the publisher.

"Joyce Cary: The Abstract Real" (Originally entitled "The Abstract Real") by Hazard Adams from *Joyce Cary's Trilogies: Pursuit of the Particular Real* by Hazard Adams, © 1983 by the Board of Regents of the State of Florida. Reprinted by permission of the University Presses of Florida.

"The Whodunit as Riddle: Block Elements in Agatha Christie" by Eliot A. Singer from *Western Folklore* 43, no. 3 (July 1984), © 1984 by the California Folklore Society. Reprinted by permission.

"Aldous Huxley and the Two Nothings" by A. E. Dyson from *The Critical Quarterly* 3, no. 4 (Winter 1961), © 1961 by *The Critical Quarterly*. Reprinted by permission.

"L. P. Hartley's *The Go-Between*: Neo-Victorian or New Novel?" (originally entitled "Hartley's *The Go-Between*: Neo-Victorian or New Novel?") by Neil McEwan from *The Survival of the Novel: British Fiction in the Later Twentieth Century* by Neil McEwan, © 1981 by Neil McEwan. Reprinted by permission of the author, The Macmillan Press Ltd., and Barnes & Noble Books.

"Liam O'Flaherty" (originally entitled "Conclusion") by John Zneimer from *The Literary Vision of Liam O'Flaherty* by John Zneimer, © 1970 by Syracuse University Press. Reprinted by permission of the publisher.

"The Creative Act: C. S. Lewis on God and Art" (originally entitled "The Creative Act: Lewis on God and Art") by Janice Witherspoon Neuleib from *The Longing for a Form: Essays on the Fiction of C. S. Lewis*, edited by Peter J. Schakel, © 1977 by The Kent State University Press. Reprinted by permission.

"Women and Language in the Fiction of Elizabeth Bowen" by Harriet S. Chessman from *Twentieth Century Literature* 29, no. 1 (Spring 1983), © 1983 by Hofstra University Press. Reprinted by permission.

"Stevie Smith" (originally entitled "Introduction") by Hermione Lee from *Stevie Smith: A Selection*, edited by Hermione Lee, © 1983 by Hermione Lee. Reprinted by permission of A. D. Peters & Co. Ltd. and Faber & Faber Ltd.

"George Orwell's Search for a Voice" (originally entitled "Introduction: Genre and Rhetoric: The Search for a Valid Voice," "The Stance of Allegory," and "Discussion") by Lynette Hunter from *George Orwell: The Search for a Voice* by Lynette Hunter, © 1984 by Lynette Hunter. Reprinted by permission of the author and Open University Press.

"Running in Circles: The Early Novels of Evelyn Waugh" by Alvin B. Kernan from *The Plot of Satire* by Alvin B. Kernan, © 1965 by Yale University. Reprinted by permission of Yale University Press.

"Reluctant Heroes: The Novels of Graham Greene" by Terry Eagleton from *Exiles and Emigrés: Studies in Modern Literature* by Terry Eagleton, © 1970 by Terry Eagleton. Reprinted by permission of the author and Chatto & Windus.

"Henry Green: Surfaces and Depths" (originally entitled "Surfaces and Depths") by Bruce Bassoff from *Toward Loving: The Poetics of the Novel and the Practice of Henry Green* by Bruce Bassoff, © 1975 by the University of South Carolina. Reprinted by permission of the University of South Carolina Press.

Index

419